# THE AMERICAN ALPINE JOURNAL
## 2012

This page: Sam Magro on pitch 1 of the Reverie, Yellowstone National Park, M̲

Cover: Cerro Torre, in the Argentine Patagonia [p. 51]. *Corey Rich-Red Bull*
Back cover: Titcomb Basin, Wind River Mountains, Wyoming [p. 16]. *Ken Driese*

D1042805

2012 VOLUME 54 ISSUE 86

# CONTENTS

**16 Recon: Titcomb Basin, by Joe Kelsey**

*Wyoming's Wind River Mountains hold some of America's favorite wilderness rock. The southern granite is famous. The north? Have a look for yourself.*

**40 The Shark's Fin Redux, by Jimmy Chin**

*Success at last on Meru Central's spectacular Shark's Fin, India.*

**45 On Darwin's Edge, by Didier Jourdain**

*The first complete traverse of the Cordillera Darwin, Tierra del Fuego, Chile.*

**51 Cerro Torre Rebooted, by Kelly Cordes**

*Forty-two years ago much of the climbing world exploded in rage when 400 bolts were added to an icon. This year it exploded again when many of those bolts were removed.*

**53 By Fair Means, by Hayden Kennedy**

*The first ascent of the southeast ridge of Cerro Torre without Maestri's bolts.*

**56 Cerro Torre Free, by David Lama**

*By an accident of timing, the long-coveted first free ascent of the southeast ridge of Cerro Torre takes place without Maestri's bolts as protection.*

**59 Venas Azules, by Bjørn-Eivind Aartun**

*An ice climber's dream line reveals itself on the south face of Torre Egger, Patagonia.*

**64 The Mausoleum, by Clint Helander**

*The first ascent of Mt. Mausolus in Alaska's little-known Revelation Mountains.*

**69 Continuing Education, by Kevin Ditzler**

*Severely tested on the first ascent of the 8,500-foot southwest spur of University Peak, Alaska.*

**76 Baba Tangi, by Pat Deavoll**

*A team of sisters makes the first ascent of the northwest ridge of Koh-e-Baba-Tangi (6,516m), Afghanistan.*

**81 The Old Breed, by Mark Richey**

*The first ascent of Saser Kangri II (7,518m) and other peaks in the Eastern Karakoram, India.*

# Climbs and Expeditions

91 Contiguous United States
112 Alaska
130 Canada
133 Greenland
144 Colombia, Venezuela
149 Peru
154 Bolivia
161 Chile
175 Argentina
194 Antarctica
201 Iran
203 Morocco
204 Norway
208 CIS (Russia, Georgia, Tajikistan)
215 Kyrgyzstan
237 Afghanistan
243 Pakistan
280 India
306 Nepal
324 China
351 Tibet
358 Mongolia
359 Indonesia
361 AAC Grants

363 Book Reviews, edited by David Stevenson

*New books by Fred Beckey, Jim Davidson, Wade Davis, Ed Douglas, Damien Gildea, Emil Henry, Sandy Hill, Joy Logan, John Long, Paul Maxim, Bernadette McDonald, John Scurlock, and Ed Viesturs with David Roberts.*

377 In Memoriam, edited by Cameron M. Burns

*Remembering Ann Brooks Carter, Steve Hackett, James W. Ebert, James Goodwin, James H. Kanzler, Victor Curt Mahler, Bonnie Prudden, and George Sainsbury.*

385 Club Activities, edited by Frederick O. Johnson

390 Index

400 International Grade Comparison Chart

*Submission guidelines, expanded reports, additional photos, topos, and comments are available at aaj.americanalpineclub.org.*

Jumaring behind Salto Tuyuren in the upper section of Kids with Guns, Amuri Tepui, Venezuela [p. 145].  *George Ullrich*

Hayden Kennedy during the descent from Deep in the Alaskan Bush, with the unclimbed south face of Xanadu behind, Arrigetch Range, Alaska [p. 112]. *Corey Rich*

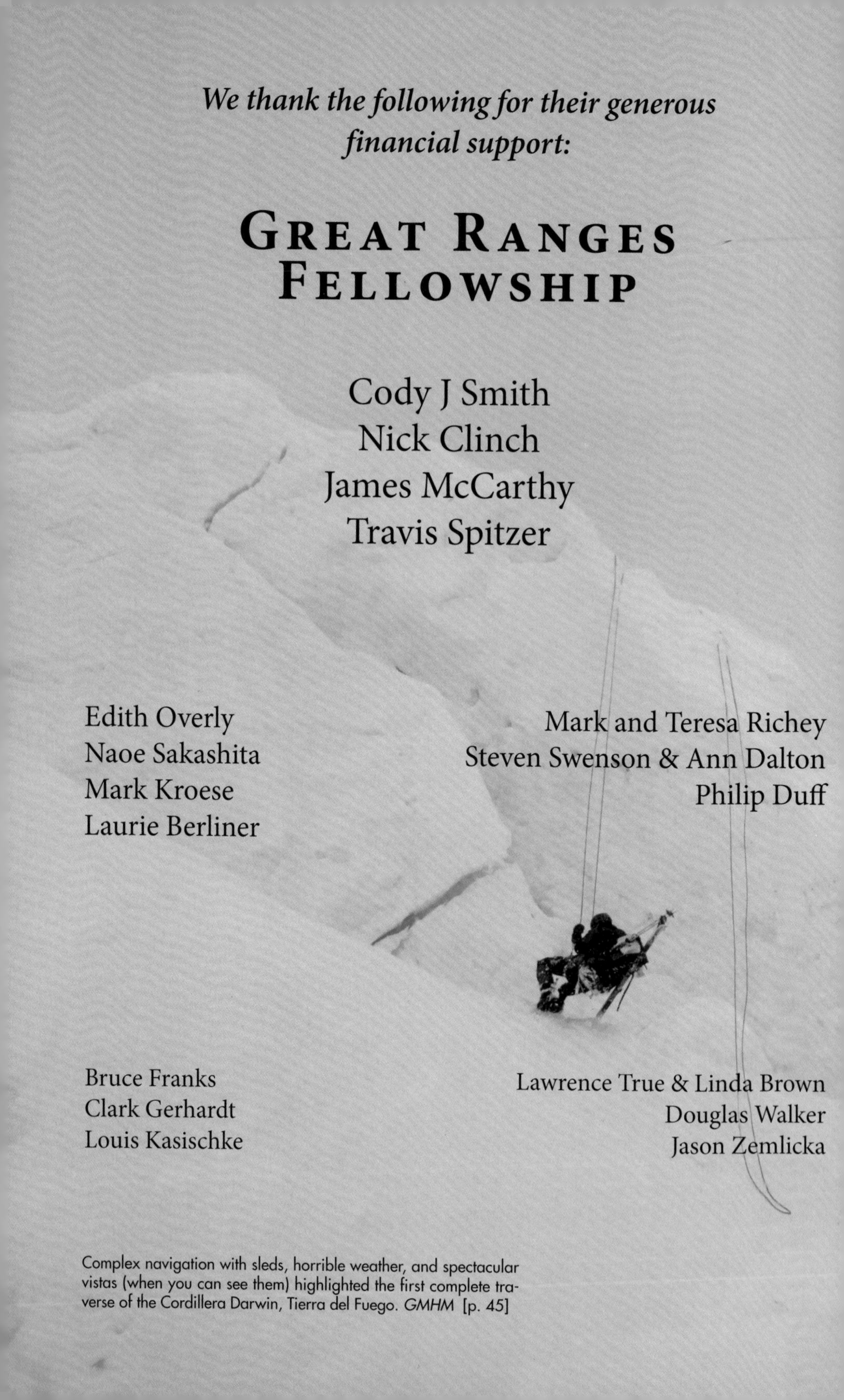

*We thank the following for their generous financial support:*

# GREAT RANGES FELLOWSHIP

Cody J Smith
Nick Clinch
James McCarthy
Travis Spitzer

Edith Overly
Naoe Sakashita
Mark Kroese
Laurie Berliner

Mark and Teresa Richey
Steven Swenson & Ann Dalton
Philip Duff

Bruce Franks
Clark Gerhardt
Louis Kasischke

Lawrence True & Linda Brown
Douglas Walker
Jason Zemlicka

Complex navigation with sleds, horrible weather, and spectacular vistas (when you can see them) highlighted the first complete traverse of the Cordillera Darwin, Tierra del Fuego. *GMHM* [p. 45]

Anonymous
John All
William Arnott
Dr. Bernhard Bach
Barry Baer
Gail Bates
Douglas Beall
Gali Beh
Laurie Bencal
Gordon A. Benner, M.D.
Tanya Bradby
William Burd
Ned and Betsy Cabot
R. J. Campbell
John Catto
Yvon and Malinda
   Chouinard
Dr. Rebecca Cole
Douglas Colwell
Kevin Cooney
Charlotte and Matt
   Culberson
John Davidge III
James Donini
Cheryl Duckworth
Jim Edwards

Ken Ehrhart
H. Newcomb Eldredge
Lee Elman
Terrence English
Roger Flahive
Charles Fleischman
Charlotte Fox
Jim Frush
Gerald Gallwas
Peter, Sam, Addis, and Gus
   Goldman
Richard Griffith
Robert Hall
Henry M. Hamlin
James Henriot
Scot Hillman
Richard E. Hoffman M.D.
James Holmes
John R. Kascenska II
Gerald Lofthouse
Jim Logan
George Lowe III
Brent Manning
Edward Matthews
David Mayer
George McCown

Peter Metcalf
Paul Morrow
Vanessa O'Brien
Marshall Peterson
Glenn Porzak
William Lowell Putnam
Verne and Marion Read
Louis Reichardt
Wolf Riehle
David Riggs
Carl Schmitt
Stephen Schofield
Steve Schwartz
Samuel Silverstein M.D.
George N. Smith
Ruth Sofield
Brian Sohn
Chris Steiner
Jack Tackle
Jack Tracy
Ronald Ulrich
Dieter Von Hennig*
   *In memory of Horst von Hennig
Kate Von Krusenstiern
Joe Yannuzzi
T. C. Price Zimmermann

## SUPPORTERS

Alta Group Inc.
H. Adams Carter American Alpine Journal Fund
James Garrett
Z. Wayne Griffin
William Kilpatrick M.D.

Michael J. Lewis Jr.
Mary Ann Matthews
John G. McCall M.D.*
   *In memory of Randall Grandstaff and Charlie Fowler
Theodore P. Streibert

The American Alpine Journal, 710 Tenth St. Suite 100, Golden, Colorado 80401
Telephone: (303) 384-0110  Fax: (303) 384-0111
E-mail: aaj@americanalpineclub.org
www.americanalpineclub.org

ISSN: 0065-6925
ISBN: 978-1-933056-75-3
ISBN: (e-book) 978-1-933056-76-0

# The American Alpine Journal

John Harlin III, *Editor*

**Senior Editor Emeritus**
Kelly Cordes

**Senior Editor**
Lindsay Griffin

**Art Director**
Daniel Gambino

**Contributing Editors**
Cameron M. Burns, *In Memoriam*
Frederick O. Johnson, *Club Activities*
David Stevenson, *Book Reviews*

**Copy Editor**
Joe Kelsey

**Translators**
Luca Calvi
Rolando Garibotti
Alex Horner
Todd Miller
Tamotsu Nakamura
Ekaterina Vorotnikova

**Indexers**
Ralph Ferrara, Eve Tallman

**Regional Contacts**
Mark Westman and Steve Gruhn, *Alaska*; Matt Perkins,
*Washington Cascades*; Doug Robinson, *Sierra Nevada*;
Drew Brayshaw, *Coast Mountains, BC*; Sergio Ramírez
Carrascal, *Peru*; Rolando Garibotti, *Patagonia*; Damien
Gildea, *Antarctica*; Rajesh Gadgil and Harish Kapadia,
*India*; Elizabeth Hawley and Richard Salisbury, *Nepal*;
Tamotsu Nakamura, *Japanese expeditions*; Peter Jensen-
Choi, *Korean expeditions*; Anna Piunova, *CIS expeditions*;
Lindsay Griffin, *Earth*

**With additional thanks to**
Eddie Espinosa, Blake Herrington, Claude Gardien,
Elena Laletina, Artur Paszczak, Randy Levensaler, Luke
Bauer, Emma Walker, and Erik Lambert

Jason Kruk on the southeast ridge of Cerro Torre during its
first ascent without using the bolts placed by Maestri 42
years ago. *Hayden Kennedy* [p. 53]

# THE AMERICAN ALPINE CLUB

## OFFICIALS FOR THE YEAR 2012
*Directors ex-officio

### EXECUTIVE COMMITTEE

**HONORARY PRESIDENT**
William Lowell Putnam

**PRESIDENT**
Charles J. Sassara III*

**VICE PRESIDENT**
Mark Kroese*

**HONORARY TREASURER**
Theodore (Sam) Streibert

**SECRETARY**
Doug Walker*

**TREASURER**
Paul Gagner*

### DIRECTORS

**TERMS ENDING 2013**
Cody J Smith
A. Travis Spitzer
George Lowe III

**TERMS ENDING 2014**
Dave Riggs
Clark Gerhardt
Jim Logan

**TERMS ENDING 2015**
Doug Colwell     Brad Brooks
Karen Daubert   John Heilprin
Rebecca Schild  Mary Hsue
Matt Culberson  Ken Ehrhart

### SECTION CHAIRS

**Alaska**
Harry Hunt & Cindi Squire
**Arizona**
Erik Filsinger
**Blue Ridge**
Simon Carr
**Cascade**
Roger Strong & Becca Vande Hei
**Deep South**
Chadwick Hagan
**Front Range**
Carol Kotchek & Bob Richards
**Great Lakes**
Bill Thompson

**Heartland**
Jeremy Collins
**New England**
Nancy Savickas & Rick Merritt
**New York**
Philip Erard
**North Central**
Mark Jobman
**Northern Rockies**
Brian Cabe
**Montana**
Kevin Brumbach & Emily Stifler
**Oregon**
John Connor & Graham Williams

**Sierra Nevada**
Lewis Richards
**Southern
Appalachian**
David Thoenen
**Southwest**
James Pinter-Lucke
**Tetons**
Brenton Reagan
**Western Slope**
Jim Donini
**Wyoming**
Don Foote

### EDITORS

**THE AMERICAN ALPINE JOURNAL**
John Harlin III

**ACCIDENTS IN NORTH AMERICAN
MOUNTAINEERING**
John E. (Jed) Williamson

### STAFF

**Executive Director** – Phil Powers
**Director of Operations/CFO** – Penn Burris
**Executive Assistant & Grants Manager** – Janet Miller
**Information & Marketing Director** – Erik Lambert
**Membership & Community Director** – John Bragg
**Conservation & Advocacy Director** – Leigh Goldberg
**Development Director** – Keegan Young
**Development Officer** – Sarah Wood
**IT Director** – Craig Hoffman
**Membership Coordinator** – Lauren Shockey
**Membership & Community Assistant** – Tricia Boomhower
**Content & Marketing Manager** – Luke Bauer

**Accountant** – Carol Kotchek
**Library Director** – Beth Heller
**Digitization Archivist** – Elizabeth Surles
**Assistant Librarian** – Alex Depta
**GTCR Ranch Manager** – Susan Garlow
**Northwest Regional Coordinator** - Eddie Espinosa
**Northeast Regional Coordinator** – Sarah Garlick
**Western Regional Coordinator** – Jeff Deikis
**Rocky Mountain Regional Coordinator** – Jenn Flemming
**Southeast Regional Coordinator** – Lisa Hummel
**Museum Director** – Shelby Arnold

# PREFACE

*Partners and colleagues.*

---

*Truth be told, Kelly Cordes didn't really want to work with me.* My very first task as the new *AAJ* editor in February 2002 was to talk Kelly into staying on in his part-time position gathering reports from new routes in North and South America. The editorial transition had been abrupt, and Kelly wasn't sure what to make of it. But he was fanatically devoted to the *AAJ*'s mission of documenting the world's new mountain routes as told directly by the world's first-ascent climbers: in their voices, no hype, no bull, no spray, all respect. And so began my courtship of Kelly, which blossomed into a friendship that yielded the most productive and enjoyable professional partnership I've been lucky enough to share.

I didn't know Kelly when I first telephoned him, though I knew I needed him. A decade younger than me, he was already an Alaskan hardcore who knew everybody (his ventures to Pakistan, Patagonia, and the Alps were still in the future). I didn't think there could be anyone more integral to mountains and climbing than Kelly.

Turns out I was wrong. Lindsay Griffin, across the Pond in Wales, has been the editor of the Mountain INFO column (for a series of magazines) since the dinosaurs roamed—that is, back when EBs were modern and sticky rubber was science fiction, not friction. Lindsay had consulted for the *AAJ*'s editors over the years, and that's how I began our correspondence. Kelly and I would ask him if we'd missed any noteworthy ascents from faraway places. Lindsay responded with multi-page treatises about how this and that "new" route had actually been climbed twice before, the first four decades previous and then again by a team from East Timbukistan, but each was really a variant and there was some doubt about this and that, and on it would go. It quickly became obvious that I needed Lindsay for "The Rest of the World" as much as I needed Kelly for the Americas. Dougald MacDonald called him "The Brain."

Which brings me to Dougald. Right from the beginning in 2002 Dougald advised me from his role on the AAC's board of directors. He had a long background in publishing, and his passion for the *AAJ* was immediately clear. A few years later I had the opportunity to bring him in professionally, editing features and consulting on everything. He moved on to other publications, but wow, did I ever benefit from his tenure at the *AAJ*. There's no one more qualified to run this globe-spanning show, and that includes me. As it turns out, Dougald will take over as executive editor. I couldn't be more pleased.

When Dougald sent manuscripts to our copy editor, Joe Kelsey, I might see a return comment from Joe about how useless he felt—there was nothing to fix. I tried hard to impress Joe myself, with little effect. But Joe sure impressed me. All of us—Kelly, Lindsay, Dougald, and I—sent our supposedly edited copy to Joe out in Bishop, where he'd read it between walks with his two golden retrievers (see their photos on page 26). The articles invariably came back leaner and clearer. You, the reader, can be thankful for Joe's sharp digital pen. But, personally, what I cherished were his between-the-lines comments that had me laughing out loud more times than I can count. Sharp plays on words and daggers to egos (what? Climbers with egos?): there should be a book of Joe's wit.

This is my last *AAJ*—my 11th—and editing this journal has been an honor and a privilege. The explorations conveyed in these pages are the heart and the soul of mountaineering, and of me. Though I'll miss the climbs and the climbers you see in these pages, above all it's my colleagues I can't imagine being without. These people are as good as they come. I wish I could do justice to the joy it's been working with them.

JOHN HARLIN III
*Editor*

Clockwise from top left: Kelly Cordes in Canyonlands. *John Harlin* Lindsay Griffin in Elbsandstein. *Hiroshi Hagiwara* Dougald MacDonald in Canadian Rockies. *John Harlin* Joe Kelsey in Wind River Mountains. *Mark Jenkins*

*If you like the AAJ, you'll love the AAJ Online. There you'll find extra panoramic photos, topos, longer reports, and more. Space in the printed AAJ is very tight, so we can't include everything. When you find a report about a place you're interested in, be sure to check out aaj.americanalpineclub.org; you might find a lot more good info. You can also leave comments and see corrections.*

# YOUR AAC: PAST, PRESENT, FUTURE

For more than a century the American Alpine Club has collected and shared unique climbing information, artifacts, and archives. We've recorded the world's most significant ascents in the *American Alpine Journal* since 1929, and today we continue to care for and grow one of the most impressive climbing libraries on earth. It is with this incredible foundation that we are now embarking on a monumental task: to make the greatest treasures in the climbing world available to you online. Here's how we're making this happen.

△ We're publishing *AAJ* reports as they happen, to give you in-depth stories online before you can read them in print.

△ Now we can store your digital files that are important to the history of climbing. Send us your diaries, notes, letters, hand-drawn topos. library@americanalpineclub.org

△ We've hired a Digitization Archivist to build a powerful database to store, organize, and deliver digital files. Scanning has already begun.

△ Look for special online coverage, and digital features to accompany future *AAJ* articles.

△ We're rescanning past *AAJ* articles to improve the *AAJ* search and online experience.

△ Take your *AAJ* with you— digitally—wherever you go. Coming soon.

Renan Ozturk jugging the "House of Cards" pitch. *Jimmy Chin* [pg.40]

Like any great expedition, there is a lot of work ahead that will require a team effort. Please help us create something great. Renew your American Alpine Club membership, introduce a friend, send us your unique material, and consider donating your time or money to the cause. This is your AAC, past, present, and future.

the
**AMERICAN ALPINE** club
WHERE CLIMBERS UNITE

**AMERICANALPINECLUB.ORG**

# RECON: TITCOMB BASIN

*Spanning 80 miles of the Continental Divide, Wyoming's Wind River Mountains hold some of America's favorite wilderness rock. The southern granite is famous. The north? Have a look for yourself.*

JOE KELSEY

Island Lake, just downstream from Titcomb Basin. *Joe Kelsey*

P rior to 1969 I'd climbed in the Sierra, Cascades, Bugaboos, Canadian Rockies, and Tetons but had only heard of the Wind Rivers. A friend had climbed its highest peak, Gannett; a Gunks lass had a gleam in her eye remembering the Cirque of the Towers; and a Vulgarian mob had been to Titcomb Basin, where they did no climbing but abused substances.

In August 1969 I finally hiked into the Cirque, to meet friends already there. The next morning I awoke certain I was where I belonged. Early the next summer I left Yosemite and headed straight for the Cirque. For a few years I spent as much time as I could there. Then, in 1973, in a three-day jaunt to get in shape for the Logan Mountains, I hiked to Island Lake and from Titcomb Basin bagged Fremont Peak. The Logans trip was a fiasco, during which I often wondered why I'd driven so far to not be in the Wind Rivers.

My most vivid early impression of Titcomb Basin was its spaciousness. I feel at home with space and distant views and am happy walking across spread-out terrain. Spaciousness, though, proved a disadvantage when recruiting partners; it translated to longer approaches. Nevertheless, I enlisted enough climbers willing to haul rock gear plus axes and crampons 12 miles to Island Lake that I got up many of the routes I had my eye on.

In the meantime I stumbled into guidebook writing. The existing guidebook too often baffled rather than enlightened, and during our early-seventies Cirque days several of us, for one another's benefit, wrote up routes we did, collecting them in a notebook I became custodian of. One winter I copied reports from *AAJs* and *Appalachias* and added them to the notebook, thus unintentionally becoming an author. My first guidebook was published in 1981.

The Cirque, with its concentration of granite spires, remains the Wind Rivers' claim to fame. Titcomb's appeal comes from its lesser renown, its wildness, and its untapped potential, for me and for everyone. I still haven't climbed many routes that I'd like to, though I may not have the youthful vigor for those highest on my list. But I've come to appreciate Island Lake, Titcomb Basin, and neighboring Indian Basin as places simply to be, the best of consolations for aging.

## A Quick Tour

Much of northwestern Wyoming constitutes an ecosystem of contiguous mountain ranges. One of these ranges, the Wind Rivers, an outlier protruding into the high plains to the east and south, contains all but a few of Wyoming's highest peaks.

The uplift that created the Wind Rivers resembled a wave breaking from east to west, so the eastern flank rises in long slopes that obscure the high peaks. The rise is more abrupt on the west side, and views are better. Most conspicuous are the massive west faces of Fremont Peak, Mt. Sacagawea, and Mt. Helen. Fremont, Sacagawea, and Helen rise above five-mile-long Titcomb Basin, a valley graced by a string of lakes and

Wind River Mountains and surroundings. (A) Wind River Mountains. (B) Wind River. (C) Lander. (D) Pinedale. (E) Green River. (F) Wyoming Mountains. (H) Grand Teton. (I) Jackson Hole. (J) Absaroka Range. (1) Gannett Peak. (2) Titcomb Basin. (3) Elkhart Park. (4) Cirque of the Towers. *Background image: Google and TerraMetrics*

Titcomb Basin and surroundings. (A) Titcomb Lakes. (B) Island Lake. (C) Lower Jean Lake. (D) Upper Jean Lake. (E) Indian Basin. (1) Stroud Peak. (2) Mt. Arrowhed. (3) Henderson Peak. (4) Gannett Peak. (5) Mt. Woodrow Wilson. (6) The Sphinx. (7) Mt. Helen. (8) Mt. Sacagawea. (9) Fremont Peak. (10) Jackson Peak. (11) Ellingwood Peak. *Background image: USDA Farm Service Agency*

drained by a stream that tumbles into Island Lake. The view from the lowlands has much to do with Titcomb Basin's rich history, the Titcomb peak's prominence enhanced by their all but hiding 13,804-foot Gannett Peak, Wyoming's high point.

The west-side rise is interrupted, at 10,000 to 10,500 feet, by a six-mile-wide terrace that distances the Wind Rivers from civilization and contributes to the modesty of the range's fame. Sprinkled with lakes and meadows and situated near treeline, the terrace adds much to the Wind Rivers' charm. With streams having carved cirques back toward the Divide, the standard base camp sites are at this elevation. Island Lake sits at 10,346 feet.

We can characterize the northern half of the Wind Rivers as alpine, the southern half as rock. The focal point of the southern end is the Cirque of the Towers, with such household names as Pingora and Wolf's Head along its jagged rim. Just south of the Cirque lies Haystack, with the Wind Rivers' densest concentration of rock routes, and just north are the range's biggest walls—on Hooker, Cathedral, Ambush, and Raid.

The focal points of the northern half are the glaciers surrounding Gannett, east of the Divide, and Titcomb Basin, west of the Divide. In Titcomb Basin, as throughout the American West, alpinism can mean as little as using an ice axe on a descent from a Grade IV rock route. It can also mean serious ice climbing, and it can mean climbing a mountain because its summit seems a worthy goal. We can most simply define Titcomb Basin's alpinism as variety of opportunity.

Fremont (13,745'), the range's second highest peak and Wyoming's third (after the Grand Teton), offers a scramble, a long snow couloir, nondescript 5.2-5.7 routes, and several Grade

IV rock routes. Sacagawea (13,569) has a 1,000-foot west face—two, since its south summit has its own face. Helen (13,620), unlike the many one-sided Wind River formations, is a real mountain, its complex architecture including three towers. Tower 1 is of particular interest to climbers, featuring the area's biggest wall and sheltering the Wind Rivers' premier ice climb.

At the head of Titcomb Basin stands elegant Mt. Woodrow Wilson (13,502). Woodrow Wilson offers climbers little besides elegance. But its sidekick, the Sphinx (13,258), is spicier, as sidekicks often are. To their east the pass variously known as Dinwoody and Bonney connects the basin with Dinwoody Glacier to the north.

Titcomb Basin is bounded to the west by the Titcomb Needles, damned with faint praise by Robert Underhill after climbing several: "The most that can be said for them is that they offer a very pleasant bit of exercise under mildly exposed conditions." Rising behind the Needles, however, is a classic three-ridge pyramid, Henderson Peak (13,115).

When we say Titcomb Basin, we mean Titcomb Basin and/or Indian Basin. Indian Basin has much to offer, though it lacks Titcomb Basin's big west faces. Its south side is dominated by Ellingwood Peak (13,052), with its north arête unlikely to be overlooked by a climber. Maps call the peak Harrower, but the name Ellingwood was established by climbers decades ago.

At the head of Indian Basin is Knife Point Mountain (13,001), whose skyline more resembles a saw blade than a dagger. North of Knife Point, between it and Jackson Peak (13,517), is Indian Pass (12,120+), a prehistoric Divide crossing reached by a trail. They say you can see evidence of prehistoric trail construction, but I only see evidence of rockfall. Indian Pass connects Indian Basin with the Bull Lake Glaciers: Knife Point, Upper and Lower Fremont, Sacagawea, and Helen. Lapping high on the east sides of their eponymous peaks, the glaciers limit climbing interest on that side, except for ice couloirs on Jackson.

## THE ROCK:

While Cirque rock is famously good granite, Titcomb's is more enigmatic. If Cirque rock is vanilla ice cream in its uniformity, Titcomb rock is many flavored, including various swirly concoctions. Most of the northern Wind Rivers is gneiss—metamorphic rock, which didn't crystallize from melt but was formed when rock below the surface was subjected to such high temperatures and pressures that it softened and flowed like chocolate in a warm pack. Titcomb's gneiss was there when granite intruded, but the emplacement of granite didn't occur as cleanly as a geologic map suggests. The magma melted nearby gneiss, further

Mark Jenkins cragging on Elephant's Foot. *Ken Driese*

metamorphosing and deforming it. Magma flowed into cracks; gneissic chunks dropped into the granitic soup. The resulting mix, called migmatite, is prominent throughout much of the northern Wind Rivers.

Geologists have described Wind River migmatite as "alternating dark and light stripes," swirling around in complex patterns," "layers…stretched and separated by flowage into lenses, wisps, and streaks," "swirly and chaotic." Different geologic maps characterize the same rock as gneiss, granite, and migmatite. Despite its lack of homogeneity, the granite-gneiss mix of Titcomb area rock is hardly inferior to Pingora granite. It's just more interesting.

## NINETEENTH-CENTURY SURVEYORS:

In 1842 a young Army engineer took a steamboat up the Missouri River, sent to survey the wagon road not yet called the Oregon Trail. Also aboard was a Rocky Mountain trapper who had returned to civilization after 16 years in the West. But after a few days in St. Louis, he had grown "tired of the settlements." Thus John C. Fremont met Kit Carson. Fremont, who later ran for president as "The Pathfinder," hired Carson as scout, adding him to a party of other experienced trappers.

Fremont's cartographer and artist was an impoverished German immigrant named Charles Preuss. Preuss never let his gratitude for the job stand between him and his disdain for the West and the man who dragged him through it. His diary, published as *Exploring with Fremont,* is a foil to Fremont's rosy *Report of the Exploring Expedition to the Rocky Mountains in the Year 1842.* Some of Preuss's entries are terse: "Murky weather, melancholy mood." Others are more detailed: "For breakfast, yesterday's dish was warmed up; it did not taste excellent"; "Had a remarkably bad night… the others lay safely under their [mosquito] nets; mine had been forgotten because of Fremont's negligence." Preuss sensed "a certain tension, not only between Fremont and myself, but also between me and the rest of the people. Only, of course, because I want to be smarter than the others."

Here is Preuss approaching the Wind Rivers:

Whoever has seen Switzerland and expects something similar here is bound for a great disappointment. An American has measured them to be as high as 25,000 feet. I'll be hanged if they are half as high, yea, if they are 8,000 feet high.

Fremont's mountain veterans were of the opinion that the Wind Rivers included the highest peak in the Rockies. According to Fremont, the height of this peak "had been a theme of constant discussion." There was, therefore, enthusiasm for getting a barometer to the top.

With 15 men on mules, Fremont led his entourage toward the high peaks of Titcomb Basin. The peaks suddenly came into view as "a gigantic disorder of enormous masses, and a savage sublimity of naked rock, in wonderful contrast with innumerable green spots of a rich floral beauty, shut up in their stern recesses." The going became rocky, so three men

One of many sketches of the first ascent of Fremont Peak, in 1842, as imagined by an artist back east.

stayed with the mules while the others proceeded on foot. Their intended peak appeared so close that, expecting to climb it and return the same day, they took little clothing and no food—except Preuss: "Only I, a more experienced mountaineer, stuck a piece of dried buffalo meat in my pocket."

Summit of Fremont's peak in real life. The Hayden Survey party in 1878 during the U.S. Geological and Geographic Survey of the Territories. *W.H. Jackson*

The next few miles are frustrating even for a modern backpacker, who should recognize the terrain described by Fremont:

> The first ridge hid a succession of others; and when with great fatigue and difficulty we had climbed up five hundred feet, it was but to make an equal descent on the other side…. We clambered on, always expecting, with every ridge that we crossed, to reach the foot of the peaks, and always disappointed, until…pretty well worn out, we reached the shore of a little lake, in which there was a rocky island.

Thus the name Island Lake. The men made what camp their scant provisions allowed on a bluff overlooking Island Lake, near the falls that drop from Titcomb Basin. Fremont's notes suggest he suffered from altitude more than most, and the wind and cold of the dinnerless, blanketless bivouac didn't improve his condition. As for Preuss, "as always, the best spots were already taken…and I can truthfully say that I did not sleep a single minute."

The next day was not a success. Fremont became progressively sicker and eventually could go no farther. Two trappers became ill and lay down on rocks. Preuss, trying to cross snow, slipped and fell a few hundred feet into rocks, where he "turned a couple of somersets" but suffered only minor bruises. Carson climbed the peak to the right of their objective but couldn't cross to the main peak and didn't consider the ascent, apparently of Jackson Peak, worth mention in his autobiography.

Men had gone back for mules, blankets, and food, and the second night at Island Lake was more comfortable than the first. Fremont, planning to leave the mountains in the morning, sent Carson out at dawn. But the remaining six men felt well enough for another try at their peak and headed up "a defile of the most rugged mountains known," probably Titcomb Basin, though it could have been Indian Basin. In either they would have been "riding along the huge wall which forms the central summits of the chain…terminating 2,000 to 3,000 feet above… in a serrated line of broken, jagged cones" and encountered "three small lakes of a green color, each of perhaps a thousand yards in diameter."

Halfway up, Fremont changed from thick-soled moccasins to a thinner pair, "as now the use of our toes became necessary to a further advance." Upon reaching the crest he "sprang upon the summit, and another step would have precipitated me into an immense snow field five hundred feet below."

The victorious climbers rammed a pole into a crevice, attached the American flag, and admired the setting:

> Around us, the whole scene had one main striking feature, which was that of terrible convulsion. Parallel to its length, the ridge was split into chasms and fissures; between which rose the thin lofty walls, terminated with slender minarets and columns. A stillness the most profound and a terrible solitude forced themselves constantly on the mind as the great features of the place.

Fremont's barometer indicated an elevation of 13,570 feet, remarkably close to the 13,745 feet on current maps. Preuss had guessed that the barometer readings "will probably correspond to almost 10,000 feet."

Preuss's diary entries after the climb suggest he was well pleased with the ascent. His one complaint is that Fremont didn't give him time to make measurements and that "when the time comes for me to make my map in Washington, he will more than regret this unwise haste."

Fremont's wife Jessie polished his journals for publication, adding much flair, but these may have been his own reflections as he left the summit:

> We had accomplished an object of laudable ambition, and beyond the strict order of our instructions. We had climbed the loftiest peak of the Rocky mountains, and looked down upon the snow a thousand feet below, and, standing where never human foot had stood before, felt the exultation of first explorers.

Fremont planting the flag on "the highest peak of the Rocky Mountains" (Fremont's Peak) from Memoir of the Life and Public Services of John Charles Frémont, 1856, as published in Appalachia Vol. XIX. *American Alpine Club Library*

Thirty years later Americans still knew little about the interior West, but four government survey parties were filling in the map. With vaguely defined domains, their leaders, Powell, King, Wheeler, and Hayden, scrambled around Washington for funding. Art attracted Congress's attention, and the surveys competed not only for turf but for artists, the most sought-after being painter Thomas Moran, photographer William Henry Jackson, and sketcher William Henry Holmes.

Ferdinand Vandiveer Hayden wandered through Colorado and Wyoming, investigating whatever interested him. Summer 1877 found Hayden's men in the Wind Rivers. A.D. Wilson, with two companions, "started for the point I then took to be Fremont's Peak." They reached the point but found themselves on 11,857-foot Mt. Baldy.

Wilson returned in 1878, bringing Jackson and Holmes to depict the landscape. They found Fremont Peak, and a group that included Wilson,

Jackson, Holmes, and Hayden climbed it. A Holmes sketch catches a triangulation team at work on Fremont's summit, with (according to its caption) a "snow capped peak north of Fremont's" visible in the background. Wilson's report and map give no hint that the surveyors found this Rum Doodle to be higher. They were establishing a triangulation network across the West, and were sighting lines to Wind River Peak (the one 13,000er in the southern half of the range) and the Grand Teton. By 1906, when that snow-capped peak was determined to be nearly 60 feet higher than Fremont, the four surveys had been consolidated as the U.S. Geological Survey, its Chief Geographer being Henry Gannett, for whom the peak was named. Nevertheless, the topographic map published in 1906 is the Fremont Peak quadrangle.

## TWENTIETH CENTURY CLIMBING:

In 1924 and 1926, Albert Ellingwood, a Colorado professor, visited the area. As a Rhodes Scholar, Ellingwood had climbed in England's Lake District and learned how to use a rope. In Colorado, in 1920, he led the first ascent of Lizard Head, in the Sangre de Cristo, perhaps then the hardest climb in America. In 1923 he made the first ascents of the Middle and South Tetons. He must have been the first climber to bring a rope to Titcomb Basin and must also have been the first of many prominent climbers who achieved renown elsewhere but parenthetically left their mark in the Titcomb area. In 1924, with Carl Blaurock and Herman Buhl (though not that one), he climbed Mt. Helen from the east and, with Buhl and Buhl's wife, the Northeast Ridge of Fremont, the first non-Southwest Slope ascent. Two years later, with various partners (or not) he climbed Helen from Titcomb Basin, Sacagawea, Knife Point, and the peak we call Ellingwood.

In 1927 Kenneth Henderson visited Dinwoody Glacier and, though he did not climb, was left with "the distinct impression that here was to be found one of the best climbing centers in the United States." He returned two years later with Robert Underhill and Henry Hall. Henderson and Underhill were becoming well known for ascents in the Tetons: East Ridge, Underhill Ridge, and North Ridge of the Grand, and the first ascent of Mt. Owen.

They climbed most everything around Dinwoody Glacier, including Gannett by its north face, the Triple Traverse of Warren, Doublet, and Dinwoody, and the Sphinx. On their last day, after traversing the Sphinx, they considered continuing to Woodrow Wilson before thinking better of it. *Appalachia* was at that time the journal of record for the Wind Rivers, and in 1932 and 1933 Henderson published long articles that may be considered the range's first guidebook.

At this time another noteworthy name appears in Wind River history: Paul Petzoldt, who a few years earlier had conceived the notion of guiding people up the Grand Teton. In 1931 Petzoldt and Gustav and Theodore Koven made the first ascents of American Legion Peak and Mt. Arrowhead, presumably from Jean Lakes.

Joe Kelsey on Ellingwood's North Arête. *Joe Kelsey Collection*

Chris Landry during a first ascent on the complex west face of Fremont in 1976. *Michael Kennedy*

Henderson returned to Titcomb Basin in 1936 with a mob, and Underhill and his wife Miriam returned in 1939. While their accomplishments lacked the significance of their earlier climbs, Henderson did get his mob up the peak now named for him.

Hans Kraus, the pioneer of numerous early Gunks classics, visited Titcomb Basin in 1945 and 1946, climbing Woodrow Wilson's South Face, the Sphinx's Southeast Ridge, and Helen's Tower Ridge—routes that not only were harder than earlier routes but two of which still qualify as classics.

After 1946 the Cirque of the Towers, 30 miles southeast, began making headlines, which helps explain Titcomb's disappearance from whatever radar the Wind Rivers have ever been subjected to. For the next two decades Titcomb Basin was not unvisited but was not where standards were being advanced.

This left a venue with such opportunities for pioneering that it inevitably attracted Fred Beckey, who made his first appearance in 1969, with Pat Callis. Sacagawea's south summit has a west face distinct from the main peak's west face, and Beckey and Callis climbed it. They also climbed the Red Tower, between Fremont's west face and southwest slope. And the North Arête of Ellingwood, though Beckey later got the worst news possible for him: that Bob Bauman, in 1967, had soloed the arête. Also on the 1969 trip, Beckey and Callis detoured to Mt. Arrowhead, which, while it doesn't overlook Titcomb Basin, has a south face often in sight during the hike to Island Lake. They climbed the first of the four routes now on the face.

In the 1970s the ripples created by Yosemite's Golden Age were spreading farther from the Valley, and Titcomb saw a flurry of activity. In 1976 Beckey, Bill Lahr, and Craig Mortinson climbed Fremont's West Buttress (now IV 5.10) and the west face of Helen's Tower 1 (V 5.10 A2). Also in 1976 Michael Kennedy and Chris Landry climbed routes on Fremont's west face (IV 5.10) and the west face of Sacagawea's main peak (III 5.9). In 1977 Landry soloed a dihedral (IV 5.9 A1) between those two Fremont routes. Also in 1977 Carla Firey and Jim M. McCarthy climbed a III 5.9 route to the left of the other Fremont west face routes.

Meanwhile, in 1971 Ray Jacquot and Bill Lindberg climbed the Wind Rivers' answer to the Grand's Black Ice Couloir (also first climbed by Jacquot): Helen's Tower 1 Gully.

There remained opportunity for a straighter line on the area's biggest wall, the west face of Tower 1. Such a line was climbed in 1981, in 11 pitches, by Greg Collins and Mike Keough—still the area's only 5.11.

## GETTING THERE AND BEING THERE:

The 12-mile hike to Island Lake begins at Elkhart Park, 14 miles of paved road from the town of Pinedale. Elkhart Park's elevation of 9,380 feet implies a gain of a mere 1,000 feet to Island Lake, which sounds too good to be true. It is too good to be true: you gain and lose those thousand feet repeatedly. The initial five miles are efficient but not scenic and bring you to the first view of the mountains, at Photographers' Point, where hikers reflexively reach for cameras and snacks. From here the trail is inefficient but scenic, as you bob up and down past many lakes before meeting the Highline Trail, coming from the south. The Highline, the Wind Rivers' answer to the Sierra's John Muir Trail, parallels the crest for 65 miles from Big Sandy Opening to Green River Lakes and coincides briefly with the Island Lake Trail before continuing north. If you've been admiring Arrowhead and its neighbors during the hike and want a closer look, follow the Highline to the Jean Lakes.

Joe Kelsey with his two golden retrievers following Mark Jenkins to Titcomb Basin in 2011. *Ken Driese*

The Island Lake Trail ascends one final rise, to what may be the classic Wind River view: lake in foreground, peaks beyond. Unless you're of stouter heart than many of us, you may be tempted to drop your pack just before the lake. There are two reasons not to: the campsites are overused, and whatever you plan to climb is farther along. If you continue another mile, rounding Island Lake, you come to the junction of the Titcomb Basin and Indian Basin trails.

The Wind Rivers offer the most luxurious campsites of any range I know. Most lie at an elevation between 10,000 and 11,000 feet, and at the Titcomb-Indian junction you can see idyllic campsites all around. During midsummer there are likely to be tents in some of these spots, and you may think this must be the place to camp. It isn't. Wilderness regulations specify that campsites be 200 feet from trails and lakes and 100 feet from creeks, but also consider privacy. In the Cirque I've seen climbers leave in the morning camped in seclusion and return to find themselves in a Zuccotti Park of tents. You can see many excellent unoccupied sites from the junction, plus there are even better ones you can't see, behind knolls, across creeks. If campers spread out, Titcomb Basin can accommodate a large number without feeling crowded.

Camping near the Titcomb-Indian junction is as good as it gets, and the day's hike from Elkhart Park may be all that most of us have in us. But if your plans include Helen, Woodrow Wilson, the Sphinx, or Dinwoody/Bonney Pass, beware of that scoundrel, foreshortening. Upper Titcomb Basin, close as it may look, is five miles away and nearly 1,000 feet higher. While upper Titcomb is austere tundra compared to Island Lake, its camping offers all the amenities. Indian Basin is much the same once you climb for half a mile from the junction, though its geography is more convoluted and its campsites more sporadic than Titcomb's.

The hospitable environment of Titcomb and Indian Basins confers the obligation on us to minimize our impact. If you're coming from certain climber-infested habitats, the

Wind Rivers may seem pristine, but they aren't. I won't reiterate the obvious misuses that trash a meadow, but I will deplore the heaving around of rocks. Rocks are inanimate objects, and there is no shortage in Titcomb Basin. But evidence has been accumulating that the main cause of deterioration of mountain meadows is campers rearranging rocks. Why move rocks? Wind River turf

New West meets Old West on the Island Lake Trail. Many climbers horsepack their gear into the Wind River Mountains. Horse-packing lets you converse rather than grunt. *Ken Driese*

takes tent stakes as well as need be; experiment before positioning your tent. Wind breaks are another unnecessary engineering feat. Despite the range's name, the Wind Rivers are no windier than other mountains of the Rockies. When situating a campsite, look for natural windbreaks, such as boulders and tree clusters.

Campfires aren't allowed above 10,000 feet, but a better reason for not making a fire at Island Lake is that every branch in reach was stripped long ago from the sparse trees. It is even more unconscionable to consume this even scarcer resource near the Titcomb-Indian Basin junction. In the upper basins your ethics are spared a trial: the nearest tree is miles away.

Your goal should be to leave a campsite looking like no one had camped there.

## ANYTHING LEFT TO DO?

After Mark Jenkins returned from his 2011 trip to the Titcomb Basin, during which he climbed new routes on Fremont and Sacagawea (see Climbs & Expeditions pages 105-110), we had an e-mail exchange that went something like this:

*Kelsey: Good job! I hope you appreciate the context in which you did those routes. The Wind Rivers are climbed out, and cool people climb only in the Cirque and at Deep Lake. But there you were in the heart of the range, on two of the most significant peaks.*

*Jenkins: You're joking about the Winds being "climbed out," aren't you? There are at least twenty routes on the East Face of Longs Peak, and there are many walls like it throughout the Winds. Half of the faces and spires of [redacted] remain unclimbed. There are dozens of 10-pitch+ routes left in the [redacted] valley, not to mention routes deeper in this watershed near the Continental Divide. What's more, many routes have yet to go free. Comparing the Winds with Yosemite Valley, there are lifetimes worth of new route potential.*

*Kelsey: In 1970, my 2nd trip to the Cirque, on the way in I passed Beckey on his way out. He'd gone to do a new route on Warbonnet, failed to find a route worth trying, and declared the Cirque "climbed out." He didn't know why people went there any more, maybe to have a good time. So, yes, I'm kidding, or at least mimicking pundits. While reminding myself to be sure my*

Top left: Oliver Deshler on pitch 8 during the first ascent of Dark Side of the Moon, west face of Fremont Peak. Below: Deshler on the 5.10 traverse on Dark Side of the Moon. *Mark Jenkins* (2) Top right: Joe Kelsey cragging in Indian Basin. *Ken Driese*

*writings don't imply an end to any Golden Age.*

*Your "deeper in the watershed" of [redacted] Creek is intriguing country— the wildest I know of in the Lower 48—and I encourage you to poke your nose farther into it, even if your routes are never repeated. Just having routes there would add to our connection with the Wind Rivers. Presumably you haven't even contemplated the [redacted] area yet.*

I've had a mantra for would-be new-routers: remote, unknown, without a prominent summit. This takes you away from the Cirque of the Towers, where adventure is diminished by popularity. But Jenkins' adventures on two of the range's most conspicuous faces, leading to prominent summits, has me revising my mantra to include peaks that have spent a generation out of the news.

The quest for the undone may be motivated by lust for renown, but, as Beckey

Chris Landry on a first ascent on the west face of Fremont in 1976. *Michael Kennedy*

conjectured, climbers do go to the Wind Rivers for a good time, not fame, and reporting is less rigorous than in more prestigious ranges. The concept of a new route depends on your definition of new. Reading reports in the *AAJ*, you get the impression that you haven't climbed something new in the Wind Rivers unless you discover fixed gear. (See Chris Barlow's Ambush report on page 108.)

You may suspect a cadre of insiders is keeping secrets. Not that I know of, and I think of myself as a historian. I've been as mystified by fixed gear as anyone, most memorably far from Titcomb Basin, near the south end of the range. In 1967 Beckey and Bob Stevenson climbed a formation they named Continental Tower. A next-door neighbor was shrouded in literary silence, so Paul Horton and I climbed it, via a five-pitch arête that led to a shoulder a few hundred feet from the top. I led a pitch, and Paul began a final one. Halfway up, he muttered unintelligibly.

"What?" I yelled up.

Bill Thompson on Ellingwood's 60° but continuously exposed North Arête.
Joe Kelsey

"A piton!" A pre-Chouinard, soft-iron piton, then another. On the summit was a cellophane bread wrapper, not preserving well a note that once must have given first ascent data, and three more trusty rusties, obviously rappel anchors.

I hoped my *AAJ* report would flush the culprits from hiding, but it didn't. The signatories of the ink-smeared pulp will achieve no recognition beyond the guidebook notation "FA: Unknown," no reward beyond memories. Far from disappointing me, our mysterious predecessors enhanced my experience—not quite up to finding a mummy on an "unclimbed" Andean volcano, but adding another dimension to our adventure.

Don't let the discovery of artifacts ruin your day. Measure not the virginity of your line but its quality and the pleasure of a day in the mountains.

The best you can do toward learning what has been climbed is to refer to my guidebook, to the *AAJ* (where occasional Wind River routes qualify for inclusion among "The World's Most Significant Climbs"), and the Internet. The scattered climbers who visit the Wind Rivers gather at such on-line sites as Mountainproject.com. Like the Internet in general, Mountainproject democratizes significance, with 5.7s standing proudly beside 5.12s.

To ascertain what has not been climbed, try the old-fashioned way: go look. The best way to find new route possibilities halfway around the world may involve research, but the best way to find a line that needs climbing in your neighborhood Wind Rivers is to seek adventure. If you spot an alluring line, and a new route happens, we'll look for your report. But even if you come upon a fixed stopper 10 feet from the top, you'll have had your adventure. I know of eight new routes done in 2011, of which six ascend rock pictured in the guidebook. The photos may show the best-known features in the range, but they show a tiny fraction of the possibilities.

To my knowledge there is only one bolt in Titcomb and Indian Basins. This scarcity can be attributed to the character of the rock, the backpack of 12-plus miles, or the outlawing of power drills in designated Wilderness. But the most important factor is climbers' reverence for the precious commodity of wilderness.

Although these may be good enough reasons for not bolting, it's worth considering that "fixed anchors" (bolts and rappel anchors) in National Forest Wilderness have been a sensitive issue. Promiscuous bolting could give the Forest Service cause to revisit fixed anchors. Climbers have been working with the Forest Service to devise a reasonable Wilderness climbing policy. Among points of the proposed policy are these: Climbing that doesn't rely on fixed anchors should be the norm. Fixed anchors are appropriate only where necessary for rappelling and no other safe means of descent is available. (No bolted rap routes simply for convenience.) This proposal reflects the attitude of nearly all Wind River climbers.

Perhaps we can define wilderness as a place where we are free to place bolts, but we refrain because it is wilderness.

Time doesn't hurry by in Titcomb Basin, and 1995 seems only a few years ago. Lorna Corson, Norm Larson, Paul Horton, and I went to Indian Basin to check out a presumably untouched formation. On Ellingwood's east ridge was a tower called Notch Pinnacle, which had been climbed a few times, and farther along another tower, unnamed, unmentioned, and perhaps overlooked. Notch Pinnacle and its neighbor stand as proudly free as several of the Cirque's towers, so it seemed a certifiable summit. Until its real name revealed itself, we referred to it as Not Notch Pinnacle.

The one reasonable line looked nice, worthwhile whether unclimbed or swarmed over by humanity. And it was nice: seven pitches, all 5.6 or 5.7, all with personality. I arrived last at the top, where Norm was already wrapping webbing around the only block suitable for a rappel anchor, and asked, "Any evidence?" My friends shook their heads. The evidence that a peak has not been climbed is never as conclusive as evidence that a peak has been climbed, but the absence of a cairn, of soggy paper crammed in a rusty tobacco tin, and of a wind-frayed, rodent-gnawed, sun-bleached remnant of rappel webbing made us as certain as we could be of being first. It isn't a summit from which you'd descend without rappelling.

No sooner had we shrugged off our ropes and racks in camp than Norm insisted that Not Notch Pinnacle was not a name. So we warmed ourselves with soup and vetoed suggestions. We looked at our formation, hoping to follow the tradition that has given the range Bear's Tooth, Camel's Hump, Shark's Nose, and Wolf's Head, but no one could see so much as an anteater's snout. Paul, who had been listening more than participating, then undid an hour's effort by wondering, "What's wrong with Not Notch Pinnacle?"

Will anyone be so lucky again? I can't say, but I can say that within sight of a few of the Titcomb area peaks is a significant formation, apparently unclimbed, whose existence only a few are aware of.

There are other Not Notch Pinnacles in the lives of men.

## NOTES, SOME PERSONAL, ON INTERESTING ROUTES:

*Ellingwood Peak, North Arête (III 5.6).* The most popular rock route in the area. Ellingwood's north and east faces intersect at a 60° arête, visible in profile from as far away as Pinedale. Notwithstanding its solo first ascent, its 1,500 feet are continuously exposed, and most climbers remain roped. A topo would be superfluous; you flow wherever looks best.

The descent of the class 4 Southwest Ridge takes time but is clean and preferable to any of the class 3 northwest-facing couloirs.

Ellingwood Peak and its neighbors, showing: (1) North Arête of Not Notch Pinnacle, 5.7 (Corson-Horton-Kelsey-Larson, 1995). (2) North Gully of Notch Pinnacle, 5.2-5.4 + Ice (Ramer-Thompson-Toombes [year unknown]) (3) North Arête of Ellingwood Peak, 5.6 (Bauman, 1967). The Southwest Ridge is the right skyline. *Joe Kelsey*

*Not Notch Pinnacle (III 5.7).* I am skeptical of a first ascent team's claim that their route is a classic. But when I am the first ascent team's spokesman, I am more credulous.

    The route deserves a better descent than ours. A rappel from an obvious horn a few feet from the summit gets you down 200 feet, but that takes you to several hundred feet of class 3 zigzagging through rubble that precludes rappelling. I reoxygenated when I finally found a solid block a ropelength above terra firma.

*Knife Point Mountain, Northwest Ridge (II 5.4).* The El Dorado of the Wind Rivers is "Another Wolf's Head"—a jagged crest like Wolf's Head's East Ridge, in the Cirque of the Towers, which features two-foot-wide, hideously exposed gangplanks and garish gendarmes circumvented by improbable horizontal cracks. Knife Point's Northwest Ridge, with its mile of shaggy silhouette, was a candidate, but as Another Wolf's Head, it fails to provoke the terror and pessimism we crave. Most of Knife Point's obstacles are too easily bypassed, and the cruxes involve downclimbing their backsides.

*Jackson Peak, North Couloirs (III 50° Ice).* There is little to differentiate two broad icy couloirs, both seven pitches, both 50°, both perhaps too wide to be called couloirs. When Jack Clinton and I went to climb one or the other late one September, they were guarded by impassable bergschrunds, so we climbed a narrow couloir between the two.

*Fremont Peak, Southwest Slope (I class 3).* A hiker's way up a well-known peak. You can reach the 11,840-foot saddle at the base of the slope from Titcomb Basin's Mistake Lake or Indian Basin's Lake 11,008, the former being more obvious, the latter far pleasanter. Routefinding up the slope is confounded by overabundant cairns.

Fremont Peak is the main summit. To its right is Jackson Peak. (1) West Face Spire, 5.10 (Kennedy-Landry, 1976). (2) West Face Dihedral, 5.9 A1 (Landry, 1977). (3) Dark Side of the Moon, 5.10 (Deshler-Jenkins, 2011). (4) West Buttress, 5.10 (Beckey-Lahr-Martinson, 1976; FFA Hansen-Toombes, 1980. (5) Red Tower, 5.6 (Beckey-Callis, 1969). (6) Red Tower Arête, 5.10 (Jenkins, 2011). (7) Southwest Slope, class 3 (Fremont et al., 1842). *Joe Kelsey*

*Fremont Peak, Five-Finger Couloir (II Snow).* A worthy way up Wyoming's third highest peak, the Five-Finger Couloir helps identify Fremont from as far south as the Cirque, but it can't be seen from the Indian Basin approach till you are beneath it. South-facing is not propitious for a snow route, but the couloir is inset deep enough to minimize direct sun. One of the five fingers into which the couloir branches deposits you at the very summit.

*Fremont Peak, West Buttress (IV 5.10).* This rib, separating the steep west face and gentle southwest slope, is Fremont's most prominent architectural feature and therefore the most obvious of the more difficult objectives.

*Fremont Peak, West Face Dihedral (IV 5.9 A1).* The west face is split by a particularly straight corner, so this route is easy to identify. We often note an aid rating attached to a route description and read no further. However, if you read the fine print—here quoting Chris Landry in the 1978 *AAJ*—it may say something like "a small amount of aid was used." If you crave significance, a FFA awaits.

*Mt. Sacagawea, West Face Right (III 5.9).* The most ambitious trip I've made to Titcomb Basin turned out to be the wettest. On our best day we squeezed in Sacagawea's West Face between three thunderstorms. While I focused on the sky, I did note a nice route underfoot. After you scramble unroped for a surprising distance, there are four pitches on the face. You then step around the face's right edge and are surprised to find four challenging pitches right of the edge.

The view southeast from Mt. Woodrow Wilson. (A) Mt. Helen. (B) Tower 1. (C) Jackson Peak, with ice climb visible. (D) Mt. Sacagawea. (E) Fremont Peak. (1) Northwest Face Right Gully (Bell-Carpenter-Haun, 1960). (2) La Mirada de la Gitana, M6 5.8 Al 3 (Pope-Tapley, 2010). (3) Tower 1 Gully, AI 3+ (Jacquot-Lindberg, 1971). (4) Northwest Ridge, 5.8 A1 (Hannibal-Turville-Wheeler, 1971). (5) West Face Left, 5.11a (Collins-Kehoe, 1981). (6) West Face Center, 5.10 A2 (Beckey-Lahr-Martinson, 1976). *Joe Kelsey*

Mt. Sacagawea, showing: (1) Indian Paintbrush, 5.10 (Deshler-Jenkins, 2011). (2) West Face Right, 5.9 (Kennedy-Landry, 1976, (3) South Summit, West Face (left: Black-Toombes-Wilson, 1976; right: Eggen, 1976). *Joe Kelsey*

*Mt. Helen, Tower Ridge (III 5.7).* The first half of Hans Kraus's route, which ascends Tower 1, mixes class 3, class 4, and easy class 5 so haphazardly as to be indescribable in terms of pitches. Bypassing Towers 2 and 3 requires either routefinding acumen or luck. I've heard of several ways up the summit tower, some 5.6 and some 5.7. Hurrying to beat an impending storm, we found a 5.8 way.

Helen, being a real mountain, involves a real descent: a few hundred feet down a class 4 ridge, Sacagawea Glacier, and interminable rubble. I was exhausted by the end of the day, with increased respect for the leather-booted, shoulder-belaying pioneers.

*Mt. Helen, Tower 1 Gully (IV WI 3+).* To anyone who has descended south from Dinwoody/ Bonney Pass, Tower 1 Gully needs no introduction. You only need reassurance that its steepness is only 60°. From the top of the gully, you can continue via Tower Ridge to the summit or work your way down from the south side of the Tower 1 col.

*Mt. Warren, Triple Traverse (III class 5).* Mt. Warren (13,722) does not quite overlook Titcomb Basin, but its satellites Doublet and Dinwoody do, and a traverse of the three, beginning with Warren, inaugurated by Henderson and Underhill, is one of the few traditional Wind River traverses. While usually done from Dinwoody Glacier, it is feasible from upper Titcomb, by way of Helen Glacier.

*Gannett Peak via Dinwoody/Bonney Pass.* Gannett is reached by the same effort from the range's west side (Elkhart Park) as from the east side (Trail Lake). However, success is far more frequent from the east. The reason must be that hiking in from the east, you get the ups

(A) Tower 1. (B) Tower 2. (C) Mt. Helen. (1) West Face Left, 5.11a (Collins-Kehoe, 1981). (2) West Face Center, 5.10 A2 (Beckey-Lahr-Martinson, 1976). (3) Tower Ridge (Kraus-Wolcott, 1946). *Joe Kelsey*

and downs out of the way during the hike in, not on the summit day. To climb Gannett from an 11,000-foot camp in upper Titcomb Basin, you hike up snow or global-warming scree to 12,800+-foot Dinwoody/Bonney Pass, then descend Dinwoody Glacier to 11,600 feet or worse, before climbing 13,802-foot Gannett—and then retrace your steps.

A classic way to traverse the range involves backpacking in from Trail Lake, climbing Gannett, crossing Dinwoody/Bonney Pass, and hiking (and perhaps peak bagging) through Titcomb Basin and out to Elkhart Park.

*The Sphinx, Southeast Ridge (III 5.7+).* Hans Kraus often asked Jim McCarthy why he didn't climb Kraus's routes when he was in the Wind Rivers. So in 1994 Jim and Laura McCarthy, Dick DuMais, and I climbed the Sphinx. The account of Kraus's first ascent devotes what seemed disproportionate attention to five "digits." I didn't know whether to treat the digits as quaint or worrisome, since the view from Titcomb Basin shows the ridge rising in two steps, separated by a horizontal break.

The lower step begins with a difficult little headwall. The route, and history, was marked by a Kraus-vintage piton. I climbed to the piton, clipped it as communion, placed a nut for safety, and found no holds. I heard Kraus's gentlemanly voice in the piton telling me that if he could climb it, I could, but I eventually climbed a crack off left, surely not the 1945 way. Jim later reminded me that in those days European free climbing included holding and stepping on pitons; this, the piton's voice neglected to mention. The lower step ends in one of those magical 5.0 pitches. This one ascends a steep face 10 feet wide, with monstrous drops to Sphinx Glacier on one side and Dinwoody Glacier on the other, over rock studded with door knobs and split by an irregular crack.

From the top of the lower step, the digits reveal themselves. The view from Titcomb

Laura McCarthy, Dick DuMais, and Jim McCarthy descending the Sphinx Glacier in 1994, with Titcomb Basin below. *Joe Kelsey*

Basin turns out to be like the view of your hand when you hold it palm-sideways. From a distance it appears that you simply climb the thumb, then the index finger. Now, seeing the ridge's upper section differently, we saw a gauntlet of five or more gendarmes, some separated by thin cracks, some by wider gaps. I passed the thumb high on its left side, but the left side of the next digit overhangs, so I traversed under its right side, then climbed the crack separating it from the digit beyond. We spent a few hours passing digits to the left, to the right, climbing cracks between them, reaching digit tips, and descending to notches.

*Henderson Peak, North Ridge (II class 4).* When I scrambled up American Legion Peak, the north ridge of Henderson Peak looked exceptionally fine, though I hadn't heard of it being climbed. Paul Horton and I approached from the Jean Lakes side, no doubt more hassle-free than a Titcomb-side approach. We came equipped for 5th class climbing. We never used the rope but, always expecting to, kept it handy. The ridge is solid, exposed, and often improbable. There are moves that could be rated easy 5th, but they are invariably just above ledges. While climbers tend to agree about a harder route's quality, our assessment of easier routes is far less consistent. Consider this subjectivity as I say that this is my all-time favorite route I've done unroped.

In the summit register were two entries recording previous ascents of the North Ridge, but there was also Kenneth Henderson's signature, dated 1936.

*G-17, Northwest Ridge (III 5.9).* When the northern Wind Rivers were first mapped, the surveyors designated peaks by a letter and numeral. G was the letter in the upper Green River drainage. The worthier peaks eventually acquired names, so that G-9 became Arrowhead and G-15 became Henderson. The peaks retaining G designations might suggest Karakoram grandeur, but actually they were the least interesting. However, a summit at the end of a spur extending from Henderson, while not of topographic significance, offers a climb of interest.

Paul Horton and Dick Olmstead first climbed the Northwest Ridge. Paul wanted to show me their route and wanted to lead

Bev Boynton on the Arrowhead's South Face original (Beckey-Callis) route (5.8). *Joe Kelsey*

Paul Horton near top of G-17's airy Southwest Ridge (5.9).
Joe Kelsey

the first pitch. This continuous pitch was unquestionably the crux, which was the problem. I led 20 feet of the second pitch, after which the route disintegrated into scrambling, until the top few hundred feet, which involved minimal fifth class on an extremely airy edge.

While I wouldn't declare the route a classic, it was a good day on rock, even if my memories of the difficult first pitch and airy but easy top pitches are as if from different climbs.

*Arrowhead, South Face (II-III 5.7-5.8).* Arrowhead's southern aspect faces just the way we rock refugees like. Moreover, the arrow is fluted, and the south face is scored by numerous systems. There are four routes, all on good rock, with not much to distinguish one from another. Might as well make the approach and decide which to climb while you change into rock shoes at the tarn at the base.

Mt. Arrowhead, showing: (1) South Face Left, 5.7 (Horton-Horton-Lang-Stolp, 2000). (2) South Face Left Center, 5.8 (Beckey-Callis, 1969). (3) South Face Right Center, 5.8 (Chouinard-Jenkins, 2001). (4) South Face Right, 5.7 (Horton-Olmstead, 1980). *Joe Kelsey*

In the old days, Wind River route names were not a problem: you climbed a south face and called your route the South Face. When there was a second route, the guidebook resorted to South Face Left and South Face Right. Four routes, however, overwhelm the system, and it may be too late to rectify. They could be the Beckey-Callis, Horton-Olmstead, Chouinard-Jenkins, and Horton-Horton-Lang-Stolp, but I am an egalitarian, and it pains me when such names are condensed to "the Beckey Route" or "the Chouinard Route," giving the more famous all the credit.

*Stroud Peak, Southeast Ridge (I class 2).* My favorite Wind River walk-up. The ideal is all grass and bedrock, no boulders or rubble, and Stroud's Southeast Ridge comes close to this ideal. Plus the view is vertiginous enough that you can imagine you've reached a significant summit.

The antediluvian definition of class 2 included "proper footwear advised." Class 2 also prescribed "occasional use of hands for balance," in contrast to class 3, where "handholds and footholds are used." I didn't originally expect to write a guidebook, and when I was compiling the first edition, I couldn't remember whether, during my peak-bagging rambles, I'd used my hands for balance or prehensily. But I could remember which peaks my golden retrievers had summited, so I differentiated class 2 and 3 according to my dogs' successes and failures. I snuck the dog-possible criterion into the introduction, supposing that no one reads introductions, forgetting that on rainy, tentbound days climbers are starved for entertainment and read anything. My definition became the most cited passage in the book. Dogs can't do Stroud's summit block, but I credit mine with an ascent because they get close enough to not whine at being abandoned.

*Cragging.* No one hikes to Island Lake and beyond for one-pitch routes or toproping. However, most Wind River cirques offer splendid cragging for days when the rain stops at 10 a.m.. Two hidden crannies in the Titcomb area are worth mentioning. At Mistake Lake, on a bench above the Titcomb Lakes, is a slab not overly challenging but great for instruction. Under Elephant Head, reached by valleys from either Island Lake or Indian Basin, is a collection of one-pitch cliffs: Elephant's Foot, of course.

A BRIEF NOTE ABOUT THE AUTHOR:

*Joe Kelsey was born two years after the first ascent of Henderson Peak and first tied a bowline around his waist in 1962, in the Gunks. Since 1972 he has based his Wind River excursions from a primitive cabin in Jackson Hole, also his base when guiding for Exum for 20 years. He winters in Bishop, California, at the base of some other mountains.*

*The third edition of his guidebook is due out in Spring 2013.*

Joe Kelsey and Mark Jenkins at Photographer's Point. *Ken Driese*

# THE SHARK'S FIN REDUX

*Success at last on Meru Central's spectacular Shark's Fin, India.*

JIMMY CHIN

Meru from Tapovan basecamp, showing the long-attempted and finally completed route on the eastern prow on Meru Central, a.k.a. The Shark's Fin. *Jimmy Chin*

The last move was merely a mantle: hands on the edge of a sharp granite ledge, a heel hook, and a press. When I pulled over the lip, I looked around, momentarily confused that there was nothing more to climb. I was sure there had to be one more obstacle, one more aid seam, one more mixed pitch, but there was only sky and swirling clouds. I stared in disbelief.

October 2 is Mahatma Gandhi's birthday, an auspicious day in India. Last year it was the day that Conrad Anker, Renan Ozturk, and I finally reached the 6,310-meter summit of the Shark's Fin, otherwise known as Meru Central. This was Conrad's third attempt on the Shark's Fin's infamous northeast buttress, and Renan's and my second.

Renan Ozturk leading on the alpine ridge. *Jimmy Chin*

Three years earlier the three of us battled for 19 days on the same route. The iconic mountain seemed intent to haze us. We were constantly humbled by the sustained nature and the diversity of its hard climbing. We also grossly underestimated how cold it would be on the northeast-facing wall. Despite weathering a weeklong storm low on the route and rationing eight days of food into 19, we pushed to within two pitches of the summit. We could see it, yet it felt far away. To push on would have required us to spend the night out, and we had already stepped far over the line. We knew that in our state we would not make it. We felt shattered, physically and emotionally, as we rappelled through the night to our hanging high camp.

Conrad's personal history with the Shark's Fin—the climber's nickname for Meru Central's blade of granite, deep in the Indian Garhwal—goes back decades. Of the peak's 25-plus attempts over the last 25 years, two were by Mugs Stump, Conrad's mentor as a climber and as a person. Mugs showed Conrad the ropes, literally and metaphorically, and this was his dream climb. Mugs died in a crevasse fall in 1992 in Alaska. Conrad wanted nothing more than to finish the route for his friend.

The Russian soloist Valery Babanov became the first to summit, in September of 2001. Babanov estimated that 15 attempts had failed before his success, including one of his own the previous spring. During his aborted attempt he'd been following the same line we climbed, up the prominent northeastern prow, but he turned back at 5,800m. In September he chose a completely different line, far to the right on the ice face (see his feature article in the 2002 *AAJ*).

Conrad's first attempt on the northeast prow came in 2003, with Doug Chabot and Bruce Miller. They attempted it in alpine style, climbing the bottom portion of the prow proper before exiting into ice flutings right of the main wall. Unconsolidated snow turned them back halfway up.

Five years later Conrad recruited Renan and me for his next attempt. The main formation, he told me, featured a long alpine climb capped by an overhanging big wall that was steep enough to BASE jump.

Renan Ozturk at the new "Center of the Universe" high camp. *Jimmy Chin*

The route was perversely stacked against alpinists, since the most technical climbing, which required the heaviest gear, was near the top. All alpine-style attempts on this line up the main face had failed at nearly the same spot, the base of the overhanging headwall that starts at roughly 5,900 meters. Conrad knew the climb would require the skills of a big wall climber as well as those of an alpinist.

After failing in 2008, we returned to our normal lives haunted by those two unclimbed pitches. Yet they were a blessing. They provided motivation, and despite telling ourselves that climbing 98 percent of the route should be good enough, we obsessed privately about the unfinished pitches.

In 2009 Silvo Karo contacted Conrad about the climb. Conrad shared everything he knew, including beta on the best style to climb it in. We hoped Silvo's team would succeed. But when Silvo didn't make it, Conrad called with the news. It was clear that we all wanted to return.

Conrad, the consummate professional, had really good notes from his first two attempts. We pored over them in preparation for the next expedition, strategizing every detail down to who would lead what pitches, how we could do it faster, lighter, and in better style. In the end we chose a hybrid alpine/capsule style. We took four ropes (two lead, two static); two haul bags; a portaledge; one stove; alpine, mixed, and aid gear; sleeping bags; and food for eight days.

Back on the route, we climbed in 48 hours what had taken us six days in 2008. Over the following few days we took advantage of an ideal cold-and-dry high pressure system. At the overhanging wall (we dubbed it the Indian Ocean Wall), which we reached after four more days of climbing, we saved time by linking aid pitches we'd done separately on our first attempt. We had a fright when one of the portaledge's bars snapped in half, but creative splinting with ice screws saved the day. Reflecting on how prior knowledge had helped our planning, we joked about our alpine redpoint attempt, how we'd fallen right at the chains but were going to send on this go. Despite the humor, doubt clouded us every day as we reclimbed tenuous A4 and hard mixed.

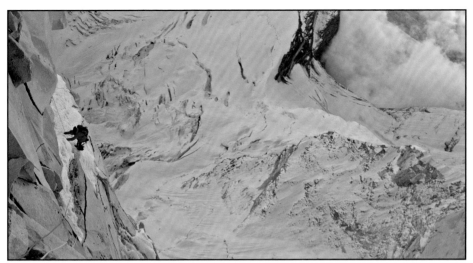

*Renan Ozturk on mixed ground. Jimmy Chin*

On the eve of our summit bid, our charmed weather broke, and it blew hard and snowed. The wind bounced our portaledge against the wall, reminding us of the days we spent stuck on the wall in 2008. We hunkered down hoping for the best. At midnight we looked out and saw stars. It was time. Launching at 2 a.m., we flew up our two fixed lines, from which Conrad led the poorly protected mixed pitch below the summit ridgeline. The force of Conrad's will had carried us in 2008, and it carried us again in 2011.

When we pulled over the ridge, we were blessed by the sun. At last we could face the final two pitches. The Gangotri Glacier shone far below. It was my lead, and I scrapped my way up, literally humping the knife-edge ridge to gain ground. After mixed climbing and 50 feet of aid, I built an anchor. Conrad came up and belayed me as Renan jugged the line below. Another 5.8 pitch, a simple mantle, and we were there.

We embraced on the summit, humbly accepting that this time Meru had allowed us passage. Our dream, Mug's dream, had been realized.

*A note from Renan Ozturk: Our 2008 near-miss was the most trying expedition of our lives. We understood that if we returned it would be with the same team. But five months before our 2011 departure, on a ski-mountaineering shoot with Jimmy, I caught an edge and tumbled off a cliff in the Jackson, Wyoming, side-country. My injuries included an open skull fracture, two fractured vertebra in my neck, as well as a severed vertebral artery. Jimmy responded fast and probably saved my life. Conrad arrived in the intensive care unit shortly after. Despite the odds, and to the horror of friends and family, I returned to Meru with the team. Having lost half the blood supply to my brain, I wasn't sure how I would do at altitude. It would have been easy for Conrad and Jimmy to find a strong partner to replace me, but they stuck with me. I really wanted to go back to be part of Conrad's two-decade dream and Jimmy and Conrad's 10-year partnership. The expedition had moved beyond climbing a mountain; it became the epitome of loyalty and trust between friends, partners, and mentors.*

Renan Ozturk belaying Conrad on the "Mugs Stump Pitch," three pitches from the summit. *Jimmy Chin*

SUMMARY:

Area: Garhwal Himalaya, India.

Ascent: *The Shark's Fin* on 6,310m Meru Central (VII, 5.10 A4 M6 WI5) by Conrad Anker, Jimmy Chin, and Renan Ozturk. They reached the summit on October 2, 2011, during a 12-day push. An estimated 25 attempts have been made on this wall since the early 1980s, including three by this expedition's members in the previous seven years. Reports on Anker and team's previous attempts can be read in *AAJ 2004* (pg 378) and *AAJ 2009* (pg 309). The 1993 British expedition led by Paul Pritchard coined the name The Shark Fin (no apostrophe) for the east pillar of then-unclimbed Meru Central.

Jimmy Chin, Renan Ozturk, and Conrad Anker on the summit at last. *Jimmy Chin*

A NOTE ABOUT THE AUTHOR:

*Jimmy Chin, from Victor, Idaho, is one of today's most successful expedition photographers. His skills as a cameraman, climber, and explorer have won him numerous awards, including National Geographic's Emerging Explorers Grant. He has made first ascents and difficult crossings on most continents and has skied Mt. Everest from the summit.*

# On Darwin's Edge

*The first complete traverse of the Cordillera Darwin, Tierra del Fuego, Chile.*

Didier Jourdain

*"Three hundred days of storm and the other 65 not pleasant."*
– Alberto De Agostini, *describing the Cordillera Darwin Range after his 1913 attempt on Mt. Sarmiento.*

*"You are raving mad to consider crossing the cordillera in its entirety."*
– Steve Ogle, *who attempted to cross the Darwin Range in 2008.*

Descending from the ridge near the end of the trip provided a good view of Darwin's complex mixture of mountains, glaciers, and sea. *GMHM*

The rare stories of those who'd been to the Darwin Range had the flavor of Homeric tales: impenetrable fogs, 200 kilometers per hour wind gusts that lift you from the earth as if with an invisible hand, virgin summits everywhere, massive glaciers tumbling into the sea, permanent rain, sketch maps all wildly different. In short, a perfect labyrinth.

Various teams over the last decades have made brief forays into the range, in order to pick off one peak or another, even to traverse the range crosswise. But to attempt a lengthwise crossing—some 130 kilometers as the crow flies—would be a different animal altogether. So we prepared according to three axioms. First, be as light as possible, because weight is time.

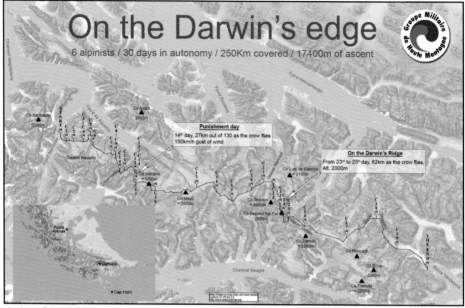

The line of the complete Cordillera Darwin traverse. *GMHM*

Second, know all that's possible to know, because so much will still be unknown. Third, train to move in bad weather, because no matter how wretched the conditions, how soaked and frozen our bodies, we must still pack and move every morning.

After some testing we determined that the maximum weight we could drag would be 75 kilograms per person. Considering the weight of the equipment, this meant we could carry 35 days of food and 40 days of stove fuel. We would not take any spare equipment—no extra skis, rope, or stove.

A drop test into a crevasse with the sleds revealed that we'd need to be at least three on a rope in order to stop the fall. So the expedition needed six people: two parties of three. Each member would know the others well and have extensive experience in cold, technical, unfamiliar places. We were from the *Group Militaire de Haute Montagne*, or, in English, the French Military High Mountain Team, a corps of soldier-experts in mountaineering and arctic conditions.

After reviewing all existing maps, it appeared that the Google Earth topo was the most accurate, although lacking in detail. The only paper map dates from 1954 and has a 1:250,000 scale, which doesn't work for navigating.

THE EXPEDITION:

After a last meal in Punta Arenas, an old fishing boat takes us toward the Cordillera Darwin. But the wind is already toying with us, the sea rages, and we are unable to cross the Strait of Magellan. After a forced landing, the next day we make it across the strait and into the maze of fjords that lead to our starting point at the west end of the Cordillera Darwin, near Mt. Sarmiento.

September 6. It's snowing as the boat drops us off with sad farewells. The sailors are disturbed about leaving us here in the land of the wind, the realm of the devil. As we say goodbye, everyone, climbers and sailors, feels a pinch in his heart, a tear in his eye.

Now the boat is gone. It's snowing. We are in the middle of nowhere.

But the weather on our second day is beautiful! Could Darwin's reputation be exaggerated? Sarmiento hovers above the sea. Everywhere massive glaciers cascade into the sea. From here to the horizon is a succession of spectacular, unknown peaks. It looks like one Mont Blanc range after another. With our feet on the glacier, we establish our strategy: one team will go forward to find the way, while the other brings up the gear and installs camp.

We seem to have picked the right season, as the snow is made to order, and we step into our skis a mere 200 meters above the sea. But three days in we learn that the weather is not a myth. Despite our plan to make progress each day, we're unable to move the camp. To make matters worse, one of our two satellite phones malfunctions. We no longer have a connection between teams.

The next day is a little better, and we move camp to the end of the previous recon and make a new one. At nightfall we discover an unexpected ramp on a wall that leads past the final serac barrier and onto the next glacier. Without this ramp we might have been stuck, as there seems to be no other possibility.

Thus far we have been moving terribly slowly as the crow flies. We're covering distance, but it's rarely in the direction we want to go.

The next day we suffer the fury of the wind as we plow through deep snow. Come morning we can barely exit the tents. However, we are developing a rhythm. Our evening routines repeat themselves: find the best snow patch, build a wall, raise the tents, prepare the food bag, take off shoes, remove snow from the tents, de-ice clothes and harnesses, melt and heat water, mop up clothes, dry clothes on our bodies, drink, eat, prepare the sleeping bags, arrange clothes and sacks to protect them while we sleep, prepare the next GPS track, load the GPS, mop, sleep. In the morning we resume our rituals: remove hoarfrost, melt snow, the bags, the shoes, the tents.... The repetition helps. Everything is done for a reason; we must forget nothing. Despite the storms, each morning we get out and go.

By the sixth day we have made only 10 straight-line kilometers of the 125 we must make. On the seventh we do a little better, but weather difficulties increase. More snow, increasing avalanche danger. The day's leader is especially stressed. Despite the weather he must find a passage through the crevasses, the snow slopes, the seracs, and the cliffs.

On the ninth day, in the pouring rain, we reach "Green Valley" the only place during the traverse that we're off glaciers. It was the first obvious objective on the map, 20 straight-line kilometers into the journey, and we're happy to reach it. And yet we're really late, and this bothers us.

As we continue over increasingly snow-loaded, avalanche-prone slopes without picking up

A new discipline: sled alpinism. *GMHM*

In the heart of Darwin: 20kg on the back and 40 in the sled, with fresh snow and strong headwinds. *GMHM*

speed, morale plummets. We are moving so slowly. There are too many difficulties, too many recons.

On the twelfth day a storm surprises us just after wevleave the bivy. We try to push on but are forced back, desperate to find our old campsite. A mere 200 meters from camp, and we still can't find it because of the wind and the whiteout. To survive we spend two hours digging a hole we can barely crouch in. But the snow still creeps in, and we are soaked. What to do? For how long will we have to stay here? We can't spend the night in these conditions. The situation is becoming critical. We feel near the end. The virtue of that snow cave is that we can now talk together and try to make the right decision.

Eventually the wind weakens and we walk 50 meters, where we find a flat enough spot to pitch the tents. It takes all six people to erect each tent. Will they hold? I've never had so much wind slamming against my tent—maybe in excess of 150 kilometers per hour. Continuing the next day would be insane, and this proves to be the only day that we spend tentbound. Even so, it is hard to rest in such a violent wind.

It took three days to cross the ridge between Mt. Shipton and Mt. Darwin, the route's long-anticipated crux. *GMHM*

The next day we leave despite the wind. We are 14 days into 35 days of supplies. We've consumed roughly one third of our food but have traveled only one fifth of the required distance. At this rate we can't complete the crossing. It's difficult to believe in our chances, but we aren't giving up.

The glaciers grow larger and easier to follow as we approach the central Cordillera, which we reach on day 16. Still, we're rationing food to make it last 40 days, just in case.

After crossing the dangerous maze of the

Marinelli Glacier on day 20, we're faced with the most technically difficult part of the expedition, the thin ridge linking Mt. Shipton (ca 2,600m) and Mt. Darwin (ca 2,400m). For three days we walk a tightrope while dragging sleds above the void. From the start our strategy has been to not attempt any peaks. It is a hard rule for a climber as he passes mere meters beneath virgin summits, but we value each second of good weather. Nevertheless, with clouds obscuring the view, we have to stick to the crest of the ridge, which takes us over the virgin summits of Mt. Gines (2,022m) and Mt. Beyond the Far (2,026m). While planning we had wondered if we could traverse that ridge, and it feels like one of my best days in the mountains when we finally descend from the ridge to the Darwin Glacier. We did it!

Setting up camp on Punishment Day required all six people on each tent in turn. The hardest part was maintaining confidence. *GMHM*

More glaciers, passes, storms, and finally moraines, and we're walking on grass again. Oh, the birds! Soon we're dining on grilled beef that our new friend, José, prepares for us. José, the only inhabitant of Darwin, hunts feral cows and horses from an old farm. His goal is to make this place completely wild again, so he rides his horse for a few days into the mountains and hunts with a lasso, bringing the animals down alive and selling them as meat to fishing boats.

Jose, the only inhabitant on the big island of Tierra del Fuego seemed a man from another time. *GMHM*

During the three days we spend waiting for a boat, we feel lost between two worlds, between two eras. This gradual return to civilization is good for us, and we're grateful to this man from another time.

In our memories this journey has been like one long day of 30, with rare moments of clear weather revealing the spectacle of Darwin: splendid, ephemeral, and barely known.

## A few words about the GMHM:

Created in 1976, the *Groupe Militaire de Haute Montagne* (GMHM) is composed of 10 alpinists, all mountain guides or aspirants. Our mission, as stated in our 2002 charter, is to "Explore the domain of extreme physical and climatic conditions on land." This generic mission can be broken down into three secondary missions: communication, experimentation, and, especially, advising the French Army.

Recruiting is done inside the armed forces but also outside for recruiting privates at the beginning of their careers. We are currently three officers, four NCOs, and three privates. Most of us stay a long time in the GMHM, so we can improve our skills and also because of the team spirit that is our strength. We're based in Chamonix at the Military High Mountain School, or EHMH.

Though we're soldiers, we're not commandos. We aren't engaged in conflicts during our stint in the GMHM, though we're part of the 27th Brigade of the Mountain Infantry, which is engaged each winter in Afghanistan. Several members of the GMHM served in the Mountain Commandos, but our GMHM role is only to advise and to train.

There are only two other countries with Military High Mountain Teams: Italy and Spain. Those teams are not structured like the GMHM, nor do they have the means and stability to carry out projects like ours, though they have made some impressive ascents. Other countries sometimes organize military mountaineering teams for a particular expedition. A few countries are thinking about creating their own GMHM.

The GMHM's first big climbing accomplishment was the second winter ascent of the Harlin Direct on the Eiger in 1978. From there the team (with changing personnel) went on to make the only free-solo ascent of the American Direct on the West Face of the Drus (Christophe Profit), numerous first ascents in the Himalaya (Nepal, India, Pakistan, China), reach six summits above 8,000m, including Everest without oxygen (1993), carry out unsupported expeditions to the North Pole (1996) and South Pole (1999), accomplish a speed-climbing record on Aconcagua (1992), and climb over 100 new or important routes in the Alps. In 2010 we completed a five-year challenge intended to demonstrate our versatility. It included climbing expeditions to Mali, Patagonia, New Zealand, Greenland, Canada, the Indian Himalaya, and Antarctica.

SUMMARY:

Area: Cordillera Darwin, Tierra del Fuego, Chile.

The GMHM team at the end, on October 5 (clockwise from top left): Lionel Albrieux, Dimitry Munoz, Sebastien Ratel, Didier Jourdain, Sebastien Bohin, François Savary. *GMHM*

Expedition: The first lengthwise traverse of the Cordillera Darwin lasted 30 days, 26 of which were roped and 22 in bad weather, with temperatures down to –25°C. It covered 130km linearly, but at least 250km on the ground, with 17,400 meters of vertical gain.

*The six team members were Captain Lionel Albrieux, Chief Warrant Officer Sébastien Bohin, Lieutenant Didier Jourdain, Mr. Dimitry Munoz, Corporal Sébastien Ratel, Staff Sergeant François Savary. Support base in France: Captain Jean-Yves Igonenc. Logistical support in Chile: Guillermo Cratcley Klenner.*

# CERRO TORRE REBOOTED

*Forty-two years ago much of the climbing world exploded in rage when
400 bolts were added to an icon. This year it exploded again when many
of those bolts were removed. Have we learned anything?*

KELLY CORDES

Cerro Torre and lenticular clouds in January, 2012. *Peter von Gaza*

In one week last January, the most beautiful spire in the world saw two historic ascents. It
also experienced more controversy than it had since 1970. What happened?

On January 16, Hayden Kennedy and Jason Kruk made the long-awaited first
"fair means" ascent of Cerro Torre's southeast ridge—eschewing the use of the hundreds of
progression bolts that had been placed in 1970 with a gas-powered compressor. A few days
later, Austrian climbers David Lama and Peter Ortner also climbed the southeast ridge, also
by fair means, with Lama freeing the route via a two and one-half pitch variation to Kennedy
and Kruk's line (which included short sections of aid). These ascents were universally lauded.

The controversy erupted because on their descent Kennedy and Kruk removed 120 bolts
from the "Compressor Route," including all the progression bolts on the headwall (they left the
anchors in place, reasoning that the alternative would become a rat's nest of webbing, pitons,
and nuts). In a few hours, the most popular route on the mountain was gone. Kennedy and

Kruk were threatened with violence, online warriors called them every conceivable name, a prominent Italian blogger compared them to the Taliban, and the police in El Chalten briefly detained them—in part, they said, to protect the climbers from harm (an angry mob had assembled around their rental apartment in town).

Nobody could have imagined this in 1968, when the southeast ridge was first attempted. Martin Boysen, Mick Burke, Pete Crew, Jose Luis Fonrouge, and Dougal Haston reached a highpoint halfway up the peak, connecting natural features without placing a single bolt. The turning point came two years later, when Italian climber Cesare Maestri placed more than 200 bolts just to equal the 1968 Argentine-British highpoint.

Maestri continued, retreating some 60 meters below the top (Steve Brewer and Jim Bridwell completed the route to the summit in 1979). He left behind his 300-pound compressor and a trail of 400 bolts.

This wasn't a matter of different standards for a different era; Maestri's antics were globally decried at the time. The use of bolts was and still is generally accepted for connecting otherwise un-protectable features. Indeed, both of the 2012 "fair means" ascents used several in-situ bolts placed during previous attempts by other parties. These multiple alternatives weave near the Compressor Route to connect natural features, features that Maestri could have used. But he chose to bolt his way up blank rock instead. That's what few climbers have defended, even in 1970.

Most climbers revere the beautiful places we venture; we respect the mountains we love. So why the controversy over removing the bolts?

One of the most strongly held views was that Kennedy and Kruk had "erased history." But how is this possible? Hasn't the removal of the bolts in fact added a new chapter to history?

Others called it vandalism. But is vandalism placing hundreds of unnecessary bolts, or is it removing them?

Many complained that they'd dreamed of summiting Cerro Torre, and now it was out of reach. But does any of us have an inalienable right to summit anything? Does the notion of personal impossibility threaten or inspire us?

Emotions flared over what is "fair." If anyone is free to place a bolt, does that leave anyone free to remove it?

Many have said that only "locals" have the right to erase a route by chopping its bolts. But who is a local in a place where international climbers have written all aspects of a mountain's history? Should the default be to leave a contentious installation or to remove it, especially when the latter is far closer to the mountain's original, non-controversial state?

Regardless of one's views on the bolt removal, this much is fact: The southeast ridge of Cerro Torre is cleaner than it has been since 1970. And this much is also fact: Last January, young climbers left their mark on one of the world's legendary peaks. Here are their stories.

A NOTE ABOUT THE AUTHOR:

*Kelly Cordes has been the* AAJ's *senior editor for 12 years. His 2007 link-up of the south face and the west ridge of Cerro Torre was a feature article in the 2007* AAJ, *written by his partner, Colin Haley. Cordes is writing a book about Cerro Torre and its 2012 de-bolting.*

# BY FAIR MEANS

*The first ascent of the southeast ridge of Cerro Torre without Maestri's bolts.*

M y mind twists in anticipation. The night is clear, and the Torres have become monsters. The moonlight provides just enough light to see the mushrooms at their tops, but the spires themselves are consumed by darkness.

The Torres rule at the top of the food chain in technical alpine climbing. They require a large skill set, from ice to mixed to snow-tunneling to steep rock. They serve it all in one heaping helping. Our goal is the southeast ridge of Cerro Torre without using Maestri's bolts for protection, while climbing as free as can be. Jason Kruk and Chris Geisler came close in late January 2011 but were shut down 40 meters below the top of the headwall. While Jason now knows the terrain up to there, those 40 unknown meters loom in our minds as if they were 1,000.

Yesterday, January 11, Jason and I left base camp at a leisurely 8 a.m. We climbed the mixed initial 300 meters of the southeast ridge to the Col of Patience slowly, trying to conserve energy for the rest

Cerro Torre's east face: (1) Bridwell-Brewer, 1979 / Alimonta-Claus-Maestri, 1970. (2) Mabboni-Salvaterra, 1999. (3) Lama-Ortner, 2012. (4) Smith-Wharton, 2007. (5) Kennedy-Kruk, 2012. (6) Anglo-Argentine highpoint, 1968. (7) Geisler-Kruk, 2011. Lines and info courtesy PataClimb.com. *Rolando Garibotti*

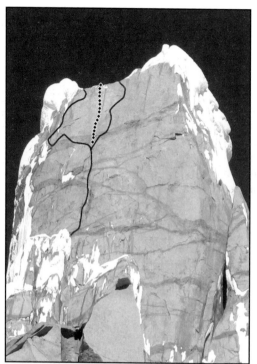

Telephoto view of Cerro Torre's headwall, showing Kennedy-Kruk on the left, the de-bolted Compressor Route in the middle, and Lama-Ortner on the right. *Rolando Garibotti*

of the route. We climbed in T-shirts under a perfectly clear sky, with unreal views of the east face, feeling pretty small below the Patagonian giants. Arriving at the col with plenty of time to rest, we set up our bivy tent to escape the mid-day heat. We planned to rest at the col and start as early as possible on the ridge proper, to give ourselves plenty of time on the headwall. As the day progressed we packed our bags, hardly able to wait to get involved with the serious climbing.

And then the alarm rings, and we are brewing coffee. The night is clear, cold, and windless. At 2:30 a.m. I start leading, short-fixing as Jason jumars. I enjoy climbing in the dark, because you can only see what your headlamp illuminates, and there is nothing else on your mind. But with the rising sun comes even more psych and speed.

By first light I've led about 10 pitches to the base of the Salvattera Variation, which avoids the first of Maestri's bolts (the 90-meter bolt traverse) by climbing a fantastic knifeblade seam at A1. The aid goes fast, and the next three pitches are marvelous face climbing on the edge of the world. With the vast south face just to the left and the equally vast east face just to the right, it's one of the coolest places I've been.

We stop at the base of the ice towers to regroup. Jason leads the ice and mixed terrain fast, placing little gear and short-fixing. From our previous climbs we know that he is the better ice/mixed climber, while I'm better on rock. The leader's job here is to get the rope up as fast as possible; the follower's job is jumaring with the pack and dealing with the rope.

Toward the end of the ice towers another bolt ladder leads to the base of the headwall, but in 2007 Josh Wharton and Zack Smith found an ice pitch that trumps most I have ever seen. It's long and steep, with the monstrous south face right below. Jason leads the pitch placing just a handful of screws, as I admire the Fitz Roy group in the morning light.

The fire is burning deep as we reach the base of the headwall at 10 a.m. We see the line of bolts that have desecrated this remarkable peak. Looking past the bolts, we begin climbing the headwall's natural features. Long flake systems make the climbing fun and athletic, but still spicy. I lead two 40-meter pitches at mid-5.11 to a ledge right in the middle of the headwall. From here bolt ladders take steep blank rock, so Jason and I forge our own path. I trend left on 5.11+ crimps and flakes to a short section of thin A1, after which we reach a bolt placed by Geisler last year.

I clip the bolt and do a "king swing" pendulum to the left side of the headwall. Here Jason and I are on new terrain. The rock quality has changed from flaky to Yosemite-buffed, a nice contrast. The next two pitches are outrageous, with incredible exposure, amazing 5.11+ face climbing, and short sections of aid due to icy cracks. I reach the top of the headwall and yell into the wind. This is our dream come true. We race to the summit and unrope for the summit mushroom. Standing on top of Cerro Torre, we are speechless. The Torres have given Jason and me much more than just a few summit photos, they have given us so much more.

Jason Kruk during the first "fair means" ascent of Cerro Torre's southeast ridge.
*Hayden Kennedy*

I think everyone has read enough about what Jason and I did on the descent. It was what we wanted to do, end of story. There is no right or wrong in this complicated controversy. Alpine climbing is an art form; therefore, people can interpret it as they wish. We chopped 120 of Maestri's bolts on the headwall in an effort to restore Cerro Torre to a more natural state. We had the right to remove the bolts, just as Maestri had the right to put them in.

Standing on Maestri's compressor during the descent. The machine is still bolted to the headwall 42 years after it was left there.
*Hayden Kennedy*

Summary:

Area: Chalten Massif, Argentine Patagonia.

Ascent: The first complete ascent of the southeast ridge of Cerro Torre without using Cesare Maestri's bolts for protection on the Compressor Route, on January 16, 2012. Hayden Kennedy and Jason Kruk climbed four new pitches (5.11+); otherwise they followed the Compressor Route and variations established by Mauro Mabboni and Ermanno Salvaterra in 1999, Zack Smith and Josh Wharton in 2007, and Chris Geisler and Kruk in 2011. (The Savaterra variation follows the first two pitches of the 1968 Anglo-American attempt.) In its entirety the route is now simply known as the Southeast Ridge. During their descent, Kennedy and Kruk chopped 120 of Maestri's bolts from the headwall.

A Note about the Author:

*Hayden Kennedy, 22, grew up in and still bases out of Carbondale, Colorado, near where he led his first multi-pitch climb, Castleton Tower, at the age of 13 with his father Michael Kennedy. That climb launched a passion that has already taken him to most of the world's continents.*

# CERRO TORRE FREE

*By an accident of timing, the long-coveted first free ascent of the southeast ridge of Cerro Torre takes place without Maestri's bolts as protection.*

DAVID LAMA

David Lama on Cerro Torre's headwall during his free ascent. *Lincoln Else-ASP Red Bull*

I returned to El Chalten on January 12. My goal of free-climbing Cerro Torre's southeast ridge hadn't changed, but over the past few years I have changed quite a bit, and so had the way I looked at my project.

To be honest, I had no idea of what was ahead of me when, in 2008, I came up with the plan. I was sitting in Chile's Cochamó Valley looking at a photo of Cerro Torre's headwall and thought, "I want to free-climb this peak." It was not like I didn't know anything about climbing. I had won several World Cup competitions and onsighted routes to 8b+. Nor was it as if I had no idea about alpine climbing. I had put up new routes in the Alps and been on a few expeditions. But I had a lot more to learn before my dream of free-climbing the Torre would come true.

My first attempt came in 2010. It was a tough year. After Patagonia's fierce winds blew me off the tower before I could summit, I was faced with a lot of criticism. The film crew that was with me had placed bolts, and their fixed lines could not be removed due to the bad weather. It took me a while to come around to my own opinion, and the discussion got out of hand. I'm not usually the kind of guy who listens much to what others say about me, but I felt that I had made a mistake.

A year later I was back in El Chalten. Despite the critique, I didn't want to give up my dream of free-climbing the southeast ridge. The film crew was with me again but this time with no bolts or fixed lines. We cleaned up everything from before. (In 2010 Argentineans removed most of the gear, while Rolo Garibotti took out most of the added bolts.) My partner, Peter Ortner, and I climbed three peaks: Aguja de la S, Cerro Poincenot, and, at the end of our trip, the Compressor Route on Cerro Torre with aid.

We arrived in Patagonia in January 2012 to the baffling inverse of everything I'd experienced before: sunshine, no wind, no rain, and no snow. It was a little surreal. If I hadn't constantly checked weather maps before arriving, I would have been shocked.

Peter, my close friend and partner from last year, joined me again. As we were walking along the road, talking about free-climbing the Torre, I knew he was as confident about our endeavor as I was. Nothing would stop us this time.

A few days before we started our attempt, we heard that Hayden and Jason had chopped most of Maestri's bolts from the headwall on the Compressor Route. This would not make free-climbing the route easier, but we were still confident. We brought a few more nuts and pitons, but it didn't otherwise affect our rack. We revised our strategy, though. Our original plan had been to climb from Niponino, the first camp, to the Col of Patience, bivy there, and climb the route the next day in a single push. Instead, for safety, we decided to climb to the Col on our first day, rest for a few hours, continue to the start of the ice towers, bivy there, and climb to the summit the next morning.

At 3 a.m. on January 20, we started from Niponino. We made good progress and reached the Col of Patience at 7:30 a.m. and rested. Peter and I had climbed from the Col to the bolt

David Lama belaying on the headwall during his free ascent. *Lincoln Else-ASP Red Bull*

traverse numerous times already. On one attempt last year the conditions were so bad that the first two pitches took us nearly two hours, and after seven hours we gave up. This time the conditions were great, and it only took three hours to reach Maestri's traverse, a line of bolts that traverses right across a blank granite wall for three pitches. There's no way to free climb this section, so I had to find a variation to the left, on the southeast ridge. After a couple of big falls on the arête left of the Salvaterra crack, I began to doubt that this section would ever go free. But I tried again—what else could I do? There is no other way up. Two more attempts (and falls) later, I figured out the sequence and sent the pitch from the belay. A few pitches higher we reached the ice towers, where we picked a small ledge on an icefield to bivy.

We crawled into our sleeping bags and sat. After a long night we started again at 6 a.m., swinging leads through the ice towers. At 9 a.m. we found ourselves at the beginning of the headwall. I put on my climbing shoes and started the first pitch. Not really difficult but demanding because of loose flakes. For two more pitches we followed Maestri's line. Then I diverged to new terrain that led the last pitch, which was probably the most difficult to protect. At first I climbed five meters straight up. There I could place some good cams and traverse right. After 10 meters I placed another good cam and climbed straight up again, into very run-out terrain. From time to time I tried to place gear, but I didn't trust it. Ten meters below the summit icefield I placed a piton (it's still there), two nuts, and a cam, which I tied together with a sling. That construction might have held a fall, but I sure didn't want to test it. I climbed onto big, loose blocks to reach crimps that led to the summit icefield. Peter and I climbed the mushroom to the very top. After 24 hours of climbing, we began to rappel down.

I have been asked a lot about rating the route, but a free ascent of Cerro Torre's southeast ridge goes far beyond grades. Everybody who has been there knows what I mean, and I think that's all that has to be said. For me this project has been a personal milestone and an emotional adventure. The experiences and memories I take from Cerro Torre are more valuable than all the other things that have happened in my climbing life so far.

SUMMARY:

Area: Chalten Massif, Argentine Patagonia.

Ascent: The first free ascent of the southeast ridge of Cerro Torre, by David Lama and Peter Ortner, summiting on January 20, 2012. They followed most of the variations to the Compressor Route taken by Kennedy-Kruk (January 12, 2012), with two new pitches on the headwall. Lama feels a route like this is beyond rating, but elsewhere he has estimated 5.13b.

David Lama. *Corey Rich-ASP Red Bull*

ABOUT NOTE ABOUT THE AUTHOR:

*David Lama, 22, was born to an Austrian mother and a Nepali father. His talent as a climber was first spotted at age 5, by Peter Habeler, who took him under his wing. A few years later he started climbing competitively and won World Cup competitions. He then turned to alpinism, including first ascents in the Alps and the Himalaya.*

# VENAS AZULES

*An ice climber's dream line reveals itself on the south face of Torre Egger, Patagonia.*

BJØRN-EIVIND AARTUN

Aartun on the way to the A1 crack on a route that was otherwise all ice. *Ole Lied*

I was suspended in the shade, clenching my upper ice tool with both hands. Behind me, the north face of Cerro Torre beamed in the sun. Deep down below me, the vast icecap met the fjords of Chile, far, far away. The ice vein that we'd followed up the south face of Torre Egger had just shut down and forced me out onto this gigantic, whale-shaped mushroom. There was no fear in me, only presence. I focused and breathed and looked up for a solution. It was a sublime moment: way above me at the end of the pitch, the steepness eased back to vertical, and a pencil-thin ice vein appeared a little to the left—an invitation to go on.

As I sat in my home back in Norway, trying to recall our climb, it became once again clear why climbing is so alluring to me. Apart from the obvious reasons—the scenery, the thrill of the void below, the ambivalence of danger and the feeling of connection to nature—there is the moment of absolute presence, the state of stillness when all my senses are aligned. It is like a well-written haiku poem; the flow of energy is clear, simple, and to the point. This feeling has, of course, to do with the severity of the situation. If we climbers do not focus and pull ourselves together, our life is in imminent danger.

The south face ice line was first commented on by Ermanno Salvaterra in 2005, first seen by Bjørn-Eivind Aartun in 2008 from the Ragni Route on Cerro Torre, and first climbed by Aartun and Ole Lied in 2012. *Bjørn-Eivind Aartun*

This state is like a drug to me. It is something I want in my life. Sometimes I feel envious thinking about people who master the art of meditation because this is what it is: a deep and meditative state. Still, at the same time, I feel that my world is richer. I feel privileged to be out in the wild, connected to something bigger than I am, and to have this experience there.

Climbing Torre Egger had been my dream for quite some time. I'd seen the line back in 2008 from the Ragni Route on Cerro Torre. It was fuel for my imagination. I like to see improbable lines. Many times, they are just fantasies that are too far out to try, but they give me energy to go climb routes that are within my reach. The south face of Egger was, to me, perfectly suspended between the realm of realistic and fantastic.

When I planned my trip to Patagonia last autumn, the Egger line was at the top of my list. Originally, I had some plans with an American friend, but when they fell through, I was lucky to convince the Norwegian Ole Lied to go. He is a great and strong partner, always willing and keen. He also knows the area well from earlier visits.

On December 22, we climbed La Silla from Paso Superior on a very cold day after a chilly bivy in the remnants of an old snow cave. We climbed the whole time in crampons and gloves, while the sparks from steel against granite ricocheted around us. Back in Chalten in the evening, we could see that a two-day weather window was due shortly. Still tired from our climb the day before, we started repacking for Egger. There was no discussion about this: two good days would give us enough time for an attempt on the Egger dream line. On the 24th, we shouldered packs and headed for the Niponino camp.

We intended to climb up to what I'd like to name the "Col of Truth" (I'm convinced that Cesare Maestri never reached this point, and I prefer to stop calling it the "Col of Conquest") via the Donini-Bragg-Wilson route of 1976 (the first ascent of Torre Egger) with El Arca de los Vientos variations to access our planned new line. We knew that some runout slabs and 5.10+ climbing awaited us on the east face of Cerro Torre and that we would need to wear rock shoes and climb with bare hands. Recalling our cold experience two days before on the other side of the valley, we slid into a 9 a.m. start on December 25—to get the best out of the morning sun.

This decision proved to be a classic mistake. The weather was now warm, and we "got the best of the sun" in an ironic way. The triangular snowfield 300 meters above the start of the route heated up quickly, turning the big dihedral into a stream of water. Small slush avalanches pounded us every five minutes.

It was a relief to get above the snowfield and onto the slabs. Eventually, my pants dried out quite well. My boots were still wet upon arrival at our bivy site, and some of the contents in our packs were affected, including our one sleeping bag. Since Ole had been jumaring with the heavy pack, he'd avoided the worst of the water and slush, but we both had wet feet. Before going to sleep, I placed the soles of my boots inside my fleece, put on dry socks, and pulled the wet ones on outside of them. Thus, I woke up the next morning with everything in reasonable condition. Spooning inside our little bivy bag, turning around in perfect sync now and then, we stayed comfortable and got some good rest. *We could probably join the national team of synchronized swimming*, I thought.

In the morning, Ole led the first block. I was so excited that I had problems standing still. "How does it look? Can you see it?" I shouted up to him several times. We couldn't see the line from the col, and there was some mixed climbing around a corner to get to it.

Finally, I heard his voice: "It looks straightforward." When I followed the pitch and arrived at the belay, I realized what an understatement he'd made. Sure, it looked possible. Actually, it looked damn fantastic, but anything other than *straightforward*. Ole had anchored himself right below the start of this enormous rime sausage. To the left was blank, vertical granite. Only a thin sheet of ice led around the rime to a possible upward path. Ole began up this tricky pitch, entering a halfpipe that spiraled out of sight. His nickname in Chalten has been "El Caballo" ["The Horse"—Ed.] ever since Rolando Garibottti met him on the headwall of the Ferrari Route on Cerro Torre. It was early in the morning, and Ole was climbing the vertical ice without gloves. Rolo was left speechless at the sight of this big, broad-shouldered Viking climbing ice barehanded—as Rolo himself was descending from a cold bivy on the headwall. Ole's big frame and strength certainly lives up to the nickname.

Above us, on what would be the third pitch, I could see an ice tongue going up a red dihedral with a small crack. The crack went at A1, steep and beautiful. While I jumared, I looked forward to taking over the sharp end. Soon we would be close to halfway. I didn't dare think about how this day would end yet. I just wanted to be in the present and climb as high as we could manage. It was impossible to get any idea of the terrain higher up. We could only see half a pitch, never more.

Aartun and Lied celebrating on the summit of Torre Egger. *Colin Haley*

It was now my lead block, and the big rime whale towered above me. I felt small, and I didn't see any good solutions yet, except to venture out into the middle of it. To do that would mean 100 meters of severely overhanging face climbing on rime-covered ice. I kept going. Up close, my heart jumped. On the right side of the mushroom, a bluish halfpipe appeared, winding its way upward. During my climbs in Patagonia, I've learned that very often, where the strong wind forms mushrooms, it also grinds out halfpipes and tunnels. I felt like singing to praise this brilliant solution. But would it go on like this?

I shouted some happy words. Ole didn't understand, and I didn't care. In a few minutes, he would be at my side on the belay anyway. Before the next curve, I stopped and searched my harness for a short ice screw. The ice was good here, and a stubbie would do. The terrain was dead vertical. Putting my body in balance with my feet in every move, I still felt relaxed. Around the bend, I saw it: the runnel shut down. Of course, it couldn't be this "easy." My heart sank a little. The runnel completely closed.

Above me, a three-meter, forty-five-degree roof of rime led out into the blue sky. Then I remembered the option I'd seen from the start of the pitch—a bluish glint on the very belly of the beast. From my now much higher position, if I ventured out onto the face, it wouldn't be long before the really steep stuff eased off. At least, that's what I thought. I shouted down for Ole to follow, and as the optimist I am, I started chopping a hole in the rime fin to my left. Leaning out as far as the belay allowed me, I could only see rime cover and steepness. I decided to traverse left and find the blue gold. We were not going down yet!

The next 15 meters may be the most exhausting bit of ice I have ever climbed. Cleaning the rime as I went and working to get good, safe placements took all my energy. Then this perfect moment came: I reached better ice and saw the inviting, thin, light blue inversion of rime that stretched way up into what would be the start of the sixth pitch.

Naïve as I am, I felt invincible and strong again. *This is the key*, I thought. Craning my neck, I even thought it looked as though there were possible exits on the seventh pitch to both the left and the right.

The thin, divine one still looked intimidating. I was a bit burnt, and I hoped Ole would take over the lead. He was also very tired. Actually, he admitted, he had, for a split second, even doubted our chances of success. Anyway, it was still my block, so I had to pull myself together. As is often the case, if you just enter into the difficulties and deconstruct them, they become manageable, and step by step, there is room for advance. I found I could stem the small rime ribs on the sides of the vein, and the narrow strip of blue ice felt solid for screws. But there was no way I could place both tools. I couldn't even cram my shoulder in there. The right side of it turned into a smooth, red rock wall. But after a few more meters, it transformed again into a work of art. Small, sloping edges for my right foot appeared in the granite one after another. The rest of the pitch was pure fun. We'd proved ourselves worthy, and now it was time for indulgence. I passed a crack and was given a perfect offset nut placement. Safe and confident, I floated to the belay. Both exits would work. The summit was now a pitch away.

A couple of tears wet my eyes. How important can a climb be to me? I was deeply touched by this one, humbled by the beauty and exposure around me, by my luck to live these moments with a friend in this place. After spending some time on the summit taking it all in, we descended by the rappels established on the Torre Traverse. Down at the col, we could enjoy a last meal in the setting sun.

Summary:

Area: Chalten Massif, Argentine Patagonia.

Ascent: After bivying on the Egger-Torre col, Norwegians Bjørn-Eivind Aartun and Ole Lied climbed a new route, Venas Azules (350m, 6b+ A1 AI6), on Torre Egger. To reach the col they followed the Donini-Bragg-Wilson Route with El Arca de los Vientos variations for a complete ascent of 950m.

A Note About the Author:

*Bjørn-Eivind Aartun (45) and Stein-Ivar Gravdal died on February 9, 2012, on a new ice route on the big wall of Kjerag in southwest Norway. They were discovered hanging upside down on their ropes, apparently having been hit by falling rock. Both climbers have reported regularly in these pages. Aartun's feature article about his new route Dracula on Alaska's Mt. Foraker appeared in the 2011 AAJ.*

Bjørn-Eivind Aartun (left) and Ole Lied on the summit of Torre Egger.

# THE MAUSOLEUM

*The first ascent of Mt. Mausolus in Alaska's little known Revelation Mountains.*

CLINT HELANDER

Scott Vincik on The Mausoleum. *Clint Helander*

From 377 to 353 B.C., the city of Halicarnassus on the shores of the Aegean Sea was ruled by a king named Mausolus. During his reign he expanded his empire, seizing control of many neighboring cities and much of southwest Asia Minor. When he died in 353 B.C., his wife Artemisia, who was also his sister, erected a large tomb, designed by six of Greece's most prominent architects and sculptors. The 148-foot-tall marble edifice was decorated with statues of gods and goddesses, warriors on horseback, lions, and spear-wielding guards. Crowning the tomb's pyramidal apex was a chariot pulled by four horses carrying Mausolus and Artemisia, all in marble. The Mausoleum was so magnificent that in 140 B.C. Antipater of Sidon declared it one of his Seven Wonders of the Ancient World. For more than 16 centuries the Mausoleum towered over Halicarnassus, even after being conquered by Alexander the Great. Now, thanks to earthquakes and pillaging, little remains of the once glorious shrine.

The photo that inspired the climb: Mt. Mausolus's 4,500' west face, showing The Mausoleum. *Cliff Cochran*

Hidden deep in Alaska's southwest wilderness, the hallowed Revelation Mountains hold more myths than truth. Rising tall and solemn against a backdrop of untrodden landscapes, Mt. Mausolus (9,170 feet) is one of the range's greatest wonders. In 1967 a party led by David Roberts spent 52 days exploring and climbing in the Revelations. On the flight in he noticed the "hopeless labyrinth of Mount Mausolus," calling it "perhaps the toughest climb in the range" (*AAJ* 1968). Like the columns of the tomb, massive granite prows soar skyward, supporting the marble-white upper mountain. An army of gendarmes on the

Dick Barber (far left) dropping off (left to right) Clint Helander, Seth Holden, and Steve Sinor during their first trip to the Revelations, in 2008. *Clint Helander*

north and south ridges guard its summit pyramid. Precarious hanging glaciers adorn towering golden walls.

As if forgotten by time, Mt. Mausolus was still unclimbed when I discovered it in 2007. Perhaps it was the Revelations' isolation, its reputation for heinous weather, and a lack of information that explained its virginity. A single photo of Mausolus's 4,500-foot west face, taken by a local pilot, brought me to the brink of obsession. The photo revealed a steel-gray dagger of ice plunging directly from the summit like a spear cast from Mausolus's soaring chariot.

In 2008 Steve Sinor, Seth Holden, and I landed northwest of Mausolus on the southwest fork of the Big River Glacier. An avalanche-prone pass kept us from seeing Mausolus. We focused elsewhere, including the first ascent of Exodus Peak (*AAJ* 2009). Seth and I returned in 2009 and encountered similar avalanche conditions to those that kept us from Mausolus. On the first ascent of the Ice Pyramid (*AAJ* 2010) we glimpsed Mausolus's spectacular west face. After two trips we had solved many of the Revelations' access problems, so we vowed to return for Mausolus the following year.

In May 2010 Dick Barber landed Seth and me on the boulder-strewn Swift Glacier on his third attempt. As in the photo, a large couloir arched up to a steep vein of ice that coursed straight to the summit. The mountain flaunted its defenses. Avalanches roared as we

cowered like slaves at the feet of a king. At dusk the mountain slumbered, and the avalanches ceased. Conditions firmed and seemed temporarily safe. Seth and I couldn't resist. That night we simul-climbed almost 2,000 feet, to the start of the real technical difficulties. Knowing that the veil of safety would soon lift with the sun, and Mausolus would awaken, we descended with heavy hearts.

On August 24, 2010, Seth died in a small plane crash not far from the Revelations. Only 30 minutes prior we had discussed our strategy for Mausolus. We had concluded that to stand any chance of success, we needed to attack before the increasingly warm spring sun reached the west face. Now I questioned whether I had the emotional tenacity for an attempt without Seth. The vision of Mausolus had been his as much as mine.

Scott Vincik on a steep bulge relatively low on The Mausoleum. *Clint Helander*

On March 13, 2011, Scotty Vincik and I flew west from Anchorage. Rob Jones' Super Cub bucked through turbulent downdrafts as we flew 160 miles toward the Swift Glacier. The infinite wilderness, frozen under Alaska's barren winter, heightened my sense of the oncoming isolation. Soon the unmistakably jagged profile of the Revelation Mountains cut the horizon. My eyes were fixed solely on Mt. Mausolus, a dozen miles southeast of the range's main spine. I had seen this view numerous times, but still my stomach twisted in knots. Without even a satellite phone, we would be completely alone.

After repeated efforts Jones landed us on the Swift Glacier. As we set up camp, the west face reared overhead with oppressive authority. Scotty and I wasted no time. An unprecedented high pressure system had been sitting over south-central Alaska for a month, but we knew it wouldn't last much longer.

We crossed the bergschrund early on March 15 and simul-climbed to the 2010 highpoint, veering slightly left to gain the most direct line

Scott Vincik following the crux pitch of The Mausoleum. *Clint Helander*

on the face. A thin WI4 smear provided narrow passage around a major slab that had looked problematic from the ground. The second was burdened with the pack, which contained two sleeping bags, pads, food, and a stove. We found that our rock rack was almost worthless, as the compact granite seldom took gear. We lamented bringing only eight ice screws, which forced us into constructing V-threads for anchors. The good news was that these would facilitate our descent.

Endless WI4–5 brought us to a lower-angle, ice-covered hourglass. As I led toward the funnel, we heard the cutting scream of a falling rock. It bounced to my left and hurtled into the void, missing Scotty by several feet. Despite the early hour, it was time to seek shelter. However, there wasn't a ledge for a thousand feet in either direction. A crappy three-foot-long snow mushroom and a sloping butt-width rock served for our semi-hanging bivy. After much work on the anchor, we improvised hammocks out of the rope and our sleeping pads. The "Shiitake Mushroom Bivy" (named for the shitty snow mushroom) made up in relative safety for what it lacked in comfort. As the evening sun hit the upper face, rockfall echoed in the gash until sunset. Without a place to set it, the stove was worthless. We ate a few bars and relished our last swigs of water before enduring the long night.

My restless thoughts were haunted by memories of Seth. The view painted our experience together. The Ice Pyramid was ghostly in the moonlight. The Angel's south ridge, which Seth and I had tried in 2010, snaked skyward in distant profile. I shivered not only from the cold but also from the reality that Seth and I would never complete our envisioned masterpiece route on the Golgotha. At one point I awoke from a dream and briefly thought Scotty was Seth.

In the morning we left most of our gear at the hanging bivy. Several steepening pitches led to the route's crux pitch, a 165-foot, dead-vertical curtain of impenetrable gray ice. With only five ice screws for the pitch, I faced numerous 30-40-foot run outs before reaching a spot to belay with two screws remaining. Toward the top of the face, we basked in the sun. More steep pitches gave way to lower-angle ice and the wind-sculpted summit. We simul-climbed 400 feet of unprotected 60-degree snow.

On the narrow summit I felt like King Mausolus riding proud in his chariot. I looked out over the western Alaska lowlands like a ruler beholding his empire. My elation, though, was somewhat dulled by the empty feeling left by Seth's absence. Yet in a way he was with me. Under the purple sky of a full moon, I cast Seth's ashes from the summit. The mountain became his mausoleum. It will be a remarkable place to spend eternity.

After a quick brew, we descended through the night. Neither of us had consumed a sip of water in over 24 hours. It took us nine hours to rappel 2,200 feet. I began hallucinating, then fighting for consciousness. At one point I shone my headlamp toward a blank wall and gazed at infinite green pastures filled with cows. We had been on the go for almost 48 hours. I fell asleep hanging from anchors as Scotty rigged the lower rappels. We reached a large natural snow cave at 7 a.m. and slept for almost 10 hours. When our food was gone, we packed up and carefully downclimbed to the glacier. Only 400 feet above the bergschrund, I discovered a Corn Nut in the snow. I had eaten a pack of Corn Nuts on Mausolus's summit, and this kernel had fallen 4,000 feet down our line of ascent.

After several days of excessive eating and coffee drinking, we skied the Swift Glacier north over the pass that had blocked access to Mausolus several years earlier. We continued down the Big River Glacier, past the Ice Pyramid and Exodus. Each mountain brought memories of Seth. After 18 miles Scotty and I camped under Mt. Hesperus's Matterhorn-like northwest face. The next day we skied the remaining 17 miles to Rob Jones' lodge on the Big River.

To this day I feel a profound sense of pride in knowing that Seth, too, would be proud. In his honor we named our route the Mausoleum.

SUMMARY:

Area: Revelation Mountains, Alaska.

Ascent: Clint Helander and Scotty Vincik made the first ascent of Mt. Mausolus (9,170 feet) on March 15–17, 2011, via the Mausoleum (4,500' V WI5) on the west face.

Clint Helander (left) and Scott Vincik after climbing Mt. Mausolus. *Clint Helander*

A NOTE ABOUT THE AUTHOR:

*Clint Helander, 27, lives in Anchorage. After graduating from the University of Alaska, he works seasonally to fund his climbing life. In 2011 he also climbed Mt. Hunter, drove 17,000 miles on a four-month climbing trip, and endured a month of bad weather in Patagonia. In March 2012 he went to his beloved Revelations for a fifth time, with great success.*

*Clint thanks the Mugs Stump Award, the AAC McNeill-Nott Award, the AAC Mountain Fellowship Award, and the Mazamas Alpine Adventure Award for making possible his trips to the Revelations.*

# CONTINUING EDUCATION

*Severely tested on the first ascent of the 8,500-foot southwest spur*

*of University Peak, Alaska.*

---

KEVIN DITZLER

I first laid eyes on 14,470-foot University Peak in 2007. Daily views of the massive south face from low on the Hawkins Glacier were like a drug that wraps itself around the base of your brain and haunts your dreams. But it was out of my league. So I did the only logical thing: I moved to Alaska. Over the next four years of living and climbing in the Wrangell Mountains I brought home aerial photos of University Peak. Its storied history slowly revealed itself as I met its pioneering climbers.

The many details of an Alaskan expedition fell into place on April 4. Once again I stood at the base of University Peak. Along for the adventure was John Kelley, an Alaskan hard man with roots in my hometown of Durango, Colorado. We have been climbing hard, scrappy lines in the Chugach together for the last two winters. The Chugach in December is a cold and dark endeavor, a place where approaches are torturous and protection is a state of mind. A handful of quiet locals have been ticking off superb modern alpine lines on the steepest faces in the range. John and I have reached that vital level where we don't need to talk much, and we've frozen our asses off enough to know the other guy can suffer and smile.

Paul Claus of Ultima Thule Lodge had landed us on a small side glacier west of the upper Hawkins Glacier and southeast of Hobbs Peak. We dug in a base camp and spent a week skiing and observing conditions. Toying with different objectives, we discovered complex faces riddled with objective hazards. Unpredictable bouts of snowfall and poor visibility weren't encouraging. In the end, however, the biggest face proved irresistible, and we began planning for the next break in the weather. We were focused on a spur that splits the southwest face. A narrow path up ice seemed the only option protected from serac falls to either side. Our descent would be the complex and broken north ridge, pioneered in 1955 by a six-man team lead by Keith Hart. The peak did not see another summiting until 1997, when Paul Claus, Ruedi Homberger, Danny Kost, and Dave Staehli landed in Beaver Basin, a high cirque at 10,000 feet, and made the second ascent of the peak, also via the north ridge.

The only people to descend this ridge without first climbing it were Carlos Buhler and Charlie Sassara, in 1997. They had just finished their 8,500-foot line on the east face, and Claus surprised them with an unexpected air drop of food on the summit. While descending the north ridge, they found a handful of wands marking the Claus party's route; their luck held when they were picked up immediately on arrival in Beaver Basin. (See AAJs 1954, 1955, and 1998 for previous climbs and good descriptions of the peak's character.) While the north ridge is arguably the best descent route, its downsides are that Beaver Basin is a dead end ringed with active serac fall, and it lies at the edge of a 4,000-foot icefall that would be a roll of the dice to descend. The first ascentionists had walked 20 miles up the Hawkins Glacier from the Chitina River and climbed the icefall into Beaver Basin before climbing the north ridge to the summit. They were either far braver than we, or the ice fall has changed since 1955. John and I were content with being "spoiled by a Supercub," as Ruedi Homberger would say.

Kevin Ditzler starting the approach to University Peak, with their route line on the southwest spur. *John Kelley*

The only other ascent by a new line was by Lorne Glick, Bob Kingsley, Lance McDonald, and John Whedon in 2002. After climbing the open south face in ideal booting conditions, the four skied the 7,000-foot run (AAJ 2003). This "day trip" earned them a remarkable virgin ski line but left them a quarter mile and 300 vertical feet shy of the summit.

On April 8 in improving weather John and I left a note in our base camp tents with route information and pick up instructions, per our agreement with Paul. We had decided to climb the line, traverse the peak, and wait a week in Beaver Basin until our scheduled pick up on April 24.

We thinned the rack, added fuel and food, and I foolishly convinced John to leave the file. We would have to carry too much gear already.

At 1 a.m. on April 11 we crossed the schrund at 6,000 feet and began simul-soloing. Soon we fell into rhythm and moved well despite the oppressing packs. Early in the day we passed through a steep gorge with bizarre echoes— we screamed various nonsenses at the walls, just to hear them repeated and magnified seven or eight times before they bounced away down the face. In the afternoon we stopped for

After 42 hours on the go, the climbers found snow soft enough to excavate camp one. *Kevin Ditzler*

our first brew. Just as we relaxed on our stomped platform and began enjoying the perfect sunny weather, a powder avalanche tore down a gully near us. We grabbed everything we could, as the powder blast hit us. When it finally passed, we were shivering. Snow packed every opening in our clothing, packs, and helmets, but we didn't lose anything. After finishing the brew, we were again soloing upward, finally putting on the rope to simul ever-steepening mixed terrain.

Three thousand feet up, at the time we should have been looking for a camp, the snow couloir ended, exiting right onto a 60-degree ice face. From there I could see the next thousand feet. I could also see the fractured face of a hanging serac leaning precariously near. I had studied it from the ground, tracing fall lines to see if we could steer clear of any debris it might fire, and convinced myself that we could safely squeak by on the right. Now, though, it was my voice that was squeaking, caught in my throat as my heart pounded. I started motoring up the ice. I could feel John at the end of the rope, out of sight in the couloir, stepping it up to meet my pace. I continued climbing until I ran out of gear, where I paused, looking from the serac to John and back to the serac. I really didn't want to stop here. I called down the face and started climbing again. When he reached the last piece of pro, he racked it, and we continued, still tied together but soloing steepening blue ice.

Finally, I pulled right of the hanging behemoth and out of the fall line. Breathing hard, I plugged my only screw and began bringing John up. Wordlessly, he pulled into the belay as twilight dwindled. Before either of us spoke, the behemoth cracked, expelling a crashing cascade of ice down the face. Startled but safe, we watched the tumbling avalanche until it faded into gray light out of sight. I traced its fall line back up the face. John and I exchanged grimaces.

We had run out of light and could see nothing resembling a ledge, nor any feature to shelter us. So we strapped on our headlamps, and I took off, hoping to find protected terrain. Soon it began to snow, which the 4,000-plus feet of 60-degree blue ice above us shed regularly. The spindrift slides increased as we continued upward, some pounding us for minutes. Sometime during that tortuous night I reached my limit. Calves on the verge of rupturing like overripe watermelons, I kneeled against the wall of ice, head bowed.

"I don't think I can lead anymore," I told John when he reached me. John replied but I didn't really listen. I knew he was telling me he couldn't lead. I closed my eyes as another spindrift slide tore into our belay. Cold powder breathed into my lungs. When the deluge stopped, I opened my eyes. The prospect of an open camp in this weather convinced us the only option was up—up to some ledge, some protection, someplace to rest away from the avalanches. In a spasm of will that I can only compare to rearranging an internal organ, I resigned myself to my fate, my penance. I stood, kicking front points into the frozen monolith.

"Fine, but I'm not carrying this fucking pack any farther."

I unshouldered it, clipped it to the near-hanging belay, and lashed a haul line to it. John and I had seen a few darkest hours together, and we could dig deep when we needed to. My light turned upward, and my hands relaxed on my tools.

We climbed through the rest of the night and the following day. Light snow continued to fall, as did the spindrift. In daylight everything seems more manageable, though there was still no protected terrain, nor anything but 60- to 75-degree blue ice. I continued with gimping slow leads.

John Kelley leaving camp two, the chopped ledge visible below. *Kevin Ditzler*

John Kelley after 40 hours on the go. *Kevin Ditzler*

Forty-two hours after crossing the schrund, we reached the relative protection of a rock band and discovered a 60-degree snow rib just deep enough for excavating a protected tent site. As we finished an hour of chopping, I saw one of my picks rattling loosely on the head of the tool. We collapsed into our small tent, made a quick brew, and within an hour fell into the nauseous coma-like sleep of the utterly exhausted. The cave-like ledge enveloped our small tent, cocooning it into the folds of the mountain.

The next morning we peeled open our eyelids and saw that the weather had improved. We brewed and ate gluttonously, lightening our packs. I took a closer look at my axe: one of the two nuts holding the pick was gone. Before the climb I had replaced the hardware, torqueing it hard. Should have used Lock-tite. We were halfway up the mountain with no spares. I went to work with pitons, chiseling stainless aircraft tie wire into the void where the nut had been and folding layers of the aluminum head back onto the bolt and remaining nut. The pick was tight again; a few test swings implied it would work.

We finished breaking camp by 4 p.m., eager to move after the delay. I took the sharp end and began traversing left on ice and mixed pitches to 75 degrees. The protection was excellent in cold, old ice, but the climbing taxed our spent calves. After only five or six pitches of traversing left under the rock band, the light began to fade. Shit. The last thing we needed was another overnight epic trying to find a ledge. Although returning to the comfort of the last camp was tempting, neither of us was willing to give up hard-earned progress. I led a pitch to the rock band above, in hope of finding a snow pocket deep enough for a ledge. Out of light and options, we settled for another steep snow rib, hoping for dense snow and névé like the previous night.

Four and a half excruciating hours later, we finished chopping through bullet-hard ice and set up our tent. We slept well and long, and the next day, under sunny skies, we slept, brewed, and ate until the sun fell away. We enjoyed our day of leisure, drinking in mountains and sky.

The next day, April 15, we were up before the sun, rested and motivated. We would end this relentless ice face. We continued traversing up and left, looking for an opening in the rock band that might take us to the snowcap at 12,500 feet. By 5 p.m. we found a path through the rock band, and I surrendered the sharp end. John took the rack and dispatched the pitch. A snow-covered rock slab with vertical bouldery rock moves through a chossy weakness took him into thin clouds and soft snowfall. Above the rock band John led through weaknesses in a labyrinth of polished overhanging ice and into a bitterly cold night. The final pitch was an unprotectable, rope-stretching, 70-degree snice face that cracked and settled as John climbed.

And then We rejoiced in all things flat and level: a small plateau at the apex of the southwest spur. Unroped we stretched tender calves (after 4,000 feet on front points), brewed, and watched the engorged blood moon quiver over an endless array of silent mountains.

The next morning we moved unroped up the massive ridge in clear, cold weather, until gaping crevasses and steepening terrain forced us to tie in and trade leads. We were soon back on our front points traversing under enormous, house-sized, rime conglomerations—hollow webs of ice, snow, and air. The 50- to 75-degree traverse was at best difficult to protect and at worst terrifying. Sometimes the ice would shoot cracks with each swing. We took to chiseling placements with our blunt tools and holding our breaths.

We were back in the routine of climbing in the dark. The thermometer on my pack read –18°F, and the wind was picking up. After a few more hours of scary rime and hollow traversing, John once again brought us to flatter ground and our next camp, at the top of the south face. This was the spot where four years earlier Lorne Glick and gang had put on their skis to descend the south face. Looking down it now, I saw nothing but smooth polished blue for 7,000 feet.

The following day brought us to the top of a twin-steepled rime pinnacle within view of the summit. It was one of those places where it feels like you're clinging to a terrestrial focal point, a soaring apex above the planet. We rapped off the other side and began a quarter-mile slog through knee-deep snow toward our goal. The snow finally firmed on a wide, wind-compacted ridge, and we walked unroped to the broad summit. Under clear mid-day skies, -10°F temps, and healthy wind, we reveled in our first 360° view.

The descent began as an enjoyable stroll down a long, gentle hill, but we soon roped up to navigate through the convoluted maze of the north ridge. Near-vertical downclimbing, avalanche slopes, leg-punching bridges, and endless gaping crevasses kept our attention. About two-thirds of the way down, the light began to fade, and a strong turbulent wind spun around us. We kicked in a platform, set up the tent, and crawled in. We spent much of that night and the following morning using our backs to brace the walls against locomotive winds. The wind stopped by mid-day on the 18th, and we sleuthed our way through the last of the maze and post-holed into Beaver Basin.

The silence and stillness of the following six days was overwhelming. The climb had been an act of will. At times it was a mind-cleansing battle and at times a saturating pleasure. Now there was only waiting. Low on food, we went into hibernation mode.

I was physically and mentally drained, powerless to stop a creeping morbidity from wrapping itself around me; I allowed it to bend my thoughts toward hopelessness. I

Ditzler at camp 3 on the apex of the southwest spur, the first flat ground since crossing the shrund. *John Kelley*

had failed my partner and myself; I had backed myself into a corner with no options. Our lives were dependent on someone far away and on the luck of flyable weather. John did what he could to raise my spirits. We joked about stretching our remaining 2,000 calories and six ounces of fuel for six days or possibly longer. We laughed about the inedibility of modern synthetic boots. John passed the time telling climbing stories, detailing mountains he'd seen that had potential. We talked excitedly when we discovered a past climb or partner in common. In the end, however, I pulled back into my brooding gloom.

Everything I have done in the mountains has been governed by a philosophy of self-reliance, of knowing that every step and every decision carries the gravity of life and death. The most difficult part about waiting was knowing that it was out of my control. I was too tired, too weak to contemplate descending the icefall. Even in perfect health, it would have been difficult and objectively dangerous. The best option now, and the decision we had made before we set foot on this peak, was to wait, knowing that Paul would eventually get the message in our tent back in base camp and show up here.

I slept in stressful fits of nightmares, unable to dial back my thoughts. Late on the sixth day, April 24, our scheduled pick up date, the clouds began to accumulate, and I zipped the tent shut like I was closing a dark curtain over my mind. That's when the faint drone of an airplane whispered through the air. Afraid to breathe, I listened and prayed. Minutes later, Paul and his Cub burst through the clouds just in front of us and landed a stone's throw away.

We piled into the Cub and glided out of the basin. John and I pressed our foreheads to the vibrating windows, studying the hideously fractured icefalls below Beaver Basin. We exchanged smiling grimaces. Maybe waiting in Beaver Basin hadn't been so bad after all.

SUMMARY:

Area: St. Elias Mountains, Alaska.

Ascent: First ascent of the southwest spur of 14,470' University Peak. Kevin Ditzler and John Kelley climbed the 8,500-foot route in seven days, summiting on April 17, 2011. The climbing was "endless grade 3 ice with the occasional grade 4 step" on 4,000 feet of 60° to

Kevin Ditzler and John Kelley on the summit of University Peak. *John Kelley*

75° ice, followed by a variously angled ice ridge to the summit. They descended the north ridge to Beaver Basin, where they waited six days for a pickup with almost no food or fuel.

A NOTE ABOUT THE AUTHOR:

*Kevin Ditzler likes imaginative adventures and aesthetic climbing lines. He and his wife Piper split their time between working in the remote Wrangell Mountains of Alaska and an arguably more "civilized" life during the winter in the city of Palmer, Alaska.*

# BABA TANGI

*A team of sisters makes the first ascent of the northwest ridge of*
*Koh-e-Baba-Tangi (6,516m), Afghanistan.*

PAT DEAVOLL

Porters on the return to the village of Kret; Baba Tangi and the route in the background. *Christine Byrch*

I'd long wanted to climb in Afghanistan's Wakhan Corridor, but with one war or another, the country had been out of bounds to climbers for more than 30 years. Finally a trickle of climbers and travelers began to return. So I thought, "Now's my chance." In 2010 I began coercing my sister Christine, also from New Zealand, and our Indian friend Satyabrata Dam into joining me. We chose Baba Tangi, which means Jade Peak in the local dialect. The highest mountain in the eastern sector of the Afghan Hindu Kush, its only ascent came in 1963, by an Italian team that included Carlo Alberto Pinelli. They climbed the west ridge with three camps, and Pinelli wrote in his book Peaks of Silver and Jade that the northwest ridge "seems to be particularly attractive ... a varied and hard route but probably not too dangerous, alternating sections of rock, mixed, and ice." So the northwest ridge it would be.

For the next 12 months we battled with embassies for visas, applied for grants, and appealed for sponsorship. We engaged an Afghan company to help with internal permits, 4WD transport, and local porters. In mid-July we flew to Dushanbe, the capital of neighboring Tajikistan, where we met Satya.

Ladies from the village of Kret and their children. *Pat Deavoll*

Dushanbe is a lovely uncongested city of elegant buildings, wide boulevards, and fountains. There was not a scrap of rubbish. But the temperature was in the 40s (Celsius), so it felt good to be on the road with the wind in our hair after a day of arranging final permits and shopping. We'd pre-booked a 4WD vehicle with Pamir Silk Travel, which arrived promptly at our hotel at 10 a.m., driven by a cheerful Tajik named Gordo, who spoke not a word of English. Though we roared out of town, within 10 kilometers the state of the roads slowed us to 20km/hour, max. We progressed at this speed for the next three days, to the border.

Gordo dropped us at a gated bridge over the Panj River. It was about 50 degrees C (120°F). Two small buildings sat in the middle of the wide, dusty riverbed: the Tajik immigration post and the Afghan immigration post. Smiling soldiers let us through the gate as we struggled with our luggage. The formalities went smoothly, but where was the representative from Wakhan Tourism who was supposed to meet us? He eventually turned up, claimed he was gravely ill, accompanied us to the small village of Ishkashim, and then disappeared to hospital. That was the last we saw of him.

When no replacement was sent, it became obvious that we'd have to do our own organizing. This turned out to be a blessing, as it saved quite a sum of money. Wandering into the middle of Ishkashim (no more than a dirt crossroads around a rough bazaar, but charming in its simplicity), Satya and I shopped for the remainder of our food, purchased a pressure cooker and two five-kilogram gas cylinders for cooking at base camp, and arranged for a 4WD to take us 120 kilometers up the Wakhan Valley to the village of Kret. From there we intended to walk to the mountain.

The locals were friendly, helpful, and not averse to having their photos taken. On the street were plenty of women and girls in the colorful Wakhi dress. And the odd burka. A young man named Adab marched us round to see the regional governor and the police to obtain the bits of paper required to enter the Wakhan. Inside the border police compound, the men had laid down their AK47s and were playing chess at a large table in the sun. We spent two nights having fun with a smattering of other western travelers in an excellent guesthouse. Then we were on the road again.

The scenery in the Wakhan Corridor is otherworldly: vast arid mountains, with brief glimpses of glaciers and snow-capped mountains up the side valleys. Villages of mud houses.

And the vast Panj River, which barricaded us from Tajikistan and the Pamir Mountains to the north. Our driver was an elderly Afghan who cheerfully dealt with a puncture and backed over a huge rock, where we were temporarily stuck. Oh well, these things happen. We arrived in Kret late in the afternoon and were invited to stay in the village guesthouse. The next day I was ill with a stomach complaint, but Satya and Christine met with a village leader, and together they organized porters. We left the next morning for base camp with eight porters and a dog.

On the first day we climbed 1,000 meters, which required great effort by our porters, who were all humping 25 kilos or more. They were a delightful team: funny, kind, and generous, sharing their tea, rice, and naan with us. We spent the first night at the toe of the glacier, after climbing a steep incline all afternoon. The next day we moved up to where an Italian team had placed base camp three years ago, when they attempted the original route up the west ridge. (They gave up at 6,000 meters, 500 meters shy of the summit.) After a final cup of tea, the porters headed back to Kret with a promise to return in three weeks.

During 10 days of acclimatizing, we scoped the northwest ridge, our goal. The route would begin with a 500-meter ice face of 60 to 80 degrees, before progressing into a narrow ice gully. From there we weren't sure what would happen, but hoped a few days would take us to the summit plateau, then the summit. We would either V-thread our way back down the route or traverse the mountain and descend the west ridge.

When the time came to climb, Satya decided not to accompany us, much to our dismay. It wasn't the altitude—he's climbed Everest without oxygen—but an injury. Christine and I devised a plan for our pack-loads should we not be able to carry them on the steepest terrain. We decided that I would lead, while Christine would jumar with the heavier pack. If this proved too strenuous, we would haul. On August 4 we waved goodbye to Satya, who promised to raise the alarm if we hadn't returned in 10 days. That night we camped under a crystal sky with beautiful views of Tajikistan and the Pamirs to the north.

The next day the ice face went surprisingly well. The bergschrund proved no problem, and after seven pitches we were perched beneath an 80-degree ice bulge. Time to try out our plan. I passed my pack to Christine, who attached hers to the end of one of our double ropes. Off I went, and it didn't seem long before I'd dispatched the pitch and Christine was seconding toward me. The pack, dangling 60 meters beneath us, duly followed. Another couple of pitches of lesser angle took us to a small col that offered a good camp. We were well on our way!

The next morning we woke at 3 a.m., in order to be away by five. We weren't sure

Pat Deavoll leads the initial ice face on day one. *Christine Byrch*

where the narrow ice gully would exit and wanted to allow plenty of time for hauling the packs. After some rotten fragile ice, it improved, and I started to enjoy myself. Here I was at last, climbing steep ice on a mountain in Afghanistan. How lucky I was! I felt confident and happy and knew that, if the weather stayed settled, and if we broke the mountain down into sections and dealt with each as it presented itself, we would climb Baba Tangi.

Christine Byrch traversing toward the top of the west ridge during the descent (day 6). *Pat Deavoll*

But during one pitch of hauling, the pack swung into the rock and lodged there. We yanked and tugged and jiggled to no avail, and Christine had to rappel to free it. By now the day was done. We chopped out a ledge at the apex of the ridge and settled in for another fine night.

When the sun rose on the third day, we could see a series of dark clouds marring the western sky. What would they bring? We were confronted with a large rock buttress and set off trudging in deep snow to round it on the left. Then we saw another steep ice slope, fringed by a nasty looking bergschrund. I tried my hardest to climb this but couldn't find any purchase in the rotten snow and kept falling in a heap. So I went around by a bridge and a nasty traverse back across the top of the schrund. Christine had an awful time jumaring, and the pitch must have taken us a good three hours. Meanwhile, the sky kept darkening.

In mid-afternoon it started to snow and the temperature dropped. Nearly at the summit plateau, we ran around looking for somewhere to camp, finally settling on an uncomfortable sloping ledge. It was still snowing at 4:30 a.m., so we gratefully settled back into our bags. However, by 8 it had started to clear, so we trudged through deep snow to the western side of the plateau until 4 p.m., when we stumbled across a perfect camp site at approximately 6,000 meters: flat and sheltered from the persistent wind. It felt good to know there would only be one more day of ascent.

We were away at 4:30 a.m., climbing mixed ice and snow slopes toward the summit ridge. It was bitterly cold and the wind hadn't let up. We were both wearing every stitch of clothing we had. At nine we were beneath what we thought was the summit. I led a moderate ice pitch, only to discover that the ridge continued up … and up some more. But an hour later the true summit appeared. We were there! We looked south into Pakistan, north into Tajikistan, and east into China. It was a magic moment, only marred by the bitter cold. We were very happy, if tired, as we headed down.

The next day we started down toward the west ridge, with hopes of returning to base camp in two days. It would be a nice touch to do a traverse of the mountain. Six a.m. found us standing at the edge of the plateau wondering which way to go. Below was a large granite buttress, and there seemed no alternative but to rappel over the edge. But things went well, and five rappels later we found a long snow/ice traverse that took us to the top of the west ridge proper. There we found cairns and an old camp site, complete with firewood. We began a scrambling descent down the 1,500-meter rocky spur. At the end of the afternoon, we came across another cleared campsite and decided to stop for the night—our seventh on the mountain. We were down to the last of our food, exhausted, hungry, and keen to be down. But it was a beautiful evening, and we didn't bother pitching the tent.

Next morning we arrived on the glacier elated. We were so excited. Then Christine spied a figure in the distance. There was Satya, waving both arms in the air, coming up the glacier to meet us.

SUMMARY:

Area: Wakhan Corridor, Hindu Kush, Afghanistan.

Ascent: On August 9, 2011 sisters Pat Deavoll and Chris Byrch from New Zealand summited Koh-e-Baba-Tangi (6,516m), via a new route up the northwest ridge, during a seven-day traverse of the mountain from base camp. Theirs was only the second ascent of the mountain, the first being in August 1963 by Italians Giancarlo Biasin, Giancarlo Castelli, and Carlo Alberto Pinelli, who placed three camps on the west ridge. In 2008 four Italian women (including World Cup Ice Climbing champion Anna Torretta)—most likely the first all-female climbing expedition to the high mountains of Afghanistan's Wakhan Corridor—attempted to repeat this route but found it more difficult than expected and retreated from 6,000m.

A NOTE ABOUT THE AUTHOR:

*New Zealander Pat Deavoll's 35-year climbing career extends from a three-month traverse of the Southern Alps in her home country to the solo first ascent of Karim Sar in northern Pakistan. In 2006 she made the first ascent of the much-coveted north face of Haizi Shan in eastern Tibet, with Malcolm Bass. She's also climbed hard in the Alaska Range and the Canadian Rockies, and taken part in 12 expeditions to the remote corners of the Greater Ranges in the past 11 years. Her book Wind From a Distant Summit was recently released.*

*Many thanks to the organizations whose support helped made this climb happen: Beattie Matheson and Berghaus; Southern Approach and Black Diamond; The Mount Everest Foundation; The New Zealand Alpine Club Expedition Fund; Icebreaker NZ.*

Pat Deavoll (left) and Christine Byrch on the summit, day 5.
Pat Deavoll

# THE OLD BREED

*The first ascent of Saser Kangri II (7,518m) and other peaks in the Eastern Karakoram, India.*

MARK RICHEY

The south side of Saser Kangri II as viewed from the summit of Tsok Kangri. The "West Peak" climbed in 1985 is clearly visible as the rounded snow shoulder far left of and below the main, east, summit reached in 2011. *Mark Richey*

When we first saw Saser Kangri, in 2001, we didn't even know its name. My partner Mark Wilford and I snapped a few photographs of four massive mountains to the north as we shivered that early dawn in our high bivouac on Yamandaka (*AAJ 2002*). Later Harish Kapadia, co-leader of our expedition with Sir Chris Bonington, informed us that the great peaks were Saser Kangri I, II, III, and IV.

The north face route on Tsok Kangri (6,585m). *Steve Swenson*

I became fascinated with these unexplored mountains in disputed Kashmir near the Actual Ground Position Line between India and Pakistan. Gaining permission to climb in this militarily restricted area can be difficult. But in 2006 Harish called and asked me, "Why not go to Saser Kangri II? The East Peak is unclimbed and higher than the West Peak and it's possible to obtain a permit."

By 2008 I had started researching the Saser Kangri peaks more seriously. Located in the Buddhist region of Ladakh in northeastern Kashmir, there was little information about this remote area, but a picture taken by Harish from the Kardung La, a high pass to the south, showed a huge rock and ice face on Sasser Kangri II (SKII). From his photo, I could see Harish was correct: the virgin East Peak of SKII was higher than the already climbed West Peak. At 7,518 meters, this made SKII East the second highest unclimbed mountain in the world. Only Ghanker Puensom in Bhutan, where climbing is prohibited, is higher.

The West Peak of SKII had been reached by a massive Indo-Japanese expedition in 1985 following a route from the north. They claimed the first ascent of SKII, declaring that the "West Peak" was similar in height to the "East Peak" but separated by a long and complex ridge. SKII fell into obscurity even though the East Peak remained unclimbed. I shared the photos with Steve Swenson, and we hatched a plan to attempt Saser Kangri II the following summer. We believed the East Peak was the true or "Main" summit and were drawn to the possibility of the first ascent of such a big and beautiful mountain.

By mid September 2009, fellow Americans Steve and Mark Wilford, with Jim Lowther from the U.K., and I found ourselves halfway up the 1,700-meter southwest face of SKII. We huddled in two tiny tents perched on a narrow ledge of ice as a storm raged and temperatures dropped well below zero. As we struggled to melt water with a failing stove, we felt our exhaustion from an open bivouac the previous night and the rigors of two months of climbing and reconnaissance. This had included six forays over a 6,000-meter pass, which was our only access to the southwest face from base camp. We retreated on our fourth day. Although unsuccessful, we learned a great deal about the mountain. The southwest face was a direct route to the "Main" summit and relatively safe from objective dangers. But the mountain had revealed a cruel secret: it offered no natural ledges big enough for a bivouac.

By 2011, Steve and I were ready for a second attempt. This time we were accompanied by Freddie Wilkinson, a top young alpine climber. Three other experienced climbers would join the expedition: Janet Bergman, Emilie Drinkwater, and Kirsten Kremer. Their plan was to share our base camp while attempting other unclimbed peaks in the region, especially a beautiful rocky peak just above base camp.

Mark Richey leading the ice gully on Tsok Kangri. *Freddie Wilkinson*

In addition to the American members, we were joined by six Indian climbers: Chewang Motup (expedition co-leader), Konchok Thinlese (sirdar), Pemba Sherpa (aka King Kong), Dhan Singh Harkotia, Jangla Tashi Phunchok, and Tshering Sherpa. Our base camp was well staffed by chief cook Santabir Sherpa and his assistants Arjun Rai, Aungchok, and Mahipal (aka Kitchen Boy). Raj Kumar, from the Indian Army, served as our liaison officer. Climbing in this restricted region requires "Joint Expedition" status, meaning that there must be an equal number of

Freddie Wilkinson leading the back side of the summit ridge on Tsok Kangri. *Steve Swenson*

Indian climbers and foreigners on foreign expeditions. Since our intent was to climb alpine style with just a three-man team of Americans, we came up with a plan to engage our Sherpa and Ladahki teammates to help establish advanced base camps for both teams as well as to manage the normal duties of base camp and cooking. This strategy proved essential to our success.

By July 11 the team was comfortably settled in a lovely base camp at 5,000 meters, above the snout of the Sakang Lungpa glacier and just three days' walk from the Nubra Valley. Wildflowers, awesome boulders, and a gurgling brook in a meadow with amazing views of unclimbed Plateau Peak and other mountains made for one of the finest base camps any of us had ever experienced. Best of all, we had it all to ourselves!

On July 23, Steve, Freddie, and I skied over the 6,000-meter pass we had discovered in 2009 and established Advanced Base Camp (ABC) on the South Shukpa Kunchang glacier. ABC was directly below the southwest face of SKII. The following day our intended recon to the 2009 highpoint ended well below, at our first camp, which we'd dubbed "The Launchpad." Extreme heat triggered major snow sloughs and rockfall in the Great Couloir—the main feature bisecting the southwest face.

It was clearly too hot to attempt SKII. We needed to wait until later in the season, when temperatures would be cooler. So we turned our attention to a spectacular cirque near ABC. There we found a beautiful line of ice runnels up a steep north face ending directly at the summit of a virgin 6,585-meter peak. We left ABC at 4 a.m. on July 31 with nothing but daypacks and climbed 12 pitches of superb grade 4+ ice to the summit ridge. After a tricky traverse around the south side we reached the top at 6 p.m., just as the final rays of sun painted the range in alpenglow. From the summit we had spectacular views north to Saser Kangri II and confirmed that our main objective, the East Peak, was considerably higher than the western point reached by the 1985 expedition.

A 22-hour round trip, including 13 rappels and a ski in the dark, brought us back to ABC exhausted but thrilled. With suggestions from our Ladakhi companions, we named the mountain Tsok Kangri, a Buddhist expression for the practice of gathering merit and wisdom in life.

On August 4, encouraged by an excellent weather forecast, we returned to ABC to attempt other first ascents in the area while we waited for the weather to cool down for SKII. The women, after encountering dangerous rock fall hazard on their peak above base camp, joined us while they looked for a safer objective. Steve meanwhile had developed a sinus infection and descended to the Nubra Valley to recover.

First to strike were Emilie and Kirsten with the first ascent of Pumo Kangri, 6,250 meters, via the west face on August 5. Assuming their route to be mainly snow, they carried only one ice screw and no bivy gear. But the snow turned out to be just a veneer over hard blue ice. Conditions slowed their progress and they arrived on the summit in the late afternoon. They made 15 V-thread rappels in the dark and passed Freddie and Janet on their way up to bag the first ascent of Saserling, a spectacular rock tower to the north. Their route follows a steep crack system in good granite for eight pitches of 5.9+ and finishes directly on a pointed summit.

After just one day of rest, everyone skied across the valley to a high camp below a 6,660-meter peak that we named Stegosaurus because of its central spine of rock towers. On August 9, all five of us climbed up steep snow just right of the towers followed by a 300-meter traverse along the exposed final ridge. Just below the top we belayed each other one at a time to the corniced summit. This was the fourth first ascent of the expedition and an altitude record for all the women. The best part was yet to come, however: a superb ski descent back to ABC from high camp. It was great fun watching pro skiers Emily and Kirsten as they effortlessly carved turns and jumped small crevasses.

Now it was time for the women to head home, so we all descended to the Nubra Valley to say farewell, check on Steve's status, which thankfully had improved, and enjoy a few days of rest, cold beer, and hot springs.

On August 16, Freddie, Steve, and I were back in BC anxious for promising weather. With less than two weeks left in the expedition, we were running out of time. On the 19th we received a forecast calling for high pressure, low winds, and light precipitation for the next six to eight days. The bad news: it would be followed by a significant disturbance. The race was on.

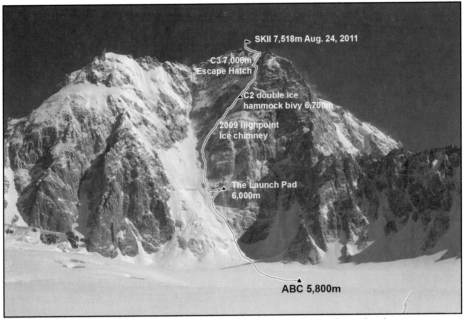

The southwest face of Saser Kangri II (7,518m), showing the line of The Old Breed. *Mark Richey*

The next morning we left BC with Thinlese, Tserring, Tashi, and Pemba helping to carry loads to ABC, which we reached early in the day. On the mountain above ABC, Steve, Freddie, and I would climb in pure alpine style carrying everything we needed to get up and down safely. We packed five days of food, mostly cheese, sausage, soups, and energy bars, six days fuel, a tiny two-man tent, and a minimal rack of eight ice screws, five pitons, and a dozen nuts and cams. To cut weight, we carried just two sleeping bags, one regular and a larger one that two could share. To address the main problem of bivouac sites we carried our own invention: two specially designed "ice hammocks" that weighed only two ounces each. These consisted of an eight-foot by three-foot sheet of fabric with sewn loops on each end that could be anchored to the slope 10 feet apart and then backfilled with snow and ice to extend a chopped tent platform on the ledge-less face.

That night my mind raced with details. Had we planned for everything? Had Steve adequately recovered? Would the weather hold long enough for a summit bid? I tossed and turned with nervous energy until the wee hours. I was worried that we were overlooking something, but I was also just eager to get on with the climb.

Morning arrived with a stiff wind as we skied to the base in darkness. Freddie, in the lead, called back to Steve and me to watch out for crevasses as they'd opened up since our last attempt. We stashed our skis in the cold pre-dawn light and, like automatons, ascended the snow funnel to the bergschrund at the base of the Great Couloir.

Freddie led the first block of 55-degree ice. After three pitches we made an encouraging discovery: hard névé had formed on top of the ice in places, allowing us to move together without belays. With the improved conditions we moved faster than on previous attempts and by late morning, just as the sun beamed over us, we reached the Launch Pad bivy. Though it

Richey and Wilkinson in the Great Couloir of Saser Kangri II. *Steve Swenson*

was colder than in mid July, we knew that the heat of the day could cause rock fall in the Great Couloir, so we set up our tent on the best ledge on route and waited until night to start climbing again.

At 3 a.m. Steve took the lead, sometimes belaying and sometimes simul-climbing, and we flew up the Great Couloir. By 10 a.m. we reached our second bivy in 2009. I took over the lead as we passed mixed rock and ice to the "Ice Chimney" pitch. Freddie hollered up encouragingly as I passed a tricky bulge and exited onto the steep ice slopes above. We were thrilled that what we learned in 2009 had helped put us above our previous highpoint so early on the second day. But finding a spot for a good bivy was the next challenge—we knew that climbing safely and successfully on such a big wall at this altitude meant we needed to set up the tent, rehydrate, and eat well. Three more pitches and a long traverse to the right placed us on top of a small, rocky buttress. As I joined Freddie at the stance he commented, "I think this is the best we're going to do," referring to the 45-degree sloping rock he was belaying from. It was time to test the "Ice Hammock."

After two hours of chopping ice and transporting snow in our packs to fill the Hammocks that slung over the rock like giant brassieres, we had the makings of a ledge just big enough to accommodate our shelter. Without the Ice Hammocks we would have been sitting exposed and upright all night.

We had climbed more than half the wall and had broken through the rock band, a section we'd feared might be the crux of the climb. What's more, the weather was calm and clear. Only one thing worried us: Steve was clearly not well. While Freddie and I chopped and prepared the bivy, Steve melted water as he was too tired for anything else. This was a bad sign. We all knew it but didn't discuss it. We feared Steve's sinus infection might be returning and it could mean the end of the climb. With almost any other climber I would have called off the ascent, but Steve is so experienced and aware of his body that when he says he can go I don't question him. That night we rested and hydrated well, and despite a lot of hacking and snorting, Steve felt well enough in the morning to move up.

Freddie took over the lead early, climbing rock to the top of the buttress and then moving diagonally up a broad gully we coined "The Ramp." Although never steep or overly technical, the relentless low angle water ice was taxing, particularly at 7,000 meters with full packs. Nonetheless, The Ramp offered an amazing passage through an otherwise imposing rock wall. After eight pitches, the Ramp dead-ended at an overhanging cul de sac. Freddie spied a weakness on the left side of the rock wall, traversed into a crack system, hooking and dry-tooling with a balancy move into a blind corner that turned out to be the technical crux of the climb. "This is f---ing awesome climbing" he screamed down, clearly enjoying himself. We named it the "Escape Hatch" pitch, a key passage to easier snow and ice slopes above. Steve and I followed, arms pumped and lungs burning as we joined Freddie at a small stance.

Since it was late in the day, we began searching for a bivouac, but wherever we excavated snow and ice we hit rock within a foot. Just as we were beginning to lose hope, Freddie lowered around a corner beneath an overhang and shouted, "I think we can chop it here, just maybe." I joined him, and we feverishly hacked at the ice while Steve melted snow again and dried his clothing that was soaked from a leaked water bottle in his pack. This time we were without the advantage of our Ice Hammocks as we had used both at previous camps and left them in place for the descent. As darkness enveloped, we squeezed into the tent, its outer corners sagging over the void. The

The second bivouac on Saser Kangri II, where Richey's two-ounce Ice Hammocks saved the night by holding snow for a level platform. *Steve Swenson*

tent was tied to an ice screw and a safety tether also snaked through a hole in the top. We filled the corners with boot shells and extra gear; it was marginal at best.

Shoehorned into the two-man tent, we shifted awkwardly about the stove as it swayed precariously in the center while Steve hacked up phlegm throughout the night. He later confided, "I was thinking I just needed to make it to the high camp, where Freddie and Mark can go for the summit while I wait for them in the tent." That team approach epitomizes Steve's character and is testament to our close friendship. Freddie and I were thinking differently. We were so close we could taste the summit, and the weather was amazingly calm and clear. We had dreamed of this mountain for three years and worked so hard that we couldn't imagine leaving Steve behind. We never even discussed it.

As we ate soup and cheese, we strategized for the next day. We would take light packs, leaving the tent and most of our equipment behind—gambling on making it to the top and back in one day. I would lead to the summit ridge, where Freddie would take over. If snow was deep, Steve suggested he could help plough, but we knew it was going to be a fight for him just getting to the top in his condition.

We woke to a fourth day of perfect weather and climbed three pitches of moderate ice to a broad shoulder on the summit ridge. Surrounding us were unclimbed mountains and unexplored glaciers as far as the eye could see. Tsok Kangri was far below us now. Freddie led us up a gentle slope and along a sharp crest and then stopped and waited for me just a rope length from the top. "Go on," he said, "you go first." When there was nowhere higher to go, emotion overcame me and I let out a long, primal scream. I have climbed many mountains over the years, but this one felt special. Perhaps because I had dreamed of this moment for three years—to be the first to summit a Himalayan giant, with best friends, and to do it in our best style—and maybe because I knew I was reaching a turning point in my climbing. At 53 I was old for this game, and there might not be another such opportunity.

Moments later we were all on top together. We cheered, embraced, shook hands, and I squeezed Steve so hard that in his weakened condition he could hardly breathe. We babbled on about our incredible fortune: a great team, a virgin 7,500-meter peak in a remote Karakoram Range on an absolutely perfect day. It seemed surreal as we gazed northwest past unclimbed peaks to the Karakoram giants in Pakistan. Steve pointed out K2, Broad Peak, and the Gasherbrums. It truly was, as Steve put it, "dreamy."

It had been anything but easy for Steve and it is proof of his tremendous will and endurance that he carried on in spite of feeling so poorly. In his words, "I have climbed other mountains that took more strength, but this one hurt the most."

Below us and half a kilometer to the west was a rounded dome of snow above a prominent rock tower that we recognized as the "West Peak" of SKII. We estimated it to be 100 to 150 meters below us and lacking any real prominence. This confirmed our suspicion that the East Peak was not only the true summit of Saser Kangri II, but also that the "West Peak" was a shoulder of the summit ridge and not an actual summit.

Eventually we had to go down. We reminded ourselves that the job is not done until all are safely in base camp. Arriving at our high camp by early afternoon, we crawled inside to rest. Steve was worse now and unable to lie down for fear of choking on his phlegm. He spent the night sitting upright at the door while Freddie and I squished into the back and did our best to make him comfortable. No one slept and in the morning we rose to cloudy skies and a light snow falling. Freddie set the first rappel as I melted water and hurriedly packed the tent.

Although we were all tired, Steve was exhausted, moving painfully slowly and beginning to lose his mental acuteness. One of our ropes had been cut by a falling stone the day before and we needed to pass the knot on each rappel. At one point Steve accidentally unclipped himself from the rappel rope without even knowing it. After that we watched him like hawks.

By midday, we had descended half the face and with shade from cloud cover we were lured into continuing down the Great Couloir rather than stopping to wait for the cool of night. Several rappels into the Couloir a thunderous crack echoed above and rocks of all sizes rained down on us. We were all tethered to a single ice screw, swaying from side to side as we dodged the deadly projectiles for what seemed like eternity. No one was hit and, amazingly, Freddie captured the whole event on video.

Thirty-five rappels, the last 12 by headlamp, delivered us to the glacier and our skis. It was insanely scary sliding down the icy surface by headlamp, accelerating toward crevasses that we could bridge with our skis but knowing that putting on the breaks at the wrong time might lead to a plunge into the abyss.

In the foggy darkness we skied right past our camp, but eventually our faithful companions, Tinless, Dhan Singh, and Pemba heard our calls and hurried to greet us with hot tea and cheers of congratulations. We drank and by midnight collapsed into our bags and fell into a comatose sleep.

That is until 3 a.m., when I awoke to a persistent tug on my leg. "Go away, let me sleep" was my first reaction. It was Steve. "I am in trouble and I need help," he whispered in a weak voice. One look in his eyes told me it was urgent. His coughing was dislodging big chunks of sticky phlegm that periodically would block his airway. With the SAT phone we called Steve's doctor friend Brownie Schoene in the United States and asked for advice. "Keep him hydrated and make sure he doesn't suffocate." Weighing the circumstances and our remote location, we placed a call to Global Rescue, our American Alpine Club rescue provider, and initiated a helicopter evacuation. Over the next 12 hours we communicated our position and situation to Chewang Motup of Rimo Expeditons, joint leader of our SKII expedition, to my wife Teresa who had joined Motup in Leh, and to the Global Rescue agent in Boston. They, in turn, contacted the Indian government to obtain the complex clearances required for the Indian Air force to send their highly trained helicopter pilots up the South Shukpa glacier for the evacuation. They had never before landed a helicopter on these glaciers.

We did our best to make Steve comfortable, but at times the waves of choking nearly overcame him and we feared for his life. Secretly, Freddie and I prepared crude tools, plastic tubes from a harness and a sterilized Swiss Army knife, for a last resort tracheotomy if it came to that. Meanwhile, Teresa and Motup worked the phones relentlessly back in Leh, badgering every government official who would take their calls to keep the pressure on and get a helicopter to BC before it was too late.

Fortunately the tracheotomy was not required and at 3 p.m. the telltale whir of rotor blades filled the air. Freddie and I felt a huge relief.

Two choppers flying low over the mountains made a big circle before putting down next to our makeshift heli pad. The second chopper was a backup in case the first would have trouble taking off from the 19,000-foot landing zone. We loaded Steve and within an hour he was at the general hospital in Leh.

Thanks to intravenous antibiotics and the expertise of great doctors and nurses, Steve made a rapid recovery. Although weak, he was able to return to our hotel after just a few days.

Meanwhile, Tashi, Pemba, Tshering, Dhan Singh, Freddie, and I broke down ABC, traversed up and over to base camp, and the next day everyone descended to the Nubra Valley where we met Teresa, her friend Lisa

Teresa Richey, Chewang Motup, and Steve Swenson in Leh after the helicopter rescue. *Steve Swenson Collection*

from the States, and Motup. After a few days we were all together in Leh for a wonderful celebration.

SKII and our other climbs were a great success for all of us and provided a remarkable adventure. Collectively, we made five first ascents including the world's second highest unclimbed mountain. All were climbed free, in alpine style, without the aid of fixed ropes or camps.

We are extremely appreciative of the support we received from our Indian team members and of the Rimo staff for helping us establish and supply our Advanced Base Camp on the South Shukpa glacier. Without that support, we would certainly not have been successful. We were delighted with the tasty meals and attention provided by our cook Santibir and his assistants in BC. Most of all, we are grateful for the friendship and camaraderie we all shared on this marvelous joint expedition.

We are also indebted to the Western Air Command of the Indian Air Force for their courage and superb skill evacuating Steve so flawlessly. Lastly I would like to acknowledge and thank my wife Teresa for being there when we needed her most.

SUMMARY:

Area: Eastern Karakoram, India

Ascents: First ascent of Saser Kangri II (7,518m), via the southwest face: The Old Breed, 1,700m, WI 4 M3, August 24, 2011, by Mark Richey, Steve Swenson, Freddie Wilkinson. First ascent of Tsok Kangri (6,585m), via the north face: 680m, WI4+, July 31, 2011, by Richey, Swenson, Wilkinson. First ascent of Pumo Kangri (6,250m), via west face: 450m, WI3, August 5, 2011, by Emilie Drinkwater, Kirsten Kremer. First ascent of Saser Ling (6,100m), via the south face: 350m, 8 pitches, 5.9+, August 6, 2011, by Bergman and Wilkinson. First ascent of Stegosaurus (6,660m), via the south glacier to south ridge: August 9, 2011, by Bergman, Drinkwater, Kremer, Richey, and Wilkinson.

2011 SKII joint Indo-American expedition members: Mark Richey, Co-leader; Chewang Motup, Co-leader; Steve Swenson, Climber; Freddie Wilkinson, Climber; Emilie Drinkwater, Climber; Janet Bergman, Climber; Kirsten Kremer, Climber; Raj Kumar, Liason Officer; Konchok Thinlese, Sirdar, Climber; Pemba Sherpa (aka King Kong), Climber; Dhan Singh Harkotia, Climber; Jangla Tashi Phunchok, Climber; Tshering Sherpa, Climber; Santabir Sherpa, Chief Cook; Arjun Rai, Cook's helper; Aungchok, Cook's helper; Mahipal, Kitchen Boy.

Mark Richey, Steve Swenson, and Freddie Wilkinson on the summit. *Steve Swenson*

A NOTE ABOUT THE AUTHOR:

*Mark Richey began rock climbing in 1972 in the Quincy Quarries of Massachusetts and continues to climb and explore wild places around the globe with his best friends.*

*When home he works in an architectural woodworking company that he owns with his wife Teresa, who often accompanies him on his adventures.*

# CLIMBS AND EXPEDITIONS

---

# 2012

*Accounts from the various climbs and expeditions of the world are listed geographically. We generally bias from north to south and from west to east within the noted countries, but the priority is on a logical flow from one mountain range to the next. We begin our coverage with the Contiguous United States and move to Alaska in order for the climbs in Alaska's Wrangell Mountains to segue into the St. Elias climbs in Canada.*

*We encourage all climbers to submit accounts of notable activity, especially long new routes (generally defined as U.S. commitment Grade IV—full-day climbs—or longer). Please submit reports as early as possible (see Submissions Guidelines at aaj.americanalpineclub.org).*

*For conversions of meters to feet, multiply by 3.28; for feet to meters, multiply by 0.30.*

**Unless otherwise noted, all reports are from the 2011 calendar year.
Longer versions, extra photos, and additional information for many of these
reports can be found at aaj.americanalpineclub.org**

## *Contiguous United States*

WASHINGTON

*Cascades summary.* It was another good snow year in the Cascades. After a stable period in February, cool and snowy conditions generally prevailed into spring. In late March, Jens Holsten and Dan Hilden climbed a new line on the northeast face of Colchuck Peak, the Hilden-Holsten (III, WI3 M6).

The Stuart Range saw the usual activity. On June 25 Jimbo Shokes and Sol Wertkin climbed a route on Colchuck Balanced Rock (Honey Badger, III 5.10- A2). On July 24 Jens Holsten and Adam Lawson climbed a new route on the northeast face of Dragontail Peak (Chasin' Tail, IV 5.10 A1). On July 31 Holsten, Sole Werkin, and Mark Westman climbed a direct finish to an existing route on Mt. Stuart (Gorillas in the Mist Direct, IV 5.11-).

Near Darrington, over the course of several visits, Chris Greyell and Darryl Kralovic established Schizophrenic (III 5.11a) on Squire Creek Wall, while Brandon Workman and friends established the Squire (III 5.10c), also on Squire Creek Wall.

Late summer saw new routes on Dome Peak and Sloan Peak. Nate Far and partner called their September 2 line on the south face of Dome Peak Indian Summer (III 5.10). Brandon Workman and Rad Roberts climbed the west face of Sloan Peak (Diamond in the Rough, III 5.10).

The fall offered excellent conditions during periods of stable weather. Rolf Larson and Eric Wherley climbed a new route on the northeast face of Tower Mountain (Tower of Babel, III 5.10-), and new lines went up in the Cascade Pass area. On October 18 Kurt Hicks and Gaston climbed the East Face Couloir on Sahale Peak (III AI3+). On October 25 Hicks, Forest McBrian, and Dave Jordan climbed the Misunderstanding (IV AI4R M4).

Sloan Peak's southwest face. (1) Diamond in the Rough. (2) Fire on the Mountain. Dashed line represents unroped scrambling to summit. (3) Descent via Corkscrew Route. *Rad Roberts*

Meanwhile, local and national climbers' organizations have been working behind the scenes on a variety of issues. The Washington Climbers Coalition had teamed with the Access Fund and the American Alpine Club to raise money for purchasing the Lower Town Wall at Index in 2010. In 2011 these groups continued to work together and with other user groups, conservation groups, and land managers to maintain access.

MATT PERKINS, *AAC*

*Pasayten Wilderness, Amphitheater Peak, Cathedral Peak, Deacon Peak, three new routes.* Alpine climbing, especially new routing, can be an uncomfortable, frightening, and challenging experience, one whose merits are only truly appreciated in hindsight, what is called type-two fun. My weeklong trip to the Pasayten Wilderness with Blake Herrington, in August, was none of these. Despite a chilly summer snowstorm and excess mosquitoes, our week of adventure and exploration on the Washington–British Columbia border was solidly type-one: fun while doing it. During our week camped on the shores of Upper Cathedral Lake, we swam, fished, rocked out to iPods (you can't

Blake Herrington following a splitter on the (Middle) Finger of Fatwa, on Amphitheater Peak. *Scott Bennett*

put a price on morale!), ate trout fried in bacon fat, drank whiskey, played cards with new friends, and, the icing on the cake, put up three stellar new routes.

First, on the south face of Cathedral Peak, we established Last Rites 300m, 5.11+). Our route wanders up the highly featured, choose-your-own-adventure face, beginning between the Beckey and Doorish routes, finally making a sharp right across the Beckey ramp to tackle a steep headwall crack (crux). We then followed the Southeast Buttress Route for its last pitch to the summit.

Second, we checked out enticing terrain on the north face of Amphitheater Peak. The biggest aspect here is called Middle Finger Buttress, so we named our route the (Middle) Finger of Fatwa. (The cirque has a religious naming theme.) Checking in at 160m and 5.11, this route was our shortest but by no means least enjoyable. It featured an incredible fingers-to-thin-hands splitter, then a series of left-leaning roofs, surmounted by hand cracks and jugs.

Finally, we checked out the north face of the Deacon, tantalized by descriptions of a face similar to Yosemite's Sentinel Rock, with the central aspect yet unclimbed.

Located just across the B.C. border, it is of course necessary to follow international laws and not simply traipse across the weirdly deforested line in the forest. The north face of the Deacon is indeed impressive. Beginning just right of the Nose (Anderson-Barnett, 1974) we followed an arcing corner to 5.10-rightward underclings. We pieced together the intricate, wandering 70m second

Cathedral Peak's Last Rights route climbs central face, joining Southeast Buttress near the end. *Blake Herrington*

pitch, connecting incipient seams and improbable traverses. The third pitch climbed a thin, mossy layback corner. This pitch necessitated some cleaning on aid but was led cleanly afterward (crux). Finally we gained the major splitter crack system we'd been shooting for and were soon reveling in alpine hand-crack heaven. Three more long pitches led us to lower-angle terrain, which we happily simuled to the summit. We'd completed our longest and best route of the trip, the Heretic (350m, 5.11).

We recommend the Pasayten Wilderness of Washington and B.C. to anyone looking for an adventurous summer trip; it's full of soft green alpine meadows, solid granite, hungry trout, and type-one fun!

SCOTT BENNETT

*Mix-up Peak, The Misunderstanding.* On October 25 Forest McBrian, Dave Jordan, and I established a new line on Mix-up Peak in North Cascades National Park. The route, which climbs the northeast face of the north summit, is partially visible from Cascade Pass. Forest and I spotted the line a week prior, while descending Sahale Arm after climbing an undocumented but excellent couloir on Sahale Peak's east face. The weather was with us; we had clear and cold temperatures, immediately following a brief warm spell that included rain up high, which created perfect conditions on the climb.

The route begins in a narrow groove 60m east of the obvious couloir that splits the face. The first pitch set the tone, with excellent sticks in perfect snice but a dearth of protection. Each of the following eight pitches stretched the rope, totaling almost 1,800' of climbing on the face. The route was longer and more difficult than we had anticipated. It is unusually sustained for a Cascades line—only two pitches didn't include 55° or steeper terrain, and all went straight up (except pitch

Forest McBrian on crux The Misunderstanding. *Kurt Hicks*

Forest McBrian on The Misunderstanding.
*Kurt Hicks*

Diggin' for Dreams, as viewed from
southeast face of South Early Winter Spire.
*Mike Pond*

5.11 fifth pitch of Diggin' for Dreams.
*Mike Pond*

two, which deviates 15m right at mid-height).

The crux was a roof draped with icicles on pitch five. It was the finest pitch we had ever climbed in the mountains, and Forest led it impeccably. Above the crux we discovered an incredible ice chimney that led to yet another ice pitch and finally a short snow slope to the crest.

Technical climbing ended at a small notch in the summit ridge, where we took in a spectacular view of Johannesberg and Formidable in evening alpenglow. It was a perfect day in the mountains. The Misunderstanding (2,200' of climbing, IV M4R AI4).

KURT HICKS, *kurthicks.com*

*Hai Tower, Diggin' for Dreams.* The Half Moon, Choi Oy, and Hai Tower massif forms a giant open book, easily visible from the nearby Liberty Bell group near Washington Pass. It was hard for us to believe that such a massive face was unclimbed. However, in speaking with several generations of local climbers, as well as Fred Beckey, we learned of no routes on the northwest face of Hai Tower. Alan Kearney and Beckey had done first ascents there, but they climbed much farther north, on Half Moon proper.

On August 25 Mike Pond, Rob Schiesser, and I climbed a prominent right-facing dihedral toward the right side of the face and then followed cracks to the summit. Of the nine pitches, seven were 5.10, one 5.11, and the "easy" one was a 5.8X lichen slab. We climbed the route onsight, in eight hours, with no bolts (1,000', IV 5.11R). There was an old sling 250' up, likely from an exploratory ascent that retreated where the corner runs out of good rock, protection, and features. We highly recommend this route; it follows high-quality, well-protected granite, except for two run-out slab pitches near the top (the R rating applies to pitches of 5.8 and 5.10, not to the 5.11). We plan to return to bolt two belays, as well as the X-rated eighth pitch, to make it safer and more enjoyable.

Diggin' for Dreams is named for pitch four, which features two body lengths of large-grained kitty litter. As Mike tossed yet another handful, groping for something solid, Rob yelled up, "You dig for that dream!"

ALAN ROUSSEAU, *AAC*

*Tower Mountain, Tower of Babble.* Rolf Larson and I bushwhacked up Swamp Creek on September 4, aiming for a new route on the northeast face of 8,444' Tower Mountain, whose shattered rock is notorious for turning back adventurers. Only one known route has been established on this face (III 5.10, Pete Doorish and Alex Cudkowicz, 1989), and that route traversed onto the face at half-height before ascending. We hoped to climb the entire face.

From our bivy at Snowy Lakes, we approached over a col on the northwest side of the mountain and descended snow along the mountain's northern arm, getting a good view of the face. In the morning light, its looming steepness had us a bit skeptical. Rolf had attempted the face before but bailed a few pitches up. Lines leading directly to the summit appeared steepest and loosest, and we turned our attention to a more moderate and solid-looking buttress on the far north side of the face.

Tower Mountain, showing (left) Cudkowicz-Doorish (1989) and Tower of Babble (2011). *John Scurlock*

We began with two simul-climbing pitches of 5.7/8 below the big ledge, then some third class on the big ledge system to reach the line we had spied. The five upper pitches were the business and went at 5.10- (50m), 5.9 (50m), 5.9 (50m), 5.6, and 4th class to the summit crest. We descended the standard West Gully route and the next day climbed the insecure Northeast Arête of Golden Horn.

ERIC WEHRLY

*Sloan Peak, Full Moon Fever.* Sloan Peak has been described as the "Matterhorn of the Cascades" because of its commanding stature. On December 12, under a full moon experiencing a lunar eclipse, Braden Downey, Will Hinckley, and I climbed a long snow and ice route on the northern aspect of its west face, above Bedal Basin. A couple of highlights included the first pitch with its full 60 meters of grade 4 ice with a texture like shampoo, and the insecure and runout ice of pitch four, which we coined "The Window" due to a large hole that revealed its delaminated status and did nothing for our confidence.

Good rock on the upper face of Tower of Babble on Tower Mountain. *Eric Wehrly*

After 950' of steep ice we bagged the ropes and carried on with an additional 1,000' of steep snow and ice to 50° that brought us to a prominent notch, followed by 40' of snow-covered 4th class

Pitch two on Full Moon Fever, Sloan Peak. *Braden Downey*

and then two rope lengths of interesting mixed climbing to the summit ridge. The final, exhausting 1,000' feet of ropeless climbing included an exposed traverse, countless false summits, and an airy down-climb into a large notch. We topped out after a feverish 12 hours. The complex descent was impeded by a whiteout, nightfall, and fading headlamps. We found our way to our cache, went into autopilot, and finished it out after 18 hours on the go. A tremendous day in the mountains. Full Moon Fever is 3,000', IV 5.8 AI4 50°.

KEVIN HOGAN, *AAC*

*Inspiration Peak, Northeast Buttress.* In August 1996 Dana Hagin and I climbed the Northeast Buttress of Inspiration Peak in the Southern Pickets but never reported it. We approached via Terror Creek, climbed to the saddle between West McMillan and Inspiration's east ridge, and rappelled and downclimbed to where we could traverse a ledge across to the buttress. From the end of the ledge we scrambled up a loose gully and gained a shallow rib that led up to the buttress. Mostly following the crest, the climbing ranged from 5.5 to about 5.8, with one pitch of 5.10-. Late in the day a perfect ledge for two, with a small snowpatch, appeared high on the route. We bivied there and made the summit the next day. The buttress joins Inspiration's upper east ridge for the last several pitches. For the complete story of our climb, go to my blog at alankearney.com. Grade III/IV 5.10-.

ALAN KEARNEY, *AAC*

*Colchuck Peak, northeast face, Hilden-Holsten.* In late January 2011 Jens Holsten and I climbed a new route on the northeast face of Colchuck Peak to the right of the Northeast Couloir during an uncommonly long period of high pressure. Two fun pitches of AI3+, a few hundred feet of 50°–60° snow trending up and left, followed by two pitches of unconsolidated snow covering moderate rock took us to a steep rock band. We traversed left 30' to climb two pitches of M6 in a chimney, followed by more steep snow and a final rock band, which brought us to a windy notch on the crest of the north ridge right at sunset. A tricky wide crack (M6) out of the notch and a traverse around to the west led to the final couloir of the North Buttress Couloir Route. Unable to find the easiest way to the top in the dark, we climbed one more short but steep mixed pitch to the windy, rime-covered summit. We decided to call it the Hilden-Holsten, sticking with the theme of the mixed routes across the way on Dragontail. IV M6 AI3+.

DAN HILDEN, *AAC*

*Dragontail Peak, Chasin' Tail.* On July 24, Adam Lawson and I picked our way through eight new pitches (two were long simul blocks) on Dragontail's northeast wall. Well right of Dragonfly, our route climbs a line of scary choss through a steep swath of stone, before intersecting the never-ending Northeast Buttress. Despite the loose rock (which I had expected) we enjoyed our adventure. At the start of the day, we were unsure if we could climb this wall via new ground in a day. It was complex, and the way was never clear. Survival trumped free-climbing, and we pulled on a few pieces along the way. Usually I'd be racing back up to a line left unfreed, but I think I will leave that improvement in style to someone else. It was one of those lines you only do once. Chasin' Tail is IV 5.10 A1.

Jens Holsten, *AAC*

*Mt. Adams, Adams Headwall variation.* It is a testament to El Niño and an open-minded approach to ice climbing that an interesting new route was enjoyed on the 4th of July. It was made possible by its high altitude, the shade of a northwest face, and a tough young lady with an eye for ice. Anastasia Blagoveshchenskaya enticed me with an e-mail alluding to steep alpine ice and my fondness for new lines on old volcanoes.

Blagoveshchenskaya-Wallace line on northwest face of Mt. Adams. *Wayne Wallace*

We made the long, snowy approach on the 3rd, and climbed the route in a brutal 22-hour day, counting the drive home. I always forget how big these monster volcanoes are. The tiny-looking cliff is actually two pitches. The whole route is over 3,000 vertical feet, with several technical pitches at the top. After climbing the first half of the Stormy Monday Couloir, we simul-soloed the first steps, then got after the middle pitches. The first was 50m and WI3+. Anastasia tackled the 30m second pitch.

After the middle pitches we struggled to find a way up the overhanging 60m rock band at the top. I began traversing left, hoping to be able to punch through to the summit snow slopes. Eventually I found a way at the end of the cliff. It was an awesome pitch: vertical ice and rock, followed by a short overhang with "good" rime (AI4) and pulling up onto the rim at 11,500'. A great finish to a long ice season.

Wayne Wallace

California

Yosemite National Park

*Liberty Cap, The Patriot Act.* Liberty Cap called us back for another round after we added Scarface in 2010. Starting halfway out the traverse ledge, in a thin corner system rising through overhanging stone, the line eventually trends right and joins the West Buttress route at the classic eighth pitch dihedral. We followed the West Buttress traverse left, then broke off to join the final pitches of Scarface to the summit. Our team consisted of Steve Bosque, Lars Johnson, and me.

We prepared for a relaxed, pitch-a-day schedule, which we strictly adhered to until the last day. The first few pitches were steep and technical. Our weapon of choice was the red Moses Tomahawk. Perfect for thin corners, they would be the staple piece for the first half of the route. High-quality rock was on the menu, pitch after pitch. Some airtime was logged, cams broken, rain gear dropped, but we moved right along.

Liberty Cap routes: (1) Passport to the Sky, V 7a A1 (Gary-Jason-Segura, 2006). (2) Scarface, V 5.8 A3 (Bosque-Mucci, 2010). (3) West Buttress, V 5.10 A3 (Bosque-Corbett, 1985). (4) The Patriot Act, V 5.9 A3+ (Bosque-Johnson-Mucci, 2011). (5) Southwest Face, V 5.8 C3 (Faint-Harding-Rowell, 1969). (6) Direct Southwest Face, VI 5.10 A3+ (Braun-Cashner, 1982). (7) Turkey Shoot, V 5.9 A3 (Bosque-Yager, 1988). (8) A Joint Adventure, V 5.9 A3+ (Barbella-Gagner-McConachie, 1979, out of sight on right). Route lines and info courtesy *Josh Mucci. Joe Hornof/qitnl.com*

After joining the West Buttress for a pitch, a long traverse left led into Scarface. We geared up for the final push up the last three pitches. I had led this path last year, so I started racking up under questionable weather. As soon as I stepped into my ladder, it started to rain. Eventually I was climbing in a low-angle waterfall from a lightning storm directly above Liberty Cap. Mildly hypothermic when I reached the belay, I was relieved that the rain turned to hail.

Our relaxed trip had suddenly turned hasty—the opposite of when we climbed these pitches in brutal heat the year before. Steve and Lars were soaked from the runoff at the belay and, having dealt with the pigs in the pool, so to speak, were inclined to let me lead to the summit, which we reached on September 24.

We spent seven days on the climb, after fixing four pitches. We drilled and filled 53 holes. At 62 Lars is the oldest person recorded as completing a big wall first ascent in Yosemite. He had also undergone cancer surgery five months prior to our climb. We named the route The Patriot Act (13 pitches, V 5.9 A3+).

JOSH MUCCI

Looking back on A2 money-pitch corner on the Patriot Act. *Josh Mucci*

SIERRA NEVADA

*Merriam Peak, north buttress, two new routes.* Late last summer Lisa Rand and I headed up from the old mine ruins in Pine Creek to the high alpine of Royce Lakes basin. The hike starts out bizarre: in a mile or so you look down on what looks like a Lord of the Rings movie set, with bombed-out buildings, rusted machinery, and creepy tunnels. Mounds of discarded crap rock look like the pooped out innards of the mountain looming above. All of which makes the peaks and snowfields feel that much more like paradise. From our lakeside base camp in late August, we watched icebergs floating like hunchbacked swans.

Merriam's north face is home to one of the classics of the range: Clevenger and Harringtons' North Buttress. Good as it is, this route follows a line left of the buttress itself. On a previous visit I'd ogled some overhanging cracks that appeared to lead up the very crest. This is what we came for.

Early next morning we stamped up sun-cupped snow to the base, arriving just behind two climbers headed for the reg route. After a long moderate pitch and a 5.11 stemming section, we arrived at the overhanging cracks. Expecting a 5.12 struggle, I instead found perfect hands in perfect rock. Above the lip the crack swept up until it pinched off below a large roof. At the last moment, edges led left to another crack and up to sling belay. A pitch higher we ran into another discontinuity: a 40' vertical headwall of orange ripples above a big ledge.

Fortunately for my nervous ankles, a few decent gear pods showed up, but I still overgripped the twisty-turny holds and huffed and puffed. Lisa, of course, made it look easy.

Merriam Peak, showing the Clevenger-Harrington North Buttress Route on the left and the two new Croft-Rands routes on the right. *Peter Croft*

From there another corner and a short traverse got us to the reg route and to the summit by 3 p.m. Lisa asked if new routing always went so smoothly. Uh, no!

After such good climbing we thought the trip was complete, but on the descent we perved out on another line on the right side of the buttress. The cracks looked to connect, but one pitch in particular looked either futuristic or impossible. Next morning we decided we at least had to check out this other line. A couple of 70m rope-stretchers led us into overhanging terrain and luckily the first of a series of perfect ledges. Above, the futuristic turned fantastic—probably the best alpine 5.11 pitch I've done. Crazy good fingers and stemming led to another cool perch. Watching Lisa follow this pitch with the ropes out in space was better than Cliffhanger. Amazingly clean fingers-to-fist led for three more

Peter Croft enjoying perfect Sierra granite on one of his north buttress routes on Merriam Peak. *Lisa Rand*

pitches to the ridge crest. If anything, this route was even better than the first.

Again on top by 3 p.m. All we had to do was the dozen-mile death march back to Mordor.

PETER CROFT, *AAC*

*Disappearing Dome, Disappearing in Plain Sight.* In July Hunter Sibbald and I climbed a new route on Disappearing Dome, in the southern Yosemite area overlooking the Middle Fork of the San Joaquin River. We called it Disappearing in Plain Sight (IV 5.11b). We climbed ground-up, placing

18 bolts, including belay anchors, from natural stances and completed the route in one day. The second pitch initially required aid (A1) to surmount a small roof, but we returned the next day to climb a free variation, which joins the original start at the top of the second pitch.

The climb starts on a dark gray exfoliation slab split by an "S" shaped chimney. This slab is near the north end of the main east face, just south of the gully that defines the northeast face—home of Do It, Don't Spew It (*AAJ 2009*). The slab is just right of a series of prominent right-facing, right-slanting corners.

The free variation starts with an awkward move (5.10a) left into the crack leading to the chimney. Belay at the top of the chimney, then climb right-facing corners to a sloping ledge on the left. The aid variation climbs the left edge of the slab and goes over a roof to a bolted belay on the sloping ledge. The route continues up and slightly left (5.11b near the start of the third pitch) following shallow corners and amazing knobs to the top of the prominent corners. Two more pitches straight up, protected by a few bolts and some gear, lead to a line of bolts coming in from the left, which is followed two more pitches to the top. We climbed five new pitches before joining an existing route for another two. The climbing is spicy in places, but well-protected in the hard sections. The rock quality is excellent.

URMAS FRANOSCH

*Dana Plateau, The Sauce Bone Arête.* In September Patrick Dougherty and I climbed a great new 800-foot route on the Dana Plateau. The 2011 *AAJ* reported a route called Butterflies and Rainbows (1,000', IV 5.10+, Brown-Finkelstein), which motivated me to have a look. From research and a call to my friend Tom Carter, I learned that Tuolumne climbers of the 1970s gave the name Bastille to the formation east of the Third Pillar, They had climbed a few routes on the wall, including a group solo up the beautiful red slab left of the wall. Carter is an excellent source of beta on unrecorded climbs in the Yosemite area. His resume includes many first and early ascents of classic routes from El Cap to Fairview Dome. Thirty-eight years after first climbing the Captain, he is still ticking off one or two El Cap routes a year. These motivated climbers left few lines unclimbed.

Dana Plateau, showing the Sauce Bone Arête. *Logan Talbott*

Patrick and I found one of those unclimbed lines, a prominent arête on the right side of the Bastille. Carter didn't think the arête had been climbed, so we had to find out for ourselves. Starting early, we approached via the well-worn Third Pillar approach trail and descent gully and continued to the base of the wall. A short walk brought us to the arête. We climbed on-sight and hammerless. After one pitch of interesting face and crack climbing over red and orange rock, the really stellar climbing started. From pitch two to the top, the route follows splitter cracks in impeccable alpine granite, from tips and hands through a chiseled squeeze chimney. Pitch three was a highlight; Patrick led a perfect 1.5" splitter for 80' on a smooth face. Pitch five revealed yet another gem: the natural line led us through a tight squeeze chimney that narrowed to an offwidth. There are great belay ledges throughout, and the climbing is not difficult as long as you enjoy a wide crack here and there.

LOGAN TALBOTT

*Bear Creek Spire, Jamaica Say You Will.* In September Mike Dahlquist and I climbed a new route on the south face of Bear Creek Spire. The route's nine pitches (5.10) trend just left of center of the tallest part of the face, following various crack and corner systems. We had come to climb the 1971 Rowell route, but, armed only with an archaic description in an old AAJ report, we were unable to find the line. Our route bore little resemblance to the description, and the upper corners had clearly not been climbed. The last three pitches required some aid but would probably go free at 5.12. After comparing notes with the climbing community, we still don't know where Rowell's route went, though the story of his solo ascent and 40-mile bicycle return to Bishop is a classic.

BRETT MARTY, *AAC*

South face of Bear Creek Spire, showing Jamaica Say You Will. *sharperblue*

Mike Dahlquist following Jamaica Say You Will. *Brett Marty*

*High Sierra, the overlooked middle.* I don't get it. The High Sierra has largely been ignored for new routes in recent years. Yeah, there is some great stuff going on at either end of the range, like Peter Croft tearing up the Incredible Hulk (lately with Lisa Rands breaking into trad leading—welcome to roped climbing, Lisa!). And down south there has been a surge of activity on the Whitney Massif. Between shifts of flipping the burgers Croft raves about at the Whitney Portal Store, Myles Moser and Amy Ness will lope up to the crest, fire a 17-pitch Grade V (such as the East Buttress of Mt. Irvine), and be back for the afternoon shift. There are also rare repeats on the south face of Lone Pine Peak. After an early ascent of the Mike Strassman Memorial Route on that wall, I can tell you that stories of flaky rock seem to be true only of the gully-type climbs. The open faces are rather nice. Unreported this year, they also put up a major first ascent on Crooks Peak (the former Day Needle) that goes at V, 5.10, A0. Details, for now, are on Supertopo.com.

An unclimbed buttress leading to a feathery ridge on the east side of Table Mountain. *Doug Robinson*

The other big activists in the Whitney region are an upstart group from San Diego who call themselves the Pullharder Alpine Club. They have been quietly pocketing one fine line after another, including the amazingly aesthetic Pipeline on Mt.Carillon and a hidden gem on the north face of Mt. Russell. This year they became the first to break onto the mouth-watering buttresses on the north face of Mt. Hitchcock. Because these routes are Grade III, they've gone unreported here, but I can tell you that those buttresses and arêtes—there are nearly a dozen—have been hiding in plain sight for too long. They are in-your-face for hours when you hike the trail from the summit of Whitney.

But there sure is a lot of terrain between Whitney and The Hulk that's being passed over. Many climbers are skeptical of my raves about hundreds of unclimbed walls in the high country. I've seen people glaze over and back away when I get on the subject. So here's a bit of proof, as a tease. Check out this photo from the north side of a ridge extending east off the summit of Table Mountain: a fine little buttress capped by a feathery ridge. I would name the creek leading there if it had a name. You'll find it if you follow the Kern River nearly to its headwaters, then turn left. And if you go look, you'll find another surprise up the same drainage. Can't miss it....

DOUG ROBINSON, *AAC*

Evolution Traverse follows ridge and tags all the summits. Photo is taken from summit of Mt. Huxley. *Shay Har-Noy*

Late afternoon on golden triangle just past summit of Mt. Darwin. *Shay Har-Noy*

*Evolution Traverse, first winter ascent.* The Evolution Traverse takes a line along the crest of the Evolution group, linking nine 13,000' peaks named after contributors to evolutionary theory. Konstantin Stoletov and we, of San Diego's Pullharder Alpine Club, made the first winter traverse of the Evolutions, from March 7 to 10, 2012. We climbed for 36 hours, over the course of four days, enduring temperatures as low as –7°F.

The Evolution Traverse is one of the four major traverses in the Sierra Nevada backcountry, first completed by Peter Croft in 1999 (VI 5.9). In summer the eight-mile route has short difficult sections but is mostly 4th and mid-5th class. In winter the route is significantly different, with mixed climbing replacing many rock sections and deep snow on other parts.

After an approach day and a tent-bound storm day, we began climbing March 7. Newly fallen snow and residual winds made climbing conditions slick and slow, allowing us only the summit of Peak 13,360+. After 10 hours we bivied under Mt. Mendel's tower. The rest of the peaks fell with various degrees of difficulty, with additional bivies on small ledges along the knife-edge ridge after Darwin and before Mt. Fiske.

March 10 saw deteriorating weather, but we were able to finish Mt. Fiske and summit Mt. Warlow before the weather set in. We then dashed up Mt. Huxley, the final summit, before descending to the toe of the ridge to complete the traverse. Deep snow in Evolution Basin made for slow going, and with wet sleeping bags and low provisions, we made one last bivy on frozen Evolution Lake.

SHAY HAR-NOY AND BEN HORNE, *Pullharder Alpine Club*

Utah

*Green River, Desolation Canyon, The Siren.* In April Josh Thompson, Andrew Gram, Lena Laakso, and I put in at Sand Wash with whitewater rafts loaded with beer, food, and camping and climbing gear. This was our approach to a tower that Andrew had seen on his first trip downriver, in 2004.

We made the Mushroom Rock camp in good time due to very high spring melt and heavy rains the day before. Along the way we passed many a bloated dead cow. We in turn were passed by two running buffalo so close we could smell them from the rafts.

Our target tower (looking from various angles like a goblin or a viper) can only be seen for five minutes while on the river, or longer from a half-mile hike to Mushroom Rock (known for its petroglyphs). The casual part of the final approach dead-ends at a series of dry waterfalls (180', loose). The first, only 20' high, was the hardest: steep choss held together by roots, mud, and salty secretions. Josh soloed it with a heel hook and a tiny tree. Some 4th class took us to more casual hiking to the base of the tower.

Andrew Gram and Lena Laasko eyeing the objective, Desolation Canyon Green River Utah. *Daniel Gambino*

We named the tower The Siren and the route Shake Wait (5.10+ A2) because Andrew shook as he waited for the next barrage of missiles launched by Josh. The rock consisted of Green River, Wasatch sandstone, limestone (2 types), basalt, and a foot of coal (yes, coal!). The route is three pitches with 20' of aid (this section could be freed; the bolts are in). Overall the vertical rock was solid; it was the ledges that held the missiles.

From an adjacent ridge I saw another unclimbed tower to the north; this one you can only see from the ridge and the summit of The Siren. It's a little smaller, but worthy.

The descent involved three days of Class 3 western whitewater to the town of Green River. Along the way many towers and walls revealed themselves—most likely all are unclimbed. I submit this report because it's so much fun to blend diverse outdoor sports with wild remoteness and a car-camping mentality.

Daniel Gambino, *AAC*

Josh Thompson climbing the steep left hand neck of the The Siren. *Daniel Gambino*

North face of Cottontail, showing Trick of the Tail. *Jeremy Aslaksen*

*Fisher Towers, Cottontail Tower, Trick of the Tail.* From September 9 to 12, Jeremy Aslaksen and I climbed a new route on the north face of Cottontail Tower in the Fisher Towers: Trick of the Tail, V 5.10+ A3. Jeremy had spent a weekend scoping the tower for new routes and eventually found a way to reach the upper cracks on the face with limited drilling.

We started 100' right of West Side Story and, after a high bolt off the ground, followed right-trending cracks for two pitches to a ledge on the route Road Kill. We followed Road Kill for 20', before again heading out right using thin Pecker seams. I led the next pitch, which started with a dicey traverse (5.10+) above a roof. The traverse ends at the start of the upper crack system that leads up the center of the face to just before the shoulder horn belay on Brer Rabbit. We followed the normal short last pitch to the top of Cottontail. As with most new Fisher Towers routes, bring lots of Peckers in all sizes.

Jeremy and I have now done new routes together on four of the five main Fisher Towers: Kingfisher, Titan, Echo, and Cottontail.

PAUL GAGNER, *AAC*

Paul Gagner on start of 5.10+ traverse on Trick of the Tail. *Jeremy Aslaksen*

The Reverie, in Yellowstone National Park. *Sam Magro*

## MONTANA

*Hyalite and Yellowstone, new ice climbs.* Hyalite Canyon is our gym here in southwest Montana, with world-class ice that's been scraped over since the 1970s. These days, to pioneer new lines, one must get scrappy on chossy rock in order to reach tantalizing drips that are few, far between, and come in and out of condition like ghosts. At the end of last season we skinned six miles and climbed 200' of chossy rock to gain a 50' drip. With a broken drill it took two days. What were we doing? Were we this desperate for new routes?

*Kyler Pallister on pitch 3 of the Reverie. Sam Magro*

Then a friend invited me deep into Yellowstone National Park. Five-hundred feet of magnificent mixed climbing later, my faith in the new route potential of southwest Montana has been reborn. Kyler Pallister, Tyler Nygard, and I climbed the Reverie, a sequence of two massive drips that poured out of a wall of mudflow rock and petrified wood. The rock is like consolidated ash in places, but it was good enough to safely climb to reach the ice. Steep rock/mixed climbing led to an overhanging curtain and a series of dagger-like drips. Pitch two's fat pillar took us to a snow shelf. The third pitch climbed vertical rock to reach the final dagger. At the top, we realized that we'd just climbed one of the best routes any of us had done in Montana (500', 5.10+ A1 WI 6). We went back a week later to free the sections that we'd aided while bolting on lead. Alas, the lower half of the route had fallen down (it was mid-April). It seemed like a good time to put away ice gear and get back on dry rock.

There may still be a handful of seldom-formed new lines in Hyalite, but Montana's real potential lies in the Yellowstone ecosystem to our south, where there is an abundance of conglomerate ice-seeping cliff bands below the seemingly endless alpine faces of the Beartooths with their melt-freeze cycles. To date Hyalite's convenience has outweighed the slog to unknown canyons and peaks, but now it seems that if we look outside the box, we will discover more reveries.

SAM MAGRO

## WYOMING

### WIND RIVER MOUNTAINS

*Titcomb Basin, new routes on Elephant Head, Fremont Peak, and Mt.* Sacagawea. Of all the ranges round the world, the Wind River Mountains, right in my backyard, remain one of my favorites. Granite walls towering above idyllic green meadows, marmots chirping, pikas braying, trout jumping, and skeeters buzzing—it simply doesn't get better. I got into the Winds twice in late summer last year.

The first trip was with legendary Winds guidebook author Joe Kelsey (72) and photographer Ken Driese. We camped on the western edge of Indian Basin and Joe regaled us with tales of his 42 years of climbing in his beloved Winds. He's been fortunate enough to miss a number of world-shaking events—Nixon resigning, Hurricane Katrina—by being in the mountains. Something we should all strive for.

North face of Elephant Head, showing Packrat. *Mark Jenkins*

Ken Driese climbing Packrat, on Elephant Head. *Mark Jenkins*

Red Tower Arête. *Mark Jenkins*

Ken and I put up a short route on the north face of Elephant Head, just right of the north arête. On the third pitch, at the belay, a loud, unknown scratching sound surprised me. Suddenly a huge packrat jumped out of the crack and began gnawing ferociously, with sharp teeth, on a sweaty, salt-soaked sling—the sling holding the belay. I beat it off before any damage was done, but for the rest of the belay I waited for it to leap from the crack and bite my face. Hence the route's name: Packrat, 6 pitches, 5.9.

On that same excursion I rope-soloed the short arête on the Red Tower, the southernmost fin on the west face of Fremont. A dangerously loose grunge pitch, several gorgeous 5.8 crack pitches, a difficult offwidth, and then, naturally, hail and lightning on the knife-point summit: Red Tower Arête, 6 pitches, 5.10.

I returned two weeks later with Class V kayaker Oliver Deshler. We camped in Titcomb Basin at the north end of Mistake Lake, directly below our objectives. The first day we attempted one of the west faces of Fremont, the first one north of the West Face Spire that Michael Kennedy climbed in 1977. After five pitches we were stymied by overhanging finger cracks and unwisely traversed right into a gully, doing two more pitches before I dislodged a 40-inch-TV size block that came within two feet of killing Oliver. We bailed.

The next day we climbed a new route on the swooping, sail-shaped main west face of Fremont, between the West Face Dihedral and the West Buttress routes. After a two-hour trod up talus, we started in a seepy black cave and did three easy pitches to vertical flakes. Two pitches of 5.9 led to an unseemly seam, so we delicately traversed right, 5.10, to a beautiful, arcing, left-facing dihedral. We did four lovely pitches of crack climbing—5.7, 5.9, 5.8 and one of the most exposed 5.10 traverses you'll want to do—before the dihedral pinched off and we rapped 40' into the next dihedral north. Two more pitches, 5.8 and 5.7, in the sun at last, and we reached the summit scramble. We descended via the standard route on Fremont, dropping west rather than east off the saddle.

Because of the face's western aspect and the north-facing dihedrals, until the last two pitches we spent the day in the shade. We climbed in our down jackets and were still trembling at every belay, goose down leaking from our torn sleeves and swirling in the air. Hence the name: Dark Side of the Moon, 12 pitches, 5.10.

We reached camp at Mistake Lake just at dark, and, true to his own twisted tradition, mad kayaker Oliver stripped and dove into the frigid water. A rest day followed, in which I lolled in the sun reading, popping ibuprofen, and drinking beer, while Oliver went for a short hike.

The following day, after another two-hour hump in the cold morning dark, we found ourselves at the base of Sacagawea. Our goal: the directissima. Starting dead center, we ascended flakes for nine

Dark Side of the Moon, on Fremont's west face. *Mark Jenkins*

Oliver Deshler warming his hands on frigid Dark Side of the Moon. *Mark Jenkins*

Indian Paintbrush, on west face of Sacagawea. *Mark Jenkins*

pitches—5.7, 5.8, 5.9, 5.9, 5.8 chimney, the obligatory sketchy 5.10 traverse, where we left a nut with a purple sling swinging in the breeze, 5.10 offwidth, 5.10 face, 5.6 gully. The north-facing dihedral then turned to an overhanging offwidth/chimney for which we had no gear, so we ramped right out onto the face and into the sun (yes!), 5.6; curled around and ascended the south ridge for two more pitches, 5.7, 5.7, then another ropelength scramble west to the summit.

Low on the route, where the climbing was easy, we found two old pins, both set up for raps, but nothing above that. Again we chose a route in the shade, so we shivered our way up some of the finest, cleanest climbing I've done in the Winds. In honor of such a beautiful line on such an elegant peak, we named the route Indian Paintbrush, 12 pitches, 5.10.

There are lifetimes worth of new routes left in the Winds just waiting for the few, the proud, the backcountry alpinists. The climbing itself is not unlike that in Colorado's Rocky Mountain National Park, although the hike in is often twice as far (15 miles), the approaches up talus twice as long (two hours), and the climbs themselves twice as tall (a dozen pitches). Which means you can't easily rap back to the base. Instead, one typically hikes down from the summit. Hence, climbing with a relatively heavy pack (approach shoes, light down jacket, rain jacket, fleece cap and gloves, two quarts of water, lunch, etc.) is often obligatory. Nonetheless, for a mere tank of gas and bag of groceries, the glory of unexplored granite is all yours.

MARK JENKINS, AAC

*Ambush Peak, I Think Therefore I Ambush.* Nestled deep in the Wind River Range at the upper end of the East Fork Valley, Ambush's east face is one of the largest faces in the Winds. Its 800' headwall is guarded

by a roof system, upwards of 30', across the middle of the wall. The face's climbing history dates to 1969, when Fred Beckey first climbed it and proposed the name Ambush. Since then the east face, which actually encompasses four distinct aspects of two summits, has seen more than a dozen new routes. Few have detailed descriptions, but they have some things in common: dubious routefinding, with significant traversing away from the intended line, and the notorious "evidence of previous ascents" (i.e., fixed gear) high on the route after many pitches of what seemed to be virgin terrain. It seems that most of the established routes on the main east face veered one way or the other to avoid the roofs. As far as we knew, only one line went through the roof itself: an unreported Chip Chace line carrying the formidable "A3+ R" rating.

Last July, after a horse-packer carried Madaleine Sorkin's and my gear most of the 12 miles from Big Sandy to Pyramid Lake, we began by climbing Ambush Plaisir (III 5.9), James and Franziska Garrett's 2006 route up the middle of the lower slabs to a rappel anchor below the largest roof. After a short reconnaissance we forged up and right through the most accessible weakness in the roof. Over a few days

Ambush Peak: I Think Therefore I Ambush is the upper (black) line; Ambush Plaisir is the lower line. The white arrow is a 4th class approach. *James Garrett* we traded long leads, as we aided, cleaned, and equipped a few pitches through the steepest part of the wall. After a rest day we went for the free ascent. The mosquitoes were thirsty, and we were antsy.

To give us more time on our route, we avoided the first several pitches of Plaisir by scrambling up a gully, which offered quicker access to the upper wall and a shorter feeding period for our blood-sucking friends. The first new pitch turned a tenuous roof to put us below the big roof. The next, crux, pitch led through a three-tiered roof system, protected by three bolts, followed by technical corner climbing.

From there we only had a vague idea of which corners and crack systems would lead to the top. Mad took the next pitch, a dicey lead through poorly protected 5.9 to a long, technical 5.11 splitter. After that I crimped left into a steep dihedral with spots of poorly protected 5.9. A benign-looking ramp almost thwarted us and necessitated another bolt. We found the requisite "evidence of previous ascents"—an old fixed stopper—in a crack near the top (from here up our line may have been climbed). The sun went down, as we scrambled the final ridge. We gave each other high-fives and hugs by headlamp on the summit. A long descent through most of the night (we had failed to scope the descent in daylight) took us back to our camp, where we resumed swatting mosquitoes. I Think Therefore I Ambush is IV 5.12-. For more on Ambush's history, see the considerable discussion on MountainProject.com.

CHRIS BARLOW, *AAC*

*Cirque of the Towers, Warrior I, The Candy Shop.* Our five-pitch variation to the Northwest Face of Warrior I stemmed from an attempt to gain the stunning right-facing dihedral at

the top of the tower while avoiding the 5.11b R traverse on the existing route. Last July we cleaned many loose blocks and broke many obvious holds, so we believe that this variation had not been climbed. Undoubtedly more unstable blocks remain; this is an adventurous route to be climbed with discretion.

The Candy Shop begins on the right side of Warrior I, in a long, wide crack visible from the meadows below (5.10 offwidth). It ends atop a pedestal. From here we followed the path of least resistance, up broken crack systems to another ledge beneath an overhanging hand crack. The next pitch ascends this superb crack to a technical roof (5.10d), a dihedral, and a short chimney to another ledge belay. The next pitch is the psychological crux, ascending a flared weakness and traversing left into a large right-facing corner, where powerful moves to a mossy undercling (5.10d) got us through the corner to a belay on

The Candy Shop on Warrior I. First five pitches are likely new. *Drew Thayer*

Nearing top of first pitch on the Candy Shop. *Drew Thayer*

another pedestal. From here we could see the upper dihedral. We traversed a slab, finding intermittent gear, and rounded a friction bulge (5.9) into a large alcove. From there we stretched the rope on easy ledges to the base of the upper dihedral and followed the existing route to the summit. The descent was an ordeal, involving several rappels off horns and old pitons into a steep gulley that spit us into the snowy col between Warriors I and II, where we found exciting rappels off boulders and snow bollards (six hours all told). The Candy Shop to the summit is 1,200', IV 5.10d and offers fun climbing up a direct line on one of the proudest features in the Cirque. We hope people will get out there and enjoy it; it will only get better with traffic!

NOAH GOSTOUT, ERIK RIEGER, and DREW THAYER, *AAC*

COLORADO
BLACK CANYON OF THE GUNNISON

*North Chasm View Wall, Hallucinogen Wall, first free ascent.* When Ben Lepesant asked if I'd be interested in climbing classic routes in the Black Canyon, I did some research and discovered that the Hallucinogen Wall hadn't been freed. Then I remembered its history and the story about the ice axes, and it became clear that we'd have to concentrate on this project. [*Editor's note: Originally climbed in 17 days in 1980 and rated A5 (Becker-Lella-Newberry-Webster), the Hallucinogen Wall was freed in 2004, except for one pitch, which was "drytooled" with specially modified ice axes. The route was re-rated 5.13- D10+ R (Nelson-Ogden) and was a feature article in the 2005 AAJ.*]

We first climbed the 16-pitch route in three days, with aid, and I realized that it could go free pretty quickly. Ben knew he wouldn't be leading any the pitches, so he gave me his complete support. I bouldered around on the crux pitches and memorized the moves.

Hansjörg Auer freeing crux pitch of Hallucinogen Wall.
©*The North Face/Cory Richards*

We rested in bad weather for three days, then set off at 5:00 am on April 22. It was snowing lightly as we descended the Cruise Gully, and then we shot up the route. I climbed every pitch first go, and Ben cleaned and jumared. Things became tough on the final pitches, as I got tired, and the pumpy crux pitch with its finishing dyno was touch-and-go. But we reached the final belay unscathed, 8 hours and 41 minutes after starting. The time was a record, but this came about completely by chance. Speed records don't really mean much to me. [In 2005 Jared Ogden and Ryan Nelson climbed it in 8h 59min—Ed.]

I had expected the crux 13th pitch would be a smooth wall with tiny crimps. But it is athletic, with good holds and cool heel-hooks. I diverged slightly from the original line three times: immediately after the belay (where I added two pegs and a copperhead); in the middle of the pitch, at the start of the bolt ladder; and just before the belay, with a leftward dyno.

The route itself isn't all that difficult (5.13+ R), but the pro is fairly alpine, with numerous copperheads, especially in the middle section. It probably had to wait 31 years for the first free ascent because the Black Canyon wasn't the place to be. I'm happy to have grabbed this little jewel, especially since there are so many talented climbers living less than five hours away, in Boulder. Climbing it free in less than nine hours, without a massive prior effort, is something pretty important to me.

HANSJÖRG AUER, Austria (based on an interview in PlanetMountain.com)

## SAN JUAN MOUNTAINS

*The Guardian, Weather Window Waltz.* In August 2011 Wesley Ashwood, Kelsey Sheely, and I put up a new line on the northeast face of the Guardian (13,617') in the East Grenadier Range of the southern San Juan Mountains. My two previous attempts on the face had been thwarted by weather (once with Jon Rezabek, once with Ashwood). Weather forecasts revealed a three-day window of sunshine, so we had to try again. We camped east of the Guardian, next to Vallecito Creek. The following morning we hiked a steep 1,200' slope to the face and began climbing, at 8 a.m., on the left side of the prominent, water-streaked dihedral. Eight pitches of surprisingly solid quartzite corners and cracks, punctuated by occasional broken sections, brought us to the high ridge, where the angle eased. We simul-climbed the ridge for 500', then strolled to the summit in the evening alpenglow. We descended the mountain's long, nontechnical south side, arriving in camp at 2 a.m. and celebrating with kipper snacks and whiskey. We christened the route Weather Window Waltz (1,700', IV 5.9).

NIC HARNISH, Durango

Weather Window Waltz on the Guardian. Nic Harnish

# Alaska

The online version of these reports frequently contains additional photos, maps, topos, and extended text. Please visit aaj.americanalpineclub.org

BROOKS RANGE

ARRIGETCH

*Deep in the Alaskan Bush.* In mid-April photographer Corey Rich asked if I wanted to join a 10-day climbing trip in the Brooks Range with the man himself, Tommy Caldwell. How could I say no? The trip came together last minute, and we didn't even know where we were going to climb. The bush pilot dropped us in the snow alongside Awlinyak Creek, and we skied 20 miles to our base camp. Snow conditions were less than ideal, but the wildlife was spectacular. We saw caribou and white wolves and even had a run-in with a grizzly. A few days of rest in base camp gave us the opportunity to scope the peaks and climbing objectives. Tommy, Corey, and I settled on a steep unclimbed wall right of the west face of Xanadu. The west face of Xanadu looks like an amazing objective but would require a portaledge and much more time.

From a bivouac two hours below the face, we scoped a good line that followed the weakness up corners to a right-trending ramp system. In the morning we left early and approached up easy mixed terrain. Tommy took the first block and led run-out 5.11 face pitches to

Deep in the Alaskan Bush seen artistically. *Cory Rich*

Looking for Arrigetch objectives from the air. West face of Xanadu (7,160′, first ascent 1974) is left of strut. Immediately right is Pt. 6,850′, the west face taken by Deep in the Alaskan Bush. Wall with horizontal snow bands further right is Melting Tower (7,068′, first ascent 1974). *Cory Rich*

a large corner. Once we reached the corner, the climbing eased to 5.10 on perfect buffed granite, and Tommy led three pitches to a large ledge. Corey and I followed with jumars. I was impressed with Corey, since this was his first time alpine climbing. He kept a positive attitude, did his share of the work, and had all of his camera gear.

Tommy Caldwell leading low on Deep in the Alaskan Bush. *Hayden Kennedy*

I started leading off the large ledge at the top of pitch seven and found an easy ramp trending right. The climbing was loose and run-out 5.9, with limited anchors. Tommy and Corey followed by climbing, because the anchors were not strong enough to jumar from. After four easy pitches on the ramp, the wall got steep again and the rock improved. I led the crux of the route up 5.11+ edges, with no gear for 50' above the anchor. At the end of the pitch, I reached a small corner, where I was able to place gear. I led one more pitch of 5.10 to a large snowy ledge just below the summit. We regrouped and found easy climbing up a ridge to the summit, having climbed 15 pitches.

The views of the Arrigetch Peaks were unreal; the west face of Xanadu looked like Half Dome. We didn't want to leave all our gear rappelling, so we climbed a knife-edge ridge toward Xanadu. The ridge took us to the base of the west face of Xanadu, where we made three easy rappels. We hiked back to base camp in the evening light, after an awesome adventure Deep in the Alaskan Bush (5.11+ X M2).

To see a short film on the expedition by Corey Rich, visit nikonusa.com and search on "Deep North."

HAYDEN KENNEDY, *AAC*

*Elephant's Tooth, north pillar; Parabola, south face, possible first ascents.* Ten years ago I tried to climb in the Arrigetch but failed to do anything, because of rain. I returned in July 2010 with Claudia Nestler and food for 32 days. Nevertheless, we had only five days without rain, operating from a base camp on Arrigetch Creek, a few hours from the climbing. On the first dry day we repeated Parabola's east ridge and continued to Parabola's west peak (22 pitches, 6b), which would be a famous route were it in the Alps. We also repeated West Maiden's north ridge, during rain. A few days previously we had climbed a new direct line from the bottom toward the crest (five pitches, 6b A0), via steep cracks and slabs, but rain stopped play, and next time we chose the original line (6a), which near the top was like climbing a waterfall.

Line climbed by Nestler and Stucki on north pillar of Elephant's Tooth. *Werner Stucki*

Line climbed by Nestler and Stucki on south face of Parabola. *Werner Stucki*

We then made the possible first ascent of the north pillar of Elephant's Tooth. The rock was not always good, but at the top we had a nice view down to our camp and Arrigetch Creek. It took six hours to climb the eight pitches, with difficulties up to 6a/b. Five rappels, and one hour later we were in camp.

The weather was still good, so we decided to try the south face of Parabola, another possible first ascent. The initial cracks and corners proved interesting and strenuous, and the rock was fantastic on each of the 15 pitches, particularly on the last five up the headwall. The climb took 12 hours, with difficulties of 6b and seven m of A1. It was a dream come true; I'd wanted to try this face 10 years earlier. When our time was up, we walked back to Circle Lake, our original drop-off, where we were delivered a canoe and six more days' food. Over the next five days we paddled down to Helpmejack Lake, where we were picked up by a Cessna from Bettles Lodge.

WERNER STUCKI, *Switzerland*

*Editor's note: It's likely several climbs in the Arrigetch are unreported, but two sources are useful for reference. In 2003 Nancy Pfeiffer and Jim Lawler compiled a summary of the mountaineering history of the Arrigetch Peaks. This 64 page report can be downloaded at: www.nps.gov/gaar/naturescience/upload/arrigetch final report compressed.pdf. In the same year a summary report was compiled by Clint Cummins and can be viewed at: www.stanford.edu/~clint/arrig/index.htm. Thanks to Steve Gruhn for help with this report.*

## HAYES RANGE

*Mt. Geist (3,269m/10,720'), northeast face, possible new route.* The idea of going to the Hayes Range developed after we did some digging on the Internet and made a trip to the (British) Alpine Club library. Scouring expedition reports, Chris Johnson, Neil Warren, and I were unable to find a report of an ascent of the west ridge of Mt. Hayes and decided it would be a great objective. It looked long, moderately difficult, committing, but possible. We were also aware that a party had been in the area the previous year, managing first ascents of the west face direct of Mt. Hayes and the northeast face of Mt Balchen. There looked to be plenty of scope for other routes on both mountains, but information was hard to come by. From discussing our proposed lines with local gurus, we learned that Hayes' west ridge had

Runnel through mixed ground on Geist's northeast face. *Guy Wilson*

been climbed from the Turkey Glacier in the 1970s. Local climbers apparently don't record many of their ascents, allowing others the pleasure of "second first ascents," a good way of keeping adventure alive. We decided to stick with our plan of climbing the west ridge from the Hayes Glacier. It would be a full-on outing, with 17km of crest if we descended the north ridge. In the end we were unsuccessful, and instead investigated several ski descents and climbed two neighbouring mountains.

The first was Skarland (3,145m/10,315'), which we climbed by the southeast ridge. Though not steep, it proved slightly precarious due to poor snow. We'd hoped to ski from the summit but at 2,800m met hard ice and left the skis there while we climbed to the top. The ski descent from 2,800m was superb. The ridge was first climbed in April 1976, by Americans Dave Davis, Dakers Gowans, and Keith Hansen, making the second ascent of this fine, pointed snow peak.

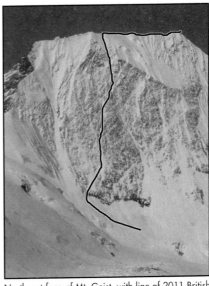

Northeast face of Mt. Geist, with line of 2011 British ascent. *Guy Wilson*

Just before our leaving date, Neil and I climbed a direct route through the mixed rocky section of Geist's northeast face. The face has been climbed several times, though the only references we found point to a line up the obvious snow slope/couloir toward the left side, originally climbed in May 1974 by Dusan Jagersky and Bill Sumner, making the first ascent of the mountain.

We completed the 1,000m face and descent of the north ridge in 22 hours from camp. The ascent involved good 55-60° névé, tricky mixed climbing through rotten schist, sections of ice, and some of the steepest snow we've encountered. Protection and belays were often poor.

On the summit ridge we met with a scary traverse over and around cornices, a little à cheval, and nothing in the way of protection before reaching the summit—similar conditions to those experienced by the 1974 party. The overall grade of the ascent was TD+. We rappelled the north ridge, from a mixture of snow bollards and Abalakovs. Next time we'll take a stove, as one liter of water wasn't enough. Many thanks to the BMC, MEF, Alpine Club, and Berghaus Adventure Challenge Award for financial assistance.

GUY WILSON, *Alpine Club, U.K.*

DENALI NATIONAL PARK

*Denali National Park and Preserve summary.* Sadly, nine climbers died in the Alaska Range during 2011, making it the third deadliest year on record. The impact of these losses is not something that can be put into words. In addition 36 climbers were stricken with injuries or illnesses that required medical intervention by NPS rangers and volunteers. While 2011 was a year of tragedy, adversity often brought out the best from the Denali climbing community. There were a number courageous acts worthy of the 2011 Mislow-Swanson Denali Pro Award, but it was given to Bobby Schnell, a paramedic who in the middle of the night carried out a life-saving operation on a climber critically injured after a long fall from Denali Pass.

On Denali 687 climbers reached the summit by a variety of routes, a success rate of just over half. On Foraker the number was just five.

After years of public engagement, a decision was reached to increase the climbing fee from $200 to $350 ($250 for age 24 and under). Though it was a difficult process that at times put the NPS at odds with members of the climbing community, the increased revenue will help sustain our program at necessary levels, particularly at a time when NPS operating budgets are shrinking. We are grateful to the American Alpine Club, the Access Fund, and the American Mountain Guides Association, which worked closely with us to help guide the process and build consensus around what was once a highly contentious issue.

Throughout the range there were several ascents, and one descent, that are not reported below but are worthy of note. British climbers Jonathan Griffiths and Will Sim climbed the Cassin Ridge on Denali in 14 hours and 40 minutes from bergschrund to Kahiltna Horn. This is about 20 minutes faster than Mugs Stump's 1991 ascent. Neither Stump nor the British visited the true summit, and the fastest time to the mountain's highest point is unknown. On May 23rd Andreas Fransson completed the first ski descent of Denali's south face, following for the most part the Haston-Scott route. Icy conditions forced him to downclimb one section, and he made four rappels.

Colin Haley and Nils Nielsen climbed Deprivation to the top of the north buttress of Hunter in just nine hours. There they were caught in a storm and unable to complete the route to the summit. Koreans Choi Suk-mun, Park Hee-yong, and Park Jong-il were the only climbers to reach the summit via the north buttress, with their mid-May ascent of the Bibler-Klewin/Moonflower—possibly only the 13th or 14th time this route has been climbed to the summit.

Over on Huntington, John Frieh and Jason Stuckey made the second winter ascent, via the West Face Couloir. Starting early on March 19, they climbed the route in a 23-hour round trip from camp. A month later Tim Dittman and Jared Vilhauer made it through most of the difficulties on the Phantom Wall, but at their high bivouac Vilhauer became violently ill with flu, and the pair retreated. This route awaits a second ascent.

The complete Mountaineering Summary can be found at www.nps.gov/dena/planyourvisit/summaryreports.htm

*Summarized from the* DENALI NATIONAL PARK AND PRESERVE MOUNTAINEERING SUMMARY

Marty Schmidt on pitch nine (Tibia) of Dad and Son, six hours into route. Foraker behind. *Denali Schmidt*

*Denali, lower southwest face, Dad and Son.* My 23-year-old son Denali felt compelled to climb his namesake. While he was studying in San Francisco, he told me over the phone (I being in New Zealand) that he was climbing Denali with or without me. I told him that I would get clients right away for the West Rib; bugger if he was going to Alaska without me.

At the last minute two clients pulled out, but I told Denali we would go anyway and be tight with our budget. Denali is a starving student, and I'm a mountain/

ski guide living out of a van. We flew to Anchorage on May 15. We climbed the upper West Rib over 10 days, made a 15-hour climb to the north summit, and climbed Foraker, via the Sultana Ridge, in a 63-hour roundtrip from Kahiltna base camp. We then skied to the northeast fork of the Kahiltna and established a safe campsite below the unclimbed buttress immediately left of West Rim Route (Southwest Rib, AK4 60° Ehmann-Morrow, 1977).

Marty Schmidt on crux pitch 10 (Patella), seven hours into route. Line continues to horizontal breaks above, then trends right to skyline. *Denali Schmidt*

Taking off early the next day, our hearts and minds were in harmony with each other and with the mountain. After swinging tools through the first section of steep snow and ice, we hooked through the lower five pitches, which brought us to the first crux: the broken glacier between what we called the Big Toe and the main body of our climb. We dubbed this section the Fungus, since it was between the big toes. In six hours of fast climbing, we reached the top of pitch 10, below the main crux of the route, a vertical rock wall split by a few cracks. I started climbing this pitch wearing the full pack but removed it for the most technical move, in a finger crack that slanted across the wall (5.10). Denali attached the packs, and I hauled. It was the only time we took them off until we stopped for a brew at hour 24.

Carrying bivouac equipment encouraged us to wish for a ledge, but none arrived. For the 29 hours we spent on the climb, no ledge appeared, so we just continued up, seeking a path through rotten

Marty Schmidt leading an ice runnel on Dad and Son. *Denali Schmidt*

snow arêtes, vertical chandelier ice pinnacles, thin vertical ice runnels, and big rock boulder moves. We belayed every pitch: Denali is my only son, and nothing was going to get in the way of our safety. Alaska offers the best and the worst of climbing. The worst comes by way of double overhanging corniced ridges, and we dealt with some of those; riding pitch 18 was like riding Brahma bulls in India, waiting for the end to happen.

The next 11 pitches, continuous, steep-angled, hard ice up the backbone of our route, went like clockwork. The final rib we called the Crowning Chakra for several reasons, one being that as the last part of the climb became clear, we finally found the first real sit-down place. We brewed the most wonderful coffees and teas, ate cereal, milk, and bars, and sat absorbing the sights, relishing the past 24 hours. Above, the climbing did not ease in angle, but we found the going easier in those last pitches. After 29 pitches and 29 hours, we reached the highest point, across from Windy Corner on the West Buttress Route.

After negotiating large crevasses between us and the Corner, we headed down the Kahiltna Glacier, following the standard West Buttress Route. We were back at our campsite on the northeast fork by midnight. We packed and were at the airstrip by 4 a.m., the first to register for a flight out. However, our last days on Denali were the longest spent in one place during our expedition. We were stuck for three days while the weather was simply Alaskan. Our route, Dad and Son (5.10 A2 WI5), was the last remaining unclimbed ridge on Denali from the Northeast Fork of the Kahiltna.

MARTY SCHMIDT, *New Zealand*

*West Kahiltna Peak (3,914m/12,835'), west ridge.* West Kahiltna Peak is just off of the Kahiltna Glacier, and every West Buttress ascensionist looks at its west ridge of as they make their home at Camp 1. It is the obvious ridge closest to the northeast fork of the Kahiltna and may have been climbed previously, but there were no recorded ascents prior to 2011.

On May 23 two Italians, Diego Giovannini and Fabio Meraldi, ascended the ridge in 12 hours and reported finding 75° ice and 5.8 on their Grade 4 route. The climbing was generally moderate and enjoyable, but the final section of the ridge was dangerously threatened by an overhanging serac. They descended the route by downclimbing and rappelling.

Japanese Yuto Inoue and Tatsuro Yamada may have climbed this line in 2008, while traversing West and East Kahiltna Peaks before ascending the Cassin Ridge. However, they perished near the summit of Denali, and as friends could not confirm their line of ascent, the truth may never be known. For now the Italians' feat stands as the first recorded ascent.

MARK WESTMAN, *Denali National Park and Preserve*

*Mt. Hunter, north buttress to Cornice Bivouac, the Cartwright Connection.* Unrelenting spindrift avalanches and gusty winds blasted and buffeted the portaledge. Our small cocoon of safety on this harsh mountain was slowly being engulfed, as we nervously watched the snow level rise up the fly walls. It had taken five of the toughest days' climbing of our lives to get to this point, and our chances of reaching the top of the north buttress were diminishing. The forecast was for more snow and stronger winds over the upcoming days.

The first day went smoothly, according to plan. Not that night, though, as Matt Helliker and I realized the perils of hanging our portaledge on a 60° ice slope. We were awakened when it collapsed and transformed into a hammock. On day two we faced many uncertainties, as we found a way through steep, complex terrain, with many overhanging snow mushrooms. Matt

fought hard in the lead all day and at 2 a.m. had us below the steepest rock band of the climb. In overcoming these difficulties our confidence had grown, and I started to think we might have a chance of getting up this climb. Day three was steep and scary—thinly iced slabs, overhanging cracks, aid on loose rock, a pitch of vertical ice, and more. We finally got to bed at 6 a.m. Day four we joined the Bibler-Klewin/Moonflower route; we just needed luck with the weather. Day five it snowed and wind blew.

Jon Bracey on belay with haul bag, Cartwright Connection. *Matt Helliker*

At 9 p.m., after being trapped on the ledge all day, we sensed a slight lull and had glimpses of the sun through the clouds. We were both thinking that this might be our only chance, and with no food left there was no point in waiting. We packed a stove, spare gloves, warm jackets, and a minimal rack, our goal being to reach the Cornice Bivouac, 500m and 13 pitches above. However, we felt the chances of success were negligible.

Two pitches later the snow started again, and we were battling against spindrift. The cold was almost unbearable, but our optimism and unwillingness to give up won through. In dream-like exhaustion we stood at the top of the face at 5 a.m. Few words were said, and we had no comprehension of what we had achieved. We only knew we had to start rappelling. Thirty-eight rappels and 14 hours later, we were back on the glacier, where we collapsed, having been awake for 36 hours. We named the route the Cartwright Connection, in memory of my good friend Jules Cartwright, whose vision it was to attempt this line.

Aerial view of eastern aspect of Hunter's north buttress. (N) North (main) summit. (C) Cornice Bivouac. (1) Northeast Ridge (1971). (2) French Route (1984). (3) Wall of Shadows (1994). (4) Cartwright Connection (2011). (5) Bibler-Klewin/Moonflower (1983), with (P) Prow and (S) Shaft. (6) West Ridge (1954). *Andy Houseman*

JON BRACEY, *France*

*Editor's note: Jon Bracey and Matt Helliker climbed very steep terrain a little left of the Bibler-Klewin/Moonflower, before joining it at the Second Ice Band, beneath the Vision Pitch. The 16 independent pitches presented difficulties of M6 AI6 5.8 A2. They rappelled the Moonflower. While some argue that the limited amount of new climbing defines this as a major variation, rather than an independent*

Steep, thinly iced, mixed grooves are characteristic of Hunter's north buttress. Here Jon Bracey tries to avoid snow mushrooms on lower part of Cartwright Connection. *Matt Helliker*

*route, it is undoubtedly a highly technical challenge, significantly harder than either the French Route or the Moonflower, and one to which future parties may try to add an autonomous finish. Jules Cartwright's original concept envisioned new ground directly to the Third Ice Band/Come Again Exit.*

Voyager Peak from southeast. (1) To the Center. (2) Attempt and high point on central rib/Nebula Arête. (3) Attempt and high point on southeast ridge/Lunar Spur. (4) Rappel descent used on all three attempts. *Mark Allen*

*Voyager Peak (12,213'), south face, To the Center.* In the first week of May, Mark Allen and I set up base camp at Kahiltna International, then headed off for the rarely visited northwest fork of Lacuna Glacier. We had learned about the Lacuna the previous winter, while digging around for objectives. An aerial photo showed big steep faces cleaved with gorgeous ice and mixed lines. We found no evidence of anyone having visited this area, so we set our sights on gaining access and sending its virgin peaks and routes.

On our first trip it took three and a half days to reach the northwest fork, due to avalanche-prone slopes and icefalls. We followed the route described by Joe Puryear in his Alaska Supertopo guide. We reached the east fork of the Lacuna, below the south face of Foraker (as for the approach to the Infinite Spur), and continued across the heads of the Lacuna, through two more major icefalls, the second of which proved the main routefinding crux. This placed us directly below the eastern aspects of the Fin, the unclimbed summit of Peak 12,213', and below the west face of Foraker.

Due to lack of objective hazard and its aesthetic lines, Peak 12,213' was the obvious choice. The following morning, May 9, we headed for what we named the Lunar Spur, which follows the right-hand margin of the south face. We spent a day and a half on this line, climbing to M5 and AI2, before being turned around on the upper ridge by bad weather and dangerous snow. Our attempt began with brilliant mixed climbing but was followed by a knife-edge choss ridge covered in two to four feet of unconsolidated powder. Concluding that conditions needed more time to become favorable for climbing, we returned to Kahiltna base camp, this time making the crossing in two days.

After a week and a half resting and climbing other objectives, we returned to the Lacuna, taking two days to reach the northwest fork. With a better handle on conditions, we opted for a central rib on the south face. On the evening of May 23 we left bivouac gear on the glacier and moved quickly up the dihedrals and flakes of a 2,500'

Graham Zimmerman on M6 crux on central rib of south face of Voyager Peak, during second of three attempts on the mountain. *Mark Allen*

granite buttress, which narrowed to a technical knife-edge ridge. We found fantastic sustained mixed climbing up to M6, with some AI2 and A1. Above, a 1,000' couloir led to a ridge that cruised another 1,000' to the summit. However, once we were on this ridge, black clouds greeted us, forcing a quick retreat. We referred to the line followed on this attempt as the Nebula Arête (after the LA band Nebula).

Next day, May 26, we woke to clear weather and found that not enough snow had fallen to create avalanche conditions. With limited food remaining, we decided to use it on one more attempt at Peak 12,213', this time via the central couloir on the south face. We left that evening, finding perfect névé, and blasted to the summit ridge in less than six hours. Passing our previous high point, we reached the summit in another hour, making the first ascent of what we named Voyager Peak, after the Voyager satellite; we named our route To The Center (4,500', AK4 AI2). We descended the southeast ridge and southeast buttress, mostly using anchors from our previous attempts.

The following day, with only four oatmeal packets between us, we skied back to Kahiltna base camp in 13 hours, motivated by the food and whiskey that awaited us. Huge thanks to the support provided by the Mt Everest Foundation, the NZAC, and Outdoor Research.

GRAHAM ZIMMERMAN, *AAC*

*Ruth Gorge, Barrill (2,332m/7,650'), northeast face, Alaskan Primer.* On May 13 Ben Gilmore and Hans Johnstone climbed a new route on the northeast face of Barrill, in a 12-hour trip from bergschrund to the summit, before descending the far side to the Mountain House. Alaska Primer (900m, AK IV 5.9+ M WI5 R) is primarily an ice and mixed climb. It follows a series of corners and ramps, with a few key traverses and a variety of climbing from squeeze chimneys to thin ice to snow mushrooms, before reaching the upper section of the northeast ridge. They had attempted the route earlier in the season but been forced back by spindrift.

MARK WESTMAN, *Denali National Park and Preserve*

REVELATION MOUNTAINS

*Mt. Mausolus (9,170'), first ascent.* From March 15 to 17 Clint Helander and Scotty Vincik made the first ascent of Mt. Mausolus. They climbed the west face via a dagger-like couloir, naming their route the Mausoleum in honor of Seth Holden, who died in 2010 in a small plane crash in the Susitna

River Valley. Helander and Holden had climbed in the Revelations together three times, including a previous attempt on Mausolus by the same line, and Helander scattered Holden's ashes from the summit. See Helander's article earlier in this *Journal*.

## Neacola Mountains

*Mystery Mountain, northeast ridge, Where's the Gas; Dog Tooth.* On May 26 Ben Chriswell, Sam Johnson, and I flew to the Pitchfork Glacier. The Neacolas are a largely unexplored group southwest of the Alaska Range. Ben and Sam had received a McNeill-Nott award for a trip and kindly let me tag along. During our 14 days on the glacier, we had little climbable weather. The first two days were the best but were mostly consumed by reconnaissance and ski-touring, exploring beautiful objectives on both sides of the Pitchfork. The next day we attempted an aesthetic peak we dubbed the Triangle. The climbing was slow, the weather was poor, and we only brought supplies for a single-push attempt. When the rain/snow and wind became more persistent, and we discovered that climbing the gorgeous 600m rock buttress would not be lightning fast, we descended.

On the 30th we climbed the northeast ridge of a peak we called Mystery Mountain (ca 2,145m/7,035'). We are guessing the mountain had not been climbed, as so few parties have been to the Neacolas, but it is not difficult, so it may have been climbed. The first half of the ridge was nontechnical, but on the second half we belayed eight pitches, including simul-climbing, with difficulties up to 5.8 (a fun step) and 70° snow. We called the moderate 900m route Where's the Gas.

We then spent a week mostly in the tent, waiting out weather. On June 2 we reconnoitered a striking rock spire and made some ski turns during a short break in the weather. This stimulated the psyche and allowed us to endure more tent time.

Dog Tooth, with line of first ascent via east ridge.
Aaron Thrasher

On the 6th we woke at 4 a.m. and set off for the spire. The temperature was -7°C and the glacier and peaks frozen. We made quick time to the base of the east ridge, where Sam led a long traverse pitch to gain sunny rock. He also led the first rock pitch (5.8), then I took over for five pitches, with climbing to 5.10 and A1, the aid in a 12m wet corner that I suspect would go free at 5.11+. With high-quality stone, we made quick progress. A headwall, which had looked questionable from the glacier, held a perfect two- to four-inch splitter. Back on the ridge Sam took over for the next block, which we did relatively quickly, booting in snow with our rock shoes between rock steps.

After five pitches (up to 5.8) and snow climbing, Ben took over for the last two pitches to the summit. The weather had been deteriorating all day, and it was gusting to probably 80-100 km/hour and snowing. Sam and I had been discussing the best descent route, and with the wind, we were concerned about pulling our ropes. I had scoped a descent off the back of the summit and rapped 60m to a rock pedestal. After rapping we decided that the wind was too strong to pull the ropes, so Sam jugged back to the summit and fixed one rope at the anchor, guaranteeing we would have a second line for the rest of the descent. Three more rappels deposited us in a snow gully, which we descended easily. We recommend this quick descent route to future parties. We took 20 hours camp to camp.

Mystery Mountain. Route of ascent and descent followed left skyline. *Aaron Thrasher*

We are calling the ca 2,180m (7,150') formation Dog Tooth. The 14-pitch, V 5.10 A1 route salvaged the trip, with its splitter cracks more like what one is likely to find in the Sierra than in obscure Alaskan mountains. On the 8th Paul Roderick flew us out, and I made it back to Anchorage that evening for an Edward Sharpe and the Magnetic Zeros show.

AARON THRASHER

## CHUGACH MOUNTAINS

*Mt. Yukla (2,297m/7,535'), north face, No Call, No Show.* In October John Kelley and I headed back to Mt. Yukla to climb the North Couloir and check out an appealing smear that intersects that route at two-thirds height. John, Ben Trocki, and I had climbed the North Couloir the previous September, but the smear wasn't formed at the time. This time, though, the smear looked to be fat. It leaves the couloir immediately after the couloir's crux, 800m above the valley floor. An early start from the infamous boulder bivouac put us at the base of the smear around mid-day, and we climbed four pitches of sustained, run-out AI4/5 before bivouacking. We each carried a light sleeping bag, but with no bivouac sack my down bag quickly turned into a sheet filled with down balls. Dawn finally arrived, and we brewed up with the last remaining fuel. That day, October 10, we climbed eight more sustained pitches, before the angle kicked back, and 180m of simul-climbing saw us on top. Our line, which went at V M5/6 X AI5 X, tops out less than 10m from the summit. We walked through the night under a great display of northern lights, returning to the

North face of Yukla. (1) North Couloir. (2) No Call, No Show. *Josh Varney*

Most People are DJs, on subpeak/shoulder of Mt. Yukla, at far left side of north face. Icicle Glacier is just off picture to left. *Aaron Thrasher*

boulder bivouac at 10 a.m. next morning, three hours after I was supposed to be at work, after a 50-hour roundtrip. We dubbed the route No Call, No Show.

JOSH VARNEY, AAC

*Mt. Yukla (2,297m/7535'), north face, Most People are DJs.* On October 10 local Anchorage climber John Kelley and I walked to the north face of Mt. Yukla, via Icicle Creek, for some early season alpine climbing. We climbed a previously tried line that shared its start with two of John's established routes, before cutting left up an obvious ramp. We soloed sticky crux alpine ice at the beginning of the route to the divergence from the other two lines, where we roped up for steep, poorly protected snow climbing. The remainder of the route consisted of moderate mixed climbing, to M4, following the ramp system to the top of the ca 6,000' sub peak of Yukla. It was a 14-hour roundtrip from the boulder bivouac, with a descent via the Icicle Glacier. We called the route Most People are DJs (2,000', IV AI4 M4), after the song by Hold Steady.

AARON THRASHER

## ST. ELIAS MOUNTAINS

*University Peak (14,470'), southwest spur.* Kevin Ditzler and John Kelley climbed this 8,500' route in seven days, summiting on April 17. They descended the north ridge to Beaver Basin, where they waited six days for a pickup with almost no food or fuel. See Ditzler's article earlier in the *Journal*.

## FAIRWEATHER RANGE

*Mt Orville (10,495'), north ridge, attempt; Peak 7,400+', northwest ridge, attempt.* In April 2011 I

Orville (on left) from east, showing route and camps on northeast spur to 8,074' foresummit. C1 (2,552', just off-picture), C2 (5,758'), and C3 (7,718'). *Paul Knott*

returned for a second visit to the Johns Hopkins glacier basin in the southern part of the Fairweather Range. In 2009 Guy McKinnon and I had been the first climbers to access the main glacier and had made two ascents. This time Vaughan Snowdon joined me, and we planned to attempt the north ridge of Mt. Orville. This is one of the awe-inspiring peaks photographed from tour boats in the Johns Hopkins Inlet. Climbers had only attempted it from the south, and only one party had summited.

As in 2009 ski-plane pilot Paul Swanstrom dropped us on the west shoulder of Mt. Abbe, at a little under 4,000', but this time in deep powder snow. A low cloud base limited our reconnaissance of Orville.

We retraced the 2009 route to 2,000' on the Johns Hopkins Glacier, finding tough snow conditions but well-bridged crevasses. We easily accessed the lower slopes of the eight km-long northeast spur, which weaves up to Orville's north ridge. The key to this spur would be a traverse of its southern slopes in the lower part. We passed the striking pinnacle (5,908') by descending, crossing its south rib, and climbing the avalanche couloir on the far side. Beyond a second rib and Point 7,803', we gained the ridge, but an awkward gendarme forced us into a steeper bowl, with a steep bergschrund to exit.

Unclimbed upper north ridge of Orville from 8,074' foresummit. *Paul Knott*

Early on our fourth climbing day, April 20, we reached a foresummit at 8,074'(GPS), with a fine view of the upper mountain. The ridge beyond became rocky on both sides and featured a cornice-encrusted knife-edge crest. This sustained, exposed ground made up half of the remaining 2.7km to the summit. We would have to rappel into a notch in front of us and could see two more deep notches beyond. Having to return the same way compounded the level of seriousness. An approaching front sealed the decision, and we retraced our steps to base camp.

Peaks south of Abbe and route followed toward Peak 7,400+'. (A) Peak 8,010'. (B) Peak 8,440', climbed by 1977 party. (C) Peak 8,290'. (D) Peak 7,100+', climbed by 1977 party. (E) Peak 7,400+' climbed by 1977 party. *Paul Knott*

After four days of damp snow showers, the sky cleared and we set off for the imposing granite peaks southeast of Mt. Abbe. Several of these summits were reached by Alan Givler, Dusan Jagersky, Steve Marts, and Jim Wickwire in June 1977, but the area has since remained untouched. We gained access to the northwest-facing bowl by traversing debris below the ice cliffs that drain the hanging glacier southwest of Abbe. We first turned our attention to an unclimbed snow summit on the southwest side of the glacier. Maps give no spot height for this sharp summit but do show a tiny ring contour of 7,400'. We rejected the northeast rib, due to avalanche risk, and instead

South face of unclimbed Peak 8,410'. *Paul Knott*

approached a col to the northwest. On the 27th we overcame the bergschrund and followed avalanche debris to a col. We continued up a snow arête to a forepeak, on which my altimeter, calibrated that morning against a GPS reading of our high camp, recorded 7,484'. A steep drop-off, a north-facing rib, and a couloir separated us from the summit pinnacle. Due to unstable powder in the couloir, we retreated.

Another potential objective was unclimbed Peak 8,410', immediately south of Abbe, via a broad couloir on the south face. However, the couloir funnels into a cliff of broken granite and is essentially inaccessible. Our final option was Peak 8,290', farther southeast, also unclimbed. It sports smooth

On east arête of Burkett Needle. *Dave Burdick*

granite pillars on the north side, but we hoped to access the southeast ridge via the col used by the 1977 party. However, we were unable to reach the col, due to a gaping bergschrund and steep powder-covered slabs. We returned to base camp and flew back to Haines that afternoon, ahead of a forecast storm. We gratefully acknowledge the financial support awarded by the Mount Everest Foundation.

PAUL KNOTT, *New Zealand*

COAST MOUNTAINS

*Burkett Needle (2,590m/8,500'), east arête, Repeat Offender.* On September 9 John Frieh, Zac West, and I flew to the Burkett Glacier in the heart of the Stikine Icecap. A rare two-day weather window had appeared between the record storms and rainfall that had been hammering the area all summer. We abandoned plans for Mt. Burkett (2,965m/9,730') after we observed the active and broken state of the hanging glacier on the approach. Instead, we turned our attention to the unclimbed east arête of Burkett Needle, the alpine tower immediately west of Mt. Burkett.

Burkett Needle, showing Repeat Offender on east arête. For lines on face to left, see *AAJ 2010*, p. 134. *Dave Burdick*

Traversing above gendarme on east arête of Burkett Needle. *Zac West*

The following day we climbed a rock rib to the icefall below the Needle's southeast face. The glacier was quite broken and required climbing into moats and up a short serac, to reach the gully that leads to the east arête. Deteriorating weather caused us to bivouac at the col.

On the 11th we ascended steep snow and low 5th-class rock on the lower arête to a gendarme, which we climbed over to reach exposed rock and mixed climbing right of the crest. This led to a false summit, beyond which we made a short rappel to the summit tower, where we joined the original route on the north ridge. Three mixed snow and rock pitches led to the summit. We rappelled and downclimbed the northeast face.

Repeat Offender (IV 5.9 M5 AI3) represents the sixth ascent of Burkett Needle. [*Previous ascents were Davis and Kor, 1964; Cauthorn, Collum and Foweraker, 1995, south pillar; Daudet and Foissac, 1999, southeast face; Hassan and Holsten, 2009, south pillar; Burdick and Frieh, 2009, west ridge.*] Many thanks to the Copp-Dash Inspire Award for supporting our trip, Dieter Klose for assistance and allowing us to climb while the Icecap was "closed for the season," and our pilot Wally, from Temsco Air.

DAVE BURDICK, *AAC*

BOUNDARY RANGES

*Traverse of Juneau Icefield, possible first ascents, and ski descents.* In April Alex Appelby, Ben Bizwell, Tom Francis, and I arrived in Haines to ski-traverse the Juneau Icefield, while making as many ascents and first descents as possible. Although all British, we were a diverse group, living in different parts of the world and using diverse planks: Ben on telemark, I on skis, and the other two on splitboards.

Devils Paw from west. In 2011 tapering central couloir was climbed to notch right of main summit, then skied. Prominent right-hand couloir, climbed in 1976 en route to first ascent of south summit, was also skied. *Oli Lyon*

We first flew to Devils Paw (2,616m/8,584'), the highest peak in the Icefield, where there are two steep 1,000m couloirs that provided the main goal of the trip. For over a year I'd visualized myself skiing these couloirs. Before us they looked even more incredible.

The weather was good on our first day, so we warmed up by climbing unnamed Peak 1,920m, to the east of the Paw, across the border in Canada. We skinned nearly the whole way, wrapping around to the north and then booting back to the summit. During the ascent I'd been staring at a 50-55° chute in the middle of the south face. It gave a 350m descent, and I named it Royal Wedding, for the celebrations going on in the U.K. at the time.

A few days later we all climbed the west couloir on Devils Paw, taking three hours to cover the 1,000m of ascent in excellent condition. In perfect weather we made a probable first ski descent, at 50-55°. Later I climbed and skied the southwest couloir, which was perhaps a little longer and steeper; 55-60°. Other members gave up at various heights during the climb. The weather was awful, with high winds and low visibility. [*Editor's note: It's not clear whether the first couloir had been climbed before, but the second was climbed in July 1976 by Fred Beckey, Dougal McCarty, Jack Tackle, and Craig Zaspel when they made the first ascent of the south summit of Devils Paw. It was first skied in the 1990s, with helicopter access, but has been climbed and skied since.*]

We moved two hours west to the base of Couloir Peak (1,898m/6,227'), waited out several days of horrible weather, and climbed the prominent 500m central couloir on the south face, first climbed by Fred Beckey and Andrew Griscom

Ben Bizwell on Meade Glacier during Juneau traverse. Mt. London in background. *Oli Lyon*

Rare perfect weather over Storm Range, adjacent to Canadian border southeast of Ogilvie. From left to right: Blzzard (2,255m/7,450'), Typhoon (2,316m/7,650'), and Gale (2,263m/7,425'). *Oli Lyon*

Camp below Couloir Peak. Prominent central couloir (skied in 2011) was climbed by Beckey and Griscom in 1949. *Oli Lyon*

Unnamed Peak 1,920m, east of Devils Paw, from south. Middle of south face was skied (Royal Wedding). *Oli Lyon*

in 1949. We didn't go to the summit but skied the 50-55° couloir in bad weather and snow conditions. [*This couloir had also been skied by Americans.*]

Our satellite phone broke, and we felt we had no choice but to start our 200km traverse of the Icefield, towing pulks. After 12 days there was a rare pocket of good weather, and we got a food drop from a pre-arranged flight near Mt. Ogilvie, on the Alaska-British Columbia border. Back onto full rations at last.

While in the area we climbed OgilvieNE4 (2,307m/7,569'), via the east ridge. We stopped at the top of a south-facing couloir 5-10m below the summit. Descending the 450m couloir gave skiing of 45-50°, with 60cm of new powder. We named this run Surprise, as it slid on me.

We continued our crossing, arriving in Skagway on the 28th day of the trip. During the last two weeks, mountain conditions really changed. Winter snow was being shed, and the pack became too dangerous to ski. We generally spent eight-hour days, starting at 4 a.m., when it was still icy. By midday the thaw started, making travel much harder. Weather was generally bad, and we often had whiteout conditions. It was almost summer at the journey's end.

It was a fantastic experience, and we loved the beauty and the people of the north.

Oli Lyon, *U.K.*

*Juneau Icefield, Taku D Peak* (*1,771m/5,810'*), *southeast face, Epic.* Some of the remotest and wildest summits on earth are located in Alaska, and climbing them is a great adventure. Our goal was to reach, climb, and exit Taku D Peak, between the Taku and Matthes Glaciers in the middle of the Juneau Icefield, without technical support. Teams climbing on the Icefield normally use helicopters, satellite phones, and GPS. Max Kirchsasser and I went without.

In mist and rain we began our first load carry from Juneau through rainforest. Four days and one storm later, all our equipment was at the edge of the Icefield. As we set off on our ski journey, pulling sledges, luck and good weather were on our side. Sunlight glistened on the Icefield in front, while behind lay the Pacific Ocean.

Epic on southeast face of Taku D. Standard route on southwest ridge is left skyline. *Florian Hill*

We crossed a ridgeline with some difficulty to reach Death Valley, where we had days of standstill, waiting for better weather. Eventually blue sky returned and, well rested, we pushed on. Finally pyramidal Taku D loomed into view. The first ascent was probably in 1952 (Robert L Schuster) by the Juneau Icefield Research Program, which 12 years later named the Taku Range. They climbed the southwest ridge, which today could be considered the standard route.

On lower granite wall of Taku D's southeast face. *Florian Hill Collection*

A phenomenon of mountains is that they appear uninviting and aloof from a distance but up close reveal possibilities of ascent. Such was the case with Taku D, as we found a weakness on the unclimbed southeast face. Through knee-deep snow we inched our way to the rock walls at the base of the face, and I led the brittle first pitch. Thick mist made way for strong morning sunshine. On the next pitch we had to move around a small roof. The cracks were full of ice, but we were carrying a large selection of pitons; more weight, but in my opinion indispensable there. We eventually exited onto a steep snow slope, where we were greeted by blue sky. High on the mountain we joined the southwest ridge, and trudged through knee-deep snow to the summit. The snow was soft and heavy, and we were afraid of a sudden slide, but we reached the top and descended the southwest ridge. We named our route Epic (550m of climbing, TD).

Months of research and preparation had come to an end. To reach our dream mountain, we'd ascended from the ocean, through rainforest and over glacial ice, to the summit of Taku D. Our adventure became complex and borderline because we reduced technical aids to a minimum.

FLORIAN HILL, *Austria*

# Canada

The online version of these reports frequently contains additional photos, maps, topos, and extended text. Please visit aaj.americanalpineclub.org

## ST. ELIAS RANGE

View east from base camp. Lower slopes of Peak 3,450m on left. Peaks in distance lie on far side of the Stairway Glacier. *Glenn Wilks*

*Stairway Glacier, Peak 3,450m, south-souteast face and southwest ridge.* Jonathan Wakefield and I arrived at Kluane Lake on May 16 and were able to fly within one and a half hours. We intended to make first ascents of peaks around the head of the Walsh-Denis Glacier confluence in Kluane National Park's icefields. Mt. Upton had been climbed some years ago, but the remaining peaks remained virgin. However, halfway into the flight strong winds forced the pilot to abort, and the following day, while we reached the area, winds prevented a landing. On the return we looked at Stairway Glacier, where I had climbed in 2009 (*AAJ 2010*), and scoped out a subsidiary glacier spotted on that trip. There seemed to be possibilities, so we returned to Kluane and discussed waiting for favorable conditions to go to the Walsh-Denis confluence. However, a party of nine was due at Kluane next day bound for Mt. Logan, and we didn't want to be waiting there for several more days, so we decided on the Stairway side glacier. This may have proven a bad decision.

That day we landed at 2,500m on the side glacier, which flows east into the Stairway. After establishing camp, clag set in, conditions that were to prove typical for the next four days. Temperatures were high, and we had only a few tantalizing views through breaks in the clouds. Over the next few days we attempted to explore the glaciers, but rising temperatures caused avalanches of both old and new snow. North-facing slopes seemed badly crevassed and seracked, while south faces were rocky and seared by avalanche. The prospect of rich picking was not favorable.

On May 21 we left camp at 4 a.m. under clear skies. It was unusually warm. The ascent of Peak 3,450m behind camp took an old avalanche track with huge debris for the lower half of the slope. The upper half of this south-southeast face (average 45°) leveled out and led to a col. We then followed a broad ridge northeast, in knee-deep softening snow of 50-55°. We eventual summited at 10:00 a.m. Views were magnificent, and we enjoyed knowing that this was a first ascent. We made our way down without incident until the final quarter of the slope, which due to the temperature was unstable. Hard debris turned to knee-deep slush in places.

From the 22nd to the 26th we made attempts on other objectives, often unseen in dense fog. Discretion overtook valor. This was my fourth trip to the icefields and by far the worst conditions I'd experienced. Back in camp on the 26th, we called for a flight out. Three hours later were back at Kluane, feeling sorry for ourselves.

There are still lower-altitude peaks in this region that remain untouched, but some appear difficult, with broken approaches and faces. Given their height, it might be necessary to go there in late April, but it could be very cold. Thanks to the Mount Everest Foundation for its support.

GLENN WILKS, *U.K.*

Jonathan Wakefield on south-southeast face of Peak 3,450m. *Glenn Wilks*

Jonathan Wakefield on final part of south-southeast ridge of Peak 3,450m. *Glenn Wilks*

COAST MOUNTAINS

*Southern Coast Mountains and Canadian Cascades.* The number of new routes reported in southwestern British Columbia has been declining since surging around 2002-2004. There are probably a number of reasons for this general decline, including the time since the last comprehensive guidebook was published, and the Internet, which guides people toward already visited places. Shifts in the forest industry have resulted in old logging roads becoming impassable while opening access to new areas. The nadir of this trend was probably 2010, when apparently only one new alpine route was put up in all southwestern B.C. There was something of a resurgence in 2011, with three notable routes.

All four routes established in 2010 and 2011 are long rock routes. In 2010, Cam Robertson, Mike Shannon, and Jeff Sherstobitoff, three motivated climbers from Kelowna, added a long, easy route at the extreme left margin of Yak Peak's southwest face. Seven One-Move Wonders of the World (III 5.7) is 15 pitches long, with several isolated moves in the 5.7 range. Much of the route consists of 4th and low 5th class slab scrambling, with bolted belays. It begins just left of Speedway, crosses the Southwest Gully around pitch nine, and possibly shares terrain with the nebulous 1987 Beckey-de Jong-Svensson. Despite its shortcomings the new route has proven popular, bridging the gap between scrambling and climbing. There was one repeat in 2010 and at least three in 2011.

In summer 2011 Justin Barnes, Jeremy Frimer, and Kat Siepmann climbed a new variation on the east face of Mt. Parkes, the subsidiary northern bump of the Mt. Slesse group. This face was already home to the 2001 route Bamboozled Buttress, which was infamously climbed in the fog by Karsten Duncan and Dan Hughes while grievously off-route attempting the more prominent Northeast Buttress of Mt. Slesse. The new route, Beached Az (III 5.9), climbs terrain near Bamboozled in the lower half (though with clearer weather allowing the choice of a less-vegetated line) but continues straight up the face where Bamboozled moves left. The climbing was said to feature lots of grassy cracks and not be particularly aesthetic.

In the Squamish area Conny Amelunxen, Jamie Chong, and Marshal German established something of a double route on the narrow south face of Mt. Dione. Both the variants of Dehydrated on Dalwhinnie are 10 pitches long, the gear variant being 5.10- and the sport variant 5.11b. The climbers established the route ground-up using trad gear and then made bolted variations to a few of the pitches, creating what was touted as a fully equipped sport line. About eight pitches are common to both, with the trad line bypassing the 5.11b crux. The sport line still has sections of loose rock and scrambling. The route seems to have been established with guiding in mind, given its visibility from and proximity to the Jim Haberl Hut.

Finally Bruce Kay with a variety of partners, but primarily Jim Martinello, spent the summer of 2011 on the east face of the Mouse's Tooth (a subsidiary rock buttress in North Joffre Creek near Pemberton, home to his winter routes Rhapsody in Floyd and Free Tibet). The result was an 11-pitch 5.11-. The rock is good overall, especially after several repeats, and Bruce went back in late summer and established higher-quality bolted variations to the first two pitches, which were said to be junky and vegetated.

These routes illustrate trends in the alpine environment of southwestern B.C.: more bolts and power drilling, more attention paid to quality, more willingness to squeeze in variations close to existing climbs, and quick repeats courtesy of the Internet. I expect these trends will become more prevalent, but the southern Coast Mountains are wild enough that the purest adventure climbing will survive well into the future.

DREW BRAYSHAW, *Canada*

# Greenland

*The online version of these reports frequently contains additional photos, maps, topos, and extended text. Please visit aaj.americanalpineclub.org*

WEST GREENLAND

*Uummannaq and Upernavik regions first ascents.* Following our successful campaign in 2010, we returned in July 2011, with a strong group mainly of Italian guides, to blitz the Uummannaq and Upernavik regions, adding a number of routes. The group operated from Mariacristina Rapisardi's super-yacht, Billy Budd. Along with Rapisardi, the main climbers were Luca Argentero, Alberto Bianchi, Marco Frezzato, Michele Maggioni, and Beppe Villa.

North face of Peak 1,600m on Alfred Wegener Halvo rises above Kangerdluarssuq Fjord. Italian attempt marked. *Michele Maggioni*

The team first visited the Uummannaq area, where on July 6 the climbers put up three new routes on south-facing slabby rock walls on Agpat Island (Umiasugssup Ilua, 70°51'90" N, 51°38'44" W): Closed on Tuesday (250m, French 5b); The First of the Sirocco (250m, 5c); and Beppe, Come Back (150m, 6a).

The following day saw two forays made onto Peak 1,630m on the peninsula of Alfred Wegener Halvo. Neither reached the summit. Argentero and Villa climbed mixed ground on the north face to 1,500m, descending unstable rock (71°09'35" N, 51°59'50" W), while Frezzato, accompanied by Augusto Scirocchi, ascended gentle ground, also reaching ca 1,500m (71°12'00" N, 51°58'70" W). On the 8th Maggioni and Villa climbed 300m up the southeast face of Upernavik O (Upernavik Island in Inukavsait Fjord, 71°16'32" N, 52°21'09" W). This huge formation is also known as the Horn. The pair attempted the slabs left of two British attempts in 2010 and overcame difficulties of 6b/c before rappelling, placing two-bolt anchors on the descent. (One of the British attempts bailed 400m from

West coast of Agparssuit. (1) Lost Images. (2) Dedicated to You. *Michele Maggioni*

the top, after 900m of climbing [*AAJ 2011* and photo *AAJ 2010*, p 152]).

The yacht then moved north to the Upernavik region, where on the 11th the group put up two parallel routes on a south-facing cliff above Tasiussaq Fjord on the large island of Nutarmiut

Iterdlagssuaq, with lines of (1) Old Man's Benefit, (2) 2006 Predan-Rapisardi, and (3) Isabella. *Michele Maggioni*

Little Auk on Red Wall of Agparssuit. *Michele Maggioni*

Pic Nic on south coast of Umiasugssuk. Dotted line is descent along grassy terraces. *Michele Maggioni*

(72°37'14" N, 55°32'53" W): You Need Cold Blood (200m, 5c) and, to its right, You Are Connected (200m, 5b). The following day the six climbers went to Qaersorssuaq Island, where a little north of Agparssuit they put up two 250m routes on a southeast-facing rock wall of Kingigtup Ilua (72°41'22" N, 55°53'90" W): Red Sam (6a) and Tic Tac (6a+).

On the 13th, on the sea cliffs on the west coast of Agparssuit at 72°40'17" N, 55°54'66" W, the whole group put up two 350m routes that intersect at two-thirds height: Lost Images (6c) and Dedicated to You (6b+). On the 15th Argentero, Maggioni, and Villa climbed the 450m Little Auk (7a) on Red Wall (72°39'24" N, 55°52'48" W). This route lies on the east face, well right of the 2010 routes, Red Chili Crackers and Seagull's Garden (*AAJ 2011*). The following day, farther west along the coast of Qaersorssuaq Island at 72°40'29" N, 55°58'38" W, all the group climbed the right side of the south-facing rounded granite dome of Iterdlagssuaq to produce Isabella (300m, 5c). This route lies well right of the corner system of Old Man's Benefit (200m, British HVS 5a, Howard-Shepton, 2009), and between this and original route on the face put up in 2006 by Gianni Predan and Mariacristina Rapisardi (200m, British Hard Severe). Members of the team also climbed the first five pitches of Arctic First Born (800m, British E3 5c A3+) on the northwest face of Sanderson's Hope, the first big wall route on this large slabby sea cliff (and the first on a large sea cliff above the Arctic Circle on Greenland's west coast). These were climbed "just for interest," but while making a rappel descent, they placed two bolts to the left of the route.

Finally, on the 18th, Bianchi, Maggioni, and Rapisardi climbed Pic Nic (200m, 6a+) on the lower walls of a southeast-facing sea cliff at 72°45'16" N, 55°56'30" W on Umiasugssuk, an almost-island rising to 620m on the north coast of Qaersorssuaq. The north coast of this almost-island holds the 2010 route Brown Balls.

Michele Maggioni during an unsuccessful attempt on the Horn. *Michele Maggioni Collection*

It is good that this area around Upernavik is at last beginning to realize something of its potential. However, as the instigator of technical climbing on the west coast of Greenland, and especially in the Upernavik area, may I make an appeal that these pristine walls be climbed without recourse to bolts. Completely blank sections on big walls may provoke an exception, but several fine, technically hard lines have been climbed without use of bolts.

BOB SHEPTON, *Alpine Club, U.K.*

EAST GREENLAND

*Saven Range, first ascents.* In May Geoff Bonney, Sandy Gregson, and I, veterans of many Greenland expeditions, were joined in the Saven Range by four younger U.K. climbers, Steve Allsopp, Vernon Needham, Steve Wilson, and Simon Yates. I had seen these beautiful, little-explored mountains, which stand just north of the huge glacier Rolige Brae from a distance of 25km during previous visits to Paul Stern Land farther south (*AAJ 2009 and 2011*). Saven means "the saw" in Danish, and the range was named by geologists for its appearance when seen from the south.

We flew to the area from Constable Pynt (Nerlerit Inaat) in a Norlandair Twin Otter skiplane, our regular pilot Ragnar Olafsson landing

Peaks of Paul Stern Land from Saven Range, 25km to north. High peak left of center is unclimbed Arken ("The Ark," 2,348m). *Jim Gregson*

Part of Saven Range from Alfheim Glacier to the north. From left to right: Peak Hymir, Peak Gymir, Breidablikk, and Ragnars Fjeld. *Jim Gregson*

Sandy Gregson and Geoff Bonney (below) on north flank of Breidablikk, with Peak Gymir behind. *Jim Gregson*

Sandy Gregson on slopes of Peak Surt. View extends southeast past Breidablikk (left) and across Rolige Brae to spiky Jomfruen ("Virgin"). *Jim Gregson*

at ca 1,900m near the west end of the Alfheim (Elfworld) Glacier. The surface was icy and bumpy, with large sastrugi, and Ragnar was not at all happy with what had been his own choice. However, by the end of the trip there had been enough snowfall and spindrift to make everything pool-table smooth for the pick-up.

In cold winds blowing off the inland ice, we established our base, Camp Jetstream, at 70°42.139' N, 29°51.241' W, and used this site for the duration of our stay. Constructing a system of spindrift-deflecting walls proved necessary.

Working in two groups we made first ascents of 13 mountains, several of which we ascended and descended by more than one route. Climbs involved a variety of ridge lines, icy north faces, and some rock of variable quality. Most days gave stunning views, highlighting the difference between blue ice-clad north slopes and immense rocky south faces falling toward the massive crevassed zones of the Rolige Brae. In the distance we could see the Inland Ice, with isolated nunataks piercing its surface, and the peaks of Paul Stern Land (many of which are unclimbed). The Alfheim Glacier was well snow-covered this year, meaning we could make ski approaches unroped. On the peaks we found plenty of bullet-hard ice, sometimes overlaid with powder, and on Hymir we chopped a rope after dispatching inconvenient loose blocks (though no humans were harmed during the making of this story). The Saven Range has more unclimbed summits in its eastern sector, but these were beyond easy skiing distance in the time available.

Summits reached were Dvalin Ridge ("Dwarf Turned to Stone," 1,995m, 70°42.349' N, 29°49.681' W); Peak Surt ("Black Giant," 2,140m, 70°40.590' N, 29°53.230' W), with three summits along its ridge); Ragnars Fjeld (2,070m, 70°40.902' N, 29°49.995' W); Valdis Topp (2,040m, 70°40.679' N, 29°49.582' W), the south summit of Ragnars Fjeld); Peak Gymir ("Frost Giant," 2,174m, 70°40.381' N, 29°43.399' W); Breidablikk ("Broad Splendor," 2,225m, 70°40.287' N, 29°46.745' W); Peak Brokk ("Dwarf," 1,980m, 70°42.292' N, 29°46.904' W); Point Gimli ("Shelter from Fire," 1,862m, 70°42.288' N, 29°44.201' W); Peak Loki ("Evil Shapeshifter," 2,002m, 70°42.721' N, 29°43.612' W); Point Idavoll ("Field of Deeds," 1,982m, 70°41.886' N, 29°59.499' W); Peak Hymir ("Giant," 2,130m, 70°40.518' N, 29°40.486' W); Glitnir North ("Hall of Silver and Gold," 2,150m, 70°41.468' N, 29°37.366' W); and Glitnir South (2,150m, 70°41.264' N, 29°37.481' W), the two Glitnirs being traversed in one outing, via Simon's Big Ridge).

All peak names, mostly derived from Norse mythology, are unofficial. Coordinates are from GPS, while heights combine of GPS and altimeter readings.

By the end of our stay, we'd had half a meter of new snow, giving the peaks a wintry look and pushing up the avalanche risk. The Twin Otter arrived for our pick-up, and in the time it took to load the gear, the undercarriage had frozen to the glacier, and even full engine power would not budge it. The pilots deployed shovels but eventually had to resort to a large soft-faced mallet to "crack" the ski runners free. After a hurried refuel at Constable Pynt, we flew to Akureyri in north Iceland. Two days later were in the air again and homeward bound to Britain when the Grimsvotn volcano blew its stack. We'd made a timely exit to close a successful expedition.

JIM GREGSON, *Alpine Club, U.K.*

Renland's alpine peaks hold great potential. These lie on south side of Edward Bailey Glacier, west of Shark's Teeth Glacier. *Alexander Ruchkin*

*Renland, Shark's Tooth (1,555m), Dance on Tiptoes.* On April 16 Mikhail Mikhailov and I arrived at Constable Pynt in poor weather after a flight from Reykjavik. The same day we left by snowmobile for Avgo, a summer fishing lodge. It took eight cold hours through the twilight. After a night sleeping on the floor (our Inuit drivers had the bunks), I awoke feeling I'd overslept. It's the same every day at this time of year in Northeast Greenland, because it is nearly always daylight. At 9:30 a.m. we were on our way again, "sailing" the fjord toward Renland over fluffy snow. Only huge blue icebergs protruding above the surface violated the black and white colour scheme.

At 3 p.m., after traveling up the Skillebugt Inlet in the southeastern corner of Renland, we were off-loaded at the end of the Apusinikajik Glacier. We were still 12km from our goal, the Shark's Tooth, but the Inuits would not take their skidoos farther, fearing crevasses on the snow-covered glacier. In around 20 days, they informed us, the fjord could melt, and we would have to return by helicopter, at more than twice the expense of skidoos.

With a temperature of -20°C, we quickly established base camp, cooked, and ate normally for the first time in two days, and then fell asleep, not forgetting to load our rifle and put it next to us

Main Shark's Tooth rises over 900m from glacier. Marked is Dance on Tiptoes with bivouac sites. *Alexander Ruchkin*

Mikhailov starts from final bivouac on northwest ridge of Shark's Tooth. Below is Edward Bailey Glacier. *Alexander Ruchkin*

Mikhailov on pitch 10 of Dance on Tiptoes, Shark's Tooth. *Alexander Ruchkin*

with the pistol and flare gun, ready for a visit from a polar bear. We stored our 15kg of fresh fish and 5kg of fresh musk ox in a box 10m from the tent; the Inuit told us that the bears' noses are so powerful, they can pick up scent from 20km away.

During subsequent days we tried to explore the area, our first impressions being that the chances of climbing anything were slim: there was too much snow, it was too cold, the humidity was high and producing frequent snowfall, and the winds were strong. Each day, as we tried to establish an advanced base on the Edward Bailey Glacier, fresh snow covered our ski trail.

Finally, on April 29, we received via satellite phone a forecast from our snowmobile provider that the weather would be good from May 1-6 and deteriorate thereafter. This seemed to be our only chance. Originally I had been attracted by the sheer north wall of the Shark's Tooth, which is split up the center by a good crack system and resembles Pik 4,810m in the Karavshin. However, weight restrictions on the air flights precluded taking a portaledge, and as there are no ledges on this 900m wall for a tent, an ascent would require sitting bivouacs, far too cold a proposition in the spring. So we chose the northwest ridge and didn't regret it. The ridge received the sun from 2:30 p.m. until 10 p.m., and we adjusted our days accordingly, sleeping until around 10 a.m.

On May 2 we left advanced base (altitude 40m) and ascended the Shark's Teeth Glacier until below the Tooth at 640m. (The Tooth lies on the ridge separating the Shark's Teeth Glacier from the Bowling Alley Glacier to the south.) Starting the 300m snow couloir right of the north face at 3 p.m., we paddled up eight pitches of unconsolidated 50° snow to a notch on the crest, where at 9:30 p.m. we erected the tent. Next day I led four-and-a-half pitches. After the first on snow-covered granite, I was able to change into rock shoes, as the temperature was no lower than -5 to -10°C.

On the 4th Misha led another four-and-a-half pitches to a flat point on the ridge where we spent our second night, though not before he had climbed two more pitches up the crest above. We decided to leave bivouac equipment here and travel light next day to the summit.

We were on our way by 10 a.m. Five pitches from 6a to 6c, followed by a gentle sixth pitch, led to the summit. On the second a few meters required aid (A1), as did a few meters on the fourth (A2). Otherwise we climbed the route free in 15 pitches from the head of the couloir. The altitude was 1,555m; we spent an hour on top soaking up the view before heading back down. We had difficulties with rope jams on the lower rappels but made it back to the tent that night and off the mountain next day.

There are many great peaks in this area, and I have to go back. This trip was spontaneous, and our desires outran our abilities. Our main mistake was going too early. In July and August you do not have to plow deep tracks in the snow, and parties can be delivered to a point not far from our base camp by boat. We named our route Dance on Tiptoes (915m, 1,210m of climbing, VI 6c A2).

ALEXANDER RUCHKIN, *Russia*

*Watkins Mountains, Mt. Augustine Courtauld (ca 3,150m).* In the second half of May, a Tangent expedition led by Ian Barker and Mark Basey-Fisher (U.K.), with Warren Allen, Julian Cooper, Mark Morrison, Sebastian Sloane (all U.K.), Andrey Pogudin (Russia), and I made the first ascent of a peak in the Gunnbjornsfjeld group.

First, though, from our base camp at 68°54.319' N, 29°43.5' W, we made the year's first ascent of the highest mountain in the Arctic, Gunnbjornsfjeld (Hvitserk, 3,694m). The usual route following the southwest ridge does not keep to the crest throughout, but skirts a rocky section by climbing out left on the west face. However, inclement weather had made these slopes dangerous, and we were forced to climb on or close to the crest (ca 50°). Pogudin and I became the first Russians to summit Gunnbjornsfjeld.

Initially we also planned to attempt the second and third highest summits, Dome (3,683m) and Cone (3,669m), but we instead became interested in a 3,000+m summit

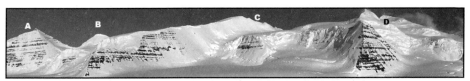

Panorama southeast to south from base camp. (A) Peak 3,175m (FA 1998). (B) Augustine Courtauld (FA 2011). (C) Peak Cappuccino (3,266m: FA 1998). (D) Deception Dome (3,526m: FA 1988). There is a minor top (hidden) between (B) and (C). *Maxim Bouev*

Looking north through to east over the Woolley Glacier from the summit of Augustine Courtauld. Fine pyramid on the left is Peak 3,175m, climbed in 1998 by Hans Christian Florian (Denmark) and an Austrian team. *Maxim Bouev*

Panorama of the highest peaks in the Arctic, seen from advanced base camp below Mt Augustine Courtauld. (A) Peak 3,369m. (B) Dome (3,683m: FA 1988). (C) Cone (3,669m: FA 1988). (D) Peak ca 3,450m (climbed). (E) Peak Osterrike (ca 3,288m: FA 1998). (F) Gunnbjornsfjeld (3,694m: FA 1935: leftskyline is southwest ridge). (G) U-Turn (3,307m: FA 1999). *Maxime Bouev*

Augustine Courtauld from the northwest, showing route of first ascent.
Maxim Bouev

southeast of the Gunnbjorns base camp. It was the last remaining unclimbed high mountain in the middle section of a tributary of the Woolley Glacier. The peak had been identified and meticulously photographed in 2009 and attempted the following year by Paul Rose's expedition, which was defeated by deep soft snow.

We attempted the mountain on May 28 from a high camp at 68° 54.336' N, 29° 37.151' W. In the lower part the route ran through a steep, heavily crevassed couloir, threatened by huge seracs. After leaving this avalanche-prone bottleneck, we reached a saddle at the base of the south-southwest ridge, where we faced another obstacle, an 18m rock tower. We climbed the left edge over snow and mixed terrain, using rock protection in cracks. We spent two hours on this section, where the angle rose to 60°. Above, an easy climb up the final, exposed crest led to the summit, which we estimate to be 3,150m.

On our return to base camp there followed a hot dispute on an (unofficial) name for our peak. Eventually we decided on Mt. Augustine Courtauld, after a hero on the 1930-31 British Arctic Air Route Expedition and member of the party that made the first ascent of Gunnbjornsfjeld in 1935.

Julian Cooper and Ian Barker (top) negotiate mixed ground alongside the rock step on Augustine Courtauld.
Maxim Bouev

From December 1930 to May 1931, Courtauld lived alone at a Greenland Icecap station, gathering meteorological data that would later be of exceptional value in establishing regular air traffic between Europe and America via a northern route. Several attempts to relieve Courtauld or replenish his food supplies by aircraft were thwarted by horrendous weather. Eventually, 150 days after Courtauld's arrival at the station, expedition leader Gino Watkins and other members of his team managed to reach the site by dog sled and relieve Courtauld, just as his food and fuel were running out.

MAXIM BOUEV, *Russia/U.K.*

## SOUTH GREENLAND - CAPE FAREWELL REGION

*Tasermiut Fjord, Hermelndal, Tininnertuup II (1,511m), east face attempt.* Our plan was to open a new rock route in Greenland, as part of my seven big walls on seven continents project. Unfortunately, when Giuseppe A. Torre Balderas and I arrived at Nanortalik in July, we had only raised 55% of the budget. We left on the 23rd with neither enough food nor resources to overcome unexpected eventualities. At 1 p.m. the boat dropped us and our 120kg of equipment at the head of the Tasermiut Fjord, agreeing to return on August 15. (We had no communication devices.)

We spent until the 26th establishing base camp in the Hermalndal, Giuseppe injuring his knee on the first day. We then made two carries to the base of Tininnertuup II and started up the east face on the 31st, climbing three long new pitches up the slabs right of Piriton Pillar (700m, British E5 6a, McManus-Tresidder, 2008) to the first terrace. On August 1st we identified a virgin dihedral and climbed four pitches to the site of our second bivouac. To this point we had climbed 375m, with pitch grades 5.8, 5.9, 5.10-, 5.11-, 5.11-, 5.10+, and 5.10+.

When we unpacked the haul bag we found our 10-liter water bottle had burst and soaked everything. Apart from wet gear, we now had only three liters of water for the remaining 600m of climbing. After an unpleasant bivouac we began a rappel descent, drilling anchors. We reached our camp that night, and with not enough food for another attempt, we spent the next five days ferrying equipment to the fjord. On August 9 we attracted the attention of a fisherman and caught a ride to Nanortalik.

LUIS CARLOS GARCIA AYALA, *Mexico*

East pillar of Tininnertuup II. (1) War Cry (Desforges-Spreyer-Stone, 2008). (2) Scorpion Grooves (Desforges-Spreyer, 2008). (3) Flying Viking (Grmovsek-Grmovsek, 2008). (4) Piriton Pillar (McManus-Tresidder, 2008). (5) 2011 Mexican attempt. (6) Anglo-Bavarian Direct (Gutzat-Vybiral, 2008). Original ascent (Irish, 1971) climbed behind the left skyline from the col between II and III. (See *AAJ 2009* for details.) *Andrej Grmovsek*

Essential protection against South Greenland's mosquitoes. In lower Hermelndal with northwest face of Hermelnberg (1,912m) behind. *Luis Carlos Garcia Ayala*

*Quvnerit Island, various ascents.* This was my third trip to Greenland. In 2001, with Gabor Berecz, Gunter Dengler, and Thomas Tivadar, I'd established a 1,000m big wall route on Pamiagdluk Island. In 2004 I found enthusiastic companions for an exploration of Quvnerit Island, where Tom Holzhauser, Caro Morel, Wanja Reichel, the Tresch brothers, Michi Wyser, and I established 10 rock routes to 7c. In early August 2011 Andreas Lietha, Holzhauser, Morel, Michi Tresch, Wyser, and I were back on Quvnerit, where due to climate change it was considerably warmer than during my previous Greenland trips. After establishing base camp at the 2004 site, we went exploring by boat; many of the walls are only accessible in this way. We could not believe that most walls and peaks are still unclimbed, and went to work on perfect granite with steep crack systems.

With great weather Via Corradojillo (6c) and Private Universe (7a+) started a wave of first ascents on the west coast of the island. Soon afterwards we climbed El Martillo (6a+), Rascana (6c), and Bondola

Dos Canones. (1) El Martillo. (2) Lucky Mushrooms. (3) Private Universe. In 2004 Holzhauser and the Tresch brothers put up first route on formation. See *AAJ 2005*. *Toni Lamprecht*

Golden Pillars. (1) Another Wallhala. (2) Waslala. *Toni Lamprecht*

Piz Rascana with (1) Coradojillo and (2) Rascana. *Toni Lamprecht*

(6a+) on perfect rock in the breathtaking setting of the Itivdliap-Pularia Fjord.

After a few rest days, Tom, Michi, and I put up Another Wallhalla (6a+) on one of the 800m crack-ridden pillars on the north coast. We traveled with a minimum of gear up this perfect route with perfect clean protection. Warm days under mosquito nets alternated with cold nights in glacier bivouacs. We climbed more "almost classic" new lines in one-day pushes. Lucky Mushrooms (6b+), Northern Comfort (6a+), and Waslala (6a+) are as good as the best granite routes in the Alps.

One highlight of the trip was the first ascent of Serratit (the Inuit word for a magic spell that may only be used in dangerous situations), above a north-facing glacier basin in the center of Quvnerit. Tom, Michi, and I climbed 12 demanding pitches between 6b+ and 7b, reaching the summit of Asiaq Tower. The constantly steep route offers face climbing, with hard bouldery sections, a dream dihedral, and cracks from finger to a 60m offwidth not far from the top.

We sat on the summit enjoying the endless views of mountains and fjords. To the south lay only the ocean. We rappelled to the 200m ice field at the foot of the face and, after another hour, arrived at the bivouac site in the middle of the glacier. It can't get any better, I thought, as I sank into my sleeping bag while the northern lights began their spectacle, and the full moon rose over our peak.

Toward the end of our stay, an incident brought home the fact that, even with a satellite phone, this is a lonely place. One day before her planned departure, Caro was injured in the hand by a falling stone. She got scant diagnosis from the hospital in Appilattoq but learned in Switzerland two days later that she had damaged metacarpal-bones and some lacerations but no tendon injuries.

The weather turned unsettled in our last week, and we lost motivation. On the last three days we bouldered. Our Inuit boat arrived to ferry us to Nanortalik, where, despite showers, extended sauna sit-ins, and culinary festivals, we were looking forward to going home. What remained were memories, and not only memories of good rock climbing.

During our five weeks on Quvnerit we climbed 10 new routes, clean and without fixed gear, and had only four days of rain and storm, during the last week. As always Nanortalik Tourism was helpful and hospitable in organizing the logistics and providing the practical and moral support needed for climbing in South Greenland, including receiving cargo, chartering boats, and booking hotels. Contact them through nanortaliktourism.com

Following is a summary of our climbs. In Itivdliap Pularia Fjord: two routes on Piz Rascana, Corradojillo (300m, 7 pitches, 6c, Morel-Lietha-Wyser, August 1) and Rascana (450m, 10 pitches, 6c, Holzhauser-Lamprecht-Tresch, August 5); two routes on Dos Canones I, Private Universe (550m 12 pitches, 7a+, Holzhauser-Tresch, August 1), and Lucky Mushrooms (600m, 10 pitches, 6b+, Morel-Lietha-Wyser, August 11); one route on Dos Canones II, El Martillo (500m, 10 pitches, 6a+, Morel-Lietha-Wyser, August 4); two routes on Bondola, Bondola (450m, 9 pitches, 6a+, Morel-Lietha-Wyser, August 7), and Northern Comfort (600m, 12 pitches, 6a+, Lietha-Wyser, August 20). In Sivinganerup ima Fiord: one route on Asiaq, Serratit (600m, 12 pitches, 7b, Holzhauser-Lamprecht-Tresch, August 15); two routes on Golden Pillars, Another Wallhalla (800m, 16 pitches, 6a+, Holzhauser-Lamprecht-Tresch, August 11), and Waslala (600m, 11 pitches, 6a+, Morel-Lietha-Wyser, August 15 and 22).

TONI LAMPRECHT, *Germany*

Bondola with (1) Bondola and (2) Northern Comfort. *Toni Lamprecht*

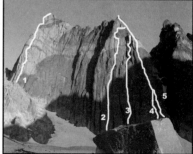

Northwest side of Asiaq Group. (1) Serratit. Line lies close to the 2004 Tresch-Tresch route (7a). (2) Chinese Gybe (Ditto-Favresse, 2010). (3) Chloé (Favresse-Villanueva, 2010). (4) Ghetto Boys (Lamprecht-Reichel-Tresch-Tresch, 2004). (5) West Pillar (Lamprecht-Reichel-Tresch-Tresch, 2004). See AAJ 2011 and AAJ 2005. *Toni Lamprecht*

Michi Tresch on first ascent of Serratit. *Toni Lamprecht*

# *Colombia*

*The online version of these reports frequently contains additional photos, maps, topos, and extended text. Please visit aaj.americanalpineclub.org*

## SIERRA NEVADA DEL COCUY

Lopez-Pfaff Direct on south pillar of Ritacuba Blanco. *Anna Pfaff*

Camilo Lopez during first ascent of Ritacuba Blanco south pillar. *Anna Pfaff*

High camp below south face of Ritacuba Blanco with approximate line of Lopez-Pfaff Direct. *Anna Pfaff*

*Ritacuba Blanco, south pillar, not to summit.* On February 21, 2012, Camilo Lopez and I climbed the south pillar of Ritacuba Blanco, naming our route Lopez–Pfaff Direct (600m, IV 5.10d AI3). We climbed to the summit of the pillar, measuring an altitude of 5,179m. The main summit (5,330m) proved unreachable, due to an unstable hanging serac above a mandatory traverse from the top of the pillar. Research prior to our trip showed no previous ventures on the south face.

We climbed alpine style, unsupported. Starting from the roadhead at Parada de Romero, Guican, we carried gear and food for three days up and down mountain passes to a base camp at Laguna del Avellanal (4,200m). From there we scoped out our project's conditions. The weather had been fairly stable for most of our approach, with only a few thick cloud formations and several drops of rain. We knew we were late in the dry season and had little time to spare. The next day we carried gear up a steep moraine to the base of the wall, dodging rockfall from the melting summit of Ritacuba Blanco. We bivouacked in a secure spot close to the face and started climbing early the next day.

We climbed fairly quickly, reaching the top at noon, with winds blowing and the sun shining. On the first three-quarters of the wall we found good steep rock with some loose stuff. Toward the top there were more broken sections, with large loose blocks. The summit ridge had blocks glued on by snow and ice and was a bit sketchy, so we retreated, rappelling the face. We left behind only pitons and tape at rappel stations and were back at base camp as the sun disappeared over the horizon.

Camilo and I spent a total of eight days in the beautiful Sierra del Cocuy, seeing only a few trekkers. It is a pristine alpine environment, full of mountains and big walls. The area is still occupied by indigenous people and is seen as a very religious and powerful place. We were fortunate to have this experience, good weather, and great climbing on the Ritacuba Blanco, one of the most exotic and magical mountains in South America.

ANNA PFAFF, *U.S.*

# *Venezuela*

*The online version of these reports frequently contains additional photos, maps, topos, and extended text. Please visit aaj.americanalpineclub.org*

*Amuri Tepui, south face, Kids with Guns.* Over 15 days during February 2012, Mason Earle (U.S.), Sam Farnsworth (U.K.), Siebe Vanhee (Belgium), and I weaved an improbable, intricate path directly behind Salto Tuyuren, topping out within a stone's throw of where the waterfall bursts from the summit plateau. Our best estimate is that the 500m wall overhangs by almost 100m. Most of our 21-pitch route crossed immaculate and wildly steep quartz-arenite (pre-Cambrian metamorphosed sandstone).

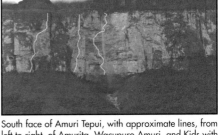

South face of Amuri Tepui, with approximate lines, from left to right, of Amurita, Wacupuro Amuri, and Kids with Guns. See photo by Nico Favresse for Belgian lines. *George Ullrich*

We met as a team for the first time in Caracas and flew in two Cessnas to Yunek, a remote Pemon Indian village, which is becoming a staging post for this rapidly developing climbing region. We hired a guide and porters to help transport our four weeks of supplies on the three-day trek to Amuri Tepui. This was a real jungle expedition, incomplete without sunglasses and a sharp machete.

We picked an audacious line up the center of the steepest section. Our base camp, to the side of the waterfall, afforded an amazing view of the wall, and we only realized later that the view came at the expense of a drenching from the fall when the wind blew in the wrong direction. A convenient cat-walk gave access to the bottom of our chosen line, so we avoided the initial jungle pitches for which the area is renowned.

From the start we were impressed by the quality of climbing. Technical face-climbing and short sections of loose rock made routefinding difficult and progress sporadic, but these were interspersed with many obvious pitches, which allowed faster progress. Twelve days after we began, we were only halfway up the face and beginning to question whether we would have the time—and enough food and water—to top out. As a result we shelved our goal of free-climbing every pitch.

A rare flat ledge on overhanging wall of Amuri Tepui. *George Ullrich*

Finally bursting through the first major roof, at half height, boosted morale, enabled faster progress, and made us realize that the top was attainable, despite steepening rock above. Every pitch resulted in a shockingly airy rappel and an invigorating morning start, swinging out 20m from the portaledges before jumaring to the previous day's highpoint. There were occasional flat ledges, unexpected but welcome.

We named our route Kids with Guns (British E6 6c or 5.13a A3, four bolts for belays and two for protection). The route would almost certainly go free, with roof sections providing wild cruxes. We were happy to establish a new line on the steepest wall any of us have ever seen, in good company, in a unique and beautiful part of the world.

The Tepui was first climbed by the Arrans in 2008. John Arran, who has spent a lot of time in the region, planted the idea for our trip with tantalizing tales of the potential for some of the steepest big-wall free-climbing anywhere. This kind of incentive meant that we were joined on this remote wall, a week or so after our arrival, by Belgians Nico Favresse, Stephane Hanssens, Sean Villanueva, and Jean-Louis Wertz, who made rapid progress on a line to our left.

GEORGE ULLRICH, *U.K.*

*Editor's note: Anne and John Arran's 2008 route, Amurita (British E7 6b), climbs steep rock some distance left of the waterfall. They decided there wasn't time to try a line directly behind the fall, but felt it had potential to be the hardest and most overhanging big-wall free climb on earth (AAJ 2009). A second route, Wacupuro Amuri (A4 5.12+), was put up over 13 days during March and April 2011 by Venezuelans Ricardo Navas, Federico Pisani, and Alfredo Rangel. It climbs farther right, much closer to the waterfall. Both routes are so steep they stay dry in heavy rain until they reach the summit.*

*Amuri Tepui, south face, Maria Rosa and Apichavai.* In March 2012, when Stephane Hanssens, Sean Villanueva, Jean-Louis Wertz, and I emerged from the jungle and saw the wall, it looked so overhanging that gravity weighed heavy on our minds. We were unsure the face behind the waterfall was free-climbable, let alone in the style we planned. There were no obvious lines, few cracks, and relentless steepness. Our friends Mason Earle, Sam Farnsworth, George Ullrich, and Siebe Vanhee, with a 10-day head start, were high one possible line. Both teams had decided to go to the same place, yet, though we are all good friends, we hadn't known of each other's plans.

The right side of the wall looked almost impossible, and our friends had taken the central line (which also looked impossible), so we first tried an appealing line to the left. We soon realized that it was very different from the big wall climbing we are used to. The climbing is steep, very featured, but mostly using horizontal holds, so it's difficult to anticipate what's next. Often you have to commit and hope for the best. Rather than climbing straight up, we often found traversing to be the most tempting solution.

Sean Villanueva redpointing pitch two after 40m fall. *Nico Favresse*

However, the line proved easier than expected, and in a mere four days we reached the base of a massive overhang near the top, where we found a perfect 10m roof crack above 400m of exposure. Unfortunately, though, gaining the crack required a boulder-problem move that shut us down. We were unable to free it but found the crack above so beautiful that we played on it for a couple of days, just for fun.

When we pushed for the summit, we split into two teams. One finished by the logical line via the roof crack, with a few moves of C1. The other climbed a completely free variation around the roof to the left, traversing for three long pitches before continuing directly to the top.

We hung out for a day on top of the tepui to enjoy the beauty of this magical place. The next day we descended farther left (looking in), down Wacupero Amuri. We thus left nothing on our route, which we named Maria Rosa (500m, 7b, no bolts, no pitons, no rap anchors), after local cookies that occasionally surprised us with their strawberry filling.

Looking steeply up south face of Amuri Tepui below Salto Tuyuren. (1) Wacupuro Amuri. (2) Maria Rosa (left-hand finish 7b; direct finish 7b and C1). (3) Kids with Guns. (4) Apichavai. Last two routes finish right of just visible waterfall. *Nico Favresse*

While making a quick trip back to Yunek for more food, we met the other team on their way home. Though we'd been climbing close to each other, we'd not been able to communicate, due to the noise of the waterfall. They encouraged us to try a free ascent of their route, Kids with Guns, but when we returned to Amuri, the call of adventure tempted us to explore another new line, this time to the right.

Only the first two pitches seemed obvious and not too steep, while the rest resembled an overhanging quartzite ocean. We encountered difficulties right away, with hard pitches, vegetation, tricky protection, and loose blocks. On an attempt to redpoint the second pitch Sean fell 40m, ripping five pieces. The ground was still 20m below, and the wall is so overhanging the only thing to hit is air, but Jean-Louis, who was belaying, got bad rope burns on both hands. We were not sure whether he should stay or go home, to avoid infection, but his hands looked better after four days, and he joined us on the wall, though he did not climb.

Sean Villanueva tackling pitch six, one of the cruxes, on Apichavai. *Nico Favresse*

Many other falls were taken on this climb, perhaps 20 among us. On pitches four, six, and seven, the route tackles the most overhanging section. These were the cruxes, with difficulties up to 8a+. We only managed to onsight four of the route's 15 pitches, the rest needing cleaning and aid in order to explore and study the pro. Amazingly, though, the line went completely free, many sections only possible due to a single hold. Eight pitches are 7b or harder. The wall didn't let go until the very end, and we were never sure we would make it. We placed three bolts for protection and two to reinforce belays. The route took 14 days, of which four were spent on the ground waiting for Jean-Louis's hands to heal. We named the line Apichavai (500m, 8a+), after the warrior who lived in Yunek and killed the Tri Tri, a giant bird that would catch people and eat them in a cave high on the tepuis.

NICO FAVRESSE, *Belgian Alpine Club*

Upigma Tepui, showing approach and Hospital Breakout. El Nido del Tirik Tirik climbs obvious pillar directly above advanced base. *Shane Houbart*

*Upigma Tepui (2,200m), south face, The Hospital Breakout.* The Gran Sabana holds some of the world's most majestic big walls, rising dramatically above rainforest. In February 2012 Cory Nauman, Alfredo Zubillaga, and I flew to the region to establish a new route on Upigma Tepui in the Canaima National Park.

Chartering a Cessna aircraft we landed at the native village of Yunek. Hiring porters we set off on the approach, negotiating grassland plateau, jungle, and river systems. Simply reaching the base of a tepui is an adventure in itself. Using machetes we cut through dense jungle. After two days of trail blazing Cory got bitten by an unknown venomous snake. His foot turned black and swelled to twice its normal size. We abandoned most of our equipment to speed up the rescue. Two days later we found ourselves back at Yunek, which had a radio. Miraculously a Cessna was passing through a neighboring valley, heard our distress call, and flew us to Santa Eleana, located on the border of Brazil. Cory received five-star treatment from the hospital staff but after three days wanted to leave for further treatment in the U.S. The hospital refused to release him, so Alfredo and I staged a hospital breakout and got Cory to Miami.

One member down, Alfredo and I went to salvage our equipment. We were now short of time but still decided to try a new line. After ferrying loads for many days, we arrived at the base of our proposed route, which was 400m high and the largest overhang I had ever laid eyes on. We eased into the complexities of routefinding on the first three pitches. After the third pitch the overhanging nature of the rock became more immediately apparent, and the climbing tested my limits as we solved the overhanging puzzle. Crack systems linked to horizontal breaks, providing well-protected climbing, though with occasional unprotected sections for up to eight m.

Alfredo handled the pressure like a heavyweight climbing champ. I'd never seen someone grin so effortlessly while cruxing out on a runout 5.12+ pitch. Most of the climbing was free, with the exception of pitch 11, a tenuous A2+ with two tension traverses, and pitch 12, C2+ with mandatory 5.11-.

It was a relief to pass the last overhang and hit thick jungle on top the tepui. That night, perched on our ledge, we celebrated The Hospital Breakout (520m of climbing, 14 pitches, V, 5.12+, A2+) with a bottle of rum. And Cory is alive and climbing, after receiving further medical attention in Miami. The Hospital Breakout turned out to be more than just a new route—an epic odyssey and adventure.

SHANE HOUBART, *Australia*

*Editor's note: Upigma was first climbed in 2007 by ubiquitous tepui explorers John Arran and Ivan Calderon, who with a BBC film team and presenter Steve Backshall established Aranas en las Nubes (300m, 5.12). The following year more tepui regulars, Kurt Albert, Bernd Arnold, and Helmut Gargitter, with Ivan Calderon, climbed El Nido del Tirik Tirik (350m, 14 pitches, 7b). El Nido was repeated in January 2009 by Venezuelans Luis Jeremias, Oliver Sevcik, and Alfredo Zubillaga. Houbart and Zubillaga established their advanced base directly below the pillar taken by El Nido del Tirik Tirik, then cut a trail through dense jungle to reach and then climb the middle of the broad wall to the left.*

# Peru

## Cordillera Blanca

*Nevado Santa Cruz (6,359m), east ridge, attempt; Santa Cruz Chico (5,800m), east face.* Italians Fabrizio Manoni, Enrico Rosso, and Paolo Stoppini attempted the long, unclimbed east ridge of Nevado Santa Cruz, which begins with a steep triangular rock buttress. They first climbed the right flank of the buttress, starting at 5,100m, and established a high camp at 5,530m, before returning to base for a rest. They regained the camp and the following day continued up the north flank of the buttress, over snow and ice to 80°, before making a 90° exit onto the ridge at 5,800m, just north of the ice-dolloped buttress top. They could see the way ahead was badly corniced and the flanks of the ridge unclimbable. However, they could also see an excellent line on the east face of Santa Cruz Chico. They changed their goal.

Despite the Santa Cruz Group being one of the most popular in the Blanca, Santa Cruz Chico (Atuncocha), which lies on the ridge between Nevado Santa Cruz and Santa Cruz Norte, has rarely been ascended. Before 2000 there was only one route on the mountain, and it is likely that no one has ever trod the highest point. Chico was first climbed during the productive 1958

In middle section of 2011 route on Santa Cruz Chico. *Enrico Rosso*

East face of Santa Cruz Chico. (1) Italian route (2011). (2) Scottish route (2002). *Enrico Rosso*

North American Andean expedition. David Michael and Irene and Leigh Ortenburger spent 12 hours on the icy northeast face, reaching the north ridge and continuing along the crest until three or four m below the huge cornice forming the summit.

In 2002 the very steep, mixed, 450-500m east face was climbed by Scots Jason Currie and Guy Robertson, on their second attempt. After 600m of climbing at TD, they were forced to stop 20m short of the highest point due to unstable cornices. Due to the rocky nature of the face, the Scots were of an opinion that a logical central line will most likely vary over time, due to changing snow/ice cover.

On June 16 Manoni, Rosso, and Stoppini climbed the next gully to the left (with a step of 90°), before moving left again onto the face. Continuous ice climbing, with one vertical section, led to the huge capping seracs. Here they were forced to make a long, intricate traverse right, crossing serac walls (90°), to join the Scottish route, which they followed to the summit ridge. The Italians too were faced with a summit meringue 10m high and stopped immediately below, as it was too unstable to climb.

LINDSAY GRIFFIN, *Mountain INFO, from information provided by Enrico Rosso*

*Chacraraju Este (6,001m), northeast ridge, direct finish; Taulliraju (5,830m), southwest face, attempt.* On June 22 Oriol Baro and Jordi Corominas from Spain reached the summit of Chacraraju Este, having completed a direct finish to the original 1962 French Route (950m, ED1/2, Dubost-Gendre-Magnone-Soubis-Terray), the hardest route in the Blanca at the time. The Spanish pair used a more direct start, climbed in 1993 by Pavle Kozjek and Grega Kresel during an attempt on a direct line up the east face. Once on the French route, they followed it up the northeast ridge to where it cuts across the east face to finish via the upper section of the southeast ridge. There, they continued directly, negotiating a short rock band (A2) and two ice pitches, the first vertical and giving fine climbing. They bivouacked twice at the same spot, once on the ascent and once during descent, grading the route ED.

Baro and Corominas also tried the well-known but unclimbed central line on the southwest face of Taulliraju, left of the Fowler-Watts East Buttress (ED3, 1982). This is a continuation of the lower section of the West Buttress Quebec Variation (TD+, Bourbonnais-Laforest, 1983), past attempts having been put off by lack of ice and the difficult central rock barrier.

LINDSAY GRIFFIN, *Mountain INFO*

*Cashan West (5,686m Peru IGM), north ridge, not to summit.* On July 25 Carlos Cabaza (Spain) and Diego Fernández (Peru) climbed the rocky north ridge of unfrequented Cashan West as far as the upper snow crest. They approached through the Rajucolta Valley and established base camp on the 21st at 4,250m. On the 24th they made a cache at the foot of the rock section and the following day climbed with only rock shoes. After an initial pitch of 5+, they simul-climbed without protection for 150m (steps of 4+). The next pitch proved the crux—a perfect 6a+ crack. Their fourth pitch was an enjoyable crack up an exposed wall (5). Above they reached the end of the granite at 5,500m and rappelled to the right of their ascent route. The climbers graded their 450m route TD/TD+.

SERGIO RAMÍREZ CARRASCAL, *Peru*

CORDILLERA CENTRAL

*Nevado Tunshu South (5,560m), southeast face, Chinita.* Aspirant mountain guide Rolando Morales and UIAGM guide Beto Pinto, who has put up 20 new routes in the Cordillera Central, climbed the southeast face of Tunshu South. Morales and Pinto entered the Reserva Paisajística Nor Yauyos, southeast of Lima, and established base camp close to Lake Azulcocha (4,400m) on October 16. Next day they cached gear near the foot of the face and on the 18th, leaving early, crossed the crevassed glacier and took a direct line up the middle of the face, beginning with a 90° section through iced rock. Subsequent pitches over rock, hard ice, and steep, time-consuming soft snow led to the top, which they reached mid-morning. They rappelled the south ridge and traversed back under the face to regain their approach route. They named the line Chinita (450m, MD, 60-90°). Pinto remarks that the Cordillera Central has excellent scope for new routes, but it is not in a national park and suffers from intensive mining.

Tunshu massif from southeast. North summit on right. Marked are ascent route on southeast face and descent of south ridge. *Beto Pinto*

SERGIO RAMIREZ CARRASCAL, *Peru*

Morales on summit of Tunshu South. Ridge behind leads toward higher Tunshu North. *Beto Pinto*

*Editor's note: the main (north) summit of Tunshu (often quoted as 5,680m or 5,650m, but 5,730m on Peru IGM) was first climbed in 1958 by the northeast ridge. It was climbed again in 1967 by Germans Jochen Edrich, Peter Mirwald, and Hans Huber, who also traversed to a subsidiary summit of "5,565m," which may have been the south summit.*

CORDILLERA ORIENTAL

*Huarancayo Sur (ca 5,200m), south face, Boys Don't Cry.* The Cordillera Oriental has been explored during the last decade by Tony Barton and various partners. It was reading about his new route in 2010 with Tom Chamberlain on the south face of Huaguruncho (Huagaruncho, 5,723m, *AAJ 2011*) that sparked our interest in the area. The area is served from the tiny town of Huachon, which boasts one hotel, where if you are lucky, you will get a room with a window.

South face of Huarancayo Sur, with snow/ice gully of Boys Don't Cry falling from just right of highest point. *Matt Balmer*

Matt Balmer on pitch four of Boys Don't Cry. *Matt Balmer collection*

During the walk to base camp Dan Fitzgerald, James Wake, and I spotted an interesting-looking gully on the south face of Huarancayo Sur. This mountain has only one previously recorded ascent, by Barton and Andy Houseman in 2006 via the southeast ridge (*AAJ 2007*). On June 5 we scrambled to the foot of the small glacier below the cirque of the south face, where we bivouacked. The following morning we made our way through a crevasse field and started up the gully. For 350m the climbing was sustained and full of interest on good névé. We perched on the summit in late afternoon, then watched with a sinking feeling as cloud rolled in. The ensuing poor weather meant a forced bivouac in an impromptu snow shelter just below the summit. At first light we continued our descent. We named the route Boys Don't Cry (350m, Scottish V, 4).

After a few days' rest, we set off for what we'd been considering our main goal, the unclimbed south face of Huaguruncho Chico (ca 5,400m). Information about climbing on this mountain is scarce, and it has possibly not been ascended since its first ascent in 1956. The south face was attempted by Barton and Houseman in 2006, but they retreated low on the central spur, due to poor snow conditions. There are two obvious ridges on the face, and while we had initially favored the right-hand one, on closer inspection the left-hand one looked slightly better, and we thought we could see a line through the rock bands and seracs. However, the unreliability of the weather was a concern. There was no clear pattern, and we were unable to see it approaching from the north.

We worked up the glacier below the left-hand ridge and found an uncomfortable crevasse, in which we got a few hours sleep. We left in the dark, taking a line through the lower rock buttress on the snow ridge. After 300m of snow and a few mixed pitches, we arrived on the crest. Higher we reached what we had identified from base camp as the "bad step": loose rock with poor protection. At the top of the ridge and below the headwall, we moved left into a gully. There we found excellent ice and the promise of a way through the fluted upper face. However, on the third pitch unconsolidated snow replaced ice, making climbing and protection far more precarious. The weather also deteriorated. Before long it was sleeting, mini avalanches were being triggered, and visibility was poor. It was time to bail. We cautiously made our way down to the ice, then started rappelling from Abalakovs. Lower we needed better visibility to negotiate the crevasse zone, so we dug a snow hole, and at first light descended the complex glacier to our first bivouac, where we lay in the sun. The walk back to base camp seemed to last forever.

In clearer weather we could see we had reached within 150m of easy ground and the summit. The weather got worse, and four days later we left. While it was a difficult decision to leave the valley and lose any chance of attempting the mountain again, it was eased by continuing poor weather.

MATT BALMER, *U.K.*

CORDILLERA CARABAYA

*Chichicapac (5,613m), south face.* After four days acclimatizing in Puno, Hamish Dunn and I arrived in Macusani (4,300m), the nearest town to the southern side of the Carabaya, to discover that nobody spoke English or understood our limited Spanish. We were lucky to bump into Daniel, an English-speaking Spanish priest on a year's exchange. After much explaining on our part, he finally understood where we wanted to go. (In Lima we had failed to locate a map to the area.) Daniel kindly drove us to the roadhead and arranged for two donkeys to carry our gear to Laguna Chambine, where we planned to camp.

Route on south face of Chichicapac. *Tom Ripley*

After acclimatizing sufficiently and making a reconnaissance of Chichicapac's unclimbed south face, we returned to base camp and sat out a period of bad weather. On August 22 we made the first ascent. The most obvious route was threatened by seracs, so we climbed a direct line up the center of the face, encountering sustained and insecure mixed climbing, until the top headwall forced us left. A short but loose rock chimney led to the upper section of the face, where a long tricky pitch, followed by easier, loose terrain, led to an easy snow slope and the summit plateau.

We summited just before 5 p.m., having spent 10 hours on the face. Anxious to get off the mountain in daylight (sunset was at 5:30), we quickly descended the west ridge and made a short rappel onto a small glacier, which led us to back to our bivouac tent. The majority of

Tom Ripley on lower section of Chichicapac's south face. *Hamish Dunn*

the face had involved mixed climbing, with powder snow on loose rock. The rock was generally terrible and protection sparse. The face is more than 600m high, and our route had an overall grade of TD, with sustained difficulties of Scottish 4/5 and two crux pitches of 6.

After this somewhat harrowing experience, neither of us felt like more dangerous climbing, but before leaving we climbed a rock route of about British VS standard on a crag above base camp.

There is much potential in the Carabaya for new routes, and it is a cheap, hassle-free place to reach. We thank the Alpine Club, British Mountaineering Council, and Mount Everest Foundation, without whose financial support the expedition would not have taken place.

TOM RIPLEY, *Alpine Club, U.K.*

*Editor's note: Chichicapac is the second highest summit in this range east of the Cordillera Vilcanota, rarely visited by climbers. It was first climbed in 1959 by the notable Italian explorer Piero Ghiglione, with Forrunaro Mautino (and repeated a few days later by a British team). In 2005 John Biggar, Pere Vilarasau, and six clients added a new route up the east glacier and northeast ridge, making what appears to be the first recorded new route in the range since 1981, a date more or less confirmed by a local farmer, who remarked that no climbers had been there for more than 20 years. In 2007 Chichicapac's south face was the main goal of a strong British team, but they judged it too dangerous and instead made the first ascent of the mountain's north ridge (AAJ 2008).*

# Bolivia

*The online version of these reports frequently contains additional photos, maps, topos, and extended text. Please visit aaj.americanalpineclub.org*

CORDILLERA APOLOBAMBA

Akuku and Orejas del Gato from southwest. *Marcin Kruczyk*

Trata Tata from northwest. High snowy peak right is Hanako. *Marcin Kruczyk*

Yagua Yagua and 2011 base camp from southwest. *Marcin Kruczyk*

*Huancasayani Valley, various ascents.* In July the second expedition of the Polish Apolobamba Exploration Project visited the Huancasayani Valley. The first, in 2009, reported in *AAJ 2010*, included Wojciech Chaladaj, Jakub Galka, and me. This time I was accompanied by Filip Drozdz, Tomasz Mucha, and Magdalena Tworek. Much geographical and historical research had already been done on this valley, and we used the map drawn by Chaladaj, published on the *AAJ* website with our report. Two years ago we had bad experiences with a local muleteer when trying to reach Puina from Pelechuco, so this time we hired a 4WD. We established base camp lower than in 2009, three hours walk up the Huancasayani Valley in a side cwm. It had the advantages of a nice stream and invisibility from the bottom of the main valley.

Acclimatizing on our first day, we walked to the 2009 base camp and found gear left under a boulder. We attempted our first peak on July 30. We chose an unnamed and likely unclimbed rock pyramid 1km east of Hucuncunca, as named on the Chaladaj and Paul Hudson sketch maps. On the west flank of a huge south rib we found a long arête and climbed it for several hours, eventually over 50° snowfields to a col. The last two pitches from col to summit were more difficult. Although the moves were not hard (UIAA IV), the rock was extremely fragile and protection difficult. We named the peak Akuku (4,975m, digital altimeter) and graded our route AD-.

On August 1 we attempted the unnamed and also likely virgin peak 500m southeast of Akuku. It is a twin-summited mountain we called Orejas del Gato (Cat's Ears). However, as we did not summit, we leave the final naming of this peak to the first ascensionists. We began to the southwest, ascending a long talus slope until 50m below the col, then worked southeast to make our first belay on the southwest ridge leading toward the north summit. We then climbed sections of UIAA V and M4, but again found very fragile rock and poor protection, the gap between placements sometimes more than 15m. For these reasons we retreated at 4,800m (two rappels, then down climbing). As far as we got, the route was AD+.

In 2009 we had climbed the two lower peaks of the Trata Tata Massif. Now we wanted to reach the highest summit. On August 3 we approached from the northwest, reaching a col on the Trata Tata ridge, where Magdalena opted to remain. Filip, Tomasz, and I continued, bypassing the first two summits on the southeast flank to reach minor difficulties below the highest point. Overall the ascent was F+, with very loose rock of UIAA II to reach the summit at 5,156m. We returned the same way, a tiring day due to large talus.

On the 7th we made our last ascent, of a peak marked as Yagua Yagua on the Hudson map. We had learned of no documented climbs, but on top, where our altimeter recorded 4,721m, we discovered a small cairn. We climbed from the southwest and reached the summit without major difficulty (F). After 12 days in the valley, we returned to Puina with the help of Juan Sulca and his llamas. By the 9th we were back in La Paz.

MARCIN KRUCZYK, *Poland*

CORDILLERA REAL

*Overview and recent new routes.* In recent years little mountaineering information has come out of Bolivia. This may partly be due to there currently being no agency or individual committed to collecting mountaineering information, particularly activity relating to new routes or notable repeats of established climbs. One of Bolivia's best known guides and archivists, Alain Mesili, has taken a break from climbing to concentrate on writing, which may have further limited the flow of information. It seems the number of climbers to Bolivia continues to decrease, despite the country

West face of Huayna Potosi from Maria Lloco. Photo taken in 2009. There was a little more snow cover in 2011, but face bears no resemblance to more snowy 1970s, when up to half a dozen lines were climbed. Marked is line followed by Beisly and Monasterio in 2011, which apart from initial section corresponds with 1970 American Direct. In 1971 an ice route was climbed up middle of rock wall on right (Via del Triangulo, 1971, D- 70°). *Gregg Beisly*

offering one of the most stable weather patterns in the mountaineering world and high scope for new route development. In recent years most activity has been on the popular and often guided peaks of the Southern Cordillera Real, easily accessible from the capital: Huayna Potosi, Condoriri, and Illimani.

In September, after a five-year break from mountaineering, I traveled home to Bolivia, joining Kiwi expat Gregg Beisly for two weeks intensive climbing. Gregg and his family work as missionaries in El Alto. In his backyard, at 4,000m, Gregg has set up what must be the highest bouldering wall in the world. After I had repeatedly failed on the easiest problems, we decided to tackle bigger, easier, and potentially achievable objectives in the Northern Cordillera Real.

Peak 5,723m of Hancopiti group with Via Santiago on north face.
Erik Monasterio

We approached the isolated eastern valleys of the Ancohuma-Illampu Massif via Cocoyu. Although there is significant scope here for new routes, expeditions have all but abandoned the eastern aspect of the Northern Cordillera Real, and there have been no reported climbs of Ancohuma from this side for a decade. Over nine days we climbed three routes. On September 1 we put up a new line on the north face of one of the Hancopitis (Peak 5,723m), an easy glacier approach, followed by five pitches of steep rock directly up the middle of the face. Climbed in a 16-hour roundtrip from base camp at 4,800m, Via Santiago was F6b.

Two days later, in an eight-hour roundtrip from the same camp, we climbed the southeast ridge of Viluyo I (5,540m), a route likely followed in 1979 by French Yvette Jupin and Jean Therisod. After a rest day we moved camp to 4,900m, from which we summited Ancohuma (6,430m) in 16 hours of sustained and at times complex climbing. We followed the established route up the northeast ridge to the north ridge and summit. Hardly acclimatized after only a week at altitude, I staggered onto the summit in a whiteout, and Gregg had to help me back down to the 6,200m col. Here I found my legs and sufficient air to get back to camp. Since my last visit to this peak 15 years ago, the characteristics of the climb have changed significantly for the worse. The route used to be a straightforward snow ascent, but now penitentes have appeared, and the summit ridge is loose rock, making for a more serious undertaking.

However, snowfall in 2011 was significantly greater than in recent years, and some traditional ice routes, which had disappeared due to climate change, reformed. On the 13th we climbed one of the longest and most sustained ice faces in Bolivia, the west face of Huayna Potosi (6,088m). We more or less followed the Direct Route, first climbed in 1970 by Americans Harthorne, Harvard, Lanney, and Thompson but often referred to as the French Direct after a 1978 repeat by Challeat, Faure, Levi, and Mesili (900m, D+/TD-). We zigzagged around a series of bergschrunds before taking the steepest, direct line to the top, reaching the summit in eight hours. In 1996 we had climbed another line on the west face and were delighted to have one final weather window this season to climb back up memory lane.

ERIK MONASTERIO, *New Zealand*

*Condoriri Massif, Piramide Blanca (5,230m), Southwest Face Direct.* In a snowstorm at the start of the rainy season, Robert Rauch and Eduardo Unzueta (Bolivia) and I (U.S.) climbed new ground on Piramide Blanca. We climbed a two- or three-pitch variation to the current Southwest Face Direct. I say current because the Southwest Face Direct was reported in Yossi Brain's 1999 guide as first climbed in 1988 (200m, D-, 80°, Bartram-Peltier-Whitelaw). However, due to the loss of much of the right side of the glacier, the route no longer exists in its original form. Also the regular route up the southwest face-southwest ridge does not resemble the photo or description in the guide; it may not be possible without mixed or rock climbing. (The original was an easy snow route.)

The line we climbed is rather more direct than the original Direct, which despite its name traversed significantly. We climbed the steepest snow/ice line on the right side of the face and then the ridge to the summit. Eduardo thinks much of our line had been followed before, though the two or three crux pitches we climbed had been avoided by moving left to reach gentler (ca 70°) snow and ice.

Our route is obvious when seen from the most popular climbing base camp in Bolivia, after Huayna Potosi's, and the Condoriri area has received much attention for decades. On the other hand, it is the more famous routes that get almost all the attention, and most climbers seem not to want to risk wasting time on an unknown objective. I'm therefore not entirely comfortable claiming our route as new, but one of the new pitches—an overhanging serac led by Robert to reach an ice cave—was really hard. It was a long day, about 10 hours tent-to-tent and 16 hours tent-to-front door, with the most dangerous part being the drive back to La Paz in the dark.

CHRIS CLARKE, *Bolivia*

*Various ascents.* In August 2009 Andy Baker, Jack Grinsted, and I climbed the obvious left-trending couloir on the southeast face of Maria Lloco (5,523m), a striking subsidiary peak west of Huayna Potosi. The finish involved three steep ice pitches up the headwall, exiting right of the rocky summit. The feature is conspicuous, and it would be a surprise to find it had not previously been climbed. However, there appears to be no recorded ascent.

Looking northeast to Serranis Murillo (Hampaturi Group). (A) Cerro Tigra Killa. (B) Unnamed peak climbed by the Beislys via southeast ridge (rocky crest descending right from summit). (C) Jati Khollu (5,421m). (D) Laguna Jachcha Khasiri. On Jati Khollu snow slopes facing camera were climbed directly to upper southeast ridge (right skyline) in 1995 by Yossi Brain and Jason Davis (400m, AD). *Gregg Beisly*

In June 2011 Baker and I climbed a new route up the south face of Point ca 5,600m on the southwest ridge of Huayna Potosi. The route is steeper and more demanding than the Yugoslav route on the left side of Huayna Potosi's west face but is much shorter. There were sustained sections of 80°, steps of 90° ice, and mixed climbing up to M4. The upper half of the face was continuously steep and nearly all the pro was good rock placements. I was surprised with the quality of the rock, although I'm sure that in leaner years there would be plenty of choss hiding in the gullies. The nine-pitch route was D+. We descended the southwest ridge, completing the roundtrip in 16 hours.

Looking north at Maria Lloco (5,522m) with 2009 Baker-Beisly-Grinsted route on southeast face. To right is Huayna Potosi with west-northwest ridge (Laba-Hudson, 1969) forming left skyline and west face to its right. *Andy Baker.*

In the Serranis Mirillo or Hampaturi Group, not far from La Paz, my wife Sal and I climbed the unnamed summit to the northeast of Cerro Tigra Killa by the rocky southeast ridge. We noticed a surprising amount of quality ice in this valley and the one immediately south, including several one- and two-pitch frozen waterfalls.

GREGG BEISLY, *Bolivia*

*Huayna Potosi (6,088m), east face, Summit or Die.* Coming up the road from tropical, mosquito-infested Zongo Valley, I saw the possibility for a new route on the east side of Huayna Potosi, far north of the normal route. In June I accessed the face by walking along the outer retaining wall of the aqueduct that runs north from Zongo Dam. It got

Looking north to (A) Pt. ca 5,600m and route on south face climbed by Baker and Beisly (descending left skyline ridge). (B) Pt. Italia (ca 5,750m). (C) Huayna Potosi (6,088m). (D) Pico Milluni (5,500m). *Gregg Beisly*

Serac-torn east face of Huayna Potosi. Summit or Die climbs through icefall left of center, before slanting up left toward summit ridge. *Robert Rauch*

narrower, and at one point I was looking down a steep rock face 400m high. It was preferable not to lose one's balance, easier said than done with a big pack. By the time I left the aqueduct for the glacier below the face, it was almost dark. I walked for two hours by headlamp and camped at the start of the glacier.

I should have stayed at this campsite for a day, to examine the face in light, but I had a guiding engagement in Chile. I don't normally climb into the unknown, but next day I made an exception. The first 200m of the face were easy, and at dawn I had arrived below the crux. Swinging axes I gained height, into a complete mess. Steep, unstable ice blocks were everywhere: I got nervous, but it was too late to go back. Succumbing to time pressure is the worst of all mistakes in alpinism. I concentrated fully; the ice was not quite vertical, but I could not trust the blocks. Finally I reached easier terrain and took a deep breath. "Done, you bastard of a wall," I said to myself. The silence was wonderful, but I knew I'd never come back to this face again.

I climbed slopes of 55°, often covered with powder snow. It was still a long way to the top. After a long, rising traverse left, I finally reached the normal route and followed a one-and-half-meter-wide track to the summit. I was soon following the track down, reaching the Casablanca Hut where I'd left the car.

At the Casablanca Hut I saw a guy in a T-shirt that said, "Summit or Die." He didn't look fit, or ready for suicide. He probably survived without summiting. It seemed a fitting route name. Summit or Die (1,100m) has a crux pitch of 60m, up to 85°. It's probably the most significant first ascent in this region for 20 years.

ROBERT RAUCH, *rauchrobert@hotmail.com, Bolivia*

*Hampaturi Group, Serkhe Khollu (5,546m), southwest face, La Venganza del Don Gringo.* The rainy season ended at the end of May, and I've returned to the Hampaturi. I pitch the tent near my vehicle and fall asleep. At 3 a.m. I set out for the southwest face, which I've been dreaming of for years: I'm well acclimatized and during the rainy season kept fit on the cliffs of Aranjuez and improved my balance and coordination by slack-lining. I start up the first vertical icefall without pausing; conditions are excellent, and I am quickly gaining height.

An Austrian pair, I think Markus Kronthaler and Michael Rechberger, were the first to climb this face. In 2001 there was almost no information about Serkhe Khollu, and they walked far to reach the mountain. An ice nose in the middle of the face led steeply to the upper glacier, the crux being an ice cave that they had to crawl through. There was steep climbing, and their line, which led directly to the summit, may have been one of the most difficult ice routes in Bolivia. The ice nose disappeared with glacial recession, and the original route no longer exists. A new mining development below the mountain has changed the character of the area, and access roads should soon be improved. These miners have caused no problem to visitors who don't bother them.

I knew the way to the mountain, because I used to visit the grasslands below to buy llamas for my restaurant. I went there almost weekly to separate llamas from the herd and kill them. When time permitted I'd walk higher to scope lines on the face and spotted a hard ice/mixed route to the right of the Austrian line.

The middle section of the face gives mixed climbing, on brittle rock (UIAA V) and 65-75° névé. A wide belt of seracs looms above. Deep powder lies to the left, so I choose a stepped, direct line—safe, elegant, but with overhangs. There is no room for fear, and my concentration is total. The key section is 125°, and I climb it quickly, then catch my breath in a small depression. The final slopes are 55° and excellent snow, leading to the ridge a short distance from the summit. I at last enjoy the warming rays of the new day. In the distance banks of cloud rise from the tropical valleys of the Yunga region. Have I ever been this alive?

I name the 700m route La Venganza del Don Gringo (Don Gringo's revenge). To make money during the quiet rainy season, I sometimes wrestle. My opponents in the pre-arranged fights are Cholitas, women in traditional dress. My fighting name, Don Gringo, has become popular, not only at the wrestling ring but also with my employees and friends. La Venganza del Don Gringo is by far the most difficult of my three first ascents on Serkhe Khollu and may be the most difficult ice/mixed climb in Bolivia. I don't think I can climb harder ice, with or without a partner.

ROBERT RAUCH, *rauchrobert@hotmail.com, Bolivia*

*Hampaturi Group, Serkhe Khollu (5,546m), southwest face, The Birthday of the Broken Leg.* Frozen gusts of thin air painfully escaping our weary lungs. Infinite stars splashing over dark velvet. "Happy birthday!" Robert Rauch screams into the Andean storm as I lean on my ice axe, panting. "Thank you," I want to tell him, but my words are violently ripped from my mouth and spiral high up into the air before they slowly drift down into silent insufficiency, somewhere between frozen cracks and ice shining with the reflection of southern stars.

It was my birthday indeed, and no words could explain what it meant to me to watch

Southwest face of Serkhe Khollu. (1) Birthday of the Broken Leg. (2) Chamaka (Berger-Hill-Rauch, 2010, incorrectly drawn in *AAJ 2011*). (3) Summit. (4) La Vengenaza del Don Gringo. The 2001 Austrian route Durch das Nasenloch climbed an ice hose, long since disappeared, between 2 and 4 to reach the upper hanging glacier. *Isabel Suppé*

once again the Bolivian Andes merge into the night. Exactly one year before, I had been climbing Ala Izquierda when one single second tore me apart from life. My imagination of the future was shattered along with my bones 300m below.

I spent the following two days and nights between my exposed bones and ghastly apparitions from the realm of hypothermia while I crawled over the ice. And yet I knew I was going to return to the magic world of ice.

I knew I had to return despite the doctors' verdicts. "You won't ever climb again," they would keep telling me. One year, 10 surgeries, and infinite sessions of painful physiotherapy later, there I was, emerging from the slightly overhanging last pitch of "The Birthday of the Broken Leg."

That day daylight had found us hiding my specially adapted "climbing crutches" in a cache before we ventured into the realm of verticality. The ice was hard as stone. The first ice shower that Robert sent down from above felt uncomfortable after such a long off-time. Then it was my turn.

On a small plateau in front of a majestic blue serac, Robert and I devoured some candy. Another 80m of steep, hard snow took us to an uncomfortable ice traverse that led to the face's last great obstacle, the final 95° ropelength, while daylight began to wane. As I followed Robert over the dreadfully hard overhanging ice, my admiration for him kept on soaring, not so much because of his ability to lead such a hard pitch without hesitation, as for his unprejudiced capacity to trust a climber on crutches. Topping off on Serkhe Khollu marked the end of our new route, "The Birthday of the Broken Leg" (TD+/ED-), dedicated to Peter, who didn't return from Ala Izquierda. But for me it also sealed a friendship.

However, another big challenge was yet to come: After walking down the normal route there remained an authentic crutch quest. I didn't doubt that we would find our cache—simply because we had to find it. I needed my crutches for the descent because the horizontal dimension does not grant my foot as much freedom as verticality does.

ISABEL SUPPÉ, *Germany/Argentina*

*Editor's note: Peter Wiesenekker died from the fall that broke Suppé's leg in 2010. The Rauch-Suppé route and the 2010 Berger-Hill-Rauch route, Chamaka, lie close together on the left side of the face and coincide for their initial ropelength (see AAJ 2011).*

*Hampaturi Group, Serkhe Khollu (5,546m,) southwest face, Tears of Pachamama.* On September 15 Robert Rauch picked me up in La Paz at 4 a.m. The first crux was driving to the trailhead for Serkhe Khollu in Robert's vehicle.

Complete southwest face of Serkhe Khollu. (1) Start of Tears of Pachamama. (2) Start of Birthday of the Broken Leg and Chamaka. (3) La Vengenaza del Don Gringo. Normal route follows snowfield at extreme left, then gentle slopes behind ridge to summit. *Chris Clarke*

The approach followed llama paths from 4,600m to 5,000m over gentle but steadily rising terrain, toward the left-hand

In 2011 Tears of Pachamama was only route on this far-left section of Serkhe Khollu's southwest face. *Chris Clarke*

end of the broad southwest face. The last few hundred meters found us in a snow storm, ascending firm snow unroped to the base of a classic water-ice gully. We followed it to the crux vertical icefall, which had options from WI5+ to WI4. We opted for the latter. Several more enjoyable ice pitches of around WI4 led to the top. Thunder and heavy snow caused us to decline walking the last few hundred feet to the summit, but this option is easily available for other parties. Descent was via standard route (the only one that gets traffic, maybe a few parties per year), which climbs a snowfield at the left end of the southwest face to gentle slopes, with no obvious crevasses, rising southeast to the summit. Tears of Pachamama (350m, IV WI4) took 11 hours car-to-car and 17 hours roundtrip from La Paz, making it a suitable warm-up climb. It seems to have little stonefall or other objective hazard.

Based on Robert's 20+ years of guiding in the Bolivian mountains, we believe that this type of ice is becoming more common in the country, where warmer temperatures are melting summit ice caps during the day and forming water ice during the night. So while Pachamama's tears allow us to enjoy ephemeral routes today, we worry for the future.

CHRIS CLARKE, *Bolivia*

# Chile

*The online version of these reports frequently contains additional photos, maps, topos, and extended text. Please visit aaj.americanalpineclub.org*

## CENTRAL ANDES

*Cajon de Maipo, various ascents.* I flew to Santiago in November with vague plans to make an excursion into the Central Andes, hoping to explore a mountain range that would be new to me. If I was lucky, I might also bag an ascent or two. After struggling to find information, I eventually met helpful local climbers and decided to focus on the region of Cajon de Maipo, southwest of the capital. Over the following weeks, I made two rewarding trips.

South face of Cerro Alto los Leones. *Ben Dare Collection*

On the first I made my way to the small village of Banos Morales and hiked up into the Quebrada Valdes, directly behind Lo Valdes Refugio Los Condores, setting up camp below the 500m south face of Retumbadero Norte (3,819m). The face made a perfect warm up and acclimatization climb, and the summit provided an impressive panorama of surrounding peaks. The climb was mostly nontechnical mixed ground, with difficulties up to M4 and AI2+. The steepest mixed sections were short and occurred at the bottom and top. I descended by a series of moderate snow gullies on the left-hand side of the face.

South face of Yamakawa. *Ben Dare*

I resupplied in Santiago and four days later trekked up the Cajon del Morado, camping on the glacier draining from the southern slopes of Cerro Cortaderas. This south face was my initial objective, but on closer inspection the upper glacier proved to be heavily crevassed and threatened by unstable ice cliffs. I reassessed and turned to two appealing faces farther down the valley.

The first was the 650m south face of Yamakawa (4,930m). Starting from the Cortaderas Glacier, I climbed through ice cliffs at the bottom of the face via a short but steep water ice step on the right-hand side. Above I followed snow slopes to the rock and mixed ground of the upper face. This proved quite sustained (up to M4+), although there were occasional snow patches and a section

South face of Peak 4,589m. *Ben Dare*

of thin water ice at half-height. More mixed climbing led to the upper snow slopes and eventually the summit. I downclimbed the original Pardo-Oyarzun Route.

The following morning I climbed the 500m south face of Peak 4,589m, via an obvious ice gully up the center. In the lower part of the face, sustained ice up to WI4 extended for four or five pitches through three prominent steps, the main difficulties involving the second and third steps. Above, the angle eased, and steep snow led to a final short mixed step and the summit ridge. I descended the same line, downclimbing the snow on the upper face and rappelling the lower gully from Abalakovs.

I only spent a short time in the area, but the potential for new alpine mixed and ice routes is undeniable. The rock was far from spectacular, but I found that with a thin coating of ice, the climbing was challenging and enjoyable. Even in the Cajon del Morado I spotted dozens of possible lines, many of which would be longer and more demanding than the climbs I completed.

This potential is far from limited to the one region. While in Santiago I was shown photos of a number of large, steep faces, such as those on Cerro Alto los Leones and Cerro Tronco, which have seen few or no ascents and offer a number of appealing lines.

BEN DARE, *New Zealand*

East flank and northeast ridge of Cerro San Gabriel. *Elvis Acevedo*

*Cerro San Gabriel (3,125m), northeast ridge; La Pala (3,647m), east face; Cerro Bello (5,239m), west face.* In September Christian Quezada, Jaime Wastavino, and I, from the Grupo de Alta Montana of the Perros Alpinos, traveled to Cerro San Gabriel, close to Santiago, to climb a new route on the northeast ridge. We followed the approach used to reach the normal route, up the southeast ridge, and established camp below the mountain. We followed the normal route for an hour, before leaving it to traverse across avalanche-exposed terrain to reach the base of the northeast ridge. We climbed the east flank of the ridge over mixed terrain and good snow to reach the corniced crest, which we followed to the beautiful summit, which caps one of the classic mountains of central Chile. Graded D-, our route had rock sections of UIAA IV.

In October Christian and I visited the Quelteheus-Las Melosas region, approaching via the Rio Claro Valley. This area has seen few mountaineers, and there are many unclimbed peaks, with potential for very difficult routes. During previous exploration and various attempts on peaks, we had seen a beautiful summit at the confluence of the Claro and unexplored Estero Godoy Valley. There was no record of this peak having been attempted.

On our first day we established base camp at a nice spot in the Claro Valley, where there is vegetation along the river. Next morning we hiked the two km to the foot of the peak in two hours. We entered the Estero Godoy ravine, then continued through loose, rugged terrain. Our route on the east face began with a wide 35°slope that we named La Pala (the Shovel) and followed to the start of the Canaleta. This couloir, five m wide, with an average angle of 60°, short

East face of La Pala. *Elvis Acevedo*

steps of 80°, and good snow, was the only way to reach the final ridge. I was hit on the head by a falling stone but was not seriously injured. Once on the east ridge we continued more easily, apart from a few gendarmes of poor rock. The final snow slopes rose to 45-50°, and after passing penetentes and several false tops, we reached the summit, where the GPS read 3,647m. The vertical gain from base camp had been 1,650m.

West face of Cerro Bello. *Elvis Acevedo*

Nightfall caught us on the descent, but we regained base camp 16 hours after leaving. We named the peak La Pala, after its most conspicuous feature. The route is D- (80° and III) and is threatened by stonefall.

In the second week of December I went alone to the Bello Glacier [north of Cerro Marmolejo, the southernmost 6,000m peak in the world]. After a two-day approach up the Rio Yeso Valley, I set up base camp on the moraine. Next day I set off for the west face of Cerro Bello. I had to start by crossing the lower half of the glacier, avoiding two large crevassed areas. The first half of the face was a 45°icefield, with sections of 55°, though at this time of year the ice is thin. Above, short 60° icefields were interspersed with sections of poor rock at IV. To reach the final ridge at 5,050m, I had to climb 20m of hard 65°ice, followed by a few easy meters of rotten rock. The final 180m was really exposed, in several places no more than half a meter wide, with drops of several hundred meters on both sides. The 1,200m ascent was TD (WI3 IV).

ELVIS ACEVEDO, *Chile, translated by Alex Horner*

NORTHERN PATAGONIA
COCHAMÓ

*Cerro Trinidad Central, La ArgenTrinidad.* In early January 2012 Jose Bonacalza, Sasha Gal, Ezequiel Manoni, Pablo Pontoriero, and I left Bariloche with a four-day good weather window. Our objective was a new route on Cerro Trinidad. To be efficient we divided into two groups. While one team

Sasha Gal underclinging on ArgenTrinidad.
*Jose Bonacalza*

climbed, the other carried loads and food to a camp at the base of the wall. The team that climbed would then go down to the refuge an hour away, to recharge power-drill batteries, sleep, pick up more equipment, and return to the base of the wall early in the morning Dividing the work, we made good progress in those short four days and put up a very good line left of Dutch Corner. We named our route ArgenTrinidad (550m of climbing, 12 pitches, followed by 100m of II/III to the summit, 7a/5.11c).

Luciano Fiorenza, *Argentina, translated by Rolando Garibotti*

*Editor's note: Much of the climbing is between 5 and 6b+, with several squeeze chimneys and off-widths, but the crux is a slab on pitch four. The climbers installed rappel anchors and reportedly did not extensively clean the line.*

Southwest face of Trinidad Central, with La ArgenTrinidad (left) and Las Manos del Dia.
*Daniel Seeliger*

Grant Simmons follows tight hands crack of pitch 10 on Las Manos del Dia. *Chris Kalman*

*Cerro Trinidad Central, Las Manos del Dia.* In early January, 2012, with support from the AAC's Mountaineering Fellowship Award, Chris Kalman and I set off for Valle Cochamo, determined to open a new route in the increasingly popular "Yosemite of South America." After a couple of days searching, we noticed a beautiful, clean headwall leading to the summit of Trinidad Central in the Upper Trinidad Valley. With advice from valley resident Daniel Seeliger, we climbed the first pitch of the ArgenTrinidad, before splitting off and following a ramp system up right. Without bolts we climbed whatever protectable ground we could, eventually linking up with the Dutch Corner [550m, 13 pitches, 7c, Katharina Saurwein-Jorg Verhoeven, 2008] for a pitch and a half, before heading up corners that led to the diamond-shaped headwall. Once on the headwall we climbed a pitch of perfect thin hands to an amazing belay ledge. Above was a splitter wide crack, but without enough big gear, we bailed only two pitches shy of the summit.

We found an independent start for the route and began working on the first pitches, cleaning vegetation and installing bolts for protection and belay stations. Joined by Daniel a few days later, we pushed to the top, cleaning as we went and bolting the rappels as we descended. Daniel's knowledge, enthusiasm, and work ethic proved invaluable, and after a few more work days, the route was ready for free-climbing.

On our first try we were defeated by weather, but on the second attempt it all came together, and Las Manos del Dia (455m,

12 pitches, 5.11+) was complete. The route follows obvious systems leading to the striking headwall. The climbing is excellent and varied, featuring delicate slabs, burly corners, a wild flake pitch, and perfect crack climbing. Only two pitches are easier than 5.10, and most are 5.11. With some folks referring to it as one of the best in the valley, we couldn't be more excited about the end result.

GRANT SIMMONS, *AAC*

*Cerro Trinidad Sur, Der Grantler.* On February 8, 2011, Mario Gilemann and I made the first ascent of Der Grantler on Cerro Trinidad Sur. The 230m route climbs close to and left of Pegadito en la Pared (7 pitches, 5.11c A0, Hartmann-Reimay, February 2006, see *AAJ 2006*), sharing the same first belay. Although the two climbs are close, Der Grantler is more than just a variation. Its six pitches vary from alpine sport climbing (pitch one), through steep face climbing (pitches three and five), to excellent crack climbing (four and six), all at around 6a/6b. Stances are equipped with stainless steel bolts.

Due to the variety of climbing, perfect rock quality, and relatively moderate difficulties, this route could become a Cochamo classic. It has already been repeated. Further information is available at Refugio Cochamo, and a topo appears with the web version of this report.

FRANK KRETSCHMANN, *Germany*

Cerro Trinidad Sur and Der Grantler. Pegadito en la Pared climbs right side of arête. *Frank Kretschmann*

*Amfiteatro, Cáscara de Huevo, A Través del Huevo.* "So you are back!" Daniel welcomed me with his huge smile. Yes, I was back. I couldn't forget the beauty of the valley, nice people, and huge amounts of unclimbed rock. Sunniva Hoel Aass (Norwegian) and I (Czech but living in Sweden) arrived on December 10 and two days later were climbing an established route in the Amfiteatro of Cochamo. Our goal was to put up a new route ground-up, onsight, with a minimum of bolts, and we spotted a nice line on the left side of the wall. It faced southwest, which was a plus, as it only caught the sun in the evening.

From the upper bivouac boulder in Amfi, we cleaned and marked a path through the jungle, then I led the first pitch, on bubbly rock that was difficult to protect. Two more pitches in grassy corners, followed by a nice traverse, brought us to a large clean dihedral cut by crack systems. We fixed our ropes and descended to the valley for more gear and food. When we returned, Sunniva led the dihedral, running it out on the face, as

Sunniva Hoel Aass starting squeeze chimmey—"6c if you are European, 5.8 if American chimney expert"—on A Través del Huevo. *Pavel Jiracek*

Cerro Gorilla from southwest. First wall is Cáscara de Huevo, with A Través del Huevo. Chimney system on wall above, followed by walking, leads to summit of Gorilla. *Sunniva Hoel Aass*

Pavel Jiracek follows first corner (about 6a) of A Través del Huevo. *Sunniva Hoel Aass*

the crack was vegetated. It was surprisingly hard to follow, with complex moves on small crimps. I passed the roof above on the right and followed a perfect hand crack in an overhanging corner, the crux a long reach past a one-m section of soil and vegetation. I belayed below a narrow squeeze chimney, into which Sunniva disappeared growling and wrestling her way up, finally reaching a big ledge 25m higher. It started to rain and as the final pitch is a funnel, we rappelled.

I went back to camp for three days, but Sunniva stayed with the birds and rain, meditating. When we returned to the route, we were unable to free climb the last crack, as it was too vegetated. Knifeblades, cams in soil, and run-out free-climbing, with only Birdbeak protection when we couldn't aid, got us to the top of what we dubbed Cáscara de Huevo (Eggshell Wall).

Two days of gardening changed the last pitch from a muddy canal to a beautiful continuous crack, with plenty of pro, save for the initial corner. After I almost hit the ledge twice on ground-up attempts, we placed a bolt. We also added a bolt higher, where fine face climbing passes a blind crack.

The top of Eggshell Wall then became our second home, with a great view and running water. After a few more days of cleaning and working the moves, we both climbed the last pitch free (Sunniva first), estimating it to be 7b+. We'd limited activities to early mornings, as it later became too hot, even at 1,500m, and the tabanos (horse flies) drove us crazy. We named the route A Través del Huevo (Through the Egg, 260m of climbing, six pitches, 7b+).

Later we continued up the face above, reached by an exposed 10-minute walk. We climbed the central chimney system in three or four pitches (5 to 6b), where from the top it is possible to walk to the summit of Cerro Gorilla to get fine views of the Trinidad Valley and distant 3,000+m volcanoes. Linking this face with A Través del Huevo gives 440m of climbing. It can also be climbed on its own, accessing the start either by an exposed walk from the Trinidad Valley or by climbing Scrambled Egg Gully to the right of Eggshell Wall. From Gorilla it is possible to make an exposed walk down to the valley or to walk down to the top of Eggshell Wall and make four 60m rappels.

We spent the last part of our stay cleaning and trying to climb several beautiful alternative pitches to the initial section of A Través del Huevo. However, the day I tried to redpoint one of the hard pitches, I fell and tore a ligament in an ankle. Sunniva injured her knees from overuse but still joined Chris Kalman and Grant Simmons on their route Las Manos del Dia. A detailed topo of A Través del Huevo and other routes can be found at www.cochamo.com

PAVEL JIRACEK, *Sweden*

*Atardecer, Al Centro y Adentro.* In February 2012 North American J.B. Haab and I opened Al Centro y Adentro (12 pitches, 5.11c) on Atardecer, a previously unclimbed wall in the Amfiteatro of Cochamo. The route follows 450m of nearly vertical splitter cracks and fun face up the center of the wall, and includes climbing behind a large flake. With this route being our baby, I encouraged recently arrived Alex Honnold to give it a try. He onsight soloed up to the crux on pitch five, before roping in with his partner Cedar Wright to complete the rest. They commented that the quality was comparable to Yosemite's Rostrum and Astroman.

Al Centro y Adentro. From top of wall it is 20 minutes scrambling to the summit. *Daniel Seeliger*

DANIEL SEELIGER, *Chile, www.cochamo.com*

*Upper Paloma Valley, Hasta la Pinky.* In the upper Paloma Valley, on February 9, 2012, Paul Mangasarian and Eli Simon put up Hasta la Pinky, cracks and chimneys accessed via two snowfields (165m of climbing, five pitches, 5.7, 5.7, 5.9, 5.10b, 5.10b).

Haab squeezing under, inside, and back out the bird-beak flake pitch. *Daniel Seeliger*

LINDSAY GRIFFIN, *Mountain INFO, from information supplied by Daniel Seeliger, Chile, www.cochamo.com*

REGIÓN DE LOS LAGOS

*Serrania Avalancha, Espiadimonis.* Serrania Avalancha is a huge, east-facing, granite wall situated eight hours, through the Valdivian forest, west of the tiny village of Puerto Cárdenas, at the northern end of Lago Yelcho. The approach requires a machete and a crossing of two wild rivers. I enlisted two Argentinian climbers to help with the haul bags, and we made two journeys, each of us carrying 25kg. The face rises from a lake, and to reach the base I used an inflatable dingy. I chose a line up the center, and after spending two weeks fixing 350m to my first camp, spent 32 days alone on the wall, from

Serrania Avalancha from southeast, with (1) Araucania
and (2) Espiadimonis. *Silvia Vidal www.vidalsilvia.com*

February 8 to March 10, 2012. After a vertical rise of 1,300m, the wall tips back, and I continued up 200m of snow and easy terrain (UIAA IV+) to the summit. I named the 1,500m route Espiadimonis (Dragonfly in Catalan, A4 6b).

Of the 32 days I spent 16 sitting out weather inside the portaledge. It rained a lot, which is normal for this area. At times the wall turned into a river, making it impossible to climb or rappel through certain sections. I frequently doubted whether I would reach the top or whether even descent would be possible. As usual I went with no means of communication, no radio, telephone, or means of obtaining weather forecasts.

Getting to the top was only half the adventure. I rappelled the route in three days, struggling with stuck ropes and twice having to cut them, despite trying my best to recover them. This counts as rubbish I have left behind, and I am not happy about it. I also came across garbage at the remains of an old fisherman's hut by the lake. This area is little frequented, and these things matter to me.

I then spent a week, alone, ferrying the haul bags back to the village (five carries of 25kg). A river we had waded on the approach, with water up to our waists, was now impassable. I had to wait four days. Three consecutive days without rain brought the level down. During nearly two months alone in this region, climbing became less important than the overall experience.

Sílvia Vidal, *Catalonia. www.vidalsilvia.com*

*Editor's note: The wall had been climbed once, in 2007 by Mariana Gallego, Martin "Fideo" Molina, and Luis Molina. Their route, Araucania (1,000m, 25 pitches, 6c A3), more or less follows the line of a rounded pillar on the left edge of the face. They climbed alpine style, with bivouacs at the top of pitch seven, pitch 16, and most likely one during the descent. They reached the top of the wall, but the late hour and snowfields discouraged them from continuing to the summit. Martin Molina had attempted the line with Matoko Erroz in 1999, climbing 15 pitches. The wall forms the flank of a ridge southwest of Cerro Cascadas.*

Asien Region

*Cordon Colmillo, Cerro Colmillo (1,896m), northeast ridge.* In February and March 2012 a NOLS semester group traveled north 125km from Laguna Tranquilo to Rio Murta. On the way we explored a number of valleys and passes, as well as crossing the glaciated and granite-spired Cordon Colmillo, north of Rio Engana. To our knowledge this range (northeast of San Valentin) had seen very little exploration. On March 10 we split into two groups, one group of 12 heading through big mountain terrain and climbing an unnamed peak of ca 1,800m, while Daren Opeka and I, with six students, attempted Cerro Colmillo, a granite tower in the middle of the range.

We left camp at 9 a.m. and traversed technical glacier terrain for an hour. After assessing the ridge above, we fixed three lines to the summit. The 110m, 5.4 ridge gave a great climb to both instructors and students. We rated the entire ascent from camp at PD. Next morning Kai Girard and I repeated the route before a communal breakfast event at 8 a.m. We left camp at 5 a.m. and returned at 7.55 a.m.

MAX FISHER

Cerro Colmillo. Northeast ridge and route of first ascent is right skyline. Rock quality in this region appears good, and there are a few attractive alpine granite walls. *Betsy Winston*

Looking northwest from summit of Meliquina, over Lagos Leones and Fiero. (A) Cuerno de Plata (3,725m). (B) Cerro San Valentin (3,910m). (C) Cerro Rendondo (1,504m). (D) Cerro Helbling (1,962m) and Explorandores region. Foreground ridge continues off-picture right to Cerro La Torre (2,337m). *Betsy Winston*

Looking northeast from Meliquina over the unclimbed La Torre Group (2,337m) to Cordon las Parvas. *Betsy Winston*

*Cordillera Meliquina, Cerro Meliquina (2,602m), northeast face.* Our group of eight NOLS instructors left Coihaique on December 24, reached Rio Leones, then turned west and traveled up the Leones Valley toward Lago Leones, as far as Rio Meliquina. We now headed south up this side valley, and after a walk of two and a half days, reached the east side of Cerro Meliquina (approximately 46°49'51" S, 73°04'12" W), where we established base camp. There appears to have been little travel in the Cordon Meliquina, northwest of the Cordon Contreras. To our knowledge Cerro Meliquina remained unclimbed, though two of the group, Michel Raab and Betsy Winston, had attempted the mountain with students.

On the 27th the group made an unsuccessful attempt on the north ridge. On the 28th we split into two groups, with one trying the south face and the other the northeast face. Again neither was successful. On the 29th, while other members of the group moved camp, Michel, Betsy, and

Northeast face of Cerro Meliquina, with route of ascent. Party descended right skyline. *Betsy Winston*

I cached our gear and made another attempt on the northeast face. The bergschrund proved to be the crux, after which moderately steep glaciated slopes led to the summit ridge and highest point. We rated the 600m route D AI2 5.7.

We descended the north ridge, to collect our gear at 1 p.m., by which time wind had started to blow Patagonia style. Wind and soft snow made for slow travel. Once united with the rest of the team, we dropped off the glacier onto rock to escape the coming weather, though it turned out to be not as harsh as anticipated. We regained our vehicles on the 31st and returned to Coihaique.

MAX FISHER

Cerro Falso Ilse, from Valle Milodon to east, showing line of ascent. *Camilo Rada*

Natalia Martinez approaching south ridge of Cerro Falso Ilse. Highest point is directly above her. North summit, to right, is slightly lower. *Camilo Rada*

SOUTHERN PATAGONIA

*Cerro Falso Ilse (2,512m GPS).* Located on the eastern periphery of the Southern Patagonian Icefield, 3.7 km northwest of Cerro Gorra Blanca, Cerro Falso Ilse is mistakenly labeled Cerro Ilse on several old maps. The correct Cerro Ilse is farther north, well within the Icefield. Because of this the double-summited, pointy, unnamed and previously unclimbed peak has recently been referred to as Cerro Falso Ilse. For the many people who access the Icefield via Paso Marconi, Falso Ilse is hidden from view behind Gorra Blanca. However, its rocky tops have attracted the attention of climbers summiting Gorra Blanca. It was Carlos Comesaña, a veteran Patagonian climber, who made us aware of this peak.

On December 2, 2008, I made a reconnaissance up Valle Milodon to assess whether the highest point was the north or south summit, but the difference was too small to be distinguished from afar. Prior to making an attempt, Natalia Martínez (Argentina) and I climbed Cerro Gorra Blanca to complete our reconnaissance. Two days later, on the 9th, we climbed Cerro Falso Ilse in exceptionally fine weather. Starting at the col below the west ridge of Cerro Gorra Blanca, we moved north to reach the south ridge of Falso Ilse. Because we were unable to tell which summit was higher, we visited the nearer (south) summit first. Following a straightforward snow arête, we arrived below the last two pitches, which provided the only serious difficulties on the route. The first crossed mixed terrain up to 60°; the second, over 5th class rock, took us to the top. We could see that the south summit was the higher but only by a meter or so.

CAMILO RADA, *Chile*

*Volcán Reclus (1,425m).* On April 13, 2008, Natalia Martinez (Argentina) and I established base camp at the head of Amalia Fjord, on the west side of the Southern Patagonian Icefield. The camp was nine km west of Volcán Reclus, one of five volcanoes in southern Patagonia (south of Taitao Peninsula). Hidden in the inaccessible and stormy western flanks of the Icefield, Reclus was found to be a volcano only in 1987. In 2005, during a period of very high temperatures, ashes were observed on satellite images, probably emanating from an eruption in the previous 12 months. It was that satellite picture that prompted us to explore the area.

Reclus is a modest mountain, with no technical difficulties. The main challenges are access, being surrounded by glaciers, and chronic bad weather. There is a poorly formed crater, the volcano being a snow-covered ash cone continually eroded by Patagonian weather. Difficult access, via the fjord, probably explains why the peak remained unclimbed. A geological expedition had flown into the area by helicopter, but no members reached the summit.

After two weeks of reconnoitering and waiting for better weather, we got a chance on April 26 and reached the summit on a rainy, misty day. A few days earlier we climbed a secondary cone three-and-a-half km west of the main summit and named it Volcán Mimi.

CAMILO RADA, *Chile*

TORRES DEL PAINE

*Cerro Paine Grande (3,050m, 2,884m GPS), first winter ascent.* On August 14 María Paz Ibarra (Chile) and I summited Paine Grande, the highest peak in the Torres del Paine Group. This was the third overall and first winter ascent.

With Sebastian Irarrazabal we established base camp on August 4 at an altitude of 70m, close

Looking northeast from plateau. (A) Peineta. (B) Torre Norte. (C) Torre Central. (D) Torre Sur. (E) Espada. (F) Hoja. (G) Paine Chico. (H) Máscara. (I) Cuerno Norte. *Sebastian Irarrazabal*

South face of upper pyramid of Paine Grande with route of first winter ascent. First ascensionists (Italians, 1957) climbed right skyline ridge. *Sebastian Irarrazabal*

to the shore of Lago Grey, west of Paine Grande. On our first attempt, in July 2010, we followed the Italian route to the plateau and climbed five pitches up the final pyramid before retreating. This time we took the same route and on the 7th, despite deep snow, managed to set up Camp 1 at 1,491m (GPS).

Strong winds then pinned us down. Although the wind in Patagonia is generally weaker in winter, and in 2010 and 2011 we certainly experienced more calm days than in summer, when it got wild the winter winds seemed every bit as strong as winds I've experienced in summer. Access to the plateau is by a couloir that normally has several sections of blue ice in winter. This time we found the couloir partly covered by hard snow, making for faster progress than in 2010. On the 12th we three made Camp 2 at the 2,311m col between Cumbre Central and Punta Bariloche (south summit).

Next day we set out at 5 a.m., reaching the final pyramid in two hours. After three pitches up the south face, Irarrazabal felt unwell and descended. Ibarra and I lowered him to the bergschrund, then resumed the climb, more or less following the same line as Rolando Garibotti and Bruno Sourzac during the second ascent in the summer of 2000. At 3 a.m. on the 14th we reached the summit, having completed eight pitches of very hard ice of 60-90°. [Garibotti and Sourzac climbed this section

Sebastian Irarrazabal climbing third pitch (60m, 70°) on south face of Paine Grande. *Camilo Rada*

in six very long pitches, up to WI5.] The last couple of pitches involved unconsolidated snow/ice on the summit mushrooms. Our GPS registered an altitude of 2,884m.

Meanwhile, once back on the plateau Irarrazabal's health improved, and he climbed to the Central Summit (2,730m)—the first winter ascent—reaching the top at 5 p.m. on the 13th. At noon on the 14th we were together at Camp 2 and began the descent next day, reaching base camp on the 17th.

Generally we experienced typical Patagonian poor weather, including heavy snow at the start and strong winds. However, our summit push was favored with perfect conditions: little wind, low temperatures (extrapolating from National Park records, possibly approaching -30°C), a full moon, and no cloud cover until midnight of the 13th, when a small cloud surrounded the summit and produced localized snowfall.

CAMILO RADA, *Chile*

TIERRA DEL FUEGO

CORDILLERA DARWIN

*Monte Buckland (1,746m),*
*northeast ridge and northeast face;*
*Monte Niebla (1,430m), northeast*
*face.* On January 29, 2012, Daniel
Gross, Markus Kautz, and I
reached the mystical and rarely
seen summit of Monte Buckland
by a new route, the northeast
ridge and northeast face (D). We
have called our line Silberkondor
after the plane piloted by Gunther
Plueschow, a German pioneering
aviator who took the first pictures
of Buckland's northeast face

Northeast ridge and northeast face of Buckland. *Markus Kautz*

during exploratory flights in 1929.
The only other reports about Buckland
come from Italian missionary Alberto
M. de Agostini, who explored the area
in 1912-13, and from the strong Italian
expedition led by Carlo Mauri, who in
1966 made, until 2012, the only ascent
of the peak (summit reached by Allipi,
Ferrari, Guidici, Machetto, Mauri, and
Pirovano). The Italians approached from
the southern Agostini Fjord and made the
ascent by the southwest face. Scarcity of

Buckland from Lago Alto to south-southeast. *Robert Koschitzki*

information, inaccessibility, nasty weather,
and impenetrable rain forest couldn't stop
us exploring the wedge-shaped mountain
of Buckland, located in the archipelago of
Tierra del Fuego.

From Punta Arenas we made a
10-hour drive on partly unpaved and rough
roads to the southwest coast of Tierra del
Fuego. To the south we caught the first
glimpses of our goal, the snow-covered
peaks of the Cordillera Darwin. Crossing
the fjord next day with two inflatable zodiacs
and passing east of Isla Dawson, we reached

Looking down on high camp from initial section of northeast ridge of Buckland. *Michael Nadler*

Fitton Bay (Bahía Fitton). After we unpacked our 450kg of equipment, the boats returned, cutting us off
from civilization for the next three and a half weeks. Due to horrible bushwhacking through dense rain
forests, which were often passable only with machetes, and negotiating open swampland, it took five long,

Approach from coast through chilly rain forest required machetes. *Michael Nadler*

hard days just to establish base camp (300m), less than five km from the beach. Plus the rain soaked us, froze us, and brought us close to despair.

Over the next few days we explored the nearby area and climbed a hiking peak south of Buckland, naming it Monte Bella Vista (825m), because of the beautiful view of surrounding peaks. Gross, Kautz, and I then made our first attempt on Buckland. From base camp we went west to the glacier beneath the east pillar. We then traversed the lower glacier, exposed to the fall of the seracs that overhang the entire east face, to reach the northeast ridge, where we set up high camp at 1,100m. The next day we climbed the first pitches of the ridge but had to return to base camp due to bad weather. On January 29 we made a second attempt from high camp, climbing mostly ice and mixed terrain to reach the upper glacial plateau below the summit headwall. Passing a difficult bergschrund (WI4), we followed the obvious central couloir (up to 65°) to the narrow summit ridge. In nearly whiteout conditions we turned south and climbed the icy summit considered to be Buckland's highest point. It was 12 hours since we'd left camp but more than four decades since this point had been reached.

Crux (WI4), crossing bergschrund below northeast face of Buckland. *Markus Kautz*

After the ascent weather worsened, with snow down to base camp. Nevertheless on February 2, with another member of our expedition Franz Goerlich, Gross, and I made the first ascent of an unnamed peak we called Monte Niebla, a tribute to the bad weather at the summit. We first followed the main valley southeast from base camp, then after two km went steeply north to a glacier west of the summit. We then reached the northeast face. A snow ridge and 30m of loose rock led to the summit (AD-). Weather now forced us to remain in our tents for the rest of the expedition, frustrated after seeing such splendid unclimbed mountains as Monte Sella. Further details are available at www.mtbuckland.com

ROBERT KOSCHITZKI, *Germany*

*Cordillera Darwin traverse.* From September 6 to October 5 Lionel Albrieux, Sébastien Bohin, Didier Jourdain, Dimitry Munoz, Sébastien Ratel, and François Savary, from the Groupe Militaire de Haute Montagne, made the first lengthwise crossing of the Cordillera Darwin. The team traveled from west to east, covered at least 250km on the ground, and ascended over 17,000m. The terrain was alpine, similar to the Mont Blanc Massif but three times as long. There were technically demanding sections, such as the narrow ridge linking Mts. Shipton and Darwin, and two new summits were climbed; Mt. Gines (2,022m) and Mt. Beyond the Far (2,026m). The story of this odyssey appears earlier in the *Journal.*

# *Argentina*

NORTHERN ANDES

PUNA DE ATACAMA

*Morro Von Rosen (5,450m), Guanuqueando.* Martin Altamirano and Martin Castillo visited the Chani Group in northern Salta during March 2010. They first climbed several short rock routes and an icefall, then on the 27th put up a new rock route on Morro Von Rosen, which they named Guanuqueando. The route began at 4,700m and finished at 5,400m, after 14 pitches up to 6a. The ascent took six hours and involved sections of vertical rock.

The Chani Group (highest summit General Belgrano, 5,949m) is the only region of relatively compact granite in northern Argentina. The Pou brothers, from Spain, climbed new routes here in 2009 (*AAJ 2010*).

MARCELO SCANU, *Argentina*

*Cerro Acay (5,716m), Como llegar a Rozarte el Alma.* In summer Cerro Acay, southeast of San Antonio de los Cobres, in the province of Salta, is generally a barren rounded hill, which was first summited by the Incas for religious purposes. However, on February 13 Gustavo González and friend, residents of Salta, climbed the then snow covered south ridge to 5,500m, at which point González descended from the ridge for 50m and reached a 200m couloir, which he climbed over ice and mixed terrain (reportedly up to 80°), then a little rock wall, to regain the ridge. He quickly reached the summit and rejoined his friend. He named the route Como llegar a Rozarte el Alma. The two got lost in a snowstorm during the descent and, once the sun came out, had to re-ascend 500m to the summit, before finally coming down easier terrain.

MARCELO SCANU, *Argentina*

*Cordon de los Pioneros, Pico Bicentenario (6,092m).* In November 2010 Guillermo Almaraz, Lelio de Crocci, Eduardo Namur, Juan Labra, Daniel Pontin, and Claudio Valva (Argentina) made the first ascent of Peak 6,092m in the northern part of the Cordon de los Pioneros, a small, isolated range of barren, unexplored volcanoes between the higher summits of Pissis (6,795m) and Bonete (6,759m). They set up base camp at 5,100m and on the 7th climbed the southwest spur to a col south of the summit and continued up the south ridge to its top. As this expedition took place during the Argentinean Bicentennial, they named the peak Pico Bicentenario (27°55'16.2" S, 68°45'12.2" W).

MARCELO SCANU, *Argentina*

Seen from Baboso to west, peaks of Cordon de los Pioneros between Bicentenario and Bonete. (A) Peak 6,243m. (B) Peak 6,152m (NW and SE summits). (C) Peak 6,150m. (D) Peak ca 6,000m. (E) Peak 6,144m. *John Biggar, www.andes.org.uk*

*Cordon de los Pioneros, various ascents.* In December our group climbed previously virgin summits in this range, south of Pico Bicentenario. None currently has a name, and all were technically easy. Italians claimed to have climbed a summit here, but no traces of a previous ascent were found. After acclimatizing in the Valle de Chaschuil, above Fiambala, we used 4WD to reach a base camp at 4,650m in the Quebrada de los Burritos Muertos. From the 2nd to the 4th, we further acclimatized and established a camp at 5,276m (27°58'21.3" S, 68°47'06.5" W), west of the Cordon. On the 5th Dante Alegria, Mike Freeman, Tim Pearce, Tom Rankin, Marcus Risdell, and I climbed Peak 6,152m (map height, 6,193m GPS, 27°57'06.5" S, 68°45'16.5" W) from the west. There are two summits of more or less identical height, situated either side of a shallow crater with no lake. No cairns were found, but we built one on the southeast summit.

On the 6th Rankin and I climbed Peak 6,243m (GPS, 27°56'23.7" S, 68°44'50.8" W) immediately to the northeast. No trace of a previous ascent was found, and we left a cairn between two lava pinnacles 30m apart; either could be the highest point. The same day Alegria and Pearce climbed Peak ca 6,150m (Google Earth estimate) by the rocky southwest face. It lies south of Peak 6,152m. They were joined by Freeman for an ascent of a smaller peak, of ca 6,000m, to the southwest.

On the 9th two previously climbed peaks in the Sierra del Veladero, west of base camp, were ascended. Rankin and I climbed Baboso (6,070m map, first ascent probably 2000), scrambling along the narrow northeast ridge, over the northeast summit (a minor point probably unclimbed prior to our visit). Our GPS read 6,070m on the northeast summit and close to 6,080m on the main summit. The same day Alegria and Risdell climbed Reclus (6,335m map, first ascent pre-Colombian).

When I got home and researched my notes from an expedition made to Bonete in 1997, I discovered I had climbed the summit marked as 6,144m on the map, immediately east of the ca 6,000m peak climbed by Alegria, Freeman, and Pearce. I climbed this from a camp due east, starting with a client who waited at 5,800m, on the east slope, after we had crossed Point 5,850m.

JOHN BIGGAR, *Alpine Club, U.K.*

CENTRAL ANDES

*Cordillera de la Ramada, Cerro Mercedario (6,770m), east face, A Contramano.* During November 2010 Fernando Daneri (Argentina) and Edgardo Liberman (Panamá, but resident in Buenos Aires) climbed a new route, A Contramano (1,300m, AD) on the east face. They had spotted the line during an evacuation of a corpse. They spent two days acclimatizing at Laguna Turqueza, a rare turquoise lake at 4,200m. They then moved up to 4,800m, where they spent three more days, before starting up the Paduszek Glacier on the east face. They began by climbing 40-50° ice, then a scree slope in the middle section, then snow and ice to an exit by the rocks of El Diente, at 6,300m on the Normal Route, just below its junction with the northeast ridge. The weather was cold and windy, and they spent three days there until they could continue to the summit via the Normal Route. They descended the Normal Route and spent a night at their top camp.

MARCELO SCANU, *Argentina*

*Cordillera de la Ramada, Pico Polaco (Cerro de los Polacos, ca 6,000m), southeast face, Acecho Felino.* While the highest peak in the Ramada is Mercedario, the most attractive is Polaco, immediately south. In January Javier Giuliani, Juan Manuel Leániz, and Fabrizio Oieni (Argentina) were active in this area. From the standard base camp at Pirca de los Polacos (3,600m), they first climbed a nice icefall (100m, three pitches, WI4) close to the col between Mercedario and Cerro Negro.

After a rest day Giuliani and Oieni started up a new route on Polaco. They established a camp at the edge of the glacier below the southeast face, where they endured a very cold night. Next day they rested and left the following morning at 5 a.m. After crossing five bergschrunds they followed obvious 40°couloirs, climbing quickly to avoid rockfall. At 5,500m Oieni gave up, leaving Giuliani to continue alone. After snow, ice, and a vertical icefall, he reached the summit, naming his 1,100m route Acecho Felino (90°). Descending the south ridge toward La Mesa (6,230m), he was involved in a small avalanche. After rappelling the bergschrund, Giuliani rejoined Oieni in camp, 14 hours after leaving.

MARCELO SCANU, *Argentina*

*Aconcagua, south face, alpine-style ascent of French Direct, with variation.* December 20 Andres Zegers (Chile) and I are at the Plaza Francia, and the weather is fantastic. We are watching the face, noting the fall lines of avalanches and seracs. There appears to be the possibility of a new variation to the 1985 French Direct. Andres would like to climb the awesome ice column, left of the French Direct, through the rock barrier. I prefer a more amenable icefall to the right. But in reality I would like to run away, like a thief in the night.

We are both nervous and admit it. We decide to follow the easiest, quickest line. We'll climb the lower slopes a little right of the French Direct, avoid the difficult pitches on the rock buttress via the icefall to the right, reach the Pasic Glacier where the 1966 Argentinean route comes in from the right, follow the latter, and finish up on the original 1954 French route.

December 22. At 3 p.m. Andres asks, "Would you mind leaving now?" At 5 p.m. we leave Plaza Francia. The approach to the face is quick. We climb the initial slopes, then the 250m WI4 icefall. Above, an easier gully leads back to the top of the buttress, where we join

South face of Aconcagua. Photo taken in 2003 but conditions similar to those in late 2011. (1) Sunline on South-southwest ridge (Sveticic-Romih, 1988). (2) Johan (Humar-Kozelj, 2003). (3) South pillar, Slovenian Route (Podgornik-Podgornik-Rejc-Zlatko, 1982). (3a) Polish start (Cichy-Kolakovski, 1987). (4) Central couloir, Medicine Buddha (Kellogg, 2009). (5) French Route (Bérardini-Dagory-Denis-Lesueur-Paragot-Poulet, 1954). (5a) Slovenian start (Biscak-Cernilogar-Skamperie-Sveticic, 1982). (5b) Messner Variants (Messner, 1974). (5c) Japanese Variant (Kamuro-Yamamoto, 1981). (6) Ruleta (Romih-Sveticic, 1988). (7) Argentinean Central (Fonrouge-Schonberger, 1966). (8) French Direct (Chassagne-Dufour-Raveneau-Vallet, 1985). (9) Slovenian Variation (Romih-Tic, 1986). (10) Argentinean (Aikes-Pellergrini, 1966). (11) East Ridge (Horak-Rocker-Sause, 1966). (12) Chilean-Italian variant (Di Donato-Zegers, 2011). *Tomaz Humar, supplied, with caption, by Peter Podgornik*

the French Direct. Just before reaching the Pasic, we bivouac on a snow slope at 5,400m. It is 10 p.m., the weather is excellent, and we manage to make contact with a friend by radio.

December 23. The night was passable, and we climb easily up the left side of the Pasic on rock and snow. A wall of hard mud and a few short gullies lead to an easy icefall. Above, after more rock/mud we arrive at a smooth section below the frightening upper glacier. We traverse right to the exposed edge of the glacier and spend five hours crossing it. One km of climbing for a vertical gain of just 200m, a fight with snow-covered penitentes. At 7 p.m., exhausted, we bivouac at 6,200m, just below the spur of the French Route.

December 24. It's difficult to get our legs moving. We climb a vertical pitch to snow/ice slopes left of the spur. A quick glance at the Messner finish: respect! Above, doubt: should we go right to a snow spur or follow a gully up left through rock? The topo mentions grade V chimneys. We go left, and below a loose chimney I find an old peg, which I remove by hand. The rock is still like hard mud. Farther on Andres suggests going right and, when I do, am surprised to find sound rock with protection. I belay on an in-situ corkscrew ice peg in the rock. Another pitch on rock and a snow slope lead to a ridge with a huge overhanging spur above and a doubtful fixed rope anchored to a Simond ice axe, buried like a deadman. Easy snow and a gully take us to the exit at 6,700m. The technical difficulties today have been a maximum of 60° and UIAA V. It is 5 p.m., and in two hours we are on the summit, 50 hours after starting up the 2,800m face. We stumble down the Normal Route to Nido di Condores, where friendly lights greet us. Argentineans, who are preparing supper, extend their hospitality. What a Christmas, guys!

ANDREA DI DONATO, *Italy, translated by Luca Calvi*

*Editor's note: In 1985 Jean Pierre Chassagne, Jean Marcel Dufour, Pierre Raveneau, and Bernard Vallet climbed a direct line through the lower face, to join the Argentinean Route, fixing rope on the lower slopes (climbed in 1966 by Fonrouge and Schonberger, as an alternate but more danger-ous start to the 1954 route), and adding 14 pitches on the rock buttress (V, with a short section of A1). The next year Slovenians Milan Romih and Danilo Tic made an alpine-style ascent, creating a variation in the lower section and adding a more direct finish, through mixed ground to the ridge right of the summit.*

*Cordon del Plata, Cerro Vallecitos (5,475m), east face, De Paso...Canazo.* On September 23 Luciano Fiorenza and Pablo Pontoriero (Argentina) opened an important new route on the impressive east face of Cerro Vallecitos. They started from Salto base camp, with high winds that prevailed during the previous night stopping when they reached the face.

Initial 60°slopes led into a couloir and to small icefalls. At 5,000m, mid-height on the face, they hit the crux, a two-pitch icefall, followed by a third pitch on snow and mixed terrain. The ground above was easier, though the snow was bad. They exited onto the summit ridge via a 60° couloir and reached the central summit, which offers an impressive view of Aconcagua. They claim that this summit is the highest but traversed the exposed ridge (one 20m rappel) to the south summit. They named the route De Paso...Canazo (1,000m, MD, WI4 M3) and descended the normal route, reaching the Salto camp 14 hours after setting out.

The south summit has a cross and is the summit normally reached by other routes. The normal route to this summit is relatively popular, due to easy access, both from Mendoza (the Cordon is an hour's drive), and the standard Salto base camp, at 4,300m. The mountain is more or less snow free in high summer, there is an easy path most of the way, and there is only a short scramble to reach the top. It is therefore often the first mountain for local aspirant climbers, and the area provides excellent acclimatization before one heads to nearby Aconcagua.

MARCELO SCANU, *Argentina*

*Cordon del Plata, Cerro Plata (5,968m), east face, Falto la Gorda.* Cerro Plata is the highest summit of the Cordon del Plata and for a long time was considered to be over 6,000m. It lies south of Vallecitos, but both normal routes are generally accessed from the Salto base camp. On September 25 Rodrigo Maique and Sebastian Ruiz (Argentina) climbed a new route on the east face. They approached on the 22nd, via Quebrada de la Angostura, and thoroughly acclimatized before setting off from camp at 3:30 a.m. Climbing through scree and penitentes, they reached a couloir. Where it split, they took the left branch. (The right branch had been climbed in 1980 by Alessio and Mon.) At first the angle was 40° over iced scree, then it steepened to 55° snow and ice. They eventually emerged onto the east ridge and reached the summit, which has marvelous views northwest to Aconcagua. They descended a couloir of less than 40° to regain camp and named the route Falto la Gorda.

MARCELO SCANU, *Argentina*

*Cerro Manantiales (5,100m), south face, Direct a la Cubetera.* In Mendoza's Tunuyán region, Diego Molina and Hernán Ortega climbed an interesting route on the south face of Cerro Manantiales during (austral) spring. From Tunuyán they went to Refugio Portinari and continued past Refugio Scaravelli (3,000m), eventually camping in an ancient ruined hotel at 3,900m. From there they reached the south face and began with 500m at 55°, followed by 180m of hard ice at 70-75°, and ending in mixed terrain on the southeast face. They continued for 100m in deep 60° snow to a foresummit, where bad conditions and cold feet forced a retreat. They made four rappels from Abalakovs. This was likely the first ascent of the south face of this rarely visited mountain, and they named their route Direct a la Cubetera (700m, D, WI3 M2 60°).

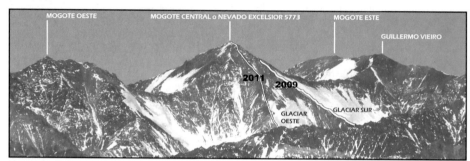

Mogote peaks from west, showing 2009 attempt and 2011 ascent on Nevado Excelsior. *Taken from blog of Pablo Gonzales*

MARCELO SCANU, *Argentina.*

*Various volcanoes, nontechnical ascents.* Shortly after the New Year Jonathan Kreiss-Tomkins (U.S.) and partner made the first ascent of Cerro Nevado (5,988m), east of the mighty El Muerto. This volcano has been referred to as El Muerito, but the true name appears on older maps. It lies in Catamarca, on the border with Chile. In the crater they found a bizarre lake that had a strange beet juice color, maybe due to algae.

In the Cordon de los Arrieros, a seldom-visited range on the Chilean border, between Ojos del Salado (6,864m) and Cerro Solo, Argentineans Glauco Muratti and Adrián Petrocelli climbed three of the four summits on the main ridge. In early December they climbed De los Grillos (5,768m IGN) and De las Chullpas (5,898m IGN), both first ascents, and De los Arrieros (5,860m), where they found evidence of the Asociación Tucumana de Andinismo ascents in 1956 and 1957.

In La Jaula Range, close to Mendoza, Pablo González and Mijel Lofti (Argentina) climbed a new route on its highest summit, Nevado Excelsior (Mogote Central, 5,733m). Before their ascent the mountain had been climbed only three times: in 1964, via the northeast ridge; in 1979, via the southeast face; and in 1985, by the south face. They spent three days on the approach up the Rio Tupungato, making base camp on November 4. The next day, carrying no ropes, they climbed a spur on the west face, close to the southwest ridge, in six hours. González, had tried the ridge in 2009 and noticed a decrease in ice cover. The angle rose to 45° at the finish, and a little easy rock led almost directly to the summit. They descended the northwest face/ridge, and returned to their tent in two hours.

MARCELO SCANU, *Argentina*

## SOUTHERN PATAGONIA

*Sierra de Sangra, Cerro Cocoví (2,155m), north flank.* The Sierra de Sangra includes an icefield of ca 100km2, east of Lago San Martin, in the province of Santa Cruz. Its highest peak, marked on the map as 2,155m, had no name. It was time it was climbed and named, so with Ramiro Calvo, a guide from Bariloche, my friends Roberta Brivio and Alessandro Moro, and Roberta's guide Giulio Signò, we began our expedition at Estancia Cocoví, across the border from the Chilean village of Villa O'Higgins. The estancia is situated at the northern tip of the northeast branch of the lake, and is the nearest point to the mountain that is reachable with 4WD.

Unclimbed peaks north of Rio Capon. San Lorenzo in far distance. *Enrico Bonatti.*

We began our approach on horseback, riding south along the east shore of the lake, then moving east up the Rio Colorado Valley. At the head of this valley, a pass leads over to the Rio Capon. It took two days to reach the head, from where it was no longer possible to continue with horses. On day three

More unclimbed peaks northwest of Capon valley. *Enrico Bonatti*

Roberta and Giulio climbed a prominent summit northwest of the pass, which they named Pico Sant'Ambroeus (1,950m), after the patron saint of Milan. Meanwhile Alessandro, Ramiro, and I crossed the pass and descended to a base camp at 1,220m, below the north side of our mountain.

Early on December 2, as the sky was turning red, we began our ascent. After crossing a small crevasse on a snow bridge, we moved up the north flank on steep scree until we reached rocks looking like the spires of a Gothic cathedral. A short snow slope led to the northeast ridge, which we followed to the summit, arriving shortly after 8:30 a.m. The day was fine, and we could see Cerro Torre and Fitz Roy to the southwest and San Lorenzo to the north. Our GPS recorded an altitude of 2,175m, and we named the peak Cerro Cocoví, after the first settler in this remote region.

ENRICO BONATTI, *Italy*

## CHALTEN MASSIF

*Various routes.* Apart from ascents reported in detail below, two new routes were climbed on the south face of Aguja De l'S. In late December Hayden Kennedy (U.S.) and Jason Kruk (Canada) climbed the lower half of Thaw's not Houlding Wright (Houlding-Thaw-Wright, 2004), then traversed right to climb a crack system parallel to and to the right of the Art of War (Davis-Robbins-Nelson, 2007). They christened their line the Gentlemen's Club (eight new pitches, 5.11+) and describe the climbing as being akin to Yosemite's Astroman. One month later, using the same approach, Josh McClure, Miranda Oakley, and John Rambo (U.S.) climbed a line farther right. Their Wormhole Theory also has eight new pitches and difficulties to 5.11+. A few days before, McClure had soloed a link-up of Aguja St. Exupéry and Aguja De l'S, via the Kearney-Harrington and the North Ridge, taking 18 hours roundtrip from the Polacos camp.

Kate Rutherford and Mikey Schaefer (U.S.) climbed a new route on the south face of Aguja St. Exupéry, starting left of Condorito (Albert-Arnold-Dosekal, 1998), then crossing it at two-thirds height. They climbed 500m of new terrain, with difficulties to 5.10 and A1. As a tribute to the quality of the rock, they named their line Astrochoss. Later they climbed a new line on the north face of Aguja Rafael Juarez. They climbed the first three pitches of Como No! (Walsh, 2005), then six new pitches, before joining Blood on the Tracks (Miyamoto-Sharratt-Tureki-Wilkinson, 2005). They christened their line Tiempo para la Playa (6c A1).

It has come to light that in late 1993 Andrew Lindblade (Australia) and Athol Whimp (New Zealand) did not repeat Chimichurri y Tortas Fritas (Locher-Pedrini, 1985), on the Goretta Pillar of Cerro Fitz Roy, in its entirety, as previously reported. They followed Pedrini's line to half-height and moved right, climbing 10 new pitches before rejoining Chimichurri. This line was repeated in 2005 by Slovenes Rok Sisernik, Aljaz Tratnik, and Rok Zalokar, who thought they were climbing virgin ground and named it Young Jerkers.

There was much activity on the southeast ridge of Cerro Torre, including a "fair means" ascent by Hayden Kennedy and Jason Kruk and a free ascent by David Lama and Peter Ortner. Feature articles regarding their activities can be found earlier in this Journal.

ROLANDO GARIBOTTI, AAC

*Editor's note: Rolando Garibotti provides more comprehensive information at his authoritative site www.pataclimb.com*

Upper south face of Standhardt, showing line of El Caracol. Dotted line shows crack system future parties should take to avoid pendulums. *Colin Haley*

*Aguja Standhardt (2,730m), south face, first complete ascent via El Caracol; other ascents.* In 1977, when Aguja Standhardt was the most compelling unclimbed peak in the Fitz Roy range, Brian Hall and John Whittle (U.K.) attempted a line that traverses ramp systems on the east face and turns the corner onto the upper south face. They were turned back only 20m below the summit, and although during the decades since several other teams had attempted the line, no one had surpassed Hall and Whittle's highpoint.

I was climbing in the Fitz Roy range for much of the 2011-2012 season, and on December 3 found myself climbing to the Standhardt Col with Jorge Ackermann (from Bariloche) for an attempt on Festerville. Winds raking Festerville would make rock climbing on the exposed ridge too cold, so we changed our objective to the south face.

We made rapid progress on the mixed pitches above the Standhardt Col and simul-climbed across the east face ramps. But when we turned the corner onto the upper south face, our progress slowed significantly. We climbed the upper south face in eight time-consuming pitches, which were typical of the Torres in that they involved ice climbing, dry-tooling, aid, free-climbing, and a bit of rime climbing. Not having photos of the face, I once chose the wrong crack and had to make two complicated pendulums to get back on track. The key to exiting the south face is that, at the point where Hall and Whittle traversed left to a point on the west face directly below the summit mushroom, we continued straight up a mixed chimney, in which a knifeblade crack allowed aid through the steepest section. One more pitch up the standard (east) side of the summit mushroom brought us to the summit at last light. We spent the night rappelling Exocet. Because of the route's spiral shape and our snail-like pace, we named the route El Caracol (500m, 5.9 A1+ M4).

I also made other climbs. On November 8 I attempted to solo Cerro

Ackermann starting up first pitch on south face of Standhardt, above snow patch. Immediately left is summit of Torre Egger. Farther left is top of Cerro Torre. *Colin Haley*

Ackermann climbing rime high on Titanic to reach easier ice slopes above. *Colin Haley*

Pollone, via the south face, but was unable to surmount the summit block, reaching my ice tool to within 40cm of the highest point but unable to get my body there. [*Editor's note: Due to glacier recession the original 1949 line is now relatively dangerous, so Haley climbed a steep gully farther east, joining the original line less than 100m below the summit.*] On December 8 I made the third solo ascent of Aguja Innominata, via the Anglo-American route. On Decemeber 14 I made the fourth solo ascent of Aguja St. Exupery, via the Kearney-Harrington route, and on the 15th soloed Aguja de l'S, via the standard north ridge, completing a several-year personal goal of making solo ascents of the seven principal summits on the Fitz Roy ridgeline (Guillaumet, Mermoz, Fitz Roy, Poincenot, Innominata, St. Exupery, and de l'S - an alternate list of the Seven Summits).

On December 25 and 26 Jorge and I ascended the east pillar of Torre Egger, via the O'Neill-Martin link to upper Titanic. On January 22 and 23 Rolando Garibotti, Doerte Pietron, and I climbed Aguja Desmochada via Golden Eagle.

COLIN HALEY, *AAC*

West faces (left to right) of Aguja Standhardt, Punta Herron, Torre Egger, and Cerro Torre. Italian attempt on Egger to just short of Col de Lux marked. *Matteo Bernasconi.*

*Torre Egger (2,850m), west face, attempt.* In December 2011 and January 2012 Matteo Bernasconi and Matteo della Bordella made attempts to climb the west face of Torre Egger. They followed the large corner system on the left side of the face, which was climbed for 300m in 1997 by Adriano Cavallaro and Ermanno Salvaterra, who retreated due to objective danger. (A previous attempt by unknown climbers reached 150m from the ground.) Bernasconi and della Bordella had tried the line during the 2010-2011 season and left ropes in place.

The pair fixed ropes, but found that the central section, starting with pitch 12, was dangerously exposed to ice falling from the vicinity of the Col de Lux (Herron-Egger Col). They tackled part of this section, before retreating to their snow cave on the glacier, where they sat out nine stormy days. Due to increasing temperatures, on their return they found the glacier changed. Enormous crevasses had opened, and it took a very long time to reach the face. They descended to Chalten and came back with an aluminum ladder to bridge gaping gaps.

Della Bordella on Christmas Day 2011 during first attempt of season on Torre Egger's west face. Walls of Punta Herron behind. *Matteo Bernasconi*

By the time of their final attempt, for which they received a forecast of four days' good weather, they had fixed ropes to pitch 17. They opted for a lightweight push to the summit, taking no real sleeping gear, just bivouac sacks and food for five days. Passing their high point they made a cold bivouac and the following day reached the top of pitch 23, 20m below the Col de Lux. They had climbed difficulties of 7a and A2 and placed two bolts. A little after 8 p.m., hoping to bivouac on the col and reach the summit the next day, della Bordella had just moved off the belay when he fell, pulling most of the anchors. Climbers and haul bags were left dangling from a 0.3 cam. Shocked and with no workable bolt kit to pass this section, they retreated, leaving ropes in place. They also abandoned the ladder.

They had planned to climb capsule style, with a portaledge, but once they saw how exposed the section from pitch 12 to pitch 17 was to falling rock and ice, they changed tactics. However, Bernasconi felt that in the prevailing conditions it was still Russian Roulette, even siege style. The two chose this line in preference to the center of the west face (attempted in 1996 by Italians) because it offers greater free-climbing potential.

LINDSAY GRIFFIN, *Mountain INFO, from information supplied by Fabio Palma and Matteo della Bordella.*

*Torre Egger (2,850m), south face, Venas Azules.* Norwegians Bjorn-Eivind Aartun and Ole Lied climbed a spectacular ice route on the left side of the steep south face of Torre Egger, overlooking the Col of Conquest. They first climbed 600m (6a A1) of El Arca de los Vientos to the col, where they bivouacked. Next day, after an initial pitch of M5, they continued for six pitches to the summit, up very steep, ephemeral rime and blue ice plastered to the granite. They rappelled the face to their bivouac. Venas Azules gains a total height of 950m, of which 350m were new, at AI6 (95°) M5 A1. This is the first time the face above the col has been climbed since the original ascent in 1976.

The ascent was one of six nominated for a 2012 Piolet d'Or, but just days before this was officially announced, the popular, well-respected Aartun was killed attempting a new ice route in his home country. Venas Azules was later awarded a special mention by the Piolets d'Or jury, which felt it achieved a new level of technical ice climbing in an alpine environment, only possible due to the team's opportunism. Aartun's account appears earlier in this *Journal*

*Cordon Adela-Cerro Torre traverse.* In a seven-day roundtrip from Chalten during January 2012, Agustin and Juan Raselli and I made a south-north crossing of the Cordon Adela to finish on the summit of Cerro Torre. We bivouacked at Laguna Toro, then, via the Rio Tunel Inferior Glacier, reached the start of a 400m, 60° ramp that led to the shoulder of the first summit on the ridge. This ice- and mushroom-covered tower, west of Punta Luca, was not named and had had no previous ascent. We've called it Mini Torre. From the shoulder a beautiful pitch of 90° ice, then a section of easy mushrooms, led to a difficult mushroom pitch. We had to clean a lot of rime on this pitch, which forced us to bivouac below it and reach the summit in the morning. It was a good warm up for the west face of Cerro Torre.

We then traversed the west flanks of Punta Luca (2,790m) and Cerro Grande (2,751m), before continuing over Cerros Doblado

South from Ragni Route on Cerro Torre. (A) Adela Sur. (B) Cerro Grande. (C) Punta Luca. (D) Mini Torre. (E) Adela Central. (F) Adela Norte, with convoluted corniced ridge descending toward camera and Col de la Esperanza. Viedma Glacier to right. *Max O'Dell*

Looking north across Rio Tunel Inferior Glacier to (A) Mini Torre, (B) Punta Luca, and (C) Cerro Grande. Access to Mini Torre was via left-slanting snow/ice slope to shoulder left of summit. *Max O'Dell*

Starting descent toward Col de la Esperanza and final goal, southwest ridge and west face of Cerro Torre (approximate line of Ragni Route marked). Left is Torre Egger. In distant right is west face of Fitz Roy. *Max O'Dell*

Final vertical ice pitch on Mini Torre. *Max O'Dell*

(2,665m) and Ñato (2,797m) to bivouac on the col before Adela Sur. Next day we crossed Adela Sur (2,840m), Central (2,938m), and Norte, then rappelled to the Col de la Esperanza. Routefinding over mushrooms and steep rock on this last section proved quite an adventure. We continued up the southwest ridge of Cerro Torre and bivouacked beneath the Helmet. On the following day we climbed the Ragni Route on the west face to the summit and descended to our bivouac, where we slept for a few hours before going down to the Circo de los Altares. We made our last bivouac at Laguna de los Esquies, before returning south along the Viedma Glacier, over the Paso del Viento, and back to Chalten, where family and friends were waiting with a big asado.

MAX O'DELL, *Argentina*

*Editor's note: In February 1958, a few days after their attempt on Cerro Torre, Walter Bonatti and Carlo Mauri climbed from the icecap to the summit of Adela Central and traversed south over Adela Sur, Cerros Ñato, Doblado, and Grande, to finish on Punta Luca. In October 1988, shortly before his death, Eduardo Brenner, with Silvia Fitzpatrick, climbed the southeast face of Adela Sur, and continued north over Central and Norte to the Col de la Esperanza, from where, after an aborted attempt on Cerro Torre, they descended west and exited via the Standhardt col.*

*Aguja Guillaumet (2,579m), west face, Patagonian Were-wolfs.* Back in Chalten, after all my compatriots from Poincenot had left, I befriended a Brazilian, Marcos Costa. Just before we were due to depart (I had a ticket to Calafate for March 10) there was a short weather window, so we went up and camped at Piedra Negra. Leaving at 3:30 a.m. on the 8th, we reached the west face of Guillaumet at 9:30 a.m. and began climbing an obvious crack system left of Dis-

A thin slab linking two crack systems on Patagonian Werewolfs. *Sergey Dashkevitch*

frute la Vida (400m, 6b A0, Pitelka-von Birckhahn, 2009).

The rock was good, and our plan was to climb free. We reached two-thirds height, then checking the time, realized that, as we had to be down that day, we needed to accelerate. The remaining third we climbed in a manner best described as "Russian competition style," using aid in places for speed. The route involved cracks of all sizes, from thin to off-width. When one crack system became impassable, we changed to another, often via a scary traverse on slabs. After 12 pitches we topped out at 7:30 p.m. on the north ridge, left of the summit, and were down to Piedra Negra by 11:30. We named the route Patagonian Werewolfs, because our ascent and descent took place under a full moon.

SERGEY DASHKEVITCH, *Russia, supplied by Anna Piunova, www.mountain.ru*

*Aguja Guillaumet (2,579m), west face, Manos al Cielo.* My friend Cheyne Lempe had never been to Patagonia. He'd never set foot on a glacier or climbed a new route. January 2012 was full of new experiences for Cheyne.

Just a few days after our arrival in Chalten, a weather window was forecast. We quickly assembled supplies and hiked up to Piedra Negra base camp, on the north edge of the Fitz Roy Massif. On the morning of the 15th, we left camp at dawn and made the short approach to the west face of Guillaumet.

I'd climbed a new route on this face the year before and remembered myriad clean crack systems cleaving the steep wall. As we hiked under my previous route, we rounded a corner and spotted an amazing line. On the left wall of a major chimney system, a hanging dihedral appeared to sport a clean hand crack over 200m long.

We were soon living the Patagonian dream: jamming clean white granite in T-shirts. The singular corner system was mostly 5.10, with brief steep cruxes up to 5.11+. After four long pitches of such bliss,

West face of Aguja Guillaumet. (1) Polish Route (350m, 6b+, Nowak-Szczotka, 2004). (2) Unknown (350m, 6c A1, ca 1980s). (3) Patagonia Werewolfs. (4) Disfrute la Vida (400m, 6b A0, Pitelka-Von Birckhahn, 2009). (5) Las Venturas (400m 6c A0, Bennett-Herrington, 2011). (6) Padrijo (400m, 6c A1, Gatt-Gatt, 1993. Direct finish - Fissure Mad Dog - climbed by Drummond and Wilkinson in 2008). (7) Tee Pitelka. (8) Manos al Cielo. (9) Rayo de Luz (400m, 6b A1, Pitelka-Von Birckhahn, 2009). *Scott Bennett. Route lines supplied by Rolando Garibotti*

Cheyne Lempe climbing fine cracks left of wide chimney, high on Manos al Cielo. *Scott Bennett*

we reached a major ledge system. Here we explored a few options but eventually continued straight up into a wide chimney. We were surprised to find a bolt, later learning that this portion of the route had been followed on the first ascent of Tee Pitelka (400m, 6b A1, Pitelka-Von Birckhahn, 2010). We avoided most of the wetness in the chimneys, by climbing thin cracks to the left, but did occasionally bridge and squirm on the final few pitches. We reached the summit in late afternoon,

Our fun route, Manos al Cielo (400m, 5.11+), was a perfect introduction for Cheyne to the joys of new-routing. The route name (Hands to the Heavens) is a tribute to Carlyle Norman, the young Canadian climber who was killed by rockfall on Aguja St. Exupéry the same day.

SCOTT BENNETT, *AAC*

*Aguja Val Biois, Mi Mundo de Contradicciones; Fitz Roy (3,405m), Pilar Goretta, Crux del Sur; Aguja de la Silla (2,938m), Destreza Criolla.* Last season, after opening Al Abordaje!, a new route on the west face of Fitz Roy's Goretta Pillar, I descended the north side of the pillar and was pleasantly surprised by the quality of the rock. I returned in February 2012, but such warm weather made it unthinkable to climb either of the gullies that lead to the Col del Bloque Empotrado. Pablo Pontoriero, Sasha Gal, and I decided to open a new access to the col, climbing Mi Mundo de Contradicciones (300m, 6b) on the west face of Aguja Val Biois. After passing below the summit of Val Biois, we dropped into the col and climbed the Casarotto, with the Kearney-Knight, variation to the summit of Fitz Roy.

Some days later Sasha and I were back. Because the weather window was short, we climbed the west couloir to the col, dodging a few falling rocks. We then climbed three pitches of the Casarotto, two of Chimichurri (without knowing where it went), and continued direct. We bivouacked halfway up, and on the second day climbed impressive dihedrals just to the side of the pillar's nose. Both the rock and the climbing were of high quality; this was one of the best routes I have done in Patagonia. At 3 p.m. we were atop the Goretta Pillar but descended rapidly, knowing the weather was supposed to take a rapid turn for the worse. We reached the bottom in the midst of

Aguja de la Silla from northwest. (1) East Ridge (250m, 6a A1, Bresba-Luthi, 1989, first ascent of peak). (2) Destreza Criolla. *Rolando Garibotti*

a snowstorm. We called our route Crux del Sur (520m, 6c).

In March Jony Jorzuk, Diego Simari, and I ventured to the northwest pillar of Aguja de la Silla, a virgin line that was on climbers' radar after Rolo Garibotti noted on his website that someone should go climb it. We approached Filo del Hombre Sentado from the north, and without a doubt the crux of the route was the approach. We did part of this traverse unroped, then followed a diagonal line left of an area threatened by stonefall. This got us to the base of the pillar, where we bivouacked, leaving everything there so as to climb light. The climbing turned out to be excellent, with many cracks and wind-worn holes. We carried photos, so as not to lose the line in a labyrinth of cracks and dihedrals that surprised us until the end. We established rappel anchors down the route, which we called Destreza Criolla (500m, 6b+).

LUCIANO FIORENZA, *Argentina, translated by Rolando Garibotti*

Crux del Sur, to summit of Goretta Pillar on Fitz Roy. *Luciano Fiorenza*

*Mermoz (2,723m) northwest ridge, to Fitz Roy (3,405m), north pillar, link-up.* I opened my eyes to see the wall above us glowing in frozen predawn. Cheyne and I had laid down at our cramped bivouac a few short hours before, sharing one sleeping bag as a blanket and huddling on a pile of ropes, packs, and squares of foam pad. Only 300m of Fitz Roy remained, but our route stretched 1,700m below and a year into the past.

Coming back to Patagonia for a second season, I had one objective, Fitz Roy. The biggest mountain hereabouts, King Fitz dominates its satellite peaks. So while climbing on Agujas Guillaumet, Mermoz, and others is a fun experience on beautiful rock, no alpinist can help but dream of touching Fitz Roy's summit.

Last year, with Blake Herrington on Cerro Pollone, we could view the entire

Luciano Fiorenza in middle section of Crux del Sur. Route follows right-hand of two arcing corners above. *Sasha Gal*

Guillaumet, Mermoz, and Fitz Roy from west, showing Mermoz's northwest ridge, Fitz Roy north pillar link-up, and bivouacs. *Scott Bennett*

Lempe following northwest ridge of Mermoz on day two. *Scott Bennett*

Fitz Roy massif from the west. From that perspective one line jumped out as the obvious line of strength: a link-up of the northwest ridge of Mermoz with the north (Goretta) pillar of Fitz. I was convinced this was the route to attempt, perhaps one of the last remaining unclimbed lines in the group.

Leaving El Chalten on January 18, 2012, with perfect weather forecast, Cheyne Lempe and I crossed Paso Cuadrado the following morning and, via the North Fitz Roy Glacier, reached the base of Mermoz's northwest ridge. Starting up a major weakness, I eventually used a pendulum and aid to gain the ridge crest, after which we enjoyed many exposed pitches on good rock. We simuled and soloed on the easy ground and pitched the many steep steps and towers, reaching a nice ledge for our first bivouac.

The second day dawned clear, as it did throughout the climb. The crest steepened above and didn't seem to offer climbable features, so we poked around to the left and found leaning cracks on the north flank. Another half-day of enjoyable, occasionally difficult, ridge climbing brought us to the junction with the main ridge of the Fitz Roy massif. We turned south, following the Care Bear Traverse. We picked a path around little gendarmes, then bypassed Aguja Val Biois on its steep west face. We made our second bivouac just below the Goretta pillar.

On day three I started up perfect splitters in a T-shirt, reveling in the morning sun, but we soon turned a corner into the shade, and I was slowed by wet, icy cracks. Halfway up the pillar Cheyne took the lead and made a diagonal rappel left onto the Casarotto Route, where he battled up wide, wet cracks. This was our longest climbing day; it wasn't until after midnight that we reached the top of the pillar and bivouacked.

The wall above glowing orange, we'd put ourselves in position for success. With 1,700m of climbing below us, and a year of planning and dreaming, we were within striking distance of the summit. However, the icy headwall looked intimidating. Cheyne, having more experience with mixed climbing, changed to boots and crampons, grabbed our tools, and started up. Kicking into brittle ice, he sent showers onto my belay. A few moments of hesitation preceded each move, as he made sure to find solid pick placements in the poor ice. He soon discovered a passage to the right, off the ice and onto rock, and we were back in business.

I led two more long pitches on perfect granite, and soon we gained the final snowfield. After scrambling to the summit, Cheyne and I stood silently, giving thanks for the opportunities, daydreams, and hard work that brought us to the summit of King Fitz.

The North Pillar Sitz Start had free-climbing up to 5.11, with numerous points of aid, pendulums, and rappels. The elevation gain is nearly 2,000m, though with rappels and downclimbing the total gain may be 300m more. We avoided the summits of Mermoz and Val Biois. We descended the Franco-Argentinean Route and, after a final bivouac at Lago de los Tres, reached Chalten on the morning of the 23rd.

Cheyne Lempe, 21, thanks the AAC for a generous Mountain Fellowship grant.

SCOTT BENNETT, *AAC*

*Editor's note: this was the first continuous ascent of the northwest ridge of Mermoz, the ridge having been climbed in two sections, during November 2001, by Zlatko Koren and Vasja Kosuta as far as a col 100m below the summit. Bennett and Lempe made a significant variation, climbing over 500m of new terrain at the start, left of the original.*

*Poincenot, southwest face, Rise of the Machines.* Over the years Jens Holsten, Mikey Schaefer, and I spent hours studying a high-resolution photo, picking out a line on this aesthetic face. It looked like high-quality, straight-in cracks to where it would join established lines. We were wrong.

We took our time on the approach and even laughed our way up the initial seven free pitches. The laughter stopped at the base of the headwall. The headwall had looked as if it would offer perfect hand cracks. However, this expectation was squashed when Jens led the first pitches of a steep, exfoliating, and all but closed crack. His high-stepping from a 000 C3 to a hook move off an ice tool and Mikey's run-out .75 Camalot crack and subsequent crack switch (read large pendulum), earned them both medals of honor. We repented our optimism often during the three days it took to complete the route.

Mikey led a huge aid block on day two. When the terrain finally broke down, Jens led into the night, arriving at an Ahwahnee Ledge at 1 a.m. The ledge was spacious and the night short.

At 5 a.m. we sat up simultaneously, after dreaming of suffocating and putting in ear plugs because of increasing wind. I led into broken crack systems, with the idea of eventually breaking right to join the established lines. We simul-climbed on moderate terrain and traversed on a red, chossy dike before seeing signs of other routes. I connected lines between tattered anchors

Southwest face of Poincenot. (1) Fonrouge-Rosasco (900M, 6c A0, 1968). (2) Southern Cross (1,000m, 6b+ A1, Copp-Tayler, 2002). (3) Benedetti-DeGregori variation start (6c, 2010). (4) El Sacrificio del Raton. (5) Rise of the Machines. (6) Judgement Day. (7) Historia Interminable (550m 6c A3, Cobo-Murcia, 1987). (8) Original Route (550m, 5+ M3, Cochrane-Whillans, 1962). *Mikey Schaefer. Route lines by Rolando Garibotti*

and found my way to the base of a right-slanting, hands-to-fists crack. This crack earned me extra credit, as did the steep crack off the following belay. I pulled into the sun on the right side of the summit and finished the spiral staircase to gain the high point. We had reached the halfway point.

We walked the knife-edge ridge individually. Jens led the initial raps and we paused to finish the gas canister before rapping the headwall. The small amount of gas melted a few liters of water and rehydrated a meal. Mikey led the raps down the headwall, rebuilding every anchor and salvaging gear from the routes that crossed. Halfway down, Jens and I looked across the Torre Valley for the source of a loud noise; it was rockfall on El Mocho, and the debris ran over the entire moraine approach, rock dust sweeping over Niponino. We had been there a few days earlier.

We called our route Rise of the Machines (900m, 650 new, VI 5.11 A2+), in keeping with the Terminator theme: Judgement Day is just right of our line. [Rise of the Machines lies between El Sacrificio del Raton (900m, ca 600 new, 5.11 A1, Sharratt-Wilkinson, 2006) and Judgement Day (900m, 650 new, 5.11 A1, Gerberding-Smith, 1992), finishing with the 1968 Fonrouge-Rosasco and the original 1962 Route]. We climbed it from December 13 to 15.

JOEL KAUFFMAN, *AAC*

*Aguja Poincenot (3,002m), southeast face, Via Russo.* In 2011 Sergey Dashkevitch (29), Arkadiy Seregin (52), and I (45) attempted a new route on the east face of Poincenot but retreated in bad weather. We returned in 2012 having as our goal the long, cold southeast face, and were joined by Eugeny Dmitrienko (37). I think it is impossible to climb this wall in a light-and-fast style, so we climbed capsule style, moving our portaledge twice.

On February 8 we established a snow cave beneath St. Exupéry and the following day took six-and-a-half hours to find a way across the glacier to the face. That day we climbed and fixed the first two pitches, both 6a M4. Next day, with heavy rain in the morning, we fixed three more pitches, the first two free, at 6a/6b, and the third A2/A3. On the 11th it rained sporadically all day, but we added four more pitches, with difficulties up to 6b A2/A3. On the 12th we placed a portaledge at the top of pitch nine and climbed one pitch above, at A3. There was heavy snow all next day, as we climbed just one 50m, A3/A4 pitch. On the following day we climbed from 8 a.m. to 1 a.m., in heavy snowfall and strong wind, adding five more pitches (mainly aid to A3/A4, with a 6a chimney) and moving a portaledge to our high point, the top of pitch 18.

On the afternoon of the 16th we climbed a pitch of 6a A1 and joined the Italian Route (Sperone degli Italiani, 1,200m, 6b A3, Bortoli-Carnati-Colombo, 1986). We then climbed three pitches (6a-6b) of this route, while also moving our other portaledge from the top of pitch three to the top of pitch 19 and stripping our gear from the face.

The 17th was a day of perfect weather, and we continued up the Italian Route and the upper section of the Original Route (550m, 5+ M3, Cochrane-Whillans, 1962) arriving on the

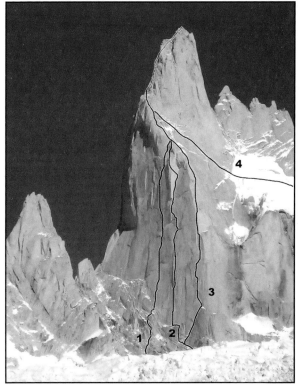

Southeast face of Aguja Poincenot. Aguja Innominata, 2,482m, left. (1) Via Russo. (2) Bagual Bigwall (750m, 6c A3, Ishibi-Maag-Portela-Schwitter, 1995, to junction with Italian route). (4) Original Route. *Arkadiy Seregin*

summit at midday. The next day was also perfect, and by 2 p.m. we had reached the glacier, having descended the Italian Route. We left no gear on our route, just slings on the way down.

We named our line Via Russo (1,200m [750m new] 6b A3/A4 M4). It is logical, safe, and solid, and the Italian Route makes a safe, logical descent.

I prefer to climb new big wall routes. Climbing for me is a leisure activity. It is about enjoyment, and I do not worry about style, speed, etc. One day on the face, in hurricane-like wind, I was jumaring and cleaning gear. Sometimes the gusts pushed me and the heavy haul bag 45° from the vertical. Loose ends of 60m rope flapped wildly. I caught myself thinking it's moments like these that make life worth living.

After only a day's rest in Chalten, we went to attempt the "new" Southeast Ridge of Cerro Torre [*the line followed by Kennedy and Kruk*]. It was not a good idea, as we hadn't time to wait for a good forecast. From the glacier beneath the Col of Patience, we climbed from 4 a.m. to 7 p.m., by which time we had reached a point beneath the headwall, where we retreated and regained the tent at 3 a.m.

MIKHAIL DEVI, *Russia, supplied by Anna Piunova, www.mountain.ru*

# *Antarctica*

The online version of these reports frequently contains additional photos, maps, topos, and extended text. Please visit aaj.americanalpineclub.org

*Damien Gildea acknowledges contributions from Simon Abrahams, Ludovic Challeat, Patrick Degerman, Bob Headland, Robert Miller, Todd Passey, Mike Roberts, Christian Stangl, and Phil Wickens.*

**Antarctica**

## ELLSWORTH MOUNTAINS

## SENTINEL RANGE

*Vinson Massif, summary.* One-hundred-and-forty-seven climbers reached the summit of Mt. Vinson (4,892m) in the 2011-12 season, with repeats by guides bringing total ascents to 158. Fourteen climbers also ascended nearby Mt. Shinn (4,660m), the continent's third highest mountain. Guides from Antarctic Logistics & Expeditions (ALE) made several ascents of Knutzen Peak, a rocky summit that lies above the Vinson normal route, and did some reconnaissance on the eastern side of the massif. American Jordan Romero, aged 15 years, 5 months, 12 days, guided by ALE's Scott Woolums, became the youngest to climb Vinson and also the youngest to complete the Seven Summits.

The major ascent of the season was the fifth ascent of Mt. Tyree (4,582m), the second highest

Tyree from northeast, seen above Patton Glacier. Previous parties approached from this direction, but Austrians came from left, crossing a low ridge to gain rocky ridge forming the right side of Grand Couloir. They climbed ridge, then traversed left into couloir above obvious serac. *Damien Gildea*

mountain in Antarctica. Austrian climbers Hans Kammerlander, Robert Miller, and Christian Stangl reached the top by making the third ascent of the northeast face, more or less following the 1997 French route up the Grand Couloir. Stangl attempted the route in December 2010 but had to retreat from very high when his partner was injured by rockfall. The three used a different approach from previous ascensionists; ALE flew them to a base camp on the Cervellati Glacier, rather than the Patton Glacier. From the Cervellati they spent the first day of 2012 climbing onto the rocky northeast ridge of Tyree, where they placed a camp in an obvious notch at 3,247 m. The next day they went a little higher on the ridge, before traversing left into the couloir (as on the second ascent, in 1997), which they followed all the way to the broad saddle between Tyree's north and south summits. Easy ground then led to the higher north summit. Their 200m, 6mm rope allowed them to make eight long rappels on the descent. Stangl joins Conrad Anker, Barry Corbet, and John Evans as the only people to have climbed Antarctica's three highest mountains.

With this ascent Kammerlander claimed to be the first person to have climbed the Second Seven Summits, a challenge thought to be considerably more difficult than the Seven Summits. However, Kammerlander's claim considers Nga Pullu, near Puncak Jaya (Carstenz Pyramid), to be the second highest in Oceania, while recent developments show that Puncak Mandala, a massif much farther east, is the second highest mountain on New Guinea, approximately 25m higher than Puncak Trikora, the third highest. Also

Kammerlander and Stangl on Tyree's Grand Couloir, 1,800m above the Cervellati Glacier (right of prominent rocky ridge behind climbers). After landing on glacier they walked around base of rocky ridge and approached face over low, sunlit, snow col, just left of center. *Robert Miller, provided by Damien Gildea*

Kammerlander plans to return to Canada's Mt Logan, as it became apparent that he did not reach the main summit on his previous expedition. There is another issue of whether Mawenzi should be considered Africa's second highest, in preference to Margherita in the Ruwenzori, given that it has sufficient prominence from Kilimanjaro. There needs to be clarification of the geographical status of these various peaks before any claims can be truly valid.

DAMIEN GILDEA, *Australia*

HERITAGE RANGE

*Mt. Spörli (2,253m), northeast face.* Climbers were again active among the small peaks around Union Glacier, due to ALE's new base near Mt. Rossman (see map in *AAJ 2011*). Probably the most notable climb in the area was the first ascent of Mt. Spörli, one of the highest peaks visible from the camp and the highest unclimbed peak in the Heritage Range. ALE guides Simon Abrahams and Todd Passey spent a few weeks touring in December with client Ralf Laier and made several first ascents. They first decided to attempt Spörli from the east but had to endure severe weather, during which they made three minor first ascents on nearby summits and one abortive try on Spörli itself. Eventually they skied to a col and climbed a rising traverse up the northeast face to the summit, topping out on December 17. Bruno Spörli was a geologist who worked in the range in the early 1960s, exploring and studying the peaks of the Heritage Range, often in the company of John Evans, first ascensionist of Vinson and Tyree.

Closer to Union Glacier camp, Abrahams, Laier and Passey made the first ascent of Guarcello Peak (2,050m), which was the highest unclimbed peak in the knot of mountains between the Union Glacier and the head of the Horseshoe Valley. They approached via the Henderson Glacier and on December 23 climbed the south face and southeast ridge. Before returning they also made the first ascent of Chappell Peak (1,860m), by the east ridge, and the second ascent of nearby Schoeck Peak (1,810m), via the north face and west ridge. A final jaunt back north to the Soholt Peaks produced the second ascent of Mt. Bursik (2,500m), the highest mountain in the Heritage Range.

The three climbed a new route, approaching from the west and ascending the north face. (The first ascensionists, 17 years previously, followed the northeast ridge.)

DAMIEN GILDEA, *Australia*

ANTARCTIC PENINSULA

*Amundsen Peak; island traverses; Mt Rendu.* To commemorate Roald Amundsen's team reaching the South Pole on December 14, 1911, the *Spirit of Sydney* transported the Spirit of Amundsen International Expedition (mostly Norwegian), to the Peninsula to make a first ascent of an unnamed peak. This they did on December 14th, climbing a summit on the southern side of the Sikorsky Glacier, which drains into Escondida Cove at the northern extremity of Gerlache Strait. The peak is ca 1,200m and unofficially named Amundsen Peak. (Amundsen already has one mountain named after him, in the Transantarctic Mountains, and some years ago another team, also unofficially, named one of the summits of Humpback Island Mount Roald.) One member, the experienced British guide Phil Wickens, returned to the Peninsula afterward, to lead the Eagle Ski Club Antarctic Expedition [*see below*].

French guide Ludo Challeat and his team made a number of notable, innovative island traverses, demonstrating the adventurous projects that can be achieved by willing guides with suitable clients. He first made the fourth ascent of Mount Friesland (1,700m), on Livingston Island, during a crossing of the main, eastern part of the island from South Bay to Moon Bay, through Aurora Gap. Picked up by *Podorange*, they sailed to the western side of Anvers Island and made another ski traverse, from Bonnier Point to near Palmer Station, stopping on the way for (unsuccessful) attempts on Mts. Français, and Agamemnon. They later landed at Rush Glacier on Brabant Island and climbed several summits at the eastern end of the Solvay Mountains (first ascended in 1984), before completing their island traverses by skiing to Terrada Point on the east coast. These trips feature committing descents, over unknown terrain, to a point on the coast where they hope they can be collected by yacht.

In January a British Services expedition reached the south coast of the Arrowsmith Peninsula. A large part of its work was scientific, but one of the highlights of its travels was the first known crossing of the Avery Plateau, ca 60km long and being up to 2,000m in altitude. It sits atop the Peninsula mainland, opposite Adelaide Island. The plateau team crossed from west to east, where they ascended a couple of peaks over 1,500m. This is the first non-government crossing of the Antarctic Peninsula (in its main section, not counting the far northern tip) and probably one of the few crossings ever.

The climbing highlight was an ascent of Mount Rendu, a bulky massif in the middle of the southern section of the Arrowsmith Peninsula. The team ascended Lliboutry Glacier to the junction of the Reid and Brückner Glaciers, and, after one failed attempt, five members climbed the north ridge. They reached the north summit (2,275m) on February 18 and continued across the plateau to measure the main summit, found to be 2,278m. In keeping with other recent GPS measurements of high Peninsula peaks, this is somewhat higher than previous estimates. Earlier survey teams had climbed lower points on Mount Rendu, but it is not known if they went to the highest point, so this ascent may well be the first. In addition two peaks, of 1,175m and 1,032m, rising to the south above Dog's Leg Fjord, on the coast of the mainland due east of Pourquoi Pas Island, were climbed.

DAMIEN GILDEA, *Australia*

*Cierva Cove, various ascents.*
During previous trips to the
Peninsula I had noticed a
number of steep and distinct
mountains east of Cierva Cove,
80km north of the areas visited
by most climbing teams. In 1999
Australians climbed several peaks
overlooking Brialmont Cove,
but the mountains of Cierva
Cove, immediately to the north,
remained untouched. Lacking
suitable anchorages the cove is
rarely visited by yachts, and its fast
currents and large amounts of ice
can make it a harrowing place to
spend the night at anchor.

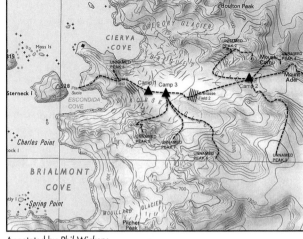

Annotated by *Phil Wickens*

Our Eagle Ski Club expedition took
place from December 28, 2011, to February
1, 2012. Members were Lucy Bound, Andy
Collins, Steve Gould, Toby Johnson, Dave
Smith, Roger Upton, David Williams, and
me as leader, transported to the Peninsula
by *Spirit of Sydney*. Before proceeding to
Cierva Cove we made a warm-up ascent of
popular Jabet Peak, and were then dropped
off at the southern tip of Anvers Island and
hauled sleds for three days to the base of the
northwest (Menelaus) ridge of Agamemnon
(2,594m). All but Gould made the ascent,
summiting in the early hours of January
9 during a brief period of clear weather.
There was only one recorded ascent of this
mountain, in 1982 by Chileans, though it is
possible it was traversed in 1955 during the
first ascent of Mt. Francais.

West ridge of Ader. Peak named in 1960 after Clement Ader
(1841-1925), French pioneering aviator. *Phil Wickens*

Cornu from south, showing route on west-southwest face.
Peak was named in 1960 after French engineer Paul Cornu.
*Phil Wickens*

Prevented from sailing farther south
by unusually heavy sea-ice, we climbed the
frequently ascended Mt. Banck (710m) and made a possible first ascent of Bruce Island (324m,
north face, F, January 15), then headed north to Cierva Cove.

Landing at Cierva Point is prohibited because it is part of an Antarctic Specially
Protected Area (ASPA No. 134), so we put ashore immediately to the south at Punta Sucia
on the north side of Escondida Cove. A slightly crevassed glacial ramp gave access to the
snowfield that borders the ASPA. While our yacht returned to Enterprise Island, we made
our way along the south bank of the Breguet Glacier and after two days established base camp

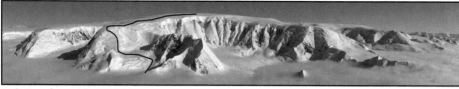

Eagle Dome from north. *Phil Wickens*

Madonna's Peaks from south. Ascent followed east ridge (right skyline) to higher east summit. *Phil Wickens*

below the striking south face of Mt. Cornu (ca 1,705m).

All the team climbed this peak on the 19th, via glaciated southwest slopes (F). During the ski descent Smith, Williams, and I traversed to a distinct double-peaked mountain to the west, where we climbed the east, slightly higher summit, initially on skis and then on foot, via the prominent east ridge (F). We unofficially dubbed this mountain Madonna's Peaks (ca 1,500m).

Next day, making the most of clear weather, Collins, Johnson, Smith, Williams, and I headed in a bitterly cold north wind to the end of the west ridge of Mt. Ader (ca 1,600m), which we climbed past one steeper section of 45°, and several ice blocks and crevasses, to the summit (PD).

After a day of bad weather, all but Williams and I climbed the unnamed fin-shaped peak between Cornu and Ader. Easy snow slopes on the west side led to a broad pass on the north side of the main peak. A short, steep step led through a small icefall onto the steep upper slope, which they followed to the summit (AD). They named it Spirit Peak (ca 1,503m). Meanwhile Williams and I attempted the broad, domed, unnamed summit to the south, marked at a little over 2,000m on the map. We reached the north spur by following a small subsidiary glacier that flows into the Breguet Glacier. This glacier led to the base of a long 45° slope, which we climbed on foot to the crest of the spur. We followed the crest south on skis for six km to reach the summit, which we named Eagle Dome and found to be 300m higher than marked on the map (ca 2,300m).

We then moved base camp west to where the Sikorsky and Breguet Glaciers join. Bound, Gould, Johnson, and Upton returned to the yacht, on the 23rd climbing from the southwest over both summits of the unnamed peak that lies at the eastern edge of the ASPA and overlooks the south side of Cierva Cove. They called it Cierva Nunatak (543m).

Collins, Smith, Williams, and I stayed for three more days to attempt unclimbed mountains that flank the southern side of the Sikorsky Glacier. The westernmost of these was climbed on December 14, 2011, by the Amundsen Antarctic Expedition. This mountain has two very separate summits, so we climbed the southeastern peak, via its northwest slopes, from the large glacial bowl that separates the two summits; We called it Amundsen East (ca 1,200m, F).

On the 24th we followed the Sikorsky east, to attempt a high, pointed summit near the head of the glacier. We found a safe, reasonably easy line by snaking around crevasse fields and serac bands to reach the 1,700m summit, naming it Missing Peak (F). Although shown on the map only as part of a spur of the Antarctic Peninsula, we found it to be a distinct and worthwhile summit.

Next day an early start allowed us to climb the last virgin summit in the area, directly south of camp. Its north face gave a fairly steep and serious route, due to the large number of sizeable crevasses. This one we named Central Peak (ca 1,300m, PD). After a superb ski descent to camp, we headed back toward the coast as the weather started to turn and arrived in thick cloud and driving snow. We were collected by *Spirit of Sydney* and spent two days on Deception Island, preparing the yacht before heading for South America.

PHIL WICKENS, *Eagle Ski Club, U.K.*

QUEEN MAUD LAND

*Overview.* Experienced Antarctic climber Patrick Degerman made his second visit to the area, climbing several minor peaks in the Wohlthat Massif with a fellow Finnish partner. The most well-known figure of Queen Maud Land climbing, Ivar Tollefsen, returned again with a Norwegian team to the iconic spire of Ulvetanna. Their flight was delayed by a week, and the remaining two weeks of unstable weather allowed no success on the east face, the steepest, coldest side of the mountain. Unsurprisingly, he plans to return.

DAMIEN GILDEA, *Australia*

EXECUTIVE COMMITTEE RANGE

*Mount Sidley (4,285m), fifth ascent and correction.* The highest peak in the range got its fifth ascent, by veteran guide Mike Roberts and party. It seems that in addition to previous reported ascents in 1990 (Bill Atkinson) and 2011 (ALE guided team, see *AAJ 2011*), there were two ascents in the early 1990s, by Bill McIntosh and partners.

DAMIEN GILDEA, *Australia*

BOUVETOYA

*Olavtoppen (774m), first true ascent.* The sub-Antarctic island of Bouvetoya is the most isolated piece of land on the planet, 1,740km from Antarctica and 2,600km from South Africa. Surrounded by rough seas and subject to severe weather, the island is 92% glaciated, rising to a high point named Olavtoppen. First sighted in 1739, set foot upon in 1822, and annexed by Norway in 1928, the island was visited numerous times during the 20th Century, though landings were rare. A meteorological station was installed in the 1970s and visited during the 1980s and 1990s by South African and Norwegian scientists, who mapped the island, often using helicopters, sometimes landing on the high point.

In February 2012 an international team approached from the west, using an inflatable to land on a small beach giving access to the plateau, which is otherwise guarded by steep ice cliffs. On February 20th William Allen, Bruno Rodi, and Jason Rodi, led by New Zealand guide Aaron Halstead, negotiated extensively crevassed, but technically straightforward, ground to make the first ascent of Olvatoppen, returning to the main ship after a round trip of nine hours. The next day Halstead led a second team of Sarto Blouin, Chakib Bouayed, Akos Hivekovics, Cindy Sampson, and Seth Sherman to the top. There is no previous record or evidence of Olavtoppen being climbed from the coast.

DAMIEN GILDEA, *Australia*

Nordenskjold, with 2011 route. To right is east summit of Roots (2,270m), climbed by British team in 2001. *Crag Jones*

SOUTH GEORGIA

*Nordenskjold (2,355m), first or second ascent.* Richard Spillett and I left the Falkland Islands in mid-November aboard Skip Novak's vessel *Pelagic Australis*, which was to deliver us to the snout of the Nordenskjold Glacier. We hoped to attempt the first complete ascent of Mt Nordenskjold (54°29.337'S, 36°21.619'W), the second highest peak on the island. Christian de Marliave, originally credited with the first ascent in 1988 after a bold solo effort, had honorably pointed out to Tim Carr that he had not reached the summit. Tim had provided me with this nugget of information some time ago, but I had been unable to obtain elaboration. Rick Armstrong, John Griber, and Doug Stoup had made an unsuccessful attempt in November 2001, and I had failed in 2009, with Julian Freeman-Attwood and Novak.

Dropped off on the coast below the Nordenskjold Glacier on November 18, it took six days to establish base camp at 1,130m on the uppermost section of the glacier. This period was characterized by cloudy and occasionally wet weather and poor visibility. A day was lost returning to the coast to collect replacement boots, after a sole became detached. Very lean conditions in 2011 meant sections of icefall proved awkward to negotiate with heavy sledges and skis, much more difficult than on my previous attempt. We left one of the sledges and our skis on the middle section of the glacier, allowing us to load carry up a steep snow field and avoid the difficult icefall guarding the upper glacier. We towed the remaining sledge, with all our gear, in tandem to the eastern end of the glacier below Nordenskjold's north face.

We took a rest day, with promising weather forecast for the following day. We set off at 4 a.m. on November 26 and moved together for the entire ascent. We already knew of a safe line skirting the lower rocks, a line protected from serac fall on the central section of the face. Above, we slanted left to reach the crest of the northeast ridge above its rocky lower section and beyond my 2009 high point. The time was 8:30 a.m. We followed the ridge in its entirety to the summit, including the crossing of a distinct hump into a saddle before the final section. Though the ridge is relatively easy-angled, its convergent faces fall away steeply north and south, and the crest consisted of glass-hard ice for nearly the entire 600m of its length. A 30cm rooster's comb was a saving respite, a ribbon of wind-packed snow glued to the crest. Continuous whiteout, combined with intermittent cornices, kept us entertained, and unusually for South Georgia the winds remained tolerable, as forecast. We reached the summit at midday after a height gain of ca 1,200m.

We descended via the same line, moving together for nearly the entire descent, which took 14hrs. We returned to our tent at 2 a.m., after a 24-hour roundtrip. After resting the remainder of the day, we set off for the coast on the 28th. We lowered the one sledge down the upper snowfield and regained our cache of sledge and skis. In the afternoon of the 29th we had reached the shore and were on the boat that evening.

Subsequent to our ascent I made contact with Christian de Marliave. He reported that he got very close to the summit, only stopping below the final ice mushroom, which was too dangerous to climb alone.

CRAG JONES, *Alpine Club, U.K.*

# Middle East

*The online version of these reports frequently contains additional photos, maps, topos, and extended text. Please visit aaj.americanalpineclub.org*

IRAN

*Alam Kuh (4,805m) and Damavand (5,610m),* AAC *exchange.* On June 5, 13 Americans, forming the second part of an exchange between the AAC and the Alpine Club of Iran (ACI), arrived in Tehran. The first part of the exchange took place in the Tetons during July 2010.

On our first afternoon we drove through the fastest, craziest traffic I'd ever seen and hiked up to the popular bouldering area of Darband, just north of Tehran. Women wore flowing robes that covered their bodies and most of their heads. Many had dyed blonde hair, make-up, and a chic look I didn't expect from such a conservative Muslim country. At one point the trail offered a view of Tehran and its seemingly endless high-rise buildings, shrouded in suffocating pollution.

Lydia Pyne on first ascent of Remembering Chris, Sangsar Sol. *Supplied by Chris Weidner*

On the 6th we split into two groups, each accompanied by ACI hosts. Stephen Alvarez, Brandon Bargo, Greg Crouch, Jim Donini, Mary Ann Dornfeld, Jennifer Flemming, Mark Wilford, and I headed to Alam Kuh, the highest peak of the Takht-e Suleyman Massif in the Alborz Mountains of northern Iran. Alum Kuh is Iran's answer to the Diamond on Colorado's Longs Peak. It's a high-altitude bastion of vertical granite more than 300m tall and the second or third highest point in Iran. It also seems to have a similar season to the Diamond, for it was plastered with snow. It looked like the Alps in winter. We'd have been better equipped with ice tools and crampons than the rock shoes and chalk bags we brought.

Nevertheless on the 8th Flemming and I climbed a new three-pitch route on Alam Kuh's North Patakht Wall—a granite buttress separate from, and lower in elevation than, the main wall. Pruchnic's Pillar (140m, 5.10c) climbs a low-angle arête to steep finger and hand cracks that weave between two large roofs on the wall's southeast face. On the 11th Mohammed Bahrevar and Wilford climbed the standard route on Alam Kuh's main face—the German Ridge—in full winter conditions. That same day Donini led a second group up a nontechnical snow route to a subpeak. The Iranians were keenly interested in learning how to jam cracks, and on two occasions Americans and Iranians top-roped together. But the weather was generally poor, with lots of snow and wind, so climbing time was limited. On our way back to Tehran, we spent half a day sport climbing on the orange granite walls of Pol-e-Khab, which has dozens of excellent routes up to 5.14a.

Meanwhile the other group, Tom Bowker, Marilyn Geninatti, Lydia Pyne, Tim Terpstra, and David Thoenen, traveled east to Damavand, a Fuji-esque volcano and the highest peak in what is traditionally referred to as the Middle East. They spent two days acclimatizing and getting established at the Bargah Sevom Hut (4,250m), where they'd hoped to stay for two nights before attempting the summit. However, an approaching storm forced the team to cut short acclimatization, and on the morning of June 9, Terpstra, Geninatti, and six members of the ACI summited Damavand in high winds and low visibility.

On the 12th the Damavand group moved farther east to the province of Semnan. On the first day here Bowker and Pyne established Remembering Chris, a 5.8 on the south-facing wall of Sangsar Sol. The next day the team hiked north of Shahmirzad, and explored the rim of an isolated canyon ringed by kilometers of beautiful unclimbed rock. This region offers a host of potential first ascents and is worthy of a return.

Our exchange set out to build an ongoing relationship between Iranian and American climbers. In this it was a huge success. Plans are in motion for a women's exchange, with 10 ACI women joining AAC ladies in Colorado during the summer of 2012. Plans are also in progress for a joint AAC/ACI climbing trip to Tajikistan in 2013. Most importantly this exchange fostered a dialogue and understanding between the *people* of our two countries—people who live half a world away but share similar hearts and minds.

Spilet Tour & Travel Co. in Tehran helped facilitate plans that we, as American, would not otherwise have been able to make. It's extremely difficult to get a visa to visit Iran. Even after two years of planning, the status of our visas was in question until the week we left the U.S. Once in Iran the government watched us closely. I highly recommend contacting Spilet Tour & Travel Co. if you're interested in climbing in the country. Thanks also to our ACI hosts, Abbas Sabetian (ACI president and participant in the Tetons event), Abbas Mohammadi (past ACI president and participant in the Tetons), Erfan Fekry (ACI secretary), and Abdolhamid Avani, Pouya Barzagar, Latifeh Boghrat, Moslem Dadashnia, Babak Doctorzadeh, Omid Ehsami, Abolgharsem Eshaghi, Rahim Gharadaghi, Nima Imani, Hossein Joudak, Parvaneh Kazemi (just returned from ascent of Manaslu), Jamal Moeini, Majid Maddah, Maziar Otoukesh, Majid Sabetzadeh (participant in the Tetons), Ali Asghar Saeedian (participant in the Tetons), Dalil Safaei, Dariush Taheri (participant in the Tetons), Hasan Yazdani, and Amir Hossein Yousefian.

CHRIS WEIDNER. *AAC*

# Morocco

*The online version of these reports frequently contains additional photos, maps, topos, and extended text. Please visit aaj.americanalpineclub.org*

### ATLAS MOUNTAINS

*Toubkal Region, Afella (4,015m), southeast face, Fountain Gully.* On January 3 James Mehigan, Olly Metherell, and Andrew Stokes-Rees made the first ascent of Fountain Gully on Afella in the Ouanoukrim chain. After a frantic evening of food shopping in Marrakesh, Mehigan and Metherell had their first scary moment when they were led into the labyrinthine streets of the medieval souk at 11 p.m., £400 of shopping piled on a hand cart, by two mischievous locals "helping" them to find their hotel. Stokes-Rees, who had previously climbed several ice routes in the region, flew in next day, and Atlas Walkers (www.atlaswalkers.com) quickly transported all three to the Neltner Hut (3,207m) below Toubkal. After an initial attempt on the 2nd, they climbed the new ice/mixed line the following day.

Crux ice pitch of Fountain Gully (continuation below hidden). *Olly Metherell*

The approach from the hut took an hour and a half on skis, following the Akoud-Afella Canyon. An initial 80m section of Scottish III led to a snow slope and belay in a corner, above which Stokes-Rees led a 40m mixed pitch of around Scottish 7 (probably about British VS 4c rock on the crux chimney, where there is an in-situ peg). Metherell then led up an ice ramp to a vertical section leading into a deep gully (40m, WI5 and some aid). A final 25m of Scottish 4 in the gully led to a large snowpatch and the finish of the route, which they rappelled. Pressurized water below the surface in the upper section made Fountain Gully seem an appropriate name.

Olly Metherell on pitch three of Fountain Gully. *Olly Metherell Collection*

This marks the final expedition of the Super 7 project, which had as its aim a new route on each continent. Metherell had climbed 24-Hour Party People, a direttissima up the south face of New Zealand's Mt. Aspiring (*AAJ 2005*); Goya Peak, in India's Miyar Valley (*AAJ 2007*); Mt. Cloos, on the Antarctica Peninsula (*AAJ 2011*); Huaytapallana II, in the Cordillera Blanca (*AAJ 2009*); Right-hand Chimney and Sioux Wall on Ben Nevis (Europe); and Tower Gully on Hut Tower in Alaska's Ruth Gorge (*AAJ 2008*).

LINDSAY GRIFFIN, *Mountain INFO, from information provided by Olly Metherell*

# Norway

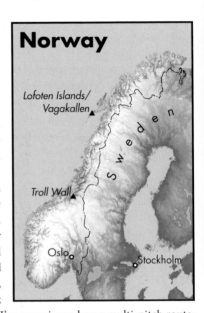

## Norway

## TROMSO REGION

Kvaloya Island, Blammanen (861m), north face, various free ascents, Peter Pan, and Febris. Last summer I had to work almost every day to finance my studies, but the sun is up all night, so I was able to climb five routes on Blammanen, all free.

Magnus Eriksson, Thomas Meling, and I began in June with a second free ascent of Ultime Thule (350m, A1/A2, Andersen-Blixt-Nilsen, 1995; FFA Aartun-Alexandersson, 2008, at 7b+; AAJ 2009), after which Per-Harald Barkost, from Tromso, and Pavel Juracek, from the Czech Republic, and I repeated Atlantis (400m, A1, Guldal-Nesheim-Nesheim, 1980, FFA Hustad-Nilsson, 1990, at 7b). I onsighted the crux pitch but found conditions on the climb the toughest I've experienced on a multi-pitch route: around 0°C and wet. It seemed harder than Ultime Thule.

Meling and I finished Tingeling to the top of the wall, naming the complete line Peter Pan. Tingeling was put up in 2010 by Hansjorg Auer and Much Mayr. It free-climbs the first two pitches of Bongo Bar, then breaks out left to climb four new pitches to a junction with Atlantis, where Auer and Mayr descended, as the final four pitches of Atlantis were too wet [see AAJ 2011]. It is not a world-class route though a logical line. We clipped the controversial bolt, but it is probably unnecessary, as the climbing on that section is no more than 6b. The crux, the second pitch of Bongo Bar, was overgraded by the first ascensionists at 7c+. We thought it 7b+, a grade confirmed by Dave Macleod.

The first time we tried the route we were tired after work. We climbed two pitches and descended, leaving a rope in place so we could practice this section. A couple of days later we climbed the route with no falls. Thomas led most of it, as I had a bad shoulder. We both climbed

North face of Blammanen near Tromso. (1) Ultime Thule. (2) Febris. (3) Peter Pan (Bongo Bar-Tingeling-Atlantis link). (4) Bongo Bar. (5) Arctandria. For other routes see AAJ 2011. Marten Blixt

every pitch free, though the upper section was partly wet.

Young guns Martin Olslund (18) and Erik Grandelius (20) and I made the third free ascent of Arctandria. (On the second, in 2007, Hansjorg Auer and Markus Haid rated the crux 8b). Each used pre-placed copperheads and a pecker on the second (crux) pitch. Prior to the ascent, although I was working seven consecutive days, I'd hike up to the wall in the evenings, powered by the midnight sun, and attempt to work the first two pitches on a jumar. Then I made phone calls, collected Martin and Erik from the airport at 10:30 p.m., and, with rain forecast for the next day, we ran up to the wall. We climbed through the night, finishing in the rain. Tired and hungry we reached the top after 15 hours on the wall and begged food from passing trekkers. Arctandria is a world-class route, and an onsight would be intense, but not life-threatening, as there is bomber protection five m below the crux.

Martin Olsund and I put up Febris, the only new route on Blammanen to be climbed without a hammer. We used aid only at the crux, which we then cleaned and redpointed. The crux took time, as it is significantly harder than anything on Peter Pan. We originally planned to try a free ascent of the aid route Lost and Found (A3 6a, 335m of climbing, Hentonnen-Karkkainen-Kurki, 2008; *AAJ 2009*) but once on the wall we saw other free possibilities. We first climbed 10m of Atlantis,

Andreas Klarstrom on crux (Pitch two, 8a+) of Arctandria. *Martin Olslund*

Erik Grandelius on fourth pitch of Arctandria—the Tromsoflaket (originally graded 8a but more like 7c). *Andreas Klarstrom*

Never mind the protection. Andreas Klarstrom climbs pitch four of Febris, a 6b dihedral. *Martin Olslund*

Andreas Klarstrom following the off-width on pitch six of Febris. *Martin Olslund*

then traversed right to Lost and Found. On pitch two we moved to new ground. Our third pitch was runout at the crux, so we cleaned it and worked it on a top-rope before the redpoint. Initially Martin couldn't do the moves, but I eventually solved the puzzle at around 7c. The next pitch was a nice surprise, a crux slab (7b+) followed by an overhanging thin-hands crack, which turned out to be easy. Above we joined the corner system of Lost and Found for one wonderful pitch (6b).

We had climbed half the wall and expected the remainder to be straightforward. Routefinding and cleaning had proved tiring, so we slept for a couple of hours on a ledge. I awoke at 2 a.m. to the sound of Martin throwing up. He had a fever and didn't improve, so we went down.

I had to leave the area for Trondheim, but on the way the car broke down, and we were brought back to Tromso. By now I had the same fever, but the weather was good, so we went back up for another try. We climbed the lower part fast and had a lot of energy left for the upper section, which was useful, as the sixth pitch proved much harder than expected—a thin, overhanging traverse leading to an off-width. Martin made an impressive onsight lead, and we finished the route with no falls or hangs, neither for the leader nor second. Pitch grades for Febris are 7b, 7c, 7b+, 6b, 6b, 7c, 6b, and 6c. I wouldn't have been able to climb this route without Martin, a mentally strong and creative climber.

ANDREAS KLARSTROM, *Norway*

Dave Macleod, pitch one, Bongo Bar. *Paul Diffley/www. hotaches.com*

*Kvaloya Island, Blammanen (861m), north face, Bongo Bar, first free ascent.* During our stay in Kvaloya, Donald King, Julia Snihur, and I climbed some established classics, which are as good as any in the world, and a few great new routes. However, it was pictures of Hansjorg Auer and Much Mayr attempting, in 2010, to free the aid route Bongo Bar, on the north face of Blammanen, that made me first think of coming to Kvaloya. They'd freed the first two pitches at a reported 7b+ and 7c+, but the overhanging third pitch through the roofs was wet, so they traversed left onto Atlantis before rappelling. *[This line was completed in 2011 by Klarstrom and Meling; see above.]*

Arriving beneath the wall, we weren't sure Bongo Bar would be possible. It looked steep and blank through the roofs, but other potential new lines looked equally desperate, with many overhanging, closed granite seams and apparently sheer, featureless sidewalls. Andreas Klarstrom and partner were 60m up a new line having an exciting time. He shouted encouragement about us having a look at Bongo Bar, so I thought we should at least give it a shot.

The 55m first pitch (British E6 6b or F7b+) was a rough warm-up, a reminder that we have little steep granite laybacking in Scotland. The following pitch was also E6 6b or 7b+ (confirmed by Klarstrom), rather then the 7c+ quoted by Auer. Perfect laybacking with spaced protection made it one of the best granite pitches I have climbed anywhere.

Next day I sent Donald up the crux third pitch (A3) with aid gear. It involved two large loose flakes. He came down part way past the first, and I half aided, half free-climbed, to the belay, to find that pitch four looked almost as hard. I then spent a couple of days working these two pitches before making a redpoint attempt with Julia. Rain threatened our chances, but the black streaks on pitch three looked fairly dry. We began with no expectations.

We climbed the two initial pitches quickly, after which Julia assured me that I'd dispatch the E8 6c/F8a pitch above. I wobbled onto the crux and began to lose my cool. The crucial thumb press and foothold were wet. There was no time for hesitation. I threw my right hand across the corner, caught the hold with two fingers, stayed on, and continued with an Elvis leg all the way to the ledge.

Dave Macleod making layaway moves on pitch two of Bongo Bar.
Paul Diffley/www.hotaches.com

Seconding this 45m diagonal pitch through roofs with razor-sharp edges was going to be one of the main hurdles on the route, not for the faint-hearted. Julia had not been on it before and was carrying a rucksack. However, the rope came in steadily. Pulling on gear where she could, to avoid weighting the rope and sawing it on the edges, Julia was up in 30 minutes, leaving me to dispatch the balancy 7c pitch above.

Layback cracks followed. Julia was keen to get out in front. She started up the long pitch six but set up a poor belay after 20m, allowing me to head around the corner and up endless cracks bathed in late evening sun. A BASE jumper flew past and touched down before we'd completed the final pitch. A long stumble down took us to a pasta meal at 1 a.m.

I have a feeling that despite the unpredictable Norwegian climate, Blammanen will evolve into one of the most famous walls in Europe for hard big-wall free-climbing. It's accessible yet impressive, with some of the best granite you'll find anywhere.

Thanks to the Gore-Tex experience tour for sending us to Norway and to the locals who helped with information and encouragement. It was a pleasure.

Bongo Bar: 400m, 7b+, 7b+, 8a, 7c, 7b, 6c, 7a+, 6b+.

DAVE MACLEOD, *Scotland*

# Russia

*The online version of these reports frequently contains additional photos, maps, topos, and extended text. Please visit aaj.americanalpineclub.org*

## CAUCASUS

*Kara-kaya West, southwest face.* I love first ascents. You climb with no hurry and in good company. You think creatively, choosing the line. You are the one who decides whether to use bolts or not. A special pleasure is to make the first ascent of a wall, finding the most beautiful line.

This fall, as is tradition, we went to the Rocky Ridge (similar to the Dolomites), north of Bezengi Village. Our aim was Kara-kaya West, a peak with no previous technical alpine routes. Even the name of the mountain was not clear to us at first. Various maps and local people give it different names. I saw this mountain in 2009, while making the first ascent of Land of Mist (6A) with Alexander Lavrinenko and Maxim Polyakov on Kara-kaya Main (3,646m). Our eyes constantly turned toward this virgin wall with a fine profile. The buttress in the center of the southwest face resembled the prow of a sailboat and led directly to the summit—a majestic and logical line.

The team was Roman Kotlyar, Eugene Timko, Alexander Zakolodny, and I, and the route went quickly: two days up the moraine, a day of fixing, two days to the summit. The wall is 500m high, and we climbed 18 pitches, at an overall grade of 5B. [The topo grade is VI and A2. In the Russian system VI does not explicitly signify a free grade but the level above which it becomes faster and safer to use aid on a first ascent.] If you go light, you can climb it in one day. We wanted to do the climb without bolts, and we succeeded, although we were unable to climb it completely free, using aid for a total of 40m.

The day after completing the route we went to look at the walls of nearby Ak-Kaya. We admired the existing routes and the potential for first ascents. However, September weather was unstable; that

evening it started raining, and lightning flashed over the main Caucasus chain, and it was time to go home.

It amazes me that in the Central Caucasus, so well explored, one can still find peaks with untouched 500m walls close to roads and villages.

EUGENE POLTAVETS,
*Russia, supplied by Anna Piunova, mountain.ru, and translated by Ekaterina Vorotnikova*

Southwest face of Kara-kaya West. *Supplied by Anna Piunova*

# Georgia

*The online version of these reports frequently contains additional photos, maps, topos, and extended text. Please visit aaj.americanalpineclub.org*

## Caucasus

*Ushba (4,710m), south pillar, Harakternik.* Ukrainians Igor Chaplinsky, Michel Formin, and Vitali Todorenko climbed directly up the famous south pillar of Ushba, adding 130m of possibly new ground on the steep central section. The center of the pillar was climbed to two-thirds height in 1960 by Monogarov and his team, who then slanted up left, leaving the final prow unclimbed. In 1962 the left flank of the pillar was climbed by Myshliaev (who joined the upper section of the Monogarov route) and the right side by the celebrated Kustovskiy route. In 2010 a Ukrainian team led by Mishel Voloshanovskiy climbed a little left of the Monogarov, joining it as it slants left, and claimed a new line. However, it appears they were close to or on a little-known route climbed in 1981 by Golubev and partners, who also slanted left at Monogarov's bolts. The climbing history of one of the most famous mountains in the Caucasus is thus complex and not well documented. In 2011 a team from Krasnoyarsk claimed a new line on Ushba, only to find it had been done before. Chaplinksky, Formin, and Todorenko followed the (possibly new) line climbed by Voloshanovskiy but, instead of slanting left, continued up the prow directly to the top of the south pillar.

The south face is ca 1,500m high. In early July the three Ukrainians first climbed 900m up easy rock (2-3) and glacial terrain, followed by 300m on the crest of the ridge to where things became difficult. About nine pitches (max 5b) led to the base of the pillar. The next three pitches gave largely free climbing, up to 6c, with short sections of A2 and A3 (skyhooks and Iron Hawks/birdbeaks). About four more pitches, up to 6c and A3, took them to an overhanging section. To this point they had followed the line climbed in 2010. The next 130m provided the crux, beginning with a 25m overhanging wall (A3). More 6b and aid took them to the top of the pillar.

On the upper section most ascents follow the right side of the final buttress, the Red Corner. These Ukrainians climbed the center in four fine pitches of 6a. They bivouacked on the final ridge and reached the summit at 8 a.m. on July 7. Starting down by the classic 1903 Heibling-Schulz Route (5A) on the southeast and east flanks, they found the snow too dangerous and bivouacked again, continuing their descent early next morning. Total time spent on the mountain was five days, and the route was named Harakternik (6A, 6c and A3). They had been lucky with the weather, which was still a bit wintry, being hampered only by a strong wind.

LINDSAY GRIFFIN, *Mountain INFO, from information supplied by Anna Piunova, mountain.ru*

Ushba from south. Northwest summit (4,694m, left) and Southeast (Main) summit (4,710m). Normal route to Northwest summit (Almer-Cockin, 1888, 4A) reaches gap between summits from far side. (1) Artsishevsiy, 1971, 5B. (2) Grigorenko-Prigoda, 1972, 5B. (3) Myshliaev, 1962, 5B. (4) Voloshanovskiy, 2010. (5) Monogarov, 1960, 5B. (6) Harakternik, 2011, 6A. (7) Kensitskiy, 1972, 5B. (8) Kustovskiy, 1962, 6B. Supplied by Anna Piunova

# Tajikistan

*The online version of these reports frequently contains additional photos, maps, topos, and extended text. Please visit aaj.americanalpineclub.org*

PAMIR

Looking north from base of the Tooth at peaks above Sidzh Valley climbed by American team. *Chris Weidner*

Mikey Church on summit of Rostam. Behind and to west, prominent rock tower in left middle distance is Shahnameh. Peak in front of it is Akvan Div. *Chris Weidner*

*Gunt and Sizdh Valleys, various ascents.* In approximately one month Darren Benton, Jesse Burkhardt, Mikey Church, Jim Donini, Jennifer Flemming, Chris Weidner, and I completed first ascents of four peaks in the Gorno-Badakshan Autonomous Oblast (GBAO) region of eastern Tajikistan. We also put up a handful of one- and multi-pitch rock climbs. The idea for the expedition arose after I moved to Khorog, a small town in southeast Tajikistan on the border with Afghanistan, to carry out a one-year research project. The mountains we visited lie above the Gunt Valley, which descends to the M41 a little east of Rivak, 35km northeast of Khorog.

Jesse and Darren, accompanied by Teo Kaye, a professional photographer based in Dushanbe, attempted Peak 5,160m in the Gunt Valley. The approach was long and difficult, and after establishing base camp the three scrambled up steep talus for 500m, then a steep snow gully, to reach a col on a ridge 200m below the summit. The way ahead looked extremely difficult, with three large gendarmes that would have to be climbed and rappelled. Considering the time of day and approaching bad weather from the north, they retreated.

In the meantime Jenn, Chris, Jim, and I made the first of two attempts on the 280m east face of a sharp granite peak located on the west side of the Gunt Valley and referred to as the Tooth. We tried two lines before rain moved in, Chris and Jenn getting 90m up after insecure 5.11a climbing.

Two days later, on June 24, both teams returned but were unsuccessful, our attempts ending 120m-130m up.

The team now focused on a side valley of the Gunt known as Sizhd (37.694866° N, 71.763264° E). A base camp at 3,800m offered good access to a large number of steep granite peaks on both sides of the valley, mostly above 4,500m.

Church-Flemming-Weidner route on west face of Rostam. *Chris Weidner*

Darren and Jesse opted for a flat-topped peak of ca 4,700m, on the right side of a snow-covered cirque. On June 28 they climbed 300m up a south-facing snow gully to a col. Above, a short section of 4th class, followed by two pitches of technical rock (5.10a and 5.4), led to a final unprotected traverse along the southeast ridge. The pair reached the summit at mid-day, naming the peak Akvan Div. Descent involved three rappels and long sections of downclimbing.

Shahnameh from approach, showing route up southeast face. *Jim Donini*

The same day Jenn, Mikey, and Chris hiked up a steep gully toward a sharp, granite peak later named Rostam (ca 4,900m). After four hours and much easy scrambling, they reached the base of the west face. Starting at the left edge, they climbed 120m of loose 4th class before roping up at the base of a chimney. Three long, right-trending pitches, with sections of vertical cracks (5.8), led to the sharp, snowy north ridge. A final steep section of verglassed rock (5.8) and a sharp arête led to the summit. Five rappels plus much downclimbing brought them back to the foot of the face, and they arrived in camp at 8 p.m., after a 14-hour day.

Jim and I left camp at 5:30 a.m. and began an arduous 600m approach up a loose, steep gully toward a 4,960m peak (altimeter) we later named Shahnameh. From a major talus field below the headwall, we saw that the southeast side gave the choice route. An obvious low-angle outcrop on the right side of the wall gave 3rd class scrambling for 180m to the headwall. Four well-protected pitches, following the path of least resistance and best rock (5.8-5.9), took us to where we could see that the remaining climbing looked long and complicated.

Jim Donini on superb granite of southeast face of Shahnameh. *Bo White*

Chris Weidner amid magnificent rock architecture on third pitch during second attempt on east face of the Tooth. *Teo Kaye*

The two lines attempted on the east face of the Tooth. *Bo White*

To the east we saw Darren and Jesse summiting Akvan Div, a little higher than us. As it was now 3p.m. and we didn't fancy an open bivouac, we opted to go down, rig rap stations, and come back after rethinking our strategy.

The following day, while we refueled and moved our camp 600m higher, Jesse, Darren, and Mikey made the first ascent of a pinnacle they named Punginella (ca 4,100m). This involved 240m of scree, followed by two moderate length 5.7 pitches. After spending some time on the precarious summit, they descended with two rappels. Later that day, Jesse and Mikey climbed a three-pitch 5.7 route on the opposite side of the valley, topping out in an obvious gully and descending before bad weather moved in.

Jim and I left the following day, the 30th, at 6:30 a.m. and embarked on 12 pitches of Sierra-style climbing. These ranged from 5.7 to 5.10, with one 8m A1 section. Routefinding was tricky, but there was good rock on the steep sections, although ledges had debris. After each headwall we expected to see the summit, but another steep face would appear. Linking these walls involved rappelling from towers or traversing (which would have to be reversed on the descent). At 4 p.m., after 600m of vertical ascent (12 pitches and two long rappels), we reached the top of Shahnameh. We descended with several rappels and two fifth-class pitches, arriving back at camp half an hour after dark. Our three major summits, Shahnameh, Akvan Div, and Rostam, relate to the epic Persian book of mythology (Shahnameh) that is the heart of Iranian, Afghan, and Tajik literature.

Bo White, *AAC with the help of Darren Benton, Jesse Burkhardt, and Chris Weidner*

*Mayakovsky (6,096m), south face, Czech Route.* On September 5 Antonin Borovka, Josef Krena, and I climbed the south face of Pik Mayakovsky (Qullai Mayakovskiy), a mountain in the southwest corner of the Tajikistan Pamir, where the north-south Ishkashim Range joins the east-west Shakhdara Range. We approached from Dushanbe on a paved road, via Khorog and Ishkashim, to the village of Darshai. From Darshai it takes at least three and a half days using donkeys or porters to reach a high camp south of the mountain at 4,900m. The 1947 Budenov Route, the original line up the peak, takes the right part of the south face. Prior to 1947 the summit had a different name, but the first ascensionists renamed it in honor of Soviet poet Vladimir Mayakovsky (1893-1930).

Panorama southeast from Pik Mayakovsky. High peaks in background form part of High Hindu Kush in Afghanistan's Wakhan Corridor. Near peaks form southern part of Ishkashim Range. (A) Koh-e-Hevad (6,849m). (B) Lhunko Massif (6,902m). (C) Akher Cioch (7,020m). (D) Koh-e-Urgunt (7,038m). (E) Saraghrar Massif (7,349m). (F) Pik Kharskhavol (Qullai Khirskhabol or Akademika Berge, 6,091m, first climbed in 1947). Snowy summit to its immediate right is Pik Imast (5,945m). (G) Koh-e-Shakhawr (7,116m). (H) Koh-e-Kishni Khan (6,755m). (I) Noshaq Massif (7,492m). (J) Pik Anbarku (5,838m). (K) Pik Kolbun (5,864m). In front of this peak and just off picture to right is Abkharv Pass. (L) Pik 5,702m. *Michal Kleslo*

We established base camp at 4,100m and high camp at 4,900m, above which we did not follow the Budenov Route (Russian 3A) but looked for an easier way. We found it toward the left side of the face, climbing through fields of penitentes, some as high as two m. We crossed three wide crevasses, where we fixed rope, and, at the final crevasse below the top section of the southwest ridge, we followed an obvious snow terrace left. Another huge crevasse (fixed rope) and a short icy section took us to the summit ridge, which we followed through more penitentes and a short rock scramble to the top. We feel this route would not have been ascended before, as few people climb this mountain, and our line is not visible when approaching the peak.

Our Czech Route (Russian 2B, 45°) is easier than the Budenov but very tiring due to the never-ending fields of penitentes. You only need to rope up when crossing the large crevasses. It took eight hours to ascend and three hours to come down. The only other (rarely climbed) routes are the 1971 Drabkin on the southwest ridge (5A, rock climbing) and the 1973 Efimov on the northwest face (5B).

South face of Pik Mayakovsky. (1) Czech Route. (2) Burdenov Route. *Michal Kleslo*

Giant penitentes on south face of Mayakovsky. *Michal Kleslo*

MICHAL KLESLO, *Czech Republic*

SHAKHDARA RANGE

*Pik Moscow Olympic Games (5,883m), south ridge.* The Saryshitcharv River flows south 20km from the Shakhdara Range to meet the Oxus River at the village of Shitcharv, directly opposite the Raij Jurm Valley in Afghanistan's High Hindu Kush. Its head is enclosed by a horseshoe of summits: Pik Moscow

View north and east from summit of Moscow Olympic Games. Karl Marx and Engels in distant right. *Zdenda Bouda*

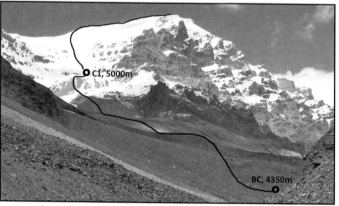

Moscow Olympic Games from south-southeast, with 2009 ascent of southeast face and south ridge. *Zdenda Bouda*

Olympic Games, Pik Marshall Grecko (6,105m), Pik Baikonur (6,091m, formerly known as Djarv), and Pik Armed Forces (6,138m, formerly Pik Soviet Army). These peaks were first climbed by Soviets in 1976, and hard routes were created on the northern flanks, notably the north face of Moscow Olympic Games, climbed in 1979.

Our 2009 expedition started from Shitcharv (2,800m, population 300) and followed a good shepherd's trail to 3,600m. We camped at 3,400m; at the confluence of the Saryshitchary and Rostoshitcharv rivers; at 3,600m where the Saryshitchary splits; and at 4,000m, on a grassy meadow; before reaching a good base camp site at 4,350m, alongside the river in the heart of the cirque. The snow line was at 4,500m.

We took five or six hours to climb over moraine slopes to a snow plateau southeast of the south ridge of Moscow Olympic Games, where we made Camp 1 at 5,000m. Next day, July 12, Vladimir Sojak and I climbed for one hour to a 300m snow face, which we followed to the crest of the ridge at 5,500m. We followed the crest up right to the rocky pyramid forming the summit. The views were extensive: Baikonur to the north, nearby Armed Forces and distant Piks Karl Marx and Engels to the east, and Mayakovsky to the west. It took two and a half hours to descend to base camp and a further two days to reach Shitcharv.

The route was Russian 2B (45-50°). There is no record of an ascent in the Clasificator, the main Russian information source, but I don't believe our route was entirely new, as it is the easiest way to the summit, and a similar line was likely followed in the 1970s. Other team members were Ruda Cerny, Marek Erban, Ladislav Szilagyi, and Fanda Ulrich. More photos, maps, and information (in Czech) are available at www.zdenda.net.

Zdenda Bouda, *Czech Republic*

# Kyrgyzstan

PAMIR ALAI

*Karavshin, Pik 4,810m, northwest face.* It was my sixth visit to the Karavshin. Our group of five arrived when the season was in full swing. The meadows were full of climbers from Zelenograd, Moscow, and Tomsk. Coming in with us was a group of 20 from St Petersburg. Taras Tsushko and I had planned to try a new route on the right side of the northwest face of Pik 4,810m, left of the 1988 Ovcharenko Route (6A). Our other three had great plans too, but an unfortunate incident while on Pik Asen's Pogorelov Route put two temporarily out of the game. The third, Max Perevalova, joined us. We took his portaledge and set off as a threesome.

Our line was perfectly logical, initially following a series of cracks to the right of a huge corner, in which were falling rocks and running water. After four pitches we crossed the corner and climbed to some roofs. In this 340m section we placed only three bolts, all for belays.

Above the roofs lay sweeping slabs, typical on the northwest face. The angle was 70°, sometimes less. There were intermittent cracks, flakes, and ledges, but features were generally poor, and we needed to search for them. Our plan was to spend a couple of days in the portaledge below the roofs, where we would be protected. We would fix ropes up the slabs toward the summit tower but had to revise our strategy when, after the first day, the portaledge broke. Actually, it didn't break; it deflated. It was an inflatable ledge designed by Eugene Dmitrienko. Our choices were to rappel to the ground or climb to natural ledges.

It was a busy day, from dawn until 1 a.m., but we reached a little sloping ledge. We'd been lucky, because there had been features on "the mirror," and we had climbed long stretches without drilling bolts. Above, a logical succession of cracks and corners, where we also found ice, led to the foresummit ridge, 60m from the main summit. On the highest point we met a team from St. Petersburg that had climbed the Kritsuk Route.

We climbed 26 pitches, up to VI and A3, all but six requiring aid (VI is not necessarily a free grade but the level above which it becomes quicker and safer to use aid). We descended to the Ak-su Valley via the Nazarov Route (5B). It is a line usually followed in ascent and proved difficult to descend with heavy sacks: hard to recover ropes and dangerous from stonefall. The 1,080m ascent took seven days; two days of preparation and five on the face.

After a rest Taras and I went to Pik Slesov (4,240m), hoping to try another new route. The peak was popular this season, with many parties climbing the famous Perestroika Crack on the southwest face. We ended up repeating the Porgorelov Route on the steeper, colder northwest face. We completed the route in five days and on the sixth rappelled the line. We found it more demanding than the Moroz Route, which I had climbed before, due to technical difficulty and lack of ledges. On the right the Klenov Route looks objectively dangerous. There are corners with much loose rock, and feathery flakes of doubtful security, seemingly ready to fall of their own accord. The weather then became poor for a week, and on August 31 we left the valley.

While the significant walls in the Karavshin have all been climbed, there are still interesting projects.

Vincent van Beek and Bas Visscher following a pitch of UIAA IV on west buttress of Pik Brokkel. *Bas van der Smeede*

Camakchay Tower from south, with the line of Yellow Submarine. *Bas van der Smeede*

An unclimbed ca 4,800m pyramid next to Pik BasBas. *Bas Visscher*

July is the preferred month: it's colder, but routes are much safer from stonefall, and there is still snow on the summits to provide drinking water.

ALEXANDER LAVRINENKO, *Ukraine, supplied by Anna Piunova, mountain.ru, and translated by Luca Calvi*

*Oibala Range, first ascents.* In July and August, Saskia Groen, Vincent van Beek, Bas Visscher, and I explored a little-known range in the eastern part of the Pamir Alai, close to the Chinese border.

This compact collection of steep alpine peaks, on a ridge running northeast to southwest, is located north of the Irkeshtam Pass at 40°07'22.79" N, 73°55'31.69" E and was noticed in 2007 by two Russian mountaineers from Omsk, who referred to it as the Oibala (Oh Boy!). Their reconnaissance trek revealed few signs of human visitation, just tracks from shepherds. It is known that the area was inspected by Soviet geologists in the 1930s, but extensive research showed no previous visit by climbers.

We accessed the mountains through Osh, though we first had trouble with our border permit and had to wait two days before the army eventually gave us permission to access the border zone. A military jeep track enabled us to drive most of the way to the mountains in a 4WD bus. A short day's walk with horses then brought us to base camp. At base camp we were enthused by the number of possible objectives. The generally stable weather allowed us to climb most of the time, and we made six ascents of previously unnamed, unclimbed peaks. The rock is limestone and mostly not good, but the peaks are steep and beautiful.

Our first climb, on July 17, was 4,750m Pik Brokkel (Dutch for Very Loose Rock). Van Beek, Visscher, and I climbed the west buttress (D UIAA IV 60°). On the penultimate pitch Visscher was hit by a rock that injured his leg. We carried on to the summit hoping for an easy descent on the far side, but there was none. We were forced to rappel our ascent route, leaving several expensive cams. Due to its loose nature, we called the route Guns of Navarone.

Next all four of us climbed Camakchay Tower (4,215m). This is not in the Oibala Range but a little

Northwest face of Pik Oibala, with Elektroshock Blues. *Bas van der Smeede*

Northwest face of Pik BasBas, showing Natte Neuzen Show. *Bas van der Smeede*

Pik Marian, with first ascent route on west face and north ridge. *Vincent van Beek*

to the northwest, across a small wild river named Camakchay. The peak was close to base camp and appeared to offer good rock. We climbed the south pillar with one bivouac over July 24 and 25, arriving on the summit at noon the second day. The rock was good, the climbing enjoyable, and we recommend this route, which we named Yellow Submarine (900m, TD+ UIAA VII-).

On the 28th Visscher and I climbed the northwest face of Pik BasBas (4,785m), via a line we dubbed Natte Neuzen Show (785m, D+/TD- UIAA VI- 50°). This route was hard to grade, as it was mostly steep snow but had a demanding finish on thinly iced loose rock. There was occasional poor weather, and on the 30th, during a three-

Pik Pewi. First ascensionists followed left skyline (south ridge). *Bas van der Smeede*

day rainy period, van Beek and I climbed the easy Pik Pewi (Peter-Wim, 4,310m), naming it after our dads. We followed the south ridge, at PD.

On August 1 van Beek and Visscher climbed Pik Marian (4,450m) by the north face and west ridge, at AD (55°). When we returned to Osh, Visscher learned that a friend had died in the Alps, so he named this peak after her.

On August 2 Groen and I climbed Pik Oibala, the highest summit in the range, via the northwest face, naming our route Elektroshock Blues (700m, TD- AI3 75°). On the

Looking south-southeast during ascent of Pik 4,815m at unclimbed peaks in northern Borkoldoy. *Mark Weeding*

Pik 4,815m in northern Borkoldoy. Ascent ridge faces camera. *Mark Weeding*

Russian map it is given a height of 4,950m, but our altimeter showed only 4,830m. Next day van Beek and Visscher made an attempt on the massive west face but retreated after 400m. On the 6th all four of us tried again, this time climbing 700m before being beaten by a blank section. We feel the Oibala range still has potential for more first ascents.

BAS VAN DER SMEEDE, *Holland*

On ascent of Pik 4,815m, northern Borkoldoy. *Mark Weeding*

TIEN SHAN

FERGANA AND BORKOLDOY,

*Various ascents.* The Northern Borkoldoy has a staggering collection of gnarly looking peaks topping out at just under 5,000m. The 4x4 journey to reach them was the hardest I have ever undertaken. The direct back roads from Naryn to Issykul feature dramatic gorges, broken bridges, crumbling single track, and a 3,940m snow-covered pass. We slithered off the road at least once.

Dave Molesworth, Tim Seel, Misha Sukhorukov, and I began my fourth trip to Kyrgyzstan in the Fergana Tau, which I visited in 2010 (*AAJ 2011*). We first climbed a peak at the head of the eastern arm of the glacier, a long slog across scree and glacier followed by a steep ice face. The final 200m provided all the delights of steep scree and broken rock, and our summit (4,710m, 40°33'07.13" N, 74°37'16.23" E, AD), proved to be part of a long broken ridge, with numerous summits for future visits.

Starting from a camp at 3,400m, we probably overdid it as a first acclimatization climb, so we moved camp higher and from this new location made two climbs. The first involved scree, snow, and a short scramble up the final ridge to a fine

Looking east at unclimbed peaks from low on Pik 4,350m, northern Borkoldoy. Pik 4,815m just off-picture left. *Mark Weeding*

summit (4,650m, 40°33'36.57" N, 74°34'55.11" E, F). The second lay east of the main col, on the watershed ridge with Osh Province. Steep snow and ice, followed by a short scramble, brought us to a forepeak, from where we traversed a snow basin to the main summit (4,685m, 40°33'02.58" N, 74°35'15.55" E, AD). Rockfall and hard ice deterred us from descending the same way, so we dropped down scree on the wrong side of the watershed, hoping to reach a glacier we had seen from the col. The farther we went, the worse it looked, and, when we saw our glacier below, we realized the immensity of the relief. All we needed to do now was re-ascend 200m to the col, but Misha wanted to traverse the ridge, which looked like at least eight hours of fun. Aged 63, he's an insatiable lad, but his internal GPS has gotten us into trouble on more than one occasion.

Looking southeast at unclimbed peaks of Borkoldoy from summit of Pik 4,350m. *Mark Weeding*

After an unsuccessful attempt on a peak above the Torugat road, we started an epic journey cross-country. Just before the Tosor Pass we saw two peaks that "needed doing." Here we met Ukrainian rafters about to descend the Rishi Naryn. From a high waterless camp, we climbed a steep face and pleasant ridge to bag summits of 4,560m (41°51'12.75" N, 77°04'43.43" E, PD) and 4,630m (41°51'11.58" N, 77°04'21.51" E, PD). I was desperately knackered, thanks to the trots leaving me badly dehydrated. Olec, our driver and cook, finished me off with a traditional cure of vodka and salt.

By the time we reached the northern Borkoldoy, we had five days left and a boatload of peaks from which to choose. A fabulous morning deteriorated into heavy snow and Tim going sick, but Dave and I reached a fantastic viewpoint (4,350m, 41°28'06.60" N, 77°31'50.01" E, F). We began to notice the approach of winter, with night temperatures dropping to -22°C.

With the return of good weather three of us decided on an ascent of the dominant peak. After a bivouac at 4,000m in biting cold and blowing spindrift, we started up an endless ridge. This led to at least four summits and an overhanging serac to traverse. The final slopes were endless, as we slogged through knee-deep snow and past a couple of unusual circular crevasses. It was 3 p.m. when we arrived on the

Looking south-southeast over Kyzyl Asker Glacier. (A) Pik Unmarked Soldier (5,352m). (B) Pik Vernyi (ca 5,250m). (C) Pik Panfilovski Division (5,290m). (1) North ridge (600m, TD+ Scottish 6, Crampton-Fyffe, 2002, repeated in 2003). (2) 2009 Krol- Sokołowski attempt. (3) Cztery Pory Roku (direct start). (4) No Shachlik (700m, 6c A3 M6, Christie-Gal-Gal-Gottefrey, 2010). (5) Belorussian-Russian Route (750m, Russian 6B, Bandelet-Malakhovskiy-Mikhailov-Nilov, 2009). (6) Original 1988 Soviet route—northwest face and south ridge. *Maria Gal*

summit (4,815m, 41°25'05.08" N, 77°41'34.15" E). We reversed the route and just finished the pinnacles when darkness fell. We stumbled down the remaining snow slopes under a full moon. It was a demanding day at AD+, but with another freezing bivouac, a bowl of cold pasta, and a tin of fish, it was overall ED, at least. We had promised to be down that evening, but the promise would be broken. Next morning Dave and Olec were relieved to see us; the tough old paratrooper and Spesnet soldier had tears in his eyes.

MARK WEEDING, *U.K.*

WESTERN KOKSHAAL-TOO

Sokolowski on pitch seven (M6). *Michel Krol*

Krol starting pitch nine. White static rope was left in 2009. *Andrzej Sokolowski*

*Pik Vernyi (5,250m), north summit, Cztery Pory Roku.* On August 13 and14 Andrzej Sokołowski and I established a new route on the north summit of Pik Vernyi. We had attempted this line in 2009, but near the end of the major difficulties, I was hit on the shoulder by a large chunk of ice that damaged ligaments.

In 2011 we traveled as before from Bishkek, but when seven km from base camp, the vehicle got stuck in a river. After extracting it the driver stated there was not enough fuel to go farther, so we lost a day carrying gear to base camp. After a rest we established an advanced base on the Kyzyl Asker Glacier and the next day climbed the first three pitches of our proposed line, to check conditions and acclimatize. The ice was good. We rappelled and returned to base.

Three days later we started up the face. An initial 120m, 50° icefield led to the face proper and the first ice runnel. In 2009 we had climbed more to the left, but now we were able to make a direct start. Two long pitches of WI4+ and 4 led to the first icefield. This was glassy and although only WI3 made our calves hurt by the time we'd reached the top. Here we rejoined the line of our 2009 attempt. A 30m pitch of WI3+ led to a chimney system. I led the next pitch and sweatily managed to reach the belay (M7 WI5).

Andrzej led the next pitch (M6). We chopped off the bolt belays here as they were partly covered in ice and damaged. Four pitches of WI4 and 5 took us to another small icefield. Down to the right we cut out a shelf and bivouacked, sitting in our sleeping bags. The night was starry and frosty, ideal weather.

Next day we climbed from the icefield (WI4) and reached an off-width, our high point of 2009. Andrzej was unable to lead the crack free, having to rest on a Camalot 6. There was no time to repeat the pitch, but we estimate this crux passage as M8- 1pa.

There were no more bolts from our previous attempt, but the climbing was easier. We climbed four pitches, up to M4 and UIAA IV+, to reach the crest of the north ridge and continued on easy ground. Below the north summit we ate and left most of our gear. We reached this foresummit (5,150-5,200m) with thick clouds forming and the sound of thunder. We were probably no more than half an hour of easy scrambling/walking from the true summit but, worried about lightning on this exposed crest, decided to skip it. We descended quickly to our gear and rappelled three successive 100m couloirs on the east face. At 11 p.m. we started down a steep, complex glacier and eventually reached advanced base.

We named the route Cztery Pory Roku (Four Seasons, M8- 1 rest point, WI5, UIAA IV+). The first 12 pitches have bolted belays. The sixth pitch has two bolts for protection, the seventh one, the eighth two, and the 13th a bolt and a piton. The weather was good throughout the expedition. It only snowed on two nights.

MICHEL KROL, *Poland*

*Editor's Note: This route lies on the north face, which drops 700m from north summit to glacier. It finishes via the upper section of the 2002 British route on the north ridge. The new line lies well left of the 2010 Swiss route, No Shachlik, and the 2009 Belorussian-Russian route, the latter incorrectly marked in AAJ 2011.*

East-facing Great Walls of China. Highest summit is on right. Arrow marks start of Border Control and Quantum of Solace. *Lindsay Griffin*

*Great Walls of China, east face, Quantum of Solace.* After two failed attempts with Wolfgang Russegger and Thomas Senf during our 2010 expedition to the southeast face of Kyzyl Asker (5,842m), I knew I'd go back. I would not have chosen the steep 1,200m line, with a variety of difficult ice and rock sections tried by many alpinists without success, were it not a real test of both my climbing skills and mental strength. But after a long winter trip to Scotland, months of endurance training, and a fast ascent of Mont Blanc, I felt perfectly prepared for the endeavor.

Spot the line. Initial section of Quantum of Solace. Iced chimney visible farthest top left is taken by Border Control. *Ines Papert*

Papert transfers from hard mixed to hanging ice on Quantum of Solace. *Ines Papert Collection*

On lower section of Quantum of Solace. *Ines Papert*

On our trip through Kyrgyzstan to base camp, I was accompanied by my 11-year-old son Emanuel. We lived modestly with nomads for several weeks, which was such a fulfilling experience. My friends Wolfgang Kurz and photographer Franz Walter accompanied us on our travels. Exploring Kyrgyzstan while riding on a horse with my son was a wonderful, intense experience.

In my luggage I brought a paraglider, flying recently having become a new passion. Getting a bird's eye view of the landscape, after climbing a mountain, and peacefully gliding down to the valley like a soaring bird is a wonderful combination. Wolfi and I climbed many mountains just so we could paraglide and land in front of our yurt camp.

We met my climbing partners, Charly Fritzer and Wolfgang Russegger, at the start of September. Already acclimatized, I was euphoric when they arrived, due to the joy of seeing them plus the anticipation of climbing the mountain.

Just before reaching base camp our enthusiasm came to a halt when our truck got stuck in swamps for several days. Intense rainfall had soaked the tracks, and there was no possibility of continuing our ride. Twenty km and 1,000m of altitude separated us from our proposed base camp site below Kyzyl Asker. Transporting our gear to the base of the mountain on foot would be an enormous challenge, but at the last minute our driver managed to free the truck. Wolfi and Franz left with my son; the pain of parting was almost unbearable. It's a pain that normally fades when the task at hand begins, but I was condemned to idleness.

My two partners became sick at camp. At an altitude of 4,000m and with the cold preventing a speedy recovery, we began the tiresome job of transporting material to advanced base. It took 10 days.

A weather check with Karl Gabl in Innsbruck promised a few days of stable high pressure, so at 4 a.m. on September 12 we began our ascent of the steep ice route. At 10 a.m., at nearly 5,300m, we reached the only feasible bivouac site. With the sun starting to melt the ice and the threat of severe ice fall, we decided to wait till the following morning, but when Charly showed signs of cerebral edema onset, we rappelled immediately.

He recovered at advanced base, but with health problems weakening the whole team, I had to accept that another attempt on the mountain of my dreams was not practicable. Should we quit and go home? No! We looked for an alternative, a reward for all our efforts. We found solace on the Great Walls of China, which rise 600m from the unnamed glacier south of Kyzyl Asker. There we discovered a very steep ice line. Wolfi and I began at first light. Steep and overhanging sections of ice and rock, with tricky protection, required all my psychological strength and climbing skills. Fragile ice pillars, overhanging rock/mixed sections alternated with waist-deep powder, where we found little stability. With great concentration I reached the crest of the watershed ridge shortly after 11 a.m. Satisfied, I belayed Wolfi, who emerged smiling. We named our route Quantum of Solace (14 pitches, WI7+ M7).

On the 29th, just before the onset of winter, the truck reached us. We drove back to civilization through a fierce snowstorm, back to a long-awaited warm shower. Franz Walter made a film of our trip to base camp: Tyndýk, Reise durch Kirgistan. See tyndyk.com for background information and trailers.

INES PAPERT, *Germany, ines-papert.de*

*Editor's note: The highest point of the Great Walls, 5,186m, is its northernmost summit. The only previ-ous route climbed on the east face is Border Control (13 pitches, ED2, WI5 Scottish VII/VIII mixed, A1, Robertson-Tresidder, 2004; see AAJ 2005). This lies on the more southerly, lower section of the walls, following a steep, icy chimney and two snow patches to the end of the hard climbing, where the pair termi-nated the route just below the watershed ridge. It was dark, they had dropped their water at the base of the climb, they had no stove, and the main summit on this section of the Walls was a long way up to the left.*

*Quantum of Solace, which reached the ridge, starts up the same initial snow slopes as Border Control but then takes a recessed line to the right, facing more or less east. Border Control faces more northeast. The prize of reaching one of the main summits of the Great Walls awaits future parties.*

*Pik Oleg (4,859m), Arbuz; Pik Byeliy (5,697m), south ridge; other ascents and ski descents.* Our group of eight was inspired by photographs provided by Paul Knott, who visited this area in 2005 (*AAJ 2006*). We had a variety of ideas of peaks to attempt and ski descents to make around the heads of the Kotur and Fersmana Glaciers. We allowed 24 days for the round trip from Slovenia, which gave little margin for error. We ended up having an adventure beyond our expectations.

The team, comprising climbers with a wide variety of age and experience, had multiple aims: to give younger members their first experience of higher altitude glaciers and mountains, to ski from summits up to 5,000m, to climb new routes up to 5,000m,

Morning sun strikes camp on 4,900m col south of Byeliy. Slovenian route follows snow and ice through buttress/ridge facing camera, over capping seracs, and left up easier snow slopes to summit. In 2000 Americans, approaching from China, attempted left ridge, completing rock section before thunderstorm forced them down from snow arête 200m below summit. *Blaz Grapar*

and to make the first ascent of Pik Byeliy, the highest unclimbed independent summit in the Western Kokshaal-too.

Deciding not to use porters, we took only a driver and cook, who would remain at base camp. We left Bishkek on July 17 and next day reached 3,500m, before being stopped by a 30-hour snowstorm. When this cleared, our Ural truck got stuck in mud, and we spent the best part of two days digging it out. It was only on the 22nd that we set up base camp north of the Kotur Glacier, already acclimatized to altitudes over 4,000m.

Next day Peter Bajec, Ursa Erman, Alenka Klemencic, Miha Lapanja, and Tina Leskosek climbed Pik Alpini (4,578m), on the east side of the entrance to the Kotur, and continued south

Pik Byeliy from southeast. Slovenian ascent on south ridge marked. (G) Gully seen from below in another photo accompanying this report. (H) Highpoint of 2008 Slovenian attempt. Southwest ridge (left skyline) was attempted in 2000 by Americans. *Paul Knott*

to Pik Lvitsa (4,631m). Klemecic and Lapanja skied from the summit. In the meantime I suffered a slipped disc, reducing our experienced climbers to two: Tadej Golob and Blaz Grapar. They ascended easy Pik Lyev (4,710m) and slept on the summit for acclimatization.

With this first phase complete, Klemencic and Lapanja walked to the next glacier system east, the Nalivkin, and set up camp below the east flank of Pik Obzhorny (5,156m). At the same time Bajec, Erman, and Leskosek skied up the Kotur to camp on the west side of Obzhorny. Over the next few days various members from both parties made ascents, and often ski descents, of Pik Greta (4,725m), Pik Lencka (4,621m), Pik Oleg by a likely new route dubbed Arbuz (450m, 60°), and Pik Obzhorny. They returned to base camp at around the same time that Golob and Grapar completed a taxing two-day, 30km walk (with 2,000m of height gain), east along the top of the range and then south up the arduous Fersmana Glacier to the Chinese border.

Approaching gully and serac barrier on south ridge of Byeliy. *Blaz Grapar*

On the 27th Golob and Grapar camped at 4,900m on the frontier ridge, at the col immediately south of Byeliy. Next day they completed the line up the south ridge attempted by a Slovenian expedition in 2008 (*AAJ 2009*). Although much of the terrain was straightforward (they only belayed two pitches), there was a significant amount of climbing beneath a large serac barrier. The 600m Slovenian Route was graded V/4.

Bad weather then settled on the range, and despite one or two attempts, the only subsequent successful ascent was another (and ski descent) of Pik Alpini. However, in brief gaps of sunshine the team did find excellent bouldering, before packing the six-wheel truck on August 3 and leaving for Bishkek.

Few parties have operated on Fersmana Glacier but Slovenians discovered large pile of inexcusably abandoned rubbish (also found and photographed by 2009 Polish team). *Blaz Grapar*

It turned out that our forced acclimatization at 3,500m during the drive to the mountains positively influenced subsequent activities above base camp. In addition we found snowshoes better suited than skis for reaching more serious climbs. We thank Turkish Airlines for flights and special treatment of our skis and acknowledge the efficiency and kindness of ITMC staff: Margarita, for solving organizational problems; Andrey, for excellent driving; and Tanya, for being the best expedition cook. We are indebted to Gregor Sluga and Janez Toni for weather forecasts.

BLAZ STRES, *Slovenia*

*Editor's note: The 2008 Slovenian high point on Byeliy was lower than inferred in AAJ 2009. It is indicated on the photo accompanying this report. Also, there now appears to be doubt as to whether this expedition reached the summit of Pik Plaza (4,912m).*

*Pik Eggemenduluk (5,210m), northeast face and north ridge; 28 Hours Later and Brothers Chechel; Pik Lyell (4,864m), east flank, Ambitious but Rubbish; Pik Georgina (4,631m) east flank; Pik Annika (4,685m), east flank.* In 2009 Edward Lemon and I formed part of a team that was the first to venture to the lower Sarychat Glacier. Problems with the drop-off location reduced our stay to only two days of climbing. We managed ascents of a number of minor peaks (*AAJ 2010*), but the major summit of the Sarychat, referred to as Fers III by the 2007 Slovenian expedition, was too big a challenge with the limited time. So in 2011, with support from the Mount Everest Foundation, we returned.

Pik Eggemenduluk showing routes followed on first ascent. Left-hand line is 28 Hours Later. Apparent peak in background lies on Kyrgyz-Chinese border but is actually a northerly shoulder of a higher summit entirely in China. Summit to right, on ridge north of Eggemenduluk, is unclimbed. *Gareth Mottram*

This time border posts and drop-off provided little drama, and we shared a beer with the Slovenian expedition that made the first ascent of Pik Byeliy. Our initial challenge was one of our team, Charlie Evans, becoming ill from drinking too much water, in an attempt to avoid AMS.

Charlie Evans starting last technical pitch (M5 and AI4) above 5,000m. *Edward Lemon*

Reaching the upper section of the Sarychat for my second time, we discovered that crevasses in the icefall had extended down the glacier several hundred meters, obstructing our access to Cwm Arwyn and high camp location. We found a way through, but it took more than two hours to negotiate the maze.

We warmed up with a second ascent of Pik Lyell, by a new route on the east flank. We named it Ambitious but Rubbish (600m, Scottish II/III), because we were hoping to use it to access Sentinel Peak on the Sarychat-Fersmana divide. On reaching the ridge we discovered the crest liberally strewn with tottering spires of shale and decided not to venture further.

Charlie Evans traversing north ridge toward summit headwall. Sarychat Glacier down to right. Peaks of Borkoldoy Range in distance. *Edward Lemon*

At 4 a.m. on August 5 we set off from high camp for the base of Fers III, where we split into two pairs, Evans with Lemon and I with Hannes Granberg, our Swedish undergraduate medic. Both teams progressed well, climbing opposite sides of a 400m ice ramp on the northeast facet. At the level of the main ridge (ca 5,000m) an overhanging 30m rock step impeded progress. Both teams passed it on the left via a descending traverse to a system of mixed gullies and ledges, which led to the ridge. This section provided the technical crux of the route, with several steps of M5 and AI4 split by narrow ledges strewn with large loose blocks. The final 300m was the same for both parties, the headwall of the summit ridge rising to 60-65° snow. From the top we reversed the route. Part way down the face, after 20 hours of climbing, ropes became stuck and had to be cut. Both teams arrived in high camp 28 hours after leaving. This led to Granberg and I naming our route 28 Hours Later, while Evans and Lemon named theirs for smoked cheese Evans carried for summit celebrations: Brothers Chechel.

We provisionally graded both routes ED1. Obligatory difficulties rated an alpine TD, but the route was remote and committing, with loose rock and the crux pitches high on the mountain. We have suggested the peak be named Eggemenduluk (which translates as freedom or independence), in honor of the August 2011 20th anniversary of Kyrgyz independence.

The major climbing phase of our expedition ended at this point, though Hannes and I climbed small peaks on the plateau above base camp, reaching Piks 4,631m and 4,685m (both PD- and located near 41°06' N, 77°31' E). We provisionally named these after our understanding girlfriends, Georgina and Annika. We reported our ascents and the provisional peak names to the Kyrgyz Alpine Club.

GARETH MOTTRAM, *U.K.*

Richard Tremellen views route ahead, south along crest to Pik Emma. He is standing on Point 4,769m, almost a summit itself, crossed en route to Emma. Pik 5,318m just off picture to left. *Alex Brighton*

DJANGART RANGE

*Pik Emma (4,783m map, 4,803m GPS), north ridge; Pik Laetitia (4,940m map, 4,952m GPS), southwest couloir and northwest face; Pik 5,318m, west face attempt.* Inspired by the 2010 Anglo-American expedition (*AAJ 2011*), Richard Tremellen and I set off in July for the remarkably unexplored Djangart region. The highest summit, Pik 5,318m, presented the most obvious goal. Alas, it remains unclimbed. However, we made two first ascents and are richer for the experience of an expedition of this nature. The unknown presented as much of a challenge as anything we faced on the mountains.

Unable to arrange horses to carry over the Djangart Pass, we set up base camp in the Kaichi Valley, two arduous days' walking from the highest mountains. Time on these peaks was limited, as we could not carry supplies for anything more than alpine-style ascents from base camp.

Our first objective was Pik 4,783, which lay above the entry to the eastern Akoguz Glacier, immediately west of Pik 5,318m. We were attracted by the possibility of a summit view toward our intended route on 5,318m, and that 5,318 formed part of a long

Pik Laetitia from west with first ascent route. *Alex Brighton*

ridge with no previous ascents of any of its summits. Though the approach to the ridge via the northwest rib was tiresome, due to poor rock (we climbed the flank of Pik 4,561m, without going to its top), the north ridge of the peak itself had a beautiful ambience, and provided interesting, though never difficult, climbing. The ridge began as a broad, gentle crest but narrowed and steepened as we moved south. Soft snow forced us to bivouac several hundred meters short of the summit, but we didn't mind spending the night in such a spectacular location. The final hour of climbing the next morning (July 22) presented mixed ground, a heavily corniced ridge, and a beautiful summit. In the prevailing conditions the grade was around AD. We named the summit Pik Emma (41.69426° N, 78.92930° E) and descended a rather dangerous gully on the west face.

Pik 5,318m from summit of Pik Emma. Left skyline is north ridge, which team planned to gain just left of foresummit. *Alex Brighton*

After a rest at base camp and an attempt at Pik 4,940m (see

Unclimbed Pik 5,041m, between the Kaichi Valley and N7 Glacier, seen from Kaichi to west. *Alex Brighton*

Richard Tremellen making steep traverse at couloir exit on the Phoenix, Pik Laetitia. *Alex Brighton*

Unnamed and unclimbed peak on west side of Kaichi Valley. *Alex Brighton*

below), we returned over the Djangart Pass, taking two days to reach the west side of Pik 5,318m, the trek over the moraines of the N1 Glacier alone taking seven torturous hours. We had taken supplies for only six days, so it was a great disappointment when our first 36 hours were spent in a cramped bivouac, watching snow pour down. With a slight clearing on our fourth day, we edged higher by means of a rock rib, in order to make a bid for the summit once the snow consolidated. The rib proved easy up to 4,750m, where a 60m snowfield separated us from another safe rib. We tentatively moved onto it, but our luck was out. Cracking of the surrounding snow stopped us. There was no need for discussion; this was the end of the climb. Pik 5,318m is achievable; the climbing as far as our high point had not been difficult, and it appeared, given good conditions, to be relatively straightforward above.

A peak that had caught our eye on our first day in the Kaichi Valley was not marked on the map, other than a tiny ring of contours reaching 4,940m on the watershed between the Kaichi Valley and N7 Glacier. Striking in appearance, it became our final project. Attempting a one-day push on July 26, via the southwest couloir and northwest face, we had met soft snow on the summit structure and bivouacked with no gear at 4,650m. We hoped to complete the ascent next morning, but a snow storm forced descent.

However, our August 5 attempt proved successful. The route began by ascending an increasingly steep snow and ice couloir in the most spectacular mountain setting. Above lay a long traverse over 70° ice, the first difficulty of a fantastic route. This was followed by a 100m step of sound rock, at UIAA III/IV, giving access to the summit block. It looked like this final section would go easily, but we were wrong. Two hundred meters of Scottish 5 and 80° mixed terrain led to the top. We named the peak Laetitia (41.64860° N, 78.81608° E) and the route the Phoenix (1,300m, TD), due to it being completed after an initial failure.

During the return home we wondered whether climbing alpine style, as we did, was the most suitable. Our attempt on Point 5,318m, for example, couldn't allow a 36-hour snow storm plus time for consolidation. However, alpine style did allow time for three other climbs, whereas a siege on one objective would not. Either way, our advice to anyone planning a similar expedition would be to expect the unexpected, be flexible, keep on smiling, and you might come home with something to show for it.

For more information visit Djangart Ascents Kyrgyzstan on Facebook.

ALEX BRIGHTON, *U.K.*

*Rakhmat (5,144m), north face and northeast ridge; Pik 4,887m, west face and south ridge; Tushunbodum (5,081m), north face.* Armed with much useful information provided by Mike Royer after his expedition to the region in 2010 (*AAJ 2011*), we traveled from Mallorca to Bishkek, arriving July 14. Two days later we started our long road trip to the mountains in the company of Alex Brighton and Richard Tremellen, with whom we would share base camp. The 25-year-old truck did not run well, and despite heroic efforts by our driver, there were many stops, and the trip took three days. On the 18th we arrived in the Kaichi Valley, and set up base camp at Sary Say, where a group of geologists, exploring for minerals, was also camped. We had wanted base camp in the Djangart Valley, but the truck could not cross the Djangart Pass, and the nomads asked for more money than the four of us had to carry our equipment on horses. As a result we had to walk an extra day each way when climbing our chosen mountains.

Pik 4,887m south summit, with route up west couloir and south ridge. *Tomeu Rubi*

Rakhmat, with ascent route up northeast ridge (left) and descent on west face and northwest flank. *Tomeu Rubi*

Our first trip was to the Djangartynbashi, a glacier with three branches. We ascended the eastern branch and on the 24th made the first ascent of Rakhmat (Kyrgyz for Thanks). After 200m of ice climbing on the north face (65°), we reached the northeast ridge. The first 200m on the crest was mixed, with isolated rock steps of UIAA IV, and a short, narrow, crux couloir of M4. The

North face of Tushunbodum. *Tomeu Rubi*

upper 300m was a snow arête at 55°. The ascent took eight hours, and we named the route Piolets Customitzats i Botes Banyades (Customized Ice Axes and Wet Boots, 700m, D, IV M4 65°), due to the transformations suffered by our axes over the years and the state of our boots after the climb. We descended west. Three rappels and a 100m traverse took us to a col, from where we downclimbed glaciated slopes northwest, regaining our high camp after four and a half hours.

After a few days rest at base camp, we again headed over the Djangart Pass and turned immediately south up the N7 Glacier. We camped the night of the 28th in a place with a good view of our next objective, Pik 5,081m. There appeared to be an obvious route, but we got a surprise next day when, after climbing an easy west-facing couloir, we reached the south ridge and discovered it

Tomeu Rubi (left) and Cati Llado on south summit of Pik 4,887m. Behind is north face of Tushunbodum. After climb of this face, pair descended northwest ridge, which faces camera. *Cati Llado*

Cati Llado on lower northeast ridge of Rakhmat. Below is junction of main eastern Djangartynbashi and subsidiary branch rising southeast to Pik 4,781m on Chinese border. Directly above Llado is Pik 4,952m, and to right, Pik 4,971m. Behind and to left is snowy Pik 5,291m. All are unclimbed. *Tomeu Rubi*

was not as we had imagined. We had to traverse back onto the west face and climb two hard vertical pitches of 6b and A1. This took us back to the crest, which was snow, but led—another surprise—to a summit northeast of our objective. The top (4,887m on the map) was a horizontal snow ridge with three small peaks. We stopped at the first—the south summit. The farthest (northeast) is probably a little higher. We named the 550m route He Perdut el Guant i les Forces (I Lost My Glove and Motivation).

During the climb we saw a good, though pushy, line on the north face of Pik 5,081m but needed to access it from the Djangartynbashi. After a few more rest days in base camp, we reached the lower central Djangartynbashi Glacier. The first 200m of the face was 65°, with short sections of 75°, and we moved together. At 4,600m we reached a 150m icefall that we climbed in three pitches of WI4. The second had an eight-m section of very thin ice and was impossible to protect. Above the icefall three pitches of mixed climbing did not allow us to relax. The last 200m on the northeast ridge was not as straightforward as expected. A cornice circled the top of the mountain, reaching to the south ridge. We found a weakness and spent 20 minutes digging through it. We emerged at the summit after 10½ hours of climbing, naming the route Si la Cornisa Vol (650m, TD+, UIAA IV+ M5 85°). It took four and a half hours to descend the northwest ridge.

We named this summit Tushunbodum (I Don't Understand You in Kyrgyz). One of us tried using this word when talking with a Kyrgyz man who offered us bread and tea in his yurt during our journey into the mountains. He laughed and repeated the word all evening.

CATI LLADO AND TOMEU RUBI, *Mallorca, Spain*

Pik Alexandra. Route of first ascent took skyline ridge. Bivouac marked. *Kristoffer Szilas*

*Pik Alexandra (5,290m), Pik Pernille (5,190m), Pik Lea (4,950m), Pik Kathryn (4,885m).* Our seven-man team was inspired to visit the Djangart region after reading a report in *AAJ 2011* by the Anglo-American expedition that climbed in the western part during 2010. We were six Danes (Sune Buur, Carsten Cooper-Jensen, Jakob Fisker, Anders Hedeager Pedersen, Simon

Lund Jensen, and I) and one British, Jim Broomhead. We explored the area from July 17 to August 3 [*Editor's note: This group of mountains on the Chinese border is split into three sectors. The western is referred to as Kaichi, the central as Djangart, and the eastern as Sauktor. While a Russian expedition inspected the Sauktor area in 2008, they did no climbing.*]

To save time and to reach the previously unclimbed-in eastern area, we chartered an old Russian helicopter to fly us to base camp. However, on our first day in the valley, it looked as though we would not be going anywhere: the gas canisters, essential for melting snow on the mountain, had not been loaded on the helicopter. We then discovered that our satellite phone was not working.

This remote region has been visited less than a handful of times, yet amazingly, the very next day a family from Moscow trekked through our base camp. They had a working satellite phone, called the helicopter company, and requested it to deliver the missing gas, thereby saving the expedition.

We split into three teams and explored four glacier basins. Jim and I made the first ascent of a 5,290m summit above the west side of the Chulaktor Glacier. We climbed the 700m east ridge over two days, with a night out at 5,000m. The lower section featured sound granite, with climbing to 5.4, while the upper section gave snow and ice up to 70°. We named the mountain Pik Alexandra and the route (rated D) Bivouac—French for Mistake.

We then hiked 15km west into the neighbouring N2 valley to attempt

Pik Alexandra from east, with route of first ascent and bivouac. *Kristoffer Szilas*

Pik Pernille from south, with route of first ascent. *Kristoffer Szilas*

Pik Lea from southwest, with route of first ascent. *Kristoffer Szilas*

the east face of Pik 5,318m, the highest summit in the range and unclimbed. This aspect of the mountain presents a serious technical challenge, with a 500m vertical wall of good granite leading to 1,000m of ice and mixed. It was too hard for us with the gear we carried, and the weather was too warm. Peak 5,318m has now been the goal of four expeditions.

We returned to base camp and climbed a 4,950m peak visible to the east, naming it Pik Lea. The 500m route on the southwest face, named Mermaid, gave tricky Scottish-style climbing in mostly white-out

Pik Kathryn from northeast, with route of first ascent. *Kristoffer Szilas*

conditions (D, M4 and 70°). While we had found Chamonix-style granite on Alexandra, Lea was poor marble. On our way down the sun came out and started to warm the face. We soon found ourselves downclimbing a dangerous avalanche trap. We were hit several times, but luckily on steep ice slopes where we could place solid screws. We were not swept off the peak and made it safely down to base camp, reuniting with the rest of the team. Carsten and Simon had made the first ascent of Pik Kathryn, west of the Kichik Sauktor Glacier, via a line on the icy northeast face they named Russian Roulette (700m, AD, 60°). Sune, Jakob, and Anders climbed Pik Pernille, east of the Kichik Sauktor, from the south via Waiting for the Tide (700m, AD, 55°). Members also made unsuccessful attempts on two border peaks, 5,112m and 5,025m, at the head of the Kichik Sauktor.

Jim Broomhead on upper ridge of Pik Alexandra. Behind is frontier ridge. In distance is broad-topped Pik 5,112m. Closer lie Pik 5,025m, Pik 4,801m and, nearest, snowy pyramid of Pik 4,881m. All unclimbed. *Kristoffer Szilas*

We found late July to be too hot. Glacier surfaces failed to freeze, even at night, and we often sank up to our hips when breaking trail. This area, and in particular an attempt on Pik 5,318m, would probably be better in September or even October. Nevertheless, we managed four first ascents in a remote region of the world and had a real adventure. What more could you ask?

KRISTOFFER SZILAS, *Denmark*

TENGRI TAG

*Pik Prezhevalskogo (6,240m), north face.* Boris Dedeshko and I reached the North Inylchek Glacier on foot from Bayancol with all our gear. Our goal was the north face of Pik Prezhevalskogo, which lies up a side branch of the main glacier. The peak was climbed twice in 1974 but never since, while the north face, a noted objective, had been attempted at least once. Using snowshoes it took 15 hours from the standard base camp to the foot of the 1,480m wall.

At 3 a.m. on July 23 we started up the face following the central couloir and climbed 21 pitches by the end of the day. Next morning was misty and, after climbing two more ice pitches, we reached the foot of the large triangular rocky headwall, where we started to work right, following a prominent mixed ramp through the triangle. The rock was shattered with only superficial cracks, but the day was warm, and we often climbed bare-handed. By the second night we had climbed a further five and a half pitches, with difficulties of 5b-6a and M4. There was no platform big enough to pitch the tent on, so we had to sit. Fortunately the night was warm.

We began the third day with the technical crux, directly above our bivouac site. We free-climbed for 15m to a large bulge and used aid for another 15m in a reasonable crack. Difficulties were 6b M5 A2. We then traversed right, at around M4, and by the day's end had completed six pitches when we spotted a good place to pitch the tent. Boris, seeing I was tired, excavated the site and collected ice for melting.

Next morning the weather was still fine. We climbed three pitches and exited the triangular headwall onto the ridge, where we left our packs and climbed 400m of easy snow to the summit, arriving at midday. There were clouds in the west but not the threatening sort. We descended west and reached a saddle, where we camped for the night. We then went down to the north and, unable to locate a possible ice couloir, made 14 rappels of 30m on rock. We reached our cached supply of food and fuel that evening and on the 27th regained the standard North Inylchek base camp.

DENIS URUBKO, *Kazakhstan, supplied by Anna Piunova, mountain.ru*

Kazakh route on north face of Pik Prezhevalskogo. *Denis Urubko Collection*

*Pik Pobeda (7,439m), north face, Dollar Rod.* After our ascent of Przhevalskogo, the plan was for Boris Dedeshko and I to traverse over Khan Tengri (6,995m) to the South Inylchek Glacier, where Gennadiy Durov would be waiting for us. From there we would attempt a new line on the north face of Pik Pobeda. Gennadiy, a guide, was acclimatized, having already climbed Khan Tengri twice during the season and slept at 6,400m. For Boris and me 6,240m Przhevalskogo was not enough.

Boris and I reached Camp 2 on Khan Tengri's normal route from the north. There Boris became ill, and he descended to

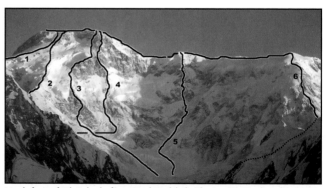

North face of Pik Pobeda from South Inylchek Glacier. (1) Northeast Face (5B, Zuravliov, 1990). (2) Original route (5B, Abalakov, 1956). (3) Dollar Route (5B, Smirnov, 1982). (4) Dollar Rod (6B). (5) Camel Buttress (6B, Gorelik-Sokolov, 2009). (6) Normal route (north spur to west ridge over 6,918m Pobeda West, 5B, Medzmariashvilli, 1961). *Denis Urubko*

Durov high on Dollar Rod, north face of Pobeda. *Denis Urubko*

Durov during the evening descent of Pobeda toward west summit. *Denis Urubko*

base camp to catch a helicopter out of the area. I continued alone, reached the summit, and camped 12m below. Next day I descended the normal southern route and met Gennadiy at South Inychek base camp, where we spent four days playing cards and eating from others' tables. We got up at 6 a.m. on August 10 and left for Pobeda.

In 1982 a Kazakh team, led by Vladimir Smirnov, climbed the Dollar Route on the north face [erroneously reported as 1986 in previous *AAJs*]. We suspect they created this route as a reaction to the Soviet expedition to Everest that year, snubbing their noses at the Himalayan climbers. A direct route up the face to the right had been on the radar of climbers since that time, and I had dreamed of completing it since 1993.

Using snowshoes Gennadiy and I climbed the Abalakov Route to 5,000m, then moved left to a snow terrace, expecting to traverse right next morning toward our proposed line. Unsurprisingly for this region, a strong snowstorm arrived after dinner, avalanches roared past on nearby slopes, and almost in a panic we ran back to the edge of the Pedestal, expecting to be swept away. The storm dropped 60cm of fresh snow. If the bottom part of the route had been less avalanche-prone, we would have returned to base camp with pleasure. However, next day the storm subsided, and we broke trail upward to our planned camp below the seracs, where we spent a leisurely day in the sun.

Late that night we ran on snowshoes under the seracs and avalanche-strewn slopes and then quickly gained height. The fact that nothing fell on us I can only attribute to divine intervention. We climbed four pitches and simul-climbed at least 800m.

We reached the first rock buttress, which we climbed for four pitches (5b-6a), then chopped out a tent site. Next day we completed the final pitch (M4) and mostly simul-climbed hard snow slopes above. We had enough confidence in our partnership that we belayed only five or six times, eventually reaching the left side of a rock rib we dubbed the Mast. At this point we swapped packs. Gennidiy, who had been following with the pack containing all our bivouac gear, now took over and climbed confidently on difficult terrain. At times I could hardly keep up and cursed my old age; he has 10 years advantage. We stopped a little early to dry our gear in the setting sun.

The following morning, after four pitches, we arrived at the foot of a rock wall. To the left it overhung, while directly above rose a beautiful buttress, which we climbed via two serious pitches (6a M4), emerging onto the upper slopes. While we could have easily traversed left to the Dollar Route, we pursued an independent finish and simul-climbed snow interspersed with rocky sections, where we occasionally belayed, for 800m to a final, unexpected, rock wall. Two pitches (5c and 5b), followed by 150m of easy snow and rock, led to the summit ridge.

We left our packs and in cloudy weather reached the top a little after 7 p.m. We were so exhausted and frozen that our only desire was to go down, and our mood was similar to the gray evening. But during the descent the sun suddenly exploded along the horizon, and the world at our feet was bathed in a golden, curling light. We inhaled new strength and by 11 p.m. had reached the west summit and tents of climbers on the normal route. Next day, August 16, we descended the normal route and were in base camp at 1:30 p.m. We called our new line Dollar Rod (2,500m, 3,200m above base camp, 6a M4-M5 WI2).

DENIS URUBKO, *Kazakhstan, supplied by Anna Piunova, mountain.ru*

*Editor's note: While the technical difficulties of the serious Dollar Rod are concentrated in the three rock barriers, much of the upper section features unprotected climbing. Bivouacs were made at 5,000m, 5,100m, 5,250m, 5,900m, and 6,700m during the ascent and at 6,900m on the descent. Urubko feels that due to its high latitude (it is the world's northernmost 7,000m peak) an ascent of Pobeda is similar to climbing close to 8,000m in the Himalaya. The route was one of six nominated for a 2012 Piolets d'Or.*

*Khan Tengri (6,995m), southeast ridge integral.* Looking through descriptions of routes on Khan Tengri, we two were surprised to find that the southeast ridge, the longest of the four ridges of this fine pyramid, was still unclimbed. Had no one tried this logical, alluring line?

The ridge had been climbed in parts in the early 1970s. In 1970 Bozhukov (leader), Kurochkin, Nevorotin, Soustin, and Zakharov climbed Pik Zholak-Too at the end of the ridge and traversed north along the "saw." On the second step a cornice collapse sent three climbers falling more than 500m, though they escaped with their lives. The remaining climbers retreated. Three years later the Uzbek Soviet Socialist Republic national team, 10 climbers led by Voronin, reached the crest at a point close to where Bozhukov had turned back. Starting on August 14 they completed the remaining ridge, reaching the summit on the 26th. No one had attempted this ridge since nor tried to complete Bozhukov's dream. We were attracted by this project, particularly because in 2010 we'd traversed Pik Communism (7,495m).

We arrived at South Inchek base camp in late July and at 5 p.m. on the 29th headed toward the start of our route. Next day we spent several hours watching stonefall in the crumbling rocky couloir leading to the top of Zholak-Too, trying to figure out the safest route. The ascent proved unexpectedly long, and we didn't reach Zholak-Too until midday on August 1. We then had to traverse the endless "saw." The first two days were demoralizing, as we didn't seem to be making progress. The traverse was spectacular and technically varied. We had to negotiate huge cornices, a knife edge, and two big rocky gendarmes and had to cross a glaciated slope with unreliable snow bridges. It took us more than six days to cover 3,000m along this ridge, which rose from 4,480m to 5,300m.

We spent the next six days traversing 2,300m of crest, to 6,250m, following the route pioneered by Voronin. The

Khan Tengri from Inylchek Glacier. Southeast ridge is right skyline, while Normal route follows glaciated slopes to col on left side of picture, then up skyline (west) ridge. Toward top of southeast ridge pair traversed left below ragged capping seracs until finding a break about midway. *Andrej Magajne*

Foreshortened view along ridge to summit. *Supplied by Anna Piunova*

weather was unstable, hampering progress, and on the 11th we were forced to remain in the tent the entire day. On other days we completed only two or three pitches. In places the ridge widened, and we moved together, but cornices became bigger, and we encountered crevasses and seracs.

Starting on the 12th we had three days of calm, warm weather. The final part of the ridge, which took a further seven days, began with a snow plateau and a rocky rib, leading to overhanging ice walls. The rib was marble, at 30-35°. We had to keep to the ice on the flanks, as it was impossible to safely belay on the crest. Dare we say it was fun? The next three days unstable weather again confined us to the tent for long periods. Near the top a three-m overhang on an icewall, leading to 60-70° ice and névé, provided the crux. Finally we reached the summit, but where was the cairn? We had to descend 50m to the first rocks to find the cherished metal tripod. It was 3 p.m. on August 19.

While the ascent of the complete southeast ridge was difficult (6A), the normal descent to the south is dangerous, despite the ridge to the col being completely fixed. Our food and fuel gone, we made drinking water by melting snow under our armpits. We barely reached the col on the 20th, and, although we'd hoped to descend to the standard Camp 1 the following day, bad weather intervened once more. Having to break trail, we only got to Camp 2. Next day we kept to the left side of the glacier, as it was safer, and erected our tent, in the dark, close to Camp 1. Normally it would take a couple of hours from there to base camp, but we didn't arrive until 5:00 the following afternoon. Fortunately, next day people were leaving, and we hitched a ride in a helicopter.

ALEKSEY IVANOV AND VLADIMIR PETLITSKY, *Russia, supplied by Anna Piunova, mountain.ru, and William Smitt, translated by Ekaterina Vorotnikova*

*Editor's note. From July 22 to August 20, 2010, the pair made an unsupported southeast-northwest crossing of Pik Communism (7,495m). They made a long approach from the south, over the Kashalayak Pass (4,281m), along the Fedchenko and Bivachny Glaciers, to the southeast side of the mountain. From there they followed the 1961 Tamm Route across the southern flanks of the southeast ridg. From the summit they descended the classic 1968 Barodkin Route to the Moskvina base camp. Total distance covered was ca 120km, and the initial weights of their rucksacks were 43kg each.*

*Paradoxically the two Russians are not considered "alpinists." In the Russian ranking lists they are "mountaineering hikers," and hence this and their Communism traverse were not registered with the Russian Mountaineering Federation.*

# *Afghanistan*

*The online version of these reports frequently contains additional photos, maps, topos, and extended text. Please visit aaj.americanalpineclub.org*

### Koh-i-Baba Mountains

Ibex Horn from north, with ascent route and bivouac site. (A) Ibex Ear East. (B) Ibex Ear West. *Mike Libecki*

*Ibex Horn, west face–north face.* In 2010 I went to the Koh-e-Baba to explore cool-looking rock towers. Though I was able to reach two summits, East and West Ibex Ears, I was denied my goal of reaching the prominent tower in the group, the Ibex Horn, and just missed being crushed by massive rockfall (*AAJ 2011*).

Redemption. In early July 2011 I flew to Bamyan and met the same friends as the previous year. In three days I was back at base camp, almost one year to the day after the rockfall incident. I'd tried two routes in 2010, on the north and west sides. Even when I was back home, I felt many strange emotions about how close I had been to death. My goal this time was to find the fastest and safest route to the summit, if such a way existed.

In 2010 I'd climbed a couloir system to the East Ear, which is connected to the ridgeline of the Ibex Horn. From this high vantage point, I saw good systems on the west side that would make a great route. It proved to be really nice. I took a couple of ropes and a rock rack and started up the couloir. There was fun climbing for 1,200', steep enough that any fall would prove disastrous, but solid conditions brought me to the stone. I left my ropes and rack and went back to base

Bivouac site on Ibex Horn. *Mike Libecki*

camp. The following day I brought up bivouac gear to my high point, and where the ice ended, I rope-soloed two pitches and bivouacked.

Next day I set off for the summit, climbing two more pitches and traversing left and north to another couloir, which went up for 400'. I found myself on easy terrain, traversing a ridge toward the summit using a combo of conventional and continuous-loop rope-soloing. I stood on top by late afternoon, having climbed a 2,500' route at V 5.9 A1 WI2.

I had to rope-solo the descent, eventually rappelling to my bivouac spot, where I spent another night. It was my third attempt on the summit, and as the saying goes, "third time's a charm." I went back to Kabul as fast as possible and bought a plane ticket to Urumqi, China, looking forward to more adventure.

MIKE LIBECKI, *AAC*

HINDU KUSH

*Introduction/Overview.* Two expeditions are known to have climbed 7,492m Noshaq by the "normal route" up the west ridge. Summiting on August 4 were Tim Wood and local guide Aziz Beg, Wood becoming the first Australian to climb the mountain. A third member, Tony Simms, stopped 200m below the top. The team left base camp (4,400m) on July 25 and spent 10 days establishing camps before making their summit attempt. Arriving at base camp on August 4 was a seven-member Polish team. They made two camps on the ridge—at 6,200m and 6,800m—and on the 13th Krzysztof Garolyna and Krzysztof Mularski reached the main summit. These are the sixth and seventh known ascents of the country's highest mountain since before the Soviet invasion.

In 2010 Mularski had attempted Noshaq, reaching 7,200m with Jakub Rybicki before retreating.

*Mandaras Valley, M3 (6,109m), south ridge.* In recent years the north side of the High Hindu Kush has again become accessible to climbers. There are beautiful peaks, untouched walls, and lonely valleys. There is also a lack of food, fuel, tourist infrastructure, mobile phone coverage and emergency services; in short, everything that makes climbers looking for adventure happy. The last ascent on a peak in the Mandaras Valley took place in 1978, a year before Soviet troops invaded Afghanistan.

 This was incentive enough for Klaudiusz Duda and me to organize an expedition to the area.

Crossing to Ishkashim from Tajikistan is currently the only safe access to the Wakhan. Reaching the area from Faizabad has become potentially dangerous, due to the appearance of the Taliban in 2011. We found the Tajikistan border closed due to a holiday and had to wait two days before crossing the river to Afghanistan, reaching Ishkashim on June 29.

Formalities for journeying onward have changed since 2010. To obtain permission to enter the Wakhan, it is now necessary to obtain a letter from the governor, to register with the

Sunrise at Camp 3 on Palane Safad, with south ridge of M3 behind. (A) Koh-e-Naser Khosraw (M2, 6,424m). (B) Koh-e-Keshnikhan (M1, 6,754m). (C) M3 (6,109m). *Klaudiusz Duda*

Panorama south over Mandaras Valley from summit of M3. *Klaudiusz Duda*

Panorama north toward Shakhawr Valley from summit of M3. *Klaudiusz Duda*

police, and to visit the border guards. The procedure can be completed in a day.

On June 30 we reached the village of Qaz-i-Deh and hired two porters to guide to the mountains. The same day we reached the entrance to the Mandaras Valley, where we encountered serious problems crossing a wild river. On July 1 we reached base camp (4,100m) and sent the porters back to the village.

Our main goal was Koh-e-Nadir Sah (M4, 6,814m) by the same route as the 1962 Polish expedition, but we wanted to do this in a lightweight alpine style, as a two-person team without fixed ropes.

At Camp 2 (5,300m) bad weather interrupted our acclimatization, but on the 6th we set off again from base camp for the summit. Back at Camp 2 I got flu, so it wasn't until the 9th that we climbed through the glacier cirque at 5,700m and started ascending snow slopes leading to the ridge connecting M3 and M3a. Once on the crest we followed it northeast over snow until we reached the junction with the west-northwest ridge of Koh-e-Nadir Sah. We walked down to the saddle, named Palane Safed (6,050m), between this peak and M3, and pitched Camp 3. That night it snowed and continued through the following day.

On the 11th we were awakened by sun, beautifully illuminating snow coating the

Route from glacier cirque to Camp 3 on Palane Safad. Final section of ascent to M3 is also visible. Original Polish route to Koh-e-Nadir Sah climbs rocky spur up and right from Camp 3, then snow ridge above. *Klaudiusz Duda*

Klaudiusz Duda on south ridge of M3. (A) M4a. (B) M5. (C) Camp 3 on Palane Safad. Snow slopes left of 3 rise toward west-northwest ridge of Koh-e-Nadir Sah. *Slawomir Kawecki*

surrounding peaks. Under these circumstances we did not have the slightest desire to approach the steep slopes leading to Koh-e-Nadir Sah. As an alternative, safe from avalanche danger, we opted for M3. The south ridge, rising from Palane Safed, had never been attempted.

Slawomir Kawecki on final section of south ridge of M3. *Klaudiusz Duda*

Klaudiusz Duda on M3 summit looking south at Mandaras peaks. See panorama south over Mandaras Valley for identification. Big mixed wall behind his left hand is 1,500m north face of Koh-e-Mandaras (M8, 6,331m)—one of the great ascents of the Hindu Kush, in 1977 by Poles Piotr Jasinski, Marek Kowalczyk, and Andrzej Zawada, and Terry King (UK). *Slawomir Kawecki*

From camp we went down a snowy depression towards the Shakhawr Valley, to bypass the first section of the jagged south ridge. We then climbed three ice-snow pitches (up to 60°) on a rocky rib to reach the main crest, which we followed for 50m to the final dome. Two pitches of mixed rock and snow led to the top. The grade was AD. We reversed the route with rappels and walked laboriously to Camp 3, worrying about the lack of time we had left. Our plane was due to depart from Dushanbe six days later. The next day we made five rappels directly from Camp 3 down the west flank of the ridge to the glacier and reached base camp in late evening. We caught our flight, very pleased that we were able to climb in such a remote, wild area during a three-week vacation.

SLAWOMIR KAWECKI, *Poland*

*Editor's note: M3 was first climbed, via the northwest ridge, in August 1962 by a predominately Polish expedition, with Henrik Dembinski, Bernard Langevin (France), Jan Stryczynski, and Stanislaw Zierhoffer reaching the top. It was not climbed again until August 1978, when a Czechoslovak expedition reached the summit via the northwest and northeast ridges. Koh-e-Nadir Sah was first climbed by the 1962 Polish expedition via the west-northwest ridge. By 1978 it had been climbed eight times, by at least two other routes.*

*Jurm Valley, Koh-e-Sauze (5,680m on Russian map), second ascent.* Only 16km wide at its narrowest, the Wakhan Corridor is an obscure panhandle of land giving Afghanistan a tiny border with China. Exploration started long before mountaineers ventured into the area. Marco Polo is reputed to have spent time here recovering from malaria, and the source of the Oxus was discovered deep in the upper Wakhan. Before the 1979 Soviet invasion, the Wakhan was a popular, if remote, mountaineering destination. Now it is an oasis of calm and relative security.

Early mountaineering expeditions concentrated on the lower Wakhan. The local people are Wakhi and follow a liberal form of Islam, known as Ismailism. With the Soviet Union to the north proving more impenetrable to Western mountaineers than the Hindu Kush, expeditions traveled overland from Kabul. Today the security situation makes this route inadvisable, and access is from Tajikistan. Expeditions have an extra visa hurdle to jump, but we found the paperwork straightforward, though getting insurance was prohibitively expensive.

James Kitson and I used Adab Shah, a 22-year-old Afghan, to organize the required permits and expedition logistics. He whisked us around the various police units and the District Governor's office in a morning. By the afternoon we were able to load the vehicle

Part of High Hindu Kush, seen from Pik Moscow Olympic Games to north. (A) Koh-e-Jamhoryat (6,170m). (B) Pegish Zom I (6,045m). (C) Koh-e-Chatal (ca. 5,500m). (D) Koh-e-Staza (ca 5,600m). (E) Koh-e-Sauze (5,680m). (F) Koh-e-Jurm (ca. 6,000m). (G) Kotgaz Zom (6,681m). (H) Akher Cioch (7,020m). (I) Koh-e-Tez (7,015m). (J) Koh-e-Urgunt (7,038m). (K) Saraghrar (7,349m). (L) Jurm Valley. (M) Urgunt Valley. *Zdenda Bouda.*

and set out on the road east. The track soon became nonexistent and meltwater rivers more difficult to ford. As the sun dipped behind the mountains, the car got stuck and started to fill with water. Unable to push it out ourselves, we gathered reinforcements from a local village and, after bailing out footwells, were on our way again. Greg Mortenson's schools were apparent in many tiny settlements.

Identification of distant peaks is an inexact science. Seen from Pik Moscow Olympic Games to the northeast, the high Afghan peaks of; (A) Koh-e-Langar (7,070m, north of Saraghrar Massif. (B) Languta-e-Barfi (6,827m). (C) Shakhawr (7,116m), (D) Koh-e-Nadir Shah (6,814m), (E) Koh-e-Keshni Khan (6,755m) and (F) Part of Noshaq Massif (7,492m). *Zdenda Bouda*

On the following day we met pre-arranged men with donkeys at the entrance to the Raij Jurm Valley. One of the animals was probably the smallest donkey I have ever seen. James and I rearranged the bags, shouldering the larger packs, but we had walked no more than 100m when the men insisted that they carry the loads. Two days later they helped establish a base camp at 4,200m.

The Jurm Valley had been visited by Italian expeditions twice, in 1972 and, unknown to us, in 1973. Unfortunately the 1972 report underestimated the heights of the peaks summited by the expedition, which misled us on the potential for first ascents.

After we negotiated unstable moraines and crevasses, our first attempt on a summit at the head of the valley was thwarted by weather. We sat it out in advanced base camp at 4,920m, but when food and fuel supplies were exhausted, we retreated down-glacier in terrible weather.

Once dried out, we made a second attempt, using the same approach. This time we continued along the glacier toward a col west of the peak. Above, we found the initial rock ridge to be loose and precarious, so we took an easier line that traversed right, below a small, stable ice cliff and went up a steady incline. After several false summits we reached the top, which consisted of a broad dome with jaw-dropping vistas across Pakistan, Afghanistan, and Tajikistan. We descended our route, which we rated PD+.

When we returned home, back issues of the 1972 *Himalayan Journal* were newly available on-line. A photograph from the 1972 Italian expedition showed that our peak was Koh-e-Sauze (Blue

Approaching Koh-e-Sauze from north. Ascent route climbed up right and back left behind skyline ridge. *Rebecca Coles*

Rebecca Coles on summit of Koh-e-Sauze. Behind and to south lie, from left to right; Akher Cioch (7,020m), Koh-e-Tez (7,015m), and various summits of Koh-e-Urgunt (7,038m). *James Kitson*

Peak), ascended via the same route in 1972. The 1973 expedition claimed in a later report that there were few further first ascents of interest to be made in the valley. However, it is a wonderful destination, and there is potential for new routes. Virgin peaks in the Wakhan will be found mainly to the east, in the upper Wakhan.

We were generally surprised at the ease with which logistics could be organized and how accommodating local people were. It seems that the mountaineering legacy in the Wakhan, from its heyday in the 1960s and 1970s, continues today, and we found it rewarding to employ local people, who were dignified, honest, and generous. Hopefully a resurgence in mountaineering can play a part in providing an income for communities. We thank the Mount Everest Foundation, Jeremy Willson Mountain Exploration Grant, and Julie Tullis Memorial Award for financial support.

REBECCA COLES, *U.K.*

*Editor's Note: Koh-e-Sauze was first climbed in August 1972, from the west, by Lino Bortolami (leader), Alfredo dal Santo, Paoli Lion, Ugo Quintily, and Elide Veronese. True heights in this area are usually a little higher than on Russian maps, making Koh-e-Sauze ca 5,730m. The Jurm Valley was visited in 1977 by Poles, who made several first ascents and repeated some Italian routes. The highest peak of the valley, Koh-e-Jurm I (ca 6,000m), lies on the western rim and was first climbed in 1969 by Japanese, approaching from the Pakistan side. Several other peaks on the rim have also been climbed from adjacent valleys. It is thought that several minor summits remain virgin.*

*Koh-e-Baba-Tangi (6,516m), northwest ridge and first traverse.* Sisters Christine Byrch and Pat Deavoll made the second ascent of Koh-e-Baba-Tangi (Jade Peak), the most easterly high peak in the Afghan Wakhan Corridor, by ascending a new route on the northwest ridge and descending the 1963 Italian route on the west ridge. This was completed in a seven-day roundtrip from base camp on the lower Kezghet Glacier. An account of the traverse appears earlier in the *Journal*.

# Pakistan

*The online version of these reports frequently contains additional photos, maps, topos, and extended text. Please visit aaj.americanalpineclub.org*

HIMALAYA

Diamir Face of Nanga Parbat. (1) Kinshofer Route (1962, original line). (1a) Line generally followed today. (2) Messner brothers 1970 descent route via Mummery Rib. (3) Messner 1978 descent route. (4) Slovenian 2011 ascent to upper southwest ridge. Bivouac sites marked. (5) Messner 1978 ascent route. (6) Upper section of 1976 Schell route (climbs Rupal Flank to Mazeno Col). There have been several variants to Schell route, e.g. in 1981 by Ronald Naar, who followed a higher traverse line to reach snowy section of ridge up and left from Slovenian high point. *Viki Groselj, provided by Irena Mrak*

*Nanga Parbat, Diamir Face, ascent to upper Mazeno Ridge.* The original goal of our seven-member expedition, supported by the University of Ljubljana, was to climb Nanga Parbat by the Kinshofer Route. Although we planned to climb in classic siege style, we wanted to use no supplementary oxygen and no high-altitude porters and leave as little trace as possible.

We established base camp at 4,250m below the Diamir Face on July 24. By August 10 we had managed partial acclimatization by reaching 5,800m on the slopes of the Mazeno Ridge and Ganalo Peak. Due to black ice and falling rock on the Kinshofer, four members abandoned the expedition and headed home. The remaining three, Viki Groselj, Mojca Svajger, and I, felt that attempting the peak in siege style was too dangerous, but an alpine-style ascent appeared reasonable, as well as more challenging. We decided to attempt the line alongside the Mummery Rib descended in 1978 by Reinhold Messner, after his solo ascent of the right side of the Diamir Face.

Mojac Svajger in lower seracs, before reaching 5,400m plateau below Messner Couloir. *Irena Mrak*

Irena Mrak in Messner Couloir during poor weather. Left is Mummery Rib; up and right Messner Serac threatens ascent. *Mojca Svajger*

On August 17 we got a weather window. Viki remained in base to coordinate logistics, while Mojca and I ascended to 4,750m, bivouacking at much the same spot as Messner. By midday on the 18th we had reached 5,800m in the couloir alongside the Mummery Rib. Here a sudden weather change forced us to find a sheltered bivouac site, where we waited for clearing. Only on the 20th were we able to continue.

Climbing over the Mummery Rib looked too dangerous, so we worked a little right of the stone-swept gully descended by Messner and reached the top of the so-called Messner Serac. We then headed right, crossing Messner's ascent route, keeping near the seracs in order to find safe bivouac sites. We spent our fourth night at 6,700m and our fifth at 7,200m, close to the point where the Schell Route traverses the face from the right. The climbing had been quite icy, but there were sections of knee-deep snow with a hard breakable crust, which made for slow going and the risk of avalanche. From 6,900m to 7,200m we tried to work left across the rock barrier giving access to the summit slopes (and the upper part of Messner's descent), but climbing thin layers of loose powder over equally loose rock was too risky, and we returned to our previous bivouac site at 7,200m.

On the 23rd we decided to complete an ascent of the Diamir Face by continuing directly to the upper Mazeno Ridge, where we would have a fine view down the Rupal Flank. The summit was no longer an option, so we traveled light, taking little protection and a 30m rope. At 1:30 p.m. we reached the crest at 7,590m. We noted that the unclimbed ridge above is very loose.

We spent the next three days descending the line, not uneventfully. While downclimbing the black-ice couloir below the Messner Serac, trying to dodge falling stones, we fell 150m. We were uninjured, though, and arrived in base camp on the 25th. Our female team had made 3,100m of ascent over slopes of 45-60°, with a section of 70°. The most dangerous part is from 4,700m to 5,800m, where the route is continually exposed to serac fall. Reinhold Messner, commenting on this ascent, said, "The summit isn't that important. The adventure counts. Eight bivouacs on such a dangerous face is worth more than a few summits by all the prepared Normal routes on 8,000m peaks."

IRENA MRAK, *Slovenia*

*Editor's Note: The Mummery Rib was the line chosen by Alfred Mummery and his Gurkha companion Rajobir for their attempt on the mountain in 1895. They retreated at 6,100m when Rajobir fell ill, after which Mummery decided to look at the northern side of the peak and set off for a fateful attempt to cross the Diamir Pass. While Messner descended the rib in 1970 (and alongside it in 1978), there appears to have been no serious attempt to climb this part of the face until 1999. In that year (previously unreported) Hungarian Zsolt Eross and three companions acclimatized by climbing Ganalo Peak (6,608m), then Eross set off alone*

Irena Mrak at 7,500m in final gully leading to upper southwest (Mazeno) ridge. Below, flowing northwest, is rubble-covered Diamir Glacier. *Mojca Svajger*

*for the Diamir Face. He followed the Messner 1978 descent route, bivouacking three times on the ascent: on the plateau below the Messner couloir (5,400m); where the route crosses left through the slanting rock barrier; and below the final headwall. Deep snow hampered progress on the upper section, but he successfully reached the summit and descended to his top bivouac. Next day he downclimbed to the valley.*

KARAKORAM

GHUJERAB MOUNTAINS

*First Koksil Glacier, Peaks 5,636m, 5,609m, and 5,626m.* From August 8 to 19 Frank Gasser, from Italy, and Katarzyna Karwecka-Wielicka, Krzysztof Wielicki, and I, from Poland, explored the Koksil (Kuksel or Kuksil) Valley.

The first expedition here took place in 1925. A small team from Holland led by Philip Visser (and including his wife Jenny

Unclimbed Peak 6,072m, at head of First Koksil Glacier, seen from northwest. *Janusz Majer*

Unvisited West Yawash Glacier (in China) from frontier ridge north of Peak 5,636m (first peak climbed by Polish-Italian team). *Frank Gasser*

Magnificent northwest face of unclimbed Yawash Sar I, at head of First Koksil Glacier. *Janusz Majer*

Visser-Hooft) crossed the Chapchingal Pass and headed south through the Ghujerab Valley to Shimshal. This trail (with certain modifications) is currently recommended as a trekking route by the Lonely Planet Guide. In 2000 Pakistani guide Karim Hayat made the first exploration of one of the Koksil side valleys, named on Jerzy Wala's 2011 sketch map [*available at the* AAJ *website*] as Third Koksil Glacier, where he made the first ascent of Jacky Chhish (5,717m, Koksil VI)). He also visited the Fourth Koksil Glacier and with two friends, Faizi Avan and Safda Karim, climbed two peaks of 5,720m. In 2003 Bernard Vaucher (France) and a Pakistani friend, Ishaq Ali, repeated Jacky Chhish (5,717m) from the Third Koksil Glacier. It has been climbed again by Karim Hayat, who has taken several Austrian trekking groups to the area. In 2011 Hayat organized both ours and the Austrian expedition [*see below*].

When we established base camp at 4,650m, at the entrance to the Third Koksil Glacier, the Austrians had climbed Koksil Sar I twice. On the 12th, after the Austrians departed, we went up to our high camp at 5,235m to attempt Koksil Sar II the following day. But the weather turned bad, with heavy snowfall, so we retreated and left to explore the First and Second Koksil Glaciers.

With the help of porters, we placed an advanced camp five hours above base camp, at 4,750m on the First Koksil Glacier. It snowed all next day but stopped at midnight, allowing Gasser and the Wielickis to traverse three 5,000+m summits to the southeast of camp on the ridge forming the Pakistan-China border. They first reached Peak 5,636m and continued north over 5,609m to 5,626m. They reversed their route, continuing south to the West Yahwash Col (5,426m), before descending west to the glacier. We were most likely the first team to visit the First Koksil Glacier (Shop Dur Glacier), at the head of which stands highly attractive Yawash Sar I (6,258m) and to its west unnamed Peak 6,072m, both unclimbed.

JANUSZ MAJER, *Poland*

*Koksil Sar I (6,176m, Polish Map; 6,152m GPS), west flank and northwest ridge; Koksil Sar II (5,909m GPS), west ridge; Koksil Sar III (5,888m GPS), southeast flank.* The Karakoram Highway is probably the longest construction site in the world. Our journey north was interrupted by the crossing of the Atabad Lake, where we found that in Hunza-speak there is no word for boat. After modest acclimatization in Shimshal, we continued up the Highway to Koksil (4,100m) on the Khunjerab River, 12km before the Khunjerab Pass. From there we walked south up the Koksil Valley, branching right at 4,500m to the Third Koksil Glacier, where we established base camp at 4,600m. From there Ulli Fechter, Harry Grün, Birgit Walk, and I

Koksil Sar II and Jacky Chhish. On first ascent of Koksil Sar II, Markus Gschwendt climbed directly to summit of Jacky Chhish, then followed skyline ridge left. *Frank Gasser*

Looking west from summit of Koksil Sar I. (A) Koksil Sar II. (B) Jacky Chhish (Koksil Sar VI). (C) Koksil Sar III, climbed by snow slopes facing camera. (D) Koksil Sar V (5,720m). *Markus Gschwendt.*

moved to a high camp at 5,300m, near the head of the glacier below Koksil Sar I. We left this camp at 4 a.m. on August 4 and started up the west flank of the northwest ridge, finding good conditions on the initial 40-50° snow face. Taking a direct line, I was soon ahead of my three friends, who had decided to follow a less direct route to a col on the ridge. I reached a rock barrier after 400m of ascent, the first place suitable for a short rest. Here I used a back rope to protect a leftward traverse over brittle rock. I then saw Harry almost level with me but separated by a rock ridge from the couloir I was in. I climbed the couloir a short distance and waited.

After half an hour there was no sign of the others. They are all experienced mountaineers, so I opted for the summit. After reaching the northwest ridge, I continued up névé to a steep ice pitch below the cornice. Here I climbed two back-roped pitches, using V-thread anchors to get past the ice and through the cornice to the summit plateau. Now all I had to contend with was knee-deep snow, and I reached the top at 3:15 p.m., my GPS reading 6,152m. I began a straightforward rappel descent and at 5,900m found rappel anchors from my three friends. When I get back to the tents, I found that Harry had injured a tendon. Two days later Ulli and Birgit made a second attempt and were successful, taking a different,

Koksil Sar I, showing (1) line of second ascent followed by Ulli Fechter and Birglt Walk; (2) line soloed by Markus Gschwendt on first ascent of west flank and northwest ridge. The Fechter-Grün-Walk attempt took a line up the snow slopes between 1 and 2 to the ridge, and then followed the crest to above the point where 1 and 2 join. *Markus Gschwendt*

lower, line to reach the crest of the ridge.

That was only the start. There were two more high, unclimbed peaks in this massif and, though not marked as over 6,000m on our sketch maps, were not much lower. On the 8th Klaus Adler, Brigitte Hantusch, and I climbed to a high camp at 5,450m in the west branch of the Third Koksil Glacier and on the following day reached the summit of Koksil Sar III, which we measured as 5,888m. We made our ascent via snow/ice slopes on the southeast flank.

While I was climbing Koksil Sar I, Klaus had attempted Koksil Sar II, retreating only 40m below the summit because he lacked the hardware he needed. On the 10th I tried this peak alone from the 5,450m high camp. The crevasse danger did not appear great, and Klaus's track was still visible. This involved climbing directly to 5,717m Jacky Chhish [a.k.a. Koksil Sar VI, first climbed in 2000, see above] west of the summit, descending east to the col between it and Koksil Sar II, then following the west ridge of the latter. Above Klaus's high point I again back-roped, as the final section was a steep, sharp, icy arête in poor condition. On the summit I had visual and radio contact with base camp, and the GPS read 5,909m.

With this phase of the expedition over, we returned to Karimabad, where all but Harry and I continued home. The two of us decided to make the trek from Hispar to Arandu, over the Nushik La (a.k.a. Nauschilak La). The trip was arduous and the crossing of the 4,990m pass far from easy: steep névé, a rotten cornice, and rockfall. English-speaking locals on the south side were amazed to see us, and subsequent research suggests we may have been the first party to complete this traverse since 1980.

MARKUS GSCHWENDT, *Austria*

*Bara Khun Group, Anbar Chhish (5,886m), west ridge-west face.* In July and August 2010 a Joint Japanese-Pakistani expedition visited the Bara Khun Valley, north of the Karakoram Highway. The team was led by Japanese cartographer Tsuneo Miyamori, and both he and Shizuo Akai carried out considerable GPS survey work. They left the Bara Khun checkpost on the KKH (36°52'33" N, 75°09'49" E, 3,603m) and headed northeast up the Rosh Dar, to establish base camp at 4,495m. From there they moved a little east, then south up the Rosh Parpik Glacier, to place Camp 1 at 5,064m (36°54'37" N, 75°20'11" E). This glacier basin lies northwest of the Khunjerab Pass and due north of Koksil.

From the same location some years ago a Japanese expedition, led by Mr Takasaki, moved west up a side branch they named D Glacier and made the first ascent of Bibitilga Chhish (5,906m), via the northeast ridge.

The 2010 expedition continued farther south up the glacier, then moved east to place Camp 2 (5,532m) below unclimbed Anbar Chhish. From there they climbed the west ridge and face to the summit (36°53'36" N, 75°22'00" E).

LINDSAY GRIFFIN, *Mountain INFO, from information supplied by Janusz Majer, Poland, and Tamotsu Nakamura, Japan.*

Looking approximately south as a climber arrives on Sun Terrace of south-southeast ridge of Koh-e-Brobar. In left middle distance are peaks of Chot Pert Group, while to right are big peaks north of Hispar Glacier. *Christof Nettekoven.*

*Koh-e-Brobar (6,008m GPS), south-southeast ridge.* Within a year Pakistan Youth Outreach has organized three expeditions and a training camp for youngsters in the peaks of the Shimshal region. Its purpose is to educate young people in mountaineering and the outdoors, to promote women's adventure, and to explore the great adventure areas of Pakistan. After two successful expeditions, the third, named Gender Equality, had as its goal an unnamed, unclimbed summit in the Ghujerab Mountains.

Starting from Shimshal on June 19, the team comprised Mirza Ali (leader), his sister, 20-year-old Samina Baig, and Arshad Karim from Shimshal; Jens Franke and Christof Nettekoven from Germany; and Malgorzata Skowronska from Poland. The foreign climbers had flown to Gilgit, traveled by jeep up the KKH, traversed the 20km-long lake caused by the catastrophic 2010 landslide, and boarded another jeep for the final leg to Shimshal, along the exposed, crumbling road completed in 2003.

The party trekked three days north, following in the footsteps of the 1925 Visser expedition, to reach the 5,090m Boesam Pass. *[Little information exists on previous ascents in this area, though in 2005 Abdullah Bei and Francois Carrel made presumed first ascents of the ca 5,700m peaks immediately northeast and northwest of the pass.]* From here the team descended to Perchod Washq in the Sok Sok-in-Dur

Koh-e-Brobar from west, showing high camp and route of ascent. *Christof Nettekoven*

Approaching col at start of Koh-e-Brobar's south-southeast ridge. West, across Sok Sok-in-Dur Valley lies Peak 6,175m, possibly unclimbed. *Christof Nettekoven*

Unclimbed northwest face of Koh-e-Brobar. *Christof Nettekoven*

Samina Baig and Mirza Ali on summit. Behind lie unnamed peaks east of Boesam Pass. *Christof Nettekoven*

Valley and, to help acclimatize and to investigate all aspects of the chosen peak, continued down to the shepherds' encampment of Mandliqshaq (Mandi Kushaq, 4,150m), close to the Ghujerab River. They returned upvalley to Perchod Washq, establishing base camp at 4,580m.

About halfway from the Boesam Pass to Mandi Kushaq, the lowest main side glacier rises east toward a col that marks the start of the south-southeast ridge of a peak they would later name Koh-e-Brobar (Mt. Equality). The summit of the peak is at approximately 36°34'08.90"N, 75°23'56.07" E (Google Earth coordinates).

On the 23rd members of the party made a reconnaissance to a site for high camp at 5,200m and, with two porters, established this camp on the 25th. Next morning they reached the foot of the mountain at 4 a.m. in perfect weather. Climbing to the col on the ridge, they continued north in snow conditions that deteriorated as the sun got higher. Passing a high plateau dubbed the Sun Terrace, the team reached the summit at 11 a.m. There were moderate difficulties on knee-deep and waist-deep snow slopes and a few falls into crevasses. Mirza led the last pitch, which proved to be the crux: steep, soft snow with a large cornice. He fixed the rope,and Samina jumared, followed by the other four. The view from the top was extensive, encompassing most great peaks of the range, from Batura in the west to K2 in the east. Franke's GPS indicated an altitude of 6,008m.

They descended quickly, as the snow was getting even worse. (According to some sources it was the hottest summer in the Karakoram for 20 years.) There were more crevasse falls before they reached camp at 1:30 p.m. All then descended to base camp in time for an evening meal, and two days later returned to Shimshal.

Samina's goal is to inspire all women, not only those of Pakistan, to become active participants in all fields of society. She hopes to encourage more women in Pakistan to take part in extreme sports and that her expeditions will encourage Pakistan youth to explore its beautiful mountains. She hopes to climb higher peaks as her technique (and support from sponsors) improves.

LINDSAY GRIFFIN, *from information provided by Mirza Ali, Pakistan Youth Outreach, and Christof Nettekoven, Germany*

BATURA MUZTAGH

*Ultar (Ultar Sar, 7,388m), southeast pillar attempt.* Giri-Giri boys Fumitaka Ichimura and Yusuke Sato made the best attempt to date on the magnificent southeast pillar of Ultar. On their alpine-style push they left 4,300m base camp on September 6, ascended the glacier, and climbed to a col below a gully at 4,500m, where they bivouacked. Next day, setting off with heavy packs loaded with one week's food, they climbed the gully. It was a hot day, and there was much melting snow and running water. Their gloves, jackets, and even inner boots soon became soaked. At 1 p.m. they reached a second col at 5,000m and after fixing one pitch above, bivouacked until 4 a.m. the following morning. This day turned out to be equally hot, and they climbed without jackets or fleeces, finally making a long traverse to a bergschrund at 5,800m, which they reached at 7 p.m.

On the fourth day they began at 5 a.m. under a starry sky, but it soon started to snow. Climbing through loose mixed terrain, with only one or two points of protection on each 60m pitch, they were finally hit by a thunderstorm and bivouacked at 6 p.m. under the upper wall, at 6,350m. Next day the weather was bad, and they remained in the tent, but the following morning they resumed climbing at 5:30 a.m. The weather was still far from perfect, and the ground above very steep. They reached 6,500m in worsening snow conditions, before retreating. They returned to the bivouac site and over the next two days made 30 rappels to the first col at 4,500m. The day after, they regained base camp shortly after noon. Sato reported the climbing was good, and they hope to return for another try.

HIROSHI HAGIWARA, *Editor ROCK&SNOW, Japan*

*Editor's Note: The first known attempt on this 3,000m "Walker Spur"took place in August 1992, when Toshio Narita and two Japanese friends retreated from a height of 5,400m. In 2000 unsettled weather stopped Frenchmen Jerome Blanc Gras, Yannick Graziani, Erwin le Lann, and Hervé Qualizza from setting foot on the pillar. Graziani returned in 2005 with Christian Trommsdorff. Noting that the main difficulties are probably located on the rock barrier at 7,000m, they planned to first climb to a small col on the pillar at 6,000m in order to acclimatize, then descend for a rest before making an alpine-style push for the top. In difficult conditions they reached 5,800m—half height on the pillar but a long way from the summit— before abandoning their attempt.*

Gulmit Tower, from Bulkish Yaz Glacier to east. 2008 attempt was by left-hand line, initial section of which is threatened by large serac to left. (Av) marks site of avalanche during rappel descent alongside couloir. *Klaudiusz Duda*

*Gulmit Tower (5,810m), southeast ridge, attempt.* Rising west from Gulmit village on the Karakoram Highway is the Bulkish Yaz Glacier, dominated at its head by an outstanding peak named Gulmit Tower, one of several summits toward the end of the long ridge running east from Ultar. The village is the administrative center of Gojal region and the former residence of the Mir of Hunza.

Klaudiusz Duda on top rib leading toward south col. Below him Bulkish Yaz Glacier runs down to distant Gulmit village and Hunza River (before 2010 landslide). *Slawomir Kawecki*

According to information collected by Polish cartographer Jerzy Wala, Gulmit Tower was first attempted in September 1988. Frenchmen Gerard Decorps and Emmanuel Schmutz approached from the Bulkish Yaz Glacier and climbed the couloir left of the peak to reach its south col at 5,500m. Bad weather prevented further progress. A second attempt was made in July 1994. Julian Freeman-Attwood and Ed Webster, approaching up the Sikardu Glacier to the southwest, climbed a south-facing couloir to the west col (5,500m). The rock on the 300m headwall of the west ridge above proved to be very loose, and the pair retreated.

In September 2006 two Poles, Tadeusz Mazeno Dziegielewski and Jakub Hornowski, made the third attempt, following the route tried by the French. They climbed a little way up the southeast ridge above the south col to the main headwall at 5,650m but then retreated. Tadeusz returned in July 2007 with Rafel Zarebski and two colleagues, but continuous bad weather and high avalanche risk prevented them climbing the couloir.

In 2008 Klaudiusz Duda and I made the fifth attempt. On June 4 we left Gulmit and the following day established base camp at 4,000m in the Balkish Yaz valley. On the 6th we discovered a way through the complex glacier and made Camp 1 in the upper reaches, at 4,300m. Over the next few days we acclimatized on a nearby ridge, then rested in base camp. We anxiously watched avalanches of heavy wet snow come down the left couloir, the only route used to reach the south col.

Kawecki at 5,650m high point below headwall on southeast ridge. *Klaudiusz Duda*

The couloir proving too dangerous, we tried a different route. On the 12th we started climbing farther left, passing below a big serac, and heading right up a snow/ice field to a rib, which was crowned by an impressive cornice. A slope of ice and rock took us to the south col, where we bivouacked. Next day we climbed the ridge to the headwall at 5,650m but, unable to find a continuation, returned to the col and rappelled alongside the couloir. Halfway down we got too close to the couloir, and a sizeable avalanche passed right over us. We escaped with just a few bruises and torn trousers. By the 14th we were back at base camp and reached Gulmit next day.

On January 4, 2010, the enormous landslide above Attabad dammed the Hunza River, forming a lake that became several kilometers long and 100m deep. Gulmit is 40 percent flooded, and the lake has isolated 25,000 people in Gojal (upper Hunza) from the rest of the country. Food has to be delivered by boats, which are also used to transport people across the landslide area.

SLAWOMIR KAWECKI, *Poland*

HISPAR MUZTAGH

*Hispar Sar (6,400m), southwest face.* Bruce Miller, Steve Su, and I left the U.S. on July 11 for an attempt on unclimbed Pumari Chhish East (ca. 6,900m). This peak and our base camp were located on the Yutmaru Glacier, a tributary of the Hispar Glacier. Steve and Pete Takeda had attempted it in 2007, and the mountain was tried again in 2009 by Slawinski, Walsh, and Welsted.

Our hopes were quickly dashed. A serac overhangs the upper cliffs, guarding the top quarter of the peak. Photos had led us to believe that we could skirt the most dangerous part, but after two days scouring the route with a spotting scope, we realized our plan was fantasy. A chunk of ice even calved off while we were watching, further sealing our decision to look elsewhere.

The choice to focus our energy on Hispar Sar was easy. It was unclimbed and showcased a striking 1,100m ice couloir that cleaved the southwest face. This line was first tried by Sean Smith and Simon Yates in 1989. Yates returned in 2004 with Andy Parkin, and the two climbed the couloir to reach the

Looking northwest from summit of Hispar Sar. (A) Khunyang Chhish East (ca. 7,400m, unclimbed). (B) Pumari Chhish Main (7,492m, Japanese, 1979). (C) Pumari Chhish South (7,350m, French, 2007). (D) Pumari Chhish East (ca. 6,900m, unclimbed). (E) Disteghil Sar (7,885m, Austrians, 1960). (F) Yutmaru Glacier. *Doug Chabot*

south ridge 300m shy of the summit but had to retreat due to bad weather and a dropped food sack. Another Brit, Rufus Duits, attempted the same line solo a few years later, but did not get much higher. Prior to this, in 1991, a team of New Zealanders had tried two routes from the north but were turned back by slab avalanches and a dangerous icefall.

On August 2 we left base camp and hiked nine hours to the base of the route. We carried enough supplies to reconnoiter and then attempt the peak. We spent the 3rd crafting a strategy and watching the

Hispar Sar, lower southwest face hidden behind foreground ridge. Route ascended prominent ice couloir, with a rocky exit onto south ridge. *Doug Chabot*

couloir. The weather was clear and forecast to remain so. With freezing temperatures we departed at midnight on the 4th, to avoid late afternoon wet avalanches and falling ice chunks. Bruce led the first block and easily crossed the bergschrund at 5,000m. By headlamp he climbed delicate ribbons of ice, as Steve and I huddled at the belays. The pitches flew by, and soon it was my turn to lead. On this section we mostly simul-climbed. Near the top of the couloir we could see a cornice threatening our exit to the ridge, so we opted for a lower traverse, which coincided with the beginning of Steve's block. He climbed seven pitches of mixed terrain to the ridge, the last in the dark. The climbing was difficult (M6), loose, and run out, but he didn't seem to mind.

On the crest we chopped snow and ice to accommodate an open bivouac. The narrow ridge wouldn't hold a tent, so we crawled into our bags, sat upright, and waited for morning. We'd climbed 20 hours to get to this point, up 1,100 meters of WI4+ and difficult mixed terrain.

The sunrise brought immediate relief from the cold. We brewed, ate, and left early. Bruce led 300m to the top, sometimes on easy snow, other times over mixed terrain. The climbing was not as easy as we had hoped. At 3 p.m. on the 5th we were as close to the top as we could safely get. A fully curled cornice was dripping, and threatening to peel away, so one at a time we got belayed to the summit for a look down the serac-choked north face. We made it back to camp before dark.

Looking steeply up 1,400m southwest face of Hispar Sar. Ascent followed prominent ice couloir that curves right to hit skyline ridge just left of a rock tower. *Doug Chabot*

Well before sunrise on the 6th we started down the couloir by rappelling from our only picket. Twenty or so raps over six hours brought us to flat ground. The climb was a gem, and we were thankful to have reached the top.

After a week of rest and bad weather, we loaded packs to explore peaks and possible routes from the Khani Basa Glacier. Two long days of hiking led into a cirque of peaks, but we had to abandon hopes of climbing due to bad snow conditions and continued snowfall. On August 23 we hiked out, our expedition finished.

Launching an expedition from the village of Hispar was problematic. We'd been warned we'd face hurdles, but hadn't appreciated how difficult they could be. Our problems included, but were not limited to, porter rates almost double than the government schedule, forced hiring of additional porters and

Steve Su exiting mixed ground onto south ridge. *Doug Chabot*

sirdars, gear being stolen; agreed prices becoming meaningless. Luckily, this type of alpine mugging seems limited to Hispar.

Doug Chabot, *AAC*

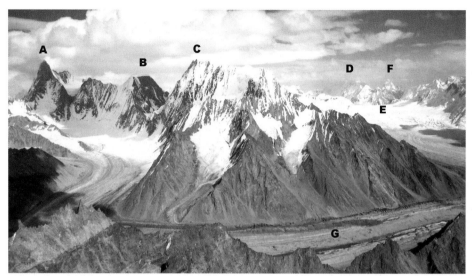

View east from Hostfjellet. (A) Tahu Rutum (6,651m). Unclimbed northwest ridge is left skyline. (B) Peak ca 6,050m. (C) Peak ca 6,500m. (D) Ogre (7,285m). (E) Hispar La (5,151m). (F) Ogre II (6,960m). (G) Khani Basa Glacier. *Magnus Eriksson*

*Hostfjellet (ca.5,500m), north-northeast face.* From August 20 to September 20 Martin Jakobsson and I, both Swedish, visited the Hispar Glacier, establishing base camp at its junction with the Khani Basa Glacier. Our goal was 6,651m Tahu Rutum by a new route, the northwest ridge [*this ridge was the aim of a young British party in 2010, but bad weather prevented them setting foot on the mountain.*] Base camp was too far away from the mountain, complicating logistics, but our porters had refused to walk farther. We took no satellite phone, radio, or GPS, in order to experience the isolation enjoyed by climbers in the past. We made two unsuccessful alpine-style attempts, reaching 5,750m, but on the approach we spotted a sharp rock pyramid in the unnamed adjacent valley between the Khani Basa and Yutmara glaciers. We thought it would make a good consolation prize.

Hostfjellet from east. Original plan was to climb gully on left to south ridge (left skyline). North-northeast face is beyond right skyline. *Magnus Eriksson*

A three-hour hike led to a nice bivouac spot on the moraine at 4,300m, just before the dry glacier. We scoped the approach and found that the snow gully leading to the south ridge, which we had seen previously, had melted out and was too dangerous. We decided to try the north-northeast face, even though we had not yet seen it.

At 3 a.m. we started up the 200m icefall guarding access to the upper basin. Here we discovered a line that would provide mixed climbing, rather than rock, and were happy that we'd carried ice gear in case. Six hundred meters

Looking north across (A) Hispar Glacier at (B) Hispar Sar (6,395m Russian map), with approach to southwest face climbed by Americans. (C) Hostfjellet. (D) Kanjut Sar (7,760m), (E) Peak 5,843m (Russian map). (F) Unnamed glacier used to approach Hostfjellet. *Lee Harrison*

of increasingly difficult climbing, with the last three pitches M5/M6, led to the summit ridge, where 100m of easy rotten rock gained the top. Our altimeters showed ca 5,400m. [*The Russian map marks the peak as 5,501m.*] We completed the climb in a 20-hour push.

As far as we can tell both mountain and glacier have no name, so we referred to the peak as Hostfjellet (Norwegian for Autumn Peak).

MAGNUS ERIKSSON, *Norway*

Martin Jakobsson on lower section of Hostfjellet's north-northeast face. *Magnus Eriksson*

PANMAH MUZTAGH

*Dom Brakk (5,830m) and panoramas.* In May 2008, when I was making my first ski traverse from Shimshal to Askole via the Lupke La, the high pass connecting the Braldu and Sim Gang Glaciers, I climbed an easy peak north of the Sim Gang Glacier (36°01'36.8" N, 75°41'41.1" W) while the other members of my group were reaching the Sim La (5,450m). I climbed the southeast flank and southwest ridge from 5,000m on the Sim Gang Glacier, the ascent featuring a 150m ice slope of 40-45°. The summit is essentially a shoulder on the southwest ridge of Peak 5,925m, but I did not continue to the main summit, which was quite far, the crest dropping slightly to a small saddle before rising again.

In May 2011, on my third Shimshal-Askole ski traverse, I repeated the ascent with four clients, again stopping at the shoulder. One of the female clients was named Dominique, so we

Dom Brakk from south, showing ascent route.  *Pierre Neyret*

Looking southwest over Sim Gang Glacier from Dom Brakk. (A) Ganchen (6,462m; Japanese, 1978). (B) Pamshe (6123m). (C) Peak 5,990m. (D) Sosbun Brakk (6,413m; Japanese, 1981). (E) Sosbun Tower (6,000m). (F) Broad Tower (6,065m). (G) Solu Peak (5,901m). (H) Solu Tower II (5,959m; British, 1987). (I) Solu Tower I (5,979m; British, 1987). *Pierre Neyret*

Identification of distant peaks is an inexact science. This wonderful panorama from northeast to southeast across the Central Karakoram was taken from the 6,220m summit of Braldu Brakk. (A) Peak 6,360m. (B) Peak 6,350m. (C) Peak 6,440m. (D) Crown (7,295m). (E) Upper (Southeast) Braldu Glacier. (F) Peak 6,410m. (G) Nobande Sobande Group. (H) Skamri Peaks (6,763m). (I) K2 (8,611m). (J) Changtok (7,045m). (K) Broad Peak (8,051m). (L) Chiring (Karpo Go, 7,090m). (M) Chiring West (ca 7,000m). (N) Gasherbrums IV (7,925m) and I (8,068m). (O) Muztagh Tower (7,284m). (P) Bobisghir North (ca 6,300m). (Q) Bobisghir (6,416m). (R) Ghent (7,401m). (S) Masherbrum (7,821m). (T) K6 (7,282m). *Pierre Neyret*

named the peak Dom Brakk. It gives a magnificent view over the entire Sim Gang Glacier. [*Editor's note: Given the location, it seems likely 5,830m and 5,925m had been climbed, but this is uncertain.*] Earlier we had summited Braldu Brakk (6,200m), largely on skis, from the Lukpa La to the south [*the first-ascent route climbed by the 1956 London University expedition*]. During our 21-day traverse we experienced 20 days of sunshine.

PIERRE NEYRET, *France*

*Latok III (6,949m), west face.* One of the Latok group's most coveted objectives, the 2,000m west face of Latok III, was finally climbed by a four-man Russian team led by Alexander Odintsov. The ascent realized an 11-year dream for the veteran leader. Considering past events on this mountain, his achievement is all the more remarkable.

Americans made strong attempts on this wall, in 1992 and 1998, before Odintsov's first attempt, in 2000. Latok III was part of an on-going program entitled "The Russian Way—Big Walls of the World," whose goal was putting up routes on 10 of the highest mountain walls in the world. By that stage his teams had already climbed large new routes on Pik 4,810m and Ak-su in the Pamir Alai, the Troll Wall, Bhagirathi III, and Great Trango Tower.

On Latok III the 2000 team bailed at 5,835m, after Yuri Koshelenko was injured by stonefall. The epic retreat, with Efimov and Ruchkin being hit by a large avalanche, Ruchkin emerging with three broken ribs and a damaged neck, and Efimov being swept 350m to the bottom of the face and escaping with only a broken leg, is well told in *AAJ 2001.*

West face of Latok III rises 2,000m above Baintha Lukpar Glacier. (1) South face of Latok I (7,145m; Matsumi, Shigehiro, and Watanabe, then Endo, Muto, and Oko, 1979). (2) 2011 Russian Route, with eight bivouacs marked. (H) 2001 attempt high point and site of Borikhin's accident. (3) 2000 Russian attempt and high point. (4) Southwest ridge. (5) Latok V (6,190m). *Alexander Odintsov, supplied by Anna Piunova*

The following year only Odintsov and Ruchkin were keen to return. Odintsov enlisted four more climbers, and this time the team reached 6,250m at a snowfield they named the Tomahawk. Next day all but Igor Barikhin, who was jumaring to remove gear, had reached a higher bivouac, when a large gendarme dropped from the

High on west face of Latok III. *Alexander Odintsov, supplied by Anna Piunova*

summit ridge. Rocks cut through Barikhin's rope, and he fell to the foot of the face.

In 2008 another Russian team, this time led by the accomplished Valery Shamalo, made another attempt, but had only climbed 500m when a stone smashed the knee of one climber and the expedition retreated to St Petersburg.

But for Odintsov the wall wouldn't go away, so in 2011 he assembled a small team of young, talented climbers who, in his words, "wouldn't know how hard it is." He also went earlier in the season; while wintry conditions would make the climbing harder, the route would be objectively less threatened. To make things even safer they would only climb in the morning, sitting out the afternoon sun, stonefall, and icefall at a protected camp.

Evgeny Dmitrienko, Ivan Dozhdev, Alex Lonchinsky, and Odintsov spent from June 10 to 25 making their largely capsule-style, 63-pitch ascent, following the 2001 line. After climbing most of the lower couloir alpine style over three days, hauling two portaledges, the team established five more camps above. Where in 2001 Alexander Klenov, leading the party, had free-climbed in rock shoes, the young guns now had to use boots, crampons, and often aid. They reached the previous high point, where Odintsov removed the bolt that had secured Barikhin 10 years earlier, so he could give it to his widow. Above they were surprised to find the final ropelengths to the summit much more difficult than expected.

During the ascent the team was inflicted by poor weather, losing several days to rain or snow, but only when they were back at base camp and the real storms began, did they realize how lucky they had been. Once again, though, they'd not escaped unscathed. During the descent a falling rock broke Lonchinsky's arm.

Latok III was the ninth of the Russian Big Walls (the five already mentioned, plus Great Sail Peak, Jannu, and Kyzyl Asker) and was awarded Russian 6B. For Odintsov it was only surpassed in difficulty by his route up the southeast face of Kyzyl Asker. Meru Shark's Fin was to be the 10th in the project, but with the American success the Russians will be looking elsewhere.

LINDSAY GRIFFIN, *Mountain INFO, from information provided by Anna Piunova, www. mountain.ru*

Battling elements during first ascent of Latok III west face. *Alexander Odintsov, supplied by Anna Piunova*

BALTORO MUZTAGH

*Great Trango Tower, southwest summit (6,237m), northwest face, Parallelniy Mir.* A new route on the huge northwest face of Great Trango, climbed by Galina Chibitok from Russia and Marina Kopteva and Anna Yasinskaya from the Ukraine, was awarded the 2011 Russian Piolet d'Or, the first time such an accolade has been bestowed on an all-female team. Parallelniy Mir (Parallel World) parallels the 2007 Krasnoyarsk Route (which completed the almost-finished 2003 line by a team from Odessa; see *AAJ 2008*), climbing the steep right flank of the prominent rounded pillar on the left side of the face.

After three days fixing ropes on the initial lower-angle section of face, the three women (a fourth female member was ill and remained in base camp) embarked on a capsule ascent, spending 32 days on the wall, before reaching the southwest summit. They climbed 49 pitches, made nine portaledge camps, and placed 75 bolts (hand-drilled 8mm) and 343 pitons but left only rappel anchors and bolts on the wall; they removed many bolt hangers. They free-climbed up to F6a,

Camp 5, at top of pitch 25, on lower section of central pillar. Two climbers can be seen working on pitch 27. *Chibitok-Kopteva-Yasinskaya collection, supplied by Elena Laletina*

largely in the lower section, the main difficulties being hard aid to modern A3. Overall they graded the route (Russian) 6B and US VI/VII. With a height of ca 2,000m and a climbing distance of 2,580m, it's difficult to think of any other all-female new route on a huge rock wall in the Greater Ranges that comes close to matching this ascent.

It appears that pitches 11-16 more or less coincide with the 1999 line Lost Butterfly, and on the final wall (from pitch 40 on) Parellelniy Mir and the Krasnoyarsk Route are identical. The three women rotated work loads daily; two climbed, while the third either rested or hauled loads. The first ca 20 pitches, leading to the base of the pillar, were largely free at F5b-6a, with many short sections of A1 and A2. The next ca 18 were largely aid, at A2 and A3 (sections of eight or more skyhook moves between bolts). To this point the weather had been generally good, but it deteriorated to almost winter conditions. The next few pitches along the shoulder to the headwall should have been straightforward, but at 6,000m and in severe weather were not. On the headwall cracks were filled with ice and gave complex

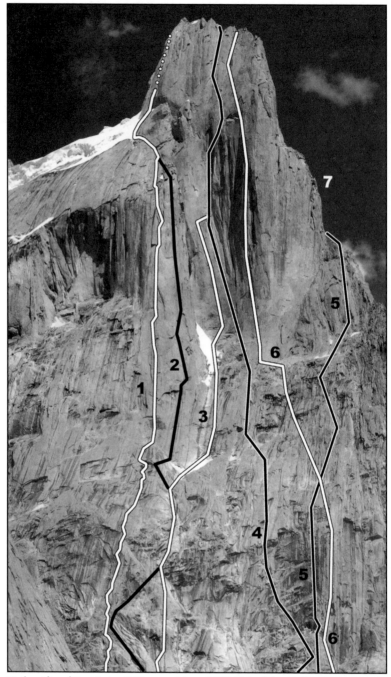

Northwest face of Great Trango. (1) Krasnoyarsk Route (2007). (2) Parallelniy Mir (2011). (3) Lost Butterfly (1999). (4) Parallel Worlds (1999). (5) Northwest Face-Soutwest Ridge (Krasnoyarsk Route, 2007). (6) Russian Route (1999). (7) Aseem (Southwest) Ridge (2004). *Vladimir Moglia, supplied by Elena Laletina, russianclimb.com*

Looking down pitch 30 to Camp 6, halfway up central pillar. *Chibitok-Kopteva-Yasinskaya collection, supplied by Elena Laletina*

aid and mixed climbing, though easier than on the pillar below. They reached the top in a blizzard at 9 pm on August 25th, having almost exhausted supplies. During the three-day descent, they ate more or less nothing. However, without the bad weather during the upper section of the climb, they would also have run out of water. Kopteva estimates that in perfect conditions the majority of pitches might be possible to free up to 7b.

LINDSAY GRIFFIN, *from information supplied by Elena Laletina, russianclimb.com and Anna Piunova, mountain.ru*

Marina Kopteva high on Great Trango after bad weather. *Chibitok-Kopteva-Yasinskaya collection, supplied by Elena Laletina*

*Trango Tower (6,239m), northwest face, No Fear.* In August Dmitry Golovchenko, Sergey Nilov, leader Viktor Volodin, and I, from the Moscow Mountaineering and Climbing Federation, planned to climb a new route on the north face of Trango Tower. However, prevailing conditions made the approach dangerous, and we opted for a new line on the northwest face.

Our route took 10 days to complete. We established three camps on the wall, living and working in pairs from two portaledges. On August 2 and 3 we fixed five ropes on the initial section and on the 5th hauled up all our gear and continued capsule style for eight days. During the first four to five days the weather was clear and relatively warm considering the altitude. Later it deteriorated, becoming colder and then snowing, and by the day of the summit push, it was quite bad. We didn't wait, as the forecast was for worse weather, and on the 12th we jumared our ropes and climbed above to the summit. We returned to our top camp and on the 13th descended to advanced base, below the wall, which was being manned by Sergey Kotachkov.

The entire route, especially the lower and middle sections, features many corners and overhangs, some of them large. The rock is mainly monolithic, and there was much aid climbing. We climbed 1,120m. We named the route No Fear (900m, 6b+ A3), the slogan of the famous Moscow climbing club Demchenko, of which we are all members.

ALEXANDER YURKIN, *Russia, Supplied by Anna Piunova, www.mountain.ru*

*Editor's Note: This route on the 900m northwest face, the first Russian route on Trango Tower, follows a large corner system to the right of Insumisioa, until joining it on a large sloping snow terrace at three-fifths height (site of the third and highest Russian portaledge camp). From here it appears to follow similar ground to Insumisioa to reach a smaller snow terrace at four-fifths height. Above, it climbs left of Insumisioa to the summit. No Fear is the first largely independent line to be established on the spire for over a decade. Insumisioa (VI 6a A3+) was put up in 1995 by Basque trio Antonio Aquerreta, Fermin Izco and Mikel Zabalza. The name is a Basque term referring to dodging the draft of the Span- ish Military Service, which remained compulsory during the 1990s. The three climbers were avoiding national service during their expedition.*

*Gasherbrum I (8,068m), first winter ascent.* The Polish Winter Gasherbrum I expedition was organized by the Polish Alpine Association (PAA) and financed by the Ministry of Sports, as well as a group of commercial sponsors. The expedition was part of an important PAA program dubbed Polish Winter Himalaism 2010-2015, the goal being for the next generation of Polish mountaineers to make first winter ascents of the remaining 8,000m peaks.

The expedition comprised four Poles. Agnieszka Bielecka (34) was base camp manager. Adam Bielecki (28, brother of Agnieszka) at 17 climbed Khan Tengri alone, has climbed more than 100 routes in the Tatras and Alps during summer and winter, and in 2011 summited Makalu without oxygen. Janusz Gołąb (44), one of the most famous Polish alpinists, was very active in the 1990s, making the first winter ascent of Manitua and the second ascent of Extreme Dream, both on the Grandes Jorasses, a new route on the west face of the Petit Dru, the first winter ascent of Arch Wall (Troll Wall), new routes on Nalumasortoq (Greenland) and Bear's Tooth (Alaska), a new line on the huge face of India's Kedar Dome, but no ascents of 8,000ers. Artur Hajzer (49, expedition leader) was a partner of the legendary Jerzy Kukuczka, making new routes on Annapurna East, Manaslu, and Xixabangma, the first winter ascent of Annapurna, and more recently three other 8,000m peaks by standard routes, all without oxygen.

The team was supported by two Pakistani climbers employed as high-altitude porters: Ali Sadpara and Shaheen Baig. Both are 8,000m summiters who have been on previous winter expeditions. Our expedition shared base camp with Gerfried Goeschl's international expedition.

The team reached base camp on January 21, 2012, after a six-day trek from Askole, and by February 9 had established Camp 3 at 7,040m on the Standard Route up the Japanese Couloir. Sadpara was frostbitten in both feet and left the expedition. From the 19th to 21st a violent storm raged at base camp, and at one point Golab, inside his tent, was lifted four m. Four tents were lost. From 25th to 27th the team made its first summit attempt but retreated from 6,650m, due to excessive wind. During the descent Golab fell into a crevasse at 5,900m and was injured. During March 4 and 5 another storm struck, this time forcing Golab, at base camp, to spend a night in his harness belayed to ice screws. On the night of the 7th, Baig, Bielecki, Golab, and Hajzer were in Camp 2, having been turned back at 6,600m by strong winds on their attempt to push through to Camp 3. Next day all except Hajzer proceeded to Camp 3. On the 9th Bielecki and Golab left at midnight and reached the summit at 8:30 a.m., descending to Camp 2 by 5 p.m. On the 10th all four climbers were back in base camp.

From the 10th to 15th the expedition tried to coordinate rescue attempts for three missing climbers from the other expedition (see below). When this was abandoned, Bielecki and Golab, both frostbitten (the former on his toes and nose, the latter only on his nose), were helicoptered to Skardu. The remaining members left on foot for Skardu the next day.

Golab reported, "I was surprised by the incredibly strong winds of the Karakoram winter. They persisted almost throughout the expedition. These winds were as strong as in Patagonia but lasted longer, almost without any quiet periods. They forced us to spend weeks at base camp without any possibility of climbing, which was probably the hardest part. It was difficult to maintain the will to climb and the belief in success. The route itself was perhaps not so technically difficult, but hard ice and little snow cover made it tiring and dangerous. Paradoxically, the section which gave me most trouble was between BC and Camp 1—a long distance, with many objective dangers.

The key to our success was not wasting energy on useless attempts but waiting until we got a weather window. This came on March 8 and 9. It was originally forecast to last three days, but eventually shrunk to one and a half, which, however, was enough for us to launch a summit push. Another key element was our decision to return to Camp II on March 7, giving up the plan to reach Camp 3. We did not waste our limited energy battling the wind, which was very strong that day. Thanks to this we reached Camp 3 the following day in pretty good shape, and this allowed us, after a half-day rest, to leave for the summit at midnight.

This was probably the most important tactical decision and an unusual one, as normally in winter night does not offer conditions for climbing. We were determined enough and departed despite a temperature of -35° C. The climb went all right, without any problems. We reached the summit in almost no wind and clear skies. By the time we got back to Camp 3, the weather was already beginning to change, so it was our last chance. At 5 p.m. the weather had deteriorated full-scale, with mist and very strong wind. We succeeded but sadly our friends from the Goeschl expedition most likely just ran out of time."

INFORMATION BY ARTUR HAJZER, *supplied by Artur Paszczak, Poland*

*Gasherbrum I (8,068m), winter tragedy.* At 10:30 a.m. on March 9, 2012, as Polish climbers Bielecki and Golab were descending from the summit of Gasherbrum I, having made the first winter ascent, Austrian Gerfreid Goeschl contacted his home country by satellite phone to say that he, Cedric Hahlen (Switzerland), and the accomplished Pakistani mountaineer Nisar Hussain Sadpara were 450m from the summit. They were close to completing a partially new line via the west-southwest face and southeast ridge. Three and a half hours later another expedition member, Alex Txikon (Spain), who was at Camp 2 (thought to be ca 6,800m), spotted them high on the peak, maybe within 250m of the top. They have not been seen since.

With Txikon and Canadian Louis Rousseau, Goeschl attempted a winter ascent of Gasherbrum I in February and March 2011. Their planned route was partially new, following the couloir and ridge close to the right edge of the triangular rock face that forms the left side of the west-southwest face of Hidden Sud (Gasherbrum South, 7,069m, see *AAJ 2011*, with route-line photo). They were stopped by bullet-hard ice at 6,650m after climbing 1,500m of new ground.

Goeschl returned in the summer and climbed the mountain by the Normal Route. In winter

2012 the team completed the 2011 line, which reaches the top of the triangle at 6,800m. From there they continued to the upper section of the southeast ridge, joining the original American Route at 7,500m. Given the conditions experienced by the Poles during their descent, it is surmised that when the bad weather struck, Goeschl, Hahlen, and Sadpara were caught by strong winds and blown off the mountain.

Although a rescue helicopter was called in immediately, continuing poor weather meant flights were repeatedly canceled, and it wasn't until the 15th that a weather window in the upper Baltoro allowed Askari Aviation to look for the missing climbers. A helicopter flew to 7,000m, studying the line of ascent, and later the Normal Route up the Japanese Couloir. There was no trace of the three, and after discussions with Wolfgang Goeschl, the brother of Gerfreid, who had arrived in Skardu that day, further searches were abandoned. The helicopter landed at base camp and evacuated the two frostbitten Polish climbers.

Goeschl came from a mountaineering family, his father having made the first ascent, in 1968, of the well-known 7,257m Karakoram peak Diran. Gerfreid had climbed seven 8,000ers, including Everest without supplementary oxygen, and in 2009 completed a partially new route on Nanga Parbat.

Hahlen, an aspirant guide, had climbed K2, Broad Peak (foresummit), and Kangchenjunga, and in 2006 made the first ascent of the north (Chinese) face of Gasherbrum II East (7,772m), with Hans Mitterer and Ueli Steck. Sadpara was one of three professional Pakistani mountaineers to have climbed all five 8,000m peaks in the country.

LINDSAY GRIFFIN. *Mountain INFO*

MASHERBRUM RANGE

La Belle Epoque on La Nariz. *Provided by Francesc Estorach*

*Various ascents and attempts from Hushe, Charakusa, Kande, and Atoshar valleys.* Between July 15 and September 3 the Federacion Espanola de Deportes de Montana y Escalada (FEDME) organized two expeditions to the Hushe Valley. The first was an all-male team of Silvestre Barrientos, Mikel Bonilla, Alex Corpas, and Martin Elias, supervised by the guide Simon Elias. The expedition served as the perfect end to FEDME's three-year High Perfomance Alpine Program. The second comprised Esther Fresneda and Berta Terres (two other women nominated for the trip were unable to go), FEDME's female national climbing team. They were accompanied by Simon Elias and another guide, Pere Vilarasau.

The groups based themselves in the comfortable refuge built two years ago in Hushe by the NGO Sarabastall. For acclimatization Barrientos and Simon Elias climbed Karpo Tower (4,630m) via the south face, naming their 360m, nine-pitch route,

Barba Roja (Red Beard) as a tribute to Spanish alpinist Daniel Crespo, who died in Peru during 2010. They reached the foot of the face after a five-hour walk from Hushe and completed the climb over two days, July 25 and 26. It is generally sustained at 6a, with the crux 7a pitch at the top.

On August 3 and 4 Corpas and Martin Elias climbed La Belle Epoque, a steep 700m rock pillar leading to the summit of La Nariz (the Nose), a 4,710m rock tower four-five hours walk from Hushe. Difficulties were 7a, 6b obl. Members of the team repeated Las Damas Primero, a route put up on the lower west flank of 5,810m Baush-ul in 2010 by a FEDME women's alpine team (*AAJ 2011*). This 850m, 16-pitch route to the top of Garidas Pillar was originally climbed at 6c+, 6b obl, with a short step of A0 (2p) near the start of pitch eight. This short bouldery section was free climbed at 7b.

The women (with Simon Elias and Vilarasau) began a series of ascents on August 3, when they completed a route on Stago Peak (4,140m), a wall on the north side of the lower

La Puerta Cerrada on Stago Peak. *Provided by Francesc Estorach*

Homboro Valley first attempted by the 2010 women's team. The 12-pitch route, with 590m of climbing, was named La Puerta Cerrada and offered difficulties of 6c+, 6b+ obl on exceptional, though often compact, granite. The route was repeated by members of the men's team.

The women's team then explored the Kande Valley, which rises west-northwest of Kande village, noting four virgin peaks above 6,000m and more than a dozen above 5,000m. On August 10 the two women and Simon Elias made the probable first ascent of Kande Peak (5,470m) at the head of the Nangrol Glacier. It provided a great viewpoint, reached over nontechnical glaciated terrain. In the meantime the men went to the Charakusa, where they summited the two previously climbed peaks Hassan Boulder Peak (5,900m) and Brethes Peak (5,860m)—short ascents without difficulty. They also attempted an interesting couloir on Farol East Peak and a new route on Farhod Brakk (ca 5,300m). The

Barba Roja on Karpo Tower. *Provided by Francesc Estorach*

Naisa Brakk, with line of e Spanish route. No More Tasty Talking follows crest of ridge throughout. *Provided by Francesc Estorach*

Northeast spur of Farhod Brakk, attempted to nearly two-thirds height by three Spanish climbers. In right background are flanks of Namika (6,325m). *Provided by Francesc Estorach*

latter was the 1,200m northeast pillar, tried by Bonilla, Corpas, and Martin Elias from August 21 to 23; they retreated from two-thirds height. After waiting out a spell of bad weather, Corpas and Vilarasau climbed the southeast ridge of Naisa Brakk (5,200m) over two days, August 25 and 26. The crest of the ridge is followed in its entirety by No More Tasty Talking (1,000m, 5.10+, Miller-Prezelj, 2004), but over the years parties have created sport routes on the lower east flank (Prezelj remembers finding bolts.) It appears the two Spanish may have climbed one of these hard pitches (7b+ or 6c and A1), though they found no gear here or anywhere else on the route. They then continued directly for several more difficult pitches, before slanting up the right flank of the ridge (6a+, 400m) to the notch. A short descent right led to a bivouac. Next day they continued up

Tasty Talking (11 pitches, 5.10+, House-Prezelj-Swensen, 2004), which climbs the upper crest.

On August 23 Terres and Simon Elias climbed Little Karim Brakk (ca 6,150m), at the head of the Atoshar Valley (a side valley flowing west into the Gondokoro, north of the Charakusa, and two valleys south of the one containing ca 5,860m Cholon). Their 22-hour ascent of the 900m south face involved difficulties up to WI5+ and M4+.

FROM INFORMATION PROVIDED BY FRANCESC ESTORACH, *Director de Comunicación, FEDME, and* SIMON ELIAS, *Spain, translated by Alex Horner.*

South face of Little Karim Brakk showing Elias-Terres route. *Provided by Francesc Estorach*

*Charakusa Valley, K7 West (6,615m), northwest face, Dreamers of Golden Caves.* You never forget your first Himalayan experience. Charakusa was mine. Our first problem was visas. We were unable to obtain these in Slovenia and eventually were forced to go to Rome. Driving home with our visas, which we received on the last possible day before the flight, I wondered if this 20-hour ordeal might be the biggest adventure of the expedition. Instead it turned into one good story in a series of many.

During the dark morning of September 6, Nejc Marcic and I heard our cook say "chapattis"

(A) K7 West. (B) K7 Middle. (C) South West Summit. (D) K7 Main. (1) 1980 British attempt and high point on unclimbed northwest ridge. (2) Dreamers of Golden Caves, with bivouacs. (3) 2007 Belgian-Polish attempt (Badal). (4) 2009 Italian attempt (Children of Hushe). (E) Around to right of this buttress is approximate start of Steve House's 2004 solo ascent of K7 Main and monumental southwest ridge integral (ca 2,400m, upper right skyline arête), attempted in 1990, 1993 and 2006. *Kelly Cordes*

Luka Strazar on short A2 section high on K7 West.
*Nejc Marcic*

and later "Inshallah," as we left base camp at 4,200m on the Charakusa Glacier. But the ascent did not begin well. Due to darkness and inattention, we lost an hour finding our way to the glacier. That made us even more nervous, until firm snow and speed restored some of our confidence. Higher up the wall steepened, and we started belaying. Searching for passages, climbing steep ice and rock, and lugging heavy packs defined our first day on the mountain. Shortly after sunset we reached the ridge and a good bivouac spot. Exhausted we quickly fell asleep.

The second day wasn't much fun. We climbed many annoying icefields, with hard ice separated by steep rock. A strong sun and dehydration slowed us, so that we only accomplished about 300m. But we found a good bivouac spot, where we melted a lot of water and prepared for the next day's push to the summit.

As we left our bivouac, we worried whether the final serac would be climbable. The weather was still good, but the forecast was for it to worsen during the day. We traversed under the huge serac, and as we approached the ridge, an easy passage revealed itself. We shouted joyfully. Heavy breathing and slow walking took us up the final slopes, and we were smiling again. It started snowing during the descent. On the fourth day we returned to base camp.

LUKA STRAZAR, *Slovenia*

*Editor's note: Marcic and Strazar, traveling with minimal equipment, initially climbed ice runnels and mixed terrain left of the monolithic, lower central spur. From their second bivouac they realized that a direct ascent of the headwall above would be too difficult, so they descended some distance and out-flanked it on the right, traversing below part of the large serac barrier that threatens the faces on each side of the spur. They reached the summit at 7 a.m. on day three. They named the route Dreamers of Golden Caves (1,600m, VI/5 M5 A2 ), because, being young and having little money, they are always dreaming of a way to finance themselves. This is only the second route to the summit of K7 West and the third ascent of the mountain. It was awarded a 2012 Piolet d'Or. The four-man Slovenian team also climbed many other routes in the valley, including a 300m variant (at the top) to the southwest ridge of Naisa Brakk (900m of climbing, 5.11-, Anderson-House-Prezelj 2007) by Marcic and Urban Novak, and a possible new route up the lefthand dihedral on Iqbal's Wall (David Debeljak and Urban Novak).*

*Charakusa Valley, Nafees Cap, west face.* What was going on? Odd-Roar was awakened by the sound of a slide coming from above. When the first ice blocks hit the portaledge, he threw himself into the wall, half on top of Ole, covering his head as best he could. A few anxious seconds later it was quiet again. A large block of ice had come through the fabric. Later he heard the story of "the last kiss" from Henki, 100m below. He and Sigurd had thought their last hour had come, and in the chaos made an intimate farewell. Before long they were all laughing, but the camp that they felt so sure was safe no longer seemed comfortable. They'd placed it at the lowest ledge on Nafees Cap, the large granite tower below K7. It was partially hidden under overhangs, though now they realized these were not as large as they'd imagined.

It was September, and Norwegians Henki Flatlandsmo, Sigurd Felde, Ole Ivar Lied, Jarle Kalland, Sindre Saether, and Odd-Roar Wiik were in the Karakoram, which only Felde had visited previously. With porters they had moved their gear from base camp to the foot of 900m-high Nafees Cap, fixing ropes to assist load carrying on difficult sections. This approach was hot and tiring and paradoxically coincided with the best weather of the trip, when ideal conditions would have been overcast and cold. Flatlandsmo, Felde, Lied, and Wiik worked on the large corner system attempted a number of years ago by Germans, while Kalland and Saether followed a line more to the right. The left-hand route gave nice aid, mostly A1-A2. The climbing was varied, needing everything from beaks to large cams, one pitch requiring Wiik to leapfrog Big Bros.

West face of Nafees Cap. K7 Central is pointed summit up left, while K7 Main is visible high on right. (1) Flatlandsmo-Felde-Lied-Wiik, 2011. (2) Kalland-Saether, 2011. (3) Naughty Daddies (Laing-Sedon, 2009, to high point a couple of pitches above junction with 4). (4) Ledgeway to Heaven (Favresse-Favresse-Pustelnik-Villanueva, 2007). *Henki Flatlandsmo*

However, cracks were filled with soil and vegetation. After climbing six pitches they placed their first portaledge camp 250m above the snow. Halfway up the wall they passed the German high point and continued up right, whereas in hindsight left would have been better. Their second camp was in an open dihedral and vulnerable to anything falling from above.

The weather became colder and more unstable, with rain every day. After 20 days and 22 pitches, up to A3, the four reached the top of the wall at midnight in a snowstorm. The gentle rock ridge to the summit was a non-issue, and they immediately began their descent. Rappelling proved demanding with four people hanging on each stance, sorting gear, surrounded by darkness and falling snow. However, by 5 a.m. they were back at the portaledges. Next day Ole removed four of the five ropes fixed above the camp, one having to be abandoned, as it was encased in ice and impossible to free.

After a day of sitting out the storm, they received a message over the satellite phone that the weather would be good the next day but bad again the day after, making getting off the wall the next day a priority. It was covered with ice, which peeled off in the sun and bombarded the climbers during their descent, but that night they reached base camp with most of their equipment.

Odd-Roar Wiik jumaring upper section of Nafees Cap. *Henki Flatlandsmo*

Kalland and Saether spent six days on their line, climbing 20 pitches up to 5.11d and A2. The route, which involved many off-widths and chimneys that made hauling difficult, lay between the first Norwegian route and Naughty Daddies (630m, 5.12 or 7b, Adrian Laing-Jon Sedon, 2009, not to summit). The first route to climb Nafees Cap, following the right edge of the wall, was Ledgeway to Heaven, put up in 2007 by Nico and Olivier Favresse, Adam Pustelnik, and Sean Villanueva (1,300m of climbing, 28 pitches, 5.12+). These four named the spire after their local guide/cook.

The Norwegians had a great if exhausting trip and to quote Wiik: "One thing for sure, I'm going back to Pakistan—a wonderful country with wonderful people, no matter what kind of impression the media and others may give."

FROM INFORMATION SUPPLIED BY HENKI FLATLANDSMO AND ODD-ROAR WIIK, *Norway*

*Editor's Note: Earlier in the summer Willi Oppenheim, Jake Tipton, and Ben Ventor, climbing in alpine style, got 14 pitches up a line to the left of the Norwegian four-man route. They made two bivouacs on ledges but retreated in heavy snowfall on their third day. On a previous attempt, this time in capsule style (and including a fourth member, Josh Beckner), they spent 10 days on the wall in mostly bad weather, making slow progress through heavy snowfall, before bailing a few hundred meters above the glacier.*

Goodman on Jenga Spur, below bivouac. *Matt McCormick*

*Fida Brakk, northwest ridge, Jenga Spur.* "Isn't there anywhere else you can climb?" "Good to have known you." Reactions to us traveling to Pakistan were not generally positive, but my experience the previous year, and that of every climber I know who has traveled there, told me otherwise. As I stepped out of the Islamabad baggage claim with Pat

Goodman and Will Meinen, I was nearly blindsided by friend and trekking agent Ghulam Muhammad, as he rushed to greet me. Similar greetings followed, as we ran into familiar faces and new ones, ecstatic at our arrival, eager to share their country with us.

Two days' walk from the stone and mortar village of Hushe, the Charakusa Valley holds a diversity of climbing that is hard to find anywhere, from granite bouldering to massive unclimbed mixed faces. However, poor weather plagued our time in the valley, snow and rime constantly forming on our rock objectives. Windows of good weather were only two or three days long.

Pat and I took advantage of the first window by climbing the north ridge (British Route) of Naisa Brakk, a classic of the valley, which provided a good acclimatization mission. After the final pitches, which resemble Matthes Crest in the Sierra, we sat on the surprisingly flat

Jenga Spur on Fida Brakk. Pointed rock summit immediately right is Farhod Brakk (5,300m). *Matt McCormick*

summit in blazing Karakoram sun, blown away by the surrounding potential.

Searching for one more acclimatization objective and an opportunity for Pat and I to climb with Will, whom we had not yet roped up with, we decided on an unclimbed granite pillar next to Farhod Brakk. As we waited for the incessant drizzle to clear, we imagined ourselves simul-climbing most of it. However, Pat and I swapped blocks on surprisingly hard climbing. A dangerously loose pitch would be followed by thin seams and cracks. One pitch found me screaming, as if at a sport crag, as I bear-hugged my way up an arête above small RPs. Pat fought his way up a finger crack that approached 5.12. With daylight waning and routefinding difficult, we rapped to a small bivouac site just below the ridgeline. After a cold night spooning on the body-width ledge, I completed my block. Pat took us out left of the arête with a delicate traverse, leading to the summit pillar. The climbing continued to be challenging right through the last pitch, which led to a small summit cone, just large enough for the three of us to perch on.

Following many rappels in fading light, we downclimbed the snow couloir as a steady rain fell, producing rockfall that narrowly missed us. We named the pillar Fida Brakk, after our friend and cook Fida Hussain, and named our climb Jenga Spur (1,050m, V+ 5.11+R A0) after the numerous loose pitches and the way the route just barely seemed to come together.

As often happens numerous factors kept us from more climbing of significance, but we left the valley content with the climbing we had done.

On our way home we visited the village of Haldi, where Fida, Ghulam, and the crew from Blue Sky Treks and Tours live. Thanks to the generosity of the Burlington, Vermont, climbing community, which donated $200 plus tons of school supplies, we delivered a full expedition duffel to the teachers and children of the village. We spent the afternoon visiting a schoolteacher who is working to develop a new primary school.

The difference between western views of Pakistan and my experiences amazes me. As Fida's son put it, "There are miscreants and dangerous areas in nearly every country." While this is true in Pakistan, the northern area of Baltistan has been a safe, welcoming place for thousands of climbers, and I imagine it will continue to be so.

We felt extremely honored to have the generous financial support of the Copp-Dash Inspire Award and the Gore Shipton-Tilman Grant. Thank you.

Matt McCormick, *AAC*

*Charakusa Valley, Hassin (Hassan) Peak (ca 6,300m).* The Charakusa Valley is an alpine-climbing candy store, offering steep rock routes and technical mixed faces on some of the most beautiful peaks in Pakistan. Kelly Cordes, Kyle Dempster, and I trekked into the Charakusa in mid-August. After acclimatizing on Naisa Brakk (5,200m) and Sulu Peak (6,000m), Kyle and I ventured toward unclimbed Hassin Peak. (Kelly was unwell.) During gear caching trips on the glacier, we scoped a nice-looking line that climbed a rock buttress on the right-hand skyline and then trended to the center of the face, where mixed steps led toward the summit.

After a few days of bad weather, Kyle and I decided it was time to give Hassin Peak a gentlemen's effort. After arriving at our gear cache on the glacier, soaked after hiking in rain, we

West buttress of Hassin Peak, with Dempster-Kennedy line. Part of K6 (7,282m) to right. *Hayden Kennedy*

dried out and started the climb. We soloed easy snow and ice to the start of the rock buttress, where we roped. Kyle led steep WI4 for a few pitches, until we reached a small ledge on the buttress. From the ledge we simul-climbed easy mixed terrain to the base of a steep crack system. I then led a few pitches of M5 on good rock, with good gear options. The buttress soon became steeper,

Kennedy on first ascent of Hassin Peak. *Kyle Dempster*

and we traversed right to find easier ice/mixed climbing that led back toward the center of the face at a large snowfield. We chopped a nice ledge on which to sleep, and hunkered down for the night.

In the morning we soloed steep snow until we reached mixed steps in the middle of the face. Kyle led interesting ice pitches through a three-hour storm that came out of nowhere. The weather cleared, and we had amazing views of the east face of K7 and the colossal massif of Masherbrum. In the evening light we chopped a less than ideal ledge and spent a cold, uncomfortable night just below the summit. For breakfast we had steep, unconsolidated snow, much better than coffee and eggs! Conditions were rather dangerous, and we triggered a few small slides. On cresting the steep snow, we found a huge overhanging serac blocking the summit. After some discussion we ventured around the right side of the serac. I led a very steep, wild WI6 pitch to the summit snow slopes.

On top we were greeted by the Norwegian Bikini team and Mojitos. After drinks and conversation, Kyle and I rappelled all the way to the glacier in one long push. Nothing but good times!

HAYDEN KENNEDY, *AAC*

*Editor's note: Hassin Peak stands on the east rim of the Charakusa Glacier, north of K6. The west buttress was attempted in 2005 by Hans Mitterer (Germany), Raphael Slawinski (Canada), and Steve Swenson. They made one bivouac but retreated from 6,000m, when the summit snow slopes became too dangerous. This team spelled it Hassin, saying it was the local term for "beautiful peak" (AAJ 2006).*

*K6 Group, Changi Tower (ca 6,500m), northwest ridge, attempt.* In July 2010 Andrzej Gluszek, Piotr Sztaba, and I, from Poland, visited the K6 group intending to make the first ascent of the prominent Changi Tower [*Editor's note: This formation is not to be confused with the much lower rock towers on the north side of the Nangma Valley, often called Changi but correctly called the Changui Towers*]. Changi Tower lies southeast of K6 (7,281m), on the watershed between the Lachit and K6 glaciers, close to the military arena of the Indo-Pakistan conflict. Our permit was issued at the last moment, and, although Changi Tower stands at the head of the Lachit Glacier, we were only allowed to approach from the neighboring Nangma Valley.

Changi Tower from Austrian Col to west. Northwest ridge is left skyline, with snowy Polish Col visible at its base. Upper Lachit Glacier in foreground. *Lukasz Depta*

Climbing last few meters to Polish Col. *Lukasz Depta*

Base camp was at 4,300m, below the junction of the East and West Nangma Glaciers, separated from the tower by 13km of densely crevassed glacier and the 5,300m Austrian Col. [*Editor's note: The col was first crossed and named by the 1970 Austrian expedition, led by Edi Koblmuller, which made the first ascent of K6 via the southeast ridge from the upper Lachit Glacier.*] Our first foray to the col convinced us that reaching our objective would be a daring task. We fixed 100m of rope and deposited gear below the col, but poor weather prevented us seeing the way ahead. We returned to base camp and waited out the bad weather, before setting off to establish an advanced base on the upper Lachit Glacier.

Back at the col, with blue skies, we saw the majestic Changi in full view. But the approach caused distress: a massive icefall festooned with seracs, followed by a few hundred meters of snow slope, barred access to the col at the foot of the Tower's northwest ridge. We crossed onto the Lachit, only the second party to do so.

We placed our modest camp below the vast south face of K6, at the site used by the Austrians 40 years before. Over the next few mornings, when the glacier surface was solid, we pushed through the labyrinth of seracs and reached a cirque filled with avalanche debris directly below the col. Another 500m up the slope above, and we were breathing hard on the saddle. Our GPS read 5,900m, and we named it Polish Col.

From here the tower looked more demanding; much mixed climbing with sections that would require rock shoes. Returning to our tent we avoided the icefall by a steep gully to the left, but it also proved exposed to avalanche, so we were relieved to get down. Crossing the squelchy glacier in midday sun was laborious, and we returned to base camp for a rest and to sit out more bad weather.

On our next attempt we reached advanced base in one day but floundered the next morning in unconsolidated snow. We moved camp to a more convenient site and the following morning re-climbed the gully, reaching the col at midday.

We had heavy loads, and progress up the ridge above was slow. After three pitches we pitched our tent on a too-small platform and with two sleeping bags for three spent a restless night. At first it wasn't too bad, but then Piotr's condition deteriorated. By morning he had a terrible headache, bad cough, and upset stomach. We had no option but to retreat and two days later were back in

South side of Khane Valley. *Nikolay Petkov*

North side of Khane Valley. *Nikolay Petkov*

base camp. Out of the 20 days we spent in the mountains, 15 had been devoted to pushing the route forward. We didn't achieve our goal but plan to return.

Lukasz Depta, *Poland*

*Tagas Group, Khane Valley exploration.* Between September 10 and 22, Doychin Boyanov, Mihail Mihaylov, and I explored the Khane Valley to investigate possibilities for big wall routes and virgin summits. It lies parallel to and immediately south of the Nangma Valley. There is almost no information about alpine ascents, and the only named summits are those that border the Nangma Valley and those visible from the village of Khane, in the Hushe Valley, and from pastures along the Khane River.

According to locals the first foreigners to visit the valley were Koreans in 2001. They came twice, making unsuccessful attempts on what we think was the southwest face of Agil (ca 5,680m). During their second visit they climbed a 250m rock wall close to their 4,450m base camp, the only route known to have been completed from the inner valley. Also, an American trekker is reported to have reached the base of Shingu Charpu (Great Tower, 5,850m, though possibly higher) on the watershed with the Nangma. In 2009 a small but beautiful pointed peak called Nauari Brakk (ca 3,250m), which lies directly above the village, was climbed by local Ali Mehmed and his son Ruhal Ali.

Access is from Khane (2,800m), on the east bank of the Hushe River, and unlike the Charakusa no special permit is required. Starting up the left bank of the Khane River, it is a five-hour walk, partly along a damaged irrigation channel, to reach a large grassy plain at 4,000m, which we called First Terrace. From here a 450m ascent leads to the Korean Base Camp (Second Terrace) at the base of the valley descending from the north cirque. Continuing upstream for one hour leads to large sandy flats at 4,650m, where we had our base camp—the last good spot with water and hard soil. It is possible to reach the Khane icefall in another one and a half hours.

Southern peaks of Khane Valley from southwest. *Nikolay Petkov*

We found the peaks impressive and took many photographs, which we hope will prove interesting to the mountaineering community. Apart from the higher peaks, there are many needles and towers immediately above the valley floor (mostly on the northern slopes) that present 300-400m high-quality granite walls.

For reference we used recent information and maps by Polish cartographer Jerzy Wala, the 2005 Year Book of the Korean Students' Alpine Federation, and local knowledge. Altitudes are GPS; approximate altitudes have been extrapolated from Google Earth. In naming features we first looked for existing local names, then those given by the Korean teams, and finally applied our own. Peak numbers have been designated by Jerzy Wala on his sketch map of the Tagas Group. A comprehensive report is available on the *AAJ* website.

Nikolay Petkov, *Bulgaria*

Tangra Tower (Peak 33, ca 5,620m), west face in profile. In sunlight to left is part of south face of Rila (Peak 36, ca 5,600m). *Nikolay Petkov*

Agil (Korean name, Peak 24, ca 5,680m), southwest face. *Nikolay Petkov*

Hidden Tower (Peak 59, ca 5,830m) from west. *Nikolay Petkov*

# India

*The online version of these reports frequently contains additional photos, maps, topos, and extended text. Please visit aaj.americanalpineclub.org*

## EAST KARAKORAM

Climber stands on summit of Junai Kangri. Behind lies great south face of Mamostong Kangri. *Jonas Cruces*

Camp I on Mamostong Glacier, with Junai Kangri (seen from northwest) behind. *Jonas Cruces*

*Junai Kangri, west face and south ridge.* On August 22 Francisco Ferrero, Juan G. Hernandez, Jose C. Llamas, and I, from Spain, with Phurbu Bhutia and Dawa Sherpa from India, made the first ascent of a 6,017m peak we have named Junai Kangri.

Our goal had been the original route on Mamostong Kangri (7,561m). The approach is from Skyangpoche, up the Mamostong Glacier and then east, crossing a col on the south ridge to reach the upper Thangman Glacier. Camp 1 was located at 5,454m, at the junction of the Mamostong Glacier and a side branch leading to the col. However, trying to descend the far side of the 5,807m col, we found a huge crevasse that proved impossible to cross. We retreated to Camp 1, from where we had noted a nice unclimbed peak immediately to the southeast.

All of us climbed the prominent central couloir on the west face and continued along the airy crest north to the summit. We named the route Sin Permiso (750m, AD+). We equipped the route for a rappel descent.

JONAS CRUCES, *Spain*

*Saser Kangri II (7,518m), southwest face.* Americans Mark Richey, Steve Swenson, and Freddie Wilkinson made the first ascent of the world's second highest unclimbed independent mountain (attempts on the highest, Gangkar Puensum in Bhutan, are banned). Saser Kangri II is also the second highest peak to receive its first ascent in true alpine style. The three climbed the southwest face by a route named The Old Breed (1,700m, WI4 M3), with the crux close to 7,000m. The ascent was awarded a 2012 Piolet d'Or, and an account of this and their other climbs in the area appears earlier in the *Journal*.

*South Shukpa Kungchang Glacier, various ascents.* In December 2009 Mark Richey e-mailed a photo of a beautiful gray granite rock peak he'd seen from base camp on an expedition to the Indian Karakoram. He was recruiting for another visit to the region and invited me to pull a team together to join him. Little did I know that the invitation was part of his plan to coerce my husband, Freddie Wilkinson, into joining him for another attempt on Saser Kangri II. Mark is a good salesman, but does that matter when it comes to good-looking granite?

Our plans for a 2010 expedition didn't pan out, so it was a year later that Mark, Freddie, Steve Swenson, Emilie Drinkwater, Kirsten Kremer, and I met in Delhi. From the village of Tigur, in the militarized zone just miles from the fabled "line of control," we trekked for three days up the Chameshan Lungpa Valley to a hanging meadow above the Sakang Lungpa Glacier, a beautiful base camp site at 5,180m that the 2009 team had reconnoitered.

There the two teams split, with the ladies continuing up the Sakang Lungpa to establish an advanced camp under Peak 6,258m, below the huge south face of Plateau Peak (which we originally misidentified as 6,135m, based on a vague map of the area).

Emilie, Kirsten, and I made two attempts on Peak 6,258m (one with a chilly open bivouac) in the high heat of July. The walls gave good quality crack climbing, but when the sun was shining, melted-out ledges and the entire summit ridge constantly bombarded us with rock and ice. With conditions that were too dangerous and only two weeks remaining, we looked for other options.

Back at base camp the guys showed us photos they'd taken from their high camp under Saser Kangri II. They'd experienced similar heat issues, even on its much higher southwest face, so we all looked for a plan B. With the help of our awesome Sherpa staff, we broke down our

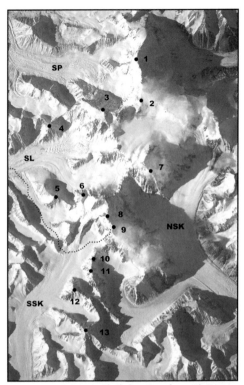

Saser Kangri Group. South Shukpa Kungchang Glacier runs north-south. American approach to Saser Kangri II marked. (SP) South Phukoche Glacier. (SL) Sakang Lungpa Glacier. (SSK) South Shukpa Kungchang Glacier. (NSK) North Shukpa Kungchang Glacier. (1) Saser Kangri IV (7,415m). (2) Saser Kangri I (7,672m). (3) Plateau Peak (7,287m). (4) Peak 6,258m. (5) Lookout Peak (6,252m). (6) Stegosaurus (6,660m). (7) Saser Kangri III (7,495m). (8) Saser Kangri II, west summit (ca 7,480m). (9) Saser Kangri II (7,518m). (10) Saserling (6,100m). (11) Pumo Kangri (6,250m). (12) Tsok Kangri (6,585m). (13) Peak 6,825m (unclimbed). *Image courtesy of Image Science & Analysis Laboratory NASA Johnson Space Center ISS022-E-7162*

Saserling (left) and Pumo Kangri from west, showing routes of first ascents. *Janet Bergman Wilkinson*

Unclimbed Peak 6,258m, showing two lines attempted during 2011. *Janet Bergman Wilkinson*

*Janet Bergman during first ascent of Saserling. Freddie Wilkinson*

high camp on the Sakang Lungpa and joined the guys on the South Shukpa Kungchang Glacier, to have a closer look at several promising unclimbed peaks.

As seems often to be the case, all our activity happened in the final week of the trip. On August 5 and 6, Emilie and Kirsten (I was in the throes of a 24-hour stomach bug) climbed the northwest face of Pumo Kangri (6,250m, PD/AD), a striking ice and snow peak across from camp. They climbed unroped for all but the final pitches and rappelled through the night with a single rope. (They'd anticipated more snow than ice but got the opposite.) Freddie and I high-fived with them on their final rappels the next morning, as we climbed the same initial ice slope to approach Saserling (ca 6,100m). We reached the summit by a beautiful south-facing, seven-pitch rock rib of IV 5.9. Finally, on the 8th and 9th Emilie, Freddie, Kirsten, Mark, and I skied across the glacier to a high bivouac, from where we simul-climbed the south ridge of Stegosaurus (6,660m, PD/AD), a dinosauresque peak west of Saser Kangri II with a 150m corniced ridge traverse to the summit.

We ladies now headed home, leaving the guys, who had two weeks remaining and were sufficiently acclimatized to have another stab at Saser Kangri II.

JANET BERGMAN WILKINSON, *AAC*

## ZANSKAR

*Reru Valley, various ascents.* Two flights, three days of bum-bruising off-road driving, and two days of scenic hiking brought us to our base camp (4,600m, 33°16'19.52" N, 76°54'20.20" E) in an arena of unclimbed mountains. It was September 1, and we were in a western branch of the Reru Valley (sometimes as Raru), known locally as the Tetleh (Tetli) Valley, and rising from Onkar. Our goal was supposedly unclimbed R6 (6,177m on the Sakamoto map and the highest in the valley; see *AAJ 2010*). The team comprised Johnny Bull, Robin Jones, Kunal Masania, Johnny Moodie, Joe Prinold, Dominic Southgate, liaison officer Anupam Mukherjee, and me. With so many of us, we split into two teams of four and approached R6 from opposite flanks. One team would go up a steep gully on the east side, while the other would climb the icy and rocky slopes of the southwest side.

Johnny B., Kunal, Robin, and I set up an advanced base camp at 5,300m. near the bottom of the gully. and next morning trudged up hundreds of meters of steep snow, moving together with thumping heads. After 400m of Scottish Grade I, the gully steepened and became icier. For the next 500m the gradient never exceeded 70°, but our energy got lower. At the cornice we played rock, paper, scissors for the finishing lead.

Peak 5,985m, with (1) Bhaio aur bheno ki khushi, and (2) descent route. *Virgil Scott*

Johnny "won," and charged up with surprising enthusiasm, reaching the summit, on which our GPS recorded 6,276m—100m higher than we expected. The other team had already summited and left 30 minutes earlier. We admired the view but noticed an old cairn and piece of faded tat that appeared to have been on this not-quite-virgin summit for at least a few years. We quickly set off down the southern slope. We suspect that the mountain had been climbed from the neighboring Temasa Nala to the north. The Tetleh Valley is known locally for the story of a lama who hundreds of years ago meditated in a cave (Lama Jimsa, Place where the Lama Sat). We named R6 Lama Jimsa Kangri.

Camp at 5,300m below east gully of Lama Jimsa Kangri. Tetleh Glacier below and approximate line of attempted route on Peak ca 5,700m, a subsidiary summit of R13, marked. *Johnny Bull*

Kunal and Johnny B. attempted a rocky ridge leading toward a summit of ca 5,700m (33°13'52.97" N, 76°53'23.05" E) below R13. They started from a camp at 5,100m on the glacier, but when 150m below the summit, came to a steep icefield, which they were unable to cross, having left crampons where they joined what had appeared to be a continuous rock ridge.

Meanwhile Johnny M., Dominic, and Robin set out to climb R2, on the west side of

R4 from east showing Prinold-Scott attempt. *Virgil Scott*

the valley. Their route took a loose gully for 800m. At 5,600m they climbed out of it, rappelled off the east ridge to an adjacent glacier, and camped at 5,500m. The following day they crossed the glacier to the south ridge of R2 and found a low-angle boulder field that circled the mountain to the summit. The GPS read 5,930m, and the peak was named Moel Kangri.

High in east gully of Lama Jimsa Kangri. *Robin Jones*

Joe and I climbed the 700m wall above base camp and a little north of R14. The nice-looking rock gave ca 20 pitches of British HS to HVS, with sections of very good climbing.

Joe and I had our minds set on an east-facing rock spur on the west side of the valley, leading to R4 (6,080m on Sakamoto map). We camped near the base of the spur at 5,000m and started climbing at 3:30am. After 200m of scrambling we arrived at the main spur just after sunrise, roped up, and moved together, occasionally belaying short sections. The climbing varied from HS to HVS. Above 800m of superb slabs, the spur steepened. At 6,000m, and at least four or five pitches below the summit, we noticed dark clouds coming down the valley. A few wisps of snow began to fall, convincing us to descend. After a cold, snowy night on a ledge at 5,700m, we continued down the following day.

On what proved to be the final foray, Kunal and Johnny B. set off for a long rock route higher up the glacier but adjusted their objective with bad weather coming from the Miyar. They chose a steep mixed line on a peak west of R13, which led onto 80° snow slopes near the top. They reached the summit (5,985m on a calibrated Suunto) at 3:45pm and didn't get down until well past dark. The difficulty rated Scottish III/IV mixed, and the 700m route had an overall alpine grade of about TD. They called it Bhaio aur bheno ki khushi. We left base camp on September 19, heavy snowfall, heralding the start of winter and making routes up the glacier out of the question. The expedition thanks Imperial College Exploration Board, Old Centralians Trust, Imperial College Trust, Mount Everest Foundation, Welsh Sports Association, The Lyon Award, and the Mountaineering Council of Scotland for financial support.

VIRGIL SCOTT, *U.K.*

GoCook peak from north. Route of ascent climbed to low col on right and followed west ridge to summit. *Yannick Flugi*

*Reru Valley, various ascents.* In August nine young climbers from Geneva, with guides Stéfane Schaffer and I, climbed three new peaks in the Reru Valley. From Leh it took three days by vehicle to reach the village of Reru, from where we took horses, yaks, and porters for our approach to base camp. We'd hoped to walk along the left bank of the Reru Nala to reach the entrance to the second side valley on the right, but after two days of trying to find a way across moraines, we gave up, came back, and started up the true right bank, eventually establishing our camp at 33°10'15.84" N, 76°59'38.16" E in the Katkar Valley at 4,470m [*see map in* AAJ 2010].

Looking southeast across Katkar Glacier during ascent of Red Apple Peak. (A) R 33 (6,128m). (B) R31 (5,962m). Big peaks on right edge of photo lie on watershed with upper Takdung Glacier, in Miyar Valley. *Stefane Schaffter/Yannick Flugi Collection*

With the help of our Nepali guide Pekma Lama Bothe and a porter, we made Camp 1 on the moraines of the Katkar Glacier at 4,983m (GPS). Many summits were available, from moderate to hard, and we could have stayed there all summer. It appeared that the best way to reach the upper glacier was to cross the lower section to the western edge and work back east once on the upper plateau.

On August 12 Laurence Di Florio, Frédéric Dupraz, Jiri Minar, Olivier Messerli, Schaffter, and Grégory Trolliet set off for a summit. Walking to the end of the moraine, they donned skis at 5,250m and in difficult snow reached a point estimated to be two hours from the top, when deteriorating weather drove them back.

Bad weather lasted for six days, and 50cm of snow were deposited. Although this was good for the team in Camp 1, who could use skis beginning at the tents, we concluded that August was too late to be climbing in this area.

On the 17th Schaffter's team set off from Camp 1 and reached the summit of Red Apple Peak (6,070m, 33° 7'42.79" N, 76°54'45.09" E) on skis and in a strong wind. The round trip took 10 hours. Meanwhile Pekma Lama Bothe, Gokul Chhantyal (Nepali cook), Sébastien Colsenet, Marc Rouiller, and I, without skis, left base camp and reached a smaller glacier basin to the east of the Katkar. [*On the left, near the entrance to this basin stands Skilma Kangri, climbed from a different valley to the north in 2009. See AAJ 2010. On the right is 6,148m R35*]. We wanted to climb the peak in the back left corner, and to reach it we crossed four km of flat glacier covered with 30cm of fresh snow. Above the bergschrund 100m of 45-50° snow led to a col west of the summit. From here the way to the top was easy and no rope was necessary. However, snow depth was often 50cm, and we kept close to rocks on the south face (a section of 45°). We named the summit GoCook Peak (6,050m, 33° 6'22.15" N, 77° 0'6.19" E ). On the way down the initial slope, we rappelled 60m, leaving one piton, and arrived in base camp after a 17-hour day.

Four days before we were due to leave, Dupraz, Messerli, Trolliet, and I made an attempt on the summit immediately south of Skilma Kangri. However, we took the wrong access couloir to the ridge, finding ourselves way too far off the summit. Two days later Dupraz and Messerli tried again, climbing a different 400m, 45-50°, snow gully and turning a loose rock wall on the right, before following another gully to the ridge. From there it was a snow and rock scramble to the summit of Tong'a Miduk Ri (Hidden Peak in Ladakhi, 6,040m, 33° 8'26.93" N, 77° 1'40.57" E).

YANNIK FLUGI, *Switzerland*

L11 (6,045m), north of Lenak Nala. *Kimikazu Sakamoto*

L15 (6,070m, left) and L14 (6,180m, highest peak in valley) south of Lenak Nala. *Kimikazu Sakamoto*

G19 (5,935m), south of Giabul Nala. *Kimikazu Sakamoto*

G22 (6,115m), at head of Namkha Tokpo. *Kimikazu Sakamoto*

*Lenak and Giabul Valleys, exploration.* In 2009 our group explored the Reru Valley, taking photographs of virgin peaks and producing a sketch map (*AAJ 2010*). We presumed there were other hidden valleys in this region, where no mountaineers had explored. I contacted Harish Kapadia about the Lenak and Giabul Valleys, southeast of the Reru. He told me he had never heard of exploration in either. We organized an expedition for 2010, but when we arrived in Delhi in early August, we found that torrential rainfall in Ladakh had caused landslides, devastating the area, so we abandoned our goal.

In 2011 Sachiyuki Hatta, Toshio Ito, Mitsuhiko Okabe, Akira Taniguchi, and I, all aged between 70 and 73, reached Leh on August 7. Three days' drive took us to Padam. From here a road is being constructed to Darcha over the Shingo La. In 2009 it was open only as far as Reru Village, but now we could drive farther, to Dorzong. On the 17th we reached Shanka (four houses and ca 20 people) at the entrance to the Lenak Nala. From the 18th to 25th we explored the Lenak Valley and from 26th to September 4th the Giabul. The latter has two large side branches, which we tentatively named Namkha Tokpo and Sachi Tokpo.

In the two valleys lie 15 peaks over 6,000m, 10 over 5,900m, eight over 5,800m, and 15 over 5,700m. In our sketch map we have labeled the mountains of Lenak L1, L2, etc. and those in the Giabul G1, G2, etc. During our stay we saw no mountaineers or trekkers and met only several women taking care of yaks. We were lucky with the weather.

These valleys are wonderful places with attractive mountains, beautiful scenery, and no garbage. We hope young climbers will attempt these virgin peaks.

KIMIKAZU SAKAMOTO, *Japan*

KISHTWAR HIMALAYA

*Cerro Kishtwar (6,155m), west face and south ridge, Yoniverse; White Sapphire (6,040m), west face, La Virée des Contemporains.* At the end of September Denis Burdet (Swiss), David Lama (Austrian), Stefan Siegrist (Swiss), and American photographer Robert Frost made the second ascent of Cerro Kishtwar. This area of the eastern Kishtwar Himalaya, untouched by the mountaineering community for almost two decades, holds many unnamed, unclimbed summits. Limited information and outdated maps made planning difficult, and after approaching up the Haptal Valley the team faced initial problems when they realized that to make an alpine-style attempt they would need to move base camp closer. They established an advanced base at 5,000m.

Cerro Kishtwar from northwest. (1) Diagonal ice ramp followed by Fowler and Sustad on first ascent. (2) Murphy-Perkins attempt. (3) Yoniverse, on west face and south ridge. *Visualimpact.ch/David Lama*

Their first idea was to link the west and northwest faces, and on September 25th all four climbed north-facing slopes of loose rock covered with snow and ice to reach a glacier terrace at 5,400m, where they placed a camp. The day was long, as 40cm of fresh snow from two weeks previous had not consolidated. Next day they saw a logical line that had not been visible from below: a thin diagonal ice ramp/couloir on the west face that curved up for 200m toward the south ridge. However, they were unable to reach the couloir that day and rappelled back to camp, to have a rest day and then set out early for the summit.

La Virée des Contemporains (solid line) on west face of White Sapphire. Arrows mark descent down south (Eagle) ridge. *Visualimpact.ch/Denis Burdet*

On the 28th the alarm went off at 3 a.m., and they left with light sacks. The first six pitches in the couloir were ice and styrofoam, good for climbing but less than ideal for placing pro. They were mostly reliant on rare rock belays. The couloir steepened to 85° before giving way to

Burdet on a crux pitch of La Virée des Contemporains, west face of White Sapphire. *Visualimpact.ch/Stefan Siegrist*

vertical rock, which gave climbing up to 6a. The temperature was -25°C but on reaching the south ridge they were able to warm their feet in the sun. The crest above, difficult at first, then with easier sections on rock and snow, led to the southeast summit, which they reached at 1:15 p.m. The GPS gave an altitude of 6,155m, rather than previously quoted heights of 6,200m and 6,220m. All except Frost traversed for 15 minutes to the northwest summit (one rappel, then an easy snow ridge), which they measured as

Starting descent of upper south ridge of Cerro Kishtwar. (A) White Sapphire. (B) Agyasol (6,200m). (C) Kishtwar Shivling (6,040m). Haptal Glacier below. *Visualimpact.ch/Robert Frost*

five meters lower. Twenty-six rappels brought them back to camp just after dark, and on the 29th they all descended to advanced base. They named the route Yoniverse (1,200m, WI5 6a).

Several days later Burdet and Siegrist left for an unclimbed peak south of Cerro Kishtwar, on the ridge leading to Sentinel Peak (5,950m). On October 4 after a long day in heavy snow, they camped at 5,200m below the western side of the mountain, the alarm set for 3:30 a.m. on the 5th. They opted for a narrow, deep gully on the west face, slanting left toward the summit. Being acclimatized, they climbed fast, and after an avalanche-prone traverse, found themselves in a chimney system similar to Exocet on Patagonia's Cerro Standhardt. There was dry-tooling, 90° ice, a difficult roof, and tricky protection. They topped out at a col to find the peak has a double summit. Leaving one sack, they traversed northwest, at first over horribly loose rock on the north flank of the crest, until after two pitches they discovered a hole leading onto the south flank, where the rock was much better. A couple more pitches led to the top, which they recorded as 6,040m GPS. Reversing their steps they continued over the southeast summit (5,980m) and down the south ridge (Eagle Ridge). Toward the end of the descent, they made four rappels down the southwest flank and reached camp at 7 p.m. They named the peak White Sapphire (33°20.532' N, 76°34.430' E) and the route La Virée des Contemporains (850m, WI5 with two crux pitches of WI6, M6, and A2).

HANS AMBUHL, *Visual Impact GMBH, and* STEPHAN SIEGRIST, *Switzerland*

---

*Editor's note: In October 1991 Brendan Murphy and Andy Perkins made a capsule-style attempt on the rounded rock pillar in the center of the northwest face. They had approached the region from Leh to the north over the Umasi La. After 17 days and 28 pitches, up to A3 and Scottish 6, they reached the north ridge, crossed to the northeast flank, and were 100m below the summit when their food ran out. Faced with more hard climbing, they bailed. In September 1993 Mick Fowler and Stephen Sustad (Fowler returning after a previous attempt with Mike Morrison in 1989) spent four days following a diagonal ice ramp left of the Murphy-Perkins line to a notch on the north ridge, where they crossed to the northeast flank and continued up mixed ground, passing the 1991 high point, to the northwest summit (1,300m, ED+). They traversed to the higher southeast summit before descending their route. The climbing was mainly ice and mixed, 25 pitches up to Scottish 6 and A3. The expedition was only allowed to approach this troubled area from the south via Manali, Udaipur, and along the Chenab River to Atholi/Gulabgarh—the route followed by the 2011 team. The mountain was named for its similar appearance to Cerro Torre.*

HIMACHAL PRADESH

MIYAR VALLEY

Mont Maudit seen from northwest, with Czech route marked. *Martin Klonfar*

*"Mont Maudit", northwest face and north ridge.* Many road blocks caused by landslides delayed arrival in the Miyar Valley, resulting in our seven-member expedition having only eight days at base camp. While five of the team ascended Masala Peak (ca 5,650m, first climbed in 2006) by a straightforward route, David Fajt and I trekked up the Chhudong Glacier. As we were not acclimatized, there was no point in attempting a serious climb. Instead we made two "acclimatization" ascents. We first climbed Grandfather Ezio Peak (often quoted as 5,750m but rather lower). We had planned to follow the 2005 Marcheggiani-Natalini route (F4c) on the southeast ridge, via the Tiziano-Cantalamessa Col, but inadvertently climbed another ridge farther right, which was probably easier.

We then climbed the mountain immediately south of Geruda Peak, via the northwest face and north ridge. This peak has sometimes been referred to as Mt. Maudit. The climbing was straightforward, about M3 and 60°. We had no altimeter but felt the summit was a little higher than Neverseen Tower (5,750m) to our north.

MARTIN KLONFAR, *Czech Republic*

Less than perfect conditions on Mont Maudit. David Fajt in couloir leading to north ridge. *Martin Klonfar.*

*Miyar Valley, various ascents.* Thanks to good preparation, a few spells of good weather, and staying healthy throughout the expedition, Ines Peschel and I made seven ascents in the Miyar, which we visited from mid-August till the end of September.

As on previous expeditions, we were stunned by the beauty of the approach, and the dignity with which the local people lead their lives had a great impact on me. Be friendly and respect everyone, but make your point and fear no one. We took three days to reach base camp. When the horsemen stopped early in the afternoon to make camp for the night, we would climb the hillside above for 500-700m, to aid our acclimatization.

We continued our acclimatization with a new line on the south face of Toro Peak (ca

Gutzele Peak. Black line is ascent on south rib and west pillar; white line descent. Unclimbed higher peak behind has been referred to as Chhudong Matterhorn. *Gerhard Schaar*

Castle Peak (ca 5,470m) from northwest, showing Four Seasons in One Day on west ridge of Iris Peak. Higher summit to left is Stefano Zvaka Peak (ca 5,300m). Main summit of Castle (Tivoli Peak) is hidden behind. *Gerhard Schaar*

(A) Korklum Gou and (B) Kurt Albert Peak from southeast. (1) Shangrila Ridge. (2) 2011 Descent. (3) Never Ending Story. *Gerhard Schaar*

4,900m). We began with a nice slab at the low point in the center of the face. Higher we traversed two big gullies to reach the right side of the headwall above the large central alcove. On the final ridge our line merged with the 2007 Slovenian and 2008 Russian routes. The result was Best of Both Sides (350m, 5.9). [*This route runs a little right of the 2008 Lopez-Pfaf Direttissima and in the upper section probably crosses the 2008 Fredell-Lampley route. See AAJ 2009*]. From the summit we saw a peak, on the east side of the Chhudong Valley, that was the lower of two distinct unclimbed summits north of Castle Peak. A few days later we were camped below it.

Leaving the tent at 3 a.m., we spent the morning climbing easy terrain up the south rib, mostly 5.6 slabs with the occasional 5.8 section. At 10 a.m. we reached a forepeak. After downclimbing to a col on the far side to reach the west pillar, we faced a section of loose rock, which I led, slowly, at 5.9R. At 1 p.m. we reached the summit, naming it Gutzele Peak. Both our altimeters read 5,500m, but we think this was too high and the height more like 5,200-5,300m. To the north lay a higher peak [*sometimes referred to as the Chhudong Matterhorn*], but we were so out of breath we never considered continuing the remaining 200m to its summit. A few rappels, followed by down-climbing a gully, took us back to camp by 5 p.m.

We returned to base, leaving the tent beneath Premsingh Peak (ca 5,200m). After refueling, we came back up with a week's food and climbed a nice east-facing rock ridge left of Pemsingh's Trident Ridge. The 450m climb took us to a summit we named Gou Gou Peak (ca 5,100m), after a strange plant (a small ball with a lot of hair

Northern flank of lower Chhudong Valley. (A) Nazomi, climbed by Sebire and Woldendorp in 2008 (*AAJ 2009*). (B) Gou Gou Peak. (C) Premsingh. Black lines mark ascent routes, Gou Gou Ridge and Trident Ridge; white lines are descents used in 2011. *Gerhard Schaar*

and dozens of blossoms on top). Our climb, Gou Gou Ridge, had much pleasant slab climbing at 5.5/5.6 and a section of 5.8/5.9 passing interesting towers. We returned next day to make the second ascent of Trident Ridge (500m, 6b+, Grmovsek-Grmovsek, 2007), which offers nice crack climbing to 5.9 in the first third, then beautiful 5.8 slabs and a nice ridge, and finally scrambling over loose rock, before climbing through strange towers (5.9R) to the summit. This last part might have been a variant of the original route.

We moved to the Chhudong Valley and tried an established line on Grandfather Enzo Peak, but the weather turned bad, and after several days we retreated to base camp.

Later we climbed a new line up the west ridge of David's 62 Nose (ca 4,850m) on Castle Peak. It is an obvious line with distinctly different sections, and we were surprised to find it had not been climbed. We started with an easy section on the west shoulder, scrambling over 5.5 terrain. This was followed by steep 5.9 cracks, above which an easy traverse led over David's 62 Nose. We then continued to Iris Peak (ca 5,200m) and soon reached a steep, loose 15m step. I climbed it on the right via a small tower of loose blocks. A long middle slabby section led to the final steep section, where two awesome 5.9 pitches up a wall led to the top of Iris Peak. We descended by scrambling north, then down big ledges to the south until we were below David's 62 Nose, after which two rappels took us to the ground. We named the route Four Seasons in One Day (650m, 5.10d).

Two days later we were back in the Dali Valley, camping just below the glacier. Our goal was an unclimbed peak just north of Korklum Gou (5,618m GPS). A long rock ridge, dividing two small glaciers, falls directly southeast from the summit. Simul-climbing as much as possible, we made progress without appearing to gain much height. The sharp ridge between the two glaciers was longer and flatter than we had thought and so loose in places it seemed to fall apart. The ridge steepened, and a series of amazing towers had to be outflanked. After eight hours we saw the top of Korklum Gou to our left and realized we must be close to topping out. Loose gullies and small steps gave way to a snow field and, just before dark, the summit. We'd spotted to the south a rappel descent we could make in the dark, but it had many flakes and boulders, so I repeatedly lowered

Gerhard Schaar negotiating tower on Never-Ending Story.
Gerhard Schaar Collection

Ines, then climbed down, until we could safely make 30m rappels. Once into the snow gully, we made 60m rappels and after a moonlit descent of the glacier, arrived at the tent 18 hours after leaving. We named the route Never-Ending Story (1,100m, 5.8) and the summit Kurt Albert Peak, as a tribute to the recently deceased influential German climber and explorer of new territories.

After a day's rest we moved downvalley to below the gully leading to the start of the south ridge (Shangrila Ridge, Grmovsek-Grmovsek, 2007) on Korklum Gou (Window Peak). This is one of the most prominent lines in the area, involves 500m of scrambling followed by 600m (5.10b R), and leads to a unique summit: a 50m rock tower with a hole through it. Local legend has it that the spirit of a great lama lives in the hole, contemplating the beauty of creation. The spirit descends to the meadows once a year to eat momos and visit its horse (a rock that looks like a saddle). Beginning at 4 a.m., we repeated the Grmovseks' line (rather than taking the direct start of a 2006 Canadian attempt, which stopped short of the summit). We reached the forepeak at 1 p.m. and the summit a little after 3 p.m. We left prayer flags and began our rappel descent of the ridge. A snow storm hit us, and the rest of the way down proved a struggle. We left much gear and were lucky the rope didn't get stuck. I was thankful I'd carried a hammer and seven pitons. Rapping through small waterfalls and downclimbing slabs with no idea where they would lead, we regained our tent 20 hours after leaving.

We always set out for a personal adventure, not to make history, having the experience as a couple, hoping we will have something to tell our grandchildren. Like the glaciers of the Miyar, which at first seem static, we flow steadily and continuously through life.

GERHARD SCHAAR, *Austria*

LAHAUL

*Chandra Bhaga Group: Daund (5,565m); Hora East (ca 5,250m); Pagoda East East (ca 5,750m), east ridge; Tara Pahar (6,227m), east ridge attempt.* Our six-member expedition from Greece originally wanted to attempt unclimbed CB33a. This would involve an approach along the Chandra River from Batal to access the Samudar Tapu Glacier, a route used by a number of previous expeditions. However, we had much difficulty crossing the main stream north of Dakka and farther on found we would have to cross the main Chandra River to access the lower glacier. This was impossible for our horses, and when local shepherds added that horses would not be able to move on the lower glacier, we changed our objective.

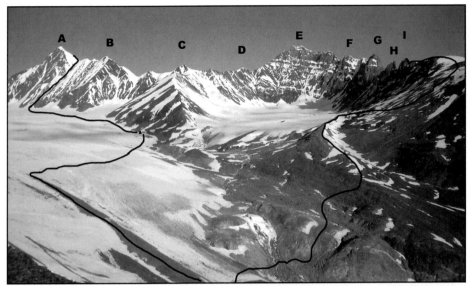

View west to northwest over Sheta Padra Glacier. (A) Tara Pahar (6,227m), with route of attempt marked. (B) Tara Pahar East. (C) Tara Pahar East East. (D) Minar South. (E) Minar (6,172m). (F) CB34 (5,913m). (G) Pagoda (ca 5,790m). (H) Pagoda East. (I) Pagoda East East, with route of ascent marked. *Christophoros Kouniakis*

Daunt from northeast with line of first ascent. *Nikolas Kroupis*

Instead Christophoros Kouniakis, Ioannis Kovanidis, Manolis Loudaros, Polychronis Sioulas, Dimitris Titopoulos, and I, with Sudipto Pal from India, attempted summits above an unnamed glacier that flows east from the Tara peaks. We named this glacier Sheta Padra (White Plateau). We made our base camp at 4,865m, three-and-a-half km east of the glacier, and explored the latter over the next few days, estimating it to be five km long, one-and-a-half broad, and with an altitude between 5,100m and 5,500m.

On July 10 Kovanidis and I left base camp, reached the glacier at 5,150m, and climbed 45° snow slopes on the left side to reach the ridge. From there we followed the crest west to a rocky point we named Daund (Tooth). The same day Kouniakis and Titopoulos climbed a peak immediately southwest of base camp, naming it Hora East.

Early the following morning Kouniakis, Loudaros, and Titopoulos crossed the glacier and reached the ridge extending east from Pagoda (ca 5,790m, southeast of CB34). By following the crest west they planned to reach Pagoda East but stopped at a nearer summit they named Pagoda East East (Pagoda EE). The ridge ahead looked narrow, and as they were short on time, they turned around, reaching base after 12 hours' climbing. There had been no previous attempts on this peak from any side.

On the 12th Korvanidis and I tried to reach Tara Pahar [*CB10, which had been climbed five times through 1984, first in 1955 by a British expedition*]. At 5,325m we found many snow-covered crevasses, forcing us to turn back, cross the glacier much lower, and camp at 5,236m. We left this camp at midnight and climbed for two hours up the right side of the glacier to the southeast couloir of Tara Pahar. We climbed the 40-55° snow couloir to a col on the east ridge at 6,031m (800m, D). A huge serac overhung the south side of the crest above, so we tried to climb the north flank, but stopped at 6,088m due to deep snow and potential avalanche risk. We rappelled to the glacier and returned to base camp. Worsening weather prevented us trying more peaks, and we left base camp on July 19.

NIKOLAS KROUPIS, *Greece*

Ache seen from C Glacier. 2009 expedition climbed peak up broad north face/ridge on left. *Supplied by Tamotsu Nakamura*

Chemma from north. Kazuo Hoshi, *Supplied by Tamotsu Nakamura*

*Ache and Chemma.* The Tokai section of the *Japanese Alpine Club (JAC Tokai)* has made 11 expeditions to the Indian Himalaya since 1988, mainly in Ladakh, Lahaul, and Spiti, where they have climbed 15 summits over 6,000m. The 10th, in 2009, planned to attempt the well-known Karcha Parvat (6,271m), in Lahaul, but found the ridge completely snow-free, so they would have been unable to melt water at camps. Instead they turned to an unnamed 6,066m peak to the south, in the upper Karcha Nala, establishing Camp 1 on July 13 at 4,700m and Camp 2 four days later at 5,200m, on what they called the C Glacier. Four main glaciers rise south from the Karcha River; they have tentatively been designated, from east to west, A, B, C, and D. The headwaters of A Glacier include Peaks

6,060m and 5,968m. B Glacier has Peak 6,105m, C has Peaks 6,066m and 5,945m, and D has Peak 6,010m. D is the largest glacier, and its head forms the watershed with the Lower Bara Shigri Glacier.

On July 19 Naoyuki Adachi (66), Ritusya Matsubara (75), and climbing leader Tsuneo Suzuki (74), with four high-altitude porters, moved south up C Glacier toward the summit. Adachi, Suzuki, and a porter gave up at 5,400m, due to deep snow, but the rest continued and reached the top in early afternoon. They called the peak Ache, which means "daughter" in Lahaul dialect. [*This ascent was briefly mentioned in* AAJ 2010, *where a proposal was noted to call the peak Lower Karcha Parvat.*]

The 11th JAC Tokai expedition took place in July and August 2011, with the aim of climbing Peak 6,150m, at the head of B Glacier. The team comprised Hitoshi Ishii (68), Katsumi Kuze, (63), Yutaka Shinohara (72), and me (60) as leader. From a 4,400m base camp in the Karcha Nala we established Camp 1 at 4,700m, Camp 2 on B Glacier at 5,250m, and Camp 3 near the head of the glacier at 5,550m. We carried oxygen cylinders for medical safety. On August 9 all members reached the summit via the northeast face and ridge. We named the peak Chemma (officially recognized by the IMF).

KAZUO HOSHI, *JAC, Japan, provided by Tamotsu Nakamura*

## KINNAUR

*Shoshala (ca 4,700m), Trishul Direct.* In spring 2010 Frederic Nicole, Bernd Zangerl, and I were exploring the Kinnaur region for new bouldering sites, when we discovered the Baspa Valley, a veritable Shangri-La for the rock climber. Returning to Switzerland I told Yannick Boissenot and Giovanni Quirici. A few minutes of description and two or three photos were enough to give birth to our project.

In April 2011 a 28-hour journey over rough roads took us from Delhi to the village of Raksham (Rakchham). The contrast of the overcrowded, overheated Indian plains with this little corner of paradise at 3,000m was extreme. Our goal was located just above the village: Shoshala, a virgin rock peak rising to ca 4,700m.

Reaching the foot of the face was complicated, and it took a week to find a feasible path for porters. We then took 18 days to climb 19 pitches up the middle of the face to the summit. We were delayed by storms, which hit almost daily and discouraged us from bivouacking on the wall. We fixed ropes and jumared to our high point each day, but this often proved slow and painful. As bad weather frequently arrived by early afternoon, it left little time to push the route forward. Lack of water was

Shoshala, with line of Trishul Direct. *Yannick Boissenot*

Giovanni Quirici on pitch 10 (7a), Trishul Direct. *Yannick Boissenot*

serious; we had to melt water from a snowfield that visibly diminished in the heat and disappeared on our last day. Our idea was to work the route and then redpoint as much as we could. We placed 39 bolts and climbed 750m at 7b, with a little A2. We completed the ascent, which we named Trishul Direct, in May. It was the last expedition that Yannick and I would have the joy of sharing with Giovanni. On August 12, 2011, he was killed in a fall on the Eiger North Face.

To see Yannick's film Shoshala, visit www.redpointmovie.fr/shoshala

ELIE CHEVIEUX, *Switzerland*

WESTERN GARHWAL

GANGOTRI

*Meru Central (6,310m), East Pillar (a.k.a Shark's Fin).* Americans Conrad Anker, Jimmy Chin and Renan Ozturk completed one of the most attempted and coveted lines in the Himalaya, when they reached the summit of Meru Central via the 1,400m east pillar (a.k.a Shark's Fin). Since the first known serious attempt in 1986, this compelling line had been tried well over 20 times by many of the world's foremost alpinists, including Anker twice, and Chin and Ozturk once. Above the initial snow/ice face, the climb involves hard free, ice, mixed and aid, with difficulties up to 6a A4 WI5 M6. It was one of six ascents nominated for a 2012 Piolet d'Or, and a full account appears earlier in the *Journal*. On an historical note, it was the 1993 British expedition, led by Paul Pritchard, that first coined the name The Shark Fin (no apostrophe), referring specifically to the east pillar of the then unclimbed Meru Central.

*Bhagirathi III, The Seed of Madness, not to summit.* Roberto delle Monache and I hoped to repeat the Spanish route, Impossible Star (1,300m, 28 pitches, UIAA VI A3+, Aldeguer-Martinez-Moreno-Tomas, 1984), on the west face of Bhagirathi III (6,454m). However, the weather proved too bad for rock climbing, so on September 13 we turned to the broad icy face to the left that leads toward the 6,050m col between Bhagirathis III and IV. We originally planned to climb the left side of this face, close to the rocks of 6,193m Bhagirathi IV, unaware that this line had been climbed by French the previous year. However, after the first pitch we found the snow too soft to go left, so we continued up right. (There was considerably less snow than during the French ascent. Their base camp was on snow; ours was more or less in the same spot but on flowers). After six pitches we reached the right side of a broad snow/ice field, where we stopped for a few hours because the snow was getting soft. It was late when we started up the steep wall above. The next 50m took three hours, and then, while aiding overhanging rock, I fell 10m when a piton pulled. I descended, leaving the rope in place, and we bivouacked. The altitude was 5,745m.

Next day I reached the top of the fixed rope and, instead of trying the overhanging rock above, made a scary traverse left on thin ice to a good belay. The next pitch was not as technical but delicate. Then Roberto led a wonderful pitch on good ice, followed by another, which included aid to pass a roof. Above, we were hit by an avalanche. For three minutes we were pummelled by spindrift while on belay. After the 12th pitch, 300m of snow (up to 60-70°), generally deep and worrisome, led to the ridge above. We climbed it roped but with no protection, following the avalanche channel, to arrive on the north ridge of Bhagirathi III at 6,178m (GPS). The ridge was covered in unstable snow and proved too thin for us to proceed farther, so we bivouacked on the crest. We'd planned to climb the face in a day and had taken little food, so we were really tired. It was 10:30 p.m. and snowing hard.

West face of Bhagirathi III-IV col. Bhagirathi IV summit on left, left side of Bhagirathi III west face to right. (1) La Fée Clochette. (2) The Seed of Madness. *Daniele Nardi*

We had planned to finish our route on the summit of Bhagirathi IV, but this was now out of the question. Next day we climbed only 50m toward this summit, when I spotted a piece of rope on the east flank. We descended from the crest, then climbed and traversed, making six rappels, across the east flank to the straightforward east ridge of Bhagirathi IV. We descended easily to the glacier and made the long walk back to base camp. That morning we had started at 7 a.m., but poor visibility, this being our third day, and our not having eaten since the first meant we didn't reach the tents until 10 p.m. Our round trip had involved 52 hours of climbing.

We named the 1,000m route The Seed of Madness (1,250m of climbing, WI5+ M6/ M7 A2+).

DANIELE NARDI, *Italy*

Daniele Nardi on overhanging mixed ground, pitch 8 of The Seed of Madness. *Roberto Delle Monache*

*Editor's note:The French route, La Fée Clochette, was briefly mentioned in* AAJ 2011. *The four climbers were Simon Duverney, Benjamin Guigonnet, Christophe Moulin, and Cédric Perillat. They finished at the 6,050m col, also finding conditions too dangerous to continue up the ridge to the summit of Bhagirathi III. They descended east, which they found easy, and walked back around the mountain. They found the crux to be the section above pitch one. Thanks to Perillat for this information.*

*Miandi Peak, correction.* In *AAJ 2008* we published a report from Pat Deavoll on the presumed first ascent of Peak 6,465m, a mountain she climbed from the west and later named Miandi Peak, as it sits above Miandi (or Maiandi) Bamak (Glacier). However, while the route was probably new, the mountain had been climbed at least once before.

Peak 6,465m was climbed on September 21, 1987, by an expedition from The London Hospital (UK), which entered the Swachand Bamak and established Camp 2 at 5,870m on the north face. From here John Sanders and Richard Stradling climbed to the summit. There were no major difficulties but interesting mixed climbing between 6,000 and 6,200m.

Upper Ronti Glacier and Trisul (7,120m). Route followed on historic first ascent of Trisul in 1907 finished up left skyline ridge. West ridge (right skyline) drops to Ronti Saddle, first crossed in 1936 by Eric Shipton. Next col west was first climbed from the far side in 1927 by Tom Longstaff and Hugh Ruttledge. From it ridge rises toward Nanda Ghunti (6,309m), well off picture to the right. *Anindya Mukherjee*

Looking southwest from Dudh Ganga Col. Corniced peak left of rocky peak in center is Nanda Ghunti (6,309m, left skyline is route of first ascent by Swiss in 1947), while peak to right is Ronti (6,063m, first climbed in 1955 from southeast) with its unclimbed northeast face in partial profile. *Anindya Mukherjee*

EASTERN GARHWAL

*Dudh Ganga Col (5,350m) and Deotoli Col (5,400m), first ascents.* Lhakpa Sherpa, Nandan Singh Negi, Pemba Sherpa, Thendup Sherpa, and I reached a previously unvisited col on the ridge north of Berthatoli Himal. West of Lata we headed south and crossed two passes traditionally used by shepherds to access the Ronti Valley. We crossed the Ronti Valley to the east and reached a col, which is on the ridge northwest of unclimbed Berthatoli North (6,352m). We named it Dudh Ganga Col. We then descended the far side to an unnamed glacier, crossed it, and climbed to a second pass on the ridge north of Berthatoli North, which we named Deotoli Col. Our route would provide an alternative into the Nanda Devi Sanctuary, but obeying the law of the land, we neither set foot on the valley floor nor entered the Sanctuary. Neither pass required climbing skills and could be reached by any seasoned Himalayan trekker. We hope the photos will encourage mountaineers to consider unclimbed objectives in this area.

ANINDYA MUKHERJEE, *India*

KUMAUN

*Changuch (6,322m), northwest ridge from south.* Before 2009 Changuch was attempted unsuccessfully three times from the south, via the Pindari Glacier. In that year Martin Moran's British expedition approached from the Lawan Valley to the north and made the first ascent via the northwest ridge (*AAJ 2010*). In spring I was asked by the IMF to organize another attempt from the south, and on May 29 we established base camp at 3,565m on the true right bank of the Pindar River. Above, 40-50° grassy slopes led to the terminal moraine of the Buria Glacier, where boulder slopes and a semi-rocky face (on which ropes had to be fixed) took us to advanced base at 4,477m, on a grassy platform the size of a helipad. After making seven carries we moved to this camp on June 5.

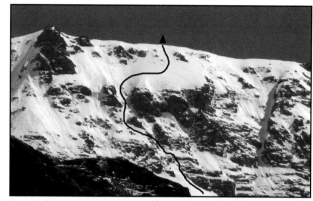

Route to Camp 1 rises at up to 50°. *Dhruv Joshi*

Route from Camp 1 to Camp 2 across the upper Pindari Glacier. Chota Changuch is small summit just left of camp. Above camp, northwest ridge, seen in profile, leads directly to Changuch's summit. *Dhruv Joshi*

A weaving route through snow and rock slopes up to 50° took us to Camp 1 at 5,380m, a few ropes being fixed on the difficult sections. From here we made a nearly horizontal traverse right for three km on the upper Pindari Glacier, above the icefall and beneath the slopes of Nanda Khat (6,611m) and Traill's Pass. This took us to below the small pointed summit of Chota Changuch on the long northwest ridge of Changuch. The last expedition to come this way met with

Approaching top of Changuch's northwest ridge. *Dhruv Joshi*

Camp 2 (Col Camp) with northwest ridge and summit of Changuch ahead. Flat-topped summit visible to left is Nanda Kot (6,861m). *Dhruv Joshi*

disaster. In September and October 2007 a joint IMF-Indian Navy team followed a similar route, establishing Camp 1 at 5,050m. They were dogged by bad weather, but eventually a party, hoping to place Camp 2 close to or on the northwest ridge, reached 5,650m (the highest altitude so far attained on the mountain) before retreating in a huge storm. Early next morning Camp 1 was hit by an avalanche, which killed two members and badly injured a third. With the route down to advanced base obliterated by snow, the survivors and injured member had to be evacuated by helicopter, though the two bodies were not recovered.

For us the upper Pindari Glacier was well covered in snow, which allowed us to cross the many crevasses easily. We climbed 250m up 45-50° slopes just right (east) of Chota Changuch, reaching the ridge above at a col. It was this col that the British expedition had reached from the opposite side. From below, the crest had appeared broad, but we discovered it was little more than two meters wide, offering an exposed site for Camp 2 or Col Camp (5,755m, two tents). The ascent from Camp 1 took 10 exhausting hours, and we decided to rest the following day, during which we collected ropes fixed on the face below.

At 12:15 a.m. on the 17th Bharat Bhushan, K Wallambok Lyngdon, Takpa Norboo, Chetan Pandey, and I roped together and set off for the summit. A 200m-long traverse on an exposed 50-60° snow/ice slope forced us to fix ropes, though we removed them during the descent. The ridge was narrow throughout, but at 9.50 a.m. we reached the summit, for its second ascent. Despite an unexpected blizzard on the way back, we were in camp at 4 p.m. We regained base camp on the 20th, cleaned up, and were back in Delhi on the 28th.

Dhruv Joshi, *India*

SIKKIM

Jopuno massif (5,936m) from northeast. Face lies above Zor Patam Valley, which has never been explored. *Anindya Mukherjee*

In the footsteps of John Claude White and photography of unclimbed peaks. From March 9 to 22 Indians Anindya Mukherjee and Thendup Sherpa made the first upstream trek along the Ronggyaong and Rukel River systems, leaving the Teesta River at Sanklang, reaching the lower Talung Glacier southeast of

Kangchenjunga, and crossing the higher Guicha La to Yoksum. This journey was completed in reverse during 1890 by John Claude White, the official in administrative charge of Sikkim. In 1920 the Scottish mountaineer Harold Raeburn, with Lt. Col. H.W. Tobin, appears to have made a similar journey, examining the Talung and neighboring Tongshiong Glaciers before retracing White's steps. Both parties traveled during the monsoon, and neither described much of the terrain nor the surrounding mountains. More importantly, apparently no photographs were taken, though White wrote, "I do not think this journey could be equalled throughout the world for its beauty and variety of scene, the magnificent gorges, with wonderful waterfalls tumbling down on all sides." Since that time permission to repeat this trek has not been granted.

North face of unclimbed Peak 5,526m, northwest of Narsing, from Zor Patam Valley. *Anindya Mukherjee*

South faces of unclimbed Peak 4,640m (left) and Peak 4,540m at head of the Ringvingram Chu, north of Sakyong. *Anindya Mukherjee*

In respect for the pioneers, Mukherjee and Thendup eschewed modern technology and navigated using only standard contour maps and a compass. They followed the Ronggyaong Valley to Sakyong, after which they took a faint poachers' trail, finding ample evidence of illegal hunting of Himalayan blue sheep and tahr (goat). Beyond

Unclimbed north face of Narsing (5,825m). *Anindya Mukherjee*

there were no paths, and they made slow progress through dense forest and undergrowth. Higher they photographed the unexplored northern and eastern sides of Tingchingkang, Jopuno, Lama Lamani, and Narsing, all except the latter Alpine Peaks now open to climbers (*AAJ 2008*), and Zemu Peak, one of the highest unclimbed summits in the world. Judging by White's description, the Talung Glacier has much

Rare view of Kangchenjunga's south summit, with unclimbed Zemu Peak (7,780m, one of highest unclimbed summits in the world) on Kangchenjunga's east-southeast ridge. Right of figure, partially obscured by foliage, is Simvu (6,812m). *Anindya Mukherjee*

receded, and the 2011 pair had no problem crossing it. Heading southwest toward the watershed, they stumbled upon a faint cairned track, which they followed to a col. This turned out not to be 4,940m Guicha La but a ca 5,100m pass to the southeast, closer to Pandim, and also inadvertently crossed by Tilman in 1938. From here it took only a day and a half to descend the Onglakthang Valley south to the roadhead at Yoksum.

Mukherjee hopes that if a trail can be established through the Ronggyaong and Rukel Valleys, the journey would appeal to adventurous trekkers, and as a by-product could put an end to illegal hunting.

LINDSAY GRIFFIN,
*Mountain INFO, from
information provided by
Anindya Mukherjee*

Sunrise on Tongshyong Glacier. Rounded dome on left is Talung. Pointed peak to right is Kangchenjunga South, with summit of Zemu Peak to its right. *Anindya Mukerjee*

Thendup Sherpa climbing final rock wall toward Zemu Gap. *Anindya Mukherjee*

*Kangchenjunga Himal, Zemu Gap (5,861m), first documented ascent from the south.* Reaching Zemu Gap from the south proved a long-standing mountaineering problem. The Gap (27°40'9"N, 88°12'53"E) lies on the high ridge extending east from the south summit of Kangchenjunga, between unnamed Peak 7,038m and the Simvu Twins (6,812m and 6,811m). From the north (Zemu Glacier) it is straightforward; from the south (Tongshyong Glacier) it is a steep icefall, though the main problem is the remote, complicated approach. Dr. Alexander Kellas was the first to reach the col, in May 1910, from a high camp above Zemu Glacier. In 1920 Tobin and Raeburn tried from the south but found the objective danger so great "the route would have been little short of suicidal." In 1925 the Greek photographer N. Tombazi claimed to have reached it from the south (and while in the region apparently made one of the earliest sightings of the yeti), but he took no photographs, and his ascent is doubted. The following year Captain Boustead said he'd reached the Gap from the south, but H.W. Tilman, in 1936, found Boustead's description completely at variance with reality. Tilman tried from the south but found the final ice wall impregnable. In the intervening years the Gap had seen another

Looking south from approach to Zemu Gap. Pandim (6,691m) distant left. Guicha La in center at foot of Pandim's west-northwest ridge. Unclimbed Peak 5,962m on right. Unclimbed Peak 5,684m in middle distance left, and between the two Tilman's snow col (5,206m). *Anindya Mukerjee*

ascent from the north, by two members of Paul Bauer's 1929 Kangchenjunga expedition. In 1937 John Hunt and Pasang Kikuli also reached the Gap from the north, as did Tilman in 1938. Tilman descended the south side, making the only crossing of the col. An Indian team failed from the south in 1975, after which bureaucratic difficulties made it impossible to visit this region until 2008, when a small British team gained a permit to cross the Guicha La to the Talung Glacier, and hence via the Tongshyong Glacier cross the Gap from south to north. They traversed the La but were turned back shortly after, as were Indians in 2010.

In November 2011 we crossed the Guicha La and continued up the Tongshyong Glacier, until five days of heavy snow thwarted our chances, and we escaped following Claude White's 1890 footsteps east to Sakyong Sanklan, Sampo, and finally Mangan.

In December I returned with Pemba

Route taken to Zemu Gap from south. *Anindya Mukerjee*

Sherpa and Thendup Sherpa, starting our trek from above Mangan on the 5th. On the 9th we put base camp on the Tongshyong Glacier at 3,750m and by the 12th had Camp 2 at 4,968m. On the 14th we placed Camp 3 at 5,250m on the moraine shelf above the first icefall on the glacier descending from Zemu Gap. Next day it took us six hours to climb the second icefall (250m) and the final headwall (200m), avoiding the overhanging blue ice that dominates the center of the Gap by the rock wall to its left. While ours is the first documented ascent from the south, and Boustead's claim is as unbelievable as Maestri's claimed first ascent of Cerro Torre, we find no reason to believe Tombazi did not reach the Gap.

ANINDYA MUKHERJEE, *India*

*Bahini Group, Tridesh (ca 5,100m), Soneri Behin (ca 5,250m), and Prabha Behin (ca 5,500m); Jopuno correction.* Between October 16 and November 3 David Kinsella (Australia), Arun Mahajan (India and US), and I explored mountains on the east side of the Thangsing Valley, climbing three summits as alpine-style one-day routes. This area, which we have named the Bahini (Sisters) Group, lies immediately south of Lama Lamani (ca 5,650m) and above the Arralang Valley. Julie-Ann Clyma and I had reconnoitered it during an October 2004 trek. The following year, after making the first ascent of Lama Lamani North, we saw a peak to the east that I later I mistook for Narsing (5,825m), an image of which was published on p.118, *AAJ 2008*. In fact this peak is unnamed and shown as 5,526m on the 1:150,000 Sikkim Himalaya map (published by the Swiss Foundation for Alpine Research, 2006). The Bahini Group is not shown on the Swiss map, and as far as we could ascertain, none of the peaks had names or been climbed. We hope the nomenclature we have used is acceptable locally, regionally, and to any interested organizations.

Bahini Group from the east. (A) Lama Lamani-Prabhu Behin Col. (B) Unnamed. (C) Prabha Behin. (D) Unnamed. (E) Kali Behin. (F) Soneri Behin. (G) Churi. (H) Kanchi Behin. *Roger Payne*

From a base camp at Thangsing, we established a comfortable advanced camp at 4,800m, below a prominent rock tower we called Chowkidar (Sentry). On October 23 we made an acclimatization reconnaissance to the col between Lama Lamani and Prabha Behin (Prabha means radiance, shine, or glow, while Behin is sister). The

Arun Mahajan on traverse during first ascent of Prabha Behin. Behind, on Nepal border, are (left to right) Koktang, Rathong, and various Kabru summits. *Roger Payne*

latter is the highest summit of the Bahini Group and is probably the one marked as 5,480m on the Swiss map.

On the 27th we climbed Tridesh (Three Lands), which is just west of the Bahini Group. Initially we had to descend from our camp to the base of the peak, which we climbed via its northeast flank on snowed-up rock (PD+, UIAA II-III). From the summit we could see that the east and south sides of the mountain had extensive rock faces, and we had good views of the lakes at Lam Pokri.

Soneri Behin (Golden Sister,) was our second peak, which we

Arun Mahajan on crux rock moves, northwest ridge of Prabha Behin. *Roger Payne*

climbed on the 28th, retracing our route of the previous day, then heading up to a hanging valley with a small glacier. We ascended this to reach the east ridge via unstable rock. The ridge itself was solider, with enjoyable rock steps (II), and the route had an overall grade of PD+. From the summit we retraced our route down the ridge, then descended a snow couloir on the north side, so making a circular route back to Chowkidar camp. The northwest ridge of Soneri Behin includes another lower summit we called Kanchi Behin (Small Sister) and remarkable rock towers we called Churi (Knife).

The third peak, climbed by Mahajan and me, was Prabha Behin, which felt higher than the map height. We climbed a snow/ice crest in the broad northwest couloir, with a leftward traverse at the top to reach the crest of the northwest ridge. This was mixed and exposed, with sections of technical rock (IV) and an overall grade of AD+/D-. The summit block is small, and required an athletic leap to reach (unnecessarily, as an easy ramp comes up from the south side). The connecting ridge west to lower summits appeared loose initially, but the lower summits look attractive, in particular Kali Behin (Black Sister), which seen from the west is an impressive black tower.

There is a correction to my report in *AAJ 2011*. On Jopuno in 2001 the climbers did not ascend the northwest face. Kunzang Bhutia, Deepak Kumar Chettri, and Sagar Raj actually climbed the right side of the southwest face, and then up the south ridge of Jopuno—a notable effort undertaken with minimal equipment. Having checked with them, it seems they reached a summit on the south ridge that may not be the highest point of the mountain. As I mentioned in *AAJ 2011*, from my knowledge of Jopuno I feel that it was not this mountain that W.W. Graham climbed in 1883. Therefore, until someone traverses the summit ridge or reaches the summit on a clear day, the ascent in 2008 by Jason Halladay and Josh Smith could be the only time the highest point of the mountain has been reached.

What is certain is that there are many summits in Sikkim that can be explored and climbed alpine-style and that access can be arranged through the tourism organizations and Sikkim state authorities in Gangtok. In eight trips since 2004, to peaks in west and north Sikkim, I have enjoyed valuable assistance from friends in the Sikkim Amateur Mountaineering Association (SAMA), and Barap Bhutia and the staff of Sikkim Holidays in Gangtok. Also the Travel Agents Association of Sikkim (TAAS) has done impressive work to increase the capacity and skills of service providers and to develop a structure for mountain rescue, working with SAMA and state authorities. You can approach organizations in Sikkim with confidence, knowing that they can make the necessary arrangements for exploratory treks and expeditions.

ROGER PAYNE, *Switzerland*

# Nepal

*The online version of these reports frequently contains additional photos, maps, topos, and extended text. Please visit aaj.americanalpineclub.org*

## FAR WEST NEPAL

## CHANDI HIMAL

*Changwatang (6,130m), east spur and northwest ridge.* The Limi Valley, in a hidden corner of northwest Nepal, is an exotic place. It has a community comprised of three ethnic Tibetan villages—Jang, Waljie, and Til. These villages are difficult to reach from Nepal and completely cut off during the long months of winter. A forgotten valley.

On September 20, 2011, a dramatic change came to Jang. For the first time a truck loaded with merchandise reached the village, marking the opening of a road from China that passes over the ca 5,000m Lapche La. Several days later a convoy of trucks and a few jeeps carrying Chinese

Changwatang from north-northwest. French party crossed small glacier and climbed long snow spur back right to crest of northwest ridge, which they followed left to summit. *Paul Grobel*

Unexplored peaks of Chandi Himal astride Tibetan border, northeast of Changwatang. These summits rise to ca 6,200m and have large glaciers on Tibetan side. Range continues east to frontier pass of Chang La. *Paulo Grobel*

officials crossed the border. An offering was made to the Jang gompa, and there was a celebration to mark the beginning of the harvest and of a new era.

For our small group heading to Changwatang, this was a considerable surprise. From our perspective as trekkers we saw the road as offensive, something marring the landscape. However, it forced us to reconsider our

Unnamed and unclimbed summit in Limi massif. *Paulo Grobel*

egocentric perception of the world and to accept other realities, to try to understand the differing values of others. One world had died, and another was born with a burst of energy. Things change, and that's how it is. Paths were never created for the small world of trekkers. Perhaps it will be necessary to create new routes for foot travel in the Limi Valley, so that tourism can develop.

Located to north, a few steps from the Chinese border, Changwatang is more interesting than its modest altitude suggests. The mountain offered several pleasant surprises, including a climbing route with alpine character. We followed a beautiful glacier along the northern flanks, then climbed an east-facing snow spur to the crest of the northwest ridge, which led easily to the summit. There was an exceptional view toward Gurla Mandhata and a region of huge unknown peaks. We descended the northwest ridge to its base, then went west around a subsidiary peak to regain base camp in the main valley [*Editor's note: Although Changwatang was not officially opened until 2002, it received an ascent two years before by four Japanese and two Sherpas, led by Tamotsu Ohnishi. It is believed this party climbed the northwest ridge integrally, approaching from the west and placing a high camp at 5,730m. In 2008 Michihiro Honda's Japanese expedition made the second ascent, via the south ridge.*]

Between Simikot and Changwatang, the Limi massif offers more than16 peaks above 6,000m and countless glaciated lower peaks and unnamed passes. Every one of these summits is unclimbed, and there is the possibility of a high-altitude traverse from here north to Changwatang. Aside from alpinism, Changwatang is an invitation to step into another world. It is a good reason to visit a rarely seen region of Nepal, where kids don't hassle you for pens or pencils as you pass.

PAULO GROBEL, *France, translated by Todd Miller*

## NALAKANKAR HIMAL

*Kanti Himal, Gojung (6,310m), west face.* In October Dave Turnbull and I, with Graham Desroy and Jonny Ratcliffe, visited West Nepal. Graham and Jonny's activity is recorded below. Dave and I made the first ascent of a mountain called Gojung. Formerly referred to as Mugu Chuli, this summit is situated in the remote Kojichuwa Valley, above the village of Mugu, a region little traveled by any foreigners, let alone mountaineers. During our three and a half weeks in the area, we saw only one other western visitor.

Route followed by Fowler and Turnbull on 1,100m (ED) west face of Gojung (right), and their descent north over Peak 6,264m and down glaciated west flank of frontier ridge. *Mick Fowler*

Looking steeply up west face of Gojung. Ascent followed obvious ice couloir, then snow and mixed slopes above. *Dave Turnbull*

As you would expect, the climbing history of this valley is sparse. The first mountaineers to carry out reconnaissance were most likely Mallorcans in 2008. Their goal was to inspect unclimbed Kojichuwa Chuli (6,439m), situated on the Tibetan border in the northeast corner of the valley, for a serious attempt the following year. However, they noticed a 6,310m peak on the frontier ridge to the south, which they described as "outstanding" and dubbed it Mugu Chuli, being unaware that it had the local name Gojung.

The Mallorcans returned in April 2009, with both peaks on their list, but were not successful. Just as they were leaving, Nick Colton, Ed Douglas, Julian Freeman-Attwood, and Rob Greaves entered the valley and proceeded to climb six peaks, between 4,900m and 5,400m. They also noted an ice/mixed line on the west face of Gojung, and Ed Douglas was kind enough to send me a photograph.

After a seven-day trek from a small airport close to Rara Lake and three days of acclimatization on peaks up to 5,300m, Dave and I set off from base camp to bivouac at the foot of Gojung's west face. Over the next four days we climbed the attractive central ice line. Benefiting from a previous heavy monsoon and very cold but stable weather, we found the initial 300m couloir in excellent condition. An icefield was then followed by steep mixed climbing and a scenic rising traverse over ice/mixed terrain, to reach the upper section of the face. A final mixed barrier gave access to summit slopes, and we made a fifth bivouac (above base camp) close to the summit.

Next day started fine, but, as we made a 10-minute ascent to the summit, a storm was building in the west. Prior to the expedition we had been unsure how to get off Gojung, but once in the valley we decided on a pleasing-looking, though long, descent to the north. Rappelling the ascent line would not have been aesthetically pleasing so, despite incoming weather, we committed to the original plan. Having made a tricky descent northeast to the col between Gojung and Peak 6,264m, we bivouacked and next day crossed the virgin 6,264m and continued north along the frontier ridge. With the weather still not clear, we were forced to bivouac again. Fortunately, we awoke to a perfect dawn and started down the previously scoped line on the west flank. After a long day we reached the valley floor and bivouacked for our eighth night. A tedious slog across glacier and snow-covered moraine then saw us reunited with the rest of the team.

Mick Fowler on scenic rising traverse on upper face. *Dave Turnbull*

In the meantime Desroy and Ratcliffe had explored the head of the valley and climbed an unnamed 5,800m peak on the frontier, west of the Kojichuwa La, which gave a loose scramble but fine views of Tibet and Kojichuwa Chuli. They also attempted unclimbed Peak 5,623m, on the east side of the valley, but retreated a few ropelengths below a col at the base of an easy-looking summit ridge, when snow and ice slopes disappeared into some of the worst rock imaginable.

MICK FOWLER, *Alpine Club, U.K.*

KANJIROBA HIMAL

*Roma (5,407m) and Danphe Sail (6,103m), attempts.* Veteran Japanese explorer Tamotsu Ohnishi, with a Japanese companion and a Sherpa, planned to attempt Roma (5,407m), southwest of Saipal, and Danphe Sail, north of Kanjiroba on the Tibet border. Ohnishi had wanted to attempt Danphe Sail during an expedition in West Nepal in 2009 (*AAJ 2010*).

Approaching Roma during April via Chainpur and Dhuli, the team was stopped at 3,800m when unable to cross a gorge. They retreated and headed for Danphe Sail. In May and June the three established base camp below the south side of the mountain at 3,900m and Camp 1 at 4,200m. Ohnishi was ill from insect bites on his feet that had become infected, and they abandoned the climb. Both peaks have been on the permitted list since 2002 but are officially unclimbed. Ohnishi's were the first recorded "attempts."

ELIZABETH HAWLEY, *AAC Honorary Member, Nepal, and* RICHARD SALISBURY,
*The Himalayan Database*

Sonia Bailiff climbing Sanctuary Peak. (A) Kande Hiunchuli (6,627m). (B) Patrasi (6,450m). (C) Peak 6,207m. *Paulo Grobel*

Eastern rim of northern Kanjiroba sanctuary. (A) Peak 5,782m. (B) Col Infranssisable (5,500m), reached by Bailiff and Grobel in 2009 from far side. (C) Peak 5,925m. (D) Hopeless Peak (6,036m). (E) Sanctuary Peak (6,025m). (F) Japanese Pass (5,831m). *Paulo Grobel*

Sonia Bailiff on glaciers below Japanese Pass. (A) Peak 6,117m (Patrasi off-picture left). (B) Peak 6,207. (C) Peak 6,313m. (D) Kanjiroba Northwest (6,289m). (E) Kanjiroba North (6,858m). *Paulo Grobel*

**Sanctuary Peak (6,025m) and Hopeless Peak (6,036m), north ridges from Japanese Pass.** Protected on all sides by Shey Phoksundo National Park, the Kanjiroba massif is wild and rarely visited. No trails or trekking itineraries go near it, but many summits are open for climbers, and currently permits are free. The route from Surket to Jumla, as well as a paved landing strip at Jumla, aid in organizing expeditions to this region, which is far removed from the usual centers of tourism.

The Kanjiroba massif is of particular interest to mountaineers in search of adventure. A visit not only allows you to discover western Nepal but brings the benefits of tourism to the residents of this area, helping to create a tourism balance between Nepal's various regions.

In November our goal was to establish a high-level route into the heart of the massif, to exit west over a high col, and follow the valley of the Chaudhabise Khola directly back to Jumla. To do this we got a permit for Patrasi (6,450m), even though we knew it would be impossible for us to reach the summit. However, a small unnamed 6,207m peak, at the northeastern head of the glacial cirque between Kanjiroba and Patrasi, offered an elegant goal that we could accomplish alpine style. We envisaged that the panorama from its summit would include a close-up of Bhula Lhasa (6,102m), a peak north of Patrasi climbed in 1961 by John Tyson during a noteworthy exploratory expedition.

The history of alpinism in the Kanjiroba massif involves a colorful cast of characters: Tichy, Tyson, an

Kanjiroba, with elegant northwest ridge falling from south summit (6,883m). Japanese climbed "northwest ridge" of Kanjiroba in 1979, but their account states they made Camp 3 (6,580m) before Kanjiroba North (rounded shoulder at left end of north ridge, 6,858m, unclimbed) and traversed below it, implying that they followed left skyline ridge in image. Other four ascents of Kanjiroba South followed south face and southeast ridge, first climbed in 1970 by Japanese. *Paulo Grobel*

all-women British expedition to Lha Shamma (6,412m), and the Japanese, who always seem to be ahead of the curve when it comes to exploration. More recently the British team of Alison and Tom Wedgewood, by chance and in bad weather, established the first route into the massif that avoids the formidable Jagdula Khola gorge. Theirs is a captivating story, which could have ended badly, but their Honeymoon Trail is the only reasonable route to Kanjiroba base camp and the sanctuary. It is used only by locals during the summer, and the initial path is gradually becoming an established trail, although it remains rocky and exposed.

The Kanjiroba massif is not a trekking destination and has no large established trails. One must be sure-footed to cross Honeymoon Pass and gain access to the Jagdula Khola and Kanjiroba sanctuary. We considered ourselves well prepared, having already been on two expeditions to different sides of the massif, scoping out new routes. But as soon as we gained access to the sanctuary, making base camp at 4,650m, we realized getting back out would be difficult. Glacier retreat had been so dramatic that the col we had gained from the far side just two years earlier was now inaccessible. We abandoned our objective of Peak 6,207m and concentrated on traversing part of the eastern rim, south of Kande Hiunchuli (6,627m), and descending to the upper Chaudhabise Khola, known locally as Bijora Khola Valley.

The weather in late fall was perfect, with hardly a breath of wind. Surrounded by beautiful peaks, we started out slowly on an exciting but only moderately difficult ridge. We named the big col at the start of our route Japanese Pass (5,831m), after the first Japanese team to visit the area back in 1958. We named the first peak on the ridge Sanctuary Peak. It was climbed on November 24, 25, and 26 by Sonia Baillif, Hugues De Varax, Kishor Gurung, Dane Magyar, Yannick Marietti, Marco Meisser, Jean-Louis Perette, Ang Dawa

Looking east up Athahra Saya Khola Valley. (A) Pt. 6,621m. (B) Fukan Glacier. (C) Hindu Himal. (D) Panbari. (E) Lilia Peak. (F) Athahra Saya Khola Himal. (G) Athahra Saya Glacier. *Paulo Grobel*

Sherpa, and me. On the 25th Bailiff, Meisser, and I continued south to the main summit on this section of ridge, which we named Hopeless Peak.

Because the cook team was waiting for us on the west side of the range, we ran out of food at base camp, and to add more spice to the adventure, one of our group injured a knee and was having trouble walking. Our sanctuary at the end of the world, so aesthetic and exceptional, had become a trap. An injured person, a long and difficult descent, the lack of food, and the fact that we were running out of time forced a quick decision. We descended to base camp in the sanctuary, and I called a helicopter to evacuate the whole group to Jumla.

It was a brutal and dissatisfying end to our trip, but we now know there is no easy way out from the Jagdula Khola valley. The Kanjiroba high-level route has yet to be established, and it may not be possible. However, this access over Honeymoon Pass to the base camps for Kanjiroba and the sanctuary is now established and mapped. It gives a much easier approach to routes on Kanjiroba, as well as many beautiful unnamed summits. And little Peak 6,207m is still unclimbed. The real exploration of the sanctuary can now begin.

PAULO GROBEL, *France. Translated by Todd Miller*

PERI HIMAL

*Athahra Saya Khola Himal (6,767m), southeast ridge over Hindu Himal (6,306m) and Lilia Peak (6,425m).* Athahra Saya Khola Himal (Mountain of 1,800 Rivers) is a bizarre name, one that evokes the feeling of a faraway place, a mythical wonderland of Buddhist culture, exotic. This is the name we gave to a previously unclimbed 6,767m summit on the Tibetan border, just north of Panbari (6,905m), in the region between Samdo and Phu, north of the Manaslu massif. Athahra Saya Khola is the Nepali name for the river that flows from the foot of the mountain and is the ancient name of the region now known as Nubri.

The Valley of 1,800 Rivers is dominated by a group of three snowy peaks called Three Brothers, or Tin Bai in Nepalese. They stand in front of Panbari, which is only just visible beyond. They are not technical peaks, nor are they particularly impressive, but they are important geographically,

North ridge of Panbari from summit of Athahra Saya Khola Himal. *Paulo Grobel*

since they control access to the vast glacial plateaus below the east faces of Nemjung and Himlung, also in the Peri Himal. The presence of major cols suggests the possibility of a lovely glaciated traverse from Phu to Samdo.

The route we established is clearly visible when heading up valley and particularly noticeable from La Chen, the col that leads to Ru in Tibet, the home village of many of the inhabitants of Samdo. It is a route that should

Three Brothers (Hindu Himal, Lilia Peak, and Athahra Saya Khola Himal) and route of ascent with high camps. *Paulo Grobel*

become classic, since Panbari, despite being 95m short of 7,000m, will likely draw alpinists seeking new and unexplored terrain. Our route also provides a nice alternative to the heavily crevassed Fukan Glacier, followed by the Japanese who made the only ascent of Panbari (*AAJ 2007*).

Initially I thought the moraine at the junction of the Athahra Saya and Fukan Glaciers would be an impenetrable labyrinth of boulders and debris. However, a base camp on the moraine is comfortable and easily accessible with pack animals. These are readily available, as the large pastures of Samdo village are near.

It snowed heavily during our autumn trip: only two short storms during a stretch of otherwise clear weather, but they dumped more than a meter of light, powdery snow, beautiful to look at but very unstable. At the high camp for Panbari, I woke in the morning and realized that we would not be going to its summit. It had snowed again the night before, and the Nepalese team that was resting at the camp below never rejoined us. However, we were overwhelmed by a bout of energy, so we got out of the tent and wallowed through the snow, eventually gaining the plateau, where we saw Panbari - the summit of our dreams - and the col to its north. The ascent to the plateau comprised huge, moderate snow slopes and a small, elegant arête. It took an entire day to gain just 100m of elevation. Above, on the windswept arête, things went better. We shoveled and shoveled, picking our way up the route with determination and persistence. On October 27 Svend Caron, Jacky Crouset, Jean Milteau, Caroline Strube, Michelle Quatrini, Benoit van

Lerberghe, and I all made it to the top of the dome of Hindu Himal. The day wasn't yet over. Caron, van Lerberghe, and I continued northwest to Lilia Peak, and then van Lerberghe and I kept going to Athahra Saya Khola Himal, reaching the summit at 2:30 p.m. From the top we could see the major col that separates Himlung and Nemjung and will perhaps be part of a future, epic trip between Samdo and Phu.

Svend Carron arriving on plateau, close to top of Hindu Himal. Behind are Athahra Saya Khola Himal (left), on Tibetan border, and Lilia Peak. *Paulo Grobel*

PAULO GROBEL, *France, translated by Todd Miller*

## MANASLU HIMAL

*Thulagi (7,059m), attempt from the south and tragedy.* In November 2010 Belarusian Nikolay Bandalet attempted unclimbed Thulagi alpine style with two Russians, climbing the far right side of the west face of Manaslu to a ridge at 6,400m, then descending the opposite flank to the upper Thulagi Glacier (*AAJ 2011*). Ahead, the northeast ridge of Thulagi looked complex, and given the committing nature of the situation, the climbers descended.

Bandalet returned in the spring with a four-man Belarusian team, and, rather than the northeast ridge, opted to climb the long, convoluted Thulagi Glacier from its base, reaching Thulagi from the south. The summit party, Bandalet and Sergei Belous, called base camp on May 8, saying they had reached the final ridge, where they had found huge amounts of snow and no safe belay points. The message implied they were not far from the summit; they had already spent a night out with no equipment.

No further word was received, and on the 14th and 15th Fishtail Air made a thorough search of the mountain. There was no trace of the climbers, though the rescue team did spot a tent at 6,300m on a glacier terrace south of the summit. The plane landed close by, and one of the rescue team found sleeping bags and equipment in the tent. Footsteps were spotted above the tent, leading to the crest of a sharp ridge.

LINDSAY GRIFFIN, *Mountain INFO*

## ROLWALING HIMAL

*Gaurishankar (7,135m), southwest face attempt.* Germans David Goettler, Stefan Glowacz, and Klaus Fengler hoped to climb a new line on the southwest face. Approaching via the Tengmarnag Gorge, they established Camp 2, in early May, at 5,050m at the foot of the face. Above, unconsolidated loose snow over wet and unprotectable rock made them abandon the climb after trying two separate lines, climbing only one pitch on each. They realized that, in the prevailing conditions, they stood no chance of climbing the face. The summit has been reached only three times, always by the southwest face.

ELIZABETH HAWLEY, *AAC Honorary Member, Nepal, and* RICHARD SALISBURY, *The Himalayan Database.*

*Pangbuk Ri (6,716m, Schneider map; 6,625m, HMG-Finn), southeast face,* Ghost Ride the Whip. In spring 2009, while climbing Jobo Rinjang with Joe Puryear, I saw for the first time Pangbuk Ri. With a massive dual summit and steep flanks on the Nepalese side, it presented an alluring objective. Two years later I had the privilege of returning to the area with Chad Kellogg. After a pleasant week acclimatizing in Rolwaling, we trekked over the Tashi Lapcha to meet Da Temba Sherpa, who had flown to Lukla with our expedition equipment. We established base camp at the toe of the Pangbuk Glacier, next to the last easily accessible water.

View of Pangbuk Ri from east-southeast. Ghost Ride the Whip marked. Boultbee and Davis climbed on far side of the left-hand skyline and may have reached, or got close to, the obvious high snow shoulder. Flat-topped summit to right is slightly lower Pangbuk Ri North, while the peak on far right is Pt 6,478m attempted by Swiss (2009) and French (2010). *David Gottlieb*

During the following week of magnificent day hikes we scouted potential lines, soon realizing that possibly two thirds of the Nepalese side of the mountain was exposed to serac and rockfall. This left an interesting direct route up the main east face. After three days of load carrying, we had advanced base pitched above the last large icefall on the main glacier, tucked below an overhanging cliff.

East face of Pangbuk Ri, showing Ghost Ride the Whip. *David Gottlieb*

We debated climbing the first pitch of steep ice just above camp and leaving ropes in place to speed up our climb. Bad style? Hard on the ropes? Faster take off for a big climb? Big mistake.

In the early hours of November 10 we set off for a single push ascent, to find the ropes frozen into the face. We'd spent a great deal of time tying them off at an angle, hoping to keep them out of the ice. Chad gazed at me with that your turn look. With a prussik for protection, I chipped them out. Seen from the belay above, pink light touched the snow on the upper slopes of Everest. We continued unroped up a couloir of névé and unconsolidated snow. After an hour, the sun hit the top of the face, and soon there was the familiar hum of falling rock and ice. A stone hit my helmet, compromising it. I wanted to take it

Kellogg climbing through runnels and flutes on first ascent of Pangbuk Ri. *David Gottlieb*

off and see the damage, but knew better and kept on climbing with improved motivation.

Higher, as we'd hoped, a more northerly change in aspect eased the rockfall and let us get back to the fun of climbing. A maze of steep snow flutings challenged Chad and me to the edge of our abilities. We led in blocks through small overhangs of unconsolidated snow and ice, reached dead ends, and made long overhanging rappels to reach climbable runnels. Day passed to night, and I went through many second winds. At 2:30 a.m. we were pushing into cold wind on a moonlight-drenched crest, a short distance across easy terrain from the summit. Anchored, we climbed down into a moat or crevasse and melted snow, as we waited for the warmth of the sun, agreeing there was no way we could go back down the route. The sun rose, and we soon stood on the summit, cameras in hand, smiling, but knowing we were merely halfway through the climb.

We descended the opposite side of the mountain. Downclimbing and making more than 20 rappels filled the rest of the day and half the following night. Our adrenalin long ago spent, we placidly cowered as rock and ice

One of several free rappels during descent. *David Gottlieb*

flew by. Our descent line was possibly not the best, yet we let gravity lead us down and by midnight were on the glacier a mere 16km from base camp.

The hike back was a blur of hallucinations and stumbling deep the world of ghosts, while a large moon lit the way. At some point we ditched the packs and at 6 a.m. stumbled into base camp, where Da Temba fed us and sent us to bed, exhausted after our 50-hour climb. It took a week to recover and collect our advanced base, then Chad and I hiked out to Jiri. We named our route Ghost Ride the Whip (1400m, VI AI5 M5). Thanks to Elizabeth Hawley, Jay Janousek, and Joseph Puryear for research support.

DAVID GOTTLIEB, AAC

*Editor's note: This was the first ascent of Pangbuk Ri, brought onto the official list of permitted peaks in 2002. In 1955 Peter Boultbee and Dennis Davis made a spirited attempt from the Menlung Glacier in Tibet. They climbed to a snow shoulder on the west-southwest ridge, but encountered great difficulties trying to get along the connecting ridge toward the main summit. It took four and a half hours to travel 120m along the crest, where they were eventually stopped by a 60m rock tower. The "official" HMG-Finn map gives an altitude of 6,625m for the main summit, but all other maps record 6,716m, and Elizabeth Hawley felt Gottlieb and Kellogg should trust the Schneider map.*

*Dingjung Ri/Rima Mancho (6,263m), first winter ascent, north face.* In mid-January Andy Parkin made a solo winter ascent of this peak above the Dingjung/Chhule Valley, via the previously unclimbed 850m north face. Parkin first spotted the north face, in profile, during his winter ascent of Dawa Peak (*AAJ 2009*). In December 2010, approaching up the Bhote Kosi, he set up base camp (a small tent at 4,550m) on Christmas Day at the entrance to the Dingjung Valley above Chhule (4,470m). The naming of peaks in this region and on existing maps has always

Looking south from Jobo Rinjang. (A) Dingjung Ri/Rima Mancho, with upper part of 2011 winter ascent marked. (B) Peak 6,293m. Fine pointed snow pyramid behind is Tangi Ragi Tau (6,938m). *Joe Puryear*

North face of Dingjung Ri/Rima Mancho. *Andy Parkin*

been confusing. A Sherpa pointed to the peak, calling it Dingjung Ri, though another Sherpa later said it was referred to locally as Rima Mancho.

After time spent acclimatizing, Parkin returned to his tent one afternoon to find clothing had been stolen. That night he was attacked: rocks, some as large as half a kilogram, were thrown through his tent. He scared off the assailant and moved down to a yak herder's house closer to Chhule, where he had no further problems.

He made an advanced camp below the face at 5,300m, but heavy snowfall at the end of the month made moving around difficult, so it wasn't until mid-January that he set off for an attempt.

The north face is steep, rather like the Grandes Jorasses but with vertical rock walls. However, to the left a steep névé line runs up the face before curving back to the central (main) summit. While access to the base proved difficult due to heavy snow, once he was on the face conditions improved.

His line gave brilliant climbing up to 85°. After two cold, windy bivouacs (5,700m and 6,050m), he traveled light to the summit—an amazing dollop of névé on pure ice that he reached early in the afternoon of January 17. Parkin made it down through the night, with frost-nipped fingers, to his lower bivouac site, where he had left a gas cylinder. Next day he reached the base of the mountain after three and a half chilly days on the face. He walked out to Namche after "one of the hardest trips I can remember." This was Parkin's fourth consecutive winter in the Khumbu, and he reports that prices continue to escalate.

Rima Mancho had been climbed at least four times before, as it presents an easy southwest flank/ridge from the upper Drolambau Glacier. During the 1952 British-New Zealand Cho Oyu expedition, Charles Evans, Alf Gregory, and Eric Shipton became the first climbers known to explore the Drolambau, from the head of which they climbed Rima Mancho, though they named it Trident. Gregory climbed it again in 1955 with Ted Courtenay during the Merseyside Himalayan expedition, as well as the higher Peak 6,293m immediately south, while other members climbed Pimu (6,344m), south of that, by the impressive southeast ridge. In 1960 Robert Sandoz's French party also repeated Rima Mancho's southwest ridge, as did two members of a German expedition in 1972.

In April 2010 a commercially organized British expedition led by Simon Yates approached from the southeast, placing an advanced base camp at 5,400m on the Chhuitingpo Glacier. A two-man reconnaissance up a couloir above the head of the glacier reached the crest of the southwest ridge at 6,000m. A later attempt by most of the members stopped when several were hit by falling stones in the couloir.

LINDSAY GRIFFIN, *Mountain INFO, from information provided by Andy Parkin, Richard Salisbury/Himalayan Database, and the Alpine Club Himalayan Index*

MAHALANGUR HIMAL - KHUMBU SECTION

*Kyajo Ri (6,186m), northeast face, attempt; Kusum Kanguru (6,370m), southwest rib and northwest ridge, attempt.* In March Steven Fortune, Mike Rowe, and I arrived in the Solu Khumbu and established base camp at 5,050m, below our first objective, the northeast face of Kyajo Ri. Initially

Southwest face of Kusum Kanguru from Thado Khoshi. (A) West peak. (B) Southwest peak. (1) 2011 New Zealand line to northwest ridge at 5,500m (and bivouac site). (2) Unclimbed southwest face. (3) 1991 British Route. In 2000 Bart Paul and Freddie Wilkinson climbed different line on 900m lower buttress, then followed 1991 route to summit ridge, where at 6,100m they retreated. (4) 2004 Alaskan attempt, which failed to gain south ridge. (HK1) New Zealand first high camp. (HK2) New Zealand second high camp. In autumn 2001 Czechs were on this side of mountain. Pavel Chiznak, Ivan Foltyn and Petr Strnadel climbed Birthday Cake (5.8 M5 80°) to Pt. 5,805m on south ridge; Roman Kamler and Slavek Vomacko put up West Buttress (5.9 90°), which leads to Pt. 5,579m on west ridge (well left of New Zealand high point). Lines taken by these two routes are uncertain. *Steven Fortune*

we attempted the standard route up the southwest ridge, starting from a high camp at 5,500m below the unclimbed south face. We retreated at just over 6,000m in deteriorating weather, when I was struck on the hand by falling ice and unable to continue climbing.

There followed a rest period at base camp, where we waited in vain for the weather and my injured hand to improve, ultimately leaving Steven and Mike to attempt our proposed new direct line up the northeast face. Early on the morning of April 15, when conditions eventually improved, the pair climbed steep ice below the hanging glacier, before making a rising traverse left on moderately angled snow to gain the glacier itself. They then tackled the upper face via the major ice gully followed in 2009 by an Italian team, gaining a

Unclimbed southwest face of Kusum Kanguru, with 1991 British route marked. (A) West peak. (B) Southwest or Main peak. *Mike Rowe*

Ben Dare and Mike Rowe traversing lower slopes of southwest face of Kusum Kanguru to reach the rib eventually climbed. Twin summits of Gonglha (5,813m, left; 5,666m) behind. *Steven Fortune*

maximum height of 5,700m before continuous spindrift avalanches forced them to abandon the climb.

*[Editor's note: In December 2009 Enrico Bonino and Nicolas Meli tried to climb directly through the lower serac barrier on the northeast face but retreated when an axe broke. They returned and climbed the rock buttress to the right at 6b with a little A1. Crossing the hanging glacier they climbed the upper face, with a section reminiscent of the Ginat on Les Droites, to reach the northeast ridge 120m below the top. Here they abandoned the climb, as it was getting late. The upper section had presented difficulties of M6+, WI5+, and A2.]*

Mike Rowe climbing under base of hanging glacier on northeast face of Kyajo Ri, with south faces of Pharilapcha (6,017m, left) and Machermo (5,766m) behind. *Steven Fortune*

Despite our lack of success, we remained quietly optimistic as we retraced our steps down the Gokyo Valley to attempt our second objective, a new direct route on the southwest face of Kusum Kanguru. Leaving the main Namche-Lukla trail at Thado Khoshi, we struck up the lower reaches of the Thado Khoshi Khola (Kusum Drangka) by a series of well-defined logging trails, camping for the night at the first major fork in the river. Above, all evidence of an established trail quickly faded, and it was only with the assistance of a local guide that we made good progress through dense bamboo forests on the true right bank of the river, to reach our proposed base camp at 3,850m.

Here we were greeted with our first close view of the face, which although largely bare of snow, still held potential in the form of an appealing gully just left of center. This contained significant ice and looked to provide access to the upper face. However, conditions quickly deteriorated, and we were again plagued by the daily snow storms

Kyajo Ri seen from high on ridge above Machermo to northeast. (1) Southeast ridge (Americans, 2005). (2) 2011 New Zealand attempt. (3) 2009 Italian attempt. *Ben Dare*

that had hampered us on Kyajo Ri. They covered the entire face in a thick layer of unconsolidated powder, triggering widespread avalanches and all but rendering our intended route unclimbable. After waiting over a week for weather and conditions to improve, during which time we made three separate climbs to our high camp at 4,900m, we abandoned our attempt and shifted focus to an alternative objective.

On April 28 we climbed a possible new line up a rock rib on the far left of the face, reaching the col on the northwest ridge where the crest begins to rise toward the west peak. We think this is left of the line climbed in 1981 by Bill Denz on the first ascent of the mountain. [*Editor's note: During early October 1981, in what is now acknowledged to be one of the most remarkable first ascents on lower Himalayan peaks, New Zealander Bill Denz spent one and a half days soloing a mixed buttress on the left of the southwest face to reach the west peak, where he bivouacked while waiting for the ridge ahead to stabilize. The following day he made a trying ascent to the main summit. He bivouacked on the summit and next day traversed the narrow connecting ridge to the 6,350m northeast summit, before descending the northwest flank and then spending a further two days bushwhacking to the standard Everest approach trail.*] We gained the base of the rib at 4,800m by a series of interlinked snow and ice fields, and then climbed 1,000m of mixed ground to the ridge, encountering difficulties up to M5.

The abundance of fresh snow insured that we progressed slowly, and on reaching the ridge, with dwindling food supplies, early on the afternoon of the second day, we opted not to continue over the west peak to the main summit as initially planned. We returned to our bivouac site

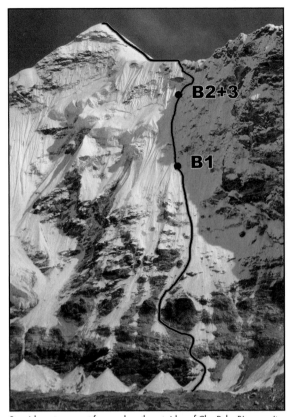

Spanish route on west face and southwest ridge of Cho Polu. Bivouac sites marked. *Jordi Corominas*

of the previous night, on a narrow snow arête just below 5,300m. Early next morning we continued down, rappelling a wide gully left of our ascent route.

We believe that, given the right conditions, the proposed direct line on the southwest face would be climbable. It remains a great challenge. There is also potential for an appealing line up the prominent prow of the left (west) buttress, directly to the west peak. We extend thanks to all our supporters and sponsors, in particular the Mount Everest Foundation, New Zealand Alpine Club, and Sport and Recreation New Zealand.

BEN DARE, *New Zealand*

*Cho Polu (6,700m), west face and southwest ridge.* Elena Parga and I spent a week in Kathmandu, waiting for the plane to Lukla. As far as Island Peak base camp the trail was full of tents and people, but then it was another world— nobody, only mountains. Beyond Lhotse Shar base camp we were forced by loose blocks on the lateral moraine to make a roped descent to the glacier. We then crossed the entire rubble-covered glacier and pitched our tent below the west face of Cho Polu, at 5,300m. The previous year we'd attempted this face, but exhaustion proved stronger than our willpower. We thought we'd find some of our gear but only came across two rappel anchors.

After a day's reconnaissance we woke in the middle of the night and set foot on the face at dawn. There was more ice than in 2010, making for faster progress, but the worst part of an ascent is always the pack, which crushes you little by little. Toward the end of the day, we arrived at some rocks, but to our disappointment they offered no shelter. We had to chop out a small ledge and, half sitting and half reclining, we held the stove between our legs.

Toward the end of November it's cold at 6,000m, and we found it hard getting moving in the morning. At first the slope was icy, but as we gained height it became unstable snow, without decreasing in angle, forcing us to make a taxing traverse. Later we cut a tent platform into a snow ridge, as the face above did not seem to offer any suitable campsite. It's a shame we were unable to photograph this site—a real eagle's nest. Despite the cold we slept and recuperated.

The following day we climbed as quickly as possible to get past the remaining difficulties and reach the col at 6,400m on the southwest ridge. We arrived at 1 p.m. From there to the summit seemed easier, so we unroped to speed things up. However, the snow was unstable, and there was more than 1,000m of air between our legs. Elena was not sure about this and, deciding there was not enough time left that day to reach the summit and return, remained on the col in the sun. I went on alone. It was a nice autumn day, with thin cloud cover and enough visibility for me to see Chomo Lonzo and Makalu, other peaks left on my list. Three hours later I was back at the col, and we began a series of ca 20 rappels down our line to the tent, arriving after nightfall. The following day we continued our rappel descent, using pitons, V-threads, rock spikes—anything was fair game to get to the bottom of the face. When we reached Chhukung, friends had prepared a fine dinner.

We rated our 1,400m route M.D., with sections of 80° ice and unstable snow in the upper section. We completed the climb itself in four days, with one sitting bivouac and two in a tent on a tiny ledge. I reached the summit on November 21.

Elena Parga on day one of first ascent of Cho Polu's west face. Lhotse Shar Glacier is directly below, with Imja Tsho glacial lake in background. *Jordi Corominas*

JORDI COROMINAS, *Spain, translated by Alex Horner*

*Editor's Note: Despite attempts dating back to the spring of 1954, when Edmund Hillary led a productive New Zealand expedition to the Barun Glacier, the first known ascent of Cho Polu took place in 1984, when it was soled by Nil Bohigas via the north face and northeast ridge. It's possible that British climber Trevor Pilling, approaching from the west, also climbed the peak from the north in 1987, shortly before his disappearance in the Annapurna Sanctuary. Both these ascents were unauthorized. The first official ascent was made by Germans in 1999 (AAJ 2000), via the north ridge and north face, approaching from the west. Corominas made the third confirmed climb of Cho Polu.*

KUMBHAKARNA HIMAL

*Jannu (7,711m), east face attempt.* Five Koreans led by Kim Hyung-il attempted the east face of Jannu (presumably Jannu East, though the exact line is unknown). On April 22 they reached 5,900m, after which heavy snowfall confined them to base camp. On May 3 they started again and on the morning of the 7th had reached 6,100m, when one member fell into a crevasse, breaking ribs. The other climbers evacuated him and abandoned the climb.

ELIZABETH HAWLEY, *AAC Honorary Member, Nepal, and* RICHARD SALISBURY, *The Himalayan Database*

# China

The online version of these reports frequently contains additional photos, maps, topos, and extended text. Please visit aaj.americanalpineclub.org

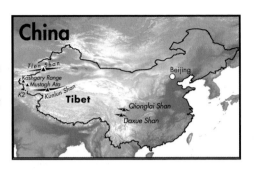

XINJIANG

TIEN SHAN

Panorama, from southwest (left) to northeast (right), from camp on an unnamed glacier south of main divide of Western Kokshaal-too. (A) Pik 5,253m. (B) Pik Byeliy, with attempted route marked. Top part of southwest spur, attempted in 2000, is rock pillar falling directly from summit. *Mike Libecki*

*Western Kokshaal-too, Pik Byeliy (5,697m), attempt from southwest.* In late July, after climbing the Ibex Horn [*see Afghanistan section*], I flew from Kabul to Urumqi, then on to Aksu, where I met local Chinese friends (liaison officer and driver). We drove for a full day to a final military check point at Akqi. I had been here a few times before, so the logistics were simple. Or so I thought. The checkpoint refused my stamped, official permission papers that I had obtained. Because my chosen mountain area is close to the Kyrgyzstan border, they would not allow me to continue. I was told I would have to meet the military person in charge of the region, an eight-hour drive away. Major frustration; eternal optimism; all good things in all good time. I had a little over two weeks for the entire trip.

We drove to the military leader, but he denied me permission. But my friend, the liaison officer from previous expeditions, had married recently, and his wife happened to have family in the military, and they happened to be from this same area. He called his wife, she made some calls, and the next day I had permission. The story is long and has to do with the Chinese Secret Service. Amazing how things work out with optimism.

We returned to Akqi, and the same day I trekked toward the mountains, using a horse to carry my equipment. I now had nine days left. Two days later I was at 4,250m, with the primary aim of reconnoitering a couple of valleys I'd seen on a previous trip. I spent two days cruising dry glaciers up to 4,900m and, yes, found endless granite alpine towers. Five days before I had to meet my driver, I decided to give Pik Byeliy a shot. It had denied Jerry Dodrill, Doug and Jed Workman, and me in 2000, when we attempted the southwest spur (*AAJ 2001*).

From a camp above 4,900m, I ascended a dry glacier with easily navigable crevasses, then reached and climbed easy terrain up the northwest ridge, the border with Kyrgyzstan. Above 5,300m I had to traverse a series of steep slopes to gain the main ridge leading to the summit. Avalanche conditions and scary seracs above made it too risky, and although tempted, I forced myself to turn back. A few hours later it started snowing, hard. I reached my tent by headlamp as the wind kicked in.

Snow continued for almost three days. This was worrying, as I was surrounded by crevasses. But on the first sunny day snow cover on the glaciers quickly began to melt. I managed to find a way through, setting only two anchors as a precaution. Embarrassingly, I fell into one narrow crevasse, though with no serious consequence. I admit it was quite frightening walking among the giant, lurking monster-mouth crevasses, which were ready to swallow me whole.

MIKE LIBECKI, *AAC*

*Xuelian Massif; Yi-ge Feng (4,420m), south face; Kundi Feng (4,601m), north face and northwest ridge; Huang Jin Feng (4,708m), southwest face and south ridge; Xuelian Northeast (6,231m), west ridge, Arête of Trust.* On July 14, with all our climbing equipment stuck in Urumqi customs, Ales Holc, Igor Kremser, and I began acclimatizing in the Xuelian Massif. With only trekking shoes we were restricted to climbing lower snowless peaks from the south. Northwest from base camp (3,600m) there was a scree-covered peak overlooking the Muzart Glacier where it bends south. We scrambled up its south face to a steeper section and climbed it (UIAA IV) to the scree-covered ridge, which we followed to the summit, where we had a superb overview of the Xuelian Massif, particularly Xuelian Northeast, our main objective. We dubbed the peak Yi-ge Feng (The First Peak). That evening we learned that the cargo had been released, and our agent, Ye Bing (David), was to bring it to base camp in the next few days.

Kundi Feng from north, with Xuelian North behind. Overnight camp marked. *Peter Juvan*

On the 18th we packed more than 30 kg each and moved slowly toward Xuelian Northeast, to set up advanced base. On the second day deteriorating weather stopped us short of our proposed site. On the right side of the glacier, a snow-covered peak, connected to another, higher peak by a long U-shaped ridge, lies north of Xuelian North and Main. Next morning we packed for two days of climbing and after a two-hour approach started up a north facing couloir on the right side of the lower peak. After two hours of climbing 60° snow unroped, we belayed the last, 70° pitch leading to a ridge. Just below the summit we negotiated a delicate, 80° pitch of snow and

Southwest face of Huang Jin Feng. *Peter Juvan*

West ridge of Xuelian northeast from summit of Yi-ge Feng. Tent sites marked. *Peter Juvan*

Second night's camp precariously sited on Xuelian northeast's narrow west ridge. East flanks of Xuelian North behind. *Ales Holc*

ice. We dubbed the peak Kundi Feng. (Kundi is Slovene for Smart Guy.) Snow and ice climbing was a smart choice for us after two weeks dealing with cargo logistics.

We pitched a tent just below the top and spent the night there for acclimatization. Next morning we climbed the scree and snow-covered ridge toward the higher, neighboring peak. From the low point of the ridge, we began traversing its left flank but, having no rock-climbing protection, were forced to stick to snow-covered terrain. The south facing couloir leading to the final ridge was completely dry and too steep for a safe ascent. We therefore descended the southeast face (600m, III) to the glacier below Xuelian North and followed it back to the Muzart Glacier and our camp.

On the 22nd, after establishing advanced base below Xuelian Northeast, we returned to base camp for food and rest. With empty packs we completed the 14km in only four hours. On the 24th we returned and moved across the glacier to a peak with a golden southwest face, situated north-northwest of Xuelian Northeast. We spent the night on the moraine and started up the golden wall at 7 a.m. Climbing unroped we reached the top in three hours. The 700m route had difficulties of M4 AI3. We descended a south facing 60°couloir, right of our ascent route, in two hours. We called the mountain Huang Jin Feng (Golden Peak).

Although snow was forecast for the night 26th-27th, there was less than expected, and, as the sun triggered no avalanches, we started up the west ridge of Xuelian Northeast at 3 p.m. The snow was compact and the slopes wide and steep. We simul-climbed 60m apart, using Ropemen on protection points. There was a vertical section before we reached the plateau at the base of the ridge. Another long section up the arête (80° max) took us to the top of a cornice, where we bivouacked. We had a good view of Xuelian Main and noted that the glacier was too broken to allow an approach from the northeast.

Next day we were forced to traverse left (M4), before regaining the ridge. It soon became a knife-edge, and we traversed the right flank, then climbed to a shoulder below the prominent rock section visible from base camp. Smooth slabs covered with fresh snow offered almost no protection (M5), but the overhanging pitch above had perfect protection and simply needed strong muscles (M5+). Ales led this section and the two pitches above to a small shoulder on a knife-edge arête, where we spent two hours chopping out an exposed perch for the tent. After 12 hours climbing we had to spend the night wearing harnesses.

Igor led the first part of the second rock barrier (M4), I led a weakness through the overhanging section (M5+), and Ales continued on mixed terrain and deep snow. The angle eased, and we progressed faster, stopping for the night below the last mixed section on the ridge. The stove failed, leaving us only half a day's supply of water.

Downclimbing beneath serac barrier on southeast face of Xuelian Northeast. *Peter Juvan*

We started early the following day, bypassing the final rock section on the left, and reached the summit from the east at 1:20 p.m., after six hours' climbing. We started down the unseen southeast face, already covered in mist. We moved together, using ice screw protection. At one point Ales lost a crampon on a 60° slope, but it stopped rolling after 50m. The cloud concealed a huge band of seracs, which we only noticed when we were well below it. In three hours we reached a plateau and were out of its range. We'd been on the go for 14 hours and were exhausted and dehydrated but were in a safe spot.

On our fifth day, again shrouded by mist and guided only by intuition, we rappelled over a serac, made a long traverse east, rappelled again, and finally reached a small but welcome stream on a 60° ice slope. At 4 p.m. we reached the glacier, covered with 30 cm of fresh snow. We embraced, and Ales cried. The 2,000m descent, on which we made only three rappels, involved difficulties of AI3, 60-80°. On the way back to advanced base, we took numerous falls into crevasses, though none deeper than our shoulders.

We called the route Arête of Trust (2,400m, ED2 AI5 M5+), as a tribute to a friend, Andrej Magajne, who had often visited the Kyrgyzstan Tien Shan and was killed the previous spring, skiing in Slovenia.

Peter Juvan, *Slovenia*

*Editor's note: Xuelian Northeast was the remaining virgin 6,000m summit of the main Xuelian Group. Its west ridge had been attempted in 2009, by Jed Brown and Bruce Normand, who retreated at 5,400m (AAJ 2010). The Slovenian ascent was one of six nominations for the 2012 Piolets d'Or*

## Sichuan

### Chola Shan

*Sejong reconnaissance.* Before our attempt on Goromity (as reported elsewhere in this section), Hitoshi Onodera and I traveled to Kangding, en route to the Gongkala Shan, where we had a permit from the Sichuan Mountaineering Association for Kawarani (I, 5,992m; II 5,928m). However, the Deputy Director of the Sports Administrative Department, a senior official in the Ganzi Tibet Autonomous Region, refused to let us continue, stating that Kawarani was holy to Tibetans. The same problem was

Unclimbed Sejong I (left) and Nobuyugya from northeast. *Takao Ohe, supplied by Tamotsu Nakamura*

Unclimbed Sejong II from northwest. *Takao Ohe, supplied by Tamotsu Nakamura*

met by British expeditions in 2005 and 2007. We moved to the northern end of the Chola Shan, where we had information that there was an unclimbed massif called Polujab, south of Zhogchen Monastery. (A preliminary reconnaissance of these mountains had been made in 2000 by Tom Nakamura, who spent three days at the monastery.) Onodera and two companions explored from the east, while another two companions and I approached from the west. Locals explained that the highest peak was named Sejong. We took photos of peaks in this massif for future attempts, concluding that the highest is Sejong I (5,816+m, not marked on the Chinese map), the second highest Sejong II (5,816m, southwest of Sejong I and marked on the map), the third highest Nobuyugya (5,594m, north of Sejong I, also marked on map), and the fourth Polujab (5,472m, west of Sejong II, marked on Chinese map).

TAKAO OHE, *Japan, supplied by Tamotsu Nakamura*

SHALULI SHAN

Acha La Ri from southwest, showing Orelletes i Cocarrois. *Sergi Ricart*

*Shaluli Shan and Daxue Shan, various ascents.* For three months I traveled alone in Qinghai, Sichuan, and Yunnan, near the Tibet border, spending time with local inhabitants and exploring unclimbed mountains and little visited valleys.

I first visited Shaluli Shan North. On the north side of the Sichuan-Tibet Highway, east of the Chola Shan Pass (Tro La, 4,910m), and directly north of the Chola Shan, is a small cirque of peaks. On October 1st I walked into the cirque, placed camp at 4,500m, and reached the top of a small pinnacle (5,050m) on the east-southeast ridge of Peak 5,358m. Next day I made the first ascent of Acha La Ri (5,000m, 31°55'40" N, 99°00'22" E), by the southwest spur, a route I named Orelletes i Cocarrois (400m, D, UIAA V). The difficulties were relatively sustained and on good rock, up short walls interrupted by snow-covered ledges. Descent by the northwest face was easy.

Peak 5,557m/5,609m, seen on approach from Sichuan-Tibet Highway. *Sergi Ricart*

I returned to the village of Manigango (Manukanggo) and took the road northwest toward Yushu for 15km, before heading south up the Sho Chen Valley to the north side of the same range, which I refer to as Tro La Range. I camped at 4,350m and on the 6th made the first ascent of Ru Chen Gangri (5,350m, 31°58'45" N, 99°00'54" E), by the north and east faces, a route I named Quan ells Nuvols Passen (400m, PD+, UIAA II 55°). This was largely easy snow climbing to an elegant summit, and I descended the same route. On the 8th I tried Peak 5,243m (31°56'59" N, 99°02'20" E) by two different gullies on the northwest face. On the second attempt I reached the northeast ridge but retreated 200m below the summit, having climbed 700m, due to soft snow over rock slabs.

Ru Chen Gangri from north, with ascent route. *Sergi Ricart*

On the 20th I took a minibus south from Kangding to Laoyuling and walked for two days up the main valley west of the northern Minya Konka massif in the southern part of the Daxue Shan. Before the Ruichi Haniya Pass, I moved east to a glacial lake at 4,600m (29°46'23" N, 101°49'37" E) in the cirque northwest of Reddomain (6,112m). On the 22nd I climbed two small rocky peaks toward the end of the long northwest ridge of Reddomain, before it terminates at the Ruichi Haniya. The first, Tso Chong Ri (5,030m, 29°46'00" N, 101°48'52" E), I climbed via the northeast face, naming the route Carne Cruda (250m, AD, III+ 65°), while the second Tso Chen Ri (5,100m, 29°45'35" N, 101°49'04" E), I climbed via the northwest ridge, a route I named El Costat Femeni (200m above the col, AD, IV+ 55°). From the summit of the

Tso Chong Ri (right), showing Came Cruda on northwest face. Tso Chen Ri showing northwest ridge (El Costat Femeni). *Sergi Ricart*

Sergi Ricart at mid-height on northwest ridge of Tso Chen Ri. Behind, past the lake of Ruiche Tongma, main approach valley leads north. *Sergi Ricart*

first I descended its southeast face easily to reach the foot of the northwest ridge of the second. Next day a storm forced me out of the area.

I then returned to the Shaluli Shan on the Sichuan-Tibet Highway, taking the bus from Batang toward Litang until south of the Xiashe massif, then jumping off about six km east of the Haizi Shan Pass (4,685m; confusingly named, as the well-known peak of Haizi Shan is much farther east in the Daxue Shan Range). On November 1st I attempted Peak 5,557m (30°21'00" N, 99°39'20" E), the north summit of Peak 5,609m on the PLA map, ca eight km southeast of Xiashe (5,833m). I climbed a 350-400m couloir on the west face, a little left of the north summit, at D-, IV+ 60°. It was a cold day, but the climbing was nice, though the rock steps were loose, and there was windslab toward the top. The northwest ridge also had windslab and dangerous cornices, so I didn't continue to the top but from my high point of 5,510m descended the 45° ridge and next day, with slightly frostbitten feet, hitched back to Batang.

SERGI RICART, *Spain*

*Ricart's topos and photos can be downloaded from the on-line version of this report. Commonly accepted names are used in this report and differ in some instances from those found in the download.*

*Nideng Gongga (5,690m), west glacier and south face.* Our initial plan was to explore valleys and the previously unattempted mountains in the Xiangqiuqieke Massif. In particular we wanted to

Nideng Gongga from north, with ascent route marked. *Yvonne Pfluger*

West face of Xiangqiuqieke. *Yvonne Pfluger*

try the second highest summit, 5,867m Xiangqiuqieke (the highest, an unnamed peak of 5,870m, lies nearly three kilometers to the southeast).

We arrived at Baige-xi, located near Batang on the G318 State Highway. Despite problems faced by a previous Japanese reconnaissance party, which was advised by the district secretary not to enter the approach valley west of the village, as the locals would prove unwelcoming, we were permitted access by Land Cruiser on a recently built gravel road. We received a friendly welcome from the villagers of Menzhen, who supplied horses to carry our gear for two short days up to a base camp at 4,500m, south of Xiangqiuqieke.

After several days of reconnaissance to find a suitable ascent route, we were preparing our last load carry when we received word that the village elders were voicing concerns about us climbing in a holy mountain range. To avoid conflict we abandoned our plans and left the valley to find other climbing possibilities.

In keeping with the spirit of our original intent, we were determined to go to another unexplored area. From Tom Nakamura's documentation we knew that Asa and Hari, south of Haga La, had not been attempted. However, we again encountered resistance by locals, who, in the light of recent mineral exploration, were sensitive to strangers.

Tim Church on summit of Nideng Gongga. Beyond him to northeast is Hati Group, while barren valley below leads off-photo left to Zhopu Pasture. Rock ribs bottom right fall from northeast ridge of Xiashe. *Yvonne Pfluger*

Finally we headed for Zhopu Pasture, which our liaison officer, Lenny, knew well from previous expeditions. We stayed four days at Zhopu Monastery, using it as a base to reconnoiter several promising unclimbed peaks in the area. Autumn was settling in, and there were snow falls each night. We eliminated two unclimbed peaks north of Zhopu Lake, as their approaches were long, and there seemed no attractive lines. Eventually we decided on an unclimbed peak to our south, immediately northwest of Xiashe (5,833m). After their successful ascent of Xiashe in 2004, Pat Deavoll and Karen McNeill had recommended this peak as one of three interesting unclimbed summits in the area. The other two, Hati and Garrapunsum (the highest point of the Jarjinjabo), had since been climbed.

We explored valley systems on the south side of the mountain and found a suitable site for base camp at 4,600m. Although the valley was stunning, the site was not so scenic, being in an area of mining exploration. The access road was too steep for our small hired vans, so several motorbikes were required to complete the load carry.

With a good weather window, we decided to make a summit attempt directly from base camp. We set off at 3 a.m. and were surprised to find the lower part of the climb, which we had seen from camp, connected with a glacier on the far side of the prominent northwest ridge. At daybreak we crossed a narrow col 400m above camp and walked onto the glacier. Roped, we negotiated a number of crevasses, most of the 1,100m of ascent being more straightforward than expected. Deep powder from recent snowfalls made progress slow, and we eventually reached the summit from the south, as rock quality on the west ridge was poor. This, combined with unconsolidated snow, made the climbing treacherous. The final 200m provided more technical snow/ice climbing, excess snow having avalanched from the slope the previous day. Finally we burrowed through a small cornice and topped out on a beautiful knife-edge ridge. We only needed to follow this for 50m before reaching the summit, nine hours after setting out. Local Tibetans call this peak Nideng Gongga, and from its top we enjoyed an amazing panorama, including the Yangmolong Massif to the southwest and our original objective, Xiangqiuqieke, to the south.

Nideng Gongga is highly prominent when viewed from the monastery and access road, but Lenny thought it was unclimbed. Subsequent research revealed one unsuccessful attempt, in October 2005 by British climber Tom Prentice. He attempted the northeast ridge while the two other members of his expedition climbed Xiashe (*AAJ 2006*). We have found no reports of subsequent attempts. Our expedition lasted from September 19 till October 20, and we received generous funding and support from the Sport and Recreation New Zealand (SPARC) Hillary Grant, and New Zealand Alpine Club.

TIM CHURCH AND YVONNE PFLUGER, *New Zealand*

*Yangmolong (6,080m GPS), north buttress.* Reaching the summit of Yangmolong was the accumulation of three years' effort. In 2009 we attempted the south side, but unseasonably warm conditions made climbing unsafe. Rocks and ice raining down on the party from the summit ridge forced a hasty retreat (*AAJ 2010*). Later we were inspired by photos of the mountain's north face published by Dave Wynne-Jones after his 2009 trip. It looked attractive but there was one small problem: locals were stopping climbers going up the main northern valley, preventing direct access to the mountain's eastern and northern sides.

We returned in 2010, this time pioneering a complex approach to the north side that would avoid ethnic problems but required traversing a difficult 5,100m col. We attempted a rock and ice spur below the summit [*inspected by Japanese and British*], but heavy snowfall prevented progress above 5,400m.

In October 2011 it took over 20 hours of driving from Chengdu, on dirt roads that were in constant repair, and two long days of walking over the pass, down 400m, and up again to the base of the route. In many ways getting to the mountain posed more challenges than the actual climb. In Chengdu Tim Boetler had become deadly ill with a supposedly blocked intestine and was in the hospital on an IV drip for three nights. This delayed our departure by a week, but Tim was miraculously with us when we left Chengdu. A couple of days later a large sand truck lost its brakes and smashed into the front of our jeep, causing further delays. Near the trailhead at Gongba, west of the mountain, I had an accident while catching a ride on a local's motorcycle, which almost put an abrupt end to my climb. (The driver was waving to friends and forgot to steer.) We contemplated turning around several times, but something kept us moving forward.

North face of Yangmolong, from 5,000m on the approach, showing American-Chinese ascent. *Jon Otto*

After a rest day at our base camp at 4,880m, Tim, Liu Yong (Daliu), Su Rongqin (Asu), and I returned to the line we all tried in 2010. The only relatively safe route is a buttress that splits the lower half of the north face. Overhanging crevasses block the rest, and in 2010 we witnessed an avalanche that took out the entire left side of the face. The technical climbing started at 5,150m.

We got onto the ridge by climbing a frozen scree and snow slope, then climbed several pitches of mixed rock and snow. The rock was loose and blocky, and it was impossible not to send chunks down on your buddies. Above 5,500m it was sustained snow and ice (up to 70°) to the summit. We camped at 5,370m and 5,780m. In the upper section we climbed with running belays, for efficiency. We reached the top mid-afternoon on day three and returned to our second camp that night. Next day we regained base camp, the roundtrip occurring in a weather window between two storms. Difficulties were probably around TD, 5.6 WI3 M4, and while established sources quote a summit altitude of 6,060m or 6,066m, our GPS read 6,080m.

Su Rongqin on Yangmolong. *Liu Yong*

Yangmolong was not the most technically challenging alpine route I've done, but it takes the cake for something I'd call discovery factor. I've never spent so much time researching and analyzing a feasible route, best time of year to climb, weather, approach, etc. There was so little known about this area. And what I found most impressive was not the climbing but the small monasteries tucked high up in the valleys, the local Tibetans' livelihood, and religious practices.

*Adapted from text supplied by* JON OTTO, *AAC*

*For the history of attempts on Yangmolong, see* AAJ 2010, *pp. 335-338, and* AAJ 2008, *p. 422.*

*Yangmolong and Jarjinjabo-Xiashe Massifs, exploration.* In May and June 2005 I undertook two treks over a six-week period, the objective being to expand on the exploration and reporting of Tom Nakamura. During these journeys I climbed a couple of small peaks above 5,000m, but more important took a large number of photos on specific bearings. I uploaded my GPS data and photos to Google Earth, where a bird's eye view of my travels, including road

In valley southwest from Yangmolong Pasture Paul Kiernan climbed the two pointed rock peaks in the center. He first ascended obvious diminishing snow couloir, then followed ridge right to northeast summit (5,213m), back left to southeast summit (5,177m), and down southeast ridge to col on left. From here he glissaded snow slope. *Paul Kiernan*

Unclimbed peaks up to 5,725m in second valley southeast of of Garrapunsum (5,818m), highest mountain in Jarjinjabo range (see *AAJ 2008*). *Paul Kiernan*

access, is visible. There is a link in the *AAJ* web report.

While the big peaks of the Yangmolong Massif more than deserve the attention they receive, there are interesting peaks of a lesser scale. These can be found southwest, southeast, and northeast of Yangmolong Pasture. I climbed a twin-summited rock peak to the southwest, via a snow couloir leading to the col between the two summits, both of which I visited. The northwest summit was 5,213m (30°01'34.3" N, 99°17'22.5"E), while the southeast registered 5,177m (30°01'34.7" N, 99°17'27.7"E).

View southeast from Peak 5,100m. These peaks are likely unclimbed. *Paul Kiernan*

In the Jarjinjabo-Xiashe region, several interesting peaks, sitting in the depths of various valleys branching off from Zhopu Pasture, have escaped the limelight. Notable are those rising to 5,725m in a valley southeast of the highest Jarjinjabo summit, Garrupunsum.

PAUL KIERNAN

DAXUE SHAN - MINYA KONKA RANGE

*Reddomain (6,112m), north face, 2010 attempt and 2011 success, Remember Chris; Jiazi (6,540m), west face, Liberal Dance; Xiao Gongga (Little Konka, 5,928m), south face, Thrill.* Zhou Peng

Remember Chris on North face of Reddomain. *Yan Dongdong*

and I spent October in the northwestern sector of the Minya Konka Range, arriving at base camp (4,300m) in the Riuche Valley on the 1st. Being National Day the valley was filled with Chinese trekkers on the popular route south over a 4,800m pass to the Moxi Valley and Konka Temple. For the next few days, with filmmaker Li Shuang, we made acclimatization and reconnaissance walks to 5,100, then went up Reddomain's northern glacier to camp below its north face at 5,111m.

In February 2010 Christina Chan, Bruce Normand, and I had attempted the icy central rib, the only line not threatened by seracs. We started too late, were too slow, and the weather turned bad before we were able to reach the top. Having little food, only one down jacket between us, and no stove, we retreated, making 10 rappels in the dark, with small avalanches coming down on both flanks of the rib every few minutes. It was 2 a.m. when, in howling winds, we finally spotted our tiny tent on the crevasse-infested glacier. Both Chris and I suffered minor frostbite from the 17-hour ordeal. Although Chris was an expert big wall climber, with many multi-day solo ascents under her belt, this was only her second alpine climb. She never once panicked but kept going with serene calmness, even at the most nerve-wracking moments. Just a few months later, she was killed while downclimbing unroped from Eichorn Pinnacle in Tuolumne Meadows.

Yan Dongdong on central rib of Reddomain north face, with southwest face of Grosvenor (6,376m) behind. *Zhou Peng*

In February the face had been mostly ice, but this time it was largely covered in October snow. Zhou and I left camp at 6:47 a.m. on the 8th, climbing on a short rope. We followed the same rib, which connects to the left bank of a couloir at 5,700m, at which point we began to use the full rope and place running belays. Four long pitches saw us on the summit at 3:42 p.m. This was the fourth ascent of Reddomain. (Chinese climbers Peng Xiaolong, Liu Yang and Su Rongqin made the third ascent in September, via a variation of the traditional west ridge route.) We named the route Remember Chris (1,000m, AI2 55° snow). The ridge proved longer and more complex than we had expected, and it was 6 a.m. when Zhou walked into base camp, past 7 a.m. when I arrived.

The ordeal left us exhausted, and we waited a week before attempting Jiazi. After retrieving the Reddomain camp on the 10th and on the 13th caching most of our climbing gear at 5,000m on the glacier below Jiazi's west face, we would have begun the attempt on 16th, but decided to wait two more days due to new snow and unstable weather. On the 18th we camped close to the face at 5,016m, there being little danger of rockfall. The wind was strong, and with tent fabric slapping we managed little sleep.

At 6:30 we left camp and headed into a chute right of the wide couloir in the middle of this face, which is more than 2km wide. We crossed a shallow couloir and traversed right, into an adjacent couloir, which led all the way to the headwall at 5,900m. There we hoped to find a decent camping spot. Except for the second pitch (M5) in the chute, we simul-climbed all day, occasionally without protection because the granite was solid, cracks hard to find, and the ice cover thin and loosely attached. When we finally reached the base of the headwall, not long after dark, we were disappointed to find no ledge, only calf-deep snow on rotten ice covering a 45° slab. It took an hour to dig a narrow bivouac at 5,914m. Fortunately we had an almost windless night, sitting in sleeping bags and wearing boots.

We left at 9:30 in the morning, hoping to reach the summit that day. Traversing right into an adjacent couloir proved relatively easy, but after slanting right onto what we believed was the exit snow ridge, we found another 100m of rocky terrain, with difficulties up to M6 where it slightly overhung. We were forced to stop at 6,407m, at the top of a steep chute rising from the right, where we chopped another sitting bivouac in a corner. The wind blew mildly but continuously, and we had to shield the stove to get a few liters of gritty water.

When we left at 9:47 a.m. on the 21st, the wind had grown stronger, blowing snow in our faces. As Zhou neared the top, the heavy cams and pitons on his rack were flying horizontally.

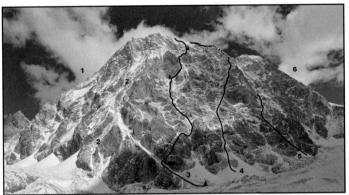

The 1,500m west face of Jiazi. (1) 1981 northwest ridge British attempt. (2) 1982 American (not to summit). (3) Liberal Dance. (4) 2009 French (not to summit). (5) 2008 French attempt. (6) 1982 American south ridge. *Yan Dongdong*

We stepped onto the summit at 12:01 p.m. This was the second ascent of Jiazi, the first being in 1982 by Americans Pat Callis, Dougal McCarty, and Richard Nolting, via the south ridge. On that same expedition Dave Stutzman and Jim Williams climbed the west face to north ridge, and in 2009 French guides Pierre Labbre and Rémi Sfilio climbed another route on the right side of the face to reach the south ridge. Our route, Liberal Dance (1,500m, M6 WI3 55°), is the first west face route to reach the summit.

The south ridge is wide, flat, long, and exposed. It was hours before we started the first of 12 rappels down the triangular south face. Zhou found an old piton,

Zhou Peng on rightward traverse between two couloirs, Jiazi west face. *Yan Dongdong*

probably from the first ascent. It was nearly dark when we reached the col and set up camp in the snow basin between Jiazi, Grosvenor, and Edgar.

Just before we left for the route, Americans and Russians arrived in the upper Riuche (see below), the Russians intent on attempting Edgar from the west. While making four rappels down a couloir on the west flank of the col, we were both delighted and surprised to see that the diligent Russians had set up a camp below the col, and two were already climbing a parallel couloir. Dima Paramonov, who had remained in the tent, gave us hot fruit tea and advice on avoiding crevasses below. By the time we met Li Shuang at advanced base, we had decided to extend the trip and attempt Xiao Gongga (Little Konka, or Tshiburongri), which had seen three ascents. Li had filmed from beneath Reddomain and Jiazi and now wanted to join us on Little Konka. Our plan was to leave gear at advanced base, go down for a rest, then move the tent farther north onto the glacier below Little Konka's south face.

We all hiked to Kangding on the 24th and resupplied. We looked up records of previous ascents, but they were conflicting. We got the impression the 1981 British first ascent team had approached from the east, while the French in 2008 and Koreans in 2010 had come from the west, likely leaving the south face unclimbed.

South face of Xiao Gongga. (1) 2010 Korean route. (2) Thrill. The two routes are not quite identical in top section. *Yan Dongdong*

We returned to base camp on the 26th with a friend, Liu Tuanxi, who brought an inflatable kayak to paddle in the small glacial lake northwest of Reddomain. On the 27th we took turns paddling. The sky was cloudy and the water freezing, but it was incredible fun. Next day we reached advanced base and on 29th moved up to the base of the south face at 5,300m, where we camped. It snowed, but after dark the sky cleared, and as there were only a few centimeters of fresh snow, we set off next day an hour before dawn.

The snow couloir in the center of the face was easy enough to simul-climb, but after moving left to avoid the steepest part, we had to belay, with Zhou, who is the superior climber, leading all technical pitches. After three pitches we unexpectedly came across white nylon fixed ropes. An empty energy gel pack with Korean printing suggested the ropes had been left by the Koreans. They were in good condition but generally didn't follow the optimal climbing route, possibly because of changing snow conditions since 2010.

We climbed three more rocky pitches, with a crux of M6, before reaching the exit ridge. We simul-climbed the last section with Zhou finishing close to the summit in the dark,

Li Shuang traversing high on south face of Xiao Gongga. *Zhou Peng*

at a Korean anchor with at least two stacks of colored dynamic rope lying frozen in the ice. There was a good ledge below one of the huge boulders that formed the base of the summit, and we camped for the night. There was another Korean anchor with a stack of woven nylon rope below. We thought about using it as a mattress, but the coils were frozen tight, so we used our own ropes, sacks, and gaiters. It snowed during the night, but with three of us in the small tent, it wasn't especially cold.

On the 31st we climbed one more pitch to the summit, arriving at 10:20 a.m. By 4:40 p.m. we had made 12 rappels down the face and were back in camp. Though it wasn't entirely new, coinciding with much of the Korean route for the last 200m (where 250-300m of rope has been abandoned), we named our line Thrill (Shuang; 600m, M6 50°) to celebrate Li's first technical alpine ascent. We continued down to base camp, arriving 40 minutes before the start of November.

Yan Dongdong, *China*

*Editor's note: the geography of Xiao Gongga has been confusing and inaccurately described in the Journal. The peak has southwest and southeast ridges separating the northwest, south, and east faces. The southeast ridge connects with Jiazi. The British Army team in 1981 approached via the glacier to the east (Tshiburongi Glacier) and climbed the right-hand of two snow gullies on the east face. The French in 2008 approached from the northwest and climbed the southwest ridge (AAJ 2009). The Koreans approached from the west, then south, and climbed the south face (AAJ 2011), with seemingly 12 members reaching the summit in three separate pushes. They had made a reconnaissance in April 2010.*

Black Wolves and Blue Poppies on west face of Grosvenor, bivouacs marked. Prominent central couloir to left was climbed in 2010 by Kyle Dempster and Bruce Normand, while first ascent of peak was made in 2003 by Julie-Ann Clyma and Roger Payne, via southwest (right skyline) ridge. *Chris Gibisch*

**Grosvenor (6,376m), west face, Black Wolves and Blue Poppies.** Grosvenor is a striking mountain, an iconic pyramid with technical faces that allow no easy way up. The west face appeared to us the most impressive and technical. It rises 1,300m and is littered with ice ribbons broken by steep rock bands. The north face, which is slightly shorter, has potential, but is topped by large seracs. The east face is shorter, with more moderate ice lines.

October 14 found Jeff Shapiro and me leaving the Buddhist community of Laouyling to spend the next three days trekking to base camp. Although initial snowfall caused concern, by the time we reached camp, the weather had improved, and conditions looked favorable. We did our best to acclimatize while scouting the west face, establishing a high camp at 5,100m, near its base.

We got weather reports from our liaison officer, who was in contact with headquarters, and the Russians who climbed the east face of Grosvenor and were e-mailing friends. On the 24th, despite conflicting forecasts, we left base camp for our high camp. Next morning we woke to a star-filled sky. Our chosen line right of the central couloir began moderately, and we simul-climbed pitches of névé and ice, protected by rock gear. Eventually I reached a belay, where I could see much steeper ground ahead. Jeff took the lead and charged up. Shortly after the rope ran out and I started climbing, Jeff

Shapiro starting last pitch below ridge. *Chris Gibisch*

reached the steepest section. His climbing slowed and he moved with precision. Unable to protect this section, he ran it out for 20m on rotten, sublimated snice, before finding solid gear. Following, I realized the significance of what I'd witnessed.

We were now on a snow/ice ramp leading to our proposed bivouac site. With the sun kissing

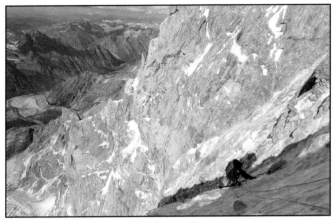

Shapiro finishing gray ice, one pitch below top of face. *Chris Gibisch*

the horizon, we made haste for what we hoped would be a reasonable ledge. To our disappointment, the site proved less than ideal, and with no other options, we placed a picket, chopped some seats, and pulled our bags over us.

First light revealed the next challenge: a 20cm strip of ice transecting the rock band above. We packed up, and I started climbing. A few delicate placements and some dry-tooling allowed access to the more moderate slope above. We again began simul-climbing, but I soon found myself faced with another intimidating challenge: more vertical, rotten snice. I did my best to not pull the pitch down on myself and was able to place a cam half-way up the strip, far off to one side.

We could now see our final mystery, a couple of pitches of gray ice that had been visible from base camp. Jeff climbed toward the ice, and our fears of fierceness were dispelled. When I reached his belay, I saw it was the best water ice we had so far encountered. However, we were at 6,200m, I was wasted, and the ice was steep. Digging deep I limped my way up for just over 60m. Half frozen, Jeff met me at the belay, carried on through, and with one more huge pull got us to the ridge above. Hopes of a bivouac on the presumed broad summit slopes were crushed when I reached him, exhausted, to find we were on a sharp knife-edge, fluting onto the west face. With the last rays of light once

North face of Edgar showing two lines attempted in 2010. Left-hand line: C1 5,200m, C2 5,400m, and C3 5,900m. Belousov-Novikov (right-hand line to northwest ridge): C1 5,100m, C2 5,560m, and C3 5,900m). ABC is at 4,400m. *Vladimir Belousov*

Edgar seen from Grosvenor to northwest. (1) 2010 attempt by Pavel Dobrinskiy and partner. (2) 2010 Belousov-Novikov attempt and descent into western cwm. (H) High point of 2011 attempt on west face. (3) Southwest ridge, climbed by Koreans Kim Jae-myung and Lee Yong-boo in 2000. (4) Peak 6,130m. (5) Peak 6,130m. (6) Peak 6,134m, climbed by Russians Mikhailov and Ruchkin in 2009. *Bruce Normand*

again gracing us, I led up the ridge to find a suitable bivouac. Near the end of the rope, all that I came up with was a good anchor and some hard ice at the base of a large overhanging boulder close to the summit. We chopped ice buckets, knowing we were in for another sleepless night.

Arctic temperatures on the morning of the 27th made us reluctant to leave our bags. But morning light was reaching the summit, so warmth awaited us there. A distant but fast-moving storm increased our motivation, so we began climbing. After some of the most exhausting easy climbing I've ever done, we stood on the summit. Winds were light, the sky blue, and the views amazing.

It took the rest of our summit day and the next to make it back to base camp. We made 12 rappels down the east face and bivouacked in the glaciated basin between Grosvenor, Jiazi, and Edgar. The following day we rappelled from the col between Jiazi and Grosvenor, then made a long slog across glaciers and moraines to reach the grassy meadows of base camp.

Once again an alpine climb had changed my perspective on my life and what I'm capable of. After working harder than either of us imagined, we came away from the experience with an entirely new outlook toward what's possible.

Our route, Black Wolves and Blue Poppies (1,300m, M5+ WI4+ AI6) was done alpine style with leave-no-trace ethics. Three unavoidable pins at rappel stations, close to the bottom of the east face, were the only gear we abandoned on the mountain. We hope the faces of the Daxue Shan will be respected by the continued absence of bolts and unnecessary fixed gear.

CHRIS GIBISCH, *AAC*

Hammered by spindrift during attempt on Edgar's west face. *Vladimir Belousov*

*Mt Edgar (6,618m), north face attempt.* In September and October 2010 our Russian team hoped to complete new routes on Edgar from the Nan Nem Guon Valley to the north. The main objective for Alexander Novikov and me was the unclimbed west face. The Nan Nem Guon is rarely visited by locals, and we trekked for two days up the valley, following overgrown tracks and building log bridges across two rivers. Our porters dropped their loads and ran away an hour below our planned base camp. It took another day to ferry our gear to base camp, which we established mid-September.

We discovered that it was more or less impossible to access the west face from there. The cwm below the face is guarded by a dangerous icefall that was active the whole time. We turned to the north face and established an advanced base below it at 4,400m. This face was huge and covered mostly with unconsolidated snow.

East face of Grosvenor, showing new Russian route. Top section probably coincides with American rappel descent, which continued down more directly than Russian route. Grosvenor-Jiazi col on right. *Vladimir Belousov*

While the weather had been fine during our approach and for several days after, it started raining at base camp and was clear only above 4,000m. As soon as we began our attempt, though, it got really bad, starting to snow at midday for two days, snowing continuously on the third.

We began on September 29 and climbed 500m before faced with poor snow and continuous powder avalanches. We headed right and climbed part way up a rocky rib, then moved right again and reached a small col at 5,900m on the northwest ridge, where we made our third bivouac. (The first two had been at 5,100m and 5,560m.) The climbing, mainly over snow-covered rock, had been unprotected. There was only one pitch of good (vertical) ice where we could place ice screws and there were no decent bivouac ledges.

West face of Edgar, showing 2011 Russian attempt and high point. *Vladimir Belousov*

We sat at the small col for two days. It was windy and snowing, with no visibility. Our only way out was to descend the left side of the west face to the cwm below. It was complicated, but after another bivouac in the cwm, we crossed the col between Jiazi and Edgar, then descended to the lower part of the icefall, which we rappelled as quickly as possible to avoid falling debris. We decided to return in 2011, having figured out a much better approach to the west face, by passing through the col between Grosvenor and Jiazi. The outcome of this attempt is described below.

VLADIMIR BELOUSOV, *Russia*

*Editor's Note: The 1981 British Army expedition explored the lower part of the Nan Nem Guon during a reconnaissance of Jiazi, but the following year another British expedition, the first with Edgar as its objective, found this approach impossible due to heavy flooding. A third British expedition, in 2004, made possibly the first exploration of the upper Nan Men Guon, with the aim of attempting Edgar's north face. However, they found a dangerous serac barrier on the approach to the face and instead unsuccessfully attempted a peak on the opposite side of the valley (AAJ 2005).*

*Grosvenor (6,376m), east face; Edgar (6,618m), west face attempt.* From mid-October to mid-November we were back in the Minya Konka Range for another attempt on Edgar by the unclimbed west face. Alexander Novikov, Dmitry Paramonov, Denis Shushko, and I spent two weeks exploring a way onto the glacier plateau between Jiazi and Edgar. To reach this we climbed to the col between Jiazi and Grosvenor from the west, fixing 200m of rope. We also acclimatized by climbing to 6,100m on the northeast ridge of Grosvenor. On October 29 we split into two parties and left base camp for our respective objectives; Dmitry and Denis for the east face of Grosvenor, and Alex and I for the west face of Edgar. It took three days for Alex and me to reach a camp below Edgar. During this period the weather became unstable, but we got a promising forecast by satellite phone. By 11 a.m. on the day of our attempt, however, the weather was bad, and we were fighting heavy spindrift. We retreated, having climbed over 400m of this 1,200m face.

The weather alternated one good day and one bad. Everything was wet, and our food was limited, but we decided to try again if the weather gave us another chance. Dmitry and Denis were lucky, as their attempt on Grosvenor was the day after, and the weather was perfect. They climbed the 700m face over steep snow and ice (14 pitches up to 70°), reaching the summit ridge at 6 p.m., just before sunset. They dug a small snow hole in the cornice and sat out the night. Next day it was still calm when they reached the summit at 9 a.m. Then the wind picked up, the clouds rolled in, and they descended. It took the rest of the day to reach camp at the foot of the face.

After two days rest at base camp, Alex and I tried the central couloir on Grosvenor's west face. However, it snowed non-stop for two days. We had run out of time and returned to pack up our base camp.

VLADIMIR BELOUSOV, *Russia*

*Daddomain (6,380m), Ame ni mo Makezu.* Giri-Giri boys Fumitaka Ichimura, Ryo Masumoto, and Takaaki Nagato made the first ascent of the east face of Daddomain, although the three originally planned a direct ascent of the imposing east face of Mt. Edgar (6,618m). After setting up base camp, the team endured 10 days of solid bad weather before heading up in drizzle for a reconnaissance. Unable to see the face on Edgar clearly, they returned but during the descent caught a glimpse of Daddomain at the head of the valley. They were captivated and decided to go for it instead.

From their advanced base at 4,100m, they left at 3:40 a.m. on April 20, crossed the bergschrund at the base of the central couloir

East face of Daddomain, with bivouacs marked. *Takaaki Nagato*

at 4,400m, and climbed snow slopes unroped to 5,100m. Above, they belayed, though generally the rock was compact, so protection was sparse. Negotiating a long, narrow, unstable snow ridge took a long time, and not until 9 p.m. could they dig a small ledge in steep snow at 5,450m and make a sitting bivouac.

On summit ridge. Broad-topped peak to left is Zhong Shan (Sun-Yat-Sen, 6,886m, second highest peak in Minya Konka Range). Pyramid is 7,556m Minya Konka; first ascent, by Americans in 1932, followed northwest ridge (right skyline). *Takaaki Nagato*

Next day the weather worsened, but the three continued their ascent at 8 a.m., climbing mostly over soft snow but with occasional vertical ice. Snowfall became heavier, and after a long day they made their second bivouac at 5,950m, keeping boots on inside sleeping bags.

The following day it snowed heavily. They started at 10 a.m. and climbed for five and a half hours to 6,100m, a little below the summit ridge. Here a serac provided shelter, and they stopped early.

On the 23rd they set out at 9:30 a.m. for the summit, but conditions proved too dangerous, so they returned to the bivouac. Weather improved on the 24th, but deeming the slopes above to be still avalanche prone, they sat tight, hoping things would settle.

On the 25th, in perfect weather, they left the bivouac at 7 a.m., climbed to the summit ridge, and continued to the top, arriving at 9:25 a.m. That day they descended the route, making 15 rappels, back to advanced base.

They have called the 1,900m climb Ame ni mo Makezu (ED1, WI4 M5R, 21 pitches), which roughly translates as "don't lose out to the rain," taken from a famous poem by Kenji Miyazawa, chosen to convey sympathy and greetings to all who suffered from the earthquake and tsunami. Daddomain's only previous ascent was in 2004 by New Zealanders Jo Kippax and Sean Waters, who climbed the West Ridge.

FROM INFORMATION PROVIDED BY HIROSHI HAGIWARA, *Editor ROCK&SNOW, Japan*

*Reddomain (6,112m), Correction.* In *AAJ 2011* we reported the second ascent of this mountain by a different (northern) approach to the west ridge from that used in 1999 by the Japanese first ascensionists. In fact this was the third ascent, the second taking place on October 4, 2006, when American Alpine Institute guide Aidan Leohr, with clients Bill Filimore and Colin Overy, reached the summit in a 17-hour round trip from their 5,000m high camp. These three followed the original Japanese route, approaching the crest of the west ridge from the south.

LINDSAY GRIFFIN, *Mountain INFO, from information provided by Mark Allen*

QONGLAI SHAN - SIGUNIANG NATIONAL PARK

*Siguniang (6,250m), northwest face, Ni Hen Piao Liang.* Climbing with a friend is great;

Ni Hen Piao Liang (right) on northwest face of Siguniang. Line of descent on north ridge. Bivouacs marked. For more routes on this face see *AAJs 2007* and *2010*. *Dimitri Messina*

Baguet on beautiful ice, with 1,000m to go before reaching north summit of Siguniang. *Dimitri Messina*

climbing with four friends even better. We inevitably come away tired from cranking and laughing. Jean-Baptiste Assier's black belt in judo allowed us to enter nightclubs without worrying about our safety. Jack-of-all-trades Sylvain Rechu also enhances our security. In spite of Fabien Suiffet's advanced age of 28, he passed our goofiness test. Maël Baguet is on the National Alpine Climbing Excellence team. Then there's me. I failed my aspirant guide's entrance exam and was deemed ridiculous, though invited to try again in 2012. This left me with more time to organize the expedition.

We arrived at base camp on October 10, after a day's travel on 4WD roads and another day hiking. On the first night I saw Jean-Baptiste in his underwear running after a herd of rutting yaks, so our nights promised to be filled with action.

We acclimatized on nearby Camel Peak (5,400m), accompanied by two canine alpinists, who even bivouacked with us on the summit ice field, at 5,300m. Our next project was Nanar (5,700m). We were roped and heading up a section of treacherous, crevassed glacier, when I saw Fabien rocketing down the slope above me, closely followed by Maël. We had been so focused on the crevasse danger that we hadn't noticed the obvious windslab, which could have been picked out by an eight-year old. Being elite-level lazies, the numerous rest days were surmounted with ease. Each member had his speciality: reading, crosswords, movies, sculpture, yak dung throwing.

On October 28 Maël and I set off for a spur on the northwest face of Siguniang, previously attempted by Americans (1981) and British (2004), while the other three headed for the unclimbed north ridge, descended by Mick Fowler and Paul Ramsden after their ascent of the Inside Line in 2002. An hour later they backed off the approach, which was heavily laden with windslab. Maël and I began at 4,950m, and things were serious from the word go. I struggled with huge amounts of snow to reach two pitches of rotten rock. These were followed by a long stretch of technical ground, with difficult protection. After 300m of 70° climbing, we arrived at the ice, late in the day. Until then we kept expecting to come to an insurmountable pitch that would force us to bail. But from where we now were, we could tell that if we got through the difficult ice pitches above, the summit would be in reach.

Baguet climbs a fine couloir high on Ni Hen Piao Liang. *Dimitri Messina*

Next day we continued on spindrift-swept ice through perfect granite. Neither of us being particularly punctual, we reached the summit ridge at 11 p.m. and chopped a 50cm ledge at 6,200m, just below the serac. The temperature that night dropped to -20°C. We crawled to the summit next afternoon. We named the route Ni Hen Piao Liang (Chinese for You Are Very Pretty, 1,300m, AI5 M6). We descended the north ridge, rappelling over cornices. At our usual time, 11 p.m., we crawled into our shelter. It looked more like a trash bag than a tent.

Getting out in the morning proved our most perilous moment. Then a rope stuck on the second rappel. Overwhelmed by fatigue, we continued the rappels with one 60m rope. Twenty Abalakovs (V-threads) and five hours later, we had finished the 600m of ice and met our friends, who had come up to advanced base. More than ever, this expedition was about our friendship. Maël's feet were a frightening shade of blue, but we turned to each other and said, "Okay guys, when are we going to do this again?"

A few practical notes: We hired the Sichuan Mountaineering Association to organize our trip. They sent us with the versatile, accommodating liaison officer Gao Wei, who is also a great cook. He speaks English, organized everything perfectly, is a mountaineer, and was resourceful (sccdgw18@126. com). You can find nearly everything you need in Chengdu: supermarkets, fast food, good Korean gas canisters, nightclubs. Unlike in some countries, people in China take little notice of you and won't try to sell you things. Take heed: there are an abnormally high number of attractive women, so bring a bib to collect the drool.

DIMITRI MESSINA, *France*

South face of Siguniang. (1) 1992 Japanese ascent of south buttress. (2) Liberation and bivouacs. (3) 2006 French attempt and approximate high point (H). For other routes on this face see *AAJ 2010* p. 347, and *AAJ 2007* p.423. *Sun Bin*

Sun Bin at 5,600m after joining south buttress. Old fixed rope from 1992 Japanese expedition visible on snow slope behind. *Sun Bin Collection*

*Siguniang (6,250m), south face, Liberation.* From November 10 to 13, Li Zhongli and I made an alpine-style ascent of the south face of Siguniang (Yaomei Feng), the highest of the Siguniang Shan (Four Girls Mountains). I first tried the line in October 2006, retreating from the base of the wall, as it was too early in the season, and rockfall was constant. In November 2008 I tried it again with Gu Jie. We reached 5,700m but gave up due to an incoming storm. In November 2009 I was back with Luo Biao, Dili Xiati, and Li Zhongli. We climbed the line to the southwest ridge, but at 6,100m the risk of frostbite from a strong, cold wind drove us down. That same day Yan Dongdong and Zhou Peng reached the top after climbing Free Spirit (*AAJ 2010*).

For my fourth attempt Li and I used porters to help establish base camp at 4,500m on November 4. From then till the 7th it snowed continuously, depositing 50cm at base camp. We waited until the 10th, then set out on our attempt, spending that night a short distance below the bergschrund, at 5,150m. Next day we set off at 4:30 a.m., following the couloir climbed by Free Spirit, to a height of 5,500m, where we slanted left up steeper, snow-covered rock to reach the south buttress above 5,600m. At the top of the buttress we slanted left below the big serac and camped above it, at a comfortable spot on the southwest ridge at 5,900m.

On the 12th a strong wind confined us to our tent, but on the 13th we set out at 4:30 a.m. for the summit. Three pitches of 60° ice were followed by three mixed pitches above 6,000m. Two pitches traversing the sharp ridge above led to the large summit crest. There we traversed right for one pitch and then climbed directly to the summit up an ice gully. We arrived on top at 11:30 a.m., discovering a huge snow hole dug by the French pair who climbed the northwest face in October. It took us five hours to regain our camp at 5,900m.

Next day we made 18 rappels straight down the south face and walked back to base camp. On the 15th we were in Rilong. We named our 1,100m route Liberation (AI3+ M4).

SUN BIN, *China*

*Editor's note: Liberation follows a similar line to the 2006 French attempt by Philippe Batoux and a Young French Alpinists Group, who fixed 500m of rope on the first section. At 5,500m, where Li and Sun slanted up to the crest of the south buttress (climbed directly in 1992 by a Japanese expedition, led by Yoshimura, which fixed 600m of rope), the French continued on the right flank of the buttress and over the top of the large serac to the crest of the southwest ridge. Here they followed the Japanese route along the crest to above 6,000m, where they were turned back by a horizontal rocky section covered with fresh snow and impossible to protect.*

*Goromity (5,609m), attempts.* Goromity (local name Riyucaibao), toward the southern end of the Siguniang Shan, is the highest unclimbed mountain in the range. In autumn 2010 two Chinese climbers, Luo Biao and Zhou Peng, approached via the Shuangqiao and Xiao Niu

(A) Goromiku (5,582m, first ascent Charlie Fowler, 1994). (B) Goromity (5,609m, unclimbed). (C) Wuse Shan (5,430m, first ascent Yan Dongdong and Li Lan, 2010). (D) Celestial Peak (first ascent Americans Lahr, Perlman, and Steck, 1983, followed a day later by Schneider, Wagstaff, and White), seen from south. *Takao Ohe, supplied by Tamotsu Nakamura*

Chang Valleys to the west, set up base camp at 4,450m, and attempted the southwest ridge. At 5,250m they retreated due to bad weather and dangerously loose rock.

Hitoshi Onodera and I attempted the peak in August 2011. After reconnoitering the access from both east and west, we dismissed the approach from the Changping Valley to the east as being far too long. We approached from the west, via the Da Niu Chang valley, which is south of the Xiao Niu Chang and leads toward Wuse Shan (5,430m). The Xiao Niu Chang is steep and narrow (as reported by the Chinese), while the Da Niu Chang has a trail. We established base camp in the latter at 4,200m and crossed the ridge north, to place advance base at 4,400m in the upper Xiao Niu Chang. This crossing took four hours.

On August 11 we set off up the couloir toward the col at the base of the southeast ridge but at 5,000m found ourselves dangerously exposed to frequent rockfall. We retreated.

TAKAO OHE, *Japan, supplied by Tamotsu Nakamura*

YUNNAN

YULONG XUESHAN

*Unnamed Peak (5,321m), attempt.* During February 2011 Darryl Kralovic and I attempted a 5,321m peak in the Yulong Xueshan. This is the easternmost prominent peak in the northern half of the chain. After hiring a car and driver in Lijiang on the 11th, we traveled to the Jade Dragon Snow Mountain Park, bought an entrance ticket, and were dropped off at the main drainage below our mountain. That night we walked west up the valley on old native trails, turned north below the peak, and went up another valley to the start of the north ridge, which appears to offer the easiest route to the summit.

We camped in the forest and spent most of next day reaching a base camp above the tree line at 4,100m. It snowed all day, and the wind was gusty, but our vantage point allowed a tantalizing view of the east side of the peaks lining the eastern edge of Tiger Leaping Gorge.

While the snow stopped early next morning, the winds continued to increase until we had no option but to retreat. Descent was by the same route until we could head east to the Yak Meadow tourist destination, from where we trekked straight down to the road.

Yulong Xueshan from south-southeast. Smaug just visible in top left corner. Shanzidou is large mountain in middle. Predominantly rocky summits on right lie on east ridge of Shanzidou. *Mike Dobie*

Northern sector of Yulong Xueshan from the southeast seen from 3,000m on road north of Lijiang. Impressive snowy peak on left is Shanzidou (Jade Dragon Snow Mountain, 5,596m). Mountain on far right is Peak 5,321m. *Mike Dobie*

MIKE DOBIE, *China*

*Smaug (ca 5,000m).* On December 17, 2010 Darryl Kralovic and I climbed a previously unnamed peak in the Yulong Xueshan, the Jade Dragon Snow Mountain area of Lijiang county. The Yulong Xueshan massif has around 14 significant peaks over 5,000m, nearly all of which are thought to be unclimbed.

Chinese advertise that the main summit, Shanzidou (5,596m) has never been climbed, and we were told by national park authorities that it is illegal to attempt it. For this reason we focused our sights on other objectives. [*Editor's note: The main summit has had one known ascent. After attempts by a New Zealand team in the 1930s, by a Japanese expedition in 1984, by Chris Jones and five other Americans, who in 1985 reached a col at the start of the north ridge, and by Eric Perlman and six other Americans, who in 1986 got within 150 vertical meters of the top via the north ridge, it was finally climbed in 1987 by Phil Peralta-Ramos and Perlman, who took a short cut to the ridge through avalanche-prone gullies and 5.7 rock climbing in crampons, before following the meter-wide crest of unconsolidated snow to the summit.*]

The range is oriented north-south, and our peak is the farthest south. We do not know if the summit has a Chinese name, but we gave it the English name Smaug to go along with the dragon theme. We carried no GPS and cannot give an altitude. However, based on information gathered from Google maps, we feel the height is ca 5,000m [*Editor's note: It is probably Peak 5,004m on a sketch map of the range.*]

We first reached the small village of Yuhu (Jade Water), where we bought tickets for 120 RMB each to enter the Jade Dragon Snow Mountain Park. We then headed up through the village

Smaug Peak, showing line of first ascent. Photo taken in dry conditions during a previous reconnaissance; at time of first ascent, snow covered scree-filled cwm. *Mike Dobie*

to a prominent horse trail/road, toward woods on the southeastern slope of the mountain. One trail seemed most obvious, and we passed a few horse stalls (used for tourism) and buildings. We went off-trail at 3,350m and headed straight up grassy slopes to an alpine basin, where we established base camp at 4,235m in a cirque below the summit.

The following morning we climbed snow-covered scree to a gully facing southeast. After entering the gully we headed up left, reaching more gully systems leading to the summit (south) ridge. We met high winds and a developing storm as we ascended a 4th

class block at the top. Our route, on which we found no evidence of previous passage, gave snow and ice climbing to 50° and class 3 and 4 rock steps. We downclimbed our ascent route. From the top it looked as though there might be other gully systems giving access to the summits farther north, between us and Shanzidou.

MIKE DOBIE, *China*

LOAJUNSHAN NATIONAL PARK,

*Rock climbing.* Austin and Laoiju Stringham have opened a sandstone trad climbing area in northwest Yunnan Province. Accessed through the town of Liming (2,100m), two and a half hours drive west of the major city Lijiang, the sandstone walls lie within Loajunshan National Park in the Three Gorges scenic region. The pair worked

Eben Farnworth on first ascent of Dancing with Dragons (FFA by Darryl Kralovic, 5.10d), Lisu East Buttress. *Darryl Kralovic*

Sandstone walls in Liming Valley. *Darryl Kralovic*

Lisu area, East Buttress. Established climbs are on left side and on pillars at base of front face. *Darryl Kralovic*

Liming Valley. (A) Orange Sky area, home to classic Orange Sky (37m, 5.11 A0), one of park's best 5.11s. (B) Cretaceous area, first sector to be climbed in Liming and home to classic Soul's Awakening (four pitches, 5.10). (C) Cave area, which currently has few established routes but loads of potential. *Mike Dobie*

tirelessly to gain access for rock climbers, which was eventually granted by the Chinese Government in November 2010.

Since then Austin, Eben Farnworth, Darryl Kralovic, and I have put up 50 new routes, documented in the guidebook Liming Rock. The potential for routes is almost limitless; sandstone cliffs up to 200m high lie throughout 10 major valleys, and the region is best described as offering a variety of crack climbing in the style of Utah's Indian Creek.

The guidebook documents approaches, potential new route information, and attractions and accommodations in the area. It can be downloaded free at junshanclimber.com. For more information you can also contact me directly.

Because the local government can now see possible financial benefits, it is totally enthusiastic about climbing development. This good news means that the park could become an example to the rest of China, opening government eyes to this type of outdoor recreation.

MIKE DOBIE, *China,*
*mdobie012@gmail.com*

# Tibet

*Gurla Mandhata (Naimona'nyi, 7,694m), first traverse.* For some years Kazuya Hiraide and I tried to visit Gurla Mandhata. We knew about ascents from the northwest, facing the holy mountain of Kailash, but never found any information about the south side. We also never received replies from the CTMA to our questions about the nearest village, Burang (first village north of the Nepalese border), or access to the south face via Ronggo Gully. With no information or permit, we went elsewhere, climbing a new route on Kamet and attempting Gauri Shankar.

Unclimbed southeast face of Gurla Mandhata. Southeast ridge forms left skyline. Hiraide and Taniguchi climbed face on right, directly beneath summit, to 6,300m before retreating. Later they climbed southwest ridge, which meets southeast ridge at distinct pointed snow summit, Naofeng Peak, in center of picture. *Kei Taniguchi*

Before leaving for Tibet in the autumn, we had only a few distant photos of Gurla Mandhata's southeast face, taken by Tamotsu Ohnishi from well south of the Tibet-Nepal border. We also had a little help from Google Earth. The CTMA had

Descending upper northwest slope of Gurla Mandhata, with Lake Rakshastal (left) and Manasarova (separated by strip of land, on which runs road from Nepalese border. Prominent peak in left distance is Kailash (6,638m). *Kei Taniguchi*

no idea as to the whereabouts of Ronggo Gully, and while our liaison officer, Tashi, had been several times to the mountain, he knew nothing of the south side.

After acclimatizing by making a circuit of Kailash, we asked a local goatherd the whereabouts of Ronggo Gully's entrance. Then we begged for horses to carry our food and equipment to the mountain, but it was harvest time, and locals were unwilling to help. The entrance to the gully looked narrow, steep, and more or less impossible. However, on September 13 a local horseman

Hiraide climbing toward southwest ridge. *Kei Taniguchi*

found a way through, although it proved difficult for the horses to get all the way to our base camp at 4,700m, halfway to the foot of the southeast face. From there we had to carry equipment to the bottom of the face, over unstable moraine and glacier. We were the first people to see it from here, and after reconnaissance, during which we watched a big serac collapse several times, we found only one safe route to the summit.

After further acclimatization we were ready to go, but due to a spell of fine, sunny weather, the face was dry, with frequent rockfall, ice fall, and avalanches. On our first day we tried to avoid falling debris, as we climbed through loose rock bands and poor snow and ice. By evening we had reached a point just below the serac, where we bivouacked. It being clear that this was not the sort of climb we like, constantly exposed to unavoidable danger, the next day we ran away from the face, a disappointing end to our attempt.

Back at base camp we rested, then we began climbing north through an unexplored valley toward the southwest ridge. On the next day we continued toward the crest, then traversed east below it on a glacier shelf, where we made our second camp, south of Point 6,992m. On the following day we reached the crest and followed it to where the southeast ridge comes in from the right. We continued, with two more camps, over previously unclimbed Naofeng Peak (Gurla Mandhata south summit, 7,422m), to reach the main summit on October 9. We made our fifth camp high on the Original Route on the northwest slope, where there were commanding views of Kailash and Lake Manasarova. We reached the base of the mountain on the 10th. Routefinding was difficult, as there is a large labyrinth of seracs, where we needed to make some rappels. On the 13th we departed for Kathmandu.

KEI TANIGUCHI, *Japan*

*Editor's note: Gurla Mandhata was first climbed by a large Sino-Japanese expedition (Katsutoshi Hirabayashi, climbing leader) in 1985, with 13 members reaching the summit via the northwest slope. Swiss Paul Tschanz and Diego Wellig repeated this route in 1990. In 1997 Charlie Fowler, Tom and Quinn Simons, and Soren Peters climbed Peak 6,912m, immediately to the north, and a 6,902m peak, Guna La, to the northeast, before Fowler, Quinn Simons, and Peters climbed the north-northeast face to the summit plateau not far from the top. They retreated when Simons' hands were frostbitten. During the descent, at 6,800m, all three fell 450m. Simons and Peters were unhurt and descended to summon local help to evacuate Fowler, with a badly wrenched leg. French repeated the Original Route in 1999, and the following year Tomoyuki Furuya, Hiroshi Iwazaki, and Ayumi Nozawai climbed onto the north ridge from the east and followed the right flank to below the summit plateau, where they slanted across the east face to reach the summit. Two Japanese and a Tibetan reached the summit in 2001 by the Original Route, for the fifth ascent of the mountain. Americans made the sixth in 2006, via the Original route. Hiraide and Taniguchi's ascent is the third new route and possibly the seventh overall ascent.*

MAHALANGUR HIMAL

*Cho Oyu, Point 7,570m, northwest face, NIL.* While climbing a new route on Palung Ri in 2006 (*AAJ 2007*), I looked at the possibility of a new route on the northwest face of Pt. 7,570m, directly opposite. In 2011 I was on Cho Oyu, guiding a group on the Normal Route. On a day off I studied Pt. 7,570m's northwest face from the Palung La (6,517m), at the head of the Gyabrag Chang Glacier, and climbed to 6,800m to check snow conditions and avalanche danger.

Cho Oyu from west. (1) North ridge over Point 7,570m (Cadiach-Ruckensteiner, 1996). (2) NIL to Point 7,570m and traverse east to Camp 2 on Normal Route. Point 7,570m was first climbed, from Cho Oyu's Normal Route, in 1954 by Jean Juge, of Raymond Lambert's expedition. (3) Normal Route (Pasang Dawa Lama-Jochler-Tichy, 1954). (4) Messner variant start (Dacher-Kammerlander- Messner, 1983). (5) Southwest pillar and west face (Gajewski-Pawlikowski, 1986). *Jordi Tosas*

When we got a weather window, I attempted the route while my clients made a summit bid on Cho Oyu. From base camp at 5,600m, I climbed with them to Camp 1 (6,400m), where they would spend the night with a Sherpa, and climb to Camp 2 the next day. I left at 8 p.m., climbed over the serac and onto the plateau above, and traversed under a large serac barrier to reach the face. I climbed the mixed face toward the right side and reached Pt. 7,570m, from where I traversed east to Camp 2 on the Cho Oyu's Normal Route. I arrived at the tents, which we had left during an acclimatization climb, between 6 and 6:30 a.m. The night had been good: relatively mild with no wind, though there was no moon. During the ascent I'd encountered 55° snow and UIAA III rock. I named the route NIL, after my son.

I waited that day for my clients to arrive, planning to set out with them the following night for the top. But we were unable to reach the top of Cho Oyu, so my new route on Pt. 7,570m does not finish on Cho Oyu's summit.

Back at base camp I got word that José Luis Quintana was at his Camp 2 (7,000m), unable to move after an unsuccessful summit

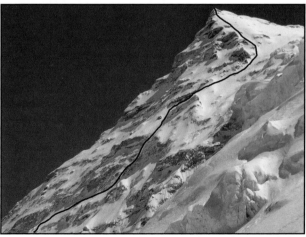

NIL on Point 7,570m. 1996 Spanish route on northwest ridge lies just behind skyline. *Jordi Tosas.*

attempt. I tried to assemble a rescue team of Sherpas and climbers, but people told me they were not interested. With two Sherpas I made an attempt to reach the camp but was driven back by a snow storm. On the third day I made another attempt, alone, and reached his tent at 10:30 p.m. He was unable to walk without assistance, and it took until 5 a.m. the following morning to get him down to Camp 1. From there I had help from Tibetan porters to bring him to base camp. [*Tosas was hospitalized with frostbite.*]

Climbing on 8,000m peaks is difficult to understand. Not the mountains but the people now attempting them. For me mountains have important human values, which it seems people have forgotten.

JORDI TOSAS, *Spain*

NYANCHEN TANGLHA WEST

*Qungmo Kangri (7,069m), southwest face; Point 6,097m, north ridge; Dhungri II (6,194m), southwest ridge; Point ca 5,980m.* In the autumn a party of climbers made four ascents in the Qungmo Kangri group at the southwestern end of Nyanchen Tanglha. They first tried the lower of two peaks referred to as Dhungri by nomads. This peak is generally known as Tangmonja and was attempted in 1999, via the southwest ridge, by a British party comprising Derek Buckle, Gary Hill, Alyson Starling, John Town, and John Whiteley. They retreated because of poor rock and bad weather but later climbed a smaller summit to the northeast named Machag. The 2011 team completed this ridge (350m, UIAA V R M3 AI3), to reach the summit of what they call Dhungri II (29°56'46" N, 90°04'55" E). Although they believed they were making a first ascent, they discovered a new rappel anchor on the top, and suspect that another party had climbed the north ridge in September.

They then turned to the southeast face of the higher peak, Dhungri I (6,328m, 29°55'58" N, 90°05'10" W), an elegant summit also referred to as Xabu. However, they failed to reach the base, as it necessitated crossing a ridge that proved to be bigger and sharper than suggested on Google Earth. Instead they soloed a predominantly rocky ridge to a point of ca 5,980m between Dhungri I and II. It was 700m of mostly walking/scrambling but with a few sections of around M4.

The team made the first ascent of the southwest face of Qungmo Kangri (29°54'12" N, 90°01'29" E), starting from the base of the glacier in the Jumu Valley, an ascent of 1,300m, with difficulties of M4/M5 and AI4. They made their first bivouac shortly before joining the south ridge. After reaching the upper ridge, they found traces of fixed rope. They descended the south ridge to the col, where they made their second bivouac. On day three they climbed the short north ridge of Point 6,097m, returned to the col, and descended first west, then south, to their camp below the glacier.

This was the fifth known ascent of Qungmo Kangri, the previous four following the south ridge. The first three (Chinese-Korean, then two Japanese) approached the ridge from the east. The fourth was a solo ascent from the west by Christian Haas (*AAJ 2006*). Point 6,097m was possibly climbed by one of the first three teams, and it was definitely climbed by Haas, from the west, who traversed it on his way to Qungmo Kangri.

LINDSAY GRIFFIN, *Mountain INFO*

NYANCHEN TANGLHA EAST

*Jiangpu Glacier, exploration.* When flying from Chengdu to Lhasa, you pass over more than 200, 6,000m peaks in the Nyanchen Tanglha East. Nearly all are unclimbed, and many are situated either side of the

Gyala Peri (7,294m) from southwest, climbed only in 1986 by Japanese expedition via west face and south ridge (between shade and sunlight). *Tamotsu Nakamura*

Southeast face of Jongpo Po Rong (6,570m) rises above middle branch of the Jiangpo Glacier. *Tamotsu Nakamura*

Yiong Tsangpo. In 2010 and 2011 Tibet became more sensitive, and access for foreigners more difficult. The situation went from bad to worse after the celebrations marking the 60th anniversary of Tibetan liberation, held in Lhasa in June 2011. Qamdo is now closed, except for Rawu (Largu) Glacier and the Midou Glacier, which are popular tourist spots. In Nyainchi Prefecture foreigners have only been allowed to visit towns along Route 318, the Sichuan-Tibet Highway. This has been strictly controlled by the Public Security Bureau, which has banned foreigners from accessing areas off the highway.

Tsuyoshi Nagai (79), Tadao Shintani (65), and I were issued a permit to visit only towns along the highway. However, to accomplish our objective, a visit to the lower Yiong Tsangpo, we couldn't acquiesce to these restrictions. In the last year and a half a vehicle road has been constructed from Yiong village to Bake, and on October 17 we drove directly to Bake, which

Southwest face of Tiba Kangri (6,846m) in Gyala Peri Group.  *Tamotsu Nakamura*

East face of San Ri Dui (6,050m).  *Tamotsu Nakamura*

Unclimbed west face of Namcha Barwa (7,782m) from Seti La (4,500m). This peak has been climbed only in 1992, by a Sino-Japanese expedition via south ridge to east ridge. West face 3,300m high. *Tamotsu Nakamura*

was originally to be the base for our exploration of surrounding mountains. When we arrived, the PSB ordered our return to Bomi County, the police there overseeing the PSB in Bake. If we had done this, we would never have been allowed to enter the Yi'ong Tsangpo. Our capable Tibetan guide, Awang, proved discreet. We drove back down the valley but turned left up a side branch north of Talu, reaching the roadhead at Wopu Village. Above, the valley leads to the Jiangpu Glacier, the second largest in Nyanchen Tanglha East and home to a number of unvisited 6,000m peaks.

Six days on horseback through Tibetan jungle brought us to a marvelous lookout, where we had magnificent views of unclimbed peaks. After 12 days of clandestine exploration, Awang received a phone call from his agent in Lhasa, explaining that the PSB was nervous about three missing Japanese, who should be reporting to Nyainchi police authorities in Bayichen. When we arrived, the talented Awang made up a consistent and plausible story for our 12 days absence, not mentioning that we had been off Route 318. He was allowed to leave, and we flew to Chengdu on the 30th.

TAMOTSU NAKAMURA, *Japan*

Aerial view of Jongpo Po Rong (6,570m) and Jonlamapo (6,605m) from southeast. *Tamotsu Nakamura*

East face of San Ri Mal (ca 6,000m). *Tamotsu Nakamura*

# *Mongolia*

*The online version of these reports frequently contains additional photos, maps, topos, and extended text. Please visit aaj.americanalpineclub.org*

ALTAI - TVAN BOGD

Changing snow cover in Mongolian Altai. North face of Naran in June 1992. 1992 Anglo-American route to left, 2011 Direct Route to right. *Lindsay Griffin*

Naran in July 2011, showing Direct Route climbed on north face. *Jeff Reynolds*

*Naran (3,884m), north face.* During the week beginning July 17 Ken Krebs and I climbed a direct line up the north face of Naran, via a prominent ice ramp, the north ridge, and the summit snow face. Earlier that week we had ascended several surrounding peaks, including Huiten (Khuiten, 4,374m), and then descended from a high camp on the Potanina Glacier to the foot of Naran. The north face is a proud, prominent statement to the entire valley, a contender for an Altai and Mongolian classic. Sustained 50-60° ice rises 600m before reaching a ridge leading to three or four pitches of packed snow on the short upper face. The overall grade was US IV.

Circumstances were not optimal. The face was very dry and much of it exposed to rockfall. This was not solely due to a dry season in the Altai. Locals have noted how far the Potanina Glacier has dropped below the lateral moraine that the trail to base camp follows, and it is also evident that the toe of the glacier has receded far beyond the lake. During our week in the area conditions changed dramatically. It snowed a little on our arrival, but warm weather then toasted the fresh snow and a 30cm more below. Reports indicate that earlier in the year a group of ski mountaineers rejected skiing Naran due to icy conditions. Perhaps this was prudent.

The direct route on the north face follows a straight, narrow line between small hanging glaciers and rock buttresses; from these there was rock and ice fall due to high midsummer temperatures. While we scoped other attractive but less evident routes west of the ice ramp, the objective hazards of a direct line up the ramp appeared manageable. Unexposed crevasses and a small bergschrund were present on the ridge and small snow face above. Looking at early summer imagery on the Internet, it's clear that Naran, like most peaks in the Altai, is best climbed late spring to early summer, but, even in midsummer, an early morning departure resulted in excellent front-pointing on the ice ramp and an amazing view of the sunrise. Getting off Naran also provided a routefinding challenge.

We descended the rocky south ridge to the lowest point of the saddle, then plunged down a 40° face to the west, crossing multiple crevasses and a bergschrund. It appeared that this descent had the least amount of exposure, and would likely form the best normal route. However, crevasses are significant and clever route finding is in order for a safe return to base camp. Altogether, we had a brilliant day.

JEFF REYNOLDS

*Editor's Note: The north face was first climbed in 1992 via a line up its eastern edge, finishing on the northeast ridge, by Julian Freeman-Attwood, Lindsay Griffin, and Ed Webster (AAJ 2003). At that time the mountain was known to them as Hadat Chajrchan (Rocky Peak).*

# *Indonesia*

BORNEO

*West Kalimantan, Mt. Batu Daya, southeast face.* In 2011, after authorities denied me a visa to return to Socotra Island, Yemen, due to war mayhem, I looked at my long list of areas to explore, with more than 20 expeditions on the docket. Batu Daya caught my eye; I had never been there. The first two weeks of December are in the rainy season, but I decided to go. I arrived at Jakarta and flew to Ketapang. A few hours drive, a few hours on a speed boat, a hitched lift on a big truck working the palm oil fields, and I was near Batu Daya, staring at its massiveness. I made this journey with a local guide and new friend, Herry, from Kalimantan. We paid locals to camp at

Mike Libecki with locals in front of Batu Daya. *Mike Libecki*

their house near Batu Daya. As in so many places, these people were wonderful and kind. I had many good meals and laughter with them, but with a roundtrip from home limited to two weeks, there was no time to lose.

Herry and I hacked through the jungle with razor-sharp machetes. It took a few days to

Unclimbed rock formation near Batu Daya. *Mike Libecki*

reach the base of Batu Daya, some of the worst suffering of my life. Hours of slogging in swamps, razor-wire bushes, 35°C, 95%+ humidity. Jungles are the worst; I would rather freeze. I have been in many jungles, always a sufferfest. Respect to all fellow jungle explorers. Of course, there is something wonderful about suffering: the pay off, survival and/or summit, seems so much better. We had a base camp near the foot of the tower, making beds out of vines and trees. The route looked like it would allow a fast ascent, and Herry asked if I could teach him some rope work, so he could follow me up, as he had always dreamed of going to the summit of Batu Daya.

We left super early and climbed all day. The rock was good and highly featured, with solid jungle foliage and vines to hold. The runouts were quite fun, as everywhere there were sweet holes and pockets in the stone. The worst part was getting to the jungle after the end of bare rock. This jungle was the thickest, most insane, I have ever seen. After four hours of being shredded by the vines and organic razor wire, we reached the summit as the sun disappeared.

Herry was able to light a fire, and we sat waiting for the sun to light our descent. It was a creepy night, and I wiped several bugs and spiders off my neck and face. Next day we reached base camp by nightfall, and the following morning got lost trying to find our way out of the jungle. I got increasingly worried as we spent all day walking through muddy swamps and razor-wire bushes and vines, but 20 minutes before full darkness we stumbled onto an old, barely visible bulldozer trail. Definitely some of the worst suffering I've experienced.

Locals say there was a team that tried to climb Batu Daya 10 or 15 years ago, and one climber died. I talked with an elder local who helped carry the body. Other than that I can find no information on attempts or successes. I graded our 650m route on the southeast face V 5.10 A1.

MIKE LIBECKI, *AAC*

# AMERICAN ALPINE CLUB GRANTS

The American Alpine Club provides resources for climbers and explorers to attempt new challenges, conduct scientific research, and conserve mountain environments. The AAC awards more than $80,000 annually, although the size and number of awards vary from year to year. For more information

Neacola Mountains, Alaska.
Aaron Thrasher

on all the grant programs, please visit americanalpineclub.org. The information below about 2011 grant recipients and objectives was accurate at the time of the grant; in some cases, recipients may have decided to attempt other objectives. Expeditions with page numbers are reported in this *Journal*.

## LYMAN SPITZER CUTTING-EDGE AWARD

**Skiy Detray, Andy Hoeckel**
*East face of Great Trango Tower, Pakistan*
$3,000

**Ben Venter, Jake Tipton, Willy Oppenheim**
*Southwest face Nafees' Cap, Pakistan [p. 272]*
$3,000

**David Anderson, Szu-ting Yi, Eric Salazar**
*Unclimbed Dkyil'khor Ri and Bka Ri, Genyen Massif, China*
$3,000

**Colin Haley, Bjørn-Eivind Årtun**
*North face of Ogre II (6,960m), Pakistan*
$3,000

## MOUNTAIN HARDWEAR MCNEILL-NOTT

**Jesse Burkhardt, Bo White, Boris Lukanov, Darren Benton**
*Peak Patkhor (6,080m), Gorno-Badakshan [p. 210]*
$3,500

**Sam Johnson, Ben Chriswell**
*Peak 8300+, Neacola Mountains, Alaska [p. 122]*
$1,500

## NIKWAX ALPINE BELLWETHER

**Seth Campbell**
*Scientific, photographic, historical exploration of West Buttress of Denali*
$1,500

**Kurt Sanderson**
*Interaction of ice, water and community survival near Santiago, Chile*
$1,500

## MOUNTAINEERING FELLOWSHIPS

**Scott Bennett (25)**
*Cerro Pollone's east peak, Argentina [p. 187]*
$600

**Tyler Botzon (21)**
*Ama Dablam, Nepal*
$400

**Christopher Carter (21)**
*Ski mountaineering, Altai Mountains, Mongolia*
$400

**Aaron Child (21)**
*Boyd Everett Fund, Bugaboos, Canada*
$500

**Sean Dormer (22)**
*REI Challenge Fund, first ascents Arrigetch Mountains, Alaska*
$1,000

**Tim Gibson (23) and Michael Wejchert (24)**
*REI Challenge Fund, Kichatna Spires, Alaska*
$800

**Hayden Kennedy (20)**
*Chamlang north face, China*
$400

**Jacon Mayer (23) and Max Talsky (23)**
*Boyd Everett Fund, Cassin Ridge, Denali*
$600

**Willy Oppenheim (24)**
*Mountain Fellowship Fund, Nafees' Cap, Pakistan [p. 272]*
$800

## ZACK MARTIN BREAKING BARRIERS GRANT

**Asa Firestone**
*Developing a climbing wall and outdoor program for children in a favela (slum) of Rio de Janeiro, Brazil*
$1,600

## SCOTT FISCHER MEMORIAL CONSERVATION GRANT

**Allen Higginbotham**
*Cleanup of fixed gear, ropes, and trash on Ama Dablam, Nepal*
$400

## LARA KELLOGG MEMORIAL CONSERVATION GRANT

**Frank Nederhand**
*Cordillera Blanca Environmental Expedition*
$1,100

## RESEARCH GRANTS

**Seth Campbell**
*Scientific, photographic, historical exploration of West Buttress of Denali*
$1,000

**Gileard Minja**
*Impact of climate change on northern circuit tourism, Kilimanjaro National Park, Tanzania*
$500

**Daniel Sturgis**
*Linking glacier outburst flood event to subglacial hydrology, Lemon Creek Glacier, Alaska*
$500

**Jon Kedrowski**
*Anthropogenic trail and route impacts from hikers on state high points, Arizona, New Mexico, Utah, Colorado, Idaho*
$1,000

**Christopher Crawford**
*Tracking abrupt temperature change across alpine environments, interior northwestern U.S.A.*
$700

**Peter Neff**
*Shallow repeating seismic events under an alpine glacier at Mt. Rainier, Washington*
$500

**Sarah Castle**
*Ecosystem succession in the earliest stages, Puca Glacier, Cordillera Vilcanota, Peru*
$500

**Frank Nederhand**
*Air pollution and global warming impacts on high mountains, Cordillera Blanca, Peru*
$500

**Lisbeth Willey**
*Long-term alpine vegetation monitoring (GLORIA), Uapsihka (Monts Groulx), Québec*
$500

**Chris Kopp**
*Shrub invasion of alpine areas, White Mountains, California*
$1,000

**Kurt Sanderson**
*Interaction of ice, water, and community survival, Santiago, Chile*
$700

**Max Stevens**
*Resolution of spatial variability uncertainty on avalanche prone slopes*
$855

## CORNERSTONE CONSERVATION GRANT

**Southeast Climbers' Coalition**
*Boat Rock Waste Management Solution Project: vault toilet for bouldering area*
$7,500

**Climbing Resource Access Group, VT**
*Bolton Quarry Driveway Restoration Project: access road rebuild after flooding, Vermont*
$2,000

**Boulder Climbing Community**
*Boulder Area Stewardship Project: human waste pack-out solution, kiosks, and education*
$1,975

**Friends of Muir Valley**
*Parking Improvements and Expansion Project: accommodating more climbers, Kentucky*
$2,500

**Las Vegas Climbers' Liaison Council**
*Red Rock Waste Bag Project: human waste pack-out solution*
$1,320

**Carolina Climbers' Coalition**
*Rumbling Bald Mapping Project: GIS services for climbing area planning, North Carolina*
$1,800

**Arkansas Climbers' Coalition**
*Sam's Throne Camping Area Project: complete camping area signage and kiosk*
$3,750

**Smith Rock Group**
*Smith Rock Spring Thing 2012 Project: trail steps improvement, Oregon*
$4,155

# BOOK REVIEWS

EDITED BY DAVID STEVENSON

*Freedom Climbers.* **Bernadette McDonald. Rocky Mountain Books, 2011. 352 pages. Color photos. Hardcover. $29.95.**

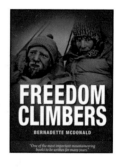

In *Freedom Climbers* Bernadette McDonald tells the story of the Golden Age of Polish Himalayan mountaineering, much of it done in winter: a 25-year period of triumph and loss. The "major Polish Himalayan climbs" catalogued in her appendix span the period from the first ascent of Kunyang Chhish in the Karakoram in 1971 to the first ascent of the northwest ridge of Annapurna in 1996. The catalog lists 40 major climbs, a high proportion of them first ascents or first winter ascents, and includes the three Poles, Kucuszka, Wielecki, and Pustelnik, who summited all the 8,000-meter peaks. While her sense of decorum doesn't let her compile a list of the deaths, she does note in her epilogue that "an astonishing 80 percent of the best [Polish] high-altitude climbers died in the great ranges in that era." Eighty percent.

McDonald performs a tremendous double service: to Polish climbers, about whom little has been published in English, and to English-speaking readers, whose access to reports of these staggering feats has been limited (mostly to the *AAJ*).

McDonald's curiosity originated from a conversation with Wanda Rutkiewicz and a plan to bring her to Banff, where McDonald directed the Mountain Film Festival. The plan was never realized because Rutkiewicz died on Kanchenjunga in 1992 while attempting her ninth 8,000-meter peak. In later conversations with Polish climbers, an "ambiguous portrait" of Rutkiewicz emerged, and McDonald became compelled to try to reconcile the warmth she experienced in Wanda with the conflicting opinions surrounding her.

While this curiosity may have been the initial driving force, the book casts a wider net. The climbing careers of Jurek Kukuczka and Yoytek Kurtka receive coverage about equal to Rutkiewicz, and others are mentioned frequently, including Krzysztof Wielecki and Andrzef Zawada.

While this book focuses on personalities and specific climbs (not a definitive history of Polish climbing, McDonald asserts), one of its strengths is historical context. "Sixty years dominated by hideous violence and oppression, massive upheaval and miraculous rebirth. The ability of this tight-knit climbing community to co-exist with such a desperate political reality, and produce the very best Himalayan alpinists in the world, was puzzling. Did the hard times forge their ambitions, or only toughen them, train them in stoicism?" This book is McDonald's answer.

McDonald resists the temptation to reduce the climbers to products of their environment. Instead she simply portrays that environment. Most of these climbers were born during the Nazi occupation and/or grew up during the Soviet occupation. All suffered poverty; some experienced work camps or relocations. Rutkiewicz's brother was killed as a child playing with an unexploded grenade in 1948, and her father was murdered. Zawada, one of the golden boys of the Warsaw Mountain Club, was imprisoned for his political views; most of his friends were executed. They all had to navigate the politics of the club system to earn even scant government support, and they created their own black-market economy to finance their climbing. They all possessed tremendous drive in the mountains, tremendous capacity for suffering, tremendous ambition. McDonald is not trying so much to explain (which is probably impossible) but to describe, an impulse arising out of curiosity and admiration. Kukuscka: "I went to the mountains and climbed them. That is all."

The deaths haunt us because there is such an air of inevitability about them. As I read I was only vaguely aware of which climbers had perished and which had survived. In the end I was happy that any of them survived. Jon Bilman has recently observed (and been criticized for saying), "... in an age when all the great firsts have been done, the new measure of adventure excellence is often the level of protracted agony." These Polish climbers set the bar damned high for "protracted agony." Alex Lowe's famous dictum, "The best climber in the world is the one having the most fun," would be hard to apply to the Poles: "fun" seems not to have been part of their alpine conversation. One finishes the book with admiration and a broken heart.

McDonald has long had an eye for little-known stories: biographies of Elizabeth Hawley, Charles Houston, and Tomaz Humar preceded *Freedom Climbers*. These are fine books, but this one rises to the level of a small masterpiece. *Freedom Climbers* has garnered for McDonald the prestigious Boardman-Tasker Award and the Banff Mountain Book Festival Grand Prize, as well as being the deciding factor in her receiving the American Alpine Club's most recent Literary Award. I can't recall alpine literary stars aligning with such unanimity, but *Freedom Climbers* deserves them.

DAVID STEVENSON

---

*Fred Beckey's 100 Favorite North American Climbs.* **Fred Beckey. Introduction by Barry Blanchard. Patagonia Books, 2011. 350 pages. Color photos. Hardcover. $79.95.**

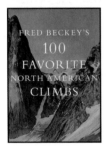

*Fred Beckey's 100 Favorite North American Climbs* is the culmination of 75 years of mountain exploration by the most prolific climber in history. This carefully curated collection of classic climbs deserves a place on every climber's coffee table.

In Seattle I had the pleasure of attended the standing-room-only signing of Beckey's new book. The first question posed to the author was how he possibly could prune his list of favorite climbs down to just 100.

That's the question. Beckey is after all climbing's original Energizer Bunny. No human has made more first ascents on North American mountains. When you gaze at aerial photos of the classics—Slesse Mountain, South Howser Tower, and Mt. Goode come immediately to mind—the sweetest lines are inevitably Beckey routes. After more than seven decades of exploring the high and wild, Fred stopped counting his first ascents long ago; the total is in the *thousands*.

I assumed this would be a collection of Beckey's 100 favorite *first ascents* and was therefore surprised to note that the majority of climbs are *not* routes he pioneered. Only 39 of the 100 are Beckey first ascents. It's an egoless compilation.

While flipping through this lavishly produced climber's bible, I realized I had stumbled upon my to-do list for the next 20 years. I started by counting the routes I've already done, and the good news is that I still have 72 of Fred's favorites remaining. More important than the number is that Beckey chose routes that mere mortals like me are capable of climbing. This is not a collection of top-end sufferfests for the modern hard man. It's an egalitarian list of timeless classics that provide realistic objectives for many of us. If you have general mountaineering skills and are comfortable on 5.9 rock, you can realistically climb 68 of Beckey's favorites. Stretching your standard to 5.9+ gets you another five, and solid 5.10 leaders belong on 94 of the 100. Only six routes involve direct aid or 5.11 climbing.

In the Foreword Beckey writes, "The span of my presented climbs ranges from the scalloped cornices of Mt. Deborah, the ice-plastered faces of Mt. Robson, the inimitable Bugaboos, the honed pinnacles on Forbidden Peak, the granite knobs of Charlotte Dome, to the dizzying sandstone of Zion."

The climbs are beautifully photographed but are not shown with route-line overlays. Despite the aesthetic appeal of clean photos, many leave the reader wondering where the route goes. The photography is generally excellent, although the book's heft suggests that many of the photos should be larger. Other than those two nits, this is an inspiring piece without equal. Beckey enriches each climb with historic perspective, and his interest in geology is evident throughout.

Beckey's favorite climbs are defined by purity of line, position, and quality of movement—not difficulty. It makes you appreciate his ability to choose nature's most beautiful lines. Surely for Beckey, thinning the list down to just 100 had to be more difficult than the toughest line in the book.

MARK KROESE

---

***The Ledge: An Adventure Story of Friendship and Survival on Mount Rainier.* Jim Davidson and Kevin Vaughan. Ballantine Books, 2011. 268 pages. Hardcover. $26.00.**

On June 21, 1992, Jim Davidson and his friend and climbing partner Mike Price summited Mt. Rainier (14,410') via Liberty Ridge. On their descent, via the Emmons-Winthrop route, they both fell through a snowbridge into a crevasse. Davidson survived; Price did not. Nineteen years later Davidson used audio records, old letters, and his memories to tell the story of their accident in *The Ledge*.

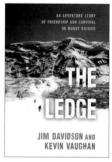

While the first few chapters are dedicated to Price's early life—his youth, his education, his work as an Outward Bound instructor, and his development as an alpine climber—the bulk of the book is Davidson's detailed first-person account of the day of the accident. After summiting, the team began their descent of "the postcard-perfect mountain." They were on the Carbon Glacier—only 1,500 vertical feet above the climbing ranger's hut at Camp Sherman—when Davidson broke through a snowbridge over a hidden crevasse. Price was unable to arrest the fall, and together they tumbled an estimated 80 feet before landing on a small ledge deep in the crevasse. (Ten feet farther, Davidson estimates, and they would have been wedged between narrowing ice walls.) Price was gravely injured upon landing, and despite Davidson's attempts at resuscitation, chest compressions, and rescue breathing, he never regained consciousness. After stopping CPR Davidson assessed his options, realized he would die in the crevasse before rescue arrived, and used his limited gear—six ice screws, ten short slings, two long runners, three Prusik cords, a belay device, and two cams—to self-rescue by aid climbing 80 feet of overhanging glacier ice. When he reached the surface, he shouted to Camp Sherman for help. Rescuers walked him back to Camp Sherman, where he was taken off the mountain by helicopter. The whole incident, from fall to rescue, took less than seven hours.

The final 50 pages cover the 19 years since the accident—the heartbreaking details of Price's memorial service, the logistics of Davidson's recovery, and, of course, his reflections. His survivor's guilt manifests in all the expected ways: fear, anxiety, doubt, sadness. He entertains the what-ifs and whys, often alone and late at night. (Strangely, though, the question that seems most natural—"Why didn't Price self-arrest?"—is only briefly discussed.) Ultimately Davidson finds solace in later climbs—notably on Cho Oyu and in Nepal—and in aspects of Tibetan Buddhism. Each of his climbs since the accident, he suggests, is "a microcosm of that repeating cycle of resilience: engage, persevere, rally."

While the final 50 pages of *The Ledge* are earnest, they're relatively predictable. But that's what's interesting: the strength of this book isn't in poetic reflection. It's in looking over Davidson's shoulder as he's figuring out how to get out of a crevasse. We hear him speak to his father, his wife, to God. We watch him struggle on overhanging ice with ripped muscles after hearing his friend's last breaths. We hear him think about inspirational stories, like Joe Simpson's *Touching the Void,* and wonder if he can pull off a similar feat. And as we witness his interior monologue during the struggle, it's impossible for readers not to wonder, "What would I have done?"

The book jacket advertises "…a heart-stopping adventure story, a heartfelt memoir of friendship, and a stirring meditation on fleeting morality and immutable nature." I disagree: I read *The Ledge* as the kind of unvarnished first-person account you'd get from a climbing partner over a beer in a dark corner of a bar. It's the kind of grossly detailed story climbers crave in a private, voyeuristic kind of way: What was that like, exactly? And therein lies the terrifying poignancy of *The Ledge*: this accident didn't happen on a new route in the Himalaya or on a wind-loaded slab in the Alaska Range. It happened to two average dudes on a well-traveled glacier on a popular mountain; one those men died and the other had to figure out how to survive. Davidson's matter-of-fact everyman perspective is terrifying—because the same thing could happen to any of us.

CHARLOTTE AUSTIN

***The Will to Climb: Obsession and Commitment and the Quest to Climb Annapurna—the World's Deadliest Peak.* Ed Viesturs and David Roberts. Crown: 2011. 304 pages. Hardcover. $26.00.**

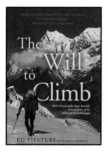

*The Will to Climb* sat in my book pile for a long time. The title turned me off, the cover announced that Roger Goodell, the Commissioner of the National Football League, wrote the Foreword, and I didn't understand why Ed Viesturs needed tried-and-true climbing writer David Roberts to help with the book. But I reminded myself of the old adage "You can't judge a book by the cover" and cracked open the pages.

The authors set the story up quickly. In April of 2000 Viesturs is hiking in to climb Annapurna, the tenth highest mountain in the world. He has climbed 10 of the 14 8,000ers without supplemental oxygen. No

American has accomplished this feat. Viesturs' wife is pregnant with their second child.

Viesturs does not climb Annapurna on this first attempt. The mountain is in horrible condition, the team retreats, and the book shifts to the history of Annapurna climbing. The story cooks through here; my palms sweat as I read about Maurice Herzog and his partner Louis Lachenal becoming the first to climb Annapurna but losing fingers and toes during their "successful" ascent. Herzog is elated, while Lachenal feels no fulfillment; instead he feels robbed of his legendary skill and grace. Here Roberts and Viesturs question the lasting rewards of mountaineering, indeed of any passionate enterprise. They repeat Maurice Herzog's famous line, "There are other Annapurnas in the lives of men."

Viesturs was 16 when he first read Herzog's *Annapurna*. He still considers this account his most important influence as a mountaineer. When he was 17, Viesturs read Chris Bonington's *Annapurna South Face*. That book further boosts his ambition to climb. The authors use Bonington's book to repeat the story of the massive English South Face Expedition, and again I breezed through the pages.

Then comes another book, *Annapurna: A Woman's Place*. In 1978 American Arlene Blum assembled 10 women to attempt the north face. The team put two women on top, while two others died trying. Viesturs and Roberts aren't inspired by Blum's tale, telling us that Blum herself didn't climb above 22,000 feet, the team used male Sherpas (who broke trail), and the summiters used supplemental oxygen for nearly the entire ascent. Viesturs tells us that he prefers to keep his thoughts about the expedition to himself.

Viesturs and Roberts also examine a host of other books by Annapurna climbers, including those by Erhard Loretan, Reinhold Messner, Jerzy Kukuczka, and Anatoli Boukreev—all books that influenced Viesturs.

Though the authors tell us up front that *The Will to Climb* is structured around obsession and commitment—and fulfillment and emptiness, triumph and failure—as revealed in the deeds of Annapurna's bravest antagonists, by the time I finished I felt I knew little about Viesturs himself except that he has some thoughts he'd rather keep private. I wondered where he got the money for all these climbs and, despite his claims to the contrary, I wasn't convinced that he wasn't in a race to become the first American to climb all the 8,000ers. When Ed Viesturs finally stands on the summit of Annapurna, his final 8,000-meter peak and exclaims, "Oh my God! It's not just my fourteenth, it's Annapurna," I'm not there. I wondered why Viesturs didn't write his own book.

JIM SWEENEY

---

*The Valley Climbers, Yosemite's Vertical Revolution.* John Long, editor. Stonemaster Press, 2011. 99 photographs, most in color. 168 pages. Hardcover. $54.95.

A coffee-table book with photos from improbable places, *The Valley Climbers* is organized around three Fs: fast, free, and first. If one can climb a big route all free, that's great. If one can climb it really fast, that's also marvelous. And, of course, to tick a first free or a first one-day ascent should get you drinks in the Mountain Room.

Four of the pieces describe solo ascents: Hans Florine linking El Cap and Half Dome, Alex Honnold ropeless on Half Dome, Dean Potter on the Rostrum with a mini-parachute on his back, and Cedar

Wright's jaunt up the Steck-Salathé on Sentinel Rock. On Sentinel Wright wanted to pass this old guy contemplating the Wilson Overhang. It turned out to be Allen Steck, 75, out for the fiftieth anniversary of his first ascent.

A fourth F, fun, isn't much in evidence, not surprising given severe pain in fingers and toes, bone-deep exhaustion from stringing together so many difficult pitches, and, to allude to an El Cap route that Beth Rodden and Tommy Caldwell climbed free, the lurking fear in a climber who's committed when his pro isn't.

All the same, these experiences are difficult to capture in words or even pictures. Crimps, piton scars, side pulls, smears, offwidths—if we have done some climbing, the book takes us part way to actual experience, but the writing tends to be more about what was done than the experience of doing it. This is not a criticism; it's just a consequence of condensing hour upon hour, day upon day, of intense physical and mental strain into a few pages. If we are told that there were only three bolts for protection in a 150-foot pitch, we can appreciate the leader's nervousness, but it isn't the same as being close to the edge of your ability 50 or 60 feet above the bolt. Often a description is reduced to numbers (5.12 seems popular, and there is quite a bit of 5.13, sometimes with an X attached). In the photos, with a few exceptions, the climbers look relaxed and completely in control, as if they were 10 feet off the ground. (Royal Robbins used to say you should climb as if you were 10 feet off the ground.) Looking at Lynn Hill coming out from under the Great Roof, you don't get the sense that she minds being 2,000 feet off the deck; she probably likes it, actually. Cool.

You have deduced by now that this book is a sequel to *The Stonemasters*. John Long seems to be the prime motivator for both books. A Stonemaster himself, he supplied a history of the Stonemasters for the first book. In this new volume's Foreword, he supplies an overview of the trends that led to the climbs described in *The Valley Climbers*. (Disclosure: Long wrote the Foreword to my book, Going Up.) Dean Fidelman was the photo editor for both books and has put together a fine collection. Cedar Wright's article "On the Shoulders of Giants" is a nice homage to Steck and his generation, but I think that old shoulder of giants saw also applies to the climbers brought to life in this fine book. Read and sweat.

JOE FITSCHEN

---

***Bold Beyond Belief: Bill Denz, New Zealand's Mountain Warrior.* Paul Maxim. Maxim Books, 2011. 303 pages. Paperback. $49.95.**

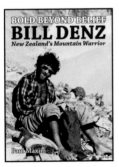

Paul Maxim has written the only biography of Bill Denz, New Zealand's luminary climber during two decades centered on the seventies. *Bold Beyond Belief* seems exhaustively researched, even though Denz died 29 years ago. It is very well written.

From a short, pudgy, fatherless beginner bonded to his mom, Denz underwent a deep transformation through 60 to 70 significant ascents worldwide, many of them firsts or early repeats. Some of the ice routes were incredibly dangerous; a few are still unrepeated. A Yosemite outsider, Denz climbed 10 grade VIs there in two seasons, including early ascents of desperate lines such as Pacific Ocean Wall, Excalibur, Tangerine Trip, Tis-sa-ack, and North America Wall.

Early in his Yosemite days he was seriously injured by rockfall, of all things. Rescued, he went through a long, crutchbound recovery in Santa Cruz. Then he sprung back. From the mid-seventies to 1980 he made four trips to Patagonia, becoming increasingly ambitious. When his intended partner, Charlie Porter, was delayed by Chilean authorities, Denz set out to solo Cerro Torre. But on the approach he lost perhaps his best friend at the time, young Phil Herron, in a crevasse, sending Denz into a funk for months.

Maxim's writing is often so detailed that it seems to exhaust its subject, but he maintains an engaging, sympathetic storyline, told chronologically. He describes personal aspects of Denz's lifestyle, including his several women companions, his flirtation with the era's drugs, and his extraordinarily dogged yet repellent charisma. Maxim acknowledges that Denz was not universally liked in his march to the top of New Zealand's climbing community. His detractors refused to be impressed, finding him rank, peculiar, and excessively competitive. But Denz worked hard to sustain his climbing and feed himself. He toiled endless frigid shifts on an Alaskan salmon boat several years running; he attempted to solo Cerro Torre 13 times, getting within 80 meters of the summit.

This is a terrific book, an important tale of an iconic climber little known outside his home country. Denz died in an avalanche on Makalu in 1983.

PETER HAAN

*Mountaineers: Great Tales of Bravery and Conquest.* **Ed Douglas et al. DK Publishing, 2011. 360 pages. Color photos. Hardcover. $40.00.**

Ignore the vulgar subtitle and open the book. It's filled with hundreds of glossy 12x10 pages and abundant photographs. There is also a good deal of text, but no "tales," except of the most abbreviated kind. Instead one finds a sweeping if anecdotal history of not only mountaineering but mountains themselves, plus geological changes and evolving climbing gear, from prehistoric times until now. As with most DK Publishing books, the emphasis is on pictures, not words.

Indeed, it is hard to learn who wrote those words, which have all the personality of an encyclopedia. No author credits appear on the dust jacket or title page; you must hunt for the attribution to Ed Douglas and associates. These writers give us brief but knowledgeable accounts of peaks and those who climbed them, or tried to. The biographies, while generally adulatory as well as accurate, can be properly critical: Oscar Eckenstein was "direct, argumentative, and quick-tempered"; Don Whillans drank too much and got fat; Paul Bauer was an especially distasteful Nazi.

Mountain descriptions (a page or two each) are well chosen, but readers will regret some omissions—in my case, Mt. Kailash, the beautiful striated sacred summit of western Tibet. The photographs, some familiar, some not, are often beautiful, although a few of the older ones aren't sharp. The pages are attractively laid out, with sidebars and boxes, and the legendary DK production is excellent, including sewn signatures, rare these days.

The book is aimed at beginners with big coffee tables. But more sophisticated readers can profit as well. How many of us know about the glaciologist Franz Josef Hugi, who made the first ascent of the Finsteraarhorn in 1828? Or the climbing monk Placidus À Spescha? Or John

Ball, the Victorian guidebook pioneer? Or the mountain interests of people famous for other achievements, including John Ruskin and J.M.W. Turner?

*Mountaineering* provides no full meals, but it is a big, tasty plate of hors d'oeuvres. Above all, it reminds (or informs) us that climbing has a rich, long history. Every climbing gym should have a copy.

STEVEN JERVIS

**Mountaineering in Antarctica: *Climbing in the Frozen South*. Damien Gildea. Éditions Nevicata, 2010. 192 pages. 200 color photos, 12 maps. Hardcover. $49.95.**

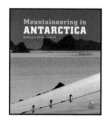

In the last three decades, private ski planes and chartered sailboats have rapidly opened Antarctica's long-forbidden mountains to growing numbers of climbers. Every season now, hundreds of mountaineers fan ever farther, finding spectacular summits, some not even named.

With the exception of a few well-documented expeditions to Mt. Vinson, to other peaks in the Ellsworth Mountains, to the otherworldly big walls of Queen Maud Land, and to surf-pounded towers along the Antarctic Peninsula, most ascents have previously received little attention. Furthermore there has never been a single go-to source where mountaineers can document and/or research what's where and who (if anyone) might have climbed nearby.

This vacuum of information has suddenly been filled with the publication of *Mountaineering in Antarctica*: Climbing in the Frozen South, a long-term labor of love by Australian explorer Damien Gildea. Although at first glance this looks like another gorgeous volume for the coffee table, it encyclopedically details virtually every expedition that has made a known first ascent below the furious fifties. In addition to the obvious locations, Gildea has included the emerging alpine paradise of South Georgia, the weather-beaten South Orkneys, and such obscure and isolated specks as the Kerguelen Islands, Peter I Island, and the Bellany Archipelago.

Judging from its span of history—and its sometimes obscure and far-flung sources—Gildea must have spent years sifting through dusty files and fading memories, getting down much that could have been forgotten. His photographic research is similarly impressive. For some places just finding anything must have been difficult, but he almost always uncovered something dramatic. (Because a few of the pictures are my own, I have to acknowledge the possibility of bias, but except for the cover photo, mine are not a significant contribution and would scarcely shape a reviewer's opinion.)

One caveat is that *Mountaineering in Antarctica* might disappoint a reader hoping for an epic polar story like *Endurance* or *Mawson's Will*. Gildea wrote this book as a resource, and in places it reads like a textbook. He presents so much information about so many people and places that even part of a chapter can suffice for a sitting. Nevertheless, he has honed an engaging style that keeps his narrative from dragging—expanding his prose when events deserve more attention or efficiently summarizing events of lesser import or about which little is known. Dense as it is with information, it is anything but boring.

The book's cast of characters is remarkable, stretching back to 19th-century explorers and sealers and marching through a who's who of science, aviation, and mountaineering right up to the present, when huge overhanging walls are being climbed, sometimes solo. It is revealing to read about familiar characters confronting such unfamiliar terrain.

Because the book is organized geographically, rather than chronologically, you can flip it open almost anywhere, encounter eye-catching pictures, and quickly read key history to give them context. One especially nice surprise is Gildea's generosity in describing special mountains that still have not been climbed. Many writers might have stayed mum.

The few big gaps in Gildea's coverage were beyond his control. Most notably, longstanding British and American protocols have precluded taxpayer funding for frivolous recreation like climbing. This includes scientists and support staffers who might want to bag accessible peaks. Some, like geologist Ed Stump and his guide/brother Mugs, skirted this by creatively choosing sites for "collecting samples." More commonly, people just climbed on the sly, leaving few records.

Secret climbing was likely most prevalent on the Antarctic Peninsula, where British Antarctic Survey teams have widely traveled for decades. Out of legions of possible first ascents, contemporary visitors can never know for certain which have already been climbed. This is a dubious destination for guaranteed "firsts."

"This lack of hard facts is not all bad," Gildea writes. "It creates a sense of mystery, a beautiful void where adventure is still possible for new travelers going south each year. Some [government-funded personnel] have deliberately maintained a silence…regardless of the authorities' views. [It has been] a means of preserving good experiences as they remember them, and not having their days of joy cast out into a world to be collected, bested and belittled by the latest record breaker."

Because Gildea often had to work from either too much or too little information, I caught a few slips, such as crediting the wrong people with first ascents of minor peaks. But nailing every detail would be nearly impossible for a work of this scope. Now that he has established himself as the Antarctic equivalent to Nepal's Elizabeth Hawley, however, I hope that he will keep track of corrections and new ascents and continue to maintain this precious resource he has created. No one else is getting it down.

My one disappointment is that although Gildea wrote sidebars about several key people, he barely mentioned Antarctica's private aviation pioneer, Giles Kershaw. Without Adventure Network, the company Kershaw founded, most of the cutting-edge climbs the author describes would not have been possible. Furthermore the harrowing story of this edge-of-the-seat "airline" is also one of the boldest, but lesser known, adventures of our time.

That minor point notwithstanding, Gildea's book is a triumph: a magnificent collection of pictures and history that may long remain the single best resource for anyone interested in the "Forbidden Continent."

GORDON WILTSIE

*Into the Silence: The Great War, Mallory, and the Conquest of Everest.* Wade Davis. Knopf, 2011. 672 pages. Black & white photos. Hardcover. $32.50.

I begin with a confession. Opening Wade Davis's *Into the Silence* for the first time, I found it difficult to believe that there was enough new left to be said about the celebrated English mountaineer George Leigh-Mallory, or about the Everest expeditions of the 1920s, to possibly justify the book's nearly 600 pages of narrative. After all, there are at least five worthy biographies of Mallory already in print, including Peter and Leni Gillman's excellent *The Wildest*

*Dream*, and any number of broader histories of Everest and/or the Himalaya that deal extensively with 1920s expeditions, including Walt Unsworth's comprehensive *Everest*. There is also a raft of more recent books inspired by the discovery of Mallory's body on Everest in 1999, including Conrad Anker and David Robert's gripping first-hand account, *The Lost Explorer.*

But I was wrong. With the publication of *Into the Silence*, Davis, a Canadian anthropologist, "explorer-in-residence" at the National Geographic Society, and prize-winning author of a dozen books about outdoor adventure, natural history, and other topics (including zombies!), steps into the front rank of mountaineering historians.

The 1920s British Everest expeditions did not succeed in climbing the mountain but were tremendously influential in shaping the history of Himalayan mountaineering. Their influence went beyond setting the pattern for the large-scale expeditions of the mid-20th century, which went forth with the double burdens of promoting national prestige and reaching for the world's highest summits. The initial British push on Everest also made Himalayan mountaineering an abiding object of popular fascination in the West, chiefly through the romantic image conjured by the disappearance into the mist on June 8, 1924, of Mallory and climbing partner Sandy Irvine, somewhere in the vicinity of the second step on the mountain's northeast ridge.

The events leading up to that dramatic tableau are part of an oft-told story. What's new and exciting about this book is that Davis begins by establishing links between the Great War of 1914–1918 and the Everest expeditions of 1921, 1922, and 1924. The typical account of Everest in the 1920s has heretofore been based on a few well-explored archives: the British Library, the Royal Geographic Society, the Alpine Club, and Mallory's correspondence from Everest with his wife, deposited at the Magdalene College library at Cambridge University. Davis mined all of these traditional sources but in addition put in many hours in hitherto ignored or underused archives, including those in London's Imperial War Museum, from which he reconstructed the military experiences of a score of British mountaineers who made their way up the Rongbuk Glacier to the North Col of Everest after the war. Except for the youngest and oldest, the mountaineers on those expeditions were almost to a man veterans of hard fighting in the ghastly trench warfare on the Western Front that killed nearly a million British and Commonwealth soldiers and wounded over two million others. As Davis writes of Canadian surveyor and mountaineer Edward Oliver Wheeler, a member of the 1921 expedition, "By the time he was twenty-eight he had witnessed the deaths of hundreds, encountered the shattered bodies of thousands. Death's power lies in fear, which flourishes in the imagination and the unknown. For Wheeler there was nothing more that death could show him, short of his own." The wartime experience of the Everest pioneers did not necessarily make them reckless climbers obsessed with the summit at all cost (a charge sometimes leveled against their German and Austrian counterparts in the inter-war era), but they certainly did share a war-bred fatalism. The three expeditions to Everest in the 1920s would cost the lives of three British and seven Sherpa climbers, deaths often keenly felt by the survivors, but accepted as necessary sacrifices in a common effort dedicated to a greater cause.

The war changed the climbers—and also shaped the perception of the public at home who eagerly followed their exploits, as conveyed through newspaper articles, expedition books, and the new medium of film. Military officer John Noel was a key figure both in launching the post-war British push on Everest and in popularizing the effort; a pioneering filmmaker, he accompanied and documented the 1922 and 1924 expeditions. Of the resulting films, *Climbing Mount Everest* (1922) and *The Epic of Everest* (1924), Davis writes, they "fed into a greater quest, embraced readily by a tired and exhausted people, to show that the life and death of an individual could still have meaning, that the war had not expunged everything heroic and inspired. The image of the noble mountaineer scaling the heights, climbing literally through a zone of death to reach the heavens, high above the sordid reality of the modern world, would emerge first from the imagination and through the lens of John Noel."

Mallory would come to epitomize the image of the death-defying mountaineer embracing a noble end; hence his inclusion in the subtitle of Davis's book. But what is striking about this Everest history is Mallory's absence until Chapter 5 (entitled "Enter Mallory"). Indeed, until the narrative reaches the 1924 expedition, nearly 500 pages in, Mallory is often a subsidiary character in the unfolding drama. That this is the least Mallory-centric history of Everest in the 1920s works to the book's advantage, for it creates room for such important but often neglected figures as Alexander Kellas (student of high-altitude physiology, champion of the Sherpas) and George Finch (champion of the use of bottled oxygen) to come into their own.

Davis seems at times a little irritated with Mallory's shortcomings in the practical skills of exploration, even as he acknowledges his stellar abilities as a climber. In 1921 Mallory repeatedly missed a key landscape feature, the mouth of the East Rongbuk Glacier, that would provide the expeditions of the 1920s and beyond a route to the North Col and potentially the summit. It was Canadian Edward Oliver Wheeler, the expedition's mapmaker and topographer, who correctly read the mountain's secrets, while Mallory floundered around pursuing dead ends. Wheeler's journals and personal correspondence, uncovered and used to good effect by Davis, will be as crucial to future accounts of the 1921 expedition as Mallory's papers have been in the past.

"The challenge from the start," Davis writes in a detailed bibliographic essay that supplements his narrative, "was to go beyond the iconic figure of George Mallory...." He has succeeded splendidly in meeting that goal.

MAURICE ISSERMAN

*Aconcagua: The Invention of Mountaineering on America's Highest Peak.* Joy Logan. The University of Arizona Press, 2011. 256 pages. Photos. Paperback. $35.00.

If you have a keen interest in mountaineering history, Joy Logan's richly researched *Aconcagua: The Invention of Mountaineering on America's Highest Peak* may be for you. This book adds to a growing list of sophisticated cultural critiques of mountaineering that do not simply recount the various exploits and drama surrounding alpine achievement and failures, but situates mountaineering within its cultural context.

As one example, this book considers the impact of Dick Bass, Frank Wells, and Rick Ridgeway's *Seven Summits*, published in 1986. As a result of this book, lots of people became interested in tagging the highest point on each continent; therefore Aconcagua became essential. But how many mountaineers who put the peak on their tick list have any knowledge of its cultural history or surroundings? All that matters about the peak is that summiting it fulfills a mountaineer's desire; in essence, the mountain is "mapped" in his imagination to conform to his own fantasies of prowess. Logan sees Bass's "Tarzan yell" on Aconcagua as symbolic: summiting Aconcagua was an act of masculine rejuvenation that prepared Bass to reenter the rough and tumble business world from which he had come.

According to Logan, the imaginative erasure of local cultural history and meaning is part of an imperial tradition in Western mountaineering. Mountains around the world fulfill masculine fantasies, she claims, just as exploring "blank spaces" in Africa, the Orient, or North America fulfilled European imperial adventurers. And when these mountaineers employ local muleteers—*arrieros*—to help transport their equipment, the locals are often treated in condescending ways that reinforce the Western sense of superiority.

Even middle-class mountaineers from Mendoza, the city that is the launching pad for expeditions to Aconcagua, tend to align themselves with the Western narrative. They, too, create hierarchical divisions between themselves and the *arrieros*. Logan traces these trends back to Argentina's rise as a nation intent on aligning itself with the Western global narrative.

Logan argues that other formulations of Aconcagua define the mountain through the lens of regional or indigenous identities. A prime example is the *Cementerio de los Andinistas*. Located five miles outside Aconcagua Provincial Park and often visited by tourists and mountaineers, this cemetery points to what Logan calls the "hybrid, fluid, postmodern identities of nation and self that Aconcagua constructs." The fact that *arrieros* who have perished on the mountain are also buried in the *cementerio* puts their stories on equal footing with those of mountaineers aligned with imperial tradition. As Logan writes, "the *Cementerio* offers a rich and complex reading of local, national, and global interactions that include images of non-Western, non-male, and non-heroic subjectivities."

Just as the cemetery offers "a rich and complex reading" of Aconcagua, so does this book. The book's style is one of academic discourse, but it remains accessible to the intellectually curious non-academic reader.

PETER L. BAYERS

---

*Triumph and Tragedy: the Life of Edward Whymper.* **Emil Henry. Matador (U.K.), 2011. 428 pages. B&W Sketches taken from Whymper's published works. Hardcover. $29.95**

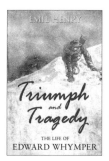

There are two justifications for a new account of a historical figure marbleized by time and previous biographies. One is new information from the attic or basement. The other is to see the life through the prism of a modern sensibility. The latter appears to be Emil Henry's intent with *Triumph and Tragedy*. Unfortunately he lacks the psychological depth or freshness for the task. As to the writing, when he deals with Whymper's late-life unhappy marriage to 21-year-old Edith Lewin, his style reminded me of women's magazines in the 40s and 50s. In the following passage Edith has just written a note to a family friend, the young American H.F. Montangier, thanking him for a present to her daughter. Henry speculates on the woman's state of mind: "Edie had made the bed she lay in, but the poignancy of her words was touching. Between the lines of her letter was a longing, a wish for more than she could give or receive in her hapless marriage to Whymper. Her joy as a new mother shone clearly but not brightly enough to conceal her loneliness. The warmly expressed thanks were tinged with sadness—for Edie's plight and from concern for the future of young Ethel herself, to whom Whymper would always seem an emotionally distant grandfather. The cautious venting of those feelings provided some relief, including the bittersweet pleasure of making contact with Montagnier, the one person she might dare include in her fantasies."

When he doesn't stray from paraphrases of letters, diaries, and Whymper's own books (*Scrambles Amongst the Alps, Travels Among the Great Andes of the Equator, and Ascent of Chimborazo and Cotopaxi*), Henry is on the solid ground provided by Whymper's superb style and force of personality. From this he weaves a capable *vade mecum* of the life and adventures, alongside classic illustrations that appeared with the original texts. One of his justifications for the book is that the last effort, F.S. Smythe's 1940 *Edward Whymper*, is out of print and unbalanced besides. Smythe "grudgingly praised the grit and determination that made Whymper's remarkable climbing career possible," Henry writes, "but painted a poorly illuminated picture of him as an arrogant, alienated loner." It's true. Smythe wrote: "A climbing Robot, egoistic, self-centered and incapable of deep feeling towards men or mountains. He was not happy, not a lover of beauty." Smythe would have liked his Whymper to be a romantic, enthralled by Ruskin and Turner—both of whom Whymper loathed.

Is Henry's character analysis any better? Well, he probably tried to be more empathic, but comes down as hard on Whymper as Smythe did. Following the words "journey to an understanding of Whymper's heart and soul, as tortuous as his most difficult mountain passages," Henry opines that "The Matterhorn tragedy seems to have aggravated an inherent depressive condition in him. His brusque manner alienated many, and he became emotionally abusive as his marriage disintegrated. But he made friends among those who refused to be intimidated, and there were times he showed kindness. He stayed, however, relentlessly self-contained. Sadness was also a part of his post-Matterhorn make up, arising out of increasing loneliness and perhaps a realization that he was his own worst enemy."

*Piffle! Merde! Poppy Cock! Fiddlesticks!! Bollocks!!* shouts a voice from a bestirred grave at the Chamonix cemetery.

JOHN THACKRAY

*Snow & Spire: Flights to Winter in the North Cascade Range.* John Scurlock. Silt, CO: Wolverine Publishing. Many color photographs. 192 pages. Hardcover. $59.95.

*Mountain.* Sandy Hill. New York: Rizzoli. 2011. 352 pages. Many color and B&W photographs. Hardcover. $85.00.

Climbers are dreamers, as well as doers, and coffee table books are dreams. The concept of the modern coffee table book is sometimes credited to none other than David Brower, who believed in "a page size big enough to carry a given image's dynamic. The eye must be required to move about within the boundaries of the image, not encompass it all in one glance." The books reviewed here are two of the best, squarely embodying Brower's criteria.

John Scurlock's *Snow & Spire: Flights to Winter in the North Cascade Range* is a showcase for a sampling of the thousands of photos the author made from his home-built aircraft, a Van's Aircraft RV-6. "The most common question I'm asked is 'who flies the plane

for you?' The answer is that all these photographs were obtained while I was piloting the plane." The photographs are gorgeous and, from a climber's perspective, simultaneously intimidating and inviting. The medium of thick, glossy paper in a large format matches the grandeur of its subjects. And though not central, the texts are always interesting: for instance, an interview with Jim Nelson on the first winter ascent of Slesse's Northeast Buttress in 1986 and Lowell Skoog's short history of winter climbing in the Cascades. Skoog added as an appendix a list of winter first ascents. Only one of Scurlock's photos features human beings; he hasn't seen many of us on his excursions. This book is a treat for any Cascades aficionado or anyone who has prematurely concluded there are no more alpine challenges in the Lower 48. Scurlock lays out for us many little-known alpine wilderness challenges, much as Washburn did in the 1960s with his photographic challenges in the Alaska and St. Elias Ranges. Or you can just sit back and marvel over the images as art.

In *Mountain* Sandy Hill has assembled the images of more than 160 photographers and artists. For every familiar iconic image—Washburn's "After the Storm, Climbers on the East Ridge" [of the Doldenhorn], Vittorio Sella's "K2 in the Evening from Southern Ridge of Staircase Peak," John B. Noel's hand-colored group photo of the 1924 Everest team, or the photo that faces it, Tom Frost's summit shot from the first ascent of the North America Wall—there are three or four others that are fresh, surprising, and sublime.

Others take iconic mountains and give us new angles or light: Devils Tower through George Grant's lens in 1933 or Katarina Stefanovi's "A New Day," revealing an unexpected Matterhorn.

Will Wissman's shot of Reggie Crist carving a line in the Takhinsha Range is my favorite ski photograph of all time. Everado Rivera captures three "climbers" on Popocateptl adorning a crucifix with flowers. I find a new favorite every time I open the book.

The endnote is by Ed Cooper, whose eye is frequently evident here and whom Hill acknowledges appropriately. I never tire of his shot of the East Face of Bugaboo Spire and was glad to see it (and others of his) included. Cooper advises us, when we see a photo we like, to not take its making for granted. "Instead," he advises, "look up the name or photographer of any mountain or photographer named here and follow the threads of information that interest you most." To this end, the acknowledgments and index are excellent.

Short essays, not by the usual suspects, separate the images. These, like the photographs, invite us to think about mountains in a way we may not have otherwise. For example, there is Robert Macfarlane: "What we call a mountain is thus a collaboration of the physical forms of the world with the imagination of humans—a mountain of the mind."

Finally, there is a generosity of spirit to Sandy Hill's introductory essay that I found utterly sincere. She discovered a way to produce a book, a kind of manifesto, about her love for mountains without personal ego.

In my little universe, mountains and books are sacred objects—of the latter, none more so than this book. I wash my hands and dry them carefully before I turn its pages.

*(Disclosure: Sandy Hill is donating her personal profits from this book to the AAC Library; this fact did not affect my review in these pages.)*

DAVID STEVENSON

# In Memoriam

*Edited by Cameron M. Burns*

## Ann Brooks Carter, 1917–2011

Ann Brooks Carter was born into a loving Quaker family in Medford, Massachusetts, on February 10, 1917. After graduation from Smith College in 1938, she taught at the Shady Hill School in Cambridge, which she had attended. In 1942 Ann married H. Adams Carter, former editor of this journal, in whose "steps she trod" for 53 years, joining him on climbs and expeditions from New Hampshire's White Mountains to Peru, Asia, and Eastern and Western Europe.

Ann and Ad Carter in the 1940s.

They attended both the wedding and the coronation of the King of Nepal, whom they had hosted in their home in Jefferson, New Hampshire, while he was studying at Harvard in 1967. In 1974 they trekked with another couple to the base of K2. Two years later Ann spent a month at a Ghandi Ashram in the foothills while Ad was on expedition. In 1988, at the invitation of the Chinese Mountaineering Federation, they became the first foreigners since the Revolution to be allowed into the Tibetan Plateau region of Yunnan Province, this in connection with a joint Chinese-American expedition. And in 1993 they joined Queen Elizabeth, to celebrate the 40th Anniversary of the first ascent of Mt. Everest.

Although Ad was the AAJ's official editor, Ann spent almost as many hours as he did editing text and reading galley proofs. In 1994 she was honored with the AAC's Angelo Heilprin Citation for this work. The side benefit for them was that they seemed to always have a place to stay with a fellow mountaineer during their world travels.

During WWII Ann and Ad were based in Washington, DC, but they both spent substantial time on Mt. Washington in the winter, testing and developing mountaineering equipment for the 10th Mountain Division. Following the war they moved to Chile for nine months, before settling for 58 years in Milton, Massachusetts. There Ad taught foreign languages, while Ann was a community volunteer and surrogate parent to countless boarding and foreign students. She was famous for her afternoon teas and ever-open heart.

Some of Ann's favorite times were spent in Jefferson, where she hosted AAC meetings, climbers, and friends, which she continued to do even after Ad's death in 1995. Last summer, at age 94, she was still sailing her beloved 1913 Catboat and swimming in Pleasant Bay.

Untroubled by the constraints of age, Ann was always willing to try something new. On last Columbus Day weekend, a few days before she was diagnosed with colon cancer, she was in Jefferson. Her son Peter called and said, "If you can get over here this afternoon, let's go up in a balloon." That afternoon they were floating a mile above the mountains of Vermont. "That was pretty typical of her," Peter recalled. "Instead of saying, 'Are you crazy?' she climbed right in, and up we went." *Parts of this obituary appeared in* The Boston Globe *and* The Valley News.

JED WILLIAMSON

## STEVE HACKETT, 1945–2011

Steve Hackett. *Tam Agosti-Gisler*

The Kachemak Nordic Ski Club and the community of Homer lost a valuable member when Steve Hackett, 65, passed away while skiing at Arctic Valley on February 26. He had been at a PSIA ski instructors workshop on a blue cold day. After completing the workshop on the last run of the day, he collapsed and passed on due to natural causes.

Steve's father had been a national park ranger, which allowed Steve to spend his childhood in the freedom of the parks of Wyoming, Montana, and Colorado, from which grew his lifelong passion for wilderness and outdoor adventure. In 1968 he graduated from the Colorado School of Mines in Golden, Colorado, with a degree in Geophysical Engineering. Shortly thereafter he moved to Alaska, where in 1977 he obtained a Masters in Geology and Geophysics from UAF. Steve's professional career was as varied as the mountains he loved. In addition to being a geologist, he worked as a trail-crew foreman in Rocky Mountain National Park, a mountaineering guide on Denali, a backcountry ranger in Denali National Park, an avalanche specialist for the Department of Transportation, an avalanche-safety instructor, a ski patrolman, a math and science teacher in rural Alaska, and a home school contact teacher for Interior Distance Education of Alaska in Soldotna. While working for the Cook Inletkeeper, he helped create the state's first agency-approved, citizen-based, water-quality monitoring program.

Steve met his wife Ann on the Ruth Glacier, where he maintained a base camp and dog-sledding service. It might have been the rarified air, but their heads were soon spinning, and they married in 1987. They worked together as teachers in Russian Mission and Seldovia and then settled on their small homestead at the head of Kachemak Bay.

He made numerous first ascents in Alaska, ascents of Denali, and took part in expeditions at home and abroad. Among his favorites were a 1972 trip to Nepal with his brother Jim, a joint Soviet expedition to the Pamirs in what is now Tajikistan, an adventurous 1974 river trip from Lake Chakachamna to Anchorage, via the Skwentna, Yetna, and Susitna Rivers, a 1976 solo ascent of Mt. Igikpak in the Brooks Range, and a 1980 ski traverse of the Bagley Icefield from Miles Lake to Yakutat. His company, Alaska Treks and Voyages, out of Moose Pass, guided remote wilderness dog-pack and river trips and sea kayaking trips in Kenai Fjords National Park.

Steve volunteered for many organizations, including the Mountaineering Club of Alaska, Alaska Backcountry Guides Cooperative, Alaska Natural History Association, Alaska Natural Resource and Outdoor Education Association, Cook Inlet Regional Citizens Advisory Council, and the Alaska Quiet Rights Coalition.

Steve will be dearly missed for his infectious enthusiasm, his generosity, his radiant smile, his perseverance in the face of all obstacles, his dedication to teaching, and his gentle spirit.

TOBY WHEELER

## James W. Ebert, 1947-2011

Jim Ebert was born and raised in the geographically oppressed Plains of the Midwest. In spite of this initial handicap, he grew into one of the most impressive climbing instructors and out-doorsmen in America.

Jim Ebert

His parents, John and Ede, started the Iowa Mountaineers Club in the 1940s and compiled an impressive record of ascents and explorations around the world, especially in North America. Jim was exposed to the mountains and climbing from an early age and as he matured became a leader in the Club and president of the Iowa Mountaineers for many years. He continued the legacy of the Iowa Mountaineers on many domestic and international outings. He was a skilled, analytic climber, but his greatest skill was teaching others to enjoy the wonders of the crags and mountains.

Jim taught thousands of us to climb through his work with the Iowa Mountaineers, University of Iowa Recreational Services, and other organizations. His greatest gift to his students was an emphasis on safety and making the mountains and rock faces fun. My life-changing moment occurred in the early 1970s when Jim convinced me as a first day rock-climbing student that, though half his weight, I could hold his practice leader fall on a belay plate. Jim's lesson led to belays of climbing buddies around the globe for four more decades.

In recent years he extended his dream of taking people to the wilderness by serving as a director of the Easter Seals Camp in Kentucky and developing Alpenglow Adventures, which takes physically challenged individuals to such spectacularly rugged places as the Grand Canyon, Kilimanjaro, and the Inca Trail.

Jim, who was always the picture of health and fitness, died while hiking with his son Justin on Mt. Whitney on July 26, 2011, at age 64. He is survived by his wife, Margie, and children, James, Jared, Justin, and Jean. He was a lifetime member of the AAC and a member of the Austrian Alpine Club.

His spirit and his love for the world's beautiful places will live on through the many of us he trained and inspired.

Chuck Huss

## James Goodwin, 1910–2011

Jim Goodwin died on April 14 in Lake Placid. To the rock and ice climbing community, he was a pioneer. But to those who knew him, especially the hundreds who joined him as children to hike Adirondack trails, Jimmy Goodwin was much more.

Jim Goodwin saw himself principally as a guide, a status he treasured not for the money but for the shared joy. Fortunately, his career began before AMGA. Jimmy tacked a notice on the bulletin board at Interbrook Lodge, in Keene Valley, when he was 11 years old. At 50 cents a day for trips to Porter Ledges and a dollar for Giant Mountain, he had lots of takers. His rates jumped when he began guiding the state's highest peak, Mt. Marcy. In 1922 it cost two dollars to

Jim Goodwin. *Ed Hale*

hire a seasoned 12-year old for a trip up Marcy. After at least 200 ascents, Goodwin wrote that Marcy had become "a holy symbol" for him. In 1995 he joined the extended Goodwin clan, children and grandchildren, for a commemorative hike.

Jim considered his 1935 winter ascent of the Trap Dike on Mount Colden to be one of his most significant climbs. Earlier, a winter ascent of Gothics caught the attention of John Case, who summered in Keene Valley. Case showed Goodwin the ropes, allowing him to make several ascents in the American and Canadian Rockies in the 1930s, ascents that gained Goodwin admission to the AAC. When the nation entered WWII, Goodwin signed up for "the ski troops," later the 10th Mountain Division. He recalled that he had then "rappelled three or four times...and driven three pitons." His AAC membership, however, got him the job as a climbing instructor, first in Colorado and later at Seneca Rocks. As an instructor he was superb.

In 1944 Jim and his wife, Jane, shared a cottage at Seneca Rocks, West Virginia, as the Face of a Thousand Pitons was earning its name. After he was called into battle as a medic, the 10th stormed Riva Ridge and took Monte Belvedere in Italy. The campaign was costly to Allies and the Germans alike, and Goodwin was proud to have paid little attention to the color of the uniform when attending to a wounded man.

After the war, Goodwin resumed his teaching career at Connecticut's Kingswood School.

In 1947 Goodwin offered Fritz Wiessner an instructor's spot in the newly formed Adirondack Mountain Club rock-climbing school. After the 1938 K2 tragedy, Wiessner's aura was tarnished to some in the AAC. But a fortuitous 1966 meeting on Indian Head, at Ausable Lake, between Wiessner and past AAC president John Case changed that.

Goodwin and Trudy Healy (who was researching the first rock guide for the Adirondacks) were on Wiessner's rope when they converged with Case and partner. It was a stem corner, declared Case. No, it was a layback, said Wiessner. It wasn't quite an argument, but neither was it friendly. Case proceeded to reinforce his claim by elegantly bridging the dihedral. Then Wiessner grabbed the edge of the crack, put his feet on the other wall, and cruised up behind. Healy and Goodwin laybacked. Goodwin invited all back to his cottage for a beer, and the tension ebbed. Wiessner later accepted an honorary membership in the AAC.

Goodwin brought people together by putting himself in the background. He'd carry two packs, if that would make a boy's day easier. If a youngster dropped a mitten, he would run back to pick it up without the troop noticing. He found more meaning in designing and cutting a trail than in putting up some high-end rock route. In fact, he'd often apologize for a climb, perhaps describing it as "a damned-fool thing to do."

Jimmy Goodwin, after 101 years in this world, has gone to the next. But he's alive in the hearts of generations of Adirondack mountaineers who know that singing makes a trail shorter and that Spam makes life richer. They know that their boots will eventually dry, even after a week in the rain in the Sewards, and that there's more joy in giving someone a skill than in flashing it for others to see.

He leaves two sons, Peter and Tony (trail builder and editor of ADK's *Trails of the High Peaks*) and five grandkids.

TONY GOODWIN

## James H. Kanzler, 1948–2011

James H. Kanzler laced up his boots for the last time and "hiked over the pass" on April 18, 2011. Born April 22, 1948, he grew up in Montana, where he began climbing with his father and younger brother in his grade school years. He became affectionately known as Rat Hole, Ratty, or R.H.

Jim Kanzler in 1977. *Terry Kennedy*

Kanzler was an important alpinist, avalanche hazard forecaster, and mountain guide. Among hs better-known climbs were his pioneering attempt (with Pat Callis) on the Emperor Face on Mt. Robson (1974) and his first ascents on the north faces of Mt. Cleveland (1976) and Mt. Siyeh (1979) in Glacier National Park. Kanz also climbed the Northwest Face of Half Dome (1971) and the Nose of El Cap (1972).

When the curved-pick ice axe revolution arrived, Kanzler heated his old straight-pick axe and hammer on his kitchen stove and hammered curves into them. Using them he made first ascents of Green Gully and Hyalite Canyon ice climbs and did routes in the Canadian Rockies before he could afford new tools.

Kanzler pioneered routes in the Beartooth Mountains with Chad Chadwick, Brian Leo, Doug McCarty, Jack Tackle, and me. He did new routes in the Wind River and Purcell Ranges with Fred Beckey. He put up numerous trad routes on local crags in southern Montana and went on expeditions to Minya Konka (1980) and Siguniang (1981) in China. Kanzler influenced many upstart climbers and ski patrolmen in Montana. Alex Lowe autographed the cover photo of *Climbing* no. 166 with "Jim, you started this nonsense—chasing you!—Alex."

He was revered for his ski patrolling and avalanche hazard forecasting. He began with the Bridger Bowl ski patrol in 1968 and was Big Sky's first ski patrol director from 1972 to 1978. He was a Jackson Hole ski patrolman from 1978 to 1999. He began avalanche hazard forecasting for Bridger-Teton National Forest and the Jackson resort in 1986 and continued until 1999. He then switched to the resort's information technology department, where he remained until his passing.

During summers he spent 22 years guiding for Exum, guiding the north face of the Grand Teton occasionally. He was a legend as a gifted, though idiosyncratic, teacher. His first rule of guiding: "Just be yourself."

Kanzler's father, Hal, died in 1967. Two years later his younger brother, Jerry, died in an avalanche with four friends on Mt. Cleveland. (I am writing a book on the incident, *In Search of the Mount Cleveland Five*.) Jim searched for them with Pat Callis and Peter Lev. During his avalanche hazard forecasting career, he took every ski patroler's death or mishap personally. He stressed fieldwork and typically dug 150 snow assessment pits a year.

Kanzler was loved by many and made a difference to the people around him, though his wit and wisdom were seasoned with sarcasm. According to a colleague, as Kanzler once walked out of an avalanche lab, he said, "We made mistakes today, but it was a good day because no one died."

Ratty often brought us to belly laughs, even ground rollers. He twice killed packrats (no relation) as they threatened climbing gear during bivouacs, demonstrating patience and quickness with a hammer.

Our friend carried on his shoulders a heavy load that most of us will never understand. He packed it farther than I would have thought possible. I am fortunate to have spent my greatest days in the mountains with Jim Kanzler, as well as nights weathering storms or gazing at the rotating heavens. We shared whacky road trips I will never forget.

Finding our way without Jim Kanzler will not be easy. Life will never be the same. We who are left behind must keep trudging. Save me a flat spot on the ledge and a place by the campfire, my friend. Until you see me coming over the ridge, be safe wherever you are.

Kanzler leaves behind his mother, his son, Jamie, and two grandchildren.

TERRY KENNEDY

## VICTOR CURT MAHLER, 1932-2011

Victor Mahler in 1972. *Courtesy Frances Wallace*

Victor passed away following a bout of pneumonia, on September 7 in New York City. An incredibly brave man, he refused to be knocked down by the loss of his sight and a stroke and continued to attend the New York Section's Annual Black Tie Dinner, with his beloved wife Mimi. Several fellow club members attended his memorial service at the only German-speaking church in Manhattan.

An alumnus of Deerfield Academy, he graduated from Dartmouth with a major in Architecture. Victor's sampling of what Dartmouth had to offer included the Outing Club and the Winter Sports Board. After graduation, he spent time in the Navy, on a destroyer.

After leaving the Navy he received a Masters in Architecture from the Harvard Graduate School of Design. His first foray into the field was with the Architects.Collaborative in Cambridge, Massachusetts. He then joined I.M. Pei in New York, before founding his own firm. In 1973 the infamous Hancock Tower problem in Boston brought Victor fame and applause. A design flaw caused the windows to fall out, and Victor diagnosed and solved the problem, which had baffled many experts. His career then took him to Hong Kong, and other exotic locations, and he was elevated to Fellow of the American Institute of Architects.

Victor climbed in the Andes, Alps, and Canadian Rockies, where he partnered with Bill Putnam on first ascents. He was a fellow AAC member of whom we can be proud.

PHIL ERARD

## BONNIE PRUDDEN, 1914–2011

Bonnie Prudden, fitness pioneer and founder of Bonnie Prudden Myotherapy, passed away at her home in Tucson on December 11, 2011. She was 97. "You can't turn back the clock, but you can wind it up again," she would tell her students and patients, and that is how she lived her life. She was born on January 29, 1914, in New York City. When she was three years old, the curious and energetic Bonnie would climb out of her bedroom window and wander the neighborhood at night. A wise doctor gave her frantic mother some advice. "There is nothing the matter with this child that discipline and exhaustion won't cure. Put her in the Russian Ballet School." It worked, and by the time she was 10, Bonnie was a professional dancer and eventually performed on Broadway with the Humphrey-Weidman concert dancers.

Bonnie equated exercising to music with happiness, and said, "body movement has a language all its own." She became an avid rock climber, skier, and fitness enthusiast. At age 23 she fractured her pelvis in four places during a skiing accident, but she wouldn't take "no" for an answer when told she would never be able to climb or ski again and that she could never have children. Bonnie bore two children and in 1943 became the first woman awarded the National Ski Patrol Badge. She has 30 first ascents to her credit in the "Gunks."

Bonnie Prudden in the Shawangunks in the 1940s.

"Bonnie holds a place in the climbing history of the Shawangunks that has yet to be superseded by any other woman," said Laura Waterman, author of *Rocks and Roses*, a book about women climbers. "Bonnie was a luminary in the climbing scene for more than a decade."

After watching her daughter's dismal gym class in the 1940s, Bonnie decided to use her background in dance and athletics to give neighborhood children "conditioning" classes. As the classes grew she used the Kraus-Weber test for minimum muscular fitness to chart student progress and noticed that new students failed the test and returning students passed. Bonnie and Dr. Hans Kraus, Kennedy's White House doctor, worked together to test thousands of children across America and in Europe and found that Americans were the least fit. The results, presented to President Eisenhower at a White House luncheon in 1955 and known as the "report that shocked the President," led Eisenhower to establish the President's Council on Youth Fitness, now the President's Council on Physical Fitness, Sports and Nutrition.

Bonnie was a columnist and advisor for *Sports Illustrated*. In 1957, in a full-length leotard of her own design, she launched a line of fitness fashions on the cover of *Sports Illustrated*. She had her own TV show in the 1960s, appeared on countless radio talk shows, and wrote 15 books and numerous articles. She also invented exercise equipment. Bonnie always felt that if individuals had the correct information and tools they could, for the most part, take care of themselves.

In 1976 she developed Bonnie Prudden Myotherapy, a non-invasive, remarkably simple method of relieving muscle pain. She went on to write *Myotherapy: Bonnie Prudden's Complete Guide to Pain-Free Living*, in which she shows how to erase and recover from muscle pain and take charge of your body. In 1980 she opened a school to train myotherapists to erase pain from muscles by pressing on the trigger points and then using appropriate exercises to keep the muscles free of pain. In 2006 Bonnie was inducted into the Fitness Hall of Fame and the Massage Hall of Fame. In November of 2007, at age 93, she received the Inaugural Lifetime Achievement Award presented by the council, which she had co-founded.

Bonnie brought hope and inspiration, laughter and play to thousands of people. She made this world a better place and the impact of her wonderful accomplishments will live on and continue to benefit us all through her teachings. "Very seldom do wonderful things happen while we wait," she said as she marched to the beat of her own drum.

ENID WHITTAKER

## GEORGE SAINSBURY, 1925–2011

George Sainsbury

George Ross Sainsbury, AAC board member, chairman of Seattle Mountain Rescue, and charter member of Olympia Mountain Rescue, passed away in Bakersfield, California, on March 13, 2011, while returning from a bird-watching trip. Sainsbury was born May 9, 1925 in Longview, Washington, and graduated from the University of Washington. His greatest passions were his family, mountain search and rescue, and scouting.

His interest in search and rescue stemmed from his attempt at a new route on Mt. Rainier's south face, during which he fell into a crevasse on the Kautz Glacier. Twenty-two hours passed before he was pulled out of the hole. Inspired by his own rescue, Sainsbury dedicated his life to the rescue of others—working with Seattle Mountain Rescue, Olympia Mountain Rescue, and the AAC to advance mountain safety.

In 1997 the AAC awarded Sainsbury the Angelo Heilprin Citation for his work in preventing mountaineering accidents in Washington State. The citation is awarded annually "to that person who has, in the opinion of the citation committee, shown exemplary service to the Club." Sainsbury was a tireless advocate for the Club's ideals.

He was also an important figure in scouting. He worked for a decade with the Boy Scouts of America, as district executive for the Chief Seattle Council and as executive for the Olympic Area Council. He spent another decade with the Girl Scouts, where he served on the national staff as financial adviser for Region 11.

Sainsbury is survived by his wife of almost 62 years, Mary Jane Sainsbury, and their daughter, Mary Ann Sainsbury.

HALE MELNICK

## NECROLOGY:

| | | |
|---|---|---|
| Ann Brooks Carter | Christian Kammer | Kathleen A Stack |
| James W Ebert | Thomas W Miller | Chris Walker |
| Kip Garre | Edward Nissen | Leon J Weil |
| James A Goodwin | Bonnie Prudden | James E White |
| Jeremy J Graczyk | George R Sainsbury | |
| John Horn | Doreen Spitzer | |

# CLUB ACTIVITIES

EDITED BY FREDERICK O. JOHNSON

*Alaska Section.* The summer of 2011 saw the completion of the AAC's newest hut, the Snowbird, located in the Hatcher Pass area of the Talkeetna Mountains about 50 miles north of Anchorage. The Section launched the Snowbird Hut project in 2005, when the original hut and land lease were purchased. Numerous fundraisers and private donations created a fund that enabled the start of construction in 2010. The hut structure was framed just in time for the winter snows, thanks to countless volunteer hours and numerous work parties led by Harry Hunt, James Brady, and "Hut Mistress" Cindy Squire. Finally, after more fundraising and work parties, 14 supporters hiked in for the official dedication of the completed Snowbird Hut on August 20. For current information, visit the AAC Web site and snowbird.com.

HARRY HUNT AND JAMES BRADY, *CO-CHAIRS*

*Sierra Nevada Section.* This was another active year for the Sierra Nevada Section, which continued to welcome many new members. Adhering to the adage of "if it's not broken, don't fix it," the Section again hosted the full slate of its annual "Climb-munity" gatherings, which continue to be well attended. In 2011 these events included an ice-climbing weekend in Cold Stream Canyon near Truckee in January; rock-climbing weekends at Pinnacles National Monument, Donner Summit, Tuolumne Meadows, and Pinecrest (with Royal and Liz Robbins and Tom Frost) from May to September; and a bouldering/sport-climbing weekend in Bishop in November. These rock-climbing weekends afforded our members not only great climbing, but also fun times with the now traditional group-camping, barbeques, parties, and raffles.

Throughout the year, the Section reached out to the climbing community and promoted the AAC. The Section continued to sponsor the year-round free climbers' coffee every Sunday morning in Yosemite with the climbing rangers where members interact with other climbers and spread the good word about the AAC. Section member and AAC Yosemite Committee Chair Linda McMillan again lead the free Saturday evening slideshow series in Yosemite as part of the climber's interpretive program, which generates further goodwill and exposure for the Club.

As for conservation activities, in September we participated in the Yosemite Facelift clean-up week, organized by the Yosemite Climbers Association. Rather than split time between community outreach and conservation at Facelift as done in past years, we focused exclusively on conservation and undertook an arduous asphalt removal project planned by the Park Service. Then in November, under the leadership of Fred Glover and in conjunction with Friends of the Inyo and the Access Fund, the Section once again organized the Fall High Ball in Bishop. This weekend event included a volunteer day of trail restoration/clean-up in the Buttermilks, a party at Mill Creek Station, and a day of bouldering/sport climbing.

Bill and Barbara Straka and Ellen Lapham participated in the AAC's 2011 Cordillera Blanca Environmental Expedition in July and contributed to its valuable research.

The year ended with our annual Holiday Dinner in Berkeley, highlighted by AAC Board

Member, Officer, Honorary Member, and Award Winner George Lowe, who presented an outstanding slideshow of his spectacular and successful alpine climbing career, including first ascents in the United States, Canada, Alaska, the Karakoram, and the Himalaya, which he modestly referred to as "Reflections On My Continuing Amateur Climbing Career." Given that George previously lived in the Bay Area and was a one of our members for several years, it was a homecoming of sorts for him. His friends and admirers came out in droves, and the banquet hall was filled to capacity. Many thanks to George Lowe for this special and successful evening

It has been my pleasure to serve as Section Chair the last three years. In January 2012, Lewis Richards of Sacramento takes over that position. No doubt the Section will be in good hands going forward under Lewis's outstanding leadership.

TOM BURCH, *Chair*

*Southwest Section.* We had four main events in 2011, finishing strongly with a successful winter dinner. The Section enjoyed good climbing and friendship January 15-16 at Joshua Tree with the Southern California Mountaineers Association. Included was a Graffiti Removal Project arranged through climbing ranger Bernadette. On April 17 eight of us met at the Mishe Mokwa Trailhead at Malibu Creek State Park, hiked into the Echo Cliffs, and enjoyed climbing in the shade on a warm day. We returned to the parking lot for a brats picnic organized by Mike and Mary Tompkins. On the weekend of October 22-23 the Section enjoyed climbs again at Joshua Tree, camping out at Sheep Pass Campground. On Sunday a few of us joined a restoration project at Indian Cove put on by the Park Service and the Friends of Joshua Tree. The Park Service organized a highly successful project, providing the tools, plants, and equipment for the volunteers and rangers to plant 50 to 60 native plants in two hours. In November the Section helped sponsor the Fall Highball in Bishop, which included a work party at the Buttermilk area and a fund raiser with beer and music that raised about $800 for conservation. In addition we gathered at Cal Tech for programs such as the Reel Rock Festival and the Banff Film Festival, sponsored by the Cal Tech Alpine Club.

Finally, 74 people attended the December holiday dinner featuring a slideshow entitled *From Patagonia to Tajikstan: A 40-Year Climbing Retrospective* by Jim Donini and accompanied by good French food at Taix French Restaurant. With the assistance of a no-host bar and appetizers, the crowd enjoyed visiting with old friends and making new ones.

JIM PINTER-LUCKE, *Chair*

*New England Section.* In February our Section helped the International Mountain Climbing School sponsor the 18th annual Ice Fest in North Conway, New Hampshire. Our members answered the call for volunteers en masse. Tim Deroehn and Robert Castro manned a booth in the mornings at IME, providing coffee and donuts to students participating in the clinics. Friday night's festivities at Cranmore Ski Area started with Jim Surrette's film of Steve House soloing Recompence and Remission, two of Cathedral Ledge's toughest mixed lines. Local hardman Freddie Wilkinson was the commentator for the indoor ice competition, which had to be seen to be believed. Saturday night's Aprés-climbing party found Rick Merritt and Nancy Savickas passing out wine and AAC information upstairs at IME. The party raged on with a slideshow by Kelly Cordes and raffle at Cranmore, where our Section donated funds for appetizers.

We hosted our 15th annual dinner at the elegant Henderson House on March 19.

Rick Wilcox provided a display of his climbing photography, which included the second ascent of the Black Dike on Cannon Mountain and several other retro-photographs, one of our own Mark Richey when he embarked on his climbing career as a 17-year-old lad. Our guest speaker was Kevin Mahoney, who treated us to a brilliant presentation entitled *Risk, Reward and Responsibility.* AAC past-president Mark Richey and two AAC Board members, Bruce Franks and John Kascenska, were on hand for the festivities, as were New Hampshire hardmen Paul Boissioneault and Tom Callaghan, and our former chair, Bill Atkinson.

The first of our two annual BBQs was held in June at my place in Albany, New Hampshire. In the fall Sarah Garlick, our Northeast Regional Coordinator, hosted the October BBQ at Echo Lake State Park near North Conway. John Bragg, the new team leader of the AAC coordinators, came out from Colorado to help. The event was a huge success with such notables present as Mark and Teresa Richey, Titoune Meunier, Freddie Wilkinson, and Doug Millen.

On November 5 Chad Hussey hosted our third annual "It Ain't Over 'Til It's Over" cragging day. Despite not having power for over a week due to the freak fall storm, Chad was up for the task of playing tour guide at one of his local crags. Connecticut was hit hard by the storm, with several trees downed and the sound of chain saws serenading us upon arrival. This year we climbed at the Owl's Lair on Ragged Mountain near Southington. Our small group was joined by new AAC member Scott Doscher, who came all the way from Manhattan for the day. Typical of Connecticut, the climbing at Owl's Lair was awesome!

Finally, a note from Bill Atkinson. Upon the re-assertion of an old shoulder injury, his 50-plus years of climbing has come to an end. He remembers not only his first climb in the 'Gunks in 1956, but his last one there as well, an ascent in 2010 of Southern Pillar with John Reppy, accomplished with a combined age of 164 years.

NANCY SAVICKAS, *Chair*

*New York Section.* The New York Section of the AAC is blessed with a strong cadre of committed volunteers who help make it one of the most active and vibrant of the AAC's regional Sections. Its Annual Black-Tie Dinner has hosted many of the world's leading alpinists of the last three decades. It has become not only an annual ritual for many out-of-town members, who combine it with a weekend in Manhattan at perhaps the best time of year, but an ongoing financial resource for the Club's Library and Journal. Our lively blog, nysaac.blogspot.com, ably edited by Conor Moran, is the preferred mode of communication for our members. The blog's lengthy 2011 archives chronicle several notable indoor and outdoor events: our first Catskills Winter Outing, in February, following our traditional January Outing in Keene, New York; our Annual June Outing at the Ausable Club, which dates back to the early 1980s; and, for the first time in several years, "*Olaf's Outing,*" held in September at Olaf and Gitta Soot's estate in Greenwich, Connecticut. With top ropes set up on the Soot's private crag, a large swimming pool to tree-dive into and, of course, delectable food and beverage provided by our affable hosts, this was one of our most relaxed and friendly events of the year. Among the many climbers in attendance were our friends from the New York branch of the Korean Alpine Club.

On the climbing front and thanks to the Section blog, we all followed 33-year-old Sophie Denis' attempt to summit five 8,000m peaks during the calendar year. Chronicling her adventure with daily images and videos, Sophie, a French-born New York banker, quickly climbed Cho Oyu and Lhotse in premonsoon, followed by Broad Peak and a brave attempt on K-2, where she managed to get to Camp IV on the south side. This was as high as anyone succeeded on that side of the peak during this difficult year. A bout of food poisoning kept her off Shishipagma, but she recovered sufficiently to summit Manaslu in October. She is continuing with her quest to summit all the remaining 14 Eight Thousanders by 2014, having already climbed Everest a few years before. A lady with boundless energy and a quick smile, Sophie has endeared herself to the whole international climbing community, and we wish her well in her ambitious efforts.

Finally, our 32nd Annual Dinner departed from the usual Himalayan theme to focus on Switzerland and its Alps. On this subject there was no more appropriate a speaker than John Harlin III, editor of this publication for many years. John embarked on a two-year odyssey to circumnavigate Switzerland by its borders, which journey he completed just a few weeks before the Dinner. Since so much of John's personal and family history is intertwined with Switzerland and the Eiger, his presentation had a depth and quality that we had rarely seen. Rounding out the program with a short, very inspirational presentation was Dr. Sherman Bull, who helped guide a group of disabled Iraq and Afghanistan veterans to the summit of Lobuche East in an Erik Weihenmayer-led expedition. As Sherman pointed out, this was one of the most personally rewarding expeditions he had ever been on. Last but certainly not least, and abetted by some spirited bidding engineered by our auctioneers, Steve Schofield and Dee Byers, the Dinner raised an all-time record sum for the *Journal*.

PHIL ERARD, *CHAIR*

*Southern Appalachian Section.* Throughout 2011, the Southern Appalachian Section focused on growing our membership base and producing relevant local club events. The Section's membership exhibited healthy growth across the region. This in turn enabled an expanded offering of local Section events.

Our success in expanding the variety and quantity of local events was due in large part to significant contributions of time and effort by committed members and regional partners such as AAC Partner Fox Mountain Guides and Climbing School. Fox guide Karsten Delap delivered AAC Self-Rescue Classes in May and September in Brevard, North Carolina. These classes were offered free to Club members. Class pricing for non-members was established in a manner that would encourage participants to join the AAC rather than pay higher tuition. Attendees came away with new or enhanced self-rescue skills, and the Club gained new members. Our thanks to Adam Fox and Karsten for their contributions.

The AAC Wilderness First-Aid classes, taught by Danny McCracken in March and November, have become a centerpiece for our annual events schedule. Danny delivered the classes to Red Cross WFA-certification standards with significant customization to focus on climbing accident first response. As with the Self Rescue classes, a graduated tuition was implemented to encourage participants to join the AAC.

Building on a strong tradition, the 7th Annual Eastern North Carolina AAC Get-Together was held on November 12 in Wake Forest. Over 30 members and their guests gathered at the home of Brigitte Weston and Keith Nangle to socialize with old climbing partners, meet new ones, and discuss over food and drink how members of the AAC community could help one another achieve our climbing goals. The featured speakers were Tracey Obeda and Danny McCracken, who entertained the audience with slides from their mid-summer adventures in the Alps, and me, who presented slides from the AAC Climber Exchange to Iran, which I helped organize. A huge thanks to Brigitte and Keith for their generous hospitality.

The Section was fortunate to receive two significant AAC grants. The Carolina Climbers' Coalition was awarded $1,800 for the GIS mapping of Rumbling Bald near Chimney Rock, North Carolina, to support future use planning. Brad Woolf was awarded a Mountaineering Fellowship Grant to support his attempt with Patrick Weaver to put up the first route on the West Face of Alaska's Mt Russell.

DAVID THOENEN, *Chair*

*Deep South Section.* The principal Section activity was the organization by Frank Nederhand and me of the 2011 Cordillera Blanca Environmental Expedition. Frank, John All, Clinton Lewis, and Brett Overcash from this Section and 13 other dedicated engineers and scientists from several other Sections, under the leadership of Ellen Lapham, joined this AAC-sponsored humanitarian and environmentally-based expedition to the high mountains of Peru. Here the various activities and experiments contributed key knowledge to both the local and global communities.

I continued to help coordinate land grants to the Southeastern Climbers Coalition through the Cornerstone Conservation Grants with Ellen Lapham, Chair of the AAC's Conservation Committee.

CHADWICK HAGAN, *Chair*

# INDEX

COMPILED BY RALPH FERRARA AND EVE TALLMAN

Mountains are listed by their official names. Ranges and geographic locations are also indexed. Unnamed peaks (eg. Peak 2,340) are listed under P. Abbreviations are used for some states and countries and for the following: Article: art.; Cordillera: C.; Mountains: Mts.; National Park: Nat'l Park; Obituary: obit. Most personnel are listed for major articles. Expedition leaders and persons supplying information in Climbs and Expeditions are also cited here. Indexed photographs are listed in bold type. Reviewed books are listed alphabetically under Book Reviews.

## A

Aartun, Bjørn-Eivind *art.* 59-63; 185
Abrahams, Simon 195
Acay, Cerro (Argentina) 175
Acevedo, Elvis 162-3
Acha La Ri (Shaluli Shan, China) **328**-30
Ache (India) **294**-5
Aconcagua (Argentina) 177-**8**
Adams, Mt. (Cascades, WA) **97**
Ader (Antarctica) 196-8, **197**
Afella (Toubkal Region, Morocco) 203
Afghanistan *art.* 76-80; 237-42
Agil "P. 24" (Pakistan) **279**
Agparssuit (Greenland) 133-5, **134**
Agpat Island (Greenland) 133-5
Akuku (Bolivia) **154**-5
Akvan Div (Tajikistan) 210-12
Alam Kuh (Iran) 201-2
Alaska (US) *art.* 64-8, 71-7; 112-29
Albrieux, Captain Lionel *art.* 45-50; 174
Alexandra, P. (Kyrgyzstan) **230**-2, **231**
Ali, Mirza 249-51
Almaraz, Guillermo 175
Altai-Tvan Bøgd (Mongolia) 358-9
Altamirano, Martin 175
Alto los Leones, Cerro (Chile) **161**
Ambuhl, Hans 287-8
Ambush P. (Wind River Rg., WY) **108**-9
Amelunxen, Conny 132
Amphitheater P. (Pasayten Wilderness, WA) 92-3
Amundsen East (Antarctica) 196-8
Amundsen P. (Antarctica) 196
Amuri Tepui (Venezuela) **145**-7
Anbar Chhish (Pakistan) 248-9
Ancohuma (Bolivia) 155-6
Andes, (Argentina, Chile) 175-80, 161-3
Anker, Conrad *art.* 40-4; 194, 296
Annika, P. (Kyrgyzstan) 225-6
Antarctic Peninsula 196-8
Antarctica 194-200

Argentero, Luca 133-5
Argentina *arts.* 51-2, 53-5, 56-8, 59-63; 175-93
Arken (Greenland) **135**
Arrigetch Peaks (AK) 112-4
Arrowhead, Mt. (Wind River Rg., WY) *art.* 37, **38**
Arrowsmith Peninsula (Antarctica) 196
Asiaq Group (Greenland) 141-**3**
Atardecer (Chile) **167**
Athahra Saya Khola Himal (Nepal) **312**-3
Atlas Mts. (Morocco) 203
Atoshar Valley (Pakistan) 266-9
Auer, Hansjörg 111
Augustine Courtauld, Mt. (Greenland) 139-**40**
Austin, Charlotte 365-6

## B

Bahini Group (India) **304**-5
Balmer, Matt 151-2
Baltoro Muztagh (Pakistan) 261-6
Bandalet, Nikolay 314
Bara Khun Group (Pakistan) 248-9
Barlow, Chris 108-9
Barnes, Justin 132
Baro, Oriol 150
Barrill (Alaska Rg., AK) 121
BasBas, P. (Kyrgyzstan) 216-**7**
Batu, Mt. (Borneo) **359**-60
Batura Muztagh (Pakistan) 251-3
Bayers, Peter L. 373-4
Bear Creek Spire (Sierra Nevada, CA) **101**
Beisly, Gregg 157
Bello, Cerro (Chile) 162-**3**
Belousov, Vladimir 340-1
Bennett, Scott 92-3, 187-91
Benton, Darren 210-12
Bergman Wilkinson, Janet *art.* 81-90; 281-2
Bernasconi, Matteo 185-6
Bhagirathi III (India) 296-**7**
Bhaio aur bheno ki khushi (India) 282-4
Bianchi, Alberto 133-5

Bibitilga Chhish (Pakistan) 248-9
Bicentenario, P. (Argentina) 175
Biggar, John 175-6
Bin, Sun 346
Black Canyon (CO) 110-1
Blammanen (Norway) **204**-7
Bohin, Sébastien *art.* 45-50; 174
Bolivia 154-60
Bonatti, Enrico 181
Bondola (Greenland) 141-**3**
Book Reviews: 363-76
    *Aconcagua: The Invention of Mountaineering on
        America's Highest Peak* by Joy Logan 373-4
    *Bold Beyond Belief: Bill Denz, New Zealand's
        Mountain Warrior* by Paul Maxim 368-9
    *Fred Beckey's 100 Favorite North American
        Climbs* By Fred Beckey 364-5
    *Freedom Climbers* by Bernadette McDonald
        363-4
    *Into the Silence: The Great War, Mallory, and
        the Conquest of Everest* by Wade Davis 371-3
    *The Ledge: An Adventure Story of Friendship
        and Survival on Mount Rainier* by Jim
        Davidson and Kevin Vaughan.* 365-6
    *Mountain* by Sandy Hill 375-6
    *Mountaineering in Antarctica: Climbing in the
        Frozen South* by Damien Gildea. 370-1
    *Mountaineers: Great Tales of Bravery and
        Conquest* by Ed Douglas et al. 369-70
    *Snow & Spire: Flights to Winter in the North
        Cascade Range* by John Scurlock 375-6
    *Triumph and Tragedy: the Life of Edward
        Whymper* by Emil Henry. 374-5
    *The Valley Climbers, Yosemite's Vertical
        Revolution* edited by John Long 367-8
    *The Will to Climb: Obsession and Commitment
        and the Quest to Climb Annapurna—the
        World's Deadliest Peak* by Ed Viesturs and
        David Roberts. 366-7
Borkoldoy (Kyrgyzstan) 218-9
Borneo 359-60
Bouda, Zdenda 213-4
Bouev, Maxim 139-40
Boundary Ranges (AK) 127-9
Bouvetoya Island (Antarctica) 199
Brabant Island (Antarctica) 196
Bracey, Jon 118-9
Brayshaw, Drew 132
Brethes P. (Charakusa Valley, Pakistan) 266-9
Brighton, Alex 226-8
Brokkel, P. (Kyrgyzstan) 216-7
Brooks Rg. (AK) 112-4
Buckland, Monte (Chile) **173**-4
Burdet, Denis 287-8
Burdick, Dave 126
Burkett Needle (Coast Mts., AK) **126**
Burkhardt, Jesse 210-12

Burns, Cameron M. 377-84
Bursik, Mt. (Antarctica) 195
Byeliy, P. (Kyrgyzstan) **223**-4
Byeliy, P. (Tien Shan, China) **324**-5
Byrch, Chris *art.* 76-80; 242

**C**

Cabaza, Carlos 150
Cajon de Maipo (Chile) 161-2
Caldwell, Tommy 112-3
California (US) 97-102
Calvo, Ramiro 181
Camakchay Tower (Kyrgyzstan) **216**-7
Canada 130-2
Cape Farewell Region (Greenland) 141-3
Carillon, Mt. (Sierra Nevada, CA) 101
Carter, Ann Brooks *obit.* 377-8
Cascade Mts. (WA) 91-7
Cashan West (Peru) 150
Castle Peak (India) 289-92, **290**
Cathedral P. (Pasayten Wilderness, WA) 92-**3**
Caucasus (Russia/Georgia) 208-209
Celestial P. (Chola Shan, China) **347**
Central Peak (Antarctica) 196-8
Chabot, Doug 253-5
Chacraraju Este (Peru) 150
Challeat, Ludo 196
Chalten Massif (Argentine Patagonia)
    *arts.* 51-2, 53-5, 56-8, 59-63
Chandi Himal (Nepal) 306-7
Chandra Bhaga Group (India) 292-4
Changi Tower (Pakistan) 275-8, **276**
Changuch (India) 299-**300**
Changwatang (Nepal) **306**-7
Chani Group (Argentina) 175
Chaplinsky, Igor 209
Chappell Peak (Antarctica) 195
Charakusa Valley (Pakistan) 266-77
Chemma (India) **294**-5
Chevieux, Elie 295-6
Chibitok, Galina 261-3
Chichicapac (Peru) 152-**3**
Chile *art.* 45-50; 161-74
Chin, Jimmy *art.* 40-4; 296
China 324-50
Cho Oyo (Tibet) **353**-4
Cho Polu (Nepal) 322-3
Chola Shan (China) 327-8
Chugach Mts. (AK) 123-4
Church, Tim 330-1
Cierva Cove (Antarctica) 196-8; *map 197*
Clarke, Chris 156-7, 160
Coast Mts. (AK, CAN) 126, 132
Cochamó (Chile) 163-7

Cocoví, Cerro 181
Colchuck Balanced Rock
  (Cascade Mts., WA) 91
Colchuck P. (Cascade Mts., WA) 91, 96
Coles, Rebecca 240-2
Colmillo, Cerro (Chile) 168-**9**
Colombia 144
Colorado (US) 110-1
Cordes, Kelly *art.* 51-2, 274
Cordillera Apolobamba (Bolivia) 154-5
Cordillera Blanca (Peru) 149-50
Cordillera Carabaya (Peru) 152-3
Cordillera Central (Peru) 150-1
Cordillera Darwin (Chile) *art.*
  5-50; 173, map 46
Cordillera de la Ramada (Argentina) 176-7
Cordillera Meliquia (Chile) 169-70
Cordillera Oriental (Peru) 151-2
Cordillera Real (Bolivia) 155-60
Cordon Adela (Agentine Patagonia) **185**-6
Cordon de los Pioneros (Argentina) 175-**6**
Cordon del Plata (Argentina) 179
Cornu, Mt. (Antarctica) 196-8, **197**
Corominas, Jordi 150, 322-3
Couloir P. (Juneau Icefield, AK) 127-**8**
Croft, Peter 98-9, 102
Crooks P. "Day Needle" (Sierra
Nevada, CA) 101
Cruces, Jonas 280

**D**

Daddomain (China) **342**-3
Damavand (Iran) 201-2
Dana Plateau (Sierra Nevada, CA) **100**
Daneri, Fernando 176-7
Danphe Sail (Kanjiroba Himal, Nepal) 309
Dare, Ben 161-2, 319-22
Dashkevitch, Sergey 186-7
Daund (India) 292-4
Daxue Shan (China) 328-43
Day Needle (Sierra Nevada, CA) *See*Crooks P.
De l'S, Aguja (Argentine Patagonia) 181-3
Deacon P. (Pasayten Wilderness, WA) 92-3
Deavoll, Pat *art.* 76-80; 242, 298, 331
Dedeshko, Boris 232-5
Degerman, Patrick 199
  della Bordella, Matteo 184-5
Dempster, Kyle 274-5
Denali Nat'l Park (AK) 115-21
Denali, Mt. (Alaska Rg., AK) 116-8
Depta, Lukasz 275-8
Desmochada, Aguja (Argentine Patagonia) 183
Desolation Canyon (UT) 103
Devi, Mikhail 192-3

Devil's Paw (Juneau Icefield, AK) **127**-8
Dhungri II (Tibet) 354
Di Donato, Andrea 177-8
Dingjung Ri "Rima Mancho" (Nepal) **317-8**
Dione, Mt. (Coast Mts., CAN) 132
Disappearing Dome (Sierra Nevada, CA) 99-100
Dittman, Tim 116
Ditzler, Kevin *art.* 69-75; 124
Djangart Range (Kyrgyzstan) 226-32
Dobie, Mike 347-50
Dog Tooth (Neacola Mts., AK) **122**-3
Dom Brakk (Pakistan) 257-9, **258**
Dome P. (Cascade Mts., WA) 91
Dongdong, Yan 334-7
Donini, Jim 201
Dos Canones (Greenland) 141-3, **142**
Dragontail P. (Cascade Mts., WA) 91, 96-7
Drinkwater, Emilie *art.* 81-90; 281-2

**E**

Eagle Dome (Antarctica) 196-8
Ebert, James W. *obit.* 379
Edgar, Mt. (China) **340**-2
Eggemenduluk, P. (Kyrgyzstan) **225**-6
Egger, Torre (Argentine Patagonia) *art.* 59-63; 183-5
Elephant Head (Wind River Rg., WY) 105-8, **106**
Elephant's Tooth (Arrigetch Peaks, AK) **113**-4
Elias, Simon 266-9
Ellingwood P. (Wind River Rg., WY) *art.* 31, **32**
Ellsworth Mtns (Antarctica) 194-5
Emma, P. (Kyrgyzstan) **226**-8
Erard, Phil 382
Eriksson, Magnus 256-7
Evolution Traverse (Sierra Nevada, CA) **102**
Executive Committee Range (Antarctica) 199

**F**

Fairweather Rg. (AK) 124-6
Falso Ilse, Cerro (Chile) **170**-1
Farhod Brakk (Pakistan) 266-9, **268**
Farol East P. (Pakistan) 266-9
Favresse, Nico 146-7
Fengler, Klaus 314-5
Fergana (Kyrgyzstan) 218-9
Fida Brakk (Charakusa Valley, Pakistan) 272-4, **273**
Fiorenza, Luciano 163-4, 179, 188-9
First Koksil Glacier (Pakistan) 245-6
Fisher Towers (UT) 104
Fisher, Max 168-70
Fitschen, Joe 367-9
Fitz Roy, Cerro (Argentine Patagonia)
  82, 188-9, 189-91, **190**
Flatlandsmo, Henki 270-2
Flugi, Yannik 284-5

Foraker, Mt. (Alaska Rg., AK) 116
Fowler, Mick 307-9
Franosch, Urmas 99-100
Fransson, Andreas 116
Fremont P. (Wind River Rg., WY) *art.* 32, **33, 34**; 105-8, **107**
Fremont, John C. *art.* 20
Frezzato, Marco 133-5
Frieh, John 116
Frimer, Jeremy 132

**G**

G 17 (Wind River Rg., WY) *art.* 37
Gagner, Paul 104
Gambino, Dan 103
Gangotri (India) 296-8
Gannett P. (Wind River Rg., WY) *art.* 35-6
Garcia Ayala, Luis Carlos 141
Garhwal Himalaya (India) *art.* **40**-4; 296-8
Garibotti, Rolando 181-2
Gasherbrum I (Pakistan) 264-6
Gaurishankar (Rolwaling Himal, Nepal) 314-5
Geist, Mt. (Hayes Rg., AK) 114-**5**
Georgia 209
Georgina, P. (Kyrgyzstan) 225-6
Ghujerab Mts. (Pakistan) 245-51
Giabul Valley (India) 286
Gibisch, Chris 338-40
Gildea, Damien 194-6, 199
Gilmore, Ben 121
Giovannini, Diego 118
Giuliani, Javier 177
Glowacz, Stefan 314-5
GoCook Peak (India) **284**-5
Goeschl, Gerfreid 265-6
Goettler, David 314-5
Gojung (Kanti Himal, Nepal) 307-9, **308**
Golden Pillars (Greenland) 141-3, **142**
González, Gustavo 175
González, Pablo 180
Goodwin, James *obit.* 379-80
Goodwin, Tony 379-80
Gorilla, Cerro (Chile) 165-7, **166**
Goromiku (Chola Shan, China) **347**
Goromity "Riyucaibao" (Chola Shan, China) **347**
Gostout, Noah 109-10
Gottlieb, David 315-7
Gou Gou Peak (India) 289-92, **291**
Grande, Cerro (Argentine Patagonia) 185-**6**
Great Trango Tower (Pakistan) 261-3, **262**
Great Walls of China (Kyrgyzstan) **221**-3
Greenland 133-43
Gregson, Jim 135-7

Greyell, Chris 91
Griffin, Lindsay 149-50, 167, 203, 209, 248-51, 259-63, 265-6, 300-2, 314, 317-8, 343
Griffiths, Jonathan 116
Grobel, Paulo 306-7, 312-3
Grosvenor (China) **338**-40, **342**
Groupe Militaire de Haute Montagne *art.* 45-50; 174
Gschwendt, Markus 247-8
Guarcello Peak (Antarctica) 195
Guardian, The (San Juan Mts., CO) **111**
Guillaumet, Aguja (Argentine Patagonia) 186-8, **187**
Gulmit Tower (Pakistan) **252**-3
Gunt Valley (Tajikistan) 210-2
Gurla Mandhata (Tibet) **351**-2
Gutzele Peak (India) 289-92, **290**
Gyala Peri (Jiangpu Glacier, Tibet) **355**

**H**

Haan, Peter 368-9
Hackett, Steve *obit.* 378
Hagiwara, Hiroshi 251, 342-3
Hai Tower (Cascades, WA) **94**
Hajzer, Artur 264-5
Haley, Colin 116, 182-3
Halstead, Aaron 199
Hampaturi Group (Bolivia) 158-60
Hancopitis (Bolivia) 155-**6**
Harnish, Nic 111
Har-Noy, Shay 102
Hassan Boulder P. (Pakistan) 266-9
Hassan P. (Pakistan) *See* Hassin
Hassin "Hassan" P. (Pakistan) **274**-5
Hawley, Elizabeth 309, 314-5, 323
Hayes Rg. (AK) 114-5
Helander, Clint *art.* 64-8; 121-2
Helen, Mt. (Wind River Rg., WY) *art.* **34, 35**
Henderson P. (Wind River Rg., WY) *art.* 37
Heritage Range (Antarctica) 195
Hermelndal (Greenland) 141
Herrington, Blake 92-3
Hicks, Kurt 91, 93-4
Hidden Tower "P. 59" (Pakistan) **279**
Hilden, Dan 91, 96
Hill, Florian 129
Himachal Pradesh (India) 289-92
Hindu Himal (Nepal) **312**-3
Hindu Kush (Afghanistan) *art.* 76-80; 238-42
Hispar Muztagh (Pakistan) 253-7
Hispar Sar (Pakistan) 253-**5, 254, 257**
Hitchcock, Mt. (Sierra Nevada, CA) 101
Hogan, Kevin 95-6
Holsten, Jens 91, 96-7, 191-2
Hopeless P. (Nepal) 310-12, **311**
Hora East (India) 292-4

Horn, The (Greenland) See Upernavik O
Horne, Ben 102
Hoshi, Kazuo 294-5
Hostfjellet (Pakistan) **256**-7
Houbart, Shane 148
Huancasayani Valley (Bolivia) 154-5
Huang Jin Feng (Xuelian Massif, China) **325**-7
Huarancayo Sur (Peru) **151**-2
Huayna Potosi (Bolivia) **155**-6, 157-**8**
Hunter, Mt. (Alaska Rg., AK) 116, 118-**9**
Huntington, Mt. (Alaska Rg., AK) 116
Hushe Valley (Pakistan) 266-9
Huss, Chuck 379
Hyalite Canyon (MT) 104-5
Hyung-il, Kim 323

**I**

Ibex Horn (Afghanistan) **237**-8
Ichimura, Fumitaka 251, 342-3
India *arts.* 40-4, 81-90; 280-305
Indonesia 359-60
Innominata, Aguja (Argentine Patagonia) 183
Inspiration P. (Picket Rg., WA) 96
Iran 201-2
Isserman, Maurice 371-3
Iterdlagssuaq (Greenland) 133-5, **134**
Ivanov, Alesey 235-6

**J**

Jackson P. (Wind River Rg., WY) *art.* 32
Jacky Chhish "Koksil VI" (Pakistan) 245-6, **247**
Jade P. (Afghanistan) SeeKoh-e-Baba-Tangi
Jannu (Kumbhakarna Himal, Nepal) 323
Jarjinjabo-Xiashe Massif (China) 333-4
Jati Khollu (Bolivia) **157**
Jenkins, Mark *art.* 27, 105-8
Jervis, Steven 369-70
Jiangpu Glacier (Tibet) 354-7
Jiazi (Minya Konka Rg., China) 334-7, **336**
Jiracek, Pavel 165-7
Jones, Crag 199-200
Jongpo Po Rong (Tibet) **355**
Jopuno Massif (India) **300**-2
Joshi, Dhruv 299-300
Jourdain, Didier *art.* 45-50; 174
Junai Kangri (India) **280**
Juneau Icefield (AK) 127-9
Jurm Valley, (Afghanistan) 240-2
Juvan, Peter 325-7

**K**

K6 Group (Pakistan) 275-8
K7 West (Charakusa Valley, Pakistan) **269**-70

Kahiltna P., West (Alaska Rg., AK) 118
Kammerlander, Hans 194
Kande P. (Kande Valley, Pakistan) 266-9
Kande Valley (Pakistan) 266-9
Kangchenjunga Himal (India) 302-4
Kanjiroba (Nepal) **311**
Kanjiroba Himal (Nepal) 309-12
Kanti Himal (Nepal) 307-9
Kanzler, James H. *obit.* 381-2
Kara-kaya West (Russia) **208**
Karakoram (India/Pakistan) 280-2, 245-79
Karavshin, Pik (Kyrgyzstan) 215
Karpo Tower (Hushe Valley, Pakistan) 266-9, **267**
Kathryn, P. (Kyrgyzstan) 230-**2**
Kauffman, Joel 191-2
Kawecki, Slawomir 238-40, 252-3
Kay, Bruce 132
Kearney, Alan 96
Kelley, John *art.* 69-75; 124
Kellogg, Chad 315-7
Kelsey, Joe *art.* 16-39
Kennedy, Hayden *arts.* 51-2,
    53-5; 112-3, 181-2, 274-5
Kennedy, Terry 381-2
Khan Tengri (Kyrgyzstan) 235-6
Khane Valley (Pakistan) **277, 278**-9,
Khunyang Chhish East (Pakistan) **254**
Kinnaur (India) 295-6
Kishtwar Himalaya (India) 287-8
Kishtwar, Cerro (India) **287**-8
Klarstrom, Andreas 204-6
Kleslo, Michal 212-3
Klonfar, Martin 289
Knife Point Mtn. (Wind River Rg., WY) *art.* 32
Knott, Paul 124-6
Koh-e-Baba-Tangi "Jade P."
    (Afghanistan) *art.* **76**-80; 242
Koh-e-Brobar (Pakistan) **249**-51, 250
Koh-e-Keshnikhan "M1"
    (Mandaras Valley, Afghanistan) **238**
Koh-e-Nadir Sah "M4" (Afghanistan) **239**-40
Koh-e-Naser Khosraw "M2" (Mandaras
Valley, Afghanistan) **238**
Koh-e-Sauze (Jurm Valley, Afghanistan) 240-2, **241**
Koh-I-Baba Mts. (Afghanistan) 237-8
Kokshaal-Too, Western (Kyrgyzstan) 220-6
Koksil Sar I (Pakistan) **247**-8
Koksil Sar II (Pakistan) **247**-8
Koksil Sar III (Pakistan) 247-8
Koksil VI (Pakistan) *See* Jacky Chhish
Korklum Gou (India) 289-92, **290**
Koschitzki, Robert 173-4
Kreiss-Tomkins, Jonathan 180
Kremer, Kirsten *art.* 81-90; 281-2

Kretschmann, Frank 165
Kroese, Mark 366-7
Krol, Michel 220-1
Kroupis, Nikolas 292-4
Kruczyk, Marcin 154-5
Kruk, Jason *arts.* 51-2, 53-5, 181-2
Kumaun (India) 299-300
Kumbhakarna Himal (Nepal) 323
Kundi Feng (Xuelian Massif, China) **325**-7
Kurt Albert Peak (India) 289-92, **290**
Kusum Kanguru (Nepal) **319**-22
Kvaloya Island (Norway) 204-7
Kyajo Ri (Nepal) **319**-22
Kyrgyzstan 215-35

**L**

La Pala (Chile) 162-**3**
Laetitia, P. (Kyrgyzstan) 226-8, **227**
Lahaul (India) 292-5
Lake District (Chile) 167-8
Lama Jimsa Kangri "R6" (India) 282-4
Lama, David *arts.* 51-2, 56-8; 182, 287-8
Lamprecht, Toni 141-3
Larson, Rolf 91, 95
Latok III (Pakistan) **259**-60
Lavrinenko, Alexander 215
Lea, P. (Kyrgyzstan) 230-2, **231**
Lempe, Cheyne 187-91
Lenak Valley (India) 286
Libecki, Mike 237-8, 324-5, 359-60
Liberty Cap (Yosemite, CA) 97-**8**
Lied, Ole *art.* 59-63; 185
Lilia P. (Peri Himal, Nepal) **312**-3
Little Karim Brakk (Pakistan) 266-**9**
Little Konka (China) *See* Xiao Gongga
Livingston Island (Antarctica) 196
Llado, Cati 229-30
Loajunshan Nat'l Park (China) 349-50
Luca, Punta (Argentine Patagonia) 185-**6**
Lyell, P. (Kyrgyzstan) 225-6
Lyon, Oli 127-8

**M**

M1 (Mandaras Valley, Afghanistan)
    *See* Koh-e-Keshnikhan
M2 (Mandaras Valley, Afghanistan)
    *See* Koh-e-Naser Khosraw
M3 (Mandaras Valley, Afghanistan) **238**-40
M4 (Afghanistan) *See* Koh-e-Nadir Sah
    MacLeod, Dave 206-7
Madonna's Peaks (Antarctica) 196-**8**
Maggioni, Michele 133-5
Magro, Sam 104-5
Mahalangur Himal (Tibet/Nepal) 319-23, 353-4

Mahler, Victor Curt *obit.* 382
Maique, Rodrigo 179
Majer, Janusz 245-6, 248-9
Manantiales, Cerro (Argentina) 179-80
Manaslu Himal (Nepal) 314
Mandaras Valley (Hindu Kush,
    Afghanistan) 238-40
Mangasarian, Paul 167
Manoni, Fabrizio 149-50
Maria Lloco (Bolivia) **157**
Marian, P. (Kyrgyzstan) 216-**7**
Marty, Brett 101
Masherbrum Rg. (Pakistan) 266-79
Maudit, Mont (India) **289**
Mausolus, Mt. (Revelation Mts.,
    AK) *art.* 64-8, **65**; 121-2
Mayakovsky, P. (Tajikistan) 212-**3**
McBrian, Forest 93-4
McClure, Josh 182
McCormick, Matt 272-4
Meliquina, Cerro (Chile) 169-**70**
Melnick, Hale 384
Mermoz (Argentine Patagonia) 189-91, **190**
Merriam P. (Sierra Nevada, CA) 98-**9**
Meru Central (Garhwal Himalaya,
    India) *See*Shark's Fin
Messina, Dimitri 344-6
Metherell, Olly 203
Miandi Peak (India) *correction* 298
Miller, Bruce 253-5
Mini Torre (Argentine Patagonia) 185-**6**
Minya Konka Rg. (China) 334-43
Missing Peak (Antarctica) 196-8
Mix-up P. (Cascades, WA) 93-4
Miyamori, Tsuneo 248-9
Miyar Valley (India) 289-92
Moel Kangri (India) 282-4
Mogote Peaks (Argentina) **180**
Molina, Diego 179-80
Monasterio, Erik (Bolivia) 155-6
Mongolia 358-9
Montana (US) 104-5
Morales, Rolando 150-1
Morocco 203
Morro Von Rosen (Argentina) 175
Moscow Olympic Games, P. (Tajikistan) 213-**4**
Moser, Myles 101
Mottram, Gareth 225-6
Mouse's Tooth (Coast Mts., CAN) 132
Mrak, Irena 243-5
Mucci, Josh 97-8
Mukherjee, Anindya 298, 302-4
Mularski, Krzysztof 238
Munoz, Dimitry *art.* 45-50; 174

Muratti, Glauco 180
Mystery Mtn. (Neacola Mts., AK) 122-3

**N**
Nafees Cap (Charakusa Valley,
    Pakistan) 270-2, **271**
Naisa Brakk (Pakistan) 266-9, **268**
Nakamura, Tamotsu 248-9, 294-5
Nalakankar Himal (Tibet-Nepal) 307-9, 351-2
Namcha Barwa **356**
Nanga Parbat (Pakistan) 243-5
Naran (Mongolia) **358-9**
Nardi, Daniele 296-7
Nariz, La (Hushe Valley, Pakistan) 266-9
Narsing (India) 300-2, **301**
Neacola Mts. (AK) 122-3
Nepal 306-23
Nettekoven, Christof 249-51
Nevado Santa Crus (Peru) **149-50**
Nevado Tunshu South (Peru) **150-1**
Neyret, Pierre 257-9
Nideng Gongga 9China) **330-1**
Niebla, Monte (Chile) 173-4
Nielson, Nils 116
Nobuyugya (China) **328**
Nordenskjold, Mt. (Antarctica) 199-**200**
North Chasm View Wall (CO) 110-1
Norway 204-7
Noshaq (Hindu Kush, Afghanistan) 238
Not Notch Pinnacle (Wind
    River Rg., WY) art. 32
Nyanchen Tanglha East (Tibet) 354-7
Nyanchen Tanglha West (Tibet) 354

**O**
O'Dell, Max 185-6
Odintsov, Alexander 259-60
Ohe, Takao 327-8, 347
Ohnishi, Tamotsu 309
Oibala Range (Kyrgyzstan) 216-7
Oibala, P. (Kyrgyzstan) 216-**7**
Olavtoppen (Antarctica) 199
Oleg, P. (Kyrgyzstan) 223-4
Orejas del Gato (Bolivia) 154-5
Ortner, Peter arts. 51-2, 56-8; 182
Orville, Mt. (Fairweather Rg., AK) 124-6, **125**
Otto, Jon 332-3
Ozturk, Renan art. 40-4; 296

**P**
P. 1,600m (Greenland) **133**
P. 1,920m (Juneau Icefield, AK) 127-**8**
P. 24 (Pakistan) See Agil
P. 3,450m (St. Elias Rg., CAN) 130-1

P. 33 (Pakistan) See Tangra Tower
P. 4,540m (Sikkim, India) 300-2, **301**
P. 4,589m (Chile) 161-**2**
P. 4,640m (Sikkim, India) 300-2, **301**
P. 4,810m (Kyrgyzstan) 215
P. 4,815m (Tien Shan, Kyrgyzstan) 218-9
P. 4,887m (Djangert Range, Kyrgyzstan) **229**-30
P. 5,041m (Djangert Range, Kyrgyzstan) 227
P. 5,177m (Yangmolong Massif, China) 333-4
P. 5,213m (Yangmolong Massif, China) 333-4
P. 5,243m (China) 328-30
P. 5,253m (Tien Shan, China) **324**-5
P. 5,318m (Djangert Range, Kyrgyzstan) 226-8, **227**
P. 5,358m (Shaluli Shan, China) 328-30
P. 5,526m (Sikkim, India) 300-2, **301**
P. 5,557m ((Shaluli Shan, China) 328-30, **329**
P. 5,609m (Pakistan) 245-6
P. 5,626m (Pakistan) 245-6
P. 5,636m (Pakistan) 245-6
P. 5,980m (Tibet) 354
P. 5,985m (India) 282-4, **283**
P. "59" (Pakistan) See Hidden Tower
P. 6,072m (Pakistan) 245-6
P. 6,097m (Tibet) 354
P. 6,258m (India) 281-**2**
P. 6,465m (India) 298
P. 6,605m (Tibet) 357
P. 6,620' (Fairweather Rg., AK) **125**
P. 7,400+' (Fairweather Rg., AK) 124-6, **125**
P. 7,570m (Cho Oyo, Tibet) **353**-4
P. 8,010' (Fairweather Rg., AK) **125**
P. 8,290' (Fairweather Rg., AK) **125**
P. 8,410' (Fairweather Rg., AK) **125**
P. 8,440' (Fairweather Rg., AK) **125**
P. ca 5600m (Bolivia)**157**
P. ca 5,700m (India) 282-4, **283**
Pagoda East East (India) 292-4, **293**
Paine, Torres del (Chile) 171-2
Paine Grande, Cerro (Chile) 171-**2**
Pakistan 243-79
Paloma Valley (Chile) 167
Pamir Alai (Kyrgyzstan/Tajikistan) 215-7, 210-3
Panbari (Peri Himal, Nepal) 312-**3**
Pangbuk Ri (Rolwaling Himal, Nepal) **315**-7
Panmah Muztagh (Pakistan) 257-60
Papert, Ines 221-3
Parabola (Arrigetch Peaks, AK) 113-**4**
Parkes, Mt. (Coast Mts., CAN) 132
Parkin, Andy 317-8
Pasayten Wilderness (WA) 92-3
Patagonia (Argentina-Chile) arts. 51-2,
    53-5, 56-8, 59-63; 171-2, 181-93
Payne, Roger 304-5

Peri Himal (Nepal) 312-3
Perkins, Matt 91-2
Pernille, P. (Kyrgyzstan) 230-2, **231**
Peru 149-53
Petkov, Nikolay 278-9
Petlitsky, Vladimir 235-6
Pewi, P. (Kyrgyzstan) 216-**7**
Pfaff, Anna 144
Pfluger, Yvonne 330-1
Pinto, Beto 150-1
Piramide Blanca (Bolivia) 156-7
Piz Rascana (Greenland) 141-3, **142**
Plata, Cerro (Cordon del Plata, Argentina) 179
Pobeda, P. (Kyrgyzstan) **233**-5
Poincenot, Aguja (Argentine Patagonia) 191-**3, 192**
Polaco, P. (Argentina) 177
Pollone, Cerro (Argentine Patagonia) 183
Poltavets, Eugene 208
Prabha Behin (India) 304-5
Preuss, Charles *art.* 20
Prezhevalskogo, P. (Kyrgyzstan) 232-**3**
Prudden, Bonnie *obit.* 382-4
Pumari Chhish East (Pakistan) **254**
Pumo Kangri (India) *art.* 81-90; 281-2
Puna de Atacama (Argentina) 175-6

Q
Qonglai Shan (China) 344-7
Queen Maud Land (Antarctica) 199
Qungmo Kangri (Tibet) 354
Quvnerit Island (Greenland) 141-3

R
R6 (India) *See* Lama Jimsa Kangri
Rada, Camilo 170-2
Rafael Juarez, Aguja (Argentine Patagonia) 182
Rakhmat (Kyrgyzstan) **229**-30
Ramírez Carrascal, Sergio 150-1
Rands, Lisa 98-9
Raru Valley "Tetleh, or Tetli Valley" (India) 282-5
Ratel, Sébastien *art.* 45-50; 174
Rauch, Robert 157-9
Reclus, Volcán 171
Red Tower (Wind River Rg., WY) **106**
Reddomain (Minya Konka Rg., China) **334**-7, 343
Rendu, Mt. (Antarctica) 196
Renland (Greenland) 137-9
Retumbadero Norte (Chile) 161-2
Revelation Mts. (AK) *art.* 64-8; 121-2
Reynolds, Jeff 358-9
Ricart, Sergi 328-30
Rich, Corey 112-3

Richey, Mark *art.* 81-90, 280-1
Rieger, Erik 109-10
Rima Mancho (Nepal) *See* Dingjung Ri
Ripley, Tom 152-3
Ritacuba Blanco (Colombia) **144**
Riyucaibao (Chola Shan, China) *See* Goromity
Roberts, Mike 199
Robertson, Cam 132
Robinson, Doug 101-2
Rolwaling Himal (Nepal) 314-5
Roma (Kanjiroba Himal, Nepal) 309
Romero, Jordan 194
Rostam (Tajikistan) **210**-2, **211**
Rousseau, Alan 94
Ru Chen Gangri (China) 328-30, **329**
Rubi, Tomeu 229-30
Ruchkin, Alexander 137-9
Russell, Mt. (Sierra Nevada, CA) 101
Russia 208
Ruth Gorge (Alaska Rg., AK) 121
Rutherford, Kate 182

S
Sacagawea, Mt. (Wind River Rg., WY) *art.* 33, **34**; 105-8, **107**
Sahale P. (Cascade Mts., WA) 91
Sainsbury, George *obit.* 384
Sakamoto, Kimikazu 286
San Gabriel, Cerro (Chile) **162**-3
San Juan Mts. (CO) 111
San Ri Dui (Tibet) **356**
San Ri Mal (Tibet) **357**
Sanctuary P. (Nepal) 310-12, **311**
Santa Cruz Chico (Peru) **149**-50
Saser Kangri Group (India) *art.* **81**-90, **85**, 280-2; *map* 281
Saser Kangri II (India) *art.* **81**-90, **85**, 280
SaserLing (India) *art.* 81-90; 281-2
Sato, Yusuke 251
Savary, Francois *art.* 45-50; 173
Saven Range (Greenland) 135-7
Scanu, Marcelo 175-7, 179-80
Schaar, Gerhard 289-92
Schaefer, Mikey 182, 191-2
Schmidt, Marty 116-8
Schnell, Bobby 115-6
Schoeck Peak (Antarctica) 195
Scott, Virgil 282-4
Seeliger, Daniel 167
Sejong I (China) **328**
Sejong II (China) **328**
Sentinel Range, Ellsworth Mtns (Antarctica) 194-5
Serkhe Khollu (Bolivia) 158-**60, 159**

Serrania Avalancha (Chile) 167-**8**
Shahnameh (Tajikistan) 210-2, **211**
Shakhawr Valley (Afghanistan) **239**
Shakhdara Rg. (Tajikistan) 213-4
Shaluli Shan (China) 328-34
Shanzidou (China) **348**-9
Shark's Fin (Garhwal Himalaya,
    India) *art.* **40**-4; 296
Shark's Tooth (Greenland) **137**-9
Shepton, Bob 133-5
Shinn, Mt. (Antarctica) 194
Shokes, Jimbo 91
Shoshala (India) **295**-6
Sichuan (China) 327-47
Sidley, Mt. (Antarctica) 199
Siegrist, Stefan 287-8
Sierra de Sangra (Argentina) 181
Sierra Nevada del Cocuy (Colombia) 144
Sierra Nevada Mts. (CA) 98-102
Siguniang (China) **344-7**
Siguniang Nat'l Park (China) 344-7
Sikkim (India) 300-5
Silla, Aguja de la (Argentine Patagonia) **188**-9
Simmons, Grant 164-5
Siren, The (UT) **103**
Sizdh Valleys (Tajikistan) 210-2
Ski Mountaineering: Cierva Cove
    (Antarctica) 196-8; Denali, Mt. (AK) 116;
    Juneau Icefield (AK) 127-8
Sloan P. (Cascade Mts., WA) 91, **92**, 95-6
Smaug (China) 348-**9**
Soneri Behin (India) 304-5
Sorkin, Madaleine 108-9
South Georgia (Antarctica) 199-200
Sphinx, The (Wind River Rg., WY) *art.* 36
Spörli, Mt. (Antarctica) 195
Squire Creek Wall (Cascade Mts., WA) 91
St. Elias Mts. (AK, CAN) *art.* 69-75; 124
St. Exupéry, Aguja (Argentine Patagonia) 182-3
Stago P. (Pakistan) 266-9, **267**
Stairway Glacier (St. Elias Rg., CAN) 130-1
Stanhardt, Aguja (Argentine Patagonia) **182**-3
Stegosaurus (India) 281-2
Stevenson, David 365-6, 377-8
Strazar, Luka 269-70
Stres, Blaz 223-4
Stroud P. (Wind River Rg., WY) *art.* 38
Stuart, Mt. (Cascade Mts., WA) 91
Stucki, Werner 113-4
Suk-mun, Choi 116
Sun-Yat-Sen (China) *See* Zhong Shan
Suppé, Isabel 159-60
Sweeney, Jim 366-7
Swenson, Steve *art.* 81-90, 280-1

Szilas, Kristoffer 230-2

**T**

Table Mtn. (Sierra Nevada, CA) 102
Tagas Group (Pakistan) 278-9
Tajikistan 210-4
Taku D P. (Juneau Icefield, AK) **129**
Talbott, Logan 100
Tangra Tower "P. 33" (Pakistan) **279**
Taniguchi, Kei 351-2
Tara Pahar (India) 292-4, **293**
Tasermiut Fjord (Greenland) 141
Taulliraju (Peru) 150
Tengri Tag (Kyrgyzstan) 232-6
Tetleh Valley (India) *See* Raru Valley (India)
Tetli Valley (India) *See* Raru Valley (India)
Thackray, John 374-5
Thayer, Drew 109-10
Thrasher, Aaron 122-3, 124
Thulagi (Manaslu Himal, Nepal) 314
Tiba Kangri (Tibet) **356**
Tibet 351-7
Tien Shan (Kyrgyzstan/China) 218-9, 324-7
Tierra del Fuego (Chile) *art.* 45-50; 173-4
Tigra Killa, Cerro (Bolivia) **157**
Tininnertuup (Greenalnd) **141**
Titcomb Basin (Wind River Rg.,
    WY) *art.* 16-39; 105-8; *map* 17
Toro Peak (India) 289-92
Torre, Cerro (Argentine Patagonia)
    *arts.* **cover**, **51**-2, **53**-5; 182, 185-**6**
Tosas, Jordi 353-4
Toubkal Region (Morocco) 203
Tower Mtn. (Cascade Mts., WA) 91, **95**
Trango Tower (Pakistan) 263-4
Trata Tata (Bolivia) **154**-5
Tridesch (India) 304-5
Trinidad Central, Cerro (Chile) 163-5, **164**
Trinidad Sur, Cerro (Chile) **165**
Tromso Region (Norway) 204-7
Tso Chen Ri (Daxue Shan, China) 328-30
Tso Chong Ri (Daxue Shan, China) 328-30, **329**
Tsok Kangri (India) *art.* 81-90, **82**
Tushunbodum (Kyrgyzstan) **229**-30
Tyree, Mt. (Antarctica) **194**

**U**

Ullrich, George 145-6
Ultar Sar (Pakistan) 251
Umiasugssuk (Greenland) 133-5, **134**
United States 91-111
University P. (St. Elias Mts., AK) *art.* 69-75, **70**; 124
Upernavik Region (Greenland) 133-5
Upernavik, O "The Horn" (Greenland) 133-5

Upigma Tepui (Venezuela) **148**
Urubko, Denis 232-5
Ushba (Georgia) 209
Utah (US) 103-4
Uummannaq Region (Greenland) 133-5

## V

Val Biois, Aguja (Argentine Patagonia) 188-9
Vallecitos, Cerro (Cordon del
Plata, Argentina) 179
Van der Smeede, Bas 216-7
Varney, Josh 123
Venezuela 145-8
Vernyi, P. (Kyrgyzstan) **220**-1
Vidal, Sílvia 167-8
Villa, Beppe 133-5
Villanueva, Sean 146-7
Viluyo I (Bolivia) 155-6
Vincik, Scotty *art.* 64-8; 121-2
Vinson Massif (Antarctica) 194-5
Voyager P. (Alaska Rg., AK) **120**-1

## W

Wakhan Corridor (Hindu Kush,
   Afghanistan) *art.* 76-80
Wallace, Wayne 97
Warren, Mt. (Wind River Rg., WY) *art.* 35
Warrior I (Wind River Rg., WY) **109**-10
Washington (US) 91-7
Watkins Mountains (Greenland) **139**-40
Weeding, Mark 218-9
Weidner, Chris 201-2, 210-12
Westman, Mark 91, 118, 121
Wheeler, Toby 378
Wherley, Eric 95
White, Bo 210-12
Whittaker, Enid 382-4
Wickens, Phil 196-8
Wiik, Odd-Roar 270-2
Wilford, Mark 201
Wilkinson, Freddie *art.* 81-90, 280-1
Wilks, Glenn 130-1
Williamson, Jed 377-8
Wilson, Guy 114-5
Wiltsie, Gordon 370-1
Wind River Rg. (WY) *art.* 16-39; 105-10
Wohlthat Massif (Antarctica) 199
Wood, Tim 238
Workman, Brandon 91
Wuse Shan (Chola Shan, China) **347**
Wyoming (US) *art.* 16-39; 105-10

## X

Xanadu (Arrigetch Peaks, AK) **112**
Xiangqiuqieke (China) **330**-1
Xiao Gongga "Little Konka" (China) 334-**7**
Xinjiang (China) 324-7
Xuelian Massif (China) 325-7
Xuelian Northeast (Xuelian
   Massif, China) 325-7, **326**

## Y

Yagua Yagua (Bolivia) **154**-5
Yak P. (Coast Mts., CAN) 132
Yamakawa (Chile) 161-2
Yangmolong (China) **332**-3
Yawash Sar I (Pakistan) 245-**6**
Yellowstone Nat'l Park (WY) 104-5
Yi-ge Feng (Xuelian Massif, China) 325-7
Yosemite Nat'l Park (CA) 97-8
Yukla, Mt. (Chugach Mts., AK) **123**-**4**
Yulong Xueshan (China) 347-9
Yunnan (China) 347-9
Yurkin, Alexander 263-4

## Z

Zanskar (India) 282-6
Zegers, Andres 177-8
Zemu Gap (India) 302-4
Zhong Shan "Sun-Yat-Sen" (China) **343**
Zimmerman, Graham 120-1

# INTERNATIONAL GRADE COMPARISON CHART

To download the complete "American Alpine Journal International Grade Comparison Chart," including alpine and ice grades, go to: aaj.americanalpineclub.org

This chart is designed to be used with the *American Alpine Journal* to help decipher the difficulty ratings given to climbs.

| YDS | UIAA | FR | AUS | SAX | CIS | SCA | BRA | UK | |
|---|---|---|---|---|---|---|---|---|---|
| 5.2 | II | 1 | 10 | II | III | 3 | | | D |
| 5.3 | III | 2 | 11 | III | III+ | 3+ | | | D |
| 5.4 | IV-/IV | 3 | 12 | | IV- | 4 | | | VD |
| 5.5 | IV+ | | 13 | | IV | 4+ | | | S |
| 5.6 | V- | 4 | 14 | | IV+ | 5- | | 4a | HS |
| 5.7 | V / V+ | | 15 | VIIa | | 5 | | 4b | VS |
| 5.8 | VI- | 5a | 16 | VIIb | V- | 5+ | 4 / 4+ | 4c | HVS |
| 5.9 | VI | 5b | 17 | VIIc | | 6- | 5 / 5+ | 5a | E1 |
| 5.10a | VI+ | 5c | 18 | VIIIa | V | 6 | 6a | 5b | |
| 5.10b | | 6a | | | | | | | E2 |
| 5.10c | VII- | 6a+ | 19 | VIIIb | | 6+ | 6b | | |
| 5.10d | VII | 6b | 20 | VIIIc | V+ | 7- | 6c | | E3 |
| 5.11a | VII+ | 6b+ | | IXa | | | 7a | 5c | |
| 5.11b | | 6c | 21 | IXb | | 7 | 7b | | |
| 5.11c | VIII- | 6c+ | 22 | IXc | VI- | 7+ | 7c | 6a | E4 |
| 5.11d | VIII | 7a | 23 | | | | | | |
| 5.12a | VIII+ | 7a+ | 24 | | | 8- | 8a | | E5 |
| 5.12b | | 7b | 25 | Xa | VI | 8 | 8b | | |
| 5.12c | IX- | 7b+ | 26 | Xb | | 8+ | 8c | | |
| 5.12d | IX | 7c | 27 | | | | 9a | 6b | E6 |
| 5.13a | IX+ | 7c+ | 28 | Xc | | 9- | 9b | | |
| 5.13b | | 8a | 29 | | | | 9c | | |
| 5.13c | X- | 8a+ | 30 | | | 9 | 10a | 6c | E7 |
| 5.13d | X | 8b | 31 | XIa | VI+ | | 10b | | |
| 5.14a | X+ | 8b+ | 32 | XIb | | | 10c | 7a | E8 |
| 5.14b | | 8c | 33 | | | 9+ | | | |
| 5.14c | XI- | 8c+ | | XIc | | | | 7b | E9 |
| 5.14d | XI | 9a | | | | | | | |

**Seriousness Rating:**

These often modify the technical grades when protection is difficult.

R: Poor protection with potential for a long fall and some injury.

X: A fall would likely result in serious injury or death.

YDS=Yosemite Decimal System; UIAA=Union Internationale des Associations D'Alpinisme; Fr=France/Sport; Aus=Australia; Sax=Saxony; CIS=Commonwealth of Independent States/Russia; Sca=Scandinavia; Bra=Brazil.